[redacted]

FODOR'S®

FLORIDA 1986

Fodor's Editor: Debra Bernardi
Area Editors: Jay Clarke; Vaughn K. Gibson; Joel A. Glass; Pam Parks; Paul C. Rapp; Joice Veselka; Fred. W. Wright Jr.
Contributing Editor: Phil Halpern
Maps and Plans: Jon Bauch; Pictograph
Drawings: Michael Kaplan; Sandra Lang

FODOR'S TRAVEL GUIDES
New York

ISBN 0-679-01234-6 (Traveltex edition)
ISBN 0-340-38431-X (Hodder & Stoughton, London, edition)

The following Fodor's Guides are current; most are also available in a British edition published by Hodder & Stoughton.

Country and Area Guides

Australia, New Zealand & The South Pacific
Austria
Bahamas
Belgium & Luxembourg
Bermuda
Brazil
Canada
Canada's Maritime Provinces
Caribbean
Central America
Eastern Europe
Egypt
Europe
France
Germany
Great Britain
Greece
Holland
India, Nepal & Sri Lanka
Ireland
Israel
Italy
Japan
Jordan & The Holy Land
Kenya
Korea
Mexico
North Africa
People's Republic of China
Portugal
Scandanavia
Scotland
South America
Southeast Asia
Soviet Union
Spain
Switzerland
Turkey
Yugoslavia

City Guides

Amsterdam
Beijing, Guangzhou, Shanghai
Boston
Chicago
Dallas–Fort Worth
Greater Miami & The Gold Coast
Hong Kong
Houston
Lisbon
London
Los Angeles
Madrid
Mexico City & Acapulco
Munich
New Orleans
New York City
Paris
Philadelphia
Rome
San Diego
San Francisco
Stockholm, Copenhagen, Oslo, Helsinki & Reykjavik
Sydney
Tokyo
Toronto
Vienna
Washington, D.C.

U.S.A. Guides

Alaska
Arizona
California
Cape Cod
Colorado
Far West
Florida
Hawaii
New England
New Mexico
Pacific North Coast
South
Texas
U.S.A.

Budget Travel

American Cities (30)
Britain
Canada
Caribbean
Europe
France
Germany
Hawaii
Italy
Japan
London
Mexico
Spain

Fun Guides

Acapulco
Bahamas
London
Montreal
Puerto Rico
San Francisco
St. Martin/Sint Maarten
Waikiki

MANUFACTURED IN THE UNITED STATES OF AMERICA
10 9 8 7 6 5 4 3 2 1

CONTENTS

FOREWORD

It can be no surprise that Florida is one of the world's most popular tourist destinations; Walt Disney World alone attracts people from everywhere. But Florida is much more than theme parks: warm winters; secluded island beaches and other, nonsecluded stretches of sand for those who want to be "where the boys are"; historic sites; lavish resorts; forests and parks for wilderness lovers and wildlife watchers; fine restaurants; great fishing. . . . We could go on and on.

Fodor's Florida is designed to help you plan your own trip based on your time, your budget, your energy, your idea of what this trip should be. Perhaps having read this guide you'll have some new ideas. We have, therefore, tried to put together the widest possible *range* of activities and within that range to offer you *selections* that will be worthwhile, safe, and of good value. The descriptions we provide are designed to help you make your own intelligent choices from our selections.

All selections and comments in *Fodor's Florida* are based on personal experiences. Some hard choices had to be made about what to include in this guide, since no one book can possibly cover all there is to see and do in Florida. We feel that our first responsibility is to inform and protect you, the reader. Errors are bound to creep into any travel guide, however. Much change can and will occur even while we are on press, and also during the succeeding twelve months or so that this edition is on sale. We sincerely welcome letters from our readers on these changes, or from those whose opinions differ from ours, and we are ready to revise our entries for next year's edition when the facts warrant it.

Send your letters to the editors at Fodor's Travel Guides, 2 Park Avenue, New York, NY 10016. Continental or British Commonwealth readers may prefer to write to Fodor's Travel Guides, 9-10 Market Place, London W1N 7AG, England.

For their help in preparing this guide, special thanks to Neil Kran, Linda Metz, and Meryl Schneider.

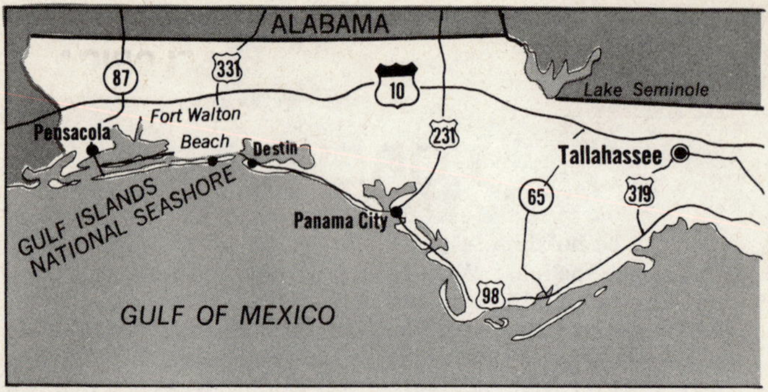
ALABAMA
87
331
10
Lake Seminole
Fort Walton
Beach
Pensacola
Destin
231
Tallahassee
65
319
GULF ISLANDS
NATIONAL SEASHORE
Panama City
98
GULF OF MEXICO

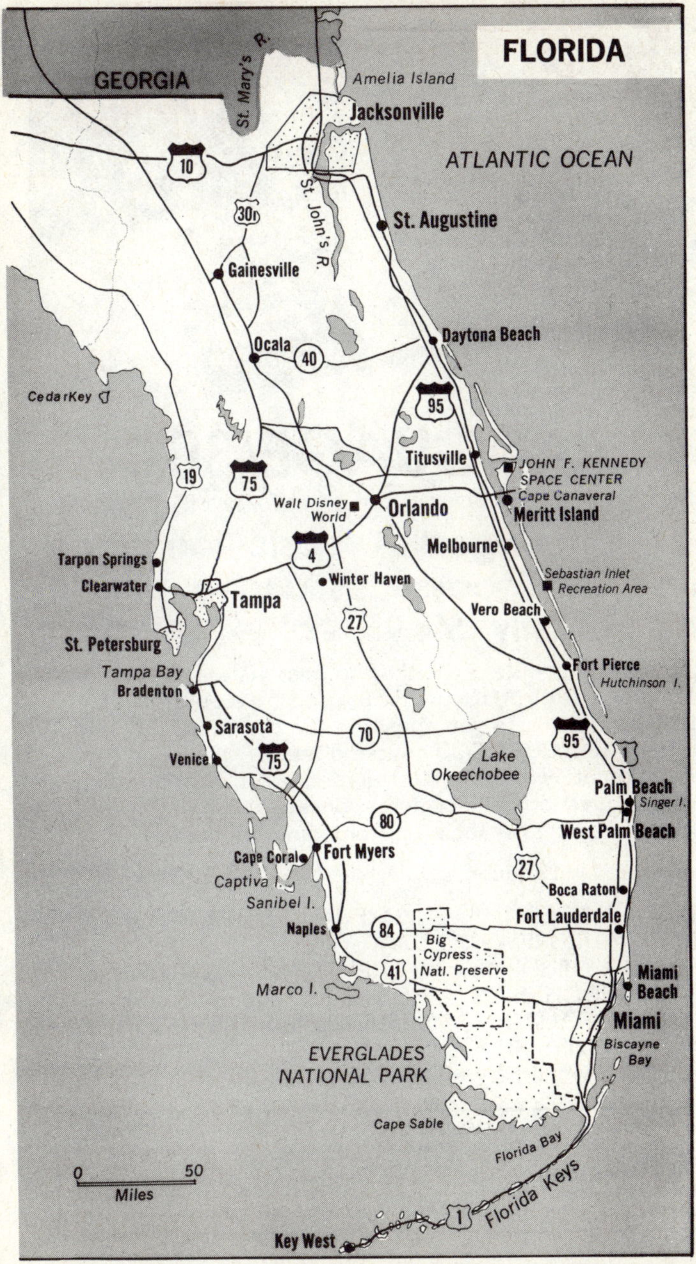
FLORIDA
GEORGIA
St. Mary's R.
Amelia Island
Jacksonville
ATLANTIC OCEAN
10
30
St. John's R.
St. Augustine
Gainesville
Daytona Beach
Ocala
40
95
Cedar Key
Titusville
JOHN F. KENNEDY SPACE CENTER
Cape Canaveral
19
75
Walt Disney World
Orlando
Meritt Island
4
Melbourne
Tarpon Springs
Clearwater
Winter Haven
Sebastian Inlet Recreation Area
Tampa
27
Vero Beach
St. Petersburg
Tampa Bay
Bradenton
Fort Pierce
Hutchinson I.
Sarasota
70
95
Venice
75
Lake Okeechobee
1
Palm Beach
Singer I.
80
West Palm Beach
Cape Coral
Fort Myers
27
Captiva I.
Sanibel I.
Boca Raton
Fort Lauderdale
Naples
84
Big Cypress Natl. Preserve
41
Miami Beach
Marco I.
Miami
Biscayne Bay
EVERGLADES NATIONAL PARK
Cape Sable
Florida Bay
0
50
Miles
Florida Keys
1
Key West

FACTS AT YOUR FINGERTIPS

WHEN TO GO. From the heights of fantasy in Walt Disney World-Epcot down to the fascinating depths of the real underwater world of John Pennekamp State Park, Florida is a state for all seasons.

Winter, for instance, is the height of the tourist season in southern Florida, and the area is crowded with "Snowbirds" flying away from the cold weather to bask in the golden sunshine. For people who need people, this is the time to make acquaintances in Florida. Hotels, bars, discos, restaurants, shops, and attractions are so crowded that you can't miss bumping into someone, both literally and figuratively. Winter is super show time, when Hollywood and Broadway celebrities appear in sophisticated supper clubs. It's the season to be cultural, as well as jolly, with opera, ballet, concerts, and drama in the spotlight. Christmas regattas, when yachts and boats are colorfully illuminated and cruise along the Intracoastal Waterways, are spectacular. Of course, decorations are everywhere and are especially beautiful when combined with tropical flowers and foliage. Right on schedule, the blazing poinsettias are in full bloom.

During the winter season, the Magic Kingdom at Disney World becomes more magical than ever. From the middle of December through January 2, the daily parade is an extravaganza of jolly giant gingerbread men, brightly uniformed soldiers seven-feet tall, and beautifully costumed characters. The Magic Kingdom's Christmas tree is a 70-foot-high fantasy with more than 3,000 scintillating lights. And the traditional Candlelight Processional with 800 carolers is unforgettable. For children especially, this is an enchanting time to visit Florida.

Fairs and festivals, art shows, parades, and fiestas happen nonstop from January through December. The Diving of the Golden Cross festivals on Epiphany in Tarpon Springs is one of the top ten annual events in the United States. During the second week in February, the swashbuckling Gasparilla Pirate Days in Tampa attract enormous crowds. Many a vacation trip is planned around a special festival. (See "Seasonal Events" in the *Practical Information* section at the end of each chapter.)

Sports enthusiasts should check the listings in the "Sports" sections in each *Practical Information* to line up vacation days at a time when their favorite activity is in the limelight. Florida's sports schedule is action-packed with nationally acclaimed yachting races, hydroplane races, car racing of all types, fishing tournaments, powerboat competitions, football, soccer, golf and tennis championships, and more.

Tennis and golf are year-around sports in Florida, boasting many of the best courts and fairways anywhere. Vacationers have the opportunity to play with famous tennis pros, such as Hall of Famer Arthur Ashe, at Miami's Doral Country Club. Florida is the national headquarters of both the PGA and U.S. Professional Tennis Association, and many of these sports' greatest players have homes here, including Chris Evert Lloyd, Martina Navratilova, Jack Nicklaus, John McEnroe, and Jimmy Connors. There are 700 golf courses and 950 tennis courts in the state.

As smart budget-minded visitors have discovered, **summer** in Florida is no hotter than summer in the Northeastern and Midwestern states. There is always a breeze at the ocean, Gulf, or bay. Every day is a beach day, and the vacationer can stay cool in pools, the ocean, bays, lakes, rivers, and the Gulf of Mexico. Summer is, in fact, the high season in northern Florida, where temperatures are cooler.

Every place is air-conditioned comfortably and the vacationer is not really aware of what the outside temperature is. Also, the pace in Florida is slow and leisurely, and the visitor finds himself relaxing and not rushing around. Another way the visitor can keep his cool is by knowing that accommodations, restaurants, and shops feature great discounts during summer months. A family can stay at a super deluxe resort, such as the Sonesta Beach Hotel and Tennis Club on Key Biscayne, for the price of a nondescript hotel anywhere else. For anyone who might think the palatial Breakers in Palm Beach is beyond their budget, a double room, costing more than $150 a day in high season, plunges down to around $60 a day from June to the end of September. With discounts of more than 50 percent everywhere, you can just imagine the unbelievable rates and weekend package specials throughout the state.

Families who want to explore Disney World-Epcot, Sea World, Busch Gardens, and the other outstanding attractions will find some crowds in summer—but fewer when the children return to school in September.

For the college crowd, **spring** vacation is the time to congregate on Daytona Beach and Fort Lauderdale Beach, or at least to go somewhere in Florida. Wall-to-wall bikinis cover the beaches and restaurants are packed. Now that beach authorities are no longer alarmed at the annual invasions and have learned that it is more pleasant to make the best of the situation, everyone is happy.

For Senior Citizens, **September, October,** and **November** often are special months for discounts to many attractions in Orlando and the Pinellas Suncoast, including special hotel packages and a series of events.

TIPS FOR BRITISH VISITORS. Passports. You will need a valid passport and a U.S. Visa (which can only be put in a passport of the ten-year kind). You can obtain the visa either through your travel agent or directly from the *United States Embassy,* Visa and Immigration Department, 24 Grosvenor Sq., London W1 (tel. 01–499 3443).

No vaccinations are required for entry into the U.S.

Customs. If you are 21 or over, you can take into the U.S.: 200 cigarettes or 50 cigars, or 3 lbs. of tobacco; 1 U.S. quart of alcohol; duty-free gifts to a value of $100. Be careful not to try to take in meat or meat products, seeds, plants, fruits, etc. And avoid narcotics like the plague.

Insurance. We heartily recommend that you insure yourself to cover health and motoring mishaps, with *Europ Assistance,* 252 High St., Croydon CRO 1NF (tel. 01–680 1234). Their excellent service is all the more valuable when you consider the possible costs of health care in the U.S.

Air Fares. We suggest that you explore the current scene for budget flight possibilities. Unfortunately there is no longer standby service on any of the major airlines; but do check their APEX and other fares which may be a considerable saving over the full price. Quite frankly, only business travelers who don't have to watch the price of their tickets fly full-price these days—and find themselves sitting right beside an APEX passenger!

CLIMATE. Although many people have the mistaken impression that the entire state is hot during the winter, the northeast part of the state and the northwest regions can be as cool as New York City in early spring. During the winter months, you may not be able to swim in the ocean from Jacksonville Beach through St. Augustine Beach, but the weather will be delightful for a brisk stroll on the sands, jogging, tennis, golf, sightseeing, etc. In Pensacola and

Tallahassee, the temperature has been known to plunge so low in the winter that it snows, therefore requiring a very heavy sweater or coat. Many tourists prefer the cool weather for walking around Disney World, Sea World, Circus World, Busch Gardens, and all the other attractions.

Furthermore, 40 or 50 degrees with bright sunshine is certainly a great improvement over the below-freezing temperatures and the snow blizzards of the past few winters in many parts of the U.S.

In St. Petersburg, 361 days of sunshine are guaranteed. Should the sun not happen to shine, the St. Petersburg *Independent* newspaper is free of charge the following day.

Summer travelers should watch out for brief but dangerous lightning storms, especially in the late afternoon. And remember that sunburn can ruin a holiday; start slowly and build your tan.

PLANNING YOUR TRIP. If you're traveling with the family, it's a good idea to sit down together and decide what everyone really wants to do. Do send for brochures and information in advance to the Office of Visitor Inquiry, 126 Van Buren St., Tallahassee, FL 32301, (904) 487–1462, and to the Chamber of Commerce in the area you are considering for your vacation (see "Tourist Information" in the *Practical Information* sections at the end of each chapter).

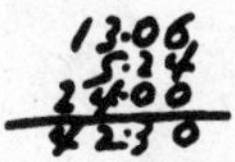

WHAT WILL IT COST? Driving to Florida, two people can expect to spend about $100 a day (not counting gasoline or other transportation costs), as you can see in the table following. In some areas you can cut expenses by traveling off-season, when hotel rates are usually lower. The budget-minded traveler can also find bargain accommodations at tourist homes or family-style YMCAs and YWCAs. Some state and federal parks also provide inexpensive lodging. And some 250 colleges in 41 states offer dormitory accommodations to tourists during vacations at single-room rates of $2–$10 per night, with meal from $0.60–$3.50. A directory of some 200 such bargains all over the U.S. is *Mort's Guide to Low-Cost Vacations and Lodgings on College Campuses, USA–Canada,* from CMG Publishing Co., P.O. Box 630, Princeton, N.J. 08540.

Over the last few years, a number of airlines have been offering very cheap fares. Also look into special fares for trains and buses.

Another way to cut down on the cost of your trip is to look for out-of-the-way resorts. Travelers are frequently rewarded by discovering very attractive areas that haven't as yet begun to draw quantities of people.

Typical Expenses for Two People

Room at *moderate* hotel or motel	$70.00 plus tax
Breakfast, including tip	6.00
Lunch at *inexpensive* restaurant	10.00
Dinner at *moderate* restaurant	20.00
Sightseeing bus tour	6.00
An evening drink	5.00
Admission to museum or historic site	4.00
	$121.00

During the summer "off-season" in Florida, especially in such resort areas as the Pinellas Suncoast (St. Pete Beach and the Holiday Isles), typical expenses for two people could be as low as $75 a day, including all seven categories above.

HOTELS AND MOTELS. Hotels and motels are divided into categories, arranged primarily by price; these are: *Super Deluxe,* where the visitor can expect all amenities as well as a special, luxurious atmosphere; *Deluxe; Expensive; Moderate; Inexpensive;* and in some areas, *Basic Budget.* Our ratings are flexible and subject to change. We should also like to point out that failure to include certain establishments in our lists does not mean they are not worthwhile—many fine hotels and motels had to be omitted for lack of space. Conversely, establishments presently listed may be dropped in the future if better accommodations in their areas surpass the old hostelries in comfort, service, and atmosphere.

Although the names of the various hotel and motel categories are standard throughout this series, the prices listed under each category may vary from area to area. This variation is meant to reflect local price standards, and take into account the fact that what might be considered a *moderate* price in a large urban area might be quite expensive in a rural region. In every case, however, the dollar ranges for each category are clearly stated before each listing of establishments.

In some instances, hotel prices reflect a certain number of meals. *Full American Plan (FAP)* includes three meals daily. *Modified American Plan (MAP)* automatically means breakfast and dinner. *Continental Plan (CP)* offers European-style breakfast (roll or croissant and tea or coffee). *European Plan (EP)* means no meals are included in the price quoted.

Hotel chains in general are becoming more cognizant of the requirements of *women guests.* Inquire at reservation time if interested in "female" amenities such as skirt hangers or "women only" floors, which may require a special key. If security is a concern, it's often wise to take rooms above the first floor and to be sure that hotel personnel do not announce your room number at the front desk. Many women prefer to stay only in rooms that do not have direct access from the outside.

Baby sitter lists are always available in good hotels and motels, and *cribs* are always on hand—sometimes at no cost, but more frequently at a cost of $1 or $2. The cost of a *cot* in your room, to supplement the beds, will be around $3 per night, but moving an *extra single bed* into a room will cost around $7 in better hotels and motels. Many properties don't charge for kids staying in the same room with their parents.

Senior citizens may in some cases receive special discounts on lodgings. The Days Inn chain offers various discounts to anyone 55 or older (September Days Club) with 10-percent discount on rooms, meals, and gift shops at their properties, and up to 50-percent discount on major theme parks. Call 800–241–5050 toll free for information. Holiday Inns give a 10-percent discount year-round to members of the NRTA (write to National Retired Teachers Association, Membership Division, 701 North Montgomery St., Ojai, CA 93023) and the AARP (write to American Association of Retired Persons, Membership Division, 215 Long Beach Blvd., Long Beach, CA 90802). Howard Johnson's Motor Lodges give 10-percent off to NRTA and AARP members (call 800–654–2000); and the ITT Sheraton chain gives 25-percent off (call 800–325–3535). Participating Quality Inns also give a 10-percent discount to AARP members. Participating Ramada Inns offer special prices to NRTA and AARP members, National Association of Mature Persons, and Golden Buckeye Club. Best Western and

Travelodge also offer discounts. (See "Senior Citizen" section below for more information.)

Resort Reservations can book accommodations in virtually any major resort in Florida: 800–327–9154; in Florida: 800–432–9809; in Canada: 800–446–5507. Reservations on duty 9 A.M.–5P.M., seven days.

There are **bed-and-breakfasts** scattered throughout Florida. These are often large, still fairly elegant old homes in quiet residential or semiresidential parts of larger towns or along secondary roads and the main streets of small towns and resorts. Styles and standards vary widely, of course; generally, private baths are less common than they are in hotels, and rates are pleasingly low. In many small towns such guest houses are excellent examples of the best a region has to offer of its own special atmosphere. Each one will be different, so that their advantage is precisely the opposite of that "no surprise" uniformity which motel chains pride themselves on. Few if any have bars. What you do get, in addition to economy, is the personal flavor of a family atmosphere in a private home. In popular tourist areas, state or local tourist information offices or chambers of commerce usually have lists of homes that let out spare rooms to paying guests, and such a listing usually means that the places on it have been inspected and meet some reliable standard of cleanliness, comfort, and reasonable pricing. Call toll free 800–872–4667 for information on these facilities. See also the *Practical Information* sections later in this book.

You might want to try two other types of accommodations, so typical of Florida's lifestyle. **Rental condominiums** are available for one week or longer. Rustic **cottages** in fishing camps are available by the day, week, or longer.

Beautifully furnished condominiums, some of them penthouses, with fully equipped kitchens (china, silver, too), are most prevalent on the Gold Coast (Miami Beach, Fort Lauderdale, Palm Beach, etc.), on Southwest Coast (Sanibel, Ft. Myers), and also on the Pinellas Suncoast (St. Pete Beach, Treasure Island, Redington Beach, Clearwater Beach, etc.). For a family, two couples vacationing together, or a group of friends, the condominium vacation could be less expensive than hotel or motel rooms or suites. And there are all the comforts of home—and more.

Local chambers of commerce and real estate offices would have listings of rental condominiums. (See *Practical Information* sections for "Tourist Information" offices; some condos are also listed in the "Hotels and Motels" sections.) Most are beachfront or adjacent to tennis and golf clubs with ultra-modern, complete resort facilities.

Since Florida has 30,000 lakes, it would be difficult to list all the lakeside fishing camps where serious bass fishermen stay. Lake County has 1,400 named lakes so it's a safe bet the angler will be lucky here, or at least meet sympathetic people to listen to fish stories. There are at least 30 fishing camps with lakeside cottages in Lake County alone (Astor, Clermont, Lady Lake, Lisbon, Leesburg, Tavares). For information, write to Lake County Chamber of Commerce, P.O. Drawer AZ, Eustis, FL 32726.

You might also want to write to the Kissimmee tourist board to inquire about fishing camps near Lake Tohopekaliga (known as Lake Toho by the locals), where the big ones are. Big bass are abundant in the Withlacoochee River if you want to look into fishing camps in Citrus, Levy, and Marion counties. Lake Okeechobee and the Everglades areas also have fishing camps. Another good contact is the Game and Freshwater Fish Commission, 620 South Meridian St., Tallahassee, FL 32301; 904–488-4676.

With increased concern about our health, **spas** are becoming popular, combining a vacation with programs to tone our body. Southeast- and west-coast areas are big on these "resorts."

Florida is a great place to **hostel,** because outdoor activities—biking, canoeing, hiking, rafting, tubing, tennis, jogging, camping—can be enjoyed year round. Some state parks reserve special youth camping sections, such as Three Rivers State Park, north of Chattahoochee and Sneads (off US 90) and Florida Caverns State Park, near Marianna.

American Youth Hostels (AYH) has five locations in Florida (more are being planned) and these are near the Ocala National Forest, a scenic, naturalist location; Camp Wewa, in a citrus grove, lakeside, about fifteen miles from Orlando with a swimming pool and tennis courts; the Riverview in New Smyrna at a beautiful beach (the old, gracious hotel is now a hostel); Epicenter, near Disney World and Sea World, with dormitories, and also a retreat facility for local churches; Young Women's Community Club, downtown Orlando, for female hostelers only.

At Lake Griffin State Park, north of Leesburg on US 27–441 at Fruitland Park, there are youth tent areas. Picnicking, fishing, boating and nature trails are the attractions here. For more AYH information, contact Tourist Bureau, Collins Bldg., Tallahassee, 32304, or write American Youth Hostel Association, Inc., National Campus, Delaplane, VA 22025.

INTERVAL OWNERSHIP VACATIONS. During the 1970s, the concept of interval ownership surfaced in Florida, although the idea had originated during the late 1960s in Europe. "Interval ownership vacation" means investing a few thousand dollars, paid in monthly installments, for a resort condominium apartment or hotel room (if the hotel has an interval ownership program) for a specified period of vacation time, which could be anything from one week to one month every year. Depending on the contract, vacations could be spent at the same place for a specified number of years, but without conveying actual ownership. Other interval vacations do convey ownership, complete with deed, for the specified vacation time period.

Of course, each property has its own variations, including some plans where time periods in one interval vacation facility can be exchanged for another.

Florida not only leads the U.S. with the interval ownership condominium phenomena but also the world. The concept has mushroomed to such dimensions that now there are two organizations exclusively for the time-swapping arrangements—Interval International of Miami (7000 SW 62nd Ave., Miami 33143–1920; 305–666–1861) and Resort Condominiums International, with an office at 4901 NW 17th Way, Fort Lauderdale 33309; 305–491–1342.

There are so many different types of interval ownership that it would be impossible to list the variations of each property in Florida. Among the resort hotels and condominiums that also offer this vacation concept are the Longboat Bay Club and White Sands, Longboat Key; Vistana and Resort World, Orlando; Eagles Nest, Marco Island; Plantation Beach Club, Hutchinson Island; Tierre Verde Resort (near St. Pete); Bayshore Yacht and Tennis Club, Indian Shores (near St. Pete Beach); Penthouse Beach Club, Treasure Island (also near St. Pete Beach); Sanibel Beach Club I and II, Lighthouse Resort, Casa Ybel and Kahlua Beach Club all on Sanibel Island.

DINING OUT. For evening dining, the best advice is to make reservations whenever possible. Most hotels and farm-vacation places have set dining hours. For motel-stayers, life is simpler if the motel has a restaurant.

Several Florida restaurants offer a Senior Citizens' menu (smaller portions at less prices). Also inquire about an extra plate and tableware for two adults who may want to share the entree. Usually this costs an extra $.50 to a dollar for the second person. Good idea for a couple with smaller appetites or who just don't want to eat too much.

The restaurants mentioned in this volume that are located in large metropolitan areas are categorized by price as well as by type of cuisine: French, Chinese, American, etc., with restaurants of a general nature listed as American-International. Restaurants in less populous areas are only divided into price categories as follows: *Super deluxe, Deluxe, Expensive, Moderate,* and *Inexpensive.* As a general rule, expect restaurants in metropolitan areas to be higher in price, but many restaurants that feature foreign cuisine are surprisingly inexpensive.

Although the names of the various restaurant categories are standard throughout the series, the prices listed under each category may vary from area to area. This variation is meant to reflect local price standards, and take into account the fact that what might be considered a *moderate* price in a large urban area might be quite expensive in a rural region. In every case, however, the dollar ranges for each category are clearly stated before each listing of establishments.

RENTAL CARS. When you read the local Florida newspapers, you can't help but notice the inexpensive rates offered by some companies. Please be aware that Florida is the only state in the nation where liability is not automatically included in the car rental price. In Florida, that means the car rental company can do whatever it wants, either provide the insurance coverage or make your insurance company responsible for any claims that might incur.

If you do not carry personal car insurance coverage, you may be asked for a cash or credit card deposit as high as $500. Others will ask a $5 to $10 a week fee to write coverage for the time you rent the car.

However, Hertz, Avis, National, Greyhound, American International, Budget, and Merlin do provide the primary coverage and will not make your insurance company primarily responsible for paying any claims.

Of course, all car rental companies do offer collision coverage with $250 to $500 deductibles. That means the person who rents the car is responsible up to that amount for any damages. The deductible can be covered with a waiver, and most car rental companies sell it for about $2.50 to $5, but it has absolutely nothing to do with your personal insurance.

Since there is so much confusion with liability and collision damage, it's advisable in Florida to rent a car from one of the top companies that at least provide the primary coverage.

The *Practical Information* at the end of each chapter will give you details about rental agencies in specific areas.

BUYING AND SHIPPING. Wherever you travel in Florida, you are sure to see sacks of oranges and grapefruits to buy or ship to friends and relatives. Most of these friendly roadside places offer free, freshly squeezed orange juice while you are selecting your purchase—even if you end up not buying anything. From winter to late spring is the best time to buy; most of the citrus shippers are closed for the summer.

Around the Orlando area, where the roads are lined with citrus groves, the fruit is less expensive. If you're sending fruit to friends, the shipping cost is figured into the price. Durable sacks are already made up into different weights, or you may handpick the fruit and they will pack and ship for you. Most are bonded shippers. During the holiday season, there is always a rush to buy fruit for out-of-state friends. So buy ahead, if you want your gift to arrive in time.

Should you be flying home and want to take sacks of fruit with you, the airlines check in the sacks with your luggage. Just make sure your nametag is on each, as you will notice just about every passenger going home has at least one sack of oranges and grapefruit. When you arrive at your airport, the sacks will be at Baggage Claim with your luggage. If not, don't worry. Some airports, such as Logan International in Boston, take the fruit aside for further protection and place the sacks on a special counter adjacent to the Baggage Claim for that particular flight. Just ask the airline porter if you miss the announcement.

Should you be vacationing in one area for a little while, you might check the yellow pages of the telephone directory for the "Citrus Fruits" listing to get a better idea where to buy. Or you might want to call ahead to ask some questions. These places usually sell citrus jams and marmalades (as well as combinations with semi-tropical fruits such as papaya), citrus candies, the famous coconut patties, even orange or grapefruit wines. If you are a stickler for drinking wine made from grapes only, the Florida fruit wines are delicious in punches and dessert sauces—and make a nice gift.

An interesting stop for citrus candy is Webb's, on US 27, Barnum City, right near Circus World, and en route to Walt Disney World and Sea World. The spacious, sparkling bright candy factory was founded nearly 50 years ago, and you can watch the candy made the old-fashioned way, and taste samples. When is the last time you ate a piece of Goat Milk Fudge? This is another delicious specialty at Webb's, attractively gift-boxed (certainly a conversation piece). The huge, classy gift shop is filled with ideas. Webb's mails and ships.

For bargain hunters, there are factory outlets of all sorts, even for clocks, in central and northeast Florida. Shell shops are everywhere in Florida. Now that interior decorators select beautiful shells to frame mirrors or to display as an artistic collection on shelves and tables, the shell has become fashionable. Jewelry artisans have also suspended unique shells on gold or silver chains or created a stunning necklace. The shell has been elevated to a prized item, and shellcraft has zoomed to popularity.

In Florida's shell shops, most profuse around beach areas, you will find everything from tiny, individual shells to enormous fighting conchs. St. Pete Beach and the Holiday Isles, Key West and Sanibel Island have good buys.

At the Shell Factory and Malacological Museum near Fort Myers, on North Tamiami Trail (US 41), anyone can get "hooked" on shells. This shop claims to be the "largest in the world," and you will agree. There is no admission, and hours can be spent in the fascinating areas. You can buy shells from Florida and from around the world, coral, sponges, fossils, shellcraft supplies, and gifts galore.

Just about every Florida gift shop features boxed miniature palm or citrus trees, weighing no more than a few ounces and all ready for mailing, if you wish. When planted at home, these flourish into attractive plants, and some bear miniature fruit, if you have a green thumb.

Although Canadian Customs are as strict as in the U.S. about taking home plants from another country, these specially packaged "trees" are allowed across the border of any foreign land. The reason is that the plants are usually potted in a synthetic substance, usually vermiculite. Other unique gift ideas: goods from Indian villages; guayaberas (cool Latin shirts); and Cuban coffee (check supermarkets).

FLORIDA FOODS AND WINES. Florida's cuisine includes more than Key lime pie, coconut patties, citrus marmalade, and fried grouper. From various parts of the world, early colonists brought their own groceries, produce, and recipes. Combined with the native Indians' expertise, the result was a delicious, interesting cuisine.

When the colonists arrived in 1565 to what is now St. Augustine, those who had lived on Spanish-ruled Caribbean islands brought along a variety of semitropical fruits, vegetables and seeds, which the Arawak Indians had taught them to prepare. Arrivals from Spain brought salt cod, Valencia oranges, olives, raisins, and even cattle. Their leader, General Pedro Menendez de Aviles, became so friendly with local Indians that the colony was founded right in an Indian village.

Although the Indians had always cultivated corn, papayas, squash, cassava, peppers, etc., they learned new ways of preparation from the colonists and traded recipes. Florida's Indians still prepare cassava for bread, fritters, or as a mashed vegetable.

The Indians taught the Spanish settlers how to barbecue, bake fish and small game encased in clay, how to color and flavor foods with annatto seeds, and introduced peppers. Sauces made with a variety of peppers became an integral part of the colonists' dishes, and the recipes eventually traveled on to other lands.

About 200 years later, after Florida became a British possession, an Englishman with a land grant arrived near St. Augustine with over a thousand colonists, mostly from Minorca, others from Italy and Greece.

The delicious blend of Indian, Spanish, and Minorcan recipes can be enjoyed in St. Augustine now. Pilau, a hearty stew, is probably the most typical, with chicken (or seafood), rice, pork, corn, beans, peppers, and piquant seasoning. Sour oranges were grown long ago here to marinate pork and they still grow in the Ribera House garden, along with other typical fruits of Florida, loquat, fig, wild cherry, plum. For dessert, little cheese turnovers (fromajardis) date back to the Minorcan-Spanish influence. Peppers, which the Indians originally grew, are important to St. Augustine menus, especially the datil pepper relish and the various sauces with seafood.

In Key West, where the heritage is Bahamian, Spanish, and Cuban, and the fishing is so great, it is fun to try the local dishes. Of course, Key lime pie originated here, made from the juice of the small limes and never, never tinted green. One of the favorite dishes is conch chowder with the accompaniment of conch fritters. In Key West, ground conch for these recipes is purchased as easily as ground beef. Just about every restaurant on the Keys serves conch in a variety of dishes. On the street, you can buy a bag of hot bollos, which are well-seasoned bean fritters.

Picadillo is as popular in Key West as it is in St. Augustine, an intriguing combination of sautéed ground beef, onion, olives, raisins and other ingredients, depending on the artisty of the cook. It is usually served with rice and black beans (note the Spanish influence) or a side dish of fried bananas or plantains.

Crispy, freshly baked Cuban bread and rolls are specialties, and warm banana bread is sold by the slice on Key West's famous Mallory Square at sunset. Look for the Banana Bread Man.

Jellies and preserves are made from calamondin, a small, tart, citruslike fruit, and calamondin-glazed cheesecake is a treat in Marker 88, a popular restaurant in Islamorada, en route to Key West.

If you like hearts of palm, you will love swamp cabbage, from the same source in the palm tree. In central Florida and bayou areas, swamp cabbage was a staple for the "Crackers."

Avocados were first cultivated after the Civil War by a Cuban farmer on Maximo Moorings, near St. Petersburg. In Dunedin, part of the Pinellas Suncoast (near Tarpon Springs), Duncan grapefruit were first cultivated by Dr. Duncan.

Miami's "Little Havana" and Ybor City (a Tampa suburb) have contributed to Florida cuisine with Spanish and Cuban specialties, everything from rich bean soups and many-layered sandwiches on crispy bread to elaborate paellas, plantains, luscious desserts, and small cups of strong black coffee. Then there are the famous cigars to top off the meal.

Seafood has been a favorite from the earliest of Indian times, as one can attest from Turtle Mound on the State Archaeological Site near New Smyrna Beach. This oldest Indian mound on the East Coast, composed of seashells which the natives discarded as they shucked their clams, scallops, and oysters for countless centuries is at least fifty feet high.

Florida lobsters are different from Maine lobsters but delicious. Blue crabs, stone crabs (Joe's on Miami Beach is world famous for serving this delicacy), grouper, snapper, calico scallops, smoked mullet, rock shrimp, pompano are distinctive. Apalachicola oysters are at their best just shucked at the many oyster bars in the Apalachicola area and around the St. Marks River near Sopchoppy. And don't miss catfish, spotted sea trout, or crawfish.

Ponce Seafoods, the largest supplier and processor of rock shrimp in the U.S., operates two restaurants where the specialty is the lobster-flavored rock shrimp. The Sand Point Inn is located in Titusville, the Pelican Point is in Cocoa Beach.

When you see "scamp" on the menu, don't think it's a typographical error and that the restaurant really wanted to list "scampi," an Italian shrimp dish. Scamp, a delicious white, flaky fish, is a member of the grouper family, and little known except on the upper Florida Gulf Coast, Local residents consider it a delicacy, and it is scarce because commercial fishermen eat most of the scamp they catch.

Mullet is sometimes called "lisa" in Florida, as that is the Spanish word for mullet. On the Pinellas Suncoast, the St. Petersburg and Holiday Isles area is famous for smoked mullet to enjoy at rustic restaurants or to "take out." The Florida fisherman calls pompano by the short term of "pomp."

On the Miracle Strip, feud cake is often listed under desserts. No one knows how this delicious concoction got its name, but it is made with finely ground pecans (pecan meal) and crowned with rich whipped cream and pecan halves.

If there's anything you want to know about Florida's fish and seafood dishes, or would like Florida seafood recipes, write to Sally Shell, Room 540, State Office Building, 525 Mirror Lake Dr., St. Petersburg 33701. Just enclose a self-addressed stamped envelope for the reply. Sally Shell, a seafood expert, was hired by Florida's Department of Natural Resources to promote the state's fish.

Should your taste buds crave the exotic, such as Florida alligator steak or perhaps whale meat, just make reservations at Bernard's Surf on Cocoa Beach, a famous long-time seafood restaurant (with their own fishing fleet). The chef can prepare sautéed alligator steak just as easily as he concocts flavorful dishes with Cape Canaveral shrimp.

If you want to drink a toast to Florida cuisine, there are citrus wines made by two wine-growers in Pensacola and Tampa, available in liquor stores and large super-markets. Florida Vineyard and Fruit Gardens, owned and operated by Esmond and Malinda Grosz, is currently experimenting with muscadine and light concords. Muscadine is a typically southern wine, mentioned in novels about the South, including *Gone With The Wind.* (Some call it "Scuppernong," but that is a muscadine wine.) The seventy-two acres of Florida Vineyard and Fruit Gardens are at Orange Lake, off US 441, between Gainesville and Ocala. By the way, they have Florida fruit to pick and purchase ten months of the year.

When purchasing Florida oranges and grapefruit, you might like to know the names for the different varieties. Early and mid-season oranges are the Navel (November to January), usually seedless, and easily peeled and sectioned. Best for "hand eating." Hamlin (October to December) is a seedless, medium-size, thin-skin orange, excellent for juice. Pineapple Orange (December to February) is very juicy, very sweet. Late oranges are the Valencia (March to July), a good juicy orange, usually seedless or with but a few and known for the delicious flavor and aroma. Temple Oranges (January to March) are easy to peel and section. Some say this is the finest eating orange grown in Florida. The skin sometimes has a pebbly appearance. Murcott (February to April) is a comparatively new variety of orange with a sweet and juicy, almost deep red interior color—very good for "hand eating." Tangelo (December to March) is a cross between the tart grapefruit and the sweet tangerine. It's very easy to peel and has a delightful flavor. Tangerine (December to February) is known as the "zipper skin fruit" because it's so easy to peel and to section. The ends are comparatively flat and the skin is a very deep orange. Duncan Grapefruit (October to May) is large with a thin pale yellow skin. Although there are clusters of seeds, the delicious, plentiful juice and the flavor are worthwhile. Seedless Grapefruit (November to June) are usually small to medium size with smooth yellow skin and a little flat at the ends. They are very easy to section and may have just a few seeds. Pink Seedless (October to May) is more glamorous because of the rosy color and similar to the yellow seedless. Other Florida citrus fruits include Key limes, Persian limes, Ponderosa lemons, kumquats, loquats, limequats, Calemondin oranges. Also try strawberries in Plant City, tomatoes in Ruskin, and in Miami, rare fruit such as sapodilla.

SENIOR CITIZENS. Florida is especially solicitous of vacationers and residents who are 55 years and over. For example, Miami Beach offers a variety of activities, including weekly dances, concerts, etc. Admission is either free or 50 cents. Check with the Parks and Recreation Department of Miami Beach for exact schedules.

Senior citizen discounts are common throughout Florida, but there are no set standards. Some discounts apply to people over 55, others to people over 60, 62, or 65. Some discounts, like those for prescriptions at the Eckerd Drug chain, require that you fill out a card and register. The best bet is simply to ask whether there is a Senior Citizen Discount available on your ticket or meal or hotel stay. Most municipal, county, state, and federal agencies (national and state parks, city bus lines, state hunting and fishing licenses) offer some sort of price break to the elderly, but definitions of this word varies. Also check with National Senior Citizens Council, 925 15th St. NW, Washington, DC 20005.

For two weeks, beginning usually about May 9, Walt Disney World observes Senior Citizen Days with a Mickey Mouse salute, parades to honor VIP senior citizens, etc. At this celebration, there is also an unlimited attraction ticket to the Magic Kingdom for those 55 years and older.

From about September 15 to December 15, Orlando area celebrates The Senior Citizen Festival with discounts at all the attractions including Disney World, hotel packages, etc. An opening ceremony at Sea World spotlights a well-known senior citizen. Contact *Sea World of Florida,* Senior Activities Director, 7007 Sea World Dr., Orlando, FL 32809.

Sanford, near the Orlando area, features the Golden Age Olympics, when the older generation demonstrates physical prowess in a variety of sports and games. The games are held annually during the second week of November. The only requirement is to be 55 years of age or over; participants can be from anywhere. Most of the week-long festivities are held at the 1,300-seat Civic Center. It all begins with the Lighting of the Olympic Torch Ceremonies, then on to a great variety from checkers and dominos to track and field events. A special trophy to the Decathalon winner, of course. Contact *Golden Age Olympics,* P.O. Drawer CC, Sanford, FL 32771 for information.

Eckerd College in St. Petersburg is part of the Elderhostel program, where senior citizens 60 years old and over study and exchange ideas with students—they are not separated into their own age group. Elderhostel participants stay on campus and Eckerd has its own marina with boats for sailing and fishing. For more information, write to Eckard College, 34th St. and 54th Ave. S., St. Petersburg 33733. Their Innovations in Education program also features advanced courses for professional, retired senior citizens (Academy of Senior Professionals).

Elderhostel headquarters are at 55 Chapel St., Newton, MA 02160.

There are excellent senior citizen recreational centers throughout Florida, especially in the larger cities. Dances, arts and crafts, shuffleboard, special lunches—there is always something going on. Contact the local Chamber of Commerce or check the yellow pages of the telephone directory. In St. Petersburg, for example, everything is listed under Senior Citizens Service Organizations, and there are telephone numbers for all the special discounts in the area, including prescriptions filled at most pharmacies.

Golden Age Passports, allowing senior citizens and companions free admission to National Parks, monuments, and recreation areas, are issued without charge to persons 62 years or older. The passport is good for a lifetime, but you do have to apply in person at National Park Service headquarters in Washington, D.C., regional National Park Service offices, or National Parklands. If you are eligible and didn't know about this before your Florida trip, the Golden Age Passport can be issued in the Everglades National Park office, less than a half hour's drive from Miami. In addition to the Everglades in Homestead, the Castillo De San Marcos Monument in St. Augustine is a National Park where you can use the Golden Passport in Florida, also the Gulf Island National Seashore near Tallahassee. You do have to show proof of age, when applying for the Passport, with a birth certificate or driver's license (Social Security and Medicare cards are not acceptable).

Avis and Hertz car rental agencies both offer AARP members a 20-percent discount on a rented car. Members have to fill out application forms to take advantage of this offer.

Usually in Spring and Autumn, Busch Gardens in Tampa has Senior Citizen Week, when seniors are admitted at reduced prices.

The Fisherman's Inn, 9595 Fourth St. N. in St. Petersburg has application forms to be filled out by persons 60 and older, who will receive a 10 percent discount on all the menu items and a senior citizen card, which has to be shown to the waitress before ordering.

Frisch's Big Boy Restaurants, known for their hamburgers, also give a 10-percent discount to persons 65 and over.

The Bounty Exhibit in St. Petersburg at the Municipal Marina gives a $.50 reduction on the admission price to AARP members who show a current card. The London Wax Museum, 5505 Gulf Blvd., St. Pete Beach, gives a $1 reduction to cardholding AARP members.

Seniors 62 years and over get good reductions on tickets to Rowdies' soccer games, wherever advance admissions are sold, such as Maas Brothers Department Stores. The championship team plays home games in Tampa Stadium.

There are "retirement community" hotels with very reasonable rates for the week, month, or year, including meals, maid service, social program, in St. Petersburg, Bradenton, Lakeland, Palm Beach, Miami Beach, Ormond Beach, etc. These are usually listed under "Retirement Apartments and Hotels" in the yellow pages of the local telephone directory. Many senior citizen vacationers have enjoyed their vacation so much at these hotels that they have decided to stay. Senior Vacation Hotels, with three properties, offers a program modeled after Club Med. For more information: 17401 Central Ave., St. Petersburg 33710.

More and more opportunities for senior citizens are being added, so always inquire, especially at the hotel front desk. (See the "Hotel and Motel" section, above, for more discount information.)

DRINKING LAWS. The drinking age in Florida is 21. Local authorities establish their own closing times; some cities are "open" until 5 A.M.

TIME ZONES. Most of Florida is on Eastern Standard Time, except for the Northwest area, which is on Central Standard Time—an hour earlier. The time zone changes at the Apalachicola River. Daylight Savings Time extends from May through October.

ROUGHING IT. If you are driving to Florida, you will notice that more and improved camping facilities are springing up each year across the country, in national parks, national forests, state parks, in private camping areas, and trailer parks, which by now have become national institutions. Farm vacations continue to gain adherents, especially among families with children. Some accommodations are quite deluxe, some extremely simple. Here and there a farm has a swimming pool, while others have facilities for trailers and camping. For a directory of farms which take vacationers (including details of rates, accommodations, dates, etc.), write to *Adventure Guides, Inc.,* 36 East 57 St., New York, NY 10022 for their 224-page book *Country Vacations U.S.A.* Their other directory, *Adventure Travel U.S.A.,* gives details on guided wilderness trips, backpacking, canoeing, rock climbing, covered wagon treks, scuba diving, and more. Same size and address. Florida has many fish camps with rustic cottages, especially in Lake County. Write to *Lake County Chamber of Commerce,* P.O. Drawer AZ, Eustis, FL 32726.

For roughing it around Lake Okeechobee (and this is really roughing it), take a tour with Leon Stem, a Lake Okeechobee wilderness guide. You will find him three miles north of Lakeport on SR 78 (on the west shore of the lake near Moore Haven) and near the Brighton Indian Reservation woodland. Look for the weather-beaten sign, Stem's Fish Camp.

The Division of Recreation and Parks established the Florida Canoe Trail, including thirty-five rivers. One of the most primitive rivers, the Wacissa, arises from cavernous springs, flowing southward some fourteen miles to meet with the Aucilla River. For Canoe Trail Information, write Crown Bldg., Tallahassee 32304.

Information on canoe trails in the Everglades and national forests can be obtained from the *U.S. Forest Service,* P.O. Box 13549, Tallahassee 32308, and Everglades National Park, P.O. Box 279, Homestead 33030.

Useful Addresses: National Parks Service, U.S. Dept. of the Interior, Washington, DC 20025; *National Forest Service,* U.S. Dept of Agriculture, Washington, DC 20025. For information on state parks, write *State Parks Dept.,* P.O. Box 1050, Tallahassee 32302. Or you can write *Dept. of Natural Resources* for a copy of *Florida State Parks Camping,* Rm. 321, Crown Bldg, Tallahassee 32304, or *Florida Campground Assoc.,* Box 13355, Tallahassee 32808, for information on private sites.

These addresses might be helpful to you should you want to stop en route to Florida: The *National Campers & Hikers Assoc.,* Box 451, Orange, NJ 07051, is an informal organization of camping enthusiasts. Commercial camping organizations include: *American Camping Assoc., Inc.,* Bradford Woods, Martinsville, IN 46151, and *Camping Council,* 17 E. 48 St., New York, NY 10017. Also write to *State Office,* P. O. Box 13355, Tallahassee 32308.

If you like rugged hiking, the *Florida Trail Association* maintains 485 miles of footpaths through backcountry. The club has 5,000 members, and visitors are welcome as guests on most hikes. Contact FTA, P.O. Box 13708, Gainesville, FL 32604.

HINTS TO HANDICAPPED TRAVELERS. Happily, more and more hotels and motels are becoming aware of those things which make traveling simpler for the handicapped. The definitive sources of information in this field are the books: *Access to the World: A Travel Guide for the Handicapped,* by Louise Weiss, available from Facts on File, 460 Park Ave. S., New York, NY 10016. These books cover travel by air, ship, train, bus, car, recreational vehicle; hotels and motels; travel organizations; travel agents and tour operators; destinations; access guides; and health and medical problems. Two other publications that give valuable information about motels, hotels, and restaurants (rating them, telling about steps, table heights, door widths, etc.) are *Where Turning Wheels Stop,* published by Paralyzed Veterans of America, 3636 16th St., N.W., Washington, DC 20010, and *The Wheelchair Traveler,* by Douglas R. Annand, Ball Hill Road, Milford, NH 03055. Many of the nation's national parks have special facilities for the handicapped. These are described in *National Park Guide for the Handicapped,* available from the U.S. Government Printing Office, Washington, DC 20402. TWA publishes a free twelve-page pamphlet entitled *Consumer Information about Air Travel for the Handicapped* to explain available special arrangements and how to get them. A central source of free information is the *Travel Information Center, Moss Rehabilitation Hospital,* 12th Street and Tabor Road, Philadelphia, PA 19141. And you may also get information from the *Easter Seal Society for Crippled Children and Adults,* Director of Education and Information Service, 2023 W. Ogden Ave., Chicago, IL 60612.

The *Florida Council on Handicapped Organizations,* Box 2027, Satellite Beach 32937, provides comprehensive information on vacation facilities for the handicapped.

An advantage of booking a trip with an ASTA travel agency is their professional handling of the handicapped. The agency has the "O.A.G. Travel Planner and Hotel/Motel Guide," with detailed information about airports and accommodations for deaf, blind, wheelchair-confined, and other handicapped persons. Where to find amplified phones in airports, special rest rooms, etc., are all included. Of course, the agent will also contact the airline's special representative to handle all boarding arrangements or other special "needs."

Congress gave permission to airlines allowing reductions for the handicapped (and senior citizens). The travel agent will explain whatever regulations pertain to this discount. If anyone requires a special diet, the agent will notify the airline. *Travel Tips for the Handicapped* can be ordered free from Consumer Information Center, Pueblo, CO 81009.

Travelers with limited mobility may take advantage of *Wheel Chair Wagon Tours,* Kissimmee (305–846–7175). Special tours of key attractions in the area are slated. Both Disney World and Sea World are barrier-free attractions with all facilities for the handicapped, rental wheelchairs, ramps, special phones, etc. Silver Springs in nearby Ocala is also ideal for handicapped visitors. Actually, just about everywhere in Florida, there are excellent facilities for the handicapped. Ramada Inns has been awarded the "Industry Achievement Award" for the elimination of architectural barriers to handicapped persons. Howard Johnson's lists the lodges in their directory which have special accommodations for the handicapped—these rooms are especially constructed on the ground floor with ramps leading from parking to the building. Master Hosts and Red Carpet Inn also have special accommodations and advance reservations are suggested.

Amtrak's new Miami station at 8303 N.W. 37th Ave. replaced the fifty-year-old station that was on 7th Avenue. The station is a barrier-free facility to make rail travel more convenient and attractive for handicapped passengers. Special telephones, ramps, an elevator, and accessible rest rooms are part of the facility. The new Orlando Airport serves the handicapped well.

Hertz provides a Ford LTD equipped with hand controls at Miami Airport. Reservations must be placed with Hertz at least ten days before arrival. Also, the car has to be returned to the airport. The cost for seven days is the same as for the conventionally equipped LTDs. Toll free number is 800–654–3131. National Car Rental (800–328–4567) in South Florida also has specially equipped vehicles.

Amtrak has some new railroad cars especially equipped for the handicapped. Both the blind person and the accompanying attendant now receive a 25-percent discount each off the regular one-way fare. A certificate is required from the American Foundation for the Blind. For information, call AMTRAK's Special Movements Desk at toll-free 800–523–5720.

Bus companies also assist the handicapped. Greyhound's Helping Hand program and Trailways' Good Samaritan program allow the handicapped person and the attendant to travel together for the price of one fare. A doctor's certificate is necessary to prove that the person absolutely could not travel without the attendant's assistance. The local bus office has the details, or contact Greyhound Lines, Director of Customer Relations, Greyhound Tower, Phoenix, AZ 85077, and Continental Trailways, 1512 Commerce St., Dallas, TX.

For the blind person, Sheraton Inns and Hotels and the McDonald's hamburger chain have menus printed in Braille.

In St. Petersburg, DART (Dial-A-Ride Transit) is available within the city limits. The city's Committee for the Assistance of the Physically Impaired has been helpful with this service. DART's vans are lift-equipped to transport wheelchair-confined passengers at special rates. Reservations are made in advance, of course, especially if someone has to be met at the train station. Two forty-five-passenger buses, already owned by the city, have been modified to handle eight to ten wheelchairs, and lifts installed. These are available for charter. Call 813–895–5571.

For the deaf, Pan Am has a special telephone number to call within Florida: 800–722–3323. Each state has a different number for this special assistance, so call Pan Am's local information number listed in the phone book. Many Florida airports have special "telephones" for travelers with hearing impairment.

Did you know that the state of Florida has a recreational park open only to the handicapped and their families? Overnight camping is allowed, and everything from picnic tables to restrooms are made-to-order for wheelchair-confined or otherwise handicapped visitors. Trout Pond (the fishing is good here, too) is in the Apalachicola National Forest, a short distance south of Tallahassee. For details, contact the *Florida Department of Commerce,* Tourism Division, 107 West Gaines St., Tallahassee 32304.

At the Kennedy Space Center in Cape Canaveral, handicapped visitors not able to leave their cars for the bus tour can contact the center at least a week in advance and a guide will be assigned to their car for the three-hour narrated tour at no extra charge. Wheelchairs are available also.

If your Florida itinerary includes the Miami, Miami Beach area, the *Wheelchair Directory of Greater Miami* will be a great help. Write for it to the Florida Paraplegic Association, 6440 S. W. 63rd Terrace, South Miami, FL 33143. The Sarasota County Society for Crippled Adults and Children issues a *Guide to Sarasota for the Handicapped,* which you can request from the society at 401 Braden Ave., Sarasota, FL 33580. The Florida Society for Crippled Adults and Children has a *Guide to the Orlando Area,* which can be ordered from 903 Lee Rd., Orlando, FL 32810.

MORE THAN THEME PARKS

An Introduction To Florida

by
JOEL A. GLASS

Joel A. Glass is a Florida-based writer who specializes in travel and tourism articles for consumer and travel-trade publications in the U.S., Canada, and Europe. A state resident for 13 years, he writes frequently about Florida and formerly served as the Miami-based Southeast Bureau Chief for Travel Weekly. *He is a former president of the Society of American Travel Writers' Atlantic/Caribbean Chapter.*

Contrary to the belief in some quarters, Florida was *not* discovered by Mickey Mouse. Nor was Mickey on hand to greet the individual who *did* discover this part of the New World, Juan Ponce de Leon, who touched foot upon Florida soil near St. Augustine shortly after Easter Sunday in 1513. In fact, the Mouse—that famous, middle-aged mouse who almost single-handedly has created an entirely "new" Florida—did not place his toe on Florida turf until October 1, 1971, when Walt Disney World first opened its marvelous doors.

Ponce de Leon named the state for its abundant flowers, but his real mission was to seek out the illusory Fountain of Youth. He never really found it, but even today, people trek to the state also in search of a magic elixir—if not youth, at least a youthful lifestyle.

Florida has come a long way in a relatively short time. It's a complex, difficult-to-understand, quixotic state not only for those from outside her boundaries but even for those residing within them. Florida's geography, culture, and values are multifaceted and very regionalized, a fact that too often keeps the state as a whole from achieving some of the desirable advances it otherwise could.

A Split Personality

Florida may be compared with states such as California and New York in that it is more than one state in reality, if not geographically. Residents of the northern and southern parts of Florida, as with northern and southern California and upstate and downstate New York, often cannot see eye-to-eye on matters of import. And as with California and New York, the State Legislature is in the northern portion and heavily influenced by politicians from that area, and as a result other parts of Florida sometimes have difficulty making their "case" in Tallahassee.

This split-personality syndrome carries over to the social side as well. Rural north Florida is a bastion of conservatism and fundamental religion, while the southern end of the long state is more developed, more liberal, and much more of an ethnic melting pot.

Today, all of Florida is known as The Sunshine State, a direct claim to its deserved fame as offering some of the finest, most consistently good weather to be found anywhere in the United States—despite a propensity to killer hurricanes, dangerous tornados, violent thunderstorms, and high winds during summer months. Weather also is one of the oddities of Florida, a result of its spanning both temperate and subtropical zones. Thus there can be vast temperature differences between north and south. On the same day, it can be 80 degrees in Miami and 42 degrees in Jacksonville. Central and even southern Florida temperatures can at times drop below the freezing mark.

Because northern Florida's climate is different from that of the state's southern portion, the tourist seasons are reversed. Northern resort areas are at their peak from late spring through fall while the southern portions are most desirable from late fall through spring. Central Florida, where the peaks and valleys of visitor arrivals are more determined by school holidays throughout the year than by quirks of weather, defies the climate.

The "Seven" Coasts

Florida has a lot of tidal coastline—more than 8,000 miles of it—and promoters seem every few years to carve out yet another slice of coast to be dubbed with an eye-catching, fancy name to lure visitors who theoretically would not otherwise come.

While Florida appears on a map to have just two coasts—the Atlantic and the Gulf—it actually has seven thanks to those promoters. The oldest and best-known is The Gold Coast, spanning that expensive piece of Florida real estate from Miami Beach to Palm Beach. The designation alludes to the enormous amount of wealth represented by residents of and visitors to the area. But there also is a lot of wealth in the Naples area on the west coast, which just couldn't take a back seat to the Miami/Palm Beach axis. Ergo, The Platinum Coast! Then there's The Space Coast, stretching from Melbourne to Cocoa as testimony to Cape Canaveral and the Kennedy Space Center, and The Treasure Coast from Stuart to Sebastian, paying homage to eighteenth-century Spanish galleons that sank off that coast with rich cargos of gold, silver, and precious stones.

More recently, three additional "coasts" have been carved out. The Emerald Coast designation was accorded the Destin to Ft. Walton Beach portion of Florida's Panhandle, presumably to honor the color of its offshore waters; The Lee Island Coast went to Lee County, which includes Ft. Myers and Sanibel and Captiva Islands, among other places; and the strip from St. Augustine to Jacksonville became The First Coast, to let people know that that is where the state's—and America's—very first tourists, the Colonial Spaniards, set foot.

Such titles make local people feel good, and, who knows, maybe they *do* entice some people who are fond of gold, platinum, emeralds, treasure, or even outer space to visit the state.

The Natural Wonders

Though some 22 million people of all ages make the pilgrimage to Walt Disney World and Epcot Center each year, the high profile of the world's largest and most sophisticated man-made attraction tends to dwarf what Florida is *really* all about. Though the concentration of sophisticated and not-so-sophisticated theme parks and attractions is probably greater in Florida than anywhere else in the world, the state first and foremost is a celebration of *natural,* not manmade, attractions: from the subtle ecology of the sprawling Everglades with its 2,000 square miles of land and water to the towering awesomeness and tranquility of the Ocala National Forest, from the underwater beauty and mysteries of the nation's only remaining living coral reef off the Florida Keys to the aqua-hued springs of the state's northern and western regions and the superb shelling on Sanibel Island.

And everywhere there are beaches, miles and miles of glorious beaches ranging from the hard-packed, drive-on sands of Daytona Beach to the reclaimed-from-the-ocean sands of Miami Beach and the rockstrewn beaches of Key West. Before Disney and since Disney, millions of people have come to Florida for what is referred to in the state as The Three S's: Sun, Sea, and Surf. That will never change.

What is changing, unfortunately, is how much of those Three S's people still can see, for what draws visitors and new residents to Florida also draws developers who seem to care more for how high they can build condominiums than for the fact that they may be destroying the aeons-old natural environment. In too many parts of Florida, from Miami Beach to St. Petersburg, white high-rises now stand virtually together, blocking from view the very expanses of Atlantic Ocean and Gulf of Mexico that made the state famous and desirable in the first place. Indeed, much of the traffic, overcrowding, and overdevelopment that led many northerners to move to Florida now has followed them to the state. And the threat from modern development extends in from both coasts, threatening some of the rare and endangered species found in such locales as the Everglades.

But despite it all, Florida remains one of the most beautiful states in the U.S., and residents take great pride in living in it—though they are the first to poke fun at its many foibles and often-amateurish handling of such things as politics, education, transportation, and development.

The Floridians

Florida has had, and still does, some notable characters. It has been home to, among others, Ernest Hemingway, whose Key West hangout, Sloppy Joe's, still is a favored watering-hole; Tennessee Williams; Marjorie Kinnan Rawlings, whose *The Yearling* and other books painted vivid pictures of northern Florida's rural ambience and mentality; and Stephen Foster, who from his White Springs home admired the 167-mile-long Suwannee River, surround by moss-encrusted oak and cypress, and felt compelled to write a song about it. And Florida has attracted its share of presidents, such as Harry S. Truman, who vacationed in Key West, and Richard M. Nixon, who did so on Key Biscayne. The state is visited often by rich and poor, famous and notorious, people from virtually every state in the nation and every corner of the globe.

Floridians by and large are a fun-loving, easy-going, and quite informal species, though their "politeness-quotient" decreases the farther south you travel in the state. It's also a state that is very much in transition. In recent years, more and more light industries, as well as individuals, have relocated to virtually all parts of Florida, bringing with them new concepts, ideas, and lifestyles. The result is that the state now is becoming more cosmopolitan and tolerant than it perhaps has been in the past. Change can be seen most everywhere in Florida; even

Miami, which just a few years ago had plunged to the deepest depths to which a city can fall, is undergoing a renaissance into a major international banking and trade center that is leading it to become a major crossroads between Europe and the Caribbean/Latin America.

Florida has strong ties to Cuba; South Florida is home to more than 250,000 refugees who fled their home island when Castro took power. In Tampa's Ybor City you still can watch old Cuban cigar-makers plying their trade, creating fine stogies entirely by hand. There are more than Cubans and Anglos (as non-Latin residents are called) in Florida. There are large concentrations of Finns in Lantana, Scots in Dunedin, Greeks in Tarpon Springs, Spaniards in St. Augustine, American Indians (Seminole and Miccosukee) in southern and western Florida, French Canadians in Surfside, English Canadians in Clearwater . . . and many more.

The impact of the various cultures' mores, cuisines, and ways of life is reflected throughout the state; they are in fact what gives Florida its wonderful mix of texture and flavor that makes it unique even beyond the uniqueness of its weather and physical accoutrements.

Because of that weather, incidentally, Floridians and visitors alike love the outdoors and sports, both spectator and participant versions. Locals and tourists pack the state's horse and dog tracks and jai-alai frontons for excitement and parimutuel betting. Residents go wild over their Miami Dolphins and Tampa Bay Buccaneers. During March, most of the major league baseball teams travel to Florida to play preseason games in what's known as the Grapefruit League, attracting fans to stadiums in sixteen different cities. For people who are outdoors-inclined, the state has provided for its over 10 million residents and 40 million annual visitors an attractive system of twenty-five riverside parks, twenty coastal parks, four garden parks, twenty-seven natural springs, and nineteen island parks to supplement the hundreds of recreation areas and facilities operated by the federal government and local municipalities and counties around Florida.

The Diversity

Because Florida is so large and so varied, it offers a bushelfull of different things for different people, but at least something for everyone.

This is a state where one day you can hob-nob with some of the world's wealthiest people on Palm Beach's Worth Avenue and next day eyeball some of the nation's outcasts along Key West's Duval Street or Daytona's beach. A state where one day you can experience the gentle rolling hills and glorious forests of the northern section, next day visit the stupendous attractions of the Orlando area and the Kentucky-like horse farms around Ocala, and spend your third day experiencing what it used to be like in pre-Castro Cuba by strolling Miami's Little Havana Calle Ocho and sipping strong Cuban coffee while trying to decipher signs printed in Spanish.

In Florida you can munch the popular local catfish on a paper plate in a broken-down, truly Southern shack one night, and spend another night eating gourmet cuisine from imported china in elegant, expensive, sometimes pretentious restaurants.

Take the time to experience north Florida's forests, lakes, rivers, hills, historic sites, and its Panhandle beaches, which many swear are the finest in the world. Move toward the south and drink in gushing springs, horse country, and even the often-crowded manmade attractions. Experience the calmness and beauty of western Florida with its thousands of untouched mangrove islands and contrast them with eastern Florida's futuristic and awesome Kennedy Space Center. Visit the fine historic sites of northeastern Florida and the snazzy shops, restaurants, and beaches of the southeast coast, even the odd mixture on Miami Beach of glitz, well-preserved historic Art Deco buildings, and senior citizens literally starving to death because their children have given up on them. Cap it all off by driving down that marvelous chain of jewellike islands known as the Florida Keys, set in emerald and sapphire seas, to the stripped-down informality and, yes, kookiness of Key West where residents and visitors swear sunsets seen from Mallory Pier excel those of anywhere else in the state—a state known for its beautiful, sparkling sunsets.

But remember, Florida is a *big* state. Distances seen on a map can be deceptive and driving on local roads can be quite slow. So come back again . . . and again . . . and again to see it all. We all promise: You'll be glad you did.

THE MIAMI AREA

by
JAY CLARKE

Jay Clarke, travel editor of The Miami Herald, *is also syndicated to more than 100 newspapers in the U.S. and Canada on the Knight-Ridder wire. He is a Florida native, raised in Miami, and his work has appeared in many magazines and virtually every major newspaper in the country.*

For 11 million visitors a year, Miami is the ultimate place in the sun. Many of them come during the winter, when the climate here is pretty close to perfect and snow and sleet make life dreary in other parts of the country. Temperatures hover in the 60s, the humidity stays comfortably low, the skies are cloudless, the vegetation green and lush, and the surf eminently swimmable. If that's not paradise—at least in wintertime—then it's a close cousin.

But Miami is not simply a winter-only resort; it shed that shackle years ago. Today, summer is just about as busy as winter, even though the summer climate makes this place something less than paradise. It is hot and humid and rainy in summer, no doubt about it, but there's always a sea breeze and Miamians live and work in an air-conditioned world.

The Birth of the Resort

A hundred years ago Miami was simply a settlement at the mouth of the Miami River, not even an incorporated city, and Miami Beach was a sandbar surrounded by mangrove swamps. It was not until Henry Flagler brought his railroad to Miami in 1896 that the city began to develop as a resort. The first big hotel, the Royal Palm, was built at the end of Flagler's line at the mouth of the river; downtown Miami's newest high-rise office buildings stand there now. On Miami Beach, Carl Fisher bulldozed the mangroves, filled in low-lying land, built roads and ritzy resting places, and created one of the greatest resorts of our time.

The New City

Today, multistory hotels and condominiums line the oceanfront as far as the eye can see, and Greater Miami has become not solely a resort but an international business hub. Miami today has more foreign banks than any other American city except New York. It is the regional headquarters for more than 100 large multinational corporations; more than 4,000 manufacturing firms are located here; Miami airport is one of the nation's busiest and second only to New York in international passengers.

The business person has the advantage of living and working in a city with splendid recreational facilities; the tourist reaps the benefits of business orientation—good hotels, restaurants, and transportation. This happy marriage is so attractive that more than a few executives have forsaken promotions that would require them to move away from Miami.

That may sound strange for a city that in recent years has suffered from a spate of unfavorable publicity. But Miamians know that living here is hard to beat. Certainly the city has its problems—among them a high crime rate, thousands of Cuban and Haitian refugees, drug smuggling—but all cities have problems. Miami's seem to have been more publicized than most, because many people did perceive it as something of an earthly paradise. Coupled with a change in tourist habits and the world-wide recession, this has resulted in a decline in tourism here. There are signs now, however, that this trend is reversing. An improved economy is bringing more people to Florida and to Miami. International tourism is picking up; Scandinavian charters have resumed and the prestigious supersonic Concorde now flies regularly out of Miami. Problems are lessening—the crime rate is down, refugees are being assimilated, and the government's efforts to crack down on drug smuggling seems to be having an effect.

The Casual Lifestyle

Miami is truly a metropolis, but the lifestyle here is casual. Outdoors is the key to Miami living, comfort is its mark. Being cosmopolitan people, Miamians can and do "dress up" as the occasion demands. But casual is the preferred state, and many a Miamian has adopted the Latin "guayabera," a decorated open-neck shirt that is regarded as suitable business attire in the tropics.

The idea, of course, is to get the most out of Miami's salubrious weather. Sunning and swimming, to be sure, rate high, but so do backyard barbecues and participant sports—and they are all-year-round activities. Consider: in a city with a population of close to two million, more than 100,000 boats are registered. Dozens of golf courses beckon, and the greens stay green throughout the year. Joggers pound along streets lined with mahogany trees, tennis players may slap away on a public court next to the likes of a Bettina Bunge, a Miami resident, and green thumbers can nurse winter vegetables in dooryard gardens. It's all part of the great outdoors here, and most Miamians take full advantage of it. So do tourists; it's a rare snowbird that doesn't return to his northern home with a tan.

EXPLORING THE MIAMI AREA

Many tourists do not realize until they get here that Miami and Miami Beach are separate and distinct places. Miami is on the mainland. It is a big, business-oriented city on the shore of Biscayne Bay with suburbs stretching out far to the south, west, and north. Miami Beach is on an island across the bay. It's tourist-oriented and linked to the mainland by six island-hopping causeways.

Miami Beach

Despite its recent decline in tourism, Miami Beach is far from a deserted resort. If you think it is, try booking an oceanfront hotel room on short notice in mid-February. The big hotels on the beach are still great tourist magnets. The biggest, the 1,224-room Fontainebleau Hilton, recently underwent a $40-million renovation that has transformed the once-garish snowbird palace of the 1950s into a sleek international resort; its one-acre, free-form pool bordered with a waterfall and stone cave is an eyestopper. The classy Doral-on-the-Ocean perennially scores tops in every guide's hotel ratings, and farther up the ten-mile-long beach, the Sheraton Bal Harbour, also recently refurbished, spreads expansively over its 800 feet of oceanfront.

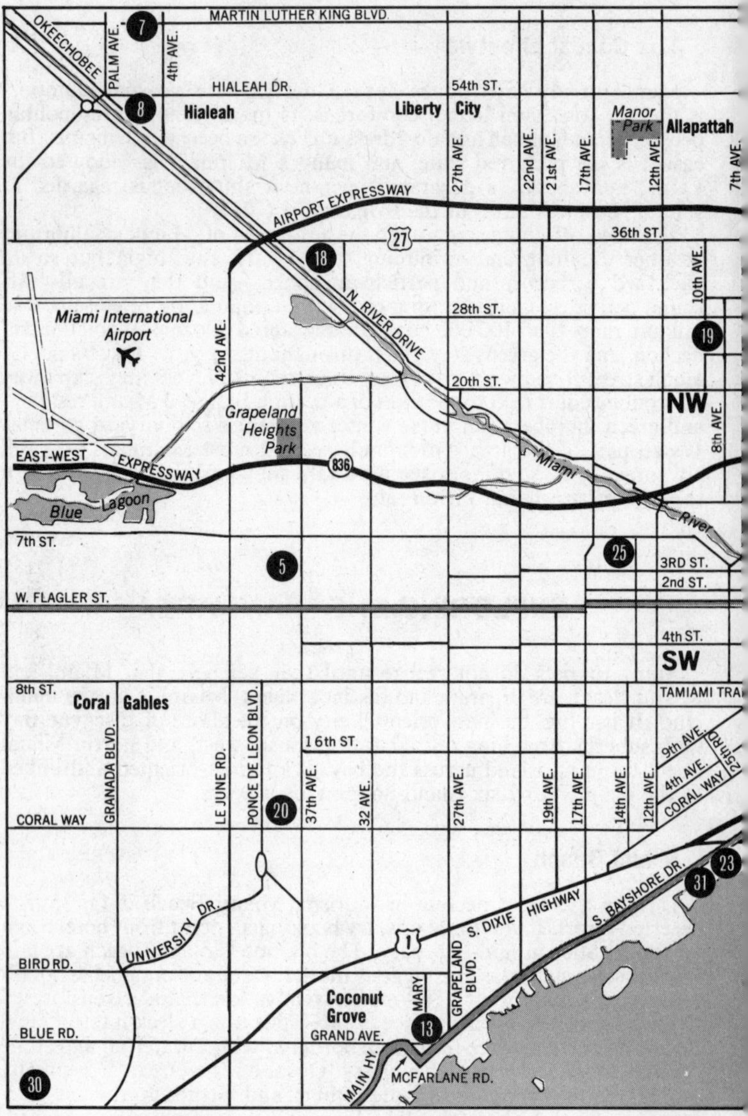
MARTIN LUTHER KING BLVD.
OKEECHOBEE
PALM AVE.
4th AVE.
7
HIALEAH DR.
54th ST.
8
Hialeah
Liberty City
Manor Park
Allapattah
27th AVE.
22nd AVE.
21st AVE.
17th AVE.
12th AVE.
7th AVE.
AIRPORT EXPRESSWAY
27
36th ST.
18
10th AVE.
N. RIVER DRIVE
28th ST.
19
Miami International Airport
42nd AVE.
20th ST.
NW
Grapeland Heights Park
8th AVE.
EAST-WEST EXPRESSWAY
836
Miami River
Blue Lagoon
7th ST.
25
5
3RD ST.
2nd ST.
W. FLAGLER ST.
4th ST.
SW
8th ST.
Coral Gables
TAMIAMI TRA
GRANADA BLVD.
LE JUNE RD.
PONCE DE LEON BLVD.
16th ST.
9th AVE.
4th AVE.
25th RD.
CORAL WAY
20
37th AVE.
32 AVE.
27th AVE.
19th AVE.
17th AVE.
14th AVE.
12th AVE.
CORAL WAY
23
31
S. BAYSHORE DR.
UNIVERSITY DR.
S. DIXIE HIGHWAY
1
BIRD RD.
GRAPELAND BLVD.
MARY
Coconut Grove
13
BLUE RD.
GRAND AVE.
MAIN HY.
MCFARLANE RD.
30

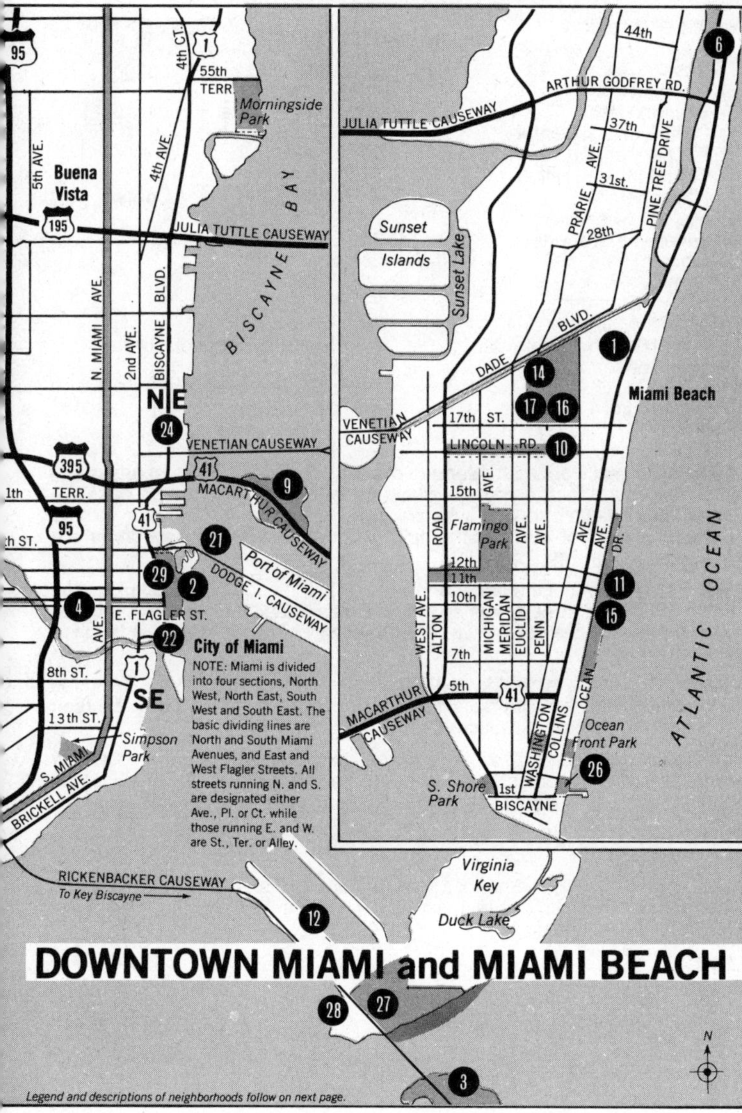
DOWNTOWN MIAMI and MIAMI BEACH
Buena Vista
Morningside Park
55th TERR.
4th CT.
4th AVE.
5th AVE.
JULIA TUTTLE CAUSEWAY
BISCAYNE BAY
N. MIAMI AVE.
2nd AVE.
BISCAYNE BLVD.
NE
VENETIAN CAUSEWAY
MACARTHUR CAUSEWAY
Port of Miami
DODGE I. CAUSEWAY
E. FLAGLER ST.
8th ST.
13th ST.
SE
Simpson Park
S. MIAMI AVE.
BRICKELL AVE.
City of Miami
NOTE: Miami is divided into four sections, North West, North East, South West and South East. The basic dividing lines are North and South Miami Avenues, and East and West Flagler Streets. All streets running N. and S. are designated either Ave., Pl. or Ct. while those running E. and W. are St., Ter. or Alley.
RICKENBACKER CAUSEWAY
To Key Biscayne
Virginia Key
Duck Lake
44th
ARTHUR GODFREY RD.
37th
31st.
28th
PRARIE AVE.
PINE TREE DRIVE
Sunset Islands
Sunset Lake
DADE BLVD.
Miami Beach
17th ST.
LINCOLN RD.
15th
Flamingo Park
12th
11th
10th
7th
5th
WEST AVE.
ALTON ROAD
MICHIGAN AVE.
MERIDAN AVE.
EUCLID AVE.
PENN
WASHINGTON AVE.
COLLINS AVE.
OCEAN DR.
Ocean Front Park
S. Shore Park
1st
BISCAYNE
ATLANTIC OCEAN
N
Legend and descriptions of neighborhoods follow on next page.

Points of Interest

1) Bass Museum of Art
2) Bayfront Park
3) Crandon Park
4) Dade Cultural Center
5) Flagler Kennel Club
6) Fontainebleau Hilton
7) Hialeah Park
8) Hialeah Speedway
9) Japanese Gardens
10) Lincoln Road Mall
11) Lummus Park
12) Marine Stadium
13) Mayfair Mall
14) Miami Beach Garden Center & Conservatory
15) Miami Beach Ocean Front Auditorium
16) Miami Beach Theatre of the Performing Arts
17) Miami Beach Convention Center
18) Miami Jai Alai Fronton
19) Miami Stadium
20) Miracle Mile
21) Miamarina
22) Miami Convention Center
23) Museum of Science
24) Omni International Mall
25) Orange Bowl
26) Pier Park
27) Planet Ocean
28) Seaquarium
29) Southeast Financial Center
30) University of Miami
31) Villa Vizcaya

Coconut Grove. Bohemian blend of the arts, shopping, and sun has made this a playground for the young and old as well as rich and not-so-rich. The "Grove" also boasts its own playhouse, making it a favorite stomping ground for artists. A word of warning: the neighborhood can get a bit rough as you move west.

Coral Gables. One of the first planned cities in the country, beautiful homes line Coral Gables' streets. It is an affluent area with fine shops, restaurants, and corporate offices downtown. The University of Miami gives it a touch of collegiate flair.

Haileah. One of the largest towns in the county with the race track being the top draw. Much of the blue-collar town is employed in light industry. Hialeah has a sizable Hispanic population.

Key Biscayne. Native Miamians retreat to immensely popular Crandon Beach. A pleasant coexistence between the commercial and resort areas has been achieved. Traffic can be overwhelming on the weekends.

Liberty City. A blue-collar region of the city and site of 1980 rioting. An area best avoided.

Miami Beach. Still the center of Miami tourism, and a favorite of the golf and glitter set. Southern tip displays art deco influence. Parks, piers, and a new boardwalk dot its coast.

The Deco District

New stars on the hotel scene are the art deco hotels, built in their distinctive streamlined style back in the 1930s and 1940s. Most of these small, aging hotels are found in the South Beach area on Ocean Drive and Collins Avenue and have been declared a National Historic District. At one point these were considered simply tacky old buildings that would better be replaced with new ones, but a growing and sophisticated coterie of travelers has been attracted to them. Now several of the hotels are being completely renovated and the art deco scene is enlivened with quarterly festivals that introduce as many as 50,000 visitors to that glittering age during a weekend of festivities.

Also new to Miami Beach, oddly, is the beach itself. Severely eroded over the years, some 10 miles of it was replenished in the past several years in a $64-million project. Now the beach is 300 feet wide, bigger than it ever was, and the city has just completed a mile-long landscaped boardwalk that promises to be a new tourist attraction.

At the north end of this new beach is Bal Harbour, one of the area's most upscale communities. Million-dollar yachts tie up at its marina, and their owners often have homes to match in this exclusive enclave. Bal Harbour Shops, with such stores as Neiman-Marcus, Ungaro, and Martha, is perhaps South Florida's most prestigious shopping mall.

Beyond Bal Harbor and Haulover Beach Park you will come upon a sector that may make you think you've stumbled upon an architect's world's fair. This is North Miami Beach's Motel Row, where gaudy facades compete frantically with each other—an Aztec motif next to Southern colonial, a Hawaiian theme opposite contemporary modern. There's good value in these low-rise, oceanfront motels, though, particularly for families who want a room with kitchen facilities. (See "Hotels and Motels" listed under "Haulover, Sunny Isles," in *Practical Information for the Miami Area.*)

Miami

Mainland Miami spreads out from the downtown bayfront all the way to the farm lands 15 to 25 miles to the west. Like a checkerboard, it is divided into many municipalities (27 total in the county) and distinct neighborhoods. Coral Gables, one of America's first planned cities, is known for its beautiful homes and streets. Acre estates cover much of Kendall. Hialeah and Opa-locka are mostly blue-collar communities. Overtown, Liberty City, and Brownsville in the northwest section are the black districts most affected in the 1980 riots.

The Grove

Two Miami enclaves are of particular interest to visitors because of their charm and distinctive personalities. Coconut Grove, on the bay just south of downtown Miami, is a beguiling amalgam of the rich and the poor, of the historical and the modern, of the Bohemian and the sophisticated. An artistic community, it attracts thousands each February to its Arts Festival. The downtown streets are illuminated with old-fashioned gas lights, the sidewalks paved with brick. In the Grove you will find the state's Coconut Grove Theater, where pre-Broadway productions may be staged; Vizcaya Museum, the magnificent Renaissance-style palace; the Museum of Science; and Miami's City Hall. Several yacht clubs, marinas, and parks line the bayfront. Mayfair, a shopping pavilion, attracts the well-heeled to its exclusive shops. Grand Bay and Mayfair House hotels cater to the discriminating traveler. Several local lounges attract the dating crowd.

Little Havana

A different but no less charming kind of atmosphere is found in Little Havana, just west of downtown, where the first Cuban refugees settled twenty-odd years ago. Visitors liken a trip through this enclave to traveling in a foreign country. Store signs are in Spanish, as is the conversation. Little knots of Cubans gather around espresso stands on Calle Ocho (S.W. 8th Street), the district's main street, as they did in their home country. A stop for the strong Cuban coffee should be on a visitor's agenda. Restaurant menus feature specialties such as palomilla steak, black beans and rice, jerked beef, and *arroz con pollo.* Miamians find that the prices are better in many Cuban markets.

Coral Gables

Coral Gables, too, to the west, has much to offer the visitor, from a downtown dotted with small, quality restaurants to the sprawling University of Miami and the bayfront Fairchild Tropical Garden, a nationally known preserve. An excellent paved bicycle trail leads visitors through some of the prettiest parts of the Gables and a marked, self-guided tour follows city streets to other points of interest.

Downtown Miami

Miami's heart, though, lies in its downtown core, easily recognized by the spikey stand of high-rises topped by the new Southeast Financial Center, the tallest building south of Manhattan and east of the Mississippi River. In recent years, some $2 billion in new office buildings and hotels has transformed the face of downtown. The county's new $70-million marble skyscraper headquarters overlooks the equally new, award-winning $42-million Cultural Center, which houses three major institutions—the Center for the Fine Arts, the Historical Museum of Southern Florida, and the main branch of the Public Library. In two years, several major hotels have risen downtown, including the Hyatt

Regency, Pavillon, Miami Marriott on the Bay, Brickell Point Holiday Inn, and the Riverparc.

Brickell Avenue, once a quiet, tree-lined boulevard of homes and estates across the river from downtown, has become the Wall Street of the South, with dozens of financial institutions housed in gleaming new high-rises. Another lure is the new Miami Convention Center next to the Hyatt. Metrorail, Miami's new rapid transit system, provides easy access from both the northern and southern suburbs.

And downtown is still growing. In a couple of years, lunchtime strollers will be able to shop, sip, and sup in a $93-million complex called Bayside, a Rouse Co. development of shops and restaurants nestled around Miamarina and similar to Baltimore's Harborplace and New York City's South Street Seaport. Still expanding, too, is the Port of Miami, the biggest cruise port in the world, just across the channel from Miamarina. On busy weekend days, you can see as many as nine sleek liners at one time taking on some of the two million passengers who sail to and from Miami every year.

Key Biscayne

On their way out of the harbor, the cruise ships pass close to several barrier islands just south of Miami Beach, the largest of which is Key Biscayne. Reached by causeway from the mainland, Key Biscayne is one of the area's most popular recreational destinations. Once a coconut plantation, the key has two major oceanfront parks—Crandon and Cape Florida—as well as hotels, residences, and a commercial sector. A commentary on Miami's postwar growth: back in the 1950s, you could buy small, VA-financed homes on Key Biscayne for as little as $10,000. Today, the same homes are called "villas" and you can't touch one for less than $150,000.

On the Outskirts

Because Miami grew so rapidly after World War II, some facilities that were then on the outskirts of town are now regarded as "close in." Suburbs now extend far beyond Miami International Airport, which used to lie on Miami's fringe, backed up against dairy farms. The busy Palmetto Expressway was criticized as being too far from town when it was built; another expressway has since been constructed well beyond it. Once, nothing but farm land lay beyond South Miami; today, Greater Miami's urban area extends many miles farther.

Miami's new Metrozoo, however, is still a considerable distance out, though it is easily reached by the Palmetto Expressway and Florida Turnpike Extension. The cageless zoo, which has won international acclaim since its opening in 1981, provides a monorail for easy viewing of its 225 acres. Residents (and some tourists) who visit the zoo often drive a little farther west to the farm lands, where they can pick fresh tomatoes, cucumbers, beans, and other winter vegetables in "U-Pick" fields at bargain prices.

Some day in the not-too-distant future, the zoo and the farm lands also may no longer be located on the "outskirts" of town. Already, developers are putting condominiums where tomatoes used to ripen, and concrete fingers of new highways are reaching into former corn fields.

Progress always has its price, but in Miami's case, the new growth seems to promise an even better and more attractive city.

PRACTICAL INFORMATION FOR THE MIAMI AREA

HOW TO GET THERE. Miami, situated on the southeastern coast of Florida, is an important transportation hub. It has the world's largest cruise port, the nation's second-busiest international airport, and is a major business and tourist destination. You can reach Miami by car, plane, bus, or train, and even by boat on certain sailings.

For short trips within the state, car and bus are the best modes of travel, but there is frequent and cheap air service between Miami, Tampa, and Orlando. For convenience and flexibility, a car is the best bet.

By air. More than 75 airlines, including every domestic trunk line, many regional carriers, and more than 35 foreign operators, serve Miami. Miami is an important gateway to the Caribbean and Latin America, with many nonstop flights available to the major South American capitals and Caribbean islands. It is also a major gateway to Europe, with nonstops to London, Frankfurt, and Madrid and direct service to a number of other European cities. Within the United States, many lines offer service to Miami. Because of this heavy concentration, many discounts are available to and from, though these change frequently. When planning travel to Miami, check not only with the larger airlines, but also with smaller ones, such as *Piedmont,* which offer deep discounts on certain flights. Between Miami and Tampa or Orlando, *Pan American* runs "air bridge" service with many flights a day at low cost. Miami does not have as many charter operations as the big cities of the Northeast, but it does offer regular charters to London and Frankfurt, Las Vegas, and Canada at fares considerably below those offered by the scheduled airlines.

By bus. Both *Greyhound* and *Trailways* serve Miami with frequent arrivals and departures, including express buses to some large cities and special destinations such as Disney World. Travel passes for unlimited or discounted travel for specified periods and/or regions are offered by both companies. Greyhound's main depot is located at 950 N.E. 2nd Ave., Miami (phone 305–374–7222), with suburban stations in Coral Gables at 2300 Salzedo St. (305–443–1664); Hialeah-Miami Springs at 93 W. Okeechobee Rd. (305–885–1413); Homestead at 5 N.E. 3rd St. (305–247–2040); Miami Beach at 1622 Collins Ave. (305–538–0381); North Miami Beach at 16250 Biscayne Blvd. (305–945–0801); and Perrine at 650 Perrine Ave. (305–251–2459). The Trailways main office is at 99 N.E. 4th St., Miami (305–373–6561), with suburban terminals at Coral Gables at 2300

Salzedo St. (305–443–1664) and in northwest Miami at 4101 N.W. 27th Ave. (305–634–6523).

By train. This is an *Amtrak* terminal served by two daily trains from New York, the *Silver Meteor* and the *Silver Star.* In addition, the *Silver Palm* operates daily between Miami and Tampa via Winter Haven and Disney World. Special rates are available. The depot is at 8303 N.W. 37th Ave., Miami. Phone 800–872–7245 for information.

By car. In summer, most tourists arrive here by car, in contrast to winter, when most arrive by airplane. Since a car is a virtual necessity for transportation within the Miami area, tourists who do not drive themselves to Miami usually rent a car once they are here. Miami lies at the southern end of Interstate 95 and of the Florida Turnpike. You can also reach Miami via US 1 from the north, US 27 from central Florida, and US 41 (the Tamiami Trail) from the Gulf coast of the state. For information on rental cars, the "How to Get Around" section, below.

By boat. Miami is the world's largest cruise port, but these sailings are round trips. A few lines, however, offer one-way passage to or from Miami or nearby Port Everglades and Europe, usually in the fall or spring, when the liners are repositioned. For information, contact individual cruise lines or the Port of Miami, 1015 North American Way, Miami (305–371–7678) or the Port Everglades Port Authority, 3360 Pan American Dr., Fort Lauderdale (Miami number: 305–945–6701).

TELEPHONES. The area code for Greater Miami is 305. Local calls cover most of the county, but those to nearby Broward County locales such as Hollywood and Fort Lauderdale are considered long-distance, and you first must dial 1. Local telephones calls cost $.25.

EMERGENCY NUMBERS. For emergency police, fire, or ambulance service in Greater Miami, dial 911. You may also dial 0 for the operator, who can assist you. Stay on the line and give information as clearly and concisely as possible. For emergency fire/police/ambulance service for deaf mutes with telecommunications devices, call 595–4749.

SECURITY. Like other large urban areas, Miami has its share of problems, though the past year has seen a substantial decrease in both violent and property crime here. Still, precautions should be taken. Hotel guests should not leave jewelry, money, or other valuables in their rooms; such items should be checked into the hotel's safe-deposit boxes. Most areas frequented by tourists are safe, but certain others should be avoided at night. Generally, these are the poorer sections of town—the Overtown and Liberty City districts in the northwest section, western Coconut Grove and parts of South Beach. Downtown Miami streets are safe in daytime, but one should be wary about wandering far from hotels at night. If in doubt, ask hotel front-desk personnel for advice and directions.

HOTELS AND MOTELS. Because this is a resort area, rates rise and fall seasonally in many hotels and motels. Most affected are properties on Miami Beach and other oceanfront areas where tourists tend to congregate. High-season rates apply from around December 15 to April 15, low season from April 15 to December 15, but there are peaks and valleys within both seasons. This means there may be great price variations during the year; at some hotels, the peak winter rate may be as much as twice the lowest summer rate. On the other hand, many hotels and motels on the mainland, which cater primarily to businessmen, have year-around rates.

Since the Miami area has hundreds of hotels and motels, the following list represents only a selection of the facilities available. Hotels are listed below by their year-round or peak-season rate, in the following categories, based on double occupancy: *super deluxe,* $100 and up; *deluxe,* $80 to $100; *expensive,* $70 to $80; *moderate,* $60 to $70; *inexpensive,* $50 to $60. In nonpeak rate periods, many hotels will drop a category or two, particularly those in oceanfront areas, where it is easy to obtain a motel room for less than $50 during the summer.

A wide variety of package plans is available both in winter and summer, which also can reduce per-day room costs. All hotels and motels listed are air-conditioned and virtually every one has a swimming pool and lounge.

Free lists of hotels can be obtained from the Metro/Dade County Department of Tourism and the Tourist Development Authority of Miami Beach (see "Tourist Information," below).

AIRPORT AREA

Super Deluxe

Doral Country Club. 4400 N.W. 87th Ave., Miami; 305–592–2000. Ten minutes from the airport. Resort complex with five golf courses, lighted tennis courts, pool, wading pool, several bars and restaurants, solarium, health club, recreation room. Free bus to Doral-on-the-Ocean hotel.

Marriott Hotel and Racquet Club. 1201 N.W. 42nd Ave., Miami; 305–649–5000. On airport periphery. Lighted tennis courts, several restaurants and bars, pool, courtesy van to airport.

Miami Airport Hilton and Marina. 5101 Blue Lagoon Dr., Miami; 305–262–1000. On airport periphery, opened 1984. Situated on lake and has marina with boating, water-skiing facilities, restaurants and bars, courtesy van to airport, pool.

Sheraton River House. 3900 N.W. 21st St., Miami; 305–871–3800, on airport periphery. Lighted tennis courts, public golf course adjacent, courtesy van to airport, restaurant, bar, pool.

Deluxe

Holiday Inn Crowne Plaza. 950 N.W. LeJeune Rd., Miami; 305–446–9000. On airport periphery, restaurant, bar, pool, sauna, limousine to airport.

Expensive

Miami Viscount Hotel. 500 Deer Run, Miami Springs; 305–871–6000. On airport periphery. Complex occupies former estate of aviation pioneer Glenn Curtiss plus other buildings. Six restaurants, five lounges, pool.

Moderate

Ramada Inn-Airport. 3941 N.W. 22nd St., Miami; 305–871–1700. On airport periphery. Restaurant, bar, courtesy van to airport.

Miami Airport Inn. 1550 N.W. LeJeune Rd., Miami; 305–871–2345. On airport periphery. Pool, bar. Has Playboy Club on premises—temporary membership for guests.

Miami International Airport Hotel. Atop Miami International Airport terminal; 305–871–4100. Only hotel on airport premises. Rooftop restaurant, bar.

Inexpensive

Miami Skyways. 2373 N.W. 42nd Ave., Miami; 305–871–3230. Restaurant, pool, bar, courtesy van to airport.

Quality Inn. 1850 N.W. LeJeune Rd., Miami; 305–871–4350. On airport periphery. Restaurant, bar, courtesy van to airport.

DOWNTOWN MIAMI

Super Deluxe

Hyatt Regency. 400 S.E. 2nd Ave., Miami; 305–358–1234. High-rise on river, attached to Miami Convention Center. Restaurants, bars, meeting rooms, pool.

Miami Marriott on Biscayne Bay. 555 N.E. 15th St., Miami; 305–374–3900. Opened 1984. High-rise with marina (sailboats for rent), restaurants, bar, pool.

Omni International. 1601 Biscayne Blvd., Miami; 305–374–0000. Occupies top 20 floors of Omni Mall, which has about 160 shops, two department stores; one block from bay. Restaurants, bars, disco, meeting rooms, tennis courts, pool.

Pavillon. 100 Chopin Plaza, Miami; 305–577–1000. Marble-encased high-rise at mouth of the river and bay, with tennis courts, health club, excellent cuisine.

Riverparc. 100 S.E. 4th St., Miami; 305–374–5100. On the river next to the Hyatt and Miami Convention Center. Small hotel, all suites, opened 1984. Restaurant, bar, pool.

Deluxe

Holiday Inn on Biscayne Bay. 495 Brickell Ave., Miami; 305–373–6000. On the bay a hundred yards from mouth of river. Restaurant, bar, pool, courtesy van to Port of Miami.

Expensive

Howard Johnson's. 1100 Biscayne Blvd., Miami; 305–358–3080. Restaurant, bar, pool, near Omni.

Moderate

Howard Johnson's. 200 S.E. 2nd Ave., Miami; 305–374–3000. Adjacent to Hyatt and Miami Convention Center. Restaurant, bar.

Marina Park. 340 Biscayne Blvd., Miami; 305–371–4400. Overlooks Bayfront Park. Restaurant, bar, pool.

Inexpensive

Dupont Plaza Hotel. 300 Biscayne Blvd. Way, Miami; 305–358–2541. On the river, across street from Hyatt and Miami Convention Center. Restaurant, bar, meeting rooms, pool.

COCONUT GROVE, CORAL GABLES

Super Deluxe

Coconut Grove. 2649 S. Bayshore Dr., Coconut Grove; 305–858–2500. Restaurant, bar, pool, entertainment, meeting rooms, tennis.

Grand Bay. 3250 Mary St., Coconut Grove; 305–858–9600. Top-class hotel, restaurants, bars, meeting rooms, health club, sauna. All rooms with bay-view, private terraces. *Regine's* club located in hotel.

Grove Isle. 4 Grove Isle, Coconut Grove; 305–858–8300. Located on island off S. Bayshore Drive. Restaurant, bar, tennis, health club, sauna, boating.

Mayfair House. 3000 Florida Ave., Coconut Grove; 305–441–0000. Opened in 1985. Luxury hotel above chic Mayfair Mall.

Mutiny at Sailboat Bay. 2951 S. Bayshore Dr., Coconut Grove; 305–442–2400. Restaurant, bar, sauna, private patios.

Deluxe

Bounty. 2585 S. Bayshore Dr., Coconut Grove; 305–854–1800. Private patios, free continental breakfast.

David William. 700 Biltmore Way, Coral Gables; 305–445–7821. High-rise with restaurant, bar, rooftop night club, health club.

Moderate

Holiday Inn. 2051 JeJeune Rd., Coral Gables; 305–443-2301. Restaurant, bar, pool, sauna, Popular *Greenstreet's* night club.

Holiday Inn. 1350 S. Dixie Hwy., Coral Gables; 305–667–5611. Opposite University of Miami. Restaurant, bar, pool, popular *Sea Shanty* restaurant.

Place St. Michel. 162 Alcazar, Coral Gables; 305–444–1666. In remodeled downtown building. Excellent restaurant.

Inexpensive

Chateaubleu Inn. 111 Ponce de Leon Blvd., Coral Gables; 305–448–2634. Downtown area motel.

Howard Johnson's. 1430 S. Dixie Hwy., Coral Gables; 305–665–7501. Opposite University of Miami. Pool and restaurant, no bar.

Riviera Court. 5100 Riviera Drive, Coral Gables; 305–665–3528. Near University of Miami, on Coral Gables canal. No restaurant or bar, efficiencies available.

KEY BISCAYNE

Super Deluxe

Key Biscayne Hotel and Villas. 701 Ocean Dr., Key Biscayne; 305–361–5431. Hotel rooms, one- to three-bedroom villas on 800 feet of oceanfront. Tennis center, 18-hole par-3 golf course, pool, bars, restaurant, beach.

Sheraton Royal Biscayne. 555 Ocean Dr., Key Biscayne; 305–361–5775. Tennis, two pools, playground, restaurant, bar, entertainment, barber, meeting rooms, tennis.

Sonesta Beach Hotel and Tennis Club. 350 Ocean Dr., Key Biscayne; 305–361–2021. Also has three-bedroom villas. Restaurant, bars, tennis center, entertainment, barber, drugstore, meeting rooms, sailing, bicycling, lawn games. On beach.

Deluxe

Silver Sands Motel. 301 Ocean Dr., Key Biscayne; 305–361–5441. Ocean front motel. All rooms have kitchenettes; two-room cottages, oceanfront apartments also available. Pool, restaurant, bar. On beach.

MIAMI BEACH, BAL HARBOUR

Super Deluxe

Doral. 4833 Collins Ave., Miami Beach; 305–532–3600. Restaurants, bars, rooftop dining, health club, solarium, sauna, pool, free bus to Doral Country Club facilities, which include five golf courses, tennis. On beach.

Eden Roc. 4525 Collins Ave., Miami Beach; 305–531–0000. Restaurant, bar, pool, sauna, disco. On beach, next to Fontainebleau.

Fontainebleau Hilton. 4441 Collins Ave., Miami Beach; 305–538–2000. Largest hotel in Miami area, with one-acre pool, cabanas, gym, solarium, restaurants, bars, night clubs, meeting facilities, drug store, barber, etc. Lighted tennis courts, jet skis, bowling alley, game room, billiards. Free bus to golf on mainland. On beach.

Konover. 5445 Collins Ave., Miami Beach; 305–865–1500. Restaurant, bar, pool, health spa, game room, barber/beauty shop. On beach.

Sheraton Bal Harbour. 9701 Collins Ave., Bal Harbour; 305–865–7511. Extensive grounds, two pools, restaurants, bars, night club with full-scale revue in winter, disco, solarium, sauna, etc. On beach.

Alexander. 5225 Collins Ave., Miami Beach; 305–865–6500. Opened 1983. All suites with full kitchens, two pools, *Dominique's* restaurant, bar. On beach.

Deluxe

Carillon. 6801 Collins Ave., Miami Beach; 305–865–4578. Restaurants, bars, health club, two tennis courts, entertainment. On beach.

Deauville. 6701 Collins Ave., Miami Beach; 305–865–8511. Restaurant, bar, pool, tennis courts, sauna. On beach.

Sea View. 9901 Collins Ave., Bal Harbour; 305–866–4441. Beachfront hotel with restaurant, bar, pool, shuffleboard, masseuse, game rooms.

Moderate

Seville. 2901 Collins Ave., Miami Beach; 305–532–2511. Restaurant, bar, lounges, gym, pharmacy, game room. On beach.

Shelborne. 1801 Collins Ave., Miami Beach; 305–531–1271. On beach. Restaurant, bar, pool, night club, game room.

Singapore Resort Motel. 9601 Collins Ave., Bal Harbour; 305–865–9931. Located on the beach. Restaurant, bar, pool, meeting rooms, efficiencies available.

Inexpensive

Art Deco Hotels. Five hotels in art deco district facing ocean, opposite beach: 1144 Ocean Dr.; 305–534–2135. Hotels in art deco style, dating to 1930s and 1940s. **Carlyle** and **Cardozo** are the best; they have restaurants, bars, and pools. These are undergoing renovation during 1985 so it's best to check which are open.

HAULOVER, SUNNY ISLES

Super Deluxe

Diplomat. 3515 S. Ocean Dr., Hollywood; 305–949–2442. Located just over the line in Broward County, but usually listed with Miami area hotels. The main high-rise building has been recently refurbished; the lower west building across the street has lower-priced smaller rooms. Three pools, nine restaurants, three lounges, two golf courses, tennis courts, solarium, beauty shop, game rooms, meeting facilities. On beach.

Deluxe

Golden Strand. 17901 Collins Ave., North Miami Beach; 305–931–7000. Pool, complete spa, restaurant, bar.

Newport. 16701 Collins Ave., North Miami Beach; 305–949–1300. Restaurant, pool lounge, entertainment, tennis, boating, boutique, sauna. On beach.

Marco Polo. 19201 Collins Ave., North Miami Beach; 305–932–2233. Pool, restaurant, lounge, dance studio, tennis courts. On beach.

Pan American. 17875 Collins Ave., North Miami Beach; 305–932–1100. On beach with restaurant, pool, bar, tennis.

Expensive

Thunderbird Resort Motel. 18401 Collins Ave., North Miami Beach; 305–931–7700. Pool, three restaurants, two lounges, Jacuzzi. On beach.

Moderate

Desert Inn. 17201 Collins Ave., North Miami Beach; 305–947–0621. Beach property. Restaurant, bar, pool, game room.

Inexpensive

Aztec. 15901 Collins Ave., North Miami Beach; 305–947–1481. Oceanfront hotel: restaurant, bar, heated pool, meeting room.

Hawaiian Isle. 17601 Collins Ave., North Miami Beach; 305–932–2121. Two pools, two restaurants, two lounges, tennis court, playground, health spa, meeting rooms. On beach.

Sahara. 18335 Collins Ave., North Miami Beach; 305–931–8335. On beach with restaurant, bar, pool.

Waikiki. 18801 Collins Ave., North Miami Beach; 305–931–8600. Beach and three pools, two restaurants, lounge.

Castaways. 16375 Collins Ave., North Miami Beach; 305–945–3461. Beach and three outdoor pools, one indoor, restaurant, bar, sauna, playground, boating, tennis court.

CAMPING. The Miami area has very few campgrounds —only two commercial facilities and one public one. *Miami North KOA,* 14075 Biscayne Blvd., Miami 33161, 800–548–7239 or 305–940–4141, has pull-through sites, heated pool, Jacuzzi, gameroom, playground. *Miami South KOA,* 20675 S.W. 162nd Ave., Miami 33187, 305–233–5300, has pull-through sites, heated pool, hot tub. *Larry and Penny Thompson Park,* at 12451 S.W. 184th St., 305–232–1049, has trailer and tent campsites, lake swimming, and picnic facilities. (See also the Everglades section at the end of this chapter.)

HOW TO GET AROUND. Miami is a spread-out city with 27 municipalities in Dade County. The downtown business district lies on Biscayne Bay. Miami generally divides into four sections—Northeast, Northwest, Southeast, and Southwest by Miami Ave. running north–south and Flagler St., running east–west. But there are exceptions, including Coral Gables and Hialeah. Miami Beach and other oceanside resort communities are on barrier islands reached by causeways from the mainland. Collins Ave. is the main thoroughfare in Miami Beach, running north–south. Newly completed *Metrorail,* the area's first rapid-transit system, runs from Hialeah through downtown to the southern suburbs. Bus service covers much of Miami, but a car is necessary to and from cities and sightseeing attractions.

From the airport: Downtown Miami is seven miles and fifteen minutes from Miami International Airport. Miami Beach is about twice as far, depending on what section you are traveling to. Taxi fares are about $12 to downtown, $16 to mid-Miami Beach, $8 to downtown Coral Gables. (See below.) Limousines, which can be found departing periodically from the airport, charge $6 per person to downtown Miami, $7 per person to Miami Beach. Bus service from the airport is extremely limited. Car rentals are available (see below).

By bus. The county-operated *Metrobus* system covers most of Miami, but may involve one or more transfers. Coral Gables has a bus terminal, but other communities do not. Bus fare is $.75 exact change. Senior citizens can travel for $.35 in non-rush hours (9:00 A.M. to 4:00 P.M.). Student fare is $.35, but those over 12 must have a bus pass from their teacher. Rush-hour express buses run between Golden Glades in north Miami and downtown business centers, and between Tropical Park in west Miami and those centers. For bus route information call 638–6700.

By rapid transit. Miami's new Metrorail opened its final leg in 1985 and now runs from Dadeland in south Dade County through downtown to Hialeah in the north. Stops are spaced about a mile apart and include South Miami, the University of Miami, Vizcaya/Museum of Science, Brickwell Avenue, Government Center, Civic Center, and Hialeah Race Track. Fare is $1. For information call 638–6700.

By taxi. Taxi rates are high in Miami—$1 for the first 1/3 mile, $.20 for each 1/6 mile thereafter. Among the larger cab companies are *Yellow Cab* (444–4444), *Super Yellow Cab* (885–5555), and *Metro Taxi* (888–8888).

By car. For most travelers, a car is a necessity here. Those who plan to spend most of their time in a resort hotel may not need a car, but South Florida does have the lowest car rental rates in the country, with compacts available for as little as $69 a week with unlimited mileage, sometimes for less during car rental wars. *Avis* (800–331–1212); *Budget* (305–871–3053); *Dollar* (800–421–6868); *Greyhound* (305–887–6000); *Hertz* (800–654–3131); and *National* (800–328–4567) all have offices at the airport and well as others throughout the county. A number of other rental firms, including *General* (305–871–3573), are located on the airport periphery. All told, there are more than 100 car-rental companies in the Miami area. Most major companies assess no drop-off charge if cars are returned to another city within Florida.

Motorists should avoid the major expressways and highways during rush hours, from 7:00 to 9:00 A.M. and 4:00 to 6:00 P.M. Certain expressways and highways also have car-pool lanes, on which only cars with two or more passengers may travel during the rush hours; these lanes are marked with a diamond and car-pool signs. The Rickenbacker Causeway from the mainland to Key Biscayne tends to become crowded on weekends, when beach-bound motorists drive to the island in the morning and early afternoon and return in the late afternoon. Limited metered curbside parking is available downtown at reasonable rates. There also are a number of parking garages, but rates may run more than $1 an hour. Elsewhere, you will encounter few problems in parking, except around the Orange Bowl during Miami Dolphin or University of Miami football games.

By tram. The *Coconut Grove Tram* takes visitors through this charming Miami suburb on weekends, operating from noon to 5:00 P.M. from Castle Harbor Sailboats at Dinner Key. Tickets are $3 adult, $1.50 for children. Call 446–1603 for information.

TOURIST INFORMATION. Several tourist offices can provide you with information. Countywide is the *Metro/Dade County Department of Tourism,* 234 W. Flagler St., Miami, 33130 (305–375–4694), which publishes brochures, maps, and other information in several languages. The *Visitor and Convention Authority of Miami Beach* offers same service for that city. It is located at 555 17th St., Miami Beach; phone 305–673–7060. *Sunny Isles Resort Association* services the north beach area. It is at 17070 Collins Ave., Sunny Isles; 305–947–5826. Chambers of commerce of various municipalities also are good sources of information. Some of them: *Greater Miami Chamber of Commerce,* 391 N.E. 15th St., Miami, 305–350–7700; *Miami Beach Chamber of Commerce,* 1920 Meridian Ave., Miami Beach, 305–672–1270; *Coral Gables Chamber of Commerce,* 50 Aragon Ave., Coral Gables, 305–446–1657; *Coconut Grove Chamber of Commerce,* 3437B Main Hwy., Coconut Grove, 305–444–7270; *Key Biscayne Chamber of Commerce,* 95 W. McIntier St., Key Biscayne, 305–361–5207. You can also contact the *Greater Miami Hotel and Motel Association,* 300 Biscayne Blvd. Way, Suite 618, Miami, 305–371–2030, and the *Southern Florida Hotel and Motel Association,* 3425 Collins Ave., Miami Beach, 305–864–2289.

SEASONAL EVENTS. January. The *Orange Bowl Festival* reaches its climax with the football classic in the Orange Bowl the night of January 1. (See December events also). The Festival also has two post-game events: the *Three Kings Parade* takes place on the Sunday nearest January 6 in Little Havana to celebrate Epiphany, the day the Three Wise Men visited the Christ child. The *Orange Bowl Marathon* is usually held in mid- or late January, running through a picturesque 26-mile course. The *Homestead Rodeo,* biggest in South Florida, is held in Homestead in late January or early February.

February. *Budweiser Miami Grand Prix* draws top drivers to race through downtown Miami streets. *Coconut Grove Arts Festival* attracts thousands to this picturesque section of town. *Doral-Eastern Golf Tournament* at Doral Country Club is a regular on the pro golf tour (sometimes in March). *Miami International Boat Show,* one of biggest in U.S., is held at Miami Beach Convention Center. *Around the World Fair* is held the first weekend of the month.

March. *Carnaval Miami* is a major festival centered on Calle Ocho (8th Street) in Miami's Little Havana section, with parades, arts, crafts, foods, and a Carnaval night in the Orange Bowl. *St. Patrick's Day Parade* is held downtown March 17. *Dade County Youth Fair,* three weeks in duration, is the biggest in the nation, at Tamiami Park. Major league baseball teams start *spring training* (Baltimore Orioles at Miami Stadium, New York Yankees in nearby Fort Lauderdale at Lockhart Stadium). *Renaissance Festival,* a medieval fair, is held on grounds of Vizcaya.

May. *Miami Home Show,* a major show with furnishings, etc., at Miami Beach Convention Center.

June. *Goombay Festival,* centering on Bahamian arts, foods, and culture, in Coconut Grove.

August. *Bowling Tournament of the Americas* attracts top bowlers from all over the hemisphere to Cloverleaf Lanes, North Miami Beach.

October. *Dinner Key Boat Show,* another major boat exhibition, is held at Coconut Grove Exhibition Center. *Baynanza,* a boat-oriented event that includes Columbus Day regatta to Elliott Key, is held over Columbus Day weekend. *Hispanic Heritage Week* highlights culture of Miami's large Hispanic population.

November. *Renaissance Fayre,* a medieval fair, is held at Crandon Gardens on Key Biscayne.

December. *Orange Bowl Festival* runs from mid-December into January, includes World Junior Tennis Championships, Intercollegiate Sailing Regatta, Fashion Show, King Orange Jamboree Parade on New Year's Eve (largest night parade in the world), and Kwanza (an African festival).

TOURS. Bay cruises. *Gold Coast Cruises* at the Haulover Park Marina (10800 Collins Ave., Miami Beach; 945-5461) sends four sightseeing vessels on a variety of cruises on Biscayne Bay, from a two-hour tour of the luxury islands (Millionaires' Row, $6.50) to all-day sailings, landside visits included, to the Seaquarium ($15.50), Vizcaya ($14), or a combination of the three ($22). Three times a week, Gold Coast runs a tour to Fort Lauderdale to board the *Jungle Queen* for a cruise up the New River ($11.50). *Haulover Park Dinner Boats,* departing also from Haulover Marina (947–6105), offer three-hour luncheon sightseeing cruises on the bay aboard its *Freedom* ($12.50); dinner cruises with music cost $15.95, last four hours. *Show Queen* (Crandon Park Marina, 4400 Rickenbacker Causeway, Key Biscayne, 361–9418) also offers dinner cruises with live music several times weekly at $18.95. *Island Queen* (Miamarina, N.E. 5th St. and Biscayne Blvd., Miami, 379–5119) operates a Millionaires' Row cruise three times daily ($6).

A newcomer is the *Reef Rover III,* which has begun cruises with Biscayne National Park, the island-dotted preserve that covers much of southern Biscayne Bay. The tours last four to five hours, include a couple of hours on Elliott Key, where interpretive programs are given. The cruises are offered on weekends, but may be expanded to other days of the week as demand indicates. Fare is $10 for adults, $6 for children. For information, write to Biscayne National Park Headquarters, Convoy Point, P.O. Box 1369, Homestead, FL 33030, or call 247-PARK.

Bus tours. *American Sightseeing* (4300 N.W. 14th St., Miami 33126; 871–2370 or 871–4992) offers a four-hour Magic City tour covering Miami Beach, Miami, Coral Gables, and Coconut Grove, with lunch in the Grove and a tour of Vizcaya. It also has tours to the Parrott Jungle, to the Seaquarium, and to Omni International Mall for shoppers. Two **night club tours** are offered, a five-hour visit to Les Violins including show and dinner, an eight-hour visit to two clubs, Les Violins and Copacabana, including shows and dinner.

Helicopter tours. *Miami Helicopter Service* (Watson Island, 1050 MacArthur Causeway, Miami; 688–6778) has nine sightseeing tours ranging from seven to forty-four minutes, covering downtown Miami, Miami Beach, Biscayne Bay, and Key Biscayne. *Gold Coast Helicopters* (15101 Biscayne Blvd., Miami; 940–1009) offer tours ranging from seven to 90 minutes ($30 to $170) covering Motel Row, downtown Miami, Miami Beach, Key Biscayne, and west to the Everglades. Price of tours is the same for one or two people; tours can be tailored to client's wishes and/or the craft can be rented on a straight time basis.

Walking tours. *Bird Walk,* a bird-watching tour, is given every Thursday at 5:00 or 6:00 P.M. at Greynolds Park (17530 W. Dixie Hwy., North Miami; 945–3425), with additional walks on Saturdays in spring and summer; the tour is free. Greynolds Park also offers an *Owl Prowl* on the third Wednesday of each month during fall, winter, and spring at 7:30 or 8:30 P.M., also free. A *Beach Walk* is given at Haulover Beach Park (10800 Collins Ave., Miami Beach; 947–3525) once a month on a Saturday at 10:00 A.M. (call for details; $1). Twice monthly, depending on tides, a *Bear Cut Exploration Walk* takes visitors out to a fossilized black mangrove reef in a wading tour. It is given in spring, summer, and fall; $2. A *Historical Trail Walk* is offered at Arch Creek Park (N.E. 135th St. and Biscayne Blvd., 944–6111) every Saturday afternoon. The free walk covers the natural history of the park and of the Tequesta Indians. In the winter season (November–March), a *Hammock Exploration Walk* ($1) is given on Saturdays at 10:00 A.M. at Matheson Hammock Park (9610 Old Cutler Rd., Coral Gables; 666–6979). A *Bayshore Walk* is given at the same park once a month in spring, summer, and fall ($2).

Art deco buffs can get an eyeful on a guided tour of *Miami Beach's National Historic District* on Saturday mornings. The tour last about an hour and costs $5.00. For information, write Miami Design Preservation League, 1300 Ocean Dr., Miami Beach 33139, or call 672–2014. (See also "Historic Sites and Houses," below.) *Redland Fruit and Spice Park* (24801 S.W. 187th Ave., Miami; 247–5727) offers guided tours of its tropical plants and trees Wednesdays and Fridays at 10:00 A.M., Sundays at 1:00 and 3:00 P.M. ($1 adults, $.50 children).

A year-around regular series of walking tours is given by the *Historical Association of Southern Florida* (101 W. Flagler St., Miami, 33131; 375–1492; contact Betty Ligae). Tours are usually on Saturdays, last two to four hours, and may also be repeated on Sundays if demand warrants. Given by knowledgeable local people, the tours cover different areas each week, among them the early settlements of downtown Miami, Key Biscayne, Lighthouse, historic homes of Coral Gables. A fee is charged, usually $8.

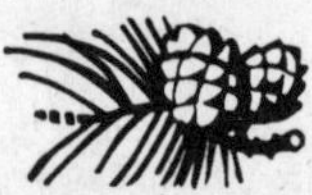

PARKS. The Miami area has two national parks, two state parks, and dozens of county and municipal facilities. Best known is *Everglades National Park,* the great wilderness preserve that encompasses more than a million acres of everglades. Here, visitors can see alligators, rare birds, and other wildlife in their native habitats. Park headquarters and the popular Royal Palm Visitor Center are about 50 miles southwest of downtown Miami. See the Everglades section at the end of this chapter.

Not as well known is *Biscayne National Park,* the nation's newest. Situated just south of Miami, it is 96 percent under water and encompasses part of the only living coral reef in the United States. About 45 keys, including 2,000-acre Elliott, lie within its boundaries. Water-related activities, obviously, are the chief attraction: the park is a popular weekend target for boaters and fishermen. A visitor center, campground, and marina are located on Elliott Key, as well as a nature trail you should avoid in warm weather, unless you enjoy being devoured by mosquitos.

A tour boat, the *Reef Rover III,* runs on weekends from park headquarters at Convoy Point in Homestead on the mainland. Fare for the four-hour trip, which includes about 2½ hours on Elliot Key for hikes, snorkeling, or sunbathing, is $10 for adults, $6 for children. For information about the park, call 247–PARK.

Key Biscayne, the resort island just south of Miami Beach, has two large and highly popular parks. *Crandon Park* there is the county's biggest and second most popular facility, drawing some 1.2 million visitors a year. The main attraction is its 2½-mile public beach on the ocean. You can set up your own beach umbrella anywhere on the sand for free (after paying the $1 parking charge on entering the park), or opt for one of the newly renovated cabanas for $12.50 a day. Also on park land is an 18-hole golf course, restaurants, a marina, and bicycle paths. For information, call 361–5421.

At the tip of the key is *Bill Baggs Cape Florida State Park,* where 406 acres shelter an ocean beach, quiet woods, bicycle and nature trails, a seawalled harbor, and picnic grounds. The Cape Florida lighthouse, with the restored lightkeeper's house, is at the tip of the key within the park. Lighthouse tours are given at 10:30 A.M. and at 1:00, 2:30, and 3:30 P.M. daily except Tuesdays; admission is $.50 per person. Admission to the park, which is open every day during daylight hours, is $.50 per person. For information, call 361–5811.

To reach Key Biscayne, take the Rickenbacker Causeway ($1 toll to enter, none to depart) from the mainland.

Several other Miami-area parks are of particular interest. Once a major race track, *Tropical Park* was taken over by the county some years ago and has become the area's most popular facility, with more than two million visitors annually. Facilities include tennis, racquetball, baseball, swimming, boating, soccer, basketball, and boxing. Also on the grounds are a Vita course, football and track stadium, equestrian center, and covered picnic facilities. For information, call 223–8710.

Another park that once was something else—in this case, an airport—is *Tamiami Park,* in the western part of the city. Now Tamiami is home for the largest youth baseball league in the U.S., the largest Youth Fair (every March), and the largest solar-heated pool. It has a football stadium and is the site for many large-scale fairs, festivals, and special events. Planned expansion includes the building of a Grand Prix race track. For information, call 223–7070.

Greynolds Park, in North Miami Beach, is a favorite nesting area for birds, the only locale in the metropolitan area with such a concentration. Late in the day, you can watch hundreds of egrets, herons, cormorants, and other birds fly to their nests in the mangrove islands of the park. Guided bird walks, offered every Thursday in late afternoon, give visitors an informative view not only of the birds but also of the plentiful wildlife here, which includes raccoons, opossums, and turtles. You can rent paddleboats for $3 a half hour on the lake, and there is also a nine-hole golf course on the grounds. For information, call 949–1741.

Bird Drive Park and Therapeutic Campground, at 3401 S.W. 72nd Ave., is a new park with special emphasis for the handicapped. It has a solar-heated pool (admission $.50) with a hydraulic lift for the handicapped, nature trails with handrails for the blind, overnight lodging, and program activities for the handicapped. For information, call 665-5319 or 665–1626 (pool).

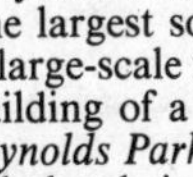

THEME PARKS AND AMUSEMENTS. **Castle Park.** When children see the distinctive turrets that mark the two Castle Parks in South Florida, they think not of knights of old but of video star wars and go-karts. Castle Parks are amusement centers, offering a potpourri of games and activities from miniature golf and video arcades to kiddie rides and batting cages. Admission is free, but each activity has its individual price. Samples: Miniature golf, $3.25 for adults, $2.25 for children 4–12; bumper boats and go-karts, $2; batting cage, $1 for 35 pitches. The original *Castle Park* in Fort Lauderdale is at 1999 S.W.

33rd Pl. (Miami phone number: 947–3253) (see *Practical Information for the Area from Fort Lauderdale North to Palm Beach*). The Miami facility is at 7775 N.W. 8th St.; 266–2100.

A great place to cool off when it gets hot here (and it does in summer) is **Six Flags Atlantis,** the world's largest water theme park. Located at 2700 Stirling Road in Hollywood, just north of Miami, the park has water flumes, wave pools, swimming pools, water-gun playgrounds, and similar activities. It is open from mid-March through January 2 from 10:00 A.M. to 5:00 P.M. daily. Admission is $9.95 for adults, $7.95 for children 3–7, with a parking charge of $1. Some attractions within the park carry additional charges, including bumper boats, paddle boats, raft rental, and sailboats. For information, call 1–926–1000.

Venetian Pool. Back in the 1920s, William Jennings Bryan sold Coral Gables lots from a podium at this pool, carved out of coral rock and built to resemble a Venetian lagoon. It has caves and stone bridges and a sandy beach. Situated at 2701 Desoto Blvd., Coral Gables, it is open 10:00 A.M. to 4:45 P.M. daily. Admission is $2.50 adults ($1.50 for Gables residents), $1 for children 12 and under. Locker fee is $1. For information, call 442–6483.

Omni Mall. Indoor amusement park with carousel, video games, midway-type attractions. 1601 Biscayne Blvd.; 371–2362.

ZOOS AND AQUARIUMS. Miami's new **Metrozoo,** opened in 1981, has already gained a national reputation as one of the best cageless zoos. With 225 acres open to the public, it far exceeds most other zoological parks in size. Biggest attractions are the white tigers, who roam on a grassy island with a Siamese temple as a backdrop, a family of gorillas, and a huge aviary—so large that the zoo's elevated monorail passes through it within a screen tunnel. Three different shows are given several times daily on the grounds. Visitors can tour the zoo by foot, by motorized tram, or by monorail (monorail cost is $2.90 for adults, $1.90 for children, and provides unlimited on-and-off privileges). Admission to the zoo is $4.50 for adults, $2 for children 3–12. Parking is free. The zoo, which draws about 750,000 visitors a year, is at 12400 S.W. 152nd St., about 20 miles south of downtown Miami, a mile west of the Turnpike Extension. It is open daily from 10:00 A.M. to 5:30 P.M. For information, call 251–0400.

When you visit the **Monkey Jungle,** you'll find you are the one in the cage, while the monkeys run free outside your screened-in walkway. A commercial attraction, the jungle has a broad collection of monkeys, apes, baboons, chimpanzees, and gorillas and presents continuous shows, including a chimpanzee performance daily. Admission to the Monkey Jungle, 14805 S.W. 216th St., Miami, is $5.50 for adults, $2.75 for children, and $4.50 for senior citizens. It is open from 9:30 A.M. to 5:00 P.M. For information, call 235–1611.

Thousands of tropical birds fly free in the **Parrot Jungle,** a beautifully landscaped commercial attraction just south of Coral Gables. Most never stray far away, but occasionally a nearby resident is startled to find a splendidly plumed parrot in his yard, talking to himself. A 40-minute trained bird show is given every hour and a half, and the beautifully landscaped grounds are a camera fan's delight. The jungle, at 11000 S.W. 57th Ave., Miami, is open from 9:30 A.M. to 5:00 P.M. daily. Admission is $6.75 for adults, $3.25 for children 6–12. Parking is free. For information, call 666–7834.

Flipper the porpoise and Lolita the killer whale do their thing at the **Seaquarium,** largest tropical marine aquarium in South Florida. More than 10,000 denizens of the deep dwell in the Seaquarium's various tanks, pools, channels, and water stadiums. Flipper, who has appeared in more than 100 television shows, is the star of one of the five shows, each of which is presented three times daily. Four-ton Lolita, the killer whale, sometimes splashes spectators as she leaps out of the water and crashes back down. Other shows feature sea lions and porpoises (dolphins). Admission is $8 for adults, $4 for children 6 to 12, $6.80 for senior citizens. Parking is free, and admission includes ride on the monorail. The Seaquarium is open from 9:00 A.M. to 6:30 P.M. It is located on Virginia Key, on the Rickenbacker Causeway. For information, call 361–5703.

GARDENS. The largest tropical botanical garden in the continental United States is *Fairchild Tropical Garden* in Coral Gables. Hundreds of varieties of palms, cycads, bromeliads, and other tropical plants are grown in this 83-acre facility. Winding paths take you through a rain forest, vine pergola, sunken garden, palm glade, rare plant house, and a hibiscus garden. Tram rides with commentary leave every hour; guided walking tours can be arranged. Admission is $3. The garden, at 10901 Old Cutler Rd., Coral Gables, is open daily except Christmas from 9:00 A.M. to 4:30 P.M. For information, call 667–1651.

On Watson Island, just opposite downtown Miami, is the one-acre *Japanese Garden,* built and donated to the city of Miami by Japanese industrialist Kyoshi Ichimura. A place for reflection, this garden has an authentic ceremonial teahouse, stone Hotei figures and pagodas, ponds, and winding paths. It is open by appointment daily from 7:00 A.M. to 10:00 P.M.; admission is free. For information, call 579–6944.

In Homestead, 25 miles south of Miami, is the *Orchid Jungle,* a commercial attraction with hundreds of varieties of orchids, some growing on oak trees in a natural Florida hammock. Admission is $3.50 for adults, $2.80 for youths 13 to 18, $1.25 for children 6 to 12, students and senior citizens $2.80. The jungle is at 26715 S.W. 157th Ave., Homestead, and is open from 8:30 A.M. to 5:30 P.M. For information, call 247–4824.

Also located in the far southern part of the county is *Preston Bird and Mary Heinlein Fruit and Spice Park.* Here visitors may see (and sometimes sample) tropical fruits such as the carambola and loquat, cashew and macadamia nuts, mangos and ponderosa lemons. Guided tours are conducted from November to May on Wednesdays, Fridays and Saturdays at 10:30 A.M. and on Sundays at 1 and 3:30 P.M. Fee is $1 for adults, $.50 for children under 12. Admission to the park, which is situated at S.W. 248th St. and 187th Ave., about 20 miles south of Miami, is free. It is open daily from 9:00 A.M. to 5:00 P.M. For information, call 247–5727.

The only formal garden in Miami is at *Vizcaya,* the Italian Renaissance-style palace built by industrialist James Deering and now a county museum. Admission, which includes a guided tour of 50 rooms of the palace, is $5 for adults, $3.50 for students and senior citizens. Sound and light shows are held in the garden on weekend evenings. Vizcaya is located at 3251 S. Miami Ave., Miami. For information, call 579–2708.

BEACHES. It was the happy meeting of ocean and shore that made Miami one of the world's biggest tourist destinations. Beaches are still the big drawing card in South Florida, the only part of the state where you can comfortably swim in the ocean the year-round.

Every beach tends to have a character of its own. Probably the most popular are those on Key Biscayne—Crandon Park and Cape Florida State Park—but by the same token these also tend to be crowded on weekends. The best bet is to rent a cabana at Crandon Park, giving you the privacy and comfort of shelter and shower by the seaside.

Miami Beach has 10 miles of beach, all replenished and broadened in the past four years under a $64-million beach nourishment project. This stretch of sand is now more than 300 feet wide and is certainly attractive, but as barefoot walkers will testify, pieces of rock were pumped up along with sand to build the beach. It takes a couple of years for the rocks to work down deeper into the sand. The city is to complete a 1¼-mile-long, $3-million landscaped boardwalk promenade on the new beach by June of 1984, expected to be an attraction for tourists. It is to run from 21st to 46th Streets and future extensions are planned. Many visitors like the new Northshore Open Space Park, but parking is limited in this area. Personal favorites are Cape Florida State Park and Northshore.

A short description of the main beaches in the Miami area follows:

Main public beaches on Miami Beach are: *Pier Park* at the southern tip of the island, popular also with surfers; *Lummus Park,* opposite the art deco hotels, also in the southern part of the city; *Northshore Open Space Park,* with wooden boardwalks, roofed pavilions, and a Vita course. Smaller public beaches are found at 21st, 35th, 46th, 53rd, 63rd, and 71st streets.

North of Miami Beach, beyond the Baker's Haulover inlet, is *Haulover Park,* with a long stretch of beach, picnic facilities, and a fishing pier. This is one of the county's most popular parks. Parking is $1. *Sunny Isles Beach,* between 163rd and 192nd streets, farther north, has two miles of beach open to the public.

Key Biscayne, south of Miami Beach but reached from the mainland via the Rickenbacker Causeway ($1 toll to the Key, free returning), has two extensive and popular beaches. *Crandon Park* (see "Parks," above) has 2½ miles of public beach with picnic facilities and rental cabanas ($12.50 per day) at one end. Cabanas have changing rooms, showers, tables and chairs. *Bill Baggs Cape Florida State Park* at the south end of the key has nature trails and the historic Cape Florida lighthouse, as well as about 1 mile of ocean beach. Crandon Park has a parking charge of $1, Bill Baggs park an admission charge of $.50 per person. *Virginia Key,* which the Rickenbacker Causeway bisects just before reaching Key Biscayne, has a less refined beach with lifeguards on duty only on weekends and holidays.

One beach here is situated on Biscayne Bay rather than the ocean. *Matheson Hammock Park* at 9610 Old Cutler Rd. in Coral Gables, has a man-made lagoon with an adjacent marina, picnic facilities, and offshore sandbar for waders. Parking is $1.

John U. Lloyd Beach State Recreation Area, 6503 N. Ocean Dr., Hollywood, is one of the most popular oceanfront parks in the area, with its 224 acres of beach, dunes, and mangroves. It is often filled with people in search of the fresh air, sunshine, and cool water. There also are picnic facilities, fishing, and canoeing. Park rangers lead periodic nature walks during the winter months.

In Florida, as elsewhere in the United States, all beaches are public between the water and the high-tide line. Access to that beach, however, may be private, as is the case with some beachfront hotels on Miami Beach. But you can enjoy any beach to which you can legally gain access. Many residents gain access to beaches at street dead-ends on Miami Beach.

PARTICIPANT SPORTS. With year-round warm weather, Miami is an ideal locale for outdoor sports, particularly when other areas of the country are shivering. Summers can be hot and muggy, but that doesn't deter the outdoors-minded. There are dozens of ways for active people to enjoy sports here. Some of the most popular are outlined below.

Bicycling. Miami has 138 miles of paved bike paths, plus many streets that are well suited for leisurely biking. One long and attractive path runs from downtown Coconut Grove through the estate area of Coral Gables, past Matheson Hammock Park and Fairchild Tropical Garden to the farm area of Perrine. Another, on Key Biscayne, winds through a mangrove swamp and into Bill Baggs Cape Florida State Park. Bike races are held in South Miami, Coconut Grove, and Key Biscayne during the year. Bikers also are welcome to join the *Wheel People Bicycle Club* at 8:00 A.M. Sundays in front of Bike One Schwinn store, 1232 N.E. 163rd St., North Miami, for an organized ride of 15 to 25 miles. Call 945–4541 for information. Bikes can be rented at a number of locations: *Dade Cycle Shop,* 3043 Grand Ave., Coconut Grove, 443–6075; *Key Biscayne Bicycle Rentals,* 260 Crandon Park Blvd., Key Biscayne, 361–5555; *Miami Beach Bicycle Center,* 923 W. 39th St., Miami Beach, 531–4161; *163rd Street Cycle Center (Bike One),* 1238 N.E. 163rd St., North Miami, 945–4541.

Boating and Sailing and Waterskiing. South Florida is one of the world's great water playgrounds, with the ocean, Biscayne Bay, and extensive waterways at its doorstep. More than 100,000 boats are registered in South Florida, and visitors can rent anything from canoes to yachts. Jet- and water-skiing are popular sports in Biscayne Bay, as is sailing on the long reaches that extend to the Florida Keys. Rental boats and recreational equipment are available at many marinas. A sampling of rates: *Castle Harbor Sailboats* at Dinner Key Yacht Basin, Coconut Grove, rents a 14-footer for $14 an hour ($50 a half day, $80 a full day) and a 27-footer for $26 an hour, with discounts for non-weekend rental. For information, call 858–3212. *Sunny Isle Boat Rentals,* 435 Sunny Isles Blvd., (944–2417), offers water-ski boats for $29 an hour plus $6 for equipment, with a $100 deposit. *Boat Rental Corp* at the Key Marina, 3501 Rickenbacker Causeway, Key Biscayne, puts you on a jet ski for $20 a half hour. For information, call 361–6611. Among the many marinas in the Miami area are *Crandon Park Marina,* Rickenbacker Causeway, Key Biscayne, 361–5421; *Haulover Park Marina,* 10800 Collins Ave., Miami Beach, 947–3525; *Matheson Hammock Park,* 9610 Old Cutler Rd., Coral Gables, 661–4010; *Miamarina,* Fifth Street and Biscayne Boulevard, Miami, (downtown), 374–6260; *Dinner Key Marina,* Coconut Grove, 579–6980; *Watson Island Marina,* MacArthur Causeway, Miami, 579–6944; *Miami Beach Marina,* 300 Alton Road, Miami Beach, 673–6000; *Plaza Venetia Marina,* 555 NE 15th St., 374–4900; and *Sunny Isles Marine Center,* 400 Sunny Isles Blvd., 947–0656. A number of public boat launching ramps are found in South Florida as well; check with marinas near you for locations.

Golf. With three dozen golf courses scattered around the county and more in next-door Broward County, it isn't hard for visitors to find a place to swing their irons and test their putting skills. About half the area's golf courses are public or semi-private, including perhaps the most famous course, the Doral Country Club's Blue Monster, site of the Doral-Eastern pro tournament every year. A sampling of area courses open to the public: *Biltmore,* 1210 Anastasia Ave., Coral Gables, 442–6485; *Diplomat Presidential,* 19650 N.E. 18th Ave., Miami, 949–2442; *Doral Country Club* (five courses), 4400 N.W. 97th Ave., Miami, 592–2000; *Kendale Lakes,* 6401 Kendale Lakes Dr., Miami 382–3935; *Key Biscayne,* Crandon Blvd., Key Biscayne, 361–9139; *Miami Springs,* 650 Curtiss Pkwy., Miami Springs, 888–2377; *Palmetto,* 9300 Coral Reef Dr., Miami, 238–2922; *Bayshore,* 2301 Alton Rd., Miami Beach, 532–3350.

Fishing. More than 2,000 kinds of saltwater and freshwater fish dwell in South Florida waters, including some of the fightingest game fish in the world.

Sailfish, marlin, swordfish, and tuna lurk in the Gulf Stream just offshore; closer in are snapper, mackerel, sea trout, snook, bluefish, and grouper.

If you're after the big ones, **deep-sea fishing** is for you. Charter fishing boats will take you out to the rich Gulf Stream for around $200–$250 a half day, $400–$500 a full day; you can price shop for better quotes, and/or share the cost with other anglers. Call these marinas for prices and details: *Crandon Marina,* 4000 Crandon Blvd., Rickenbacker Causeway, Key Biscayne, 361–5421; *Miamarina,* 333 N.E. Miamarina Pkwy., Miami, 374–6260; *Sunny Isles,* 435 Sunny Isles Blvd., Sunny Isles, 944–2417; *Haulover Marina,* 10800 Collins Ave., Miami Beach, 945–3801.

If that's too expensive, try the party boats, larger vessels that accommodate up to 50 or so anglers on trips to the coral reef offshore for snapper, grouper, yellowtail, and other bottom fish. Party boats, also known as drift boats, are available at several marinas, among them: *Miamarina,* Miami (see above), with two boats that can accommodate up to 49 persons at $22 a day with equipment furnished ($19 if you bring your own), or $17 for half day ($14 with own tackle); *Haulover Marina,* Miami Beach (see above), has five party boats at $17 a half day ($14 with own equipment).

Another way to fish is from piers, bridges, and causeways. Many Biscayne Bay bridges are equipped with special fishing catwalks that are particularly popular at night, when the bay fishing is at its best. Some locales: MacArthur, Rickenbacker, North Bay, and Sunny Isles causeway bridges.

One ocean-fishing pier also is open to anglers. *Haulover Beach Fishing Pier,* 10880 Collins Ave., Miami Beach, extends 1,100 feet into the Atlantic and is open 24 hours a day. Admission is $2 adult, $1 children up to 16. Spectators are charged $.75, and there is a parking charge of $1. You can rent tackle on the pier, which attracts 500,000 visitors a year. Another pier, without bait-shop facilities, is located at the south end of Miami Beach in Pier Park; admission is free.

Horseback Riding. Several ranches offer riding, hayrides, and similar activities. Among them are *Golden Eagles Ranch,* 41 S.W. 122nd Ave., Miami, 221–4312—riding at $8 an hour; *Quail Roost Ranch,* 15400 Quail Roost Dr., Miami, 253–3308—$8 an hour on weekdays, $9 on weekends; *Country Gentleman Stables,* 15500 Quail Roos Dr., Miami, 233–6615—trail rides $10 an hour.

Tennis. Flamingo Park is the site of the World Junior Tennis Championships here every December, but it is only one of a number of tennis centers open to the public. Here are several sites (some hotels permit outside guests to play also); Miami Beach: *Flamingo Park,* 1000 12th St. (673–7761); *North Shore Center,* 501 72nd St., 673–7754. Key Biscayne: *Calusa Park,* Crandon Blvd., 361–2215; Miami: *Henderson Park,* 961 N.W. 2nd St., 325–8359; *Continental Park,* 10001 S.W. 81nd Ave., 271–0732; *Tropical Park,* 7900 S.W. 40th St., 223–8710; *Tamiami Park,* 11201 S.W. 24th St., 223–7072; *Palmetto Tennis Center,* 9300 Coral Reef Dr., 232–1920; *Moore Park,* 765 N.W. 36th St., 635–7459. Coral Gables: *Biltmore Tennis Center,* 1150 Anastasia Ave., 442–6565; *Salvadore Park Tennis Center,* 1120 Andalusia Ave., 442–6562. North Miami: *North Miami Tennis Center,* 16851 W. Dixie Hwy., 948–2947.

Racquetball. Courts, both private and public, are scattered over the county. Biggest of the private organizations is *Sportrooms,* which has four locales in Miami, at 1500 Douglas Rd., Coral Gables, 443–4228; Hialeah, 1900 W. 44th Place, 556–4545; North Miami, 444 N.W. 165th St. Rd., 944–8500; and South Dade, 10680 S.W. 113th Pl., 596–2677. Racquetball courts can be rented at several parks, including *Tropical* (553–3161), *Coral Reef* (235–1593), and *Miami-Dade Community College* (596–1140).

Skeet and Trap Shooting. *Trail Glades Range,* 17601 S.W. 8th St., Miami (266–1823), open Thursday through Monday, various hours (call for information). You can rent a rifle ($2 a day) or shot gun ($1 a day). Shooting is $3.50 adults, $1.50 for youths 16–17.

Jogging. More than 20 Vita courses are located in the county. Among the more popular are *David T. Kennedy Park,* 220 S. Bayshore Dr., Coconut Grove; *Greynolds Park,* 17530 W. Dixie Hwy., Miami; *Morningside Park,* 750 N.E. 55th St.; *Miami and Tropical Park,* 7900 S.W. 40th St., Miami.

Windsurfing. Most windsurfers gather along the Rickenbacker Causeway that leads from the mainland to Key Biscayne. Some resort hotels also rent windsurfing equipment. Some dealers and hotels with facilities and/or rentals are: *Windsurfing Place,* 6043 N.W. 167th St., Miami, 557–5217; *Upwind Surfing,* 3001 Grand Ave., Coconut Grove, 373–7245; *Sonesta Beach Hotel,* Key Biscayne, 361–2021; *Suez Motel,* 18215 Collins Ave., North Miami Beach, 932–0661; *Dinner Key Marina,* Coconut Grove, 579–6951.

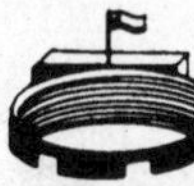

SPECTATOR SPORTS. There's always something going on in sports in this outdoor-minded city. For up-to-date information on sports events, turn to page 3 of *The Miami Herald's* sports section, which carries a daily listing of sports events, both televised and local.

Baseball. In the spring, the major league teams come to Florida for spring training, playing "Grapefruit League" exhibitions in a number of cities. The *Baltimore Orioles* are Miami's "home" major-league team during this period, playing at Miami Stadium, 2301 N.W. 10th Ave., Miami; 635–5395. The stadium is also the base for Miami's minor-league team, the *Marlins.* The *University of Miami Hurricane Nine,* perennial challengers to the national collegiate baseball championship, plays at its own 6,000-seat Mark Light Stadium in Coral Gables at Hurricane Drive and San Amaro. For ticket information, call 284–2655.

Football. The professional *Miami Dolphins* play home games at the Orange Bowl, 1400 N.W. 4th St., Miami; 579–6971. Dolphins tickets can be purchased there; call 643–4700 for information. The *University of Miami Hurricanes,* the number 1 college football team in the country in 1983, also plays at the Orange Bowl. For ticket information, call 284–2655.

Golf. The *Doral-Eastern Golf Open,* held in late February or early March, is one of the top tournaments on the pro tour. It is held at the Doral Country Club, 4400 N.W. 87th Ave., Miami; 592–2000.

Jai alai, a Basque game that uses a hard ball played on a three-walled court, attracts visitors to the *Miami Jai Alai Fronton,* N.W. 36th St. and 37th Ave., Miami, 633–9661, during the winter months. Pari-mutuel betting is permitted.

Racing (automobile). Biggest event of the year is the *Budweiser Grand Prix* race, usually held the third weekend in February on Biscayne Boulevard in downtown Miami. Tickets are sold through various outlets, including BASS Ticket Office, 174 E. Flagler St., Miami; 372–0925. Various other auto races at held at *Hialeah Speedway,* 3300 W. Okeechobee Road, Hialeah, 821–6644, during much of the year.

Racing (boat). Motorboat races are held at various times of the year at Miami Marine Stadium, 3601 Rickenbacker Causeway, Key Biscayne; 361–6732. Biggest race of the year is the *Champion Spark Plug Unlimited Hydroplane Regatta* in June, which attracts some of the nation's top drivers. Another big event is the *Lee Evans Memorial Regatta* in October.

Racing (greyhound) is conducted at *Flagler Kennel Club,* N.W. 37th Ave. and 7th St., Miami, 649–3000, and at *Biscayne Kennel Club,* 320 N.W. 115th St., North Miami, 754–3484, on a rotating basis. Pari-mutuel betting permitted.

Racing (horse). Wagering is permitted at horse tracks and as well as at dog tracks and jai-alai games. Horse racing here reaches its peak in the winter months, but one of the three tracks in the Miami area is open during most of the year. Racing dates are rotated among the three tracks—*Hialeah Park,* 105 E. 21st St., Hialeah, 885–8000; *Gulfstream Park,* US 1 and Hallandale Beach Blvd., 944–1242, just north of the Dade County line; and *Calder Race Course,* 210th St. and N.W. 27th Ave., Miami, 625–1311. Biggest stakes races are Hialeah's Widener, Turf Cup, and Flamingo, Gulfstream's Gulfstream Park Handicap, Florida Derby, and Pan American Turf Handicap.

Tennis. *Ilie Nastase Hamptons Invitational,* a December event, is played at the Hamptons at Turnberry Isle, 20281 E. Country Club Dr., Miami; 932–3044. Another December event of note is the *Orange Bowl Junior Tennis Championships,* which showcase stars of the future (Bjorn Borg and Chris Evert Lloyd were junior winners here). It is staged as part of the Orange Bowl Festival, at Flamingo Park Tennis Center, 1000 12th St., Miami Beach; 673–7761.

BABYSITTING SERVICES. Miami has long been a happy destination for families, so just about every hotel and motel has a list of babysitters. Contact front desk for information and rates. Two agencies you can contact directly: *Babysitting Employment Service,* 688–7677, $3.50 an hour, four-hour minimum daytime, five-hour minimum at night, plus $4 transportation. Rate for babysitting two children is $4 an hour, $4.50 for three. The agency is bonded.

Central Sitting Agency, 856–0550, is licensed and in business for 14 years. Charges are $3 an hour with a four-hour minimum daytime, five-hour minimum at night, plus $3 transportation. The charge for two children is $5 an hour.

HISTORIC SITES AND HOUSES. See also "Museums," below. Rapidly becoming a star attraction is Miami Beach's **Art Deco District,** a National Historic District. More than 800 buildings in the district are done in the 1930's–1940's art deco style, with strong lines, porthole windows, heavy use of chrome and etched glass, and other architectural marks of the genre. Many of the buildings are run down, and parts of the area are not safe at night. Several oceanfront art deco hotels, however, have been renovated and draw visitors both day and night. Special events, including an annual art deco festival weekend every January, are held from time to time. Guided tours are offered every Saturday at 10:30 A.M., starting from various locations; fee is $5. For information, contact the Miami Design Preservation League, Cardozo/Carlyle Hotel, 1300 Ocean Dr., Miami Beach; 672–2014.

The Barnacle. Now a state historic site, this bayfront home was built by Coconut Grove pioneer Ralph Monroe in 1891, which makes it ancient by Miami standards. Tours are given at 9:00 A.M., 10:30 A.M., 1:00 P.M., and 3:30 P.M. Wednesday through Sunday. Admission is $.50. The Barnacle is located at 3485 Main Highway in downtown Coconut Grove. For information, call 448–9445.

Coral Castle. This commercial attraction has an unusual and appealing romantic history. It is a house and garden built of enormous monolithic coral stone by a Latvian immigrant stone-mason over a 20-year period from 1920 to 1940. The eccentric Edward Leedshainin hoped his creation would induce his estranged fiancée to come live with him. It still is not know how he managed to raise and balance the huge stones—some of which weigh more than a ton—as he worked completely alone. The castle at 28655 S. Federal Hwy., Homestead, is open from 9:00 A.M. to 5:00 P.M. daily. Admission is $5.50 adult, $4 for children 5–10. For information, call 248–6344.

Coral Gables House. Also known as Merrick Manor, this was the family homestead of the founder of Coral Gables, George Merrick. Once it was the only home on the 3,000-acre fruit and vegetable plantation that became this affluent city. The house, at 907 Coral Way, Coral Gables, is open from 1:00 P.M. to 4:00 P.M. Sunday and 10:00 A.M. to 4:00 P.M. Wednesday. Admission is $1 adult, $.50 children. For information, call 442–6447.

Hialeah Park Race Track. When the horses aren't running (all but 60 days of the year), this fashionable track is open to allow visitors to look around. A National Historic Site, its clubhouse was built in distinctive French style, and the infield is populated with dozens of pink flamingos, who nestle around the lake and palms. An aquarium is on the premises, as are displays of historic carriages and thoroughbred racing silks. Hialeah is an Audubon Bird Sanctuary and shelters many rare and unusual tropical birds. The track, at 79th St. and E. 4th Ave., Hialeah, is open from 9:30 A.M. to 4:30 P.M. daily except during racing dates in the winter. Admission is free. For information, call 885–8000.

Spanish Monastery. Visitors are amazed to learn that young Miami has the oldest building in the Western Hemisphere, built in 1141. There's a catch, of course: the building, the Cloisters of the Monastery of St. Bernard de Clairvaux, was built in Spain and only came to Miami in the twentieth century, when William Randolph Hearst admired it in 1925 during a visit to Spain. He bought it, had it dismantled stone by stone, and shipped to the United States, where its stones and statues remained in a warehouse for 20 years. Set up in Miami in the 1950s, the cloister is situated at 16711 W. Dixie Hwy. in North Miami Beach and is open from 10 A.M. to 5:00 P.M. Monday through Saturday and noon to 5:00 P.M. Sunday. Admission is $3 for adults, $2 for senior citizens, $1 for students, $.75 for children 6–12. For information, call 945–1461.

Cape Florida Lighthouse. Built in the 1830s during the Seminole Wars, this is the oldest structure to actually be constructed in South Florida. It was attacked by Tequesta Indians, who set a fire within the tower to roast the keeper and his helper, who had fled to the top of the light. The keeper survived the ordeal. The light and the restored keeper's home are open daily except Tuesdays. Tours are conducted at 10:30 A.M., 1:00 P.M., 2:30 P.M. and 3:30 P.M.; tour fee is $.50. There is also a $.50-per-person charge to enter Bill Baggs Cape Florida State Park, in which the lighthouse is situated. For information, call 361–5811.

Miami Biltmore Hotel. In the 1920s and 1930s, this was the fashionable hotel of south Florida, visited by the famous and the wealthy of the era. Today the hotel is a National Historic Landmark, its distinctive 250-foot-high replica of the Giralda Tower in Sevilla, Spain, soaring high above the Coral Gables residences that surround it. The hotel was converted to a hospital during World War II, but has been closed for many years. Plans have been approved, however, to restore the building and reopen it as a hotel and apartment complex, preserving its architecture. Visitors currently can visit only two parts of the structure—the Biltmore Restaurant, the walls of which are paneled in 50 different kinds of woods, and the Metropolitan Museum, which occupies the hotel's former country-club building. An 18-hole golf course lies behind the hotel and the award-winning Biltmore Tennis Center is adjacent. Both are public. The Biltmore is at 1212 Anastasia Ave., Coral Gables.

INDIANS. *Miccosukee Indian Village.* You can see how the Indians of this region live at this village, a tourist attraction, some 25 miles west of Miami on the Tamiami Trail (US 41). Indian craftsmen exhibit patchwork, basketry, and other items, and visitors are shown family "camps" with the Seminole chickee (a thatched-roofed, open-sided structure, in which Indians of today and yesterday lived). A Culture Center showcases Indian art. Alligator wrestling and airboat rides are featured. During the annual Miccosukee Indian Art Festival in December, Indians from 40 tribes in the United States, South America, Central America, and Canada show their work. The village is open from 9:00 A.M. to 5:30 P.M. daily. Admission is $3 for adults, $1.75 for children 3–12. Parking is free. Airboat rides are $5 per person for 15 minutes, $6 for 30 minutes.

MUSEUMS. Bass Museum. A permanent collection of paintings, sculpture, graphics, and textiles from the fourteenth through twentieth centuries is on view at this municipal Miami Beach museum. The collection of Oriental bronzes is among the best in the nation, as are two large Belgian tapestries. Located at 212 Park Ave., Miami Beach, the museum is open Tuesday through Saturday 10:00 A.M. to 5:00 P.M. and 1:00 P.M. to 5:00 P.M. Sunday. Admission is $1, except on Tuesdays, when it is free. Call 673–7533 or 673–7530.

Center for the Fine Arts. The county's new art museum is housed in a massive new downtown cultural complex designed by famed architect Philip Johnson. The center is not a traditional museum in that it will not have a permanent collection, but will mount rotating exhibits. Admission is $3 for adults, $2 for children 6–12. There is metered curbside parking as well as a new parking garage adjacent to the center, located at 101 W. Flagler St. For information, call 375–1700. The center is open from 10:00 A.M. to 6:00 P.M. Monday, Tuesday, Wednesday, and Friday; 1:00 P.M. to 9:00 P.M. Thursday; 10:00 A.M. to 5:00 P.M. Saturday, and noon to 5:00 P.M. Sunday.

Lowe Art Museum. This facility, part of the University of Miami, has rotating exhibitions, as well as permanent collections of Renaissance paintings, pre-Columbian, Oriental, early American and modern art, plus a good collection of American Indian blankets. Located at 1301 Miller Dr. on the UM campus in Coral Gables, the museum is open Tuesday through Friday from noon to 5:00 P.M.; Saturday from 10:00 A.M. to 5:00 P.M.; and Sunday from 2:00 P.M. to 5:00 P.M. Admission and parking are free. For information, call 284–3535.

Metropolitan Museum and Art Center. This private museum is located within the historic Biltmore Hotel and Country Club in Coral Gables. It presents traveling exhibitions as well as a permanent collection of Latin American, Oriental, and pre-Columbian art, photography, and historic costumes. At 1212 Anastasia Ave., Coral Gables, the museum is open from 10:00 A.M. to 5:00 P.M. Tuesday through Saturday; 7:00 P.M. to 10:00 P.M. Wednesday evening; and noon to 5:00 P.M. Sunday. Admission is $1 adult, $.50 for children 12–18, students, and senior citizens. Metered parking is available. For information, call 442–1448.

SCIENCE AND HISTORY

Florida Pioneer Museum. Three railroad structures—an agent's house, the old Homestead depot, and a caboose—make up this museum, which houses artifacts of South Florida at the turn of the century. Situated at 826 N. Krome Ave., Florida City, about 25 miles southwest of Miami on the road to Everglades

National Park, the facility is open daily except Christmas and New Year's Day from 1:00 to 5:00 P.M. Admission is $1.50 for adults, $.75 for children. For information, call 246–9531.

Historical Museum of Southern Florida. Just moved into its new quarters in the downtown Dade Cultural Center, this facility houses a chronological history of south Florida covering a 10,000-year span. In addition to exhibits, the museum sponsors outings such as canoe trips and nature treks. It is open from 9:00 A.M. to 5:00 P.M. Monday through Saturday and noon to 5:00 P.M. Sunday. There's an admission charge. For information, call 375–1492.

Museum of Science. In 1983, the museum completely redid its main exhibit section, adding many hands-on displays and an animal exploratorium. More than 75 exhibits in natural history, light, sound, chemistry, biology, fossil history, and technology are on display here. Major traveling exhibitions are mounted periodically. The museum, at 3280 S. Miami Ave., Miami, is open 10:00 A.M. to 6:00 P.M. Monday through Friday; 10:00 A.M. to 10:00 P.M. Saturday and Sunday. Admission is $2 for adults, $1 for children, $1.25 for seniors. Parking is free. For information, call 854–4242.

Planet Ocean. You can touch an iceberg and walk through a simulated hurricane. Planet Ocean is an ocean-oriented theme attraction on Virginia Key on the Rickenbacker Causeway, Miami. A heavily hands-on museum, the facility has exhibits such as a yellow submarine children can climb into, a real iceberg, and water turbines that produce electricity, as well as several films. It is open from 10:00 A.M. to 6:00 P.M. daily. Admission is $5.50 for adults, $2.75 for children 6–12. Forinformation, call 361–9455.

South Cross Observatory. This small facility, atop the Museum of Science, offers star-gazing through powerful telescopes on Friday and Saturday nights from 8:00 P.M. to 10:00 P.M. and on Sunday from 2:00 P.M. to 5:00 P.M. Free.

Space Transit Planetarium. This award-winning facility with a 65-foot dome is headed by Jack Horkheimer, who has a syndicated television science show. The planetarium presents two kinds of shows: temporary shows daily at noon, 1:30 P.M., 3:00 P.M., 4:30, and 7:00 P.M., with an 8:00 P.M. show on Mondays, Tuesdays, and Wednesdays (admission $4 adult, $2 children); and laser shows, given Thursday, Friday, Saturday, and Sunday at 8:30 P.M., with late shows Friday and Saturday at 10:00 P.M. and 11:30 P.M. (admission is $4 for adults, $2 for children). For information, call 854–2222.

Villa Vizcaya. A magnificent Italian Renaissance-style palace, industrialist James Deering built this as a winter home in 1914–1916. Fifty of its rooms, all furnished in European and Oriental antiques, are open to the public on guided tours. Sound and light shows are held in the formal gardens on weekend evenings, and there are also gondola rides at this bayfront villa. Vizcaya is open from 9:30 A.M. to 4:30 P.M. daily except Christmas. Admission is $5 adults, $3.50 for students and senior citizens. For information about the museum, which is situated at 3251 S. Miami Ave., Miami, call 579–2813.

ART GALLERIES. Several galleries are concentrated on Kane Concourse in Bay Harbor Islands, an island municipality in the North Beach area. Two galleries that show Florida artists as well as national and international ones are *Barbara Gillman Gallery,* 2886 Biscayne Blvd., Miami (573–4898), and *Artspace,* 169 Madiera Ave., Coral Gables (444–4493). Other respected galleries include *Galerie 99,* 1088 Kane Concourse, Bay Harbor Islands (865–5823); *Gloria Luria Gallery,* 1033 Kane Concourse, Bay Harbor Islands (865–3060) and *Gallery at 24,* 2399 N.E. 2nd Ave., Miami (861–2424), which specializes in ethnographical art. *Netsky Gallery* (448–6163) (crafts works, no paintings) is moving from its current South Miami location to another in 1984. See also the Miami Yellow Pages for other listings.

MUSIC. *The Opera Guild of Greater Miami* books important stars from the Continent, the Met, and elsewhere. Its seasonal openings bring out a socially conscious, conspicuously gowned and furred crowd. Rehearsals are year round, the chorus members are paid just as the stars are. The company keeps engagements as far off as Fort Lauderdale. Family operas are booked as late as spring and make a memorable musical occasion. A number of leading families lend their support to the Opera Guild. Call 854–1643 for up-to-date information. The Company usually appears at Dade Auditorium, 2901 W. Flagler St., 545–3395, and Miami Beach Theatre of the Performing Arts, 1700 Washington Ave., 673–8300.

Although the *Florida Philharmonic* has disbanded (there are plans to have an orchestra soon to replace it), the Miami area is the site of numerous, diverse concerts by internationally renowned artists. There are outstanding facilities, including Gusman Hall (formerly the ornate, old Olympia Theatre) 174 E. Flagler in the heart of downtown Miami (358–3338), Dade Auditorium, Miami Beach halls, as well as theaters at universities in the area.

Miami Beach also has a symphony, with a season extended into the warmer months with a *Summer Pops series.* Alfredo Munar directs both the winter symphony and the summer program. The Miami Beach Theater of the Performing Arts box office at 1700 Washington Ave. will provide current information (673–8300).

The *Youth Symphony of South Florida,* the *Chamber Music Society in Greater Miami,* the *Miami Little Orchestra* and dozens of other groups are active in the resort area. The *Miami Herald* is a good source for information on current performances.

For music with a Latin beat, the July annual *Fiesta Latina* (since 1977) features South American stars performing inside and outside the Miami Beach Convention Center. Free.

STAGE. The Greater Miami area cannot yet compete with New York in legitimate theater, but it is doing quite well in its own right. Visitors who love theater will find a variety of excellent productions.

Coconut Grove Playhouse, 3500 Main Hwy., Coconut Grove, 442–4000, is the home of the *Players State Theatre,* where lesser-known Broadway shows and pre-White Way productions are staged. Aesthetically and technically, the theater is an improvement on many of Broadway's more famous houses, with fine seats, good acoustics, excellent restaurant service attached, and an upstairs art gallery.

The Miami Beach Theatre of the Performing Arts, 1700 Washington Ave., 673–8300, is the chief outpost of Broadway hits with major casts. Audiences, including many socialites, are attracted from all over the world. The $6-million facility also hosts outstanding concerts, ballets, and other cultural events.

The *Ring Theater,* 1380 Miller Dr., Coral Gables, at the University of Miami, 284–3355, offers presentations of such high quality they could compare with Broadway performances. Other area colleges also have good theater, especially Florida International University and Miami-Dade Community College.

The *Merry-Go-Round Playhouse and Drama Studio,* 235 Alcazar, Coral Gables, 445–8331, has continuous *Children's Theater;* also presents amateur Shakespeare and contemporary plays. Spanish plays may be seen at *Teatro America,* 2173 S.W. 8th St., 325–0515.

Ruth Foreman Theatre, Florida International University, N.E. 151 St. and Biscayne Blvd., North Miami, 891–1830, presents both legitimate and children's theater, Saturday matinees.

SHOPPING. Values are so good here for South Americans that they flock to Miami with empty suitcases, which they fill up at the area's stores. It's not quite the same kind of bargain bonanza for American visitors, but the shopping here is varied and just about every department store in the nation has an outlet here. Many international shops also have a branch in South Florida.

Most stores here are gathered in shopping malls. Some of the top malls are listed below, with examples of the stores located in each.

Bal Harbour Shops. Probably the most exclusive mall in the area, this mall a block from the ocean in Bal Harbour has a *Neiman-Marcus, Ungaro, Rive Gauche, Martha,* and *Brooks Brothers* branches, to name a few. The mall is open Monday, Thursday, and Friday from 10:00 A.M. to 9:00 P.M.; Tuesday, Wednesday, and Saturday from 10:00 A.M. to 6:00 P.M.; and Sunday noon to 5:00 P.M. For information, call 866–0311.

Mayfair. Running a hot second to Bal Harbour Shops is Mayfair, situated in trendy Coconut Grove. Mayfair houses *Ralph Lauren, Berenka,* and *Charles Jourdan*—among other shops—and is adding a new wing. Mall hours are Monday and Thursday from 10:00 A.M. to 9:00 P.M.; Tuesday, Wednesday, Friday, and Saturday from 10:00 A.M. to 6:00 P.M. On Sundays, only the restaurants and one or two shops are open. For information, call 448–1700.

Dadeland. Anchoring this mall, one of the largest in the nation, are *Burdines, Jordan Marsh, J.C. Penney,* and *Saks Fifth Avenue.* There are hundreds of other shops and boutiques. Operating hours are Monday through Saturday from 10:00 A.M. to 9:30 P.M.; Sunday from noon to 5:30 P.M. For information, call 665–6226.

Aventura Mall. Located in the north end of the county, Aventura has the area's first *Macy's,* as well as a *Lord and Taylor, J.C.Penney,* and *Sears,* and 150 other shops. Hours are Monday through Saturday from 10:00 A.M. to 9:30 P.M., Sunday from noon to 5:30 P.M. For information, call 935–1110.

Omni International Mall. This downtown mall, situated in a fortresslike complex, has 165 shops and is anchored by a *Jordan Marsh* and a *J.C. Penney.* Operating hours are Monday through Saturday from 10:00 A.M. to 9:00 P.M., Sunday noon to 5:30 P.M. A small indoor amusement park is situated within the mall. For information, call 374–6664.

The Falls. This southwest area complex, built around a winding waterway and waterfalls, has added a new wing with a *Bloomingdale's,* the area's first. The Falls has about 60 shops, with 20-odd more in the new wing. Hours are Monday through Saturday from 10:00 A.M. to 9:00 P.M., Sunday from noon to 5:00 P.M. For information, call 255–4570.

Two other shopping locales that are not malls deserve mention. Coral Gables' *Miracle Mile* is a four-block-long street of shops with a Sears at one end. Downtown Miami is full of small discount shops that are a favorite target of Latin bargain hunters; you'll find good values here, but cash only and no returns. Miami Beach's *Lincoln Road Mall,* once a premier shopping area, has declined in recent years.

DINING OUT. As befits a melting-pot city, Miami offers a world's fair of dining experiences, from Continental and standard American to Vietnamese and Hungarian. The huge influx of Cuban exiles to Miami, of course, put a definite imprint on dining styles here. Miamians were soon introduced to traditional Cuban dishes such as arroz con pollo and paella, not to mention frituras de sesos (fritters of brains), sopa de ajo (garlic soup), jerked beef, and chatinos (fried green plantains). Then along came the refugees from Southeast Asia, and presto, soon there were restaurants serving mee grob (crisp rice noodles, shrimp, and scallions) and pad Thai (noodles, shrimp, pork, egg, and bean sprouts). Add to this an already superior collection of good restaurants and you have a city with a range of quality, diversity, and price that compares favorably with other large American metropolises. Tip: Because of the high concentration of multinational business offices in Coral Gables, you will find a number of excellent restaurants of various cuisines there.

Price Classifications and Abbreviations. The price classifications of the following restaurants, from inexpensive to deluxe, are based on the cost of an average three-course dinner for one person for food alone; beverages, tax and tip would be extra. *Inexpensive* means less than $10; *Moderate,* $10 to $14; *Expensive,* $14 to $22; and *Deluxe,* over $22. Abbreviations for credit cards are: A, American Express; D, Dinners Club; M, MasterCard; and V, Visa.

Abbreviations for meal codes are: L, Lunch; D, dinner. As restaurant hours and days of closing often change, you should call first to confirm the hours they are open. (Restaurants are in Miami, proper, unless otherwise noted.)

AMERICAN

Expensive-Deluxe

Christy's. 3101 Ponce de Leon Blvd., Coral Gables; 446–1400. It has functioned under different names, but is always popular with businessmen and the well-heeled Coral Gables crowd. Masculine decor—red walls, red gaslight sconces. Habitués swear it has the best beef in town (prime rib costs $15.75). Reservations. L and D. All credit cards.

Cye's Rivergate. 444 Brickell Ave.; 358–9100. On river downtown, popular with businessmen. D Monday–Saturday, L Monday–Friday. All credit cards.

David Harrison's Secret Garden. 4100 N.E. 2nd Ave.; 573–3331. Flowers, marble floors, mirrors give this restaurant a flamboyant touch. Elegant dishes complement the setting, Try the roast duck with California plums or conch fritters served on a conch shell. L Monday–Friday, D Monday–Saturday. All credit cards.

New York Steak House. 17985 Biscayne Blvd., North Miami; 932–7676. If you are homesick for that restsaurant ambiance back in the northeast you are going to feel right at home here. Caricatures of local celebrities on the walls; warm and hospitable welcome. Thick steaks and Maine lobsters. Live entertainment by a pianist. Fresh baked bread. L and D. All credit cards.

The Palm. Seacoast Towers East, 5151 Collins Ave., Miami Beach; 868–7256. This is an offspring of The Palm in New York, one of the Beach's more elegant dining spots. The steaks ($20) and pasta are popular, but the house delicacy is the lobster, flown in daily from Maine and Iceland ($11 a pound at the table.) The dining room features caricatures of local and national celebrities. Wednesday–Monday. Reservations. D. All credit cards.

Peppermill. 8800 S.W. 56th St.; 274–8800. This quiet, suburban restaurant is located in the heart of some of Miami's most beautiful homes where the ambitious middle class holds sway. Food includes Italian cuisine with veal, the pride of the house. Restaurant was once a golf course clubhouse and the ambiance still lingers. For that tucked away, quiet place to dine, this is the place. L and D, daily. All credit cards.

Port of Call. 14411 Biscayne Blvd.; 945–2567. The parking lot is always filled here and the lure is seafood. This is one of Miami's most popular seafood restaurants, although there is no water around. Clam and conch chowder are popular selections and try the yellowtail and swordfish. L and D daily. All credit cards.

The Rusty Pelican. 3201 Rickenbacker Causeway, Key Biscayne; phone 361–5753. Miamians know this restaurant has the best sunsets in town. Sit close to the water's edge outside and watch the Miami skyline sink into a golden glow in the west. Hold an exotic drink while you are doing it—the kind with little parasols in them, served in coconuts. Food won't excite you, but the view's great. L and D daily. All credit cards.

Moderate

Arthur's Eating House. 1444 Biscayne Blvd.; 371–1444. Popular with downtown businessmen for lunch; prices moderate (London broil for $5.95). Homemade soup and bread. Owner Arthur Horowitz has build up a comprehensive selection of the best California wines. Live entertainment in the evenings. L and D. All credit cards.

Coco's. 9700 Collins Ave., Miami Beach; 864–2626. This ritzy little place is located in the Bal Harbour world of shops like Martha's Saks, Bonwit Teller and Neiman-Marcus, so it's great place for people-watching indoors and out. No big deal about the cuisine; many customers settle for tasty snacks and desserts. Prices reflect the class of the area. L and D. All major credit cards.

English Pub. 320 Crandon Blvd., Key Biscayne; 361–5481. Pewter tankards hang from the ceiling (one belonged to ex-President Richard Nixon, who had his summer White House on the key), and oak beams and memorabilia make transplanted Britons nostalgic. L and D. All credit cards.

94th Aero Squadron. 1395 N.W. 67th Ave.; 261–4220. This is a franchised restaurant developed along the theme of a World War I farmhouse that headquarters a fighter squadron. But don't let that bother you. Here's a chance to look out on one of the nation's busiest airports, Miami International, which is on view from the restaurant's windows. They don't take reservations, however, so you take your chances. Strive for that table by the windows. L and D daily. All credit cards.

Roney Pub. 2305 Collins Ave., Miami Beach; 532–3353. On the site of the former Roney Plaza Hotel, an early Miami Beach establishment. As the name suggests, the decor is somewhat Tudor, but the food is solidly American. Ample portions. Prime rib is popular. Diners receive three loaves of fresh bread and if you can't eat it all, don't be afraid to ask for a doggie bag even if there isn't a dog at home. L and D. All credit cards.

Inexpensive

Cafe Brasserie. Coconut Grove Hotel, 2649 S. Bayshore Dr., Coconut Grove; 858–2500. The atmosphere is laid-back; has the apperance of a superior coffee shop with some tables overlooking the pool. Most food items under $10. After-theater crowd settle for hamburger and salad. L and D. All credit cards.

Cafe Cardozo. Cardozo Hotel, 1300 Ocean Dr., Miami Beach. 534–2135. Due to reopen in 1985 after extensive renovation. There's no better place to sample the sentiment for art deco in the Miami Beach area than Cafe Cordozo. Light snacks and tempting salads are more the vogue here than full meals. L and D. All credit cards.

Marshall Majors. 6901 W.W. 57th Ave., South Miami; 665–3661. Deli-type sit-down restaurant. L and D daily. M, V.

Mr. Clyde's. 16780 N.W. 67th Ave.; 825–7139; and 7700 N. Kendall Dr.; 595–4141. Miamians like their barbecued baby back ribs and many a fan says the best in town are right here—especially because of the sauce. Barbecued chicken and pork and beef sandwiches are also on hand, of course. Not real "ya'll Southern," but good. L and D daily. All credit cards.

Raffles. 163rd St. Shopping Center; 944–0853; and 7437 Dadeland Mall; 665–3987. If you are on a shopping outing at either of these first class malls, you'll be tempted to drop in at one of these restaurants. Put those shopping bags down and order yourself a Dagwood Grinder, or—Gad!—fried ice cream. L and D daily. All credit cards.

Shorty's. 9200 S. Dixie Hwy.; 665–5732. A South Miami tradition: a log cabin with family-style barbecue tables. Chicken and ribs specialties; new this year is catfish. L and D daily. No credit cards.

CHINESE

Deluxe

Two Dragons. 350 Ocean Dr., Key Biscayne; 361–2021. Breaded, clicking curtains hint of sweet intimacies inside the lanterned booths with their blue-tiled, pagoda-like roofs; muted Oriental music comes from somewhere. The food is exquisite: Moo Shoo Pork ($10.50) with bamboo shoots, mushroom, egg and scallion wrapped in thin crepes. Many of the vegetables are imported from China. Reservations. D. All credit cards.

Moderate

Christine Lee's Gaslight Restaurant. 18401 Collins Ave.; 932-1145. The enchanting and seemingly perdurable Miss Lee adds her own enchantment to her restaurant, which she has run for 15 years. Her favorite servings: coconut shrimp appetizeres ($6.50), lemon chicken ($10.95), Szechuan dumplings ($6.25), and her Cantonese eggplant Imperial ($9.50). D. All credit cards.

Tiger Tiger Teahouse. 5716 S. Dixie Hwy.; 665–5660. Modest prices, but excellent Mandarin and Szechuan food. Dinners start at $6.95. L and D. A, M, V.

Inexpensive-Moderate

Mandarin Garden. 3268 Grand Ave., Coconut Grove; 446–9999. If you're in artistic Coconut Grove, this is the only place for Chinese food, especially Szechwan. The Peking duck is $12.95, the Chef Tai chicken, with hot sauce and watercress, $9.25. You can also take out. L and D. M, V.

Inexpensive

Canton. 6661 S. Dixie Hwy.; 666–9198. Very popular. Giant portions of food—Cantonese, Szechuan, Mandarin—served. A Cantonese steak ($15) serves two or three persons; newcomers usually find they over order. L and D. M, V.

CONTINENTAL

Deluxe

Esplanade. 400 S.E. 2nd Ave.; 358–1234. Located in the downtown Hyatt Regency Hotel, and a favorite with concertgoers and the cocktail crowd. Specialty is Fettuccine Esplanade—homemade spinach pasta with shrimp, scallops, broccoli in sherry cream sauce, $13.95. Reservations. L and D. All credit cards.

The Forge. 432 Arthur Godfrey Rd., Miami Beach; 538–8533. This Continental institution is replete with Art Deco decor—chandeliers, an ornate carved ceiling, stained glass. International favorites are Singapore snapper and java steak. The service is excellent, and there is a superb wine cellar. The Forge has been here since 1929, and its reputation never falters, Reservations. Lounge/entertainment (no cover). D. All credit cards.

Vinton's Town House. 116 Alhambra Circle, Coral Gables; 445–2511. A prize-winner located in La Palma Hotel, built during World War I. Food always good, but Monday is gourmet night. An expert's wine list. L and D. All credit cards.

Expensive

The Bistro. 2611 Ponce de Leon Blvd., Coral Gables; 442–9671. Small and intimate. Try the homemade soups in this congenial owner-managed restaurant. Swiss/Continental cuisine. D daily. All credit cards.

Charade. 2900 Ponce de Leon Blvd., Coral Gables; 448-6077. Here are ferns, wicker chairs, and terracotta tiles in what used to be a Spanish furniture factory. Most popular dish is veal, prepared in several different ways. Gracious atmosphere. L and D. A, M, V.

Comme Chez Soi. 235 N.W. 37th Ave.; 649–4999. run by a Belgian couple, who don't care much about external appearances (the green exterior looks like a small, rather dreary apartment house), but offer wholesome food like carbonade flamode (beef with onion and black beer) for $9.25. L and D. All credit cards.

Melody Inn. 108 Aragon Av., Coral Gables; 448–0022. Swiss/Continental cuisine, specializing in veal dishes. L Tuesday–Friday, D daily. All credit cards.

La Paloma. 10999 Biscayne Blvd., North Miami; 891–0505. Austrian chef serves excellent and reasonably priced Continental food. D daily. A, M, V.

Prince Hamlet. 19115 Collins Ave., Miami Beach, 932-8488. Conceived, unsurprisingly, by a Dane, the restaurant's main attraction is a 40-item all-you-can-eat cold buffet including caviar, shrimp, and pickled herring. But available only after you order an entree, such as snapper in a paper bag ($17.95). D. V, M.

Rogers on the Green. 4000 Crandon Blvd., Key Biscayne; 361–9460. It's open for lunch (light meals), but more patronized at dinnertime, so people can watch the sun set behind the golf course. Lobster tails $16.50. All credit cards.

Whiffenpoof. 2728 Ponce de Leon Blvd., Coral Gables; 445–6603. French/Continental cuisine, reservations required weekends. Closed Mondays. All credit cards.

Moderate-Expensive

Piccadilly Hearth. 35 N.E. 40th St.; 576–1818. English pub atmosphere in Miami's design district. The menu runs from breast of chicken Florentine to steak au poivre flambe, which is about as imaginative as they come. L and D. All credit cards.

Village Inn. 3131 Commodore Plaza; 445–8721. In a delightful setting of wood and plants amid a small world of boutiques. You go for the ambiance rather than the food, though the veal Francaise and chicken tetrazzini are satisfying. Very attentive service. L and D. All credit cards.

CUBAN/SPANISH

Expensive

Cervantes. 2121 Ponce de Leon Blvd., Coral Gables; 446–8636. This is very much Spanish; indeed, the decor reflects the spirit of Don Quixote with wood-carved ceilings, arches, porcelain plates. The menu has entrees like cordero Segovia (lamb in sherry) and vaga Secilia (shrimp in wine with hollandaise sauce). The tapas appetizers, eaten at the bar, are delicious. Spanish singers nightly, flamenco show at weekends. L and D. All credit cards.

El Cid. 117 N.W. 42nd St.; 541–3514. This is a Latin glamour restaurant with strolling musicians, expensive food and a romantic atmosphere. It is tremendously popular and somewhat on the dressy side. It's worth the visit, however, for the Latin ambiance, the hum of excitement that makes the place lively, and the flamenco dancers in the lounge. L and D. All credit cards.

Moderate

Bilbao. 5910 SW 8th St., West Miami; 266–2010. Basque cuisine, music and dancing in lounge. Closed Mondays. All credit cards.

El Gaucho. 3494 S.W. 8th St.; 444–6968. Argentine cuisine, emphasis on steaks. Closed Tuesdays. All credit cards.

Juanito's Centro Vasco. 2235 S.W. 8th St.; 643–9606. Spanish cuisine, specialties are paella and seafood. L and D daily. Major credit cards.

Malaga. 740 S.W. 8th St.; 858–4224. This is a traditional Cuban restaurant popular with non-Spanish speaking patrons as well as with Latin clientele. Paella, a wonderful seafood and rice "stew" that includes many other ingredients is worth the wait. Also consider the white bean soup, a Cuban delicacy and the arroz con pollo (chicken and rice.) You are going to try the latter dish at one time or another if you dine Cuban in Miami and this is a good place to start. L and D. All credit cards.

Los Ranchos. 135 S.W. 107th Ave., Sweetwater; 552–6767. Char-broiled steaks are the specialty of this Nicaraguan restaurant. Try the Nicaraguan dessert, très-leches, made of three kinds of milk. L and D daily. All credit cards.

La Tasca. 2741 W. Flagler St.; 642–3762. Its next door to the Dade County Auditorim, where most concerts and recitals are held in Miami, so it's a favorite with the 6–6:30 P.M., before-the-event crowd (not after, because it closes at 9:30 P.M.). You can get anything from roast chicken with black beans and plantains for $5, to a $15 lobster. Don't linger if you want to get there for curtain time. They take early reservations. L and D. All credit cards.

Inexpensive

La Carreta. 3632 S.W. 8th St.; 444–7501. The influx of Cubans into Miami brought with it the Cuban sandwich. It's a meal in itself prepared on crispy Cuban bread. A good place to get your teeth into one is at this restaurant. It's also a popular late night spot, so if you want to catch Latins in a festive, late evening mood, this is a good place to go to catch a glimpse of what goes on after hours. L and D. All credit cards.

La Esquina de Tejas. 101 S.W. 12th Ave.; 545–5341. President Reagan catapulted this modest restaurant into local fame by having lunch here during a tour of Miami aimed at wooing the Latin vote. The result was an incredible growth of popularity for the eating establishment. You can enjoy the same things that the president did by ordering roast chicken, moros (black beans and rice prepared together), fried plantains, flan (custard), and Cuban coffee. L and D. All credit cards.

Islas Canarias. 285 N.W. 27th Ave.; 649–0440. This has become a gathering place for a mixed bag of personalities—writers, singers, bankers, actors, and painters—all of whom know where to find excellent Cuban food at very moderate prices (the Fantasia Canaria, which is crabmeat in white sauce, goes for $5.95). The menu changes daily, so even if Fantasia Canaria isn't available one day, there'll be enough optional temptations. L and D. No credit cards.

El Minerva. 265 N.E. 2nd St.; 374–9420. This is probably Miami's oldest Cuban restaurant, established long before the coming of refugees. It has long been a popular eating spot for Miamians and continues to be so despite the enormous growth of other Latin restaurant attractions. Food is solidly traditional. Try the pork and chicken in almost any form. You will know that you are getting the real thing if you elect to lunch or dine here. All credit cards.

El Segundo Viajante. 2846 Palm Ave. Hialeah; 888–5465; 1676 Collins Ave., Miami Beach, 534–2101; 7390 W. Flagler St., Miami, 261–6444. Authentic, although basic, Cuban food (seafood paella is the best). Because of low prices (entrees range from $3.95 to $11), it's crowded at lunchtime. All credit cards.

FRENCH

Deluxe

Cafe Chauveron. 9561 E. Bay Harbor Dr., 866–8779. The Mobil Guide five-star award-winner, and recommended by every gourmet magazine, serves classic French cuisine, expertly served. The service is elaborate and the wines superb. And it's expensive. Reservations a must. All credit cards.

Dominique's. Alexander Hotel, 5225 Collins Ave., Miami Beach; 861–5252. This mostly French specialty restaurant, owned by Dominique D'Ermo of Lyon, France, tempts the more adventurous diner with its rattlesnake and alligator dishes; others will probably settle for the superb rack of lamb ($22), which is the house specialty. Reservations essential. L and D. All credit cards.

Pavillon Grill. 100 Chopin Plaza; 577–1000. This one is located in one of Miami's newest and most impressive hotels on the bay front, The Pavillon, which accounts for the mahogany walls, leather chairs, Irish linen, and Italian silver. Get braised pigeon ($26) or sweetbreads with crayfish ($22.50). L and D. All credit cards.

Expensive

Brasserie de Paris. 244 Biscayne Blvd.; 379–5461. Situated in Miami's venerable Everglades Hotel, the Brasserie offers Choucroute Alsacienne, pot-au-feu, and a white bean stew served by black-tied waiters by candlelight. One of the great French experiences in Miami—a gourmet's delight. L and D. All credit cards.

Chez Vendome. David William Hotel, 700 Biltmore Way; 443–4646. There are red velvet booths and framed paintings on the walls of this eating place that has retained its reputation for quality over a couple of decades. A romantic place for anniversaries. Try the oysters Florentine. There is an extensive wine cellar. L and D. All credit cards.

Le Festival. 2120 Salzedo St., Coral Gables; 442–8545. Simple setting and pricey, but consistently good food like red snapper Duglere and frogs' legs. Reservations. L and D. A, M, V.

French Connection. 2626 Ponce de Leon Blvd., Coral Gables; 442–8587. Try the Long Island duck, and beef Wellington (Saturday nights only). L Monday–Friday, D daily. All credit cards.

Le Manoir. 2534 Ponce de Leon Blvd.; 442–1990. Friday is bouillabaisse night ($18.75), but the rest of the week, take consolation in the duck a l'orange,

$12. There's a delicious rice cake dessert. There are luncheon specials for $6.95. L and D. All credit cards.

Restaurant St. Michel. 2135 Ponce de Leon Blvd.; 446–6572. In an elegant old hotel, which the new owners are restoring to the atmosphere of the 20s with the intestines of demolished old movie theaters. Famous for its crepes, but offers a selection of other items. L and D. All credit cards.

INDIAN

Moderate

House of India. 22 Merrick Way, Coral Gables; 444–2348. Recorded sitar music while you dine on fish, curry and vegetarian dishes. Smooth Indian atmosphere in a long-established eating place. L and D. All credit cards.

ITALIAN

Deluxe

Gatti's. 1427 West Ave., Miami Beach; 673–1717. Undistinguished decor, somewhat on the lines of Joe's Stone Crabs, but who cares, because the quality of the northern Italian food has made this popular Beach landmark a must for the local winter regulars. Seafood to pasta, but the menu is strictly a la carte. Jackets requested, which may tell you something, considering the casual area. Reservations suggested. D. All credit cards.

La Scala. 951 Crandon Blvd., Key Biscayne; 361–2436. Northern- and Southern-style cooking available. One of the best entrees: red snapper with shrimp stuffing, $13.50. L and D. All credit cards.

Raimondo's. 4612 Lejeune Rd.; 666–9919. Raimondo is a legend, and has scooped up numerous awards for his Northern cooking (his fettuccini Alfredo doesn't bear comparison). The decor is modest, but the pastas are superb—and Super-superb when Raimondo himself is in town. Reservations. D. A, C, D.

Tiberio. Bal Harbour Shops, 9700 Collins Ave.; 861–6161. You can enjoy your cannelloni and pasta rolls stuffed with veal and mozzarella ($10.95) at an elegant table while surveying fine art. Service excellent. All credit cards.

Expensive

Pappagallo. 11500 Biscayne Blvd., North Miami; 895–3730. Specialties here include braciola di manzo (stuffed beef rolls), filettini di cappone alla Piemontese (sliced capon in wine and mushroom sauce), and its own tetrazzini Pappagallo. Strolling guitarists add atmosphere. D Monday–Saturday. All credit cards.

Valenti's. 9101 S. Dixie Hwy.; 667–0421. Long-established Italian restaurant used to be in northwest section, moved south a few years ago. L and D daily. All credit cards.

Moderate

Bellina's. 1559 Sunset Dr., South Miami; 661–3035. Dining amid original art and classical music. Northern Italian cuisine. L weekdays, D daily. Major credit cards.

D'Andrea's Restaurant. 8745 Sunset Dr.; 271–4745. Owner chef Joe D'Andrea prepares lusty southern Italian dishes with some northern touches, while his daughter manages the dining room. Unlike many Italian chefs, D'Andrea is easy on the garlic. Try the gnocchi (tiny potato dumplings), $4, the dolphin fra diavolo ($15.95), and one of his inspirations, vitello—thin, sauteed veal slices with tomato and cream sauces, topped with ricotta-stuffed sauteed eggplant rolls. ($15.95.) D. All credit cards.

Inexpensive-Expensive

Capriccio. 12313 S. Dixie Hwy.; 255–3422. More tuxedoed waiters in simple surroundings. Specialty of the house: shrimp and lobster scampi on a bed of linguini for $15.95. Good selection of Italian and California wines. Reservations. D. A, M, V.

JAPANESE

Expensive

Japanese Steak House. Miami Viscount Hotel, 500 Deer Run; 871–6000. Costumed hostesses offer choice of chicken, sirloin, or jumbo shrimp prepared at the table. D. All credit cards.

Samurai Steak House. 8717 S.W. 136th St.; 238–2131. The $17.95 dinner here is guaranteed to satisfy a Samurai warrior: filet and lobster or steak and chicken, chicken liver or shrimp appetizer, soup, salad, vegetable, rice and dessert. (Early bird special 5:30–7 P.M.; $7.45). L and D. All credit cards.

Toshi. 5759 S.W. 40th St.; 661–0511. Choice of a la carte sushi, tempuras, teriyakis, or sashimis served by kimono-clad waitresses. Sit on floor or at tables. D. A, M, V.

Inexpensive

Shibui. Sunset Dr. and S.W. 102nd Ave.; 274–5578. Modestly hidden behind a shopping center, Shibui fast earned a reputation for knowledgeable treatment of sushi, tempura and teriyaki, at similarly modest prices starting at $6.95. D. A, D, M, V.

MEXICAN

Inexpensive

Coco Loco. 3500 Main Hwy., Coconut Grove; 446–4562. It's right next to the Playhouse, so theater-goers pop in afterwards to its vast confines for chicken mole, tostadas, and enchiladas. There's a huge bar from which emerge huge margaritas. A mariachi band keeps the place jumping. From 11 A.M. to 2 A.M. A, M, V.

Mexico Lindo. 61 Giralda Ave., Coral Gables; 446–2360. Traditional Mexican specialties. D daily except Mondays. A, M, V.

El Torito. Falls Shopping Center, 888 Howard Dr.; 255–6506. Popular with younger crowd, specialty is fajitas—sauteed, marinated chicken and beef. L Monday–Saturday; brunch with mariachis Sunday; D daily. All credit cards.

NATURAL

Inexpensive

Granny Feelgood's. 190 S.E. 1st Ave.; 358–6233 and 555 N.E. 15th St., Miami Beach; 371–2085. "Granny" is a shrewd gentleman named Irving Fields, who loved his grandmother. Health-conscious downtown office workers swarm all over Granny's first Avenue spot (the Plaza Venetia restaurant is less frenetic) for budget-priced fruit salads or baked stuffed potato florentine with spinach, cheese and salad ($3.95), raw vegetable sandwiches ($2.25), spinach pie (95 cents), or lobster salad sandwich ($3.95). Lately, Granny has added fresh fish and chicken. L and D. All credit cards.

The Good Earth. 11740 N. Kendall Dr.; 279–5513. Homemade soups, salads and sandwiches with dinner entrees $5.45–$9.95 in a rustic setting of plants, brass fans, and linens. Great carrot cake. L and D. AMV.

The Spiral. 1630 Ponce de Leon Blvd., Coral Gables; 447–0646. Simple setting, but generous salads and seafood and vegeterian dishes. Good value in the wines. L and D. A, M, V.

The Unicorn. 16454 N.E. 6th Ave.; 944–5595. Tofu lasagna, broccoli-noodle parmesan, vegetable cheddar nut loaf, and fish and poultry dishes beautifully presented. No alcohol. L and D. M, V.

SEAFOOD

Deluxe

Grand Cafe. 2669 S. Bayshore Dr.; 858–9600. In one of Miami's spanking new hotels in Coconut Grove, the Grand Bay, the restaurant has pink and burgundy decor and a profusion of flowers. The grilled swordfish ($17.50), pompano en Papillote ($18.50), and other delicacies are done Continental-style. Entertainment in the evenings. L and D. All credit cards.

Expensive

Joe's Stone Crabs. 227 Biscayne St., Miami Beach; 673–0365. Of all the restaurants in the Miami area, none is as popular as Joe's Stone Crabs, a local institution if ever there was one. The name says it all. Stone crabs, dipped in a buttery lemon sauce, are a local legend, and for many nobody does them better than this restaurant. Be prepared to stand in line; no reservations. But there's many a native who will attest that the wait is worth it. Many other seafoods, too, of course. L and D. All credit cards.

JP's, 3360 Pan American Dr., Coconut Grove; 858–7510. Raw bar; seafood buffet Wednesday nights (all you can eat, $13.95). View of Biscayne Bay. Closed Mondays. Major credit cards.

Monty Trainer's. 2560 S. Bayshore Dr.; 858–1431. You sit outdoors at wooden tables and gaze out on Biscayne Bay, or, if you're more refined, take refuge from the sun in the air-conditioned dining room. One of the liveliest places in town, with excellent bouillabaise ($15.95) and conch, that shellfish delicacy from these waters, in chowder or salad. Good outside raw bar. Popular with the T-shirt and cufoff jeans crowd. Forget about reservations. L and D. All credit cards.

Moderate

The Crab House. 1551 79th St., Causeway; 868–7085. They give you wooden mallets to crack the garlic crabs here. All-you-can-eat crab specials for $10. There's also a raw bar and salad bar. L and D. A, M, V.

East Coast Fisheries. 360 W. Flagler St.; 373–5515. The clientele is mostly Latin in this fish warehouse. Raw bar and only Florida seafood, but fresh—grouper, conch, squid, stone crabs, sea trout. It's also a seafood market in case the experience makes you want to take away. L and D. No credit cards.

The Sandbar. 301 Ocean Dr., Key Biscayne; 361–1049. The Silver Sands Motel, a relic from the 50's, once was practically the only such establishment on the Key Biscayne waterfront; now it is dwarfed by giant hotels and condominiums. But old-time regulars still like to sit on the terrace of its restaurant, The Sandbar, and watch the waves roll in. Good basics in Florida fish, jolly atmosphere. L and D. A, M, V.

NIGHT LIFE. Gone are the days when Miami and Miami Beach were the entertainment capitals of the U.S., with night clubs and hotel cabarets abounding with big name entertainers. The growth of hundreds of condominium high rises pushed most of them out of business.

However, you can still get night life on the plush side today, much of it with a Latin beat. The Latin influx into Miami and Miami Beach brought with it the nostalgia of such famous night clubs as the Tropicana in Havana. The Cubans who have arrived on south Florida's shores haven't allowed their love of staying up late for supper and flashy night club revues to die out entirely. There are three major Latin clubs that entertain in their tradition, all of them on the Miami side of Biscayne Bay. The entertainment they offer combines both Latin and American music, particularly Broadway show tunes for the latter. You will also catch some flamenco and folklorico styles of dancing.

To attend one of these supper clubs is to catch a glimpse of Miami's cosmopolitan *Latin* life. All of the revues offered at these clubs are lavish and present singers, variety acts, and chorus lines. Topless showgirls, however, are never seen in classy Latin clubs.

Copacabana, newest of Miami's Latin supper clubs, 3600 S.W. 8th St. in Little Havana; 443–3801. Lavish decor. Expensive. Major credit cards.

Flamenco Supper Club, 991 N.E. 79th St.; 751–8631. Folklorico and flamenco are popular with the choreographers here. Expensive. Colorful dance routines and staging. Major credit cards.

Les Violins is the oldest established Labin club in Miami, 1751 Biscayne Blvd.; 371–8668. Lavish revue. Expensive. Remember Latins like to dress for late night outings. Major credit cards.

American-style night life in Miami and Miami Beach is a little more subdued with the exception of the Las Vegas-style revue at the **Sheraton Bel Harbour Hotel,** 9701 Collins Ave., Bal Harbour (which natives think of as part of Miami Beach); 865–7511. The revue in the hotel's Bal Masque Room is seasonal, usually running from November through April. Topless dancers, first rate singers, and choreography. Expensive. Major credit cards.

Konover Hotel (5445 Collins Ave., Miami Beach, 865–1500) and **Deauville Hotel** (6701 Collins Ave., Miami Beach; 865–8511) also have seasonal revues.

Arthur's Eating House, 1444 Biscayne Blvd., Miami; 371–1444. Beautiful lounge; excellent art collection. Sophisticated piano jazz. Moderate. Casual. Dinner served. Major credit cards.

Ciga Lounge, Grand Bay Hotel, 2669 S. Bayshore Dr., Coconut Grove; 858–9600. One of Miami's newest and most elegant hotels with one of Regine's famous private clubs occupying the top floor. Trios usually play the Ciga. Expensive. Major credit cards.

Club Mystique, Airport Hilton Hotel, 5101 Blue Lagoon Dr., Miami; 262–1000. Dance music alternates with DJ. Informal. Major credit cards.

Club Top Draw, 1850 79th St. Causeway, Miami; 868–6800. Popular spot to see and be seen. Middle-aged patronage. Food, music, and lively bar scene. Recently reopened and redecorated. Major credit cards.

Currents Lounge, Hyatt Regency Hotel, 400 S.E. 2nd Ave. Large bands, plus reggae music. This is one of Miami's newest hotels and lounges. Casual. Contemporary decor; colorful. Major credit cards.

Daphne's, Sheraton River House, 3900 N.W. 21st St.; 871–3200. Popular Miami spot; sleek atmosphere. Casual attire. Major credit cards.

Doral Hotel, 4833 Collins Ave., Miami Beach; 532–3600. Rousseau's and the Downstairs Lounge have entertainment nightly.

Fanny's Lounge, Holiday Inn, 495 Brickell Ave.,Miami; 373–6000 Piano music, both popular and jazz. View of the Miami River. Casual. Major credit cards.

Flynn's Ocean 71, 6985 Collins Ave., Miami Beach; 865–4098. Rock, pop. Shows 9 P.M. to 4 A.M. nightly, doors open at 7. Cover varies.

Follies International Restaurant and Lounge, 3301 W. Okeechobee Rd., Hialeah; 557–2221. For those who want a little walk on the wild side. Nude dancers are featured but quality is high and food is good. Moderate. Major credit cards.

Fontainebleau Hilton Hotel, 4441 Collins Ave., Miami Beach; 538–2000, has shows in its Poodle Lounge.

The Forge, 432 Arthur Godfrey Road, Miami Beach, 538–8533. One of the top clubs in area, with Latin and disco bands; shows 9:30 P.M.–4:30 A.M. nightly.

Greenstreet's, Holiday Inn, 2051 LeJeune Rd., Coral Gables; 445–2131. Piano bar in tropical setting. Moderate. Major credit cards.

Manhattan Club, 6600 Red Rd., South Miami; 666–1375. Video dance club. Informal. Moderate. Major credit cards.

Marco Polo Hotel and Resort, 19201 Collins Ave., Miami Beach; 932–2233. The hotel's several lounges are usually active, especially with musical revues, most all of which are produced locally and feature nostalgia themes. Moderate. Major credit cards.

Miami Playboy Club. 1550 N.W. LeJeune Rd., Miami; 871–5200. The lounge features entertainment nightly and is open 6 P.M.–3 A.M. Monday through Saturday.

Monty Trainer's Bayshore Inn, 2560 S. Bayshore Dr., Coconut Grove; 858–1431. Jazz sessions for a youthful crowd. Restaurant and lounge. Moderate. Major credit cards.

Newport Beach Resort, 16701 Collins Ave., Miami Beach; 949–1300. There's almost always something going on here, usually a musical revue. Name entertainers are sometimes featured, and road shows come in occasionally. Informal. Moderate. Major credit cards.

New York Steak House, 17985 Biscayne Blvd., North Miami Beach; 932–7676. Nightly shows (contemporary, jazz) 9 P.M.–2 A.M., later on weekends.

The Place at Palm Bay, 6815 Biscayne Blvd., Miami; 758–8755. Soul and jazz. Restaurant adjoining. Moderate. Casual. Major credit cards.

The Place for Steak, 1335 79th Street Causeway, North Bay Village, 758–5581. Harbor Lounge has shows 9 P.M.–2:30 A.M. weekends, 8:30 P.M.–2:30 A.M. other nights except Mondays. Pianist on Mondays.

Porter's Lounge, Miami Airport Marriott Hotel, 1201 LeJeune Rd.; 649–5000. Piano bar. Attractive, romantic setting. Casual. Major credit cards.

Rick's Cafe, 5859 S.W. 73rd St.; 666–8223. Top 40 band, popular with young professionals. Cover on weekends.

Rollo's, 9100 S. Dixie Hwy., Miami; 665–0025. Rock and roll for a young crowd. Inexpensive. No credit cards.

Ronnie's, Miami Skyways Hotel, 2373 LeJeune Rd., Miami; 871–3230. Lots of fun, lots of music. Audience participation encouraged. Popular with airline personnel. Moderate. Major credit cards.

Rumcake Lounge, Howard Johnson's Motor Lodge, 16500 N.W. 2nd Ave.; 945–2621. Active crowd; loud rock-and-roll and pop music. Informal. Major credit cards.

700 Club, David William Hotel, 700 Biltmore Way, Coral Gables; 445–7821. Piano bar atop prestigious hotel with good view of the city of Coral Gables, particularly at night. Food available. Moderate. Major credit cards.

Stefano's, 24 Crandon Blvd., Key Biscayne; 361–7007. Pop, swing, jazz. Nightly entertainment. $5 cover without dinner.

Suzanne's in the Grove, 2843 S. Bayshore Dr., Coconut Grove; 441–1500. Nightly entertainment (jazz, swing, pop).

Tobacco Road, 626 S. Miami Ave.; 374–1198. Jazz and popular piano music in two different rooms. Setting is in older part of Miami, and site has local history to go with it. Very informal. Inexpensive. Major credit cards.

Ziegfield's, at the Holiday Inn Airport Lakes, 1101 N.W. 57th Ave.; 261–8500. One of Miami's newest night clubs with ambiance based on a 20's razzle dazzle theme. Not to be confused with Florenz Ziegfield. Dancing, dinner. Moderate. Major credit cards.

"Z." 1235 Washington Ave., Miami Beach; 538–0888. An old art deco theater restored as a dance club. A laser light show is the centerpiece of the club's $1.6 million sound and light system. VIP lounges are on the top floor of the two story club, above a spacious dance floor. Doors open at 10 P.M. and close at 5 A.M. Open weekends only. Admission is $12.

EXPLORING THE EVERGLADES

Everglades National Park is the largest subtropical wilderness in the United States. In 1979, the United Nations declared the Everglades a World Heritage Site. This 1,400,000-acre area thereby joined the Serengeti Plain in Africa, the Galapagos Islands, and Mt. Everest as a unique preserve.

This vast park at the southwest tip of Florida is the protected habitat of alligators, crocodiles, and the shy, harmless manatee ("sea cow"), which weighs close to a ton and is 15 feet long and feeds on plants. Bird life includes the great white heron, roseate spoonbill, reddish egrets, southern bald eagle, peregrine falcon, short-tailed hawk, and osprey. The Everglades's famous "River of Grass" is a slow-moving river only 6 inches deep but 50 miles wide; its mangrove islands, swamp, and jungle team with the fish and wildlife. Park rangers will lead you on tours for an intimate look at the wildlife. The Everglades has coastal prairie, pinelands, cypress, jungle, swamp.

Canoe trips, hiking trails, saltwater and freshwater fishing are all available. You can rent boats, stay at Everglades Park campgrounds, attend campfire programs, and drive your car within the park. The Everglades National Park is open 24 hours a day, including holidays. The main entrance is just 50 miles from Miami.

PRACTICAL INFORMATION FOR THE EVERGLADES

HOW TO GET THERE. From Miami, take US 1 to Homestead, where a sign directs you to the Everglades entrance and *Main Visitor Center.* Or, if you are coming from Florida's west coast, you can enter the park at Everglades City, 40 miles from Naples.

At the *Main Visitor Center,* you'll find exhibits, orientation programs, detailed maps, and other information, as well as an introductory film that is shown regularly. An entrance fee of $2 per car is charged at the Main Visitor Center only; it is good until noon the next day, and you can leave by any exit.

MOTELS AND COTTAGES. *Flamingo Lodge,* at Flamingo on Florida Bay, 38 miles from the Main Entrance, has the only overnight accommodations, aside from camping, in the Park. Air-conditioned motel rooms and full-service cottages are available year-round. The Flamingo Lodge offers a restaurant and lounge, swimming pool, full-service marina, gift shop, grocery store, and sunset cruises and other Everglades trips. Flamingo is also a park-ranger station.

To Flamingo Lodge rates below, add 5 percent Florida sales tax: Winter (Nov.1–May 31), standard double room and private bath: $55–$65 (for two people). Summer rate, $33. Standard cottage, winter rate: $63 (for two people), $6 for each additional person. Summer: $50, plus $3 for each additional person. Reservations advisable. Also available for rent are boats, canoes, and bicycles. For additional information or reservations, write: Flamingo Inn, Flamingo, 33030; 813–695–3101 or 305–253–2241.

CAMPING. You can camp at two National Park Service campgrounds. *Long Pine Key Campground* is 5 miles inside the main entrance and has 108 sites. *Flamingo* is 38 miles from the main entrance and has 300 sites. Flamingo also has walk-in sites. Hookups are not available at either campground, but both have modern comfort stations, drinking water, picnic tables, fire grills, and tent and trailer pads. Rates for both areas: trailer and tent sites, $5 per night; walk-in sites (at Flamingo only), $4 per night. Campsites are available on a first-come, first-serve basis; no reservations. But *group* campsites can be reserved in advance.

You may also camp, without charge, at other designated sites—on beaches or in the backcountry, areas reached by foot or boat. You must first obtain a free back-country use permit at the park entrance station or at a ranger station. For further camping information, write to: Everglades National Park, Box 279, Homestead 33030.

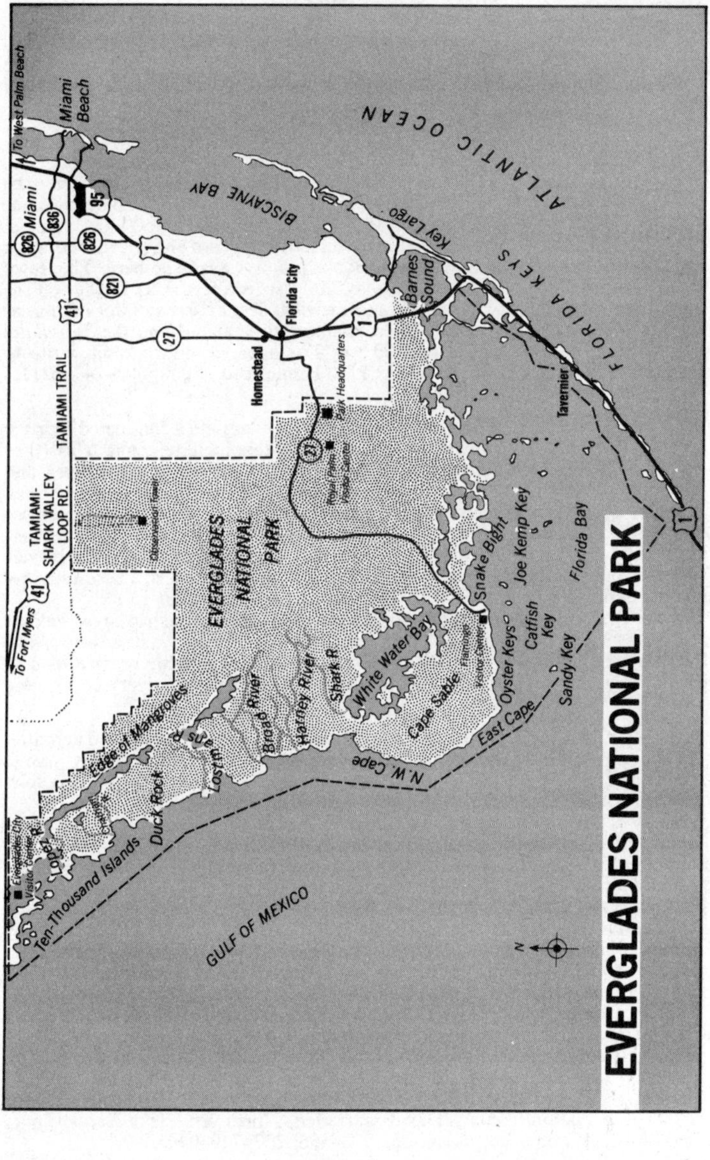
EVERGLADES NATIONAL PARK
To West Palm Beach
Miami Beach
Miami
ATLANTIC OCEAN
BISCAYNE BAY
Key Largo
FLORIDA KEYS
Barnes Sound
Florida City
Homestead
Park Headquarters
Royal Palm Visitor Center
Tavernier
TAMIAMI TRAIL
TAMIAMI-SHARK VALLEY LOOP RD.
Observation Tower
To Fort Myers
EVERGLADES NATIONAL PARK
Edge of Mangroves
Lost Man's R.
Broad River
Harney River
Shark R.
White Water Bay
Cape Sable
Flamingo Visitor Center
Snake Bight
Joe Kemp Key
Florida Bay
Oyster Keys
Catfish Key
Sandy Key
East Cape
N.W. Cape
Duck Rock
Ten-Thousand Islands
Lopez R.
Everglades City Visitor Center
GULF OF MEXICO
N
95
1
41
27
826
836
821

HOW TO GET AROUND. There is no public transportation within the park. You can drive a car or RV, hike, or bicycle. Bicycle rental is available at Flamingo and Shark Valley centers. The park has trails marked as being accessible to handicapped people in wheelchairs. There are also rental boats and canoes, and sightseeing tours by boat or open-air tram (see below). Marked maps at the visitor centers show trails and points of interest.

TOURIST INFORMATION. *Visitor Centers* are open daily. At the *Main Visitor Center* (near the park entrance on State Road 27), open 8:00 A.M. to 5:00 P.M., you can see an 18-minute introductory film and learn about park trails, tours, camping, and activities. Books are also available here. The *Royal Palm Visitors' Center,* open 8:00 A.M. to 5:00 P.M., is a few miles farther on the main road through the Everglades and provides less extensive information, as do the *Flamingo Visitor Center,* open 8:00 A.M. to 5:00 P.M., and the *Everglades City Center,* open 8:00 A.M. to 5:00 P.M. For advance information, write to Everglades National Park, P.O. Box 279, Homestead 33030; 305–247–6211.

FREE ACTIVITIES. Free activities conducted by park rangers at the visitor centers include **canoe trips** (they furnish the canoes, except at *Everglades City Center,* and Flamingo, where you must bring your own or rent one), **campfire programs, demonstrations, hikes** (wear your oldest clothes), **sunrise bird walks,** and **moonlight night prowls.** You can go on a four-hour ranger-guided car caravan (you provide your own car), take part in a ranger-led bicycle trip, see slides, or be led on a "wet" walk through the swamps. These activities change daily, so ask at the visitor centers for the schedules.

Note: Because of the popularity of the ranger-guided canoe trips, reservations are necessary, but they will be taken no more than three days in advance. The Park wants to offer this program to as many people as possible, so visitors may attend only one ranger-guided canoe trip per Visitor Center every two weeks.

TOURS. In addition to the free ranger-guided activities mentioned above, sightseeing tours provided by private concessioners are available. Add 5-percent Florida sales tax to the fares below:

Air Boat Rides of Cooper Town (22700 S.W. 8th St., Miami, 226–6048, about 15 miles west of the Palmetto Expressway) cost $6, and you usually see an alligator or two in the propeller-powered craft that skim over swamp water.

Everglades Air Boating offers rides from near the main entrance to Everglades National Park for $7.50 for half an hour.

Mangrove Wilderness Trip, available at Park Docks, Chokoloskee Causeway on Rte. 29, near Everglades City. This is a 1¾ hour boat trip through the Park's mangrove jungle—accessible only by boat—where birdlife is plentiful. For rates and information: Sammy Hamilton, Box 119, Everglades 33929; 813–695–2591.

There are also 4- to 12-day Everglades trips, available from *North American Canoe Tours.* These expert canoe trips include all food and equipment, accept no more than 10 people on a trip, and have skilled, knowledgeable guides. Four-day adventure, $225; 12-day Everglades exploration (for the seasoned canoeist), $545 per person. Two six-day trips, $345 and $395 per person. For further information, contact David Harraden, North American Canoe Tours Inc., 65 Black Point Rd., Niantic, CT 06356; 203–739–0791.

Sunset Cruise. At Flamingo. An hour-and-a-half cruise among the Everglades islands at day's end when the great herons, egrets, and ibis return to their island nests and roosts. Cocktails available on board. Adults, $5.50; children 6 to 12, $2.75; under 6, free. Open daily, approximately November to May.

Ten Thousand Island Boat Trip, available at Park Docks, Chokoloskee Causeway, on Rte. 29, near Everglades City. A 2½ hour trip through the outer mangrove islands bordering the Gulf of Mexico. Includes a brief stop for exploration and shelling. Fares range from $5 to $8 for adults; approximately half price for children. For further information, contact Sammy Hamilton, Box 119, Everglades 33929; 813–695–2591.

Whitewater Bay Cruise (year-round), at Flamingo Lodge. A two-hour boat trip with a naturalist guide through the wilderness, along canal banks, to Whitewater Bay, home of the manatee (sea cow) and bottlenose dolphin. Daily. Adults, $7.25; children 6 to 12, $3.60; under 6, free.

Wilderness Tram, at Flamingo. An open-air "tram" with a naturalist driver takes you on a two-hour trail that includes orchids and cacti, animal life, alligators, rare birds daily. Adults, $6; children 6 to 12, $3; under 6, free. Open approximately from November to May.

FISHING. The inland and coastal waters of the Everglades are popular fishing grounds. There are largemouth bass in freshwater ponds. Saltwater species include snapper, redfish, and trout. Saltwater fishing does not require license, but you need a Florida state fishing license for freshwater fishing. Florida fishing regulations apply. In addition, special federal regulations apply within the Park boundary. Ask at visitor centers or ranger stations for a copy of the park's fishing regulations. Charter fishing boats are available at *Flamingo Marina,* 813–695–3101 or 305–253–2241. The marina also has rental skiffs, motors, and canoes year-round. At Everglades City, canoe rental is available November 1 through April 30, through *Sammy Hamilton,* Box 113, Everglades 33929; 813–695–2591.

NORTH OF MIAMI

Fort Lauderdale to Palm Beach

by
JOEL A. GLASS

The portion of Florida's Gold Coast heading north from Miami is anchored at either end by two of the most beautiful—and distinctively unusual—cities in the state, perhaps in the entire country.

Fort Lauderdale, at the southern end, likes to call itself "The Venice of America" because of its distinctive 165-mile system of navigable inland waterways and canals and its annual Venetian Festival of Food and Fashion. The original canal-laced Venice is in fact Fort Lauderdale's sister city.

At the northern extremity of the Gold Coast sits legendary Palm Beach, playground of the wealthy, offering some of the world's most expensive pieces of real estate, many of the largest yachts, and the most chic shopping street this side of Paris.

The roughly 45-mile strip of coastal Florida connecting the two is a continual series of beaches, which become increasingly less crowded the farther north you travel, and strings of mostly small residential communities ranging from the Spanish-Mediterranean, heavily landscaped beauty of Boca Raton to the near-harsh ugliness of communities such as Lantana.

Fort Lauderdale

Water, water everywhere . . .

With its population of 154,000, Fort Lauderdale is the second largest city of Florida and the largest in Broward County, which encompasses twenty-nine municipalities boasting a total population of 1.1-million. Testimony to its transient nature is the fact that roughly 75 percent of the county's now-permanent residents came from elsewhere. Along Florida's stretch of east coast, Fort Lauderdale in recent years has become the most developed city after Miami.

Greater Fort Lauderdale is very oriented toward water: the area boasts 27 miles of sandy white beach along the Atlantic Ocean. There are more than 30,000 boats permanently registered, supplemented by at least 10,000 more that join the fleet each winter from home bases in colder northern climes. Fishing is a top priority and even Fort Lauderdale's snowless Christmases are water-oriented. The annual Boat Parade is one of the world's more unusual celebrations of the holiday period, featuring well over 100 small boats and ocean-going yachts vying for prizes by decorating and lighting their boats and costuming onboard guests in the holiday spirit.

Locals love to boast to their friends back north about the weather; with a year-round average temperature of 75.5 degrees, there's quite a bit to boast about! Tourism officials claim that Greater Fort Lauderdale is bathed in 3,000 hours of sunshine a year—more than any other place in the continental U.S. Despite high temperature and humidity during summer, weather *is* one of the area's greatest attributes. And that weather leads many to play golf on the area's 50 courses and tennis on its 550 courts, as well as to swim or sail off its fine oceanfront beaches and to indulge in boating activities.

When not indulging in sports and other outdoor activities that stimulate appetites, locals and visitors alike enjoy dining out. The area offers more than 2,500 eating establishments to sate their appetites. Unfortunately, this passion for dining away from home or hotel often leads to long waits at the more popular eateries, especially between December and April.

Behind Fort Lauderdale's readily apparent outward beauty and high-quality lifestyle, the city is one in transition. While still welcoming and accommodating some 3.1 million tourists a year, it is striving to become a center of business, finance, and clean light industry and has been making progress toward that goal by rebuilding its small downtown core. The city also has partially restored Himmarshee Village, a historic area along the New River that includes the city's two oldest structures, the Stranahan Home and the King-Cromartie House.

Fort Lauderdale boasts one of the country's most convenient airports, less than a 20-minute ride from the majority of hotels and motels, restaurants, and the beach. Just two miles from the airport is Port Everglades, which offers the deepest water between Norfolk and New Orleans. Port Everglades officials love to boast that their facility attracts the highest-priced ocean liners in the world while its arch-competitor, the Port of Miami just 25 miles south, is home to the lower-priced, mass-marketed cruise ships.

Where the Boys Are . . .

. . . and the girls too! Ever since Connie Francis portrayed Fort Lauderdale as *the* place to be during spring college break in her 1960 film *Where the Boys Are,* the city is flooded each year by an estimated 250,000 high school and college students during the late-February through spring-break period. Nobody's quite sure exactly how many come for the annual rites of spring because they arrive packed into vans and often stay six or more to a room in hotels and motels near the beach. Nor can anyone accurately gauge the economic benefits of the annual invasion, but there is one existing piece of hard evidence: The Button, one of the most popular spring-break watering holes, pours into thirsty young mouths an incredible 72 kegs of beer each day during that period.

The area most favored by the students is called The Strip, which runs along the beachfront highway called State Road A1A, between Las Olas and Sunrise Boulevards. That same area and nearby streets also cater to gay residents and visitors. Early in 1984, a leading publication for gays identified Fort Lauderdale as one of the most popular destinations for gay travelers, ranking it right up there with New York, San Francisco, and Provincetown. And indeed, the city's official attitude of "live-and-let-live," which applies to the sometimes-rowdy students, applies equally to gays.

The Strip also has its sad side. It serves a third sub-culture, teenage runaways from around the country, who find they can panhandle, obtain drugs, and pursue prostitution in this area with minimal police interference.

A Long History

The city has come a long way since its earliest recorded beginnings when the aboriginal Tequesta Indians roamed the New River area as early as 1450 B.C. The stretch of calm water became one of the first rivers in the New World to be charted when Spanish explorers arrived in the sixteenth century, and it's suspected that youth-seeker Ponce de Léon set an aging foot in the area around 1513. The city derived its name from Major William Lauderdale, who in 1837 led his band of

Tennessee Volunteers in building a stockade on the banks of the New River to protect the few pioneers from marauding Indians during the Seminole Wars.

When Henry Flagler extended his Florida East Coast Railway south from Palm Beach in 1896, the stage was set for a series of real land booms in Fort Lauderdale. During the early 1920s, the water-surrounded artifical islands that led to the city's dubbing as "Venice of America" were created to lure those who could afford to spend their winter vacations in the area. Fort Lauderdale really entered the modern era of tourism and development when military personel stationed in local hotels during World War II returned home and spread the word. Many continued to return on vacation each year and quite a few moved to the city to start new lives and families.

Elsewhere in the Area

Greater Fort Lauderdale has some other notable aspects. The world's largest water-theme park, Six Flags Atlantis in Hollywood, offers 65 acres of nonstop fun for the entire family. That city also has its own Indian Reservation, a Seminole tribal facility with shops and tourist attractions, as well as a *very* popular high-stakes Bingo Hall providing payouts that have exceeded $100,000 for a single game! (Florida law prohibits all but nonprofit Bingo but because this hall is on a Federal Reservation, it's exempt from that law.)

Pompano Beach has its claim to fame: an unusual horse farm that boasts a collection of 60 performing miniature thoroughbreds and gives kids the chance to pet the 17- to 31-inch-tall Arabians, Clydesdales, and other species. Dania is known as the "Antiques Center of the Southeast" because of its more than sixty-five antiques shops on and about Federal Highway (US 1), and in Davie, the "Wild West" still lives. Here, residents favor jeans, cowboy shirts, and boots, and there are lots of horse farms and even a weekly rodeo.

Fort Lauderdale Today

Fort Lauderdale remains Broward County's largest and most important city, yet its population has remained stagnant at just over 153,000 for the past few years. On the other hand, suburbs of the city have blossomed dramatically. Davie, for example, has seen its population explode in just three years from 20,515 to more than 35,000. Predictably, all the rapid growth has taken its toll on the area. The county's 4,263 miles of roadway are extremely overburdened by the more than 785,000 licensed drivers. A car is virtually mandatory in this part of the country because the public bus system is woefully inadequate.

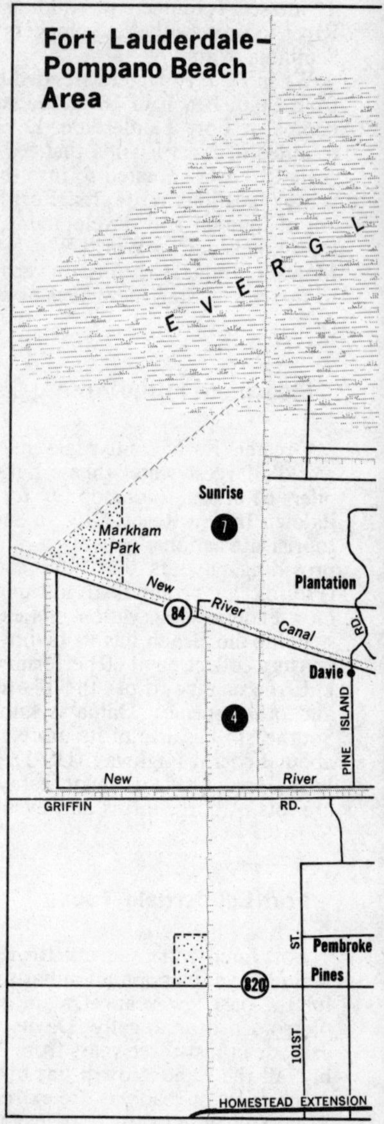

Points of Interest (Ft. Lauderdale-Pompano Beach)

1) Bahia Mar Marina
2) Birch State Recreation Area
3) Dowdy Field (Baseball)
4) Flamingo Grove Botanic Gardens
5) Ft. Lauderdale Executive Airport
6) Ft. Lauderdale Stadium
7) Sunrise Musical Theatre
8) Gulfstream Park (Horse Racing)
9) Hollywood Dog Track
10) Indian Mound Park
11) Jai Alai Fronton
12) Atlantis Water Park
13) Municipal Amphitheater
14) Municipal Stadium (Baseball)
15) Nova University
16) Ocean World
17) Playhouse
18) Pompano Park (Harness Racing)
19) Roger Brown's Miniature Horse Farm
20) Scenic Railroad
21) Seminole Okalee Indian Reservation
22) Swimming Hall of Fame
23) Yankee Stadium

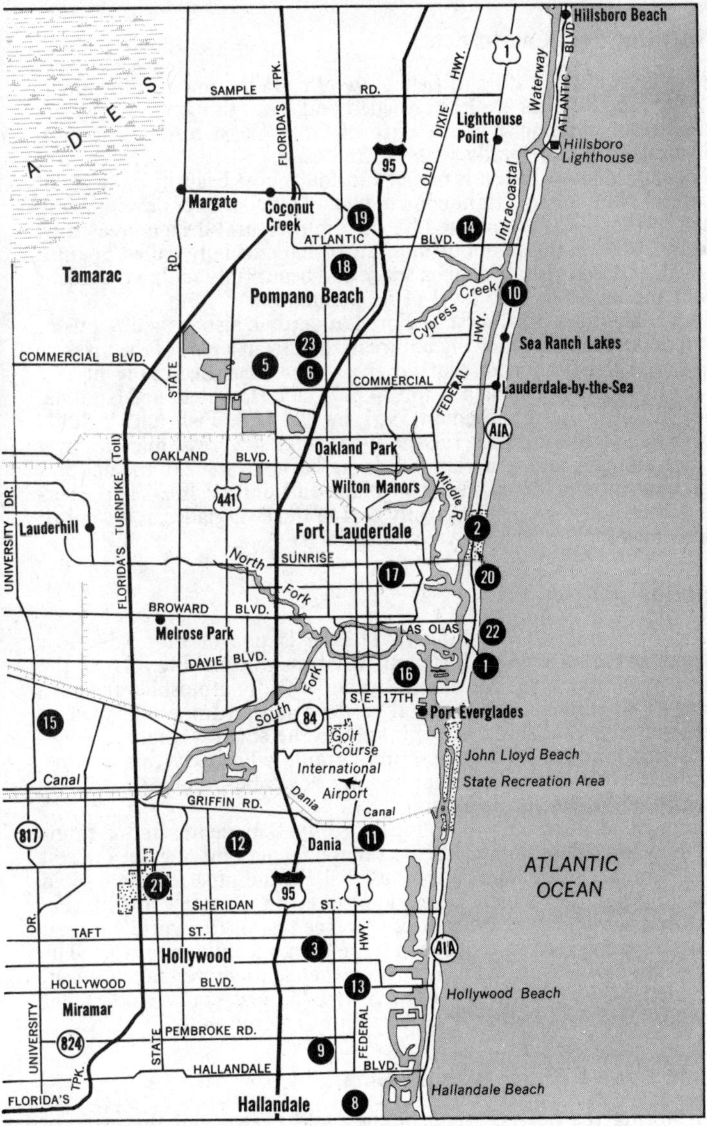
Hillsboro Beach
Lighthouse Point
Hillsboro Lighthouse
Intracoastal Waterway
ATLANTIC BLVD.
OLD DIXIE HWY.
SAMPLE RD.
FLORIDA'S TPK.
Margate
Coconut Creek
ATLANTIC BLVD.
Tamarac
Pompano Beach
Cypress Creek
Sea Ranch Lakes
COMMERCIAL BLVD.
COMMERCIAL
Lauderdale-by-the-Sea
FEDERAL HWY.
STATE RD.
OAKLAND BLVD.
Oakland Park
Wilton Manors
Middle R.
Fort Lauderdale
Lauderhill
UNIVERSITY DR.
FLORIDA'S TURNPIKE (Toll)
North Fork
SUNRISE
BROWARD BLVD.
Melrose Park
LAS OLAS
DAVIE BLVD.
South Fork
S.E. 17TH
Port Everglades
Golf Course
John Lloyd Beach
State Recreation Area
International Airport
Canal
Dania Canal
GRIFFIN RD.
Dania
ATLANTIC OCEAN
SHERIDAN ST.
TAFT ST.
Hollywood
HOLLYWOOD BLVD.
Hollywood Beach
Miramar
PEMBROKE RD.
HALLANDALE BLVD.
Hallandale Beach
FLORIDA'S TPK.
Hallandale
1
95
441
84
817
824
A1A
1 2 3 5 6 8 9 10 11 12 13 14 15 16 17 18 19 20 21 22 23

North of Fort Lauderdale

As you head toward Palm Beach, two things become readily apparent. One, the beaches are less crowded and, two, things to see and do become less common. Yet the strip of Gold Coast toward the bejewelled island is not totally without interest.

The city of Boca Raton is one of Florida's most beautiful, the result of careful planning and tight control by city officials over development. Much of the city is punctuated by the architectural design created by Addison Mizner (more about him later) that's usually called Spanish Revival, and there is lots of open space and beautifully sculpted gardens to suit the upper-income level of its population.

The inland area northwest of Fort Lauderdale also provides a wonderful opportunity for viewing nature in the raw in a part of the massive Everglades that is not all that far from the coast. Beginning just 12 miles west of Boyton Beach is the 145,635-acre Loxahatchee National Wildlife Refuge, established in 1951 by the U.S. Fish and Wildlife Service to protect and preserve the Everglades sawgrass, marshes, wet prairies, sloughs, and tree islands that are home to some of the nation's most unusual and rarest forms of plant and animal life. (The Everglades National Park, which is only part of the Everglades, is described at the end of "The Miami Area" chapter.)

Florida's Orient

About six miles west of Delray Beach is one of Florida's most unusual attractions, the Morikami Museum. Sitting literally in the middle of nowhere, the Morikami's other-worldly atmosphere is pure Japan, a 140-acre oasis of Oriental gardens and an Imperial Japanese house-museum that stand as testimony to the small Yamato Colony, which was founded by Japanese immigrants who early this century attempted to raise pineapples and winter vegetables under the leadership of George Sukeji Morikami.

Lantana, an extremely uninteresting city that claims more Finns than most anywhere in the U.S., becomes a focal point of great interest each December. That interest is focused about the supermarket tabloid *National Enquirer,* which is headquartered in Lantana and during Christmas season erects in front of its office one of the world's largest Christmas trees, each year drawing more than one million visitors. The tree, usually a Douglas fir from Oregon that soars more than 100 feet, is far higher than the famed Christmas tree in New York's Rockefeller Plaza and is lighted with 280,000 brightly colored bulbs.

Palm Beach: Glitter without Glitz

Anchoring the northern end of the Gold Coast, and the primary reason for that appellation, sits one of the world's most famous—and most expensive—cities, Palm Beach. Writers and other observers for years have used phrases such as "genteel grace," "palatial," "exclusive," and "playground for the wealthy" so often in describing Palm Beach that those words literally have become cliches. Yet, they all do *indeed* apply!

If you don't already know about the city's fame for its sprawling mansions owned by the wealthiest and most prominent members of Society, industry, and politics, recent testimony came in 1984 when Mar-a-Largo, the 118-room, vintage-1927 digs owned by the late Marjorie Merriweather Post (of the cereal family) on a 17-acre piece of prime beachfront property was sold for more than $12 million (fully furnished, of course!). That was believed to have been one of the highest prices ever paid for residential property in U.S. history.

While other mansions on the city's Atlantic Ocean beachfront may not be quite as expensive, mansion-looking is a prime activity for visitors, even though many of the homes cannot be seen because of high fences and lush landscaping. To catch glimpses of some of the finest mansions built during Palm Beach's 1920s and '30s heyday, just cruise slowly on Ocean Boulevard (State Road A1A) between Seabreeze Avenue and Southern Boulevard.

All of Palm Beach is literally one grand, open-air museum of architecture, particularly of the earth-tone and white Spanish-Mediterranean style that was so fashionable in the area during the 1920s. There are at least 200 examples, large and small, of the island's architectural glories still standing and in use, including the famed Breakers Hotel completed in 1926 and today the area's more expensive and most formal resort.

All that, plus scores of fantastic restaurants, dozens of hotels, and countless fancy shops and boutiques are squeezed into an island-city just 14 miles long and less than a half-mile across at its widest point, squeezed by the Atlantic Ocean on the east and Lake Worth on the west.

Welcome to Fantasy Island

Palm Beach is a rather curious place. During the peak season months of November through April, socialites flock to the island, joined by some 35,000 tourists—more than three times its permanent population of 10,000. But during summer, Palm Beach comes eerily close to resembling a ghost town as a number of the finer shops and restaurants close down, their owners fleeing to outlets they own in the more comfortable, northern summer resorts such as Bar Harbor and Southhampton.

Wherever the well-to-do flock, there's got to be more than just super-plush homes, hotels, and restaurants; there also must be a variety of spiffy shopping opportunities. In that arena, Palm Beach shines, glistens, and satisfies.

Worth Avenue

Worth Avenue is one of the most famous streets in the world. Packed into just four blocks of what locals refer to as "The Avenue" are more than 200 unique and pricey shops, art and antiques galleries, and gourmet restaurants, sporting such heady names as Brooks Brothers, Cartier, Van Cleef & Arpels, Ungaro, Georgette Klinger, St. Laurent, Sotheby Parke Bernet, and Gucci.

One of the reasons so many shops have been able to locate in just four blocks, and one of the things that help make The Avenue so charming, is its vest-pocket "Vias," accessible through short, fashionable alleys leading into courtyards embellished in true Mediterranean style with fountains, wrought iron, and greenery, around which are clustered off-street shops. Worth Avenue not only is a shopping and architectural delight, but is also a visual sensations, all abloom with bougainvillea hanging from balconies and archways, neatly trimmed evergreens, and potted plants along its tiled walks, in doorways, and windows. And one of the most interesting and least expensive things to do on Worth Avenue is, simply, people-watching, for it's along this street and in its shops that one can eyeball some of the most-famous, classiest, best-dressed women and men in the world.

The Sporting Life

When they're not planning or attending the many luscious balls held during the winter "social season," Palm Beachers head for the only places in Florida where professional polo matches are played: the Palm Beach Polo & Country Club in West Palm Beach, the Gulfstream Polo Club in nearby Lake Worth, the Royal Palm Polo Club in Boca Raton, or at one of the 20 private polo clubs on the island.

Golf also is a big number in the Palm Beach area, which is home to the Professional Golfers Association. The PGA headquarters, four golf courses, and the plush PGA Sheraton Resort sit on a 2,340-acre complex in nearby Palm Beach Gardens. Palm Beach County is said to have more golf courses than any county in the U.S., averaging one every 10 miles, though the overwhelming majority are private.

Palm Beach History: Flagler and Mizner

Henry Morrison Flagler and Addison Mizner are two names you'll see and hear quite often around Palm Beach because of their tremendous significance to the area's early development and fame.

Flagler, who joined forces with John D. Rockefeller and others to form the Standard Oil Company, visited St. Augustine in the 1880s and fell in love with Florida. He began building hotels for the social set in that historic city and others south of it, then connected them toward the turn of the century with his Florida East Coast Railroad. The rail link opened up Palm Beach as the new resort playground for society, replacing St. Augustine. In 1894, Flagler built Palm Beach's first hotel, the Royal Poinciana, which at the time was the world's largest wooden hotel. In 1895, he started The Palm Beach Inn, predecessor of The Breakers. In 1901, he built himself a lovely white 73-room mansion named Whitehall, which today serves as a museum of the era and area.

The other strong influence on Palm Beach was Mizner, who conceived and created the character of the island. An architect without a degree and known for his eccentricities, he designed the lavish early-1900s homes of wealthy families on New York's Long Island. Mizner fell ill and moved to Palm Beach in 1918 to live out his last days. But instead of dying he flourished in the tropical sunshine and went on to introduce his entirely new, and at the time highly controversial, Spanish-Mediterranean design, which in years to come was to become a standard, sprouting up all over Palm Beach and other Florida cities.

There are nearly 30 Mizner-designed structures still standing in Palm Beach, including his first, The Everglades Club, at 356 Worth Ave.; one of his most famous, The Bath & Tennis Club at 1170 S. Ocean Blvd.; and virtually all of Worth Avenue, which he converted from an alligator farm into the most fashionable shopping boulevard this side of Rodeo Drive.

While Palm Beach caters to the wealthy and socially prominent clientele, West Palm Beach, on the western end of Lake Worth, is a rather mundane, business-oriented, urbanized city that holds relatively little of interest for the casual visitor.

Inland Areas: Lake Okeechobee

Well inland, west of the area stretching roughly from West Palm Beach to Stuart, is one of Florida's most wonderful natural attractions, Lake Okeechobee. Filling more than 730 square miles and surrounded by nearly a half-million acres of outdoor recreation areas, it's the second largest freshwater lake in the country. Often called "The Bass Capital of the World," the lake is a fisherman's delight, where the Florida largemouth black bass is caught year-round, as are crappie, catfish, bream, and other finned delights. Hunters enjoy the area for its pintails, blue bills, teal and mallard ducks, quail, dove, turkey, squirrel, and deer.

The lake area boasts two other titles: "Winter Vegetable Capital of the World," for the 37 different varieties produced annually, and "Sugar Cane Capital of the World," for its 350,000 producing-acres of cane and its six sugar mills. The focal point of the sugar industry is Clewiston, with 12,000 population; the other major lakeside city is Belle Glade, a town of just over 22,000 people, most of whom are engaged in agriculture or fishing.

If you plan to visit the lake for fishing or hunting, contact the Florida Game and Fresh Water Fish Commission, Farris Bryant Bldg., Tallahassee, FL 32301, for its detailed list of fishing camps and other facilities that surround the lake.

PRACTICAL INFORMATION FOR THE AREA FROM FORT LAUDERDALE NORTH TO PALM BEACH

HOW TO GET THERE. By air: The entire area is served by two of the busiest airports in Florida, Hollywood/Fort Lauderdale and Palm Beach International, yet the vast majority of visitors arrive by car. However, during peak holiday periods, such as Easter and Christmas, most arrive by air and the scene at both airports is nothing short of chaotic: terminals are packed, parking lots jammed, taxis difficult to secure, rental cars impossible to obtain without advance reservation. Hollywood/Fort Lauderdale International Airport is served by *American Airlines, Braniff, Continental, Delta, Eastern, Florida Express, Midway Express, Northeastern, Northwest, Ozark, Republic, TWA, United,* and *USAir* from domestic points; from international points, meaning the Bahamas, the city is served by *Bahamasair, Pompano Airways, Trans Air,* and *Chalk's,* which operates only seaplanes. Commuter lines serving the airport include *Aero Coach, Air Sunshine, Caribbean Express, Gull Air, Jetstream International,* and *Southern Express.* Palm Beach International Airport is served by *American, Delta, Eastern, Midway Express, Northeastern, Northwest, Ozark, People Express, TWA, United,* and *USAir.* Among commuter lines are *Aero Coach, Caribbean Express, Gull Air, PBA,* and *Trans Air.* For information on getting from the airport, see "How to Get Around," below.

By bus. Broward County: *Trailways* serves only Fort Lauderdale; *Greyhound* stops at Hollywood, Fort Lauderdale, Pompano Beach, and Deerfield Beach. Palm Beach County: *Trailways* serves Boca Raton and West Palm Beach; *Greyhound* stops at Delray Beach, Boynton Beach, Lake Worth, and West Palm Beach. There are a number of special fares available from various cities to these areas. Check your travel agent or nearby Trailways or Greyhound office for information on fares and special tours to these cities.

By train. *Amtrak* provides daily service in this area with stops at Hollywood, Fort Lauderdale, Deerfield Beach, Delray Beach, and West Palm Beach. The upgraded *Silver Palm* service also stops at those cities daily on its Miami to Tampa route, offering deep, reclining seats in modern coaches, and sandwiches and beverages in its Cafe Lounge.

By car. The major access highways to the area from the south or north are Florida's Turnpike, I–95, US 1, US 441, and, for a more scenic though slower drive, Highway A1A, which generally parallels beach areas. The primary access to Broward County from the west is State Road 84; to Palm Beach County, US 98.

TELEPHONES. The area code for the entire region is 305. However, calls between Broward and Palm Beach counties are considered long distance, so you must first dial "1" then your number. Local pay-telephone calls cost $.25.

HOTEL AND MOTELS in this area cater to a wide variety of tastes and pocketbooks, and vary widely in size, location, price range, facilities, and degree of formality. They very top-of-the-line hotels usually are on or quite close to the beaches, but there are nice, more reasonably priced accommodations to be found in some cases within walking distance to beaches as well as along major highways, where all chain motels are represented. During the winter months in general, and particularly around Easter and Christmas, hotels are very heavily booked, so you should reserve as far in advance as possible.

BROWARD COUNTY

(Fort Lauderdale Area)

Broward County hotel rates are based on double occupancy, European plan, reflecting peak-season rates in effect generally between December and mid-April. Rates are lower during other months of the year. Categories, determined by prices, are: *Super Deluxe,* $120 and up; *Expensive,* $90 to $120; *Moderate,* $75 to $90; *Inexpensive,* $50 to $75; and *Basic Budget,* under $50. State sales tax of 5 percent plus a 2-percent resort tax are added to all hotel bills.

Super Deluxe

Marriott's Harbour Beach. 3030 Holiday Dr., Fort Lauderdale 33316; 305–525–4000. The area's newest—and most expensive—hotel offers 645 rooms and suites with ocean or Intracoastal Waterway views. Though high-priced, rooms are disappointingly small, but public areas are spectacular, including an 8,000 sq. ft. free-form pool with waterfall, 1,000 feet of beach, four upscale restaurants, three lounges, pool bar, five tennis courts, and all watersports and exercise equipment. Sitting on 16 acres, the resort is very popular with business travelers and conventioneers.

Pier 66. 2301 S.E. 17th St. Causeway, Fort Lauderdale 33316; 305–524–0566. The area's original high-rise luxury hotel had become quite seedy, triggering owner Phillips 66 to spend more than $25-million between 1981 and 1983 to totally refurbish. The result is a truly tropical feeling throughout, with light woods, greenery, and large expanses of windows overlooking tropical gardens. With 200 rooms and 56 suites, all quite spacious, the hotel sits on the eastern bank of the Intracoastal, across from the Marriott. With its 17-story octagonal tower and rooftop cocktail lounge, which offers the best views of the area as it slowly rotates, the hotel is popular for conventions as well as families.

Expensive

Bahia Mar Hotel & Yacht Center. 801 Seabreeze Blvd., Fort Lauderdale 33316; 305–764–2233. This 297-room hotel is situated on the Intracoastal Waterway, across from the beach and at the area's largest marina. The entire building, keyed to nautical themes, is in a small, upscale shopping plaza. An elevated walkway goes from the hotel over traffic-heavy Hwy. A1A onto the beach. It's an airy hotel, with lots of blues and browns, but often can be noisy because it's a popular convention location.

Bonaventure Inter-Continental Hotel. 250 Racquet Club Rd., Fort Lauderdale 33326; 305–474–3300. This is a massive, sprawling resort with all possible amenities, set in the middle of a large condominium development close to the Everglades. Sitting 22 miles west of Fort Lauderdale's beach via State Road 84, the luscious resort offers pools, spa, two championship golf courses, 23 tennis courts, and some very fine dining in its restaurants.

Fort Lauderdale Beach Hilton Inn. 4060 Galt Ocean Dr., Fort Lauderdale 33308; 305–565–6611. The main attributes are its site directly on the beach, a great steak restaurant and lounge, and a snazzy though modestly sized lobby with lots of marble. The 226 rooms are standard size, with balconies, and are recently refurbished.

Hollywood Beach Hilton Resort. 4000 S. Ocean Dr., Hollywood 33019; 305–458–1900. Originally built to be a condominium apartment building, this former Holiday Inn is lusher, plusher, and offers far larger rooms (320 of them) than you'll usually find at a Holiday Inn. Décor is different on each floor; the pool is very large and surrounded by a massive sun deck area. The lobby is enormous, with lots of marble and restaurants and specialty shops surrounding the sunken center portion. The beach is across the street.

Holiday Inn-Fort Lauderdale Beach. 999 N. Atlantic Blvd., Fort Lauderdale 33304; 305–563–5961. This is not your standard Holiday Inn. It's part of an upscale chain of Holiday Inns operated by JP Hotels, and offers 242 large rooms, all with ocean view, in a high-rise building, with all facilities, a pool, shops, and restaurants. It's across the street from the beach and a short walk from the Galleria shopping center.

Marina Bay. 2175 State Road 84, Fort Lauderdale 33312; 305–791–7600. This is a unique resort because all 135 of its units are in multilevel houseboats sitting on the New River. They're a bit small, as they must be, but light and airy. Restaurant, two discos, pool, tennis, and other facilities are on shore, surrounded by lush tropical foliage.

Ocean Manor. 4040 Galt Ocean Dr., Fort Lauderdale 33308; 305–566–7500. This 150-room hotel is very European in style and ambience, a bit stuffier than most in the area, yet highly sophisticated. Rooms are a good size, each decorated somewhat differently. Public areas are beautifully done in subtle, elegant style.

World of Palm-Aire. 2501 Palm-Aire Dr. N., Pompano Beach 33060; 305–972–3300. Sitting just off Powerline Road, well inland from the beach, this is the area's original luxury spa resort. While it offers a lot of special spa programs for those who need them, you can stay as a regular guest in good-sized rooms, many with kitchen facilities, and play golf and tennis on this sprawling resort.

Moderate

Ireland's Inn. 2220 N. Atlantic Blvd., Fort Lauderdale 33305; 305–565–6661. This most delightful hotel offers 90 very large rooms, some with kitchenettes, in an immaculately kept property sparked by décor that's a bit old-fashioned but elegant. A lot of people who discover this place return year after year. Its restaurant is quite popular and its pub-style lounge and piano bar are often filled with locals. The best rooms are in the main building, which is on the beach; those in an annex across the street are priced lower.

Sheraton Yankee Clipper. 1140 Seabreeze Blvd., Fort Lauderdale, 33304; 305–524–5551. It's hard to miss this place at the south end of the city's beach because it's tall and in the shape of a glistening white ship. Inside, the sizable lobby is nautically themed, as are lounges and restaurants. The 505 rooms are comfortable, though not overly large. There are most facilities you'll need, except tennis courts; if that's your game, you can play at the sister hotel one mile north, the *Yankee Trader.*

Inexpensive

Bahia Cabana. 3001 Harbor Dr., Fort Lauderdale 33316; 305–524–1555. This small, 80-room hotel is almost hidden, nestled at the point where Highway A1A turns west as it leaves the beach and heads inland. Across the street from the *Yankee Clipper,* this place is highly informal and very tropical Florida, which gives it a most welcome appearance when compared with the many untropical hotels in this area. Rooms are modest but comfortable. The dockside patio and raw bar overlooking the Intracoastal Waterway is a favorite gathering spot for locals.

Oakland Park Inn. 3870 N. Andrews Ave., Fort Lauderdale 33309; 305–563–1351. This is well inland, on one of the city's major north-south streets, but if the beach is not vital to your existence, you'll enjoy the cozy informality that's popular with families. The ambience is of Mediterranean Europe, with grillwork and architecture carrying out that theme. You can stay in one of the 32 hotel rooms, which are modest, but it's far nicer and more comfortable in one of the 105 poolside villas, which offer living rooms, dining rooms, and bedrooms. There's also a putting green.

Riverside Hotel. 620 E. Las Olas Blvd., Fort Lauderdale 33301; 305–467–0671. The 115-room Riverside is one of the city's oldest structures, though it's been totally remodeled and refurbished while retaining a lot of its original, elegant charm. The large lobby is luscious with chandeliers, armchairs, wicker, marble, mirrors, and fireplace. The rooms are pretty basic, though comfortable. Clientele is primarily an older crowd that's been coming for years. The hotel, which also has beautiful gardens out back along the New River, is conveniently situated right on the posh Las Olas shopping street and a short ride from both the beach and the downtown city center.

Basic Budget

While these hotels are lower in price than the majority of those near the beach areas, they're nicer than their "budget" categorization may make them appear and therefore represent good value for money.

Anacapri Inn. 1901 N. Federal Hwy., Fort Lauderdale 33305; 305–563–1111. Considering the fact this place is only about a five-minute drive from the beach, it's a good find. The 120 rooms are nicely maintained, as are the public areas. Staffers are friendly and accommodating to the families that stay here.

Beach Plaza Hotel. 625 N. Atlantic Blvd., Fort Lauderdale 33304; 305–566–7631. This hotel is on the ocean and was recently redecorated to spiff up its 43 rooms and efficiencies. The tropical private courtyard gives a bit of an Old Florida feeling.

PALM BEACH AREA

Palm Beach County hotel rates are based on double occupancy, European plan, unless otherwise noted. Categories determined by price are: *Super Deluxe,* $150 and up; *Deluxe,* $130 to $149; *Expensive,* $100 to $129; *Moderate,* $90 to $99; and *Inexpensive,* under $90. Five-percent state sales tax and 2-percent resort tax are added to all bills.

Super Deluxe

The Breakers. So. County Rd., Palm Beach 33480; 305–655–6611. Room rates are based on Modified American Plan. This grand hotel on 140 beachfront acres opened in 1926 and has been going strong ever since. A tradition in a traditional town, its Italian Renaissance palatial design, with features such as the classic lobby loggias, was created by Leonard Schultze, who also designed New York's Waldorf-Astoria. New life has been pumped into this grand dame of Florida resorts in recent years, and the results are obvious in the overall fresh, stylish appearance. There are 568 rooms and suites (some standard rooms are disappointingly small), a very formal dining room, two more-casual dining facilities, a poolside patio bar and snack bar, and a Moorish-inspired show lounge. Recreational facilities are extensive, including two 18-hole golf courses, 14 tennis courts, lawn bowling, health club, and croquet. There also is an arcade with *chi-chi* shops and boutiques. This hotel's formality is not for everyone. For example, the strictly enforced dress code requires that men—and even little boys—wear a jacket and tie after 7:00 P.M., even if they're just crossing the lobby. Women and girls must wear a dress or evening suit.

Deluxe

The Brazilian Court Hotel. 300 Brazilian Ave., Palm Beach 33480; 305–655–7740. Don't be misled by the unassuming outside appearance of this hotel. Several Mediterranean-style buildings form a lovely, quiet tropical courtyard with a fountain, umbrella-shaded tables and chairs. The 108 rooms, suites, and penthouses are large and tastefully furnished. The windowed, elegant, oval dining room is a locally popular spot. Other facilities include a cozy bar, library, and secluded pool. Rates include breakfast and a service charge. Closed after sale in late 1984. Refurbishing was to be done with hotel reopening scheduled for October 1985.

Palm Beach Hilton. 2842 S. Ocean Blvd., Palm Beach 33480; 305–586–6542. An oasis for families, this oceanfront resort offers 136 warmly decorated rooms with balconies, a contemporary lobby, restaurant, oceanview lounge, pool, and two tennis courts. It's several miles south of the Worth Avenue downtown part of Palm Beach. Children of any age who share their parents' accommodations stay for free.

Palm Beach Polo & Country Club. 13198 Forest Hill Blvd., West Palm Beach 33414; 305–793–1113. What makes this 1,650-acre resort community that's four miles west of Florida's Turnpike unique are its world-class polo facilities. A number of major tournaments are held on them each year. There are nine polo fields, facilities for more than 3,000 horses, and a clubhouse, in addition to extensive riding trails. Accommodations are in 200 privately owned villas, ranging from studios to three-bedroom units. Recreational facilities also include two 18-hole golf courses, a John Gardiner Tennis Center with 17 courts, two croquet fields, eight pools, three restaurants, and two lounges.

Radisson Hotel Palm Beach. 235 Sunrise Ave., Palm Beach 33480; 305–659–2255. This distinctive hotel, an example of Addison Mizner architecture, originally opened in 1925. More recently, it was closed for a one-year, multimillion-dollar refurbishing before reopening in October 1985. The building's original character has been retained but updated with stylishly decorated and spacious public areas, including an Art Deco-inspired restaurant, upgraded patio loggia overlooking a courtyard pool, and 150 guest rooms and suites modernized with paneling and restful, contemporary appointments. There is a small shopping arcade.

Expensive

Boca Raton Hotel & Club. 501 Camino Real, Boca Raton 33432; 305–395–3000. This magnificent pink hotel, situated on the Intracoastal Waterway, traces its beginnings back to The Cloister Inn built by Addison Mizner in the 1920s, which today is one portion of the main building. This is an elegant resort of tremendous diversity, offering over 900 rooms: 340 in the Cloister, 242 in the

Tower, 213 in its nearby Beach Club, and 88 villas. Recreational facilities include an 18-hole golf course, 22 tennis courts, five swimming pools, a 23-slip marina, seven restaurants, and three lounges. Additional facilities, including four golf courses and 27 tennis courts, are available at the Boca West Resort & Club, four miles west. The style of this resort is classic, like that of *The Breakers,* but it's more casual, with dress code applying only in the main dining rooms at night.

The Colony Hotel. 155 Hammon Ave., Palm Beach 33480; 305–655–5430. This prestigious hotel, situated midway between Worth Avenue and the ocean, offers 100 smallish, unexceptional rooms, suites, and penthouses; a pink, latticed restaurant and lounge with nightly dancing to a combo, and a pool-patio area. The real find here is the two-story Colony Maisonette annex across the street. Accommodations there, consisting of just four rooms and 16 suites, are larger, more modern, and more stylishly decorated. If you stay at the Maisonette, continental breakfast is included in the room rate and is served in your room.

PGA Sheraton Resort. 400 Ave. of the Champions, Palm Beach Gardens 33410; 305–627–2000. This mecca for sports enthusiasts at PGA Boulevard and Florida's Turnpike is part of the 2,340-acre PGA National Headquarters and home of the World Tennis Association. Thus, there are top-notch facilities, such as four 18-hole golf courses, including the Champion Course, which hosts many major events, and a 19-court Tennis & Sports Center with health-club facilities. The resort offers 336 spacious rooms, three restaurants, two lounges, and two swimming pools.

Moderate

Hyatt of the Palm Beaches. 630 Clearwater Park Rd., West Palm Beach 33401; 305–833–1234. This commercial hotel at Australian Avenue and Okeechobee Boulevard is not one of Hyatt's more notable properties, but it's quite nice and comfortable. It offers 349 rooms, two restaurants, a cozy lounge, swimming pool, and two tennis courts.

Palm Beach Ocean Hotel. 2770–2830 S. Ocean Blvd., Palm Beach 33480; 305–582–5381. This casual resort several miles south of the center of the city offers 267 larger-than-average rooms, efficiencies, and suites in citrus colors, all with terraces facing either pools or the ocean. Some rooms include steam baths. Facilities include a restaurant, lounge, pool bar and grill, four pools, and three tennis courts.

Palm Beach Plaza Hotel. 215 Brazilian Ave., Palm Beach 33480; 305–655–7101. The new owner of this spotless little 50-year-old gem has updated and refurbished the lobby and 48 guest rooms and baths, all of which have small refrigerators. There is a small, sedate cafe offering nightly specials with two complimentary glases of wine; a pool and parking lot. The hotel is situated on a quiet residential street four blocks north of Worth Avenue. Rates include Continental breakfast served in the café.

Inexpensive

Heart of Palm Beach Hotel. 160 Royal Palm Way, Palm Beach 33480; 305–655–5600. This conveniently located property offers 88 standard motel-style rooms in two wings set back from busy Royal Palm Way and overlooking a pool and sundeck. Facilities include a basic coffee shop, a cute little nautically themed pub adjoining the pool, and an underground parking garage. Rooms in the newer wing are nicer and priced slightly higher, but well worth it.

Testa's Hotel. 215 Royal Poinciana Way, Palm Beach, FL 33480; 305–832–2672. This small, family-operated, 25-room hotel was built in 1921 and is next to the famous *Testa's Restaurant.* It's a boarding-house-type operation, ideal for those on a limited budget who insist on staying in Palm Beach and are willing to forego some of the usual amenities. The undersized rooms are immaculate; décor is functional. Not all rooms have private baths. The hotel is open only from mid-December through April, after which the Testa family moves its operation to Bar Harbor, Maine.

BED-AND-BREAKFAST TREASURES. This part of Florida does not offer historic, small, colorful old inns, such as may be found in New England or even North Florida. However, there are a few comfortable, somewhat colorful, small bed-and-breakfast places, including some near ocean areas of this region. Prices average about $35 per day, double; only cash or traveler's checks are accepted. For specific details, contact Joan E. Hopp, *Bed & Breakfast of the Keys, Inc.,* 5 Man-O-War Dr., Marathon, FL 33050; 305–743–4118.

HOW TO GET AROUND. From the airport. Fort Lauderdale Airport is four miles south of that city's center; three miles north of Hollywood. Palm Beach International Airport is about three miles from downtown West Palm Beach and six from Palm Beach. At Fort Lauderdale International, Broward Transit's bus route No. 1 operates between the airport and its main terminal at Broward and Andrews avenues in the center of Fort Lauderdale. Fare is $.50. There is no bus service to or from Palm Beach International. *Gray Line,* 739–1200, operates limousines from Fort Lauderdale International to all parts of Broward County. Fares range from $5 to $9 per person, depending on distance; fares to most Fort Lauderdale beach hotels are in the $5 range. Pick-up points are at the Delta, Eastern, and United baggage claim areas. At Palm Beach International, limos must be arranged for in advance for pickup. *County Limousine Service,* 968–6300, charges $22.50 for one or two to Palm Beach; *Blair Limo* provides the same service for $30 (up to five persons) in Lincoln Continentals. If you prefer a chaufeurred Cadillac, *American Coach,* 659–7777, will pick you up for a flat rate of $25 for the car. If you want to rent a car, see "By car," below.

By bus. Most of the Fort Lauderdale area is covered by *Broward County Transit,* whose bus fare is $.50, but they also sell special seven-day tourist passes for $5 that are good for unlimited use on all county buses. These are available at most major hotels. For routing and other information, call 357–8400. Palm Beach County is covered by *CoTran,* whose bus's basic rate is $.75. For routing and information, call 686–4555.

By taxi. You can hail them on the street, but it's often difficult. The best places to find them are at major hotels and restaurants, or you may phone for one; they usually come quickly. Fares are not budget level. In Broward County, meters run at the rate of $1.75 for the first mile and $1.50 for each additional mile. Major companies are *Yellow Cab,* 527–8600, and *Broward Checker,* 485–3000. In Palm Beach County, metered rates vary somewhat. Major companies are *A & A Yellow Cab,* 689–2222, which charges $1.25 per mile, and *Captain's Cab,* 747–1363, whose rate is $1.20 per mile.

By car. Rush hour times generally are from 8:00 to 9:00 A.M. and from 4:00 to 6:00 P.M. During those hours, expect in Broward County to hit heavy traffic on I–95, US 1, and 441, Commercial Boulevard, Oakland Park Boulevard, Sunrise Boulevard, Hollywood Boulevard, and Hallandale Beach Boulevard. Some of the worst traffic in the Palm Beach area is along Worth Avenue during shopping hours and between 4:30 and 5:30 P.M. on Southern Boulevard as shops close and people head across to the mainland. Also heavy during rush hours are US 1 and Okeechobee Boulevard.

Fort Lauderdale houses dozens of rental car companies, from the major national firms to regional operations and even some that are operated by new-car companies. Two national firms, *Alamo* (305–522–0000) and *General* (800–327–7607), are headquartered in the city, on US 1 near the airport. Those with counters in the airport terminal are *Hertz* (800–654–3131), *Avis* (800–331–1212), *National* (800–328–4567), *Budget* (305–921–8585), and *Value* (800–327–2501). All the national firms and a few regional ones can be found in Palm Beach County as well. Those with counters at Palm Beach International are *Avis, Budget, Hertz,* and *National.* At both airports and in both areas, it's always advisable to reserve cars in advance; during winter months and holiday periods, it's crucial. Keep in mind that auto rentals in Florida are a major bargain; rates are the lowest in the entire country because of keen competition.

TOURIST INFORMATION. Both counties have highly organized Tourist Development Councils, whose budgets are supplied by the 2-percent tax placed on all hotel bills. These TDCs can provide virtually anything you may need such as local and area tourist guides and maps, brochures for hotels and attractions, restaurant information, books, event calendars, etc. The *Broward County TDC,* 201 S.E. 8th Ave., Fort Lauderdale 33301, 305–765–5508, is open Monday through Friday, from 8:30 A.M. to 5:00 P.M. The *Palm Beach County TDC,* 324 Datura St., West Palm Beach, FL 33401, 305–837–3890, is open Monday through Friday, from 8:30 A.M. to 5:00 P.M. *Travelers Aid* maintains a counter at Palm Beach Airport's main terminal, Monday–Friday, 9 A.M. –6 P.M.

Helpful chambers of commerce are: *Belle Glade,* 540 S. Main St., Belle Glade, 33430; 305–996–2745. Open Monday through Friday, from 9:00 A.M. to 5:00 P.M. Executive Secretary Jewel Crane has been in this Lake Okeechobee community for more than a quarter-century; sitting down with her to chew the fat produces some marvelous stories about the area's history. *Clewiston,* West Sugarland Hwy., Clewiston, 33440; 813–983–7979. Open Monday through Friday, from 9:00 A.M. to noon and 1:00–3:00 P.M.

Foreign Currency Exchange. Broward County: The main office of *Landmark Bank,* 1 Financial Plaza, at the corner of East Broward Blvd. and Federal Highway, 765–2373, is open Monday through Thursday, from 9:00 A.M. to 5:00 P.M. and from 9:00 A.M. to 7:00 P.M. on Friday. *Barnett Bank* branches located closer to the beach and hotel areas are at 2929 E. Commercial Blvd., 473–0591, open Monday through Friday, from 8:00 A.M. to 6:00 P.M.; 2455 E. Sunrise Blvd., 765–1751, open Monday through Friday, from 9:00 A.M. to 5:30 P.M.; and 2745 E. Atlantic Blvd., Pompano Beach, 785–6800, open Monday through Thursday, from 9:00 A.M. to 5:00 P.M. and Friday, from 9:00 A.M. to 7:00 P.M.

Palm Beach County: The *First National Bank* in Palm Beach at 255 S. County Rd. and 2875 S. Ocean Blvd., Palm Beach, 655–7111, is open Monday through Friday, from 9:30 A.M. to 3:00 P.M. Their branches at 5400 So. Dixie Hwy., West Palm Beach, 585–8100, and 4600 N. Ocean Blvd., Boynton Beach, 272–2687, are open Monday through Friday, from 9:00 A.M. to 3:00 P.M. The *Sun First National Bank* at 1277 W. Palmetto Park Rd., Boca Raton, 392–1300, and 302 E. Atlantic Ave., Boynton Beach, 737–8925, is open Monday through Thursday, from 9:00 A.M. to 2:00 P.M. and Friday, from 9:00 A.M. to 2:00 P.M. and 4:00 to 6:00 P.M.

SEASONAL EVENTS. Each **January,** Fort Lauderdale honors its sister city in Italy at the *Las Olas Venetian Festival,* with outdoor stalls of chef-prepared foods and fashions brought directly from Italian designers' shops lining chic Las Olas Boulevard. There also are entertainers to keep the kids happy and various Venetian artisans working on their wares. In West Palm Beach, the month comes roaring in as car nuts flock to the Village Green at Lion Country Safari for the annual *Mustang Auto Show,* at which more than 50 museum-quality specimens of the favored Ford compete in a "people's choice" judging for trophies. In West Palm Beach the annual *Music & Dance Festival* is held Jan.–March. See "Music" and "Dance," below.

February brings an Oriental flavor to Delray Beach when such Japanese arts as drum ensembles, dance troups, martial arts, bonsai, food and crafts of that Far Eastern nation are offered up at the weekend-long outdoor *Hatsume Fair* on the grounds of the Morikami Museum. In West Palm Beach, Western arts draw crowds to the Safari Village at Lion Country Safari for the annual *arts and crafts festival* benefiting the Bambi Wildlife Sanctuary. More than 40 artists and craftsmen from Florida guilds and associations display and sell their work to benefit the area's injured bird and wildlife refuge. Lake Worth also attracts craftsmen this month to its *Poinsettia Arts & Crafts Festival,* which honors the blooming of the beautiful red flowers throughout the city.

In **March,** Fort Lauderdale's Las Olas Boulevard comes alive with the always-crowded *Las Olas Art Festival,* where the works of area artists are lined up and down the famed shopping street and street performers keep spirits up. March generally comes in like a lion, but at West Palm Beach's Lion Country Safari, it comes in like an elephant, as the wildlife park hosts its most unusual event of the year, the *Great Elephant Weigh-In,* on March 3. A team of weights-and-measures officials enter the park to count the pounds, or tons, of each of Lion Country's elephants to celebrate the birthdate of the first African pachyderm to be born in Florida—Bulwagi, who arrived on March 3, 1981, at the attraction. The *Palm Beach Festival of the Arts* is usually held from mid-March to mid-April. See "Music" and "Dance," below.

During **April,** all of Broward County celebrates the *Week of the Ocean,* honoring the Atlantic with various sorts of water-related activities, particularly along Fort Lauderdale Beach and in the Galleria shopping mall. Hugging contests, beauty contests, floats, street dances, a 10K run, rodeo events, an old-fashioned carnival, hot-air baloon races, and lots of other highlights are part of the week-long *Davie-Cooper City Orange Blossom Festival,* which usually draws some 50,000 people to the cowboy part of the county for one of Florida's biggest annual events. April doesn't bring many showers in Delray Beach, but it does bring loads of arts and crafts to the sidewalk arts and crafts festival called the *Delray Affair.* More than 500 exhibitors and 50,000 browsers and buyers crowd the sidewalks of Atlantic Avenue, which is bedecked with all imaginable forms of crafts and artworks. The artists from around the state flock to the Boca Raton Museum of Arts for the *Annual All-Florida Competitive Art Exhibit,* while on Easter Sunday, children of all ages comb the Safari Village picnic area, reptile park, and miniature golf course in Lion Country Safari's annual *Easter Egg Hunt.*

In **May,** the person who catches the biggest fish of any type from the famed Pompano Fishing Pier during the weekend-long *Pompano Beach Fishing Rodeo* takes home a grand prize of $75,000—and lots try! Also this month, the AAU-sanctioned *International Hall of Fame Diving Meet* in Fort Lauderdale draws large crowds because of the event's significance as a training ground for Olympic competition. Music is this month's theme in West Palm Beach as *Sunfest* comes alive with a jazz show featuring prominent musicians, a food festival, an outdoor art show, and even a beer hall on a barge to celebrate the imminent arrival of summer. And, once again, antique autos emerge in Lake Worth as 40 or more *classic cars* are driven in procession from Bryant Park out to Lion Country, where they're put on display at the Village Green.

On the Fourth of **July,** Fort Lauderdale and environs celebrate *Independence Day* with an aquatic display of superb *fireworks,* fired from boats cruising up and down the Atlantic Ocean, a few hundred yards from the shore. During the last weekend of the month, the Sunrise Kiwanis Beach Festival in Delray Beach offers a variety of fun events for the entire family, including boat racing, a marathon, sandcastle-building contests, and so on.

August may be the dregs of summer, but in two Palm Beach County cities it's a highly cultural time of year. The *Boca Raton Festival* runs the entire month, bringing visitors and residents a continuous series of sporting, theatrical, literary, and arts events throughout the manicured city, while in Delray Beach, the unusual Morikami Museum is site of the unique *Bon Odori.* Delray's sister city of Miyazu, Japan, is famous for its Bon Odori folk dance festival, and it's re-created in the Morikami's Japanese Garden by area residents dressed in traditional costume, performing traditional dances.

October is beer time in many parts of the world, and so it is here. Fort Lauderdale's Snyder Park resembles a little bit of Munich as the city celebrates its *Old World Oktoberfest* with bands, beer, dances, and various competitions, while residents and visitors of Lake Worth do pretty much the same in Bryant Park.

During **November,** one of the nation's largest boat shows, the *Fort Lauderdale International Boat Show,* draws thousands to the Bahia Mar Yachting Center to see some of the most luscious floating objects in the world. Also during the month, Gulfstream Race Track in Hallandale is the site of the *Broward County Fair,* the single event that draws more participants and observers than any other in the area. It's a combination agricultural and cultural music fair. Horse lovers, meanwhile, flock out to the Davie Rodeo Grounds to watch the *Florida Championship Rodeo,* filled with fun and thrills galore.

There's no snow in this area in **December,** but that doesn't take away the holiday spirit at all. One of the most unusual celebrations in the world of the Christmas holidays is the week-long *Winterfest & Boat Parade of Greater Fort Lauderdale,* which each year attracts close to 500,000 people for parties, concerts, beauty pageants, and special sports contests. Capping off the week is the unique Christmas Boat Parade in which more than 150 boats and yachts compete in their lighting and decorations during the Intracoastal Waterway parade from Port Everglades to Pompano Beach; thousands line both banks to watch the uncommonly beautiful procession. In Lantana, more than one million visitors come during the month to see the massive Christmas tree in front of the National Enquirer Building. It's usually a Douglas fir from Oregon that soars more than 100 feet, lighted with more than 280,000 brightly colored bulbs. And in Lake Worth, parades, floats, band concerts, games, exhibits and other fun-filled activities take place throughout the city as part of the month-long *Wonderland of Fantasy* celebration.

TOURS. See also "Special Interest Sightseeing," below. **By boat.** Fort Lauderdale Area: With its 165 miles of navigable inland waterways, the Fort Lauderdale area is most attractively, and leisurely, seen from the water, and there are several opportunities to do so by cruising the Intracoastal Waterway. *Paddlewheel Queen* departs from 2950 N.E. 32nd Ave., Fort Lauderdale, 564–

7659, for its three-hour Starlight Steak Dinner Cruise on most nights at 7:30 P.M. (Sometimes it's unavailable because a group has chartered the boat, so it's vital to check and reserve in advance.) Payment must be in advance at the box office, open daily from 9:00 A.M. to 5:00 P.M., until 7:00 P.M. sailing nights. Along with dinner, you get to see some of the most fashionable residential areas of the city, as well as some of its fine waterside parks and Port Everglades. Price is $21.50 for adults, $17.50 for children 3 to 11. Afternoon sightseeing cruises daily at 1:00 P.M., priced at $4.50 adults, $3.50 children. Food available. *Jungle Queen* departs nightly at 7:00 P.M. from the Bahia Mar Yachting Center, 800 Seabreeze Ave., Fort Lauderdale, 462–5596, for a four-hour dinner cruise with vaudeville-style entertainment and singalongs while cruising a path similar to *Paddlewheel Queen.* Price is $15.95 adults or children. This boat also conducts daily daytime cruises at 10:00 A.M. and 2:00 P.M. for three-hour trip that includes a one-hour stop at the Seminole Indian Village. Prices for these are $4.95 for adults and $3.00 for children 3 to 12.

Palm Beach County: the *Island Queen,* a genuine Mississippi Paddlewheeler, goes on 1½-hour cruises to and around Lake Worth, which separates Palm Beach from the mainland, while the Captain relates tales of early Florida history along with narratives about Palm Beach, Singer Island, and other nearby sites of interest. Cruises depart daily, except Monday, at 10:00 A.M., noon, 2:00, and 4:00 P.M., from the east side of Blue Heron Bridge on Singer Island. Cost is $6 for adults and $3 for children 3 to 12. For information, call 842–0882.

By tram. If you're strictly a landlubber, try the *Voyager Sightseeing Train,* a rubber-wheeled "train" that follows an 18-mile circuit through old and new Fort Lauderdale, the city's "Millionaire's Row," residential areas, and Port Everglades. The 1½-hour rides leave from 600 Seabreeze Blvd. daily at 10:00 A.M., noon, 2:00, and 4:00 P.M. Prices are $4.75 for adults and $2.25 for children 3 to 12. For information, call 463–0401.

By air. If you'd like to see the Greater Palm Beach area from the air, *Glider Rides of America* will take you up for a spin in a sailplane (glider) or old-time, open-cockpit biplane. Cheapest and shortest ride (20 mins.) on either plane is $29.95 per person, minimum of two required. Longest and highest (one-mile up) ride is the Fantastic Journey of nearly 45 minutes, priced at $59.95 per person. If booking for a weekday, you get a 20 percent discount. The planes depart from Lantana Airport, 2633 Lantana Rd., Lantana, one mile west of I–95. If you're planning to fly on a weekend, it's wise to reserve in advance. For information, call 965–9101.

By balloon. Captain Chuck Rohr is a professional hot-air ballooning champ who claims to have more hours in the air than anyone in the world. He'll take you on a two-hour ride over the Broward County area while explaining all the sights and scenes as well as provide informal "lessons" on what makes the big things operate. There are two flights a day, early morning and late afternoon (exact times depend on wind and weather). The early flight is usually best because wind currents are most stable in the morning. You can take the Champagne Flight for two, which includes the flight, champagne, and a chase car down below, for $200. Group flights for five to seven persons are priced at $90 per person. Reservations are absolutely necessary, particularly during the winter months. If you're thinking of a weekend flight, book at least seven days ahead; for weekday flights, two to three days in advance. *Rohr Balloons* is based at Hanger 1-E, Fort Lauderdale Executive Airport, 5500 N.W. 21st Terrace, but you usually don't have to go there. When making a reservation, you'll be directed to the launching site nearest you. For information, call 491–1774.

By limo. If you really want to tour in high style, consider *Classic Motor Tours,* which will whisk you about Palm Beach in an unmarked 1958 white Rolls

Royce as the driver tells you about the island's history, architectural highlights, real-estate values, and, most fascinating of all, Palm Beach's unusual lifestyles. You can do it for one hour at $40 a couple or for two hours at $80 per couple (second hour is a tour of Whitehall Flagler Museum). For information, call 655–8933.

SPECIAL INTEREST SIGHTSEEING. Nature walks. The Broward County Parks & Recreation Department sponsors a different nature walk each weekend during the winter season. For current schedule and departure places and times, call 765–5920. In Hollywood, rangers lead periodic nature walks through the 224-acre John U. Lloyd Beach State Recreation Area during winter months. For current schedule, call 923–2833. There is a one-mile interpreted walkway through a Florida pine forest at the Morikami Museum, 4000 Morikami Park Rd., Delray Beach, open daily from sunrise to sunset.

Horseback riding. The Broward County Parks & Recreation Department leads 1½-hour guided horseback rides through the trails of Tradewinds Park, 4400 N.W. 39th Ave., Pompano Beach, on Saturday, Sunday, and holidays at 10:00 and 11:30 A.M.; 1:00, 2:30 and 4:00 P.M. For information, call 971–8521.

PARKS. To enjoy the unusual situation of a lush, tropical area that is just across the street from the Atlantic Ocean, visit *Hugh Taylor Birch State Park,* 3109 E. Sunrise Blvd., Fort Lauderdale. Aside from wandering through this 180-acre cool oasis of shade trees, you can picnic, play ball, hike, or go canoeing. The park is open daily, from 8:00 A.M. to 5:30 P.M. Admission is $.50.

Everglades Holiday Park, 21940 Griffin Rd., 30 minutes west of Fort Lauderdale, is the eastern entrance to 750,000 acres of the Everglades. Here you can observe the wildlife, swamps, and mangroves of the protected ecological area by airboat, special tours, power boat, or recreational vehicle. Fishing and hunting also are permitted during certain times of the year. Open 24 hours a day. No admission charge. For information, call 434–8111. (See "Everglades" section in "Miami and Miami Beach" chapter.)

C.B. Smith Park, 900 N. Flamingo Rd., Pembroke Pines, is heavily family-oriented, offering 160 acres of waterslides and tube rides, tennis courts, racquetball, canoe trails, picnic areas, and a sandy, freshwater beach. Open daily, from 8:00 A.M. to sunset. Admission is $1. Children under six are free. For information, call 435–2500.

Toppekeegee-Yugnee Park, 3300 N. Park Rd., Hollywood, just off I–95 at Sheridan Street, offers 150 acres of palm trees, swimming in a large lake with beach, boating and canoeing, hiking, biking, and miniature golf, as well as what's said to be Florida's fastest waterslide. Open daily, from 8:00 A.M. to sunset. Admission is $1. For information, call 961–4430.

The *Loxahatchee National Wildlife Refuge,* sitting at the eastern fringe of the Everglades and just 14 miles from the nearest Atlantic Ocean beaches, is comprised of 145,635 acres of shallow water flats and dense stands of sawgrass cover in which 252 species of birds have been identified, as well as dozens of rare and endangered wildlife such as the Everglade kite, American alligator, Florida panther, bald eagle, and Florida sandhill crane. In addition to its natural beauty, which may be seen by walking the refuge's trails, there are extensive fishing opportunities for such catches as largemouth bass, bream and crappie, hunting for waterfowl, boat launching docks, rental boats, and airboat tours. The refuge is open daily from 1½ hours before sunrise to one hour after sunset. Admission is free. The shortest, most direct route from the coastal area is from Boynton Beach, driving west on Boynton Beach Road (Hwy 804). For more information, call 399–3187.

The *Dreher Park & Zoo,* 1301 Summit Blvd., West Palm Beach; 585–2197, offers 20 acres of lush botanical gardens, the Betty Cardinal Nature Trail inhabited by unique plant life from around the world, special free weekend programs on wildlife and conservation, and a zoo. Open daily, from 9:00 A.M. to 5:00 P.M. Admission is $2 for adults and $1 for children 3 to 12.

Other parks of interest, most of which are open from one hour before sunrise to one hour after sunset and are free, include *John Prince Park,* 2700 Sixth Ave., Lake Worth; 964–4420, offering 665 acres of camping, biking, ballplaying, fishing, picnicking, watersports, and a Vita course for joggers; *Lake Ida Park,* N.E. 9th Ave., off Linton Blvd., Delray Beach; 964–4220, with a 300-acre lake, boating, picnicking, fishing, and a children's playground; *Spanish River Park,* Camino Real at Highway A1A, Boca Raton; 393–7810, with 46 acres of woods, children's playground, nature trail, picnicking, showers, grills, a tunnel to the nearby beach, open daily from 8:00 A.M. to sunset. The 180-acre *Morikami Japanese Park,* 4000 Morikami Park Rd., Delray Beach; 495–0233, offers up a lavish Japanese Garden, a nature trail through extensive pine woods, picnicking, and a museum. Open daily from sunrise to sunset. No charge.

THEME PARKS AND AMUSEMENTS. Malibu Castle Park, 1999 S.W. 33rd Pl., Fort Lauderdale; 462–8110, which is almost impossible to miss with its "castle" rising from the middle of the grounds, surrounded by two waterslides, bumper boats, and other amusements, including 125 video and other games inside the castle. Also surrounding the structure are three 18-hole miniature golf courses, which wend their way through a series of interesting, miniature structures such as Taj Mahals, haunted houses, carousels, and candy stores. Rides are open Monday through Thursday, from 8:00 A.M. until 11:00 P.M.; Friday through Sunday until midnight. The golf courses are open daily, from 10:00 A.M. to 11:00 P.M. There's no admission to the park, but there are charges of $2 to $3.25 for each thing you do while in it.

Back in 1969, a well-to-do West Palm Beach resident named Paul Dreher, who owned a 32-acre piece of property a bit east of I–95, decided to donate his land for use as a city zoo and park. Since then, the **Dreher Park & Zoo,** at 1301 Summit Blvd., between I–95 and Parker Ave., has carved out space for some 200 different animals, including 15 rare or endangered species, for visitors to enjoy. The facility also includes a rehabilitation center for injured birds and animals and an area where children may pet some of the animals. See "Parks," above.

Lion Country Safari, West Palm Beach; 793–1084, is ideal for kids, with 350 acres of preserve over which bears, lions, giraffes, elephants, zebras, and rhinos roam at will as you drive through and observe them from the safety of your car. The park also offers a Safari Village, boat rides, jeep tours, a petting zoo, aviaries, a reptile yard, prehistoric monster park, rides, and a carousel. Open daily, from 9:30 A.M. to 4:30 P.M. Admission is $7.95 per person; children under 3 are free. The most direct route to Lion Country from coastal areas is west on Southern Boulevard. The park is 15 miles west of Florida's Turnpike.

Ocean World, 1701 S.E. 17th St. Causeway, Fort Lauderdale, 525–6611, provides continuous two-hour aquatic shows daily, from 10:00 A.M. to 6:00 P.M.; the last show starts at 4:15 P.M. Water shows feature trained sea animals such as porpoises, as well as sharks, alligators, sea lions, and turtles. Admission is $7.95 for adults, $3.95 for children 6 to 12, and free for those 5 and under accompanied by a paying adult. There are two optional activities as well: a tour boat ride, priced at $3 for adults and $2 for children 3 to 12; and three hours of deep-sea fishing, which costs $15 per person, all equipment included.

Quiet Waters Park, 6601 N. Powerline Rd., Pompano Beach, 421–3133, is a large, water-oriented 427-acre park that is the area's newest. It offers just about anything your kids could ever want: five lakes with canoes, paddleboats, and fishing boats, a beach for swimming, "cable-tow" skiing and instruction, bike paths, an 18-hole golf course, picnic facilities, restaurant, and snack bars. Open daily, from 8:00 A.M. to 6:00 P.M. Admission is free Monday through Friday; $.50 on Saturday and Sunday. Children under four are free at all times.

A full day of fun in the sun and water can be enjoyed at **Rapids Minigolf & Waterslide,** also in West Palm Beach. The park offers 19 holes of miniature golf in a nicely landscaped, tree-shaded area, and a gigantic waterslide with four super-fast flumes. There also are refreshment stands, sundecks, and dressing rooms. The golf facility is open daily from noon to 10:00 P.M.; the slide from noon to 5:00 P.M. The cost for golf is $3 per person; the waterslide is $4, or you can buy a combination ticket for $5. The park is on Military Trail, between 45th Street and Blue Heron Boulevard. For information, call 848–6272.

World of Horses, 1000 N.W. 31st Ave., Pompano Beach, 971–9000, is a fairly new and most unusual attraction, offering 60 miniature Arabian, Appaloosa, Clydesdale, and Fallabella horses less than two-feet high. Shows featuring such activities as steeplechasing, swimming, dancing, and mathematical problem-solving are continuous daily, from 11:00 A.M. to 4:00 P.M. Children also may visit the attraction's two barns and pet the tiny animals. Gates open daily at 10:00 A.M. and close at 5:00 P.M. Admission charge is $6.45 for adults and $4.45 for children 3 to 11.

Six Flags Atlantis, 2700 Stirling Rd., Hollywood, adjoining I–95; 926–1000, is said to be the world's largest water-theme park, and it sure seems to be. Stretching over 65 acres, it offers one mile of waterslides, an Olympic pool, a wave pool, giant inner tube rides, bumper boats, and a large grassy park area to relax between rides. There are also more than 80 rides, shows, and attractions here, highlighted by an 82-foot-long mosaic of King Neptune made of 6,000 tiles. Indoors, there are 5,000 square feet of video games to keep already busy kids even busier. The park operates daily, from 10:00 A.M. to 5:00 P.M., from March through December. Admission is $9.95 for adults and $7.95 for children three to seven.

At **Spyke's Grove & Tropical Gardens,** 7250 Griffin Rd., Davie, 583–0426, the entire family can hop aboard an hourly 15-minute, tractor-pulled tram through working citrus groves complete with tropical animals and birds in their natural environment. Open daily, from 9:00 A.M. to 5:30 P.M. Admission is free.

ZOOS. There is unfortunately only one in Broward County, and it's a bit on the modest side. But *Gator World Zoo,* 3782 Flamingo Rd., Fort Lauderdale; 472–4433, does offer a good perspective on how tropical animals live in a natural environment that's changed little over the centuries. There are crocodiles and alligators, monkeys, flamingos, and other exotic birds to see, along with a petting zoo, a mini-botanical garden, 200 acres of orange groves, antique car and historical museums, and a tram ride. Open daily, from 9:00 A.M. to 5:00 P.M. Admission to the park is free, but there is an all-inclusive charge of $4 for adults, $2.50 for children 4 to 17, for Gator World, petting zoo, and tram ride.

GARDENS. Though it's quite small, roughly about one-quarter acre, there is a most unusual complex of gardens at the *Society of the Four Arts complex* in Palm Beach's Four Arts Plaza, one block east of Lake Worth, via Royal Palm Way. The garden is in three contiguous parts. One is heavy with tropical foliage, fountains, and an occasional tiled bench on which to sit and relax in an other-wordly surrounding. The second part is a Chinese Garden containing such unusual delights as tenth-century foo dogs, a sixteenth-century Buddha from the Winter Palace Gardens in Peking, and entrance gates from an old Chinese Jade House. The final portion is a relaxing garden of herbs, gardenias, roses, and other plants, along with chairs and tables beneath a portico. All three portions are connected by a small, winding path. The gardens, which are next to the Four Arts Library building, are open Monday through Friday, from 10:00 A.M. to 5:00 P.M. Between January and April, they're also open on Sunday, from 2:30 to 5:00 P.M.

In West Palm Beach, there is a most unusual garden—one that is comprised not of flora and fauna, but of sculpture, all the work of one well-known sculptress, Ann Norton. Ms. Norton's works have appeared in such prestigious venues as the Museum of Modern Art and the Whitney Museum of American Art in New York. The *Anne Norton Sculpture Gardens* were conceived to present a natural area of beauty amid the clutter of modern high-rise buildings; it now represents a small, yet effective, oasis of tranquility. Birds have been encouraged to return to the overbuilt area by a ban on the use of sprays and insecticides on the berry bushes and other plants in the garden. The facility is divided into three parts: the largest segment contains five monumental brick sculptures surrounded by a heavily-foliaged, junglelike environment and three ponds often visited by waterfowl; the second garden contains a group of seven granite figures, each measuring some 12 feet in height; the final portion contains just one structure, but it's truly monumental—a 47-foot long horizontal sculpture of hand-made Mexican brick set in water filled with lotus blossoms and exotic fish. The Garden may be visited by appointment only. To arrange a visit, call 832–5328. There is no charge. The garden is six blocks north of Belvedere Road, between Olive Avenue and Flagler Drive, which parallels Lake Worth.

The Morikami Museum in Delray Beach offers a delightful and traditional *Japanese Garden* surrounding an Imperial Japanese home that houses the museum. The two-acre landscaped garden includes various flowers and plants, a small Japanese-style pond with bridge, and a traditional rock garden. The Garden is open Tuesday through Sunday, from 10:00 A.M. to 5:00 P.M. There is no charge. Between October and April, a traditional Japanese tea ceremony is held in the Garden on the third Saturday of each month. Charge is $2. the Morikami is at 4000 Morikami Park Rd., Delray Beach, about seven miles west of the city center. The best approach from coastal areas is west on Linton Boulevard to Carter Road, then south to the Morikami. For information, call 499–0631.

BEACHES. The Fort Lauderdale area boasts an average temperature of 75.5 degrees and 27 miles of oceanfront beach, so obviously there is swimming everywhere. The area's entire beachfront is contiguous and open to the public. Parking is readily available. At the southern end, *John U. Lloyd State Beach Recreation Area,* 6503 N. Ocean Dr., Hollywood, offers not only beach for swimmers and sunners, but 224 acres of mangroves, picnic facilities, fishing, and canoeing as well. Elsewhere, you just jump in wherever you wish. The most crowded portion of beach in this area is along the Fort Lauderdale "strip,"

which runs from Las Olas to Sunrise Boulevards. Swimming is good all along the area's beachfront, though there is an offshore reef at the northern end of the city. When heavy thunderstorms are in the area, there are actually some surfing possibilities (generally not available in this area) but the threat of being hit by lightning keeps most sensible people out of the water. In Palm Beach County, the region is virtually one long, continuous stretch of sand, just about all of it open to the public.

There are an assortment of facilities and parking areas that pop up through the area; parking is alongside the road where there are no facilities. Generally, beaches are supposed to be used from one hour before sunrise to one hour after sunset, but that's not always followed.

In Palm Beach, most of the beach area is restricted for use of nearby residents or hotel guests. The sole public ocean area in the central portion of the city is between Australian Avenue and Hammon Avenue (just south of Worth Avenue). Many locals prefer to do their beaching and swimming along Lake Worth, which is one continuous circular beach spanning the cities of Lake Worth, Palm Beach, and Lantana. There are parking facilities and lifeguards at most of the popular portions of beach, which are open daily, from 8:00 A.M. to 11:00 P.M.

PARTICIPANT SPORTS. Bicycles can be rented from the *Bicycle Exchange,* 619 E. Sunrise Blvd., Fort Lauderdale, 523–0150, and by the week from *Ray's Cyclery,* 647 N. Federal Hwy., Pompano Beach, 942–6866. Bicycling paths are available at *Quiet Waters Park,* 6601 N. Powerline Rd., Pompano Beach. There are a number of other biking possibilities around Broward County. For details of where and when, call the Broward County Parks & Recreation Department at 765–5920. Palm Beach offers three wonderful bicycle trails. The longest is five miles, beginning at the western end of Worth Avenue, heading north on Lake Trail along Lake Worth, and ending near the northern end of the island. A 1½-mile trail begins at Wells Road and N. County Road (nine blocks north of The Breakers Hotel) and runs south along N. County to the Palm Beach Country Club. A three-mile trail begins at Ibis Isle, south of the Southern Boulevard Bridge and opposite Phipps Ocean Park, and runs down Highway A1A along Lake Worth to Lantana. Bikes can be rented from *Palm Beach Bicycle Trail Shop,* 105 N. County Rd., 659–4583.

Boat rentals and instructions, including sailing and windsurfing, are available from *Bill's Sunrise Boat Rentals,* 301 Seabreeze Ave., Fort Lauderdale, 467–1316 and 2025 E. Sunrise Blvd., 763–8962. Also in Fort Lauderdale: *Susi's Watersports, Inc.,* 2000 E. Sunrise Blvd., 463–7874.

Diving equipment rentals and lessons are available through *Under Seas Sports, Inc.,* 1525-C N. Federal Hwy., Fort Lauderdale, 564–8661; *Pro Dive Sail, Surf & Ski,* 2507 N. Ocean Blvd., Pompano Beach, 942–3000; *Nautilus Dive, Surf & Ski,* 877 E. Palmetto Park Rd., Boca Raton, 368–0555; *Coastal Sport & Dive Shop,* 2407 10th Ave. N., Lake Worth, 965–0524.

Fishing is always a big pastime in this area. You can cast off from the 875-foot-long *Pompano Beach Fishing Pier,* on the ocean two blocks north of E. Atlantic Blvd., any time of day or night; shops on the pier rent any equipment you need. If deep-sea angling is your pleasure, there are quite a few charter boat operators at the *Bahia Mar Yachting Center,* 800 Seabeeeze Ave., Fort Lauderdale, next to the Bahia Mar Hotel. Rates generally run about $200 for a half-day; $400 for full-day charter. Contact the Dockmaster at 525–7174 for specific details and rates. There is also deep-sea fishing at *Ocean World.* See "Theme Parks and Amusements," above. In Palm Beach County, try the *Shamrock,* 336 E. Blue Heron Blvd., Riviera Beach, 842–4850; the *B-Love Fleet,* 314 E. Ocean

Ave., Lantana, 588–7612; or Ric-A-Rue, *Sailfish Marina,* Palm Beach Shores, 848–9085. For information on fishing and hunting facilities in the Lake Okeechobee area, contact Florida Game and Freshwater Commission, Farris Bryant Bldg., Tallahassee 32301.

Among **golf** courses open to the public in Broward County are *Bonaventure,* 200 Bonaventure Blvd. (State Road 84), Fort Lauderdale, 389–8000, which offers two 18-hole courses, one 6,400 yards, the other 7,200 yards; *Rolling Hills Golf Resort,* 3301 S.W. 82nd Terrace, Davie, 475–3010, with 18 holes on a 7,145-yard course; and *American Golfer's Club,* which is closer to beaches and oceanfront hotels at 3850 N. Federal Hwy., Fort Lauderdale, 564–8760, offering an 18-hole Executive course with four par-4 holes and 14 par-3s on a total course of just over 3,000 yards. In Palm Beach County, the *West Palm Beach Country Club,* 7001 Parker Ave., 582–2019, offers 18 holes over 6,400 yards; the *Breakers East* provides an 18-hole, 6,008-yard course at The Breakers Hotel on S. County Road, Palm Beach; and the *Palm Beach Lakes Golf Club,* 1101 N. Congress Ave., West Palm Beach, 683–2700, has an 18-hole course of 5,505 yards.

You can try your hand at **horseback riding** through the ranch and farm country of the Davie area at *Bar-B Ranch,* 4601 S.W. 128th Ave.; 434–6175. Charge is $10 an hour. Broward County operates guided trail rides on horseback at Tradewinds Park in Pompano Beach (see "Special Interest Sightseeing," above).

Among public **tennis** courts are those at *Holiday Park,* 701 N.E. 12th Ave., Fort Lauderdale, 761–2301; *C.B. Smith Park,* 900 N. Flamingo Rd., Pembroke Pines, 435–2500; *Seaview Avenue Tennis Courts,* 340 Seaview Ave., Palm Beach, 655–5341; *Currie Park,* 2400 N. Flagler Dr., 832–9448, *Howard Park,* 1309 Lake Ave., 832–1544, and *Phipps Park,* 4301 S. Dixie Hwy., 833–9269, all in West Palm Beach.

If you're a **runner** and want to keep up your pace while on vacation in this area, check out the Vita courses at *Markham Park,* 16001 W. State Rd. 84, Fort Lauderdale, 472–5882, and *West Lake Park,* 1200 Sheridan St., Hollywood, 925–8377.

Swimming is readily available from most all beaches, but if you prefer pools, try the Olympic one at the *International Swimming Hall of Fame,* 501 Seabreeze Blvd., Fort Lauderdale; 761–2451. This pool is the scene of a number of championship diving and swimming contests, but when there isn't one going on, the public can swim daily, from 10:00 A.M. to 4:00 P.M. Admission is $2 for adults and $1 for children up to 18.

If **waterskiing** is your avocation, *Mike Seipel's Barefoot International* will bring you out onto Lake Worth at a cost of $20 for 30 minutes or $40 for a full hour, daily during sunlight hours. Reservations required 24 hours in advance. Mike is located at 5917 Via Vermilya, West Palm Beach, just off Lantana Road, one-half mile west of I–95. For information, call 964–3346.

If you like to play **volleyball** and other sports in the buff, you're welcome to do so at the *Seminole Nudist Resort,* 3800 S.W. 142nd Ave., Davie; 473–0231. Couples only!

SPECTATOR SPORTS. This area has quite a bit of action and variety to offer the sports fan. If **baseball** is your thing, March is Grapefruit League time in Florida when major-league teams play pre-season games. The *New York Yankees* play at Fort Lauderdale Stadium, 5301 N.W. 12th Ave., 776–1921; the *Texas Rangers* at Pompano Beach Municipal Stadium, 1700 N.E. 8th St., 786–4113; the *Atlanta Braves* and *Montreal Expos* at West Palm Beach Municipal Stadium, 715 Hank Aaron Dr., which is near the intersection of

Congress Avenue and Palm Beach Lakes Blvd. Call 683–6100 for the Braves; 684–6801 for the Expos.

Bingo is generally a penny-ante game most anywhere; in Florida, the law permits it to be played only for nonprofit purposes and payoffs cannot exceed $75 a day. But through a fluke of law, there is one place in this area where you can play the game and win $100,000 or more. It's permitted because the *Seminole Bingo Hall* sits on a Federal Reservation deeded to the Seminole Indians, and thus is exempt from local laws. The Bingo Hall seats 1,400 and is almost always filled during nighttime hours as busloads of people come to play. Nighttime Bingo is played daily, from 6:45 P.M. to 1:00 A.M. Matinee games are Monday through Saturday, beginning at 11:15 A.M. Admission price is $15, except when stakes are higher, Monday and Thursday nights, when admission is $20. Both prices include your first 12 Bingo cards. The hall is at 4150 N. State Rd. 7, at the corner of Sterling Road, Hollywood, 961–5140.

There's also betting at the high-speed game of **jai-alai** imported from the Basque country of Spain. Though vaguely similar to lacrosse, it's different and balls often zip through the air at speeds up to 188 miles per hour. You can get in on the action from December through April and June through November at *Dania Jai-Alai Fronton,* 301 E. Dania Beach Blvd., Dania, 428–7766, and at *Palm Beach Jai-Alai Fronton,* 1415 45th St., West Palm Beach, one-quarter mile east of I–95, 844–2444, during the late-October through March season.

Palm Beach County is the only place in Florida where you can watch professional **polo.** The island of Palm Beach alone has more than 20 polo clubs, but they're strictly for members. However, you can watch the action at two places open to the public. The *Palm Beach Polo & Country Club* offers polo matches year round, but the really professional matches are during the winter season, from December to May. The 1½-hour matches are Saturdays and Sundays at 3:00 P.M. Additional midweek games are sometimes scheduled during summer months. General admission is $4, reserved seats $6, boxes $10 on Sunday. On Saturday, reserved seats are $5 and boxes $8. Among the major events at Palm Beach Polo are the Cadillac Cup in January, the Boehm International Challenge Cup in February, the U.S. Polo Association Rolex Gold Cup, and the Cartier International Open in March. The club is at 13198 Forest Hill Blvd., 10 miles west of West Palm Beach. For information, call 793–1440. The *Royal Palm Polo & Sports Club* offers matches every Sunday and Wednesday at 1:00 and 3:00 P.M. between January and April, and at 5:00 P.M. during other months. General admission is $4, box seats are $8, children under 17 pay $1.50. The club is at 6300 Clint Moore Rd., at the corner of Powerline Road, Boca Raton. For information, call 994–1876.

Racing. There is thoroughbred **horse racing** from January to March at *Gulfstream Park* on US 1, near Hallandale Beach Blvd., Hallandale, 454–7000; harness racing from mid-November to mid-April, and quarter-horse racing from May through July are at *Pompano Park Harness,* 1800 S.W. 3rd St., Pompano Beach, 972–2000. **Greyhound dog racing** has long been popular in Florida. You can see it from December 26 through April at *Hollywood Greyhound Track,* 831 No. Federal Hwy., Hallandale, 454–9400, and at the *Palm Beach Kennel Club,* Belvedere Road and Congress Avenue, just west of I–95, West Palm Beach, 683–2222, from late December through April. All horse and dog tracks permit parimutuel betting.

You can watch a real "Wild West" **rodeo** every Friday night at 8:00 P.M. at the *Davie Rodeo Grounds,* S.W. 65th Avenue (Rodeo Way) and S.W. 41st St., near State Rd. 84, Davie, 434–7062.

BABY SITTING SERVICES. In Broward County, *Lul-A-Bye Sitters Registry,* Inc., 565–1222, has been operating since 1946 and is fully licensed. The agency provides local mothers and grandmothers to sit with your children; no teenagers are used. Office hours are daily, from 9:00 A.M. to 9:00 P.M., but sitting services are available any time, day or night. A basic flat rate of $19 for a minimum of four hours is charged, with an additional $2.50 per hour for each hour over four. There's no transportation charge for the sitter unless she's asked to take the child out somewhere. Then, the charge is $.21 per mile. If you'd rather leave your child in a supervised center, *Children's Kingdom,* 1016 N.E. 7th Ave., Fort Lauderdale, 764–2933, will be happy to receive them Monday through Thursday and Sunday from 6:30 A.M. until midnight; Friday and Saturday until 2:00 A.M. Children are entertained and supervised by certified teachers who also take them on day trips during the summer months. The charge to leave your child at the center is $2 per hour. If you want to leave the child for a full week, there's a $37.50 charge for a minimum of 45 hours if the child is 3 or older; $47.50 for infants and toddlers. Each additional hour over that is $1.

In Palm Beach County, *Pinch Hitters,* 2934 Forest Hill Blvd., West Palm Beach, 439–6111, has been operating for four years and is licensed and bonded. Charges are $5 per hour, minimum four hours, plus transportation costs. If you're going to be away overnight, the charge is $70.

CHILDREN'S ACTIVITIES. There is no lack of them. See "Zoos" and "Theme Parks and Amusements," above.

Kids always seem to enjoy the *Rodeo* in Davie (see "Spectator Sports," above).

The famed *Goodyear blimp Enterprise* shows up quite often on TV, particularly when it hovers over football games played at Miami's Orange Bowl. You'll also often see the blimp cruising above the Fort Lauderdale area beaches, sometimes flashing commentary or advertisements with lights along its sides. Visitors no longer may take flightseeing tours on the blimp, but your kids may get a kick out of seeing it up close. You can do that by visiting the *Enterprise's* base at 1500 N.E. 5th Ave., Pompano Beach. There's no charge, but before going, call 946–8300, to find out if the blimp is on the ground.

There also are what you might call "rainy-day activities" that are in fully enclosed structures. Kids, and their parents, can obtain "hands-on" educational experiences in scientific, artistic, and historic matters at the *Discovery Center,* 231 S.W. 2nd Ave., Fort Lauderdale; 462–4115. Situated in one of the downtown area's historic buildings, there are laser games, a computer lab, glass-enclosed beehives and anthills, mathematical problem-solving, optical illusions, and other things to keep the kids entertained while they learn. Open Tuesday through Friday, from 2:00 to 5:00 P.M.; Saturday, from 10:00 A.M. to 5:00 P.M.; Sunday, from 1:00 to 5:00 P.M. Admission is $2. Children under three are free.

Buehler Planetarium, on the Broward Community College campus, 3501 S.W. Davie Rd., Fort Lauderdale, 475–6680, offers astronomy shows that change with the season, on Sunday at 2:30 and 3:30 P.M. and Thursday at 7:30 P.M. There is viewing of the heavens through a telescope following the Thursday show, weather permitting. There is no charge. There also is a planetarium at Dreher Park, 1141 W. Lakewood Rd., West Palm Beach; 832–1988. There are daily shows at the *Aldrin Planetarium,* 4801 Dreher Trail N., West Palm Beach at 3:00 and 7:00 P.M. on Fridays. Laser-light shows are daily at 8:00 and 9:00 P.M. Special astronomy shows for children are Saturday and Sunday at 1:00

P.M.; laser-light at 2:00 P.M. The observatory opens Friday at 8:00 P.M. for viewings, weather permitting. Admission is $2 for adults and $1 for children enrolled in grades 1 through 12. You can also buy a family ticket for $8, which admits two adults and up to three children. See also "Museums," below.

HISTORIC SITES AND HOUSES. Fort Lauderdale's downtown *Himmarshee Village* historic district offers four restored homes built by Edwin Thomas King, who helped build the Florida East Coast Railroad extension from Palm Beach to Fort Lauderdale in 1895. An accomplished builder, he was the city's first building contractor, developing the hollow, concrete block that even today is used in most South Florida residential construction. The first president of the City Council, King built its first hotel, in 1908, the 40-room New River Inn, which now is the *Discovery Center* at 231 S.W. 2nd Ave. (See "Children's Activities.") One year earlier, he built a residence for his family next door at what today is 229 S.W. 2nd Ave. Known as the *King-Cromartie House,* the two-bedroom house boasted the city's first indoor bathroom and acetylene lighting. When electricity became available in 1911, King immediately installed receptacles for this new miracle of the modern age. The same year, he added a second floor with two bedrooms and a bath. The combination name derives from its builder and Bloxham A. Cromartie, the husband of King's daughter, Louise. The home's furniture is representative of turn-of-the-century South Florida furnishings. Some pieces are original to the home; others were moved to it from other nearby homes. Tours are conducted irregularly, about three times a day, depending on how many volunteer-guides are around at any given time. Tickets are given out on a first-come, first-served basis in the Discovery Center, 231 S.W. 2nd Ave. While the King-Cromartie tours are free, you've got to pay the $2 per person admission to the Discovery Center to get them. For tour information, call 462–8803 between 10:00 A.M. and 1:00 P.M., Tuesday through Friday.

The *Stranahan Home* at 355 S.E. 6th Ave., dates to 1902, but was not opened as a public historic site until the middle of 1984. Frank Stranahan was Fort Lauderdale's first ferry operator, going into business on the New River in 1893. Nine years later, he and his wife built a Dade pine building by hand that became the New River Camp & Trading Post, a social center for the community, which then numbered just 52, and a trading center for travelers on the river and nearby Seminole Indians. In 1906, the trading post was converted by Stranahan into his family home. He lost all his money in The Great Crash and committed suicide. For nearly 40 years after his death, the old home was operated as the Pioneer House Restaurant, until being taken over in 1979 by the Fort Lauderdale Historical Society, which then began several years of renovation. Much of the two-story home and its furnishings are original. Hours are Wednesday, Friday, and Saturday, from 10:00 A.M. to 4:00 P.M., and Sunday, from noon to 4:00 P.M. Admission is $2. For information, call 524–4736.

The *Old Bryan Homes,* 301 S.W. 3rd Ave., are two houses dating from 1905–06 that in late 1983 were bought by a restaurateur, refurbished, joined by a covered walkway, and converted into one of Fort Lauderdale's most expensive restaurants, serving unusually prepared American cuisine.

The island of Palm Beach is a virtual open-air, living museum of historic houses, more than 200 of them. The vast majority were built during the island's heyday 1920s and 1930s, and many are in the mode originated by Addison Mizner—the so-called Spanish Revival architecture and design. One can hardly wander on most any street of the city without running into historic houses. Among the most famous is one of Mizner's own homes, at 3 Via Mizner, just off Worth Avenue. The five-story villa was built in 1924 for his use both as a personal residence and a studio. Now a private home, the *Villa Mizner's* exterior reflects the typical Spanish-Italian touches for which he became famous: wrought-iron stairway, graceful arches, large Moorish windows with stained glass, the tiled roof, white stucco walls in pastel tints, and weathered cypress woodwork. In front is a typical Mediterranean courtyard, now surrounded by chic little shops. Perhaps the most magnificent part of the Villa Mizner is inside; however, since it is a private residence, visitors are not permitted. But it's still worth wandering into Via Mizner to see the beautiful structure and lush patio out front.

Whitehall, Henry Morrison Flagler's 73-room mansion, is on Whitehall Way just off Cocoanut Row near Lake Worth. It was built by the railroad magnate who opened Palm Beach to the world. It's considered a fine example of Southern plantation form translated into nineteenth-century Beaux-Arts style, with some Renaissance and Victorian touches added in. It's open Tuesday through Saturday, from 10:00 A.M. to 5:00 P.M. and Sunday, from noon to 5:00 P.M. (see "Museums," below).

Though some visitors assume that the *Breakers Hotel* was built by Mizner because it's true to his style and form, it actually was designed by a New York firm called Schulze and Weaver, who also did New York's Waldorf-Astoria and the Los Angeles Biltmore. The current Breakers, constructed in 1925, is on the site of an earlier hotel built by Flagler in 1895. It burned down, was rebuilt in 1903, then burned again. With the exception of a few alterations and extensions, the exterior of the hotel's main building is as it was when it opened 60 years ago.

If you'd like to see the oldest house still standing in Palm Beach, go to 561 N. Lake Way, where you'll find "*Duck's Nest,*" believed to have been assembled in two sections in New York and shipped to the island by barge in 1891. The original sections today form the two outside gabled structures, which are shingled. The central gable, which is false, was added later. The walls are of board and batten and the porch roof and eaves have large boards. The house is named for a large freshwater lake at the east side of the house, where birds are said to have roosted years ago, before the lake was filled in.

If you've got a serious interest in historic homes and sites, particularly of the Palm Beach variety, you could spend weeks on the island. The best guide for such investigation is Barbara D. Hoffstot's *Landmark Architecture of Palm Beach,* (Ober Park Assoc., Pittsburgh, 1980), a marvelous, well-researched book with photos and descriptive copy about all the historic homes of the island, including those that have been demolished.

MUSEUMS. (For information on Planetariums, see "Children's Activities," above.) The museums in this area can only be called eclectic, in every way. They span the range from art facilities to historic and unusual, from multifaceted museums to one honoring the works of a single artist. They come in all shapes and sizes, from quite small and modest to fairly large and imposing.

The **Fort Lauderdale Museum of Art,** which since its opening in 1958—in a remodeled 5,000-square-foot hardware store at 426 E. Las Olas Blvd.—has been woefully inadequate because of its small size, is able to show only about 2 percent of its collection at any one time. But the situation is due to improve soon. At press time the facility is preparing to move to its new $7-million, 57,000-square-foot showcase at 1 E. Las Olas Blvd. Experts expect the new facility to become the finest art museum in the region. Some 40,000 square feet of gallery space and a rooftop sculpture deck are planned. Until the opening, the old facility remains open Tuesday through Saturday from 10:00 A.M. to 4:30 P.M. and Sunday from noon to 5:00 P.M. Check about summer hours. 463–5185. Small admission charge.

The **Hollywood Art and Culture Museum,** 1301 S. Ocean Dr., Hollywood, 921–3274, offers contemporary paintings and sculpture by international, national, and regional artists in both permanent and traveling shows. Open Tuesday through Saturday from 10:00 A.M. to 4:00 P.M. and Sunday from 1:00 to 4:00 P.M. Admission is free. Sunday concerts at 2:30 P.M. cost $2 each.

The **Museum of Archaeology,** 203 S.W. 1st Ave., in downtown Fort Lauderdale, 765–5965, shows exhibits relating to the now-extinct Tequesta Indians of eastern Florida, as well as models, casts, artifacts from area archaeological digs. Open Tuesday through Saturday from 10:00 A.M. to 4:00 P.M. and Sunday from 1:00 to 4:00 P.M. Admission is free.

The **Swimming Hall of Fame Museum,** 501 Seabreeze Blvd., Fort Lauderdale, 462–6536, is totally aquatic in nature, with memorabilia and swimming lore from 107 nations and a swimming-related library. It adjoins the Olympic pool used for collegiate and international swimming and diving competitions. Open Monday through Saturday from 10:00 A.M. to 5:00 P.M. Sunday from 11:00 A.M. to 4:00 P.M. Admission is $1.25 for adults and $.50 for children 3 to 12.

Palm Beach area residents are inveterate museum-goers, and there are several very professional facilities to satisfy them.

The **Boca Raton Museum of Arts,** 801 W. Palmetto Park Rd., offers a small collection of permanent and traveling exhibitions of eclectic paintings, photography, and sculpture, mostly 20th-century Americana. The Soyer Brothers' works are part of the permanent collection. The museum is open Tuesday through Friday from 10:00 A.M. to 4:00 P.M. and Saturday and Sunday from 1:00 to 4:00 P.M. Admission is free, but donations are requested.

Whitehall, the **Henry Morrison Flagler Museum** on Cocoanut Row just east of Lake Worth, was built in 1901 by Flagler, whose Florida East Coast Railroad "opened" Palm Beach and other Florida east coast resorts to world society. The mansion, which is architecturally significant (See "Historic Sites," above), was built by the pioneer for his wife, Mary Lily Kenan. The 73-room home was sold in 1925 and became an annex to a nearby luxury hotel. It was acquired by the Henry Morrison Flagler Museum in 1959, restored to its original condition, and reopened to the public in 1960. The museum has a heavy emphasis on the decorative arts representative of the way the mansion was furnished and decorated when the Flaglers lived in it. Many of the opulent furnishings to be seen today were in their original home. Often referred to as one of the most opulent homes in the U.S., Whitehall includes more than $1 million worth of treasures in a series of "period rooms," special collections of paintings, silver, glass, dolls, lace, costumes, and family memorabilia, ceiling art panels and graceful sculpture, and mementos of early Florida and the lavish heyday of Palm Beach. Out back is The Rambler, an exquisite private railroad car built for Flagler in 1886 and completely restored in 1967. The car's carpeting, upholstery, and drapery have been reproduced to the exact specifications of the originals, utilizing small scrap samples found scattered about the car. The museum is open Tuesday through Saturday from 10:00 A.M. to 5:00 P.M. and Sunday from noon to 5:00 P.M. Guided tours begin about every 30 minutes until 3:15 P.M. Admission is $3 for adults and $1 for children 3 to 12. For information, call 655–2833.

The **Hibel Museum of Art,** 150 Royal Poinciana Plaza, was opened in January 1977 as a tribute to the American artist Edna Hibel. The beautifully laid-out facility was funded by two or the world's foremost collectors of Hibel works, Ethelbelle and Clayton B. Craig, to serve as a repository for their world-famous collection. The museum is not only that; it also functions as a resource for the study and appreciation of a comprehensive collection of the works of an artist who has contributed in a major, unique way to America's art heritage. The museum's collection of Hibel paintings, lithographs, and porcelains may be seen Tuesday through Saturday from 10:00 A.M. to 5:00 P.M. and Sunday from 1:00 to 5:00 P.M. Admission is free. For information, call 833–6870.

The **Morkiami Museum of Japanese Culture** is a most unusual facility for Florida, devoted entirely to permanent and traveling collections of the Japanese folk arts, both traditional and modern. The collection is housed in a traditional Imperial Japanese house, separated into a series of small rooms, each of which houses works pertaining to a particular theme. As in a Japanese home, visitors must remove their shoes to walk on the tatami mats. The museum, a tribute to the Japanese Yamato Colony that existed on the site earlier in this century, sits amid 180 acres that include a traditional Japanese Garden, pine forests with a one-mile-long interpreted nature walk, and sheltered picnic facilities. The museum is open Tuesday through Sunday from 10:00 A.M. to 5:00 P.M. There is no charge, but donations are requested. Between October and April, there is a traditional Japanese tea ceremony held the third Saturday of the month, for which there is a $2 per person charge. The facility is at 4000 Morikami Rd., about seven miles west of the center of Delray Beach. The best approach from coastal areas is west on Linton Boulevard to Carter Road, then south to the museum. For information, call 499–0631.

The **Norton Gallery & School of Art,** 1451 S. Olive Ave., West Palm Beach, calls itself "one of the foremost small museums in the United States," and its collection is indeed impressive and well displayed. The French Collection includes nineteenth- and twentieth-century paintings by such important artists as Gauguin, Cezanne, Renoir, Monet, Matisse, Picasso, and Braque. Its American collection includes such painters as O'Keeffe, Hopper, Shahn, and Pollock. The Chinese Collection includes some 200 archaic bronzes and jades, Buddhist sculpture, later jade carvings, and ceramics. There also are a number of important sculptures both within the museum and in its lovely outdoor landscaped patio garden. The permanent collection is supplemented by rotating shows of high caliber; the best art is usually shown during the winter months. During summer, private collections of Palm Beach socialites are often loaned to the museum. The Norton is open Tuesday through Saturday from 10:00 A.M. to 5:00 P.M. and Sunday from 1:00 to 5:00 P.M. Admission is free, though donations are requested. For information, call 832–5194.

The **Science Museum of Palm Beach County,** 1141 W. Lakewood Rd., West Palm Beach, presents a learning experience in an airy, well laid-out building with permanent displays relating to chemistry, physics, biology, space science, adaptive anatomy, and marine science. There also is a continuing series of educational films and lectures. The *Aldrin Planetarium* provides daily shows and one-night-a-week viewings of the heavens, weather permitting. The museum is open Monday from 1:00 to 5:00 P.M.; Tuesday through Saturday from 10:00 A.M. to 5:00 P.M.; Sunday from 1:00 to 5:00 P.M.; and Tuesday and Thursday from 6:30 to 10:00 P.M. Planetarium shows are presented daily at 3:00 P.M. and Friday at 7:00 P.M. The observatory opens Friday at 8:00 P.M. Admission is $2 for adults and $1 for children enrolled in school grades 1 through 12. You also can purchase a family ticket for $5, which admits two adults and up to three children. The museum is in Dreher Park, which is accessible from coastal areas via Forest Hill, Southern, and Okeechobee Boulevards or Belvedere Road. For information, call 832–1988.

The **Society of the Four Arts** was incorporated in 1936 by a small group of local citizens who believed that the arts should play an important part in community life. They created this museum to encourage art appreciation not only through its small permanent collection, but also with traveling exhibitions, lectures, concerts, and films. The gallery is large, with ample space for fine displays of art and sculpture. The Four Arts is open from December through mid-April only, weekdays from 10:00 A.M. to 5:00 P.M. and Sundays from 2:00 to 5:00 P.M. It is in Four Arts Plaza, just off Royal Palm Way and one block east of Lake Worth. There is no admission charge, but donations are requested.

MUSIC. Music is popular in this area, particularly around Greater Palm Beach, though the Fort Lauderdale region is not exactly devoid of good music. Most of the performances come during the winter season, from about mid-December to April.

Broward County: The *Fort Lauderdale Opera Guild* schedules one major production each month during January, February, and March. Performers are drawn from major international and national companies, such as New York's Metropolitan Opera. They're usually given at 8:00 P.M. at the War Memorial Auditorium, 800 N.E. 8th St. Tickets may be obtained at Guild offices, 1040 Bayview Dr., Monday through Friday from 9:00 A.M. to 5:00 P.M. For information, call 566–9913.

The *Fort Lauderdale Symphony Orchestra* puts forward 10 productions a year during its October to May season. Each production is performed twice and each performance features one or more guest soloists; several offer guest conductors. Performances are usually on Tuesday and Wednesday at 8:15 P.M. in the War Memorial Auditorium, 800 N.E. 8th St., Fort Lauderdale. For information and tickets, the Symphony's office at 1430 N. Federal Hwy., 561–4973, is open Monday through Friday from 9:00 A.M. to 5:00 P.M., except on performance days, when tickets may be purchased at the auditorium, beginning at 7:30 P.M.

One of the highlights for Fort Lauderdale-area residents is the monthly free concert given by the *Hollywood Philharmonic Orchestra* at the Young Circle Band Shell in Hollywood. The best approach is via Hollywood Boulevard from the east or west. Performances, which usually begin at 8:00 P.M., are on a different day each month, so call 920–8580 to find out when the next one is scheduled.

Palm Beach Area: *The Stages Foundation for the Performing Arts* in Boca Raton usually features at least a few musical performances during its annual November-through-May season. Events include at least one opera and a country/western jamboree. Performances are at the Boca Raton Community Center, 201 W. Palmetto Park Rd., and at Red Reef Park, Highway A1A about 1 mile north of Palmetto Park Road. Tickets are $5. For information about performances, times, and prices, call 393–7806, Monday through Friday, from 10:00 A.M. to 5:00 P.M.

One of the annual highlights north of Fort Lauderdale is the *Palm Beach Festival of the Performing Arts,* usually held from mid-March through mid-April. The festival includes performances of all the arts. On the music side, there is usually a chamber orchestra series, a series of classical concerts that are often highlighted by well-known soloists, pops concerts, and a Renaissance series of music and musical theater of that early period. Performances are given in the West Palm Beach Auditorium, the Royal Poinciana Playhouse, and the Henry Morrison Flagler Museum. For updated information, call 686–6800 Monday through Friday, from 9:00 A.M. to 5:00 P.M. The box office is open Monday through Friday from 10:00 A.M. to 4:00 P.M.. You must call 686–6841 in advance to reserve tickets.

The *Palm Beach Opera* stages three performances each of three major productions during its December to March season. Each performance, which includes stars drawn from major opera companies, is at 8:00 P.M. in the West Palm Beach Auditorium. For information and tickets, call 833–7888.

The annual *Music & Dance Festival* held from January through March by the Regional Arts Foundation is also very popular. The varied programs are presented at the West Palm Beach Auditorium, Palm Beach Lakes Boulevard and N. Congress Avenue. The festival includes two series, the "At Eight" and the "At Two" (meaning performances are either at 8:00 P.M. or 2:00 P.M.). Scheduled for the 1985–86 season are the Atlanta and Montreal symphony orchestras, Zagreb Philharmonic, Cleveland String Quartet, Polish Chamber Orchestra, Solisti New York Chamber Ensemble, the Beaux Arts Trio, and solo performances by Nathan Milstein, Alexander Toradze, Itzhak Perlman, and Leontyne Price. For information, call 684–3444.

DANCE. The Regional Arts Foundation's annual *Music & Dance Festival* includes several major ballet companies and dance theater troupes during its January through March season at the West Palm Beach Auditorium. For information, call 684–3444. Performances by such noted companies as the National Ballet of Canada also are included in the annual *Palm Beach Festival of the Performing Arts,* from mid-March to mid-April. For current information, call 686–6800, Monday through Friday, from 9:00 A.M. to 5:00 P.M. You must reserve tickets in advance by calling 686–6841, Monday through Friday, from 10:00 A.M. to 4:00 P.M.

STAGE. Cities in this area may be small in comparison with New York or Los Angeles, but they boast more than their fair share of professional theater, and performances are often given by stars of Broadway and Hollywood. Most of the best theater, however, comes during peak tourist season, roughly between November and April. There is also an active scene among local repertory companies, which give performances on an irregular schedule either seasonally or occasionally throughout the year.

Broward Community College, Central Campus, 3501 S.W. Davie Rd., Fort Lauderdale, offers its International Showcase from October through April. The Showcase is a mixture of Broadway productions with name stars, dance companies, jazz bands of national stature, and individual concerts of various types. Performances are held in several different halls, usually on Saturdays and Sundays at 12:15 P.M. and 8:15 P.M. For current schedule and information on reservations and tickets, call the Cultural Affairs Office, 761–7412. Less-costly Broadway productions are performed in a highly professional manner by students in the college's nationally known Theatre Department, also at Bailey Hall. Two or three major productions are mounted each year, usually in spring and fall, with at least nine performances of each. There also is children's theater during the spring. Ticket prices are kept low intentionally and usually cost about $5. To obtain tickets, go to Room 178 in Building 4 or Bailey Hall (Building 6) on the Central Campus Monday through Friday from 9:00 A.M. to 3:00 P.M. For information, call 475–6840.

The Fort Lauderdale area's major showplace for theater is the *Parker Playhouse,* 707 N.E. 8th St., 764–0700, where Broadway shows and occasional pre-Broadway shows are performed by name stars during the late November through late April season. Performances are Monday through Saturday at 8:00 P.M. and Wednesday and Saturday at 2:00 P.M. Tickets may be obtained at the box office Monday through Saturday from 10:00 A.M. to 9:00 P.M. and Sunday from noon to 4:30 P.M.

The *Sunrise Musical Theater,* 5555 N.W. 95th Ave., Sunrise, 741–7300, offers Broadway musicals, some dramatic plays with name stars, and individual concerts by well-known singers throughout the year. Tickets may be obtained at the box office Monday through Saturday from 11:00 A.M. to 6:00 P.M. or at Spec's Music Store, near the beach area at 2400 E. Sunrise Blvd., 565–7706, Monday through Saturday, from 10:00 A.M. to 8:30 P.M. and Sunday from noon to 5:30 P.M. The theater is 14 miles west of Fort Lauderdale beach via Commercial Boulevard.

Among experimental theater groups performing in the Broward County area from time to time are the *Black Renaissance Theater,* 963–4092; *Encore Players,* 581–8673; *One-Way Puppets,* 491–4221; and *WO/MAN'S Showcase,* 772–9962. Call for schedule information.

The *Caldwell Playhouse,* 286 N. Federal Hwy., in the Boca Raton Mall, is a small, 245-seat facility that serves as the city's resident professional theater. Four different shows performed during the November through April season usually include a few classic drama and comedy productions and at least one new Broadway release or a world premiere. All seats are excellent; the last row, in fact, is only 50 feet from the stage, and there are no obstructed seats. Tickets are $12. The box office is open Monday from 10:00 A.M. to 5:00 P.M., Tuesday through Saturday from 10:00 A.M. to 8:00 P.M., and Sunday from 11:00 A.M. to 7:00 P.M. For information, call 368–7509.

Some good children's theater is presented from September through June by the *Little Palm Theatre* players in the Royal Palm Dinner Theatre, Boca Raton. Curtain is Saturday at 9:15 A.M. Tickets, which may be purchased at the door beginning at 8:45 A.M., or at Spec's Music Store, Towne Center Mall, are $4.25, adults or children. For schedules and information, call 395–7975.

The major theater of Palm Beach County is the *Royal Poinciana Playhouse,* 70 Royal Poinciana Plaza, Palm Beach; 659–3310. During its late December through March season, a variety of Broadway and pre-Broadway shows are presented, often with "name" stars. Productions here are Zev Buffman-produced, meaning most are the same that appear during the season at the Miami Beach Theatre of the Performing Arts and Fort Lauderdale's Parker Playhouse. The box office is open Monday through Saturday from 10:00 A.M. to curtain time (usually 8:00 P.M.) and Sunday from noon to 4:30 P.M.

The *Royal Palm Dinner Theatre,* 303 Golfview Dr., just off US 1, Boca Raton, operates year-round with Broadway and other productions, sometimes featuring special guest stars. Tuesday through Sunday dinner is at 6:00 P.M., show at 8:00 P.M. Price is $28.75. Luncheon matinees begin at noon, Wednesday and Saturday priced at $25.60. For information, call 426–2211. Dinner theater also is offered at the *Musicana,* 1166 Marine Dr., off Belvedere Road and two blocks west of Southern Boulevard, in West Palm Beach. Shows vary between old-fashioned musicales, classic productions, and nostalgic musicals from Broadway. The theater operates Tuesday through Sunday, with dinner at 6:00 P.M., show at 7:30 P.M. Prices are $13.95 to $19.95, depending on entree selected. For information and reservations, call 683–1711.

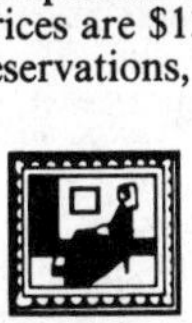

ART GALLERIES. The art gallery scene in this area consists, to a large degree, of shops selling lithographs, graphics, posters, and inexpensive oils that either are mass-produced or dashed off by local amateurs. Many so-called galleries are really framing shops in disguise. Nonetheless, there are some very good galleries to be found, primarily along Las Olas Boulevard in Fort Lauderdale and on and near Worth Avenue in Palm Beach. Among the more interesting galleries and their specialties are:

Edna Hibel works: *Edna Hibel Gallery,* 200 Worth Ave., Palm Beach, 655–2410, specializes in oil paintings, limited-edition lithographs, and collector's plates by the famed American artist. Open Monday through Saturday from 10:00 A.M. to 4:30 P.M.

French Impressionists and Post-Impressionists: *Wally Findley Galleries International,* 165 Worth Ave., Palm Beach, 655–2090. This gallery, with outlets in New York, Paris, Chicago, and Beverly Hills, specializes in extensive collections of well-known French Impressionists and Post-Impressionist artists and modern masters. Open Monday through Saturday from 9:30 A.M. to 5:30 P.M.

Contemporary art: The *Hokin Gallery,* 245 Worth Ave., Palm Beach, 655–5177, includes the works of such well-known artists as Avery, Calder, Dubuffet, Nevelson, and Warhol. Open Monday through Saturday from 10:00 A.M. to 5:00 P.M. The *Holsten Galleries,* 206 Worth Ave., Palm Beach, 833–3403, features American *objets d'art* and offers monthly exhibitions by major American artists. Open Monday through Saturday from 10:00 A.M. to 5:30 P.M. Closed May through October. *Deligny Art Galleries,* 709 E. Las Olas Blvd., Fort Lauderdale, 467–9303, offers original, contemporary American and international oil paintings, bronzes, and sculptures in precious stones such as onyx and alabaster. Open Monday through Saturday from 10:00 A.M. to 5:30 P.M.

Early American: *Mary Douglas Gallery,* 1219 E. Las Olas Blvd., Fort Lauderdale, 522–5222, specializes in eighteenth- and nineteenth-century American paintings, antiques, and *objets d'art.* Open Monday through Saturday from 10:00 A.M. to 5:00 P.M.

Eclectic: *Elsie Orfuss Ltd. Fine Art Galleries,* 155 Worth Ave., Palm Beach, 655–8885, offers a lot: Old Masters, American artists, Impressionists, modern painting, lithographs, and pastels. Open intermittently. Call for appointment. *Helena Rubenstein Gallery,* 125 Worth Ave., Palm Beach, 659–1711, offers up a *soupçon* of outstanding contemporary American painting and sculpture, glass, classic prints, posters, and photographs. Open Monday through Saturday from 10:00 A.M. to 6:00 P.M.

Sporting art: *Ashley Gallery,* 353 Peruvian Ave., Palm Beach, 659–5150, is quite unusual because it specializes in paintings and prints relating to sporting scenes, particularly hunting. Open Monday through Saturday from 10:00 A.M. to 5:30 P.M.

Southwestern art: The Canyon Gallery, 619 E. Las Olas Blvd., Fort Lauderdale, 522–2011, concentrates entirely on original, contemporary art and sculpture created in America's Southwest. Open Monday through Saturday from 10:30 A.M. to 5:00 P.M.

SHOPPING. As with most of Florida, the majority of shopping in this area is done in regional shopping malls, of which there are quite a few of the large variety. The malls generally contain at least four major department stores and scores of shops and boutiques running the gamut from tacky to very upscale. Aside from the malls, this area offers two major, trendy shopping streets, which are lined with pricey shops and boutiques. Prices generally are at the upper end of the scale, but it may well be worth it because they offer top-of-the-line, *au courant* items that are not often seen in run-of-the-mill stores and shops of Florida. In Fort Lauderdale, East *Las Olas Boulevard* is a well-manicured, pretty street with plants, benches, and dozens of chic little shops and boutiques. While parking is not permitted in front of most shops, there is ample space in the streets behind Las Olas, both at meters and in municipal or private parking lots.

The situation is quite different on Palm Beach's *Worth Avenue,* one of the most famous—and most crowded—shopping streets in the world. "The Avenue," as locals refer to it, stretches just about three blocks, though it's been extended at bit at its eastern end by the addition of the two-story Esplanade, adding yet more shops to the more than 200 on Worth Avenue. During the winter season, from about mid-December to April, traffic on the relatively narrow street is quite heavy and on-street parking space at a premium. If you're lucky enough to actually land a space, you're usually limited to 30 or 60 minutes—and it's *very strictly* enforced! That leaves you with just a few possibilities for dumping the family gas-guzzler while you go shopping: valet-parking in The Esplanade or public parking lots on Hibiscus Avenue, between Worth and Peruvian avenues, or on Peruvian, just east of Hibiscus. However, don't be surprised to find those facilities full much of the time. As for parking on city streets within a seven-block radius of Worth Avenue—forget it, unless you get there at about 7:00 in the morning!

If you're Worth Avenue-bound, you also should be aware of the fact that a number of its shops close down for all or part of the period between May and October because business is rather slow then, and most of the shopowners have outlets in such northern resort areas as Bar Harbor, Maine, and Provincetown, Massachusetts.

There's another difference between Worth Avenue and Las Olas Boulevard: on the Palm Beach street, all shops are very closely supervised by the Worth Avenue Association to make sure they maintain high standards. It's not all that easy to open up on this street and equally difficult to stay on it if you don't measure up. Salespersons are as well-dressed as their upscale customers, who come from High Society, industry, finance, and the entertainment world. Shops are never permitted to display "Sale" signs during the winter months, referred to locally as "the social season."

Shops along both streets generally are open Monday through Saturday from 10:00 A.M. to 5:00 P.M. Sales tax is 5 percent.

Among the malls, the fanciest, and newest, in the Broward County area is *Galleria,* which stretches for a half-mile along East Sunrise Boulevard, from the 2300–2600 blocks, just west of the causeway to Fort Lauderdale Beach; call 564–1015 for information. The first phase of this mall opened in August 1978, but new shops still are being added. The 1.3-million-square-foot facility is believed to be the world's most expensive mall in terms of construction cost, which topped $150-million. There's another claim to fame: it's the only place in the world where you'll find three highly competitive specialty stores nearly side by side—*Nieman-Marcus, Lord & Taylor,* and *Saks Fifth Avenue.* Other major chain department stores are *Burdine's* and *Jordan Marsh.* There also are 130 shops and boutiques of all types. Hours are Monday through Saturday from 10:00 A.M. to 9:00 P.M. and Sunday from noon to 5:30 P.M.

The area's second major mall, nearly as big with 1.1-million square feet, is *Broward Mall,* well inland at West Broward Boulevard and University Drive (US 441) in suburban Plantation; call 473–8100. Major department stores are *Burdine's, Jordan Marsh, Sears,* and *JCPenney.* Among the 132 shops are some very fashionable clothing stores, jewelers, photographic outlets, electronic and computer stores, and bookshops. Hours are Monday through Saturday from 10:00 A.M. to 9:00 P.M. and Sunday from noon to 5:30 P.M.

Shopping that's a bit more down-to-earth than it is along Worth Avenue may be found at the *Palm Beach Mall,* 1801 Palm Beach Lakes Blvd., adjoining I-95, West Palm Beach; 686–3513. This 1.3-million-square-foot mall is the largest such facility in Palm Beach County, and it's only about seven minutes' drive from the beach. The mall contains 100 shops of virtually all types, and five department stores—*Lord & Taylor, Burdine's, Jordan Marsh, JCPenney,* and *Sears.* Hours are Monday through Saturday from 10:00 A.M. to 9:00 P.M. and Sunday from noon to 5:30 P.M.

Oakbrook Square, 11594 US Hwy. 1, at the corner of PGA Boulevard (Highway A1A), Palm Beach Gardens; 626–3880. This mall truly delights the eye. Its 47 shops and stores are spread out around sculptured fountains, patio dining nooks, and lush gardens. It's the only mall included here that is not fully enclosed, which makes it seem more of a tropical Florida locale than the others. Shops are in the brown-and-beige Mediteranean style of architecture that's so popular in this area. The north end of the linear mall is anchored by *Jacobson's,* an upscale department store. Among the high-level shops to be found here are those with names such as *Lily Pulitzer* and *Pappagallo,* along with art galleries, gourmet shops, and restaurants. Hours are Monday through Saturday from 9:30 A.M. to 5:30 P.M.

DINING OUT. This area in general, and Fort Lauderdale and Palm Beach in particular, is well known for its distinctive restaurants. There are several thousand eating places in the area, from diners and fast-food chains to internationally acclaimed gourmet restaurants that are top-flight, with prices to match. Palm Beach, in particular, has many famous restaurants, which are quite expensive—but since they offer some of the finest food, ambience, and service to be found most anywhere in the world, many people consider them well worth the price. Seafood is a most popular dish among natives and visitors, but the full spectrum, from Continental to Thai, is available and enjoyed. Because both locals and visitors dine out a lot, it's always advisable to make a reservation for most restaurants, especially during the winter season, from November through April. The most-popular, top-of-the-line restaurants often book tables a week in advance during the season. Virtually all restaurants in the area are relatively informal, though some of the more expensive ones request that gentlemen wear jackets and slacks for dinner. Very few require it.

The price classifications of the following restaurants are based on the cost of an average three-course dinner for one person for food alone; beverages, tax, and tip would be extra: *Deluxe,* more than $30, *Expensive,* $25 to $30; *Moderate,* $20 to $25, and *Inexpensive,* less than $20. Sales tax is 5 percent.

Abbreviations for credit cards are: AE, American Express; CB, Carte Blanche; DC, Diners Club, MC, MasterCard; V, VISA. Most restaurants will accept travelers' checks; very few will take personal checks.

Abbreviation for lunch is L, for dinner is D.

What follows is only a very selective list of the many dining possibilities available in this area:

AMERICAN

Deluxe

Historic Bryan Homes. 301 S.W. 3rd Ave., Fort Lauderdale; 523–0177. American dishes prepared in most creative and unusual ways are served in two of the city's oldest homes, joined together and turned into a series of intimate dining nooks along the New River. L,D, Tuesday–Sunday. All major credit cards.

Moderate to Expensive

Chuck & Harold's. 207 Royal Poinciana Way, Palm Beach; 659–1440. A popular, trendy eatery with tile floors, a large blond-wood bar, lots of greenery, and dining in the enclosed sidewalk café area or in the spacious Garden Court Cafe dining room in the rear. The staff is young and friendly. Entertainment nightly. L,D, Monday–Sunday. All major credit cards.

Moderate

Doherty's. 288 S. County Rd., Palm Beach; 655–6200. An upscale saloon with a long bar on one wall, mirrors and black banquettes on the other, and paddlefans overhead. Crowded and noisy at both lunch and dinner; especially so once the piano player gets going at about 9:00 P.M. L,D, daily. AE, MC, V.

Harrison's on the Water. 3000 N.E. 32nd St., Fort Lauderdale, 2 blocks west of Highway A1A; 566–9667. Interesting variety of dishes plus all the standards are served in a large room overlooking the Intracoastal Waterway. A number of booths provide comfortable dining. Popular with families. Waitresses are old-fashioned friendly. L,D, daily. AE, MC, V.

Inexpensive

The Sly Fox. 3537 Galt Ocean Drive, 1 block east of Highway A1A, Fort Lauderdale; 565–1666. The menu is rather limited, but all the food is good home cooking, served by friendly waitresses in this neighborhood favorite that's small, cozy, and very publike. There's entertainment at night around the piano bar. L,D, daily. AE, MC, V.

This Is It Pub. 424 24th St., West Palm Beach; 833–4997. The only authentic pub in the area, this place is decorated with nostalgic memorabilia and is a favorite hangout for businessmen at lunch. The Pub is famous for its authentic conch chower and conch fritters, which are flown in fresh from the Bahamas every Friday. The soup kettle, steaks, and general seafood are all demand-items. L,D, Tuesday–Saturday. All major credit cards.

BARBEQUE

Inexpensive

Bobby Rubino's. 1430 S.E. 17th St. Causeway, Fort Lauderdale, 522–3006; 4100 N. Federal Hwy., Fort Lauderdale, 561–5305; 1901 Palm Beach Lakes Blvd., Palm Beach Lakes, 686–1770. This chain is always the most popular in its town for the leanest, juiciest barbecued ribs and chicken plus a most amazing fried onion ring loaf that sticks with you. Large and comfortable, but often noisy, rooms have booths and tables, wood and greenery. L,D, daily. AE, MC, V.

Tom's Place. 1198 N. Dixie Hwy., Boca Raton; 368–3502. This is no chain; it's purely one-of-a-kind, and locals swear by this no-frills, no-nonsense ribs place that is always crowded with elbow-to-elbow customers. The neighborhood-type, small restaurant has become a legendary institution in this area, thanks largely to its secret-recipe barbecue sauce. L,D, Tuesday–Saturday. No credit cards.

CHINESE

Expensive

Christine Lee's Northgate. 6191 Rock Island Rd., a half-block north of Commercial Boulevard, Tamarac; 726–0430. This place may not look all that Oriental, but it's world-famous for its gourmet Oriental cuisine served amid polished woods, greenery, and muted lighting. Some of the dishes are rather unusual for this type of restaurant. Surprisingly, it also serves some of the best steaks in town. D, daily. All major credit cards.

Inexpensive

Hong Kong Island. 1000 US Hwy. 1, North Palm Beach; 622–3223. This large, standard-in-appearance Chinese restaurant offers the big three: Cantonese, Mandarin, and Szechuan cuisines. There's a cocktail lounge as well. L, Monday–Saturday; D, daily. AE, MC, V.

Moy Lee's. 2321 N. Federal Hwy., Fort Lauderdale; 565–6604. Large selection of Szechuan and Cantonese dishes that are consistently good, served in a large, brightly lit, often noisy room. Six tables in the lounge are quieter and cozier, but the bartender almost always has the TV on. L, Monday–Saturday; D, daily. All major credit cards.

CAJUN

Moderate

Lagniappe Cajun House. 230 E. Las Olas Blvd., Fort Lauderdale; 467–7500. Cajun cookery began arriving in this area only recently, but it's caught on fast. This relatively small place simply "reeks" of the Cajun bayous of southern Louisiana. The menu is a bit unusual if you're not accustomed to this version of spiced-up French food, but it's interesting. Live jazz nightly from about 9:00 P.M. L, Monday–Friday; D, daily; Brunch, Saturday, Sunday. AE, MC, V.

CONTINENTAL

Deluxe

Down Under. 3000 E. Oakland Park Blvd., Fort Lauderdale; 564–6984. This luscious place got it's name from the fact that it's almost hidden under the small bridge crossing over the Intracoastal Waterway. The restaurant is beautifully decorated in brick and greenery to resemble an old house. There are some turn-of-the-century posters adorning the walls. You also can sit outside and dine overlooking the Intracoastal and watching the yachts that pass by. The menu offers a very wide selection of gourmet food, served in a friendly manner. The only slight drawback is that tables are rather close together. Even hamburgers at lunch are quite expensive. L, Wednesday–Friday; D, daily. All major credit cards.

Petite Marmite. 315 Worth Ave., Palm Beach; 655–0550. An enchanting restaurant that long has been a Palm Beach institution, it's hidden just off Worth Avenue down one of the Vias. The restaurant features a garden atmosphere with skylight, brickwork, wrought-iron tables and chairs, and lots of plants. The ambience is rather formal, and jackets are required after 6:00 P.M. L,D, Monday–Saturday. All major credit cards.

Providencia. 251 Royal Palm Way, Palm Beach, on the lobby level of the Palm Beach Plaza office building; 655–2600. Forest-green and pink appointments, oil paintings, mirrors, and trellis panels contribute to the stylish and elegant appearance of this relative newcomer. There are two dining rooms, a small cocktail lounge with live music nightly, and an intriguing menu. L, Monday–Friday; D, daily. All major credit cards.

Windows on the Green. In the Pier 66 Hotel, 2301 S.E. 17th St. Causeway, Fort Lauderdale; 525–6666. Hidden on the lower level of this centrally located hotel, Windows is relatively new but was an instant success from the day it opened, even though it's one of the most expensive restaurants in the area. The sophisticated, elegant service and gourmet food served by candlelight is imaginative and delicious. Allow about three hours to work your way through dinner because everything is made to order and served leisurely. D, Monday–Saturday. All major credit cards.

Expensive to Deluxe

Capriccio's. 330 Royal Poinciana Plaza, Palm Beach; 659–5955. The sophisticated décor of browns and beiges, stained-glass panels and mirrors sets the mood for elegant dining. Rooms are large, but the mood is intimate and quiet. There's a stunning lounge and outdoor dining patio overlooking the Plaza's gardens and fountains. Jackets are required. L, Monday–Saturday; D, daily. All major credit cards.

Ta-boo. 221 Worth Ave., Palm Beach; 655–5562. This restaurant and lounge offer a large, dimly lit dining room with mirrored walls lined with banquettes, chandeliers made of large bunches of grapes, and twinkling lights. Out of place on Worth Avenue? Not at all: it's very popular with shoppers and business people for lunch and large enough so you don't have to wait for a table. At dinner, though, it gets quite crowded once the live music for dancing begins at about 8:00 P.M. Jackets are required after 6:00 P.M. L, Monday–Saturday; D, daily. All major credit cards.

Expensive

Brazilian Court. 300 Brazilian Ave., Palm Beach; 655–7740. A formal, pastel-pretty, oval-shaped dining room with windows looking onto a tropical courtyard make for a very popular dining experience, particularly among the older set who know and like the Brazilian Court Hotel, in which this restaurant is situated. A cozy, clubby cocktail lounge adjoins the dining room. B, L, D, daily. AE, MC, V.

La Reserve. 3115 N.E. 32nd Ave., Fort Lauderdale; 563–6644. This is truly a beautiful restaurant with a gourmet menu to match. Half the restaurant offers tables along picture windows overlooking the Intracoastal Waterway; the other half are booths on a raised level so you can see the water from there as well. Consistently courteous service and consistently great food. D, daily. All major credit cards.

Nando's. 221 Royal Palm Way, Palm Beach; 655–3031. A tradition in the Palm Beaches for 40 years, this New York-style restaurant is crowded and noisy, yet intimate. The two front rooms with brick walls, wrought-iron accents, bar, and piano bar are the most desirable. The two back rooms are more subdued, with back-lighted stained-glass windows. An enormous menu makes your selection a challenge. Strolling musicians visit the tables during dinner. D, daily. All major credit cards.

Moderate

Bentley's. 730 US Hwy. 1, North Palm Beach; 842–6831. A popular place and one of the first restaurants in the area to capitalize on the casually elegant atmosphere provided by lots of polished woods, stained glass, and greenery. There is a large bar and several dining rooms that range from crowded and noisy to intimate and relatively private. L, Monday–Friday; D, daily. Major credit cards.

ENGLISH

Inexpensive to Moderate

Rose & Crown. 3680 W. Commercial Blvd., Fort Lauderdale; 485–8560. The only relatively authentic pub in South Florida serves up such traditionals as Shepherd's pie and bangers and mash from its small kitchen. A variety of

English beers and ales add authenticity, as does the dart board—often the scene of area tournaments. Quite popular with the area's growing British community. A small adjoining grocery sells English specialty items, best of which is fresh sausage. L and D, daily. AE.

FRENCH

Deluxe

Cafe L'Europe. 150 Worth Ave., Palm Beach; 655–4020. With meteoric speed, this restaurant at The Esplanade has joined the ranks of Palm Beach's epicurean landmarks. It's stunning in appearance, with rich woods, brick archways, flowering plants, and tables set with salmon-pink tablecloths, Coalport Ming Rose china, silver, and crystal stemware. A young staff provides attentive, properly paced service, complementing the classical and innovative selections on the menu. Jackets are required. D, Monday–Saturday. All major credit cards.

Le Monegasque, 2505 S. Ocean Blvd., in the Palm Beach President condominium, Palm Beach; 585–0071. This hard-to-find restaurant (only a small, unobtrusive sign marks its location) is in a residential area several miles south of Worth Avenue. A classic, small one-room, *very* French-style restaurant, it offers white banquette seating along both walls, tables that are close together, and a well-lit atmosphere. The sumptuous menu is an epicurean's dream come true. Jackets are required. D, Tuesday–Sunday. AE.

Petitbon. 4711 N. Dixie Hwy., Oakland Park; 771–7792. Almost hidden in the Bauder Plaza mini-shopping center, this is one of the Fort Lauderdale area's newer additions. The owner, Alain Petitbon, is also the chef, a factor that usually guarantees good food—and it certainly does here. Ambience is delightful in this relatively small place with starched white tablecloths and candles. D, Monday–Saturday. All major credit cards.

La Vielle Maison. 770 E. Palmetto Park Rd., Boca Raton; 391–6701. This award-winner, situated inside a Mizner-era mansion that's elegantly furnished with period furniture, decorative tiles, and original artwork, provides a very special ambience in which to enjoy an equally special dining experience. Tables are exquisitely set with French china and Austrian crystal. In character with everything else, the wine list is superior. Two seatings nightly. Jackets are required. D, daily. All major credit cards.

Moderate

The French Place. 360 E. McNab Rd., Pompano Beach; 785–1920. Though more than a decade old and almost totally lacking in décor and ambience, this delightful classical French restaurant was relatively unknown to outsiders until a restaurant critic discovered it. Since then, it's not uncommon to have to wait in line to enjoy the friendly service and well-prepared meals. L, Monday–Friday; D, daily. All major credit cards.

La Ferme. 1601 E. Sunrise Blvd., Fort Lauderdale; 764–0987. Highly original preparations of traditional nouvelle cuisine are prepared and served by Marie-Paul and Henri Terrier amid a cozy, French Provincial home décor, complete with lace tablecloths. The service and food are consistently good, and Madame Terrier is constantly looking over your shoulder with a smile to make sure you're enjoying the meal. D, Tuesday–Sunday. AE, MC, V.

Inexpensive

The Magical Inn. 800 S. Federal Hwy., Hallandale; 456–4451. This small, family-owned and operated place almost makes you feel as though you're sitting in somebody's home kitchen, with baskets and utensils hanging on the white-washed walls. The food is as well prepared as it would in fact be in your best friend's home, and the service is keenly attentive, friendly, and low-key. D, daily. MC, V.

GERMAN

Expensive

The Wine Cellar. 199 E. Oakland Park Blvd., Fort Lauderdale; 565–9021. Its high popularity forced this formerly small gourmet German/East European restaurant to move into what used to be an Indian eatery. Though now larger, it retains its charm and intimacy. L, Monday–Friday; D, Monday–Saturday. All major credit cards.

Moderate

Bavarian Village. 1401 N. Federal Hwy., Fort Lauderdale; 922–7321. This isn't your large, rowdy-Bavarian-beer-hall kind of place, but it does have the feeling of old Germany. In a family-style setting, you munch away at specialties such as sauerbraten, rouladen, and pork shank chosen from among 30 entrées. L, Monday–Friday; D, daily. All major credit cards.

Brauhaus. 1701 E. Sunrise Blvd., Fort Lauderdale; 764–4104. Southern Germany really comes to life here, not only via the menu that features eight kinds of schnitzel, among other things, but also with its periodic shows of traditional Bavarian slap-dancing and cowbell-ringing. It's quite a vivid sight to add to an evening's enjoyment. Thursday is suckling-pig night. Shows are Wednesday, Thursday, and Sunday at 7:30 P.M., and Friday and Saturday at 8:15 and 9:30 P.M. D, Tuesday–Sunday. AE, MC, V.

INDIAN

Inexpensive

Punjab. 1001 W. Oakland Park Blvd., Oakland Park; 565–2522. Sort of hidden away in the Oakland Mall, next to Movie 10, this relative newcomer is rather large, a favorite with families, and offering attentive service. They offer the area's only selection of the Moglai cuisine of North India. L, Monday–Saturday; D, daily. AE, MC, V.

ITALIAN

Deluxe

Casa Vecchia. 209 N. Birch Rd., Fort Lauderdale; 463–7575. Just west of Highway A1A, this is one of the area's most famous, and most popular, restaurants. The setting is a home dating from the 1920s, in Mediterranean-Italian style, with patio, wrought-iron, fountains, tiles, and greenery, overlooking the Intracoastal Waterway. The menu of Northern Italian specialties is superb; service is quite formal and, often, somewhat stuffy, and the prices quite high. But despite it all, the food makes it more than worthwhile. D, daily. All major credit cards.

Expensive

Frankie's. 3333 N.E. 32nd St., Fort Lauderdale; 566–7853. An absolutely delightful place in a beautiful setting overlooking the Intracoastal Waterway through large picture windows. Lighting is subdued and candlelit, tables a bit too close together, but service and cuisine are consistently excellent. L, Monday–Friday; D, daily. All major credit cards.

Moderate

La Perla. 1818 E. Sunrise Blvd., Fort Lauderdale; 765–1950. It's kind of easy to miss this small storefront squeezed next to the Gateway Theater, but the search is worthwhile. This elegantly decorated brick-and-greenery place is a true find. The menu of Italian dishes, with seafood preparations a specialty, is superb, served in a friendly, neighborhood manner. D, daily. AE, MC, V.

La Scala. 1620 N. Federal Hwy., Fort Lauderdale; 563–0660. Intimate dining from a large selection of Italian specialties amid candlelight and, most evenings, quiet dancing to a small orchestra, in an elegant room. D, daily. DC, MC, V.

Raffaello's. 725 E. Palmetto Park Rd., Boca Raton; 392–4855. This is a popular restaurant of stylish design, with green flowered wallpaper contrasting warmly with salmon tablecloths. There is a small cocktail bar and several dining areas separated by dividers. Jackets are required. D, daily. AE, MC, V.

Testa's. 221 Royal Poinciana Way, Palm Beach; 832–0992. Open from mid-December through April only. Since 1921, the Family Testa has been feeding visitors and residents alike with hearty food accompanied by friendly, unpretentious service. Fresh pasta dishes and strawberry pie are the specialties on the rather lengthy menu. There are three dining areas, an enclosed sidewalk café, a clubby room filled with dark-wooden booths, and a large, well-lit patio room landscaped with live trees and plants. B,L,D, daily. All major credit cards.

Inexpensive

Juliano's. 2528 N. Federal Hwy., Fort Lauderdale; 564–6788. Very homey, neighborhood-style, relaxed family setting of brick, greenery, and overhead fans. Everything is cooked to order and served by some of the friendliest waitresses around. All the standard Italian pasta and meat, fish, and chicken dishes are served. D, daily. All major credit cards.

MEXICAN

Moderate

Acapulco. 1666 E. Oakland Park Blvd., Fort Lauderdale; 566–6436. A large, popular restaurant that's bedecked with serapes, sombreros, and piñatas; seating is at glass tables with wicker chairs. Mostly Mexican specialties, but there also are some Cuban offerings such as fried pork and beans. Mariachis play Tuesday through Sunday evenings. L, Monday–Friday; D, daily. AE, MC, V.

Inexpensive

Carlos & Pepe's 17th St. Cantina. 1302 S.E. 17th St., Fort Lauderdale; 467–7192. This is a large place with Mexican touches via sombreros, tiles, and serapes, in a highly informal atmosphere. All the standards such as tacos, tostados, nachos, enchiladas, plus some quite unusual combinations, are washed down with giant margaritas. L,D, daily. All major credit cards.

MIDDLE EASTERN

Moderate

Marrakech. 2980 N. Federal Hwy., Fort Lauderdale; 561–4764. If you don't believe you're in the middle of Morocco in this place, it's a miracle, for it's got all the standard elements: tented ceiling, red, green, and gold velvet walls, banks of pillows and banquettes. Waiters are garbed in caftans and provide attentive service as they bring everything from couscous to beef tajine. D, daily. All major credit cards.

POLYNESIAN

Expensive

Mai-Kai. 3599 N. Federal Hwy., Fort Lauderdale; 563–3272. This place has been a landmark for more than 30 years. It's large and surrounded by Polynesian-style tropical gardens and waterfalls. The largest room offers Polynesian shows nightly at 7:30 and 10:30 P.M. The early show comes with dinner; the later one can be watched without dinner, but you've got to pay a $5.95 cover charge either way. Waitresses are garbed in Tahitian outfits and tend to rush you when the place is crowded, which it often is. D, daily. All major credit cards.

SEAFOOD

Expensive

Busch's. 5855 N. Ocean Blvd., Ocean Ridge; 732–8470. Once a local "find," people now come from miles around to dine in this place south of South Palm Beach, making it often quite crowded. Operated by the Lambrakis family, the restaurant offers a bar that's often packed with customers waiting for tables, and two dining areas: the more-casual Porch (where jackets are not required) and the French country-style dining room (where they are). Décor is unusually nice for a seafood house, though the Porch is far more intimate. D, Tuesday–Sunday. All major credit cards.

Charley's Crab. 456 S. Ocean Blvd., Palm Beach; 659–1500. This extremely popular restaurant (the line for dinner starts forming at about 4:00 P.M.) is under the same ownership as Chuck & Harold's. Informal and noisy, the front dining room overlooking the ocean houses a crowded raw bar. Dining is somewhat less harried but less atmospheric in the nautically decorated rear dining rooms. L, Monday–Saturday; D, daily. All major credit cards.

15th Street Fisheries. 1900 S.E. 15th St., Fort Lauderdale; 763–2777. This large, sophisticated place is 100 percent oriented to the sea in its décor, with old photos of the city's early fishing industry adorning the walls. The setting is nice—on the water—and the selection of fresh seafood dishes expansive. L,D, daily. All major credit cards.

Fin & Claw. 2502 N. Federal Hwy., Lighthouse Point; 782–1060. Relocated from New Jersey where it had been since 1945, this place just north of the Pompano Fashion Square is popular with families from the area, as well as with visitors. The main room is large, well-lit, and often noisy; a smaller room between the large one and the tiny cocktail lounge offers a few booths, dimmer lighting, more intimacy. The seafood offerings are top-notch. Recently, some German-style dishes such as schnitzel have been added to the list of nearly 50 entrées. D, daily. All major credit cards.

Moderate to Expensive

Burt & Jack's. Port Everglades (take Rte. 84E and follow the signs); 522–5225. Fort Lauderdale's busy port is an unlikely setting for a full-service restaurant, yet it's become one of the area's "hottest" new dining spots, probably because of its "silent" partner, Burt Reynolds. The cozy, European-style villa offers candlelight, white tablecloths and casual service, with seafood items the specialty and a selection of beef dishes. Picture-window views of the Intracoastal Waterway and the port are sensational. D, daily. All major credit cards.

Moderate

Old Florida Seafood House. 1414 N.E. 26th St., Wilton Manors; 566–1044. This place is certainly off the beaten track, a bit over a half-mile west of US 1, but it's been found by a lot of locals and visitors. The reason is its exceptionally fine, fresh seafood, a very popular raw bar, and friendly service in three rooms, all sporting standard nautical décor. Unfortunately, popularity takes its toll; waits for tables can be up to an hour, especially during winter months. L, Monday–Friday; D, daily. AE, MC, V.

Port of Call. 701 S.E. 17th St., Fort Lauderdale; 761–1116. Owned and operated by professional fishermen, this place offers top-flight fresh seafood most of the time, but occasionally falls down on the job. It's a friendly, cozy, informal place with one large well-lit room and another that's cozier and quieter with candle-lit booths. L, Monday–Friday; D, daily. All major credit cards.

The Crab Pot. 386 E. Blue Heron Blvd., Riviera Beach; 844–2822. This popular waterfront restaurant under the Riviera Bridge offers a small rustic bar and informal dining areas. Customers dine on newspaper-covered tables with mallet in hand to crack the blue crabs. Steamed shrimp and home-grown catfish also are specialties. L, D, daily. AE, MC, V.

Inexpensive

Cap's Place. Lighthouse Point; 941–0418. If you want to see what a true, informal old Florida restaurant is like, don't miss this place; it's one of the few remaining examples of its genre. Cap's is housed in two rambling old wooden buildings are on a palm tree-covered island not far from shore. Inside, extremely fresh dishes made with local catches are served up in friendly style in booths and tables along split-wood floors. It's a bit tricky getting to this place, but well worth the effort. Just past Pompano Fashion Square, turn east at N.E. 24th Street and follow signs to the Marina at 2765 N.E. 28th Court. Then, you hop on an open boat for the slow, short trip to the island as the "captain" regales you with jokes and tales of Old Florida. D, daily. AE, MC, V.

STEAK

Expensive

Charcoal Pit. 825 E. Sunrise Blvd., Fort Lauderdale; 763–4262. If you want to see the way restaurants looked in the 1940s, this is the place to go—with its Art Deco touches, large chandelier, and etched mirrors. Steak is cooked on an open hearth in view of patrons, who sit either in the large, well-lit Deco room or the smaller, more intimate adjacent room sporting windows overlooking lighted gardens. The blackboard menu changes daily. D, Tuesday–Sunday. All major credit cards.

Moderate

Tropical Acres. 2500 Griffin Rd., Dania; 761–1744. One mile west of I–95, this is another area landmark, open since 1949. It's a classic, no-nonsense steak house where the portion size and food quality is more important than the atmosphere of the large, noisy room usually filled by the family trade. The style and the waitress staff are strictly old-fashioned, meaning nice, helpful, and courteous. An organ is played during dinner hours. D, daily. All major credit cards.

SWISS

Moderate to Expensive

Cafe de Geneve, 1519 S. Andrews Ave., Fort Lauderdale; 522–8928. The area's last remaining Swiss restaurant specializes in cheese and meat fondues, duck and scallops, among the 36 items on its eclectic menu. Decor is pure Swiss chalet with tropical touches such as palm trees. Very friendly, accommodating service is provided in this popular restaurant. L, Monday–Friday; D, daily. All major credit cards.

THAI

Inexpensive

Chiang Mai of Siam. 3341 N. Federal Hwy., Fort Lauderdale; 565–0855. This tiny storefront restaurant next to the Coral Ridge Theater is cozy and all the food cooked to order and served up in quite large portions to a thankful audience. Dishes range from mild to extra hot. L, Monday–Friday; D, daily. AE, MC, V.

Siam Curry House. 2010 Wilton Dr., Wilton Manors; 564–3411. This is a small, basic restaurant specializing in mild to very hot Siamese curries and a few other unusual dishes. L, Monday–Friday; D, daily. All major credit cards.

NIGHT LIFE. Many of the hotels and motels in this area offer some form of nighttime entertainment, ranging from piano bar to band, singer, and/or comic. Many locals and residents tend to spend their evenings simply eating a nice dinner and going home, or perhaps attending theater or dinner theater, rather than plunking themselves down at a nightspot. There are not a tremendous number of nighttime places in this area that would be of particular interest to the visitor, but there are enough to provide after-dark entertainment for those who seek it.

Broward County

Some old-time, big-name stars as well as noted Big Bands are found December–April at the *Galt Ocean Mile Hotel,* 3200 Galt Ocean Dr., Fort Lauderdale, 1 block north of Oakland Park Boulevard and just east of Highway A1A. There are a large number of nightspots that cater to tastes of all ages; mostly situated in the central area of Fort Lauderdale, along the Intracoastal Waterway, Federal Highway (US 1), and Sunrise and Commercial boulevards.

The mature set goes to dance to easy-listening music bands at *Stan's,* 3300 E. Commercial Blvd. College kids and young professionals head for three side-by-side places along the Intracoastal Waterway's eastern bank, just south of Oakland Park Boulevard: The newest and most popular is *Shooter's,* 3033 N.E. 32nd Ave.; the other two are *Bootlegger's,* 3033 N.E. 32nd Ave., whose outdoor pool is very popular; and *Durty Nellie's,* 3051 N.E. 32nd Ave. Many customers shuttle back and forth between the three. Also popular with young professionals are *Christopher's,* 2857 E. Oakland Park Blvd., on the Intracoastal's western bank, and the trendy *Mr. Laff's,* 1135 N. Federal Hwy.

Jazz buffs head for *Musician's Exchange,* 729 W. Broward Blvd., while those in search of disco are found at the *Riverwatch* in the Marriott Hotel, 1881 S.E. 17th St. Causeway; *Playpen South,* 3411 N. Federal Hwy; *Confetti's,* 2660 E.

Commercial Blvd.; and *Penrod's,* 303 N. Atlantic Blvd. (Highway A1A). Late-night disco fans head for the only place in the area open until 4:00 A.M., *City Limits,* 2520 S. Miami Rd., Hollywood, just south of Port Everglades. The high school and college crowd hang out at *The Candy Store,* 1 N. Atlantic Blvd.; *The Button,* 3000 E. Las Olas Blvd; and *The Parrot,* 907 Sunrise Lane. All three are wall-to-wall during the spring college break period.

Country music and dancing can be found at *Club Texas,* 1495 S.E. 17th St. Causeway.

Comedy clubs have been starting to appear and are gaining in popularity. The two most popular are *The Comic Strip,* 1432 N. Federal Hwy., which showcases comics from Los Angeles and New York, and *A Comedy Nightclub,* 1960 S. Ocean Dr., Hallandale, which specializes in the Los Angeles variety. Both also have amateur nights.

Particularly nice piano bars boasting friendly, neighborhood ambience can be found at the *Edgewater Lounge* in Ireland's Inn, 2220 N. Atlantic Blvd., on the ocean, and in the *Sly Fox,* 3537 Galt Ocean Dr., one block east of Highway A1A.

Palm Beach County

In the Palm Beach County area, the most elegant pursuit to be found is dancing at *The Breakers,* S. County Rd., Palm Beach, where formal ballroom dancing takes place nightly in the gorgeous and opulent Florentine Room, and, in a somewhat more upbeat tempo, in the smaller, Spanish-decorated Alcazar Lounge. After 7:00 P.M., men must wear jacket and tie; women, suitable dress or pant suit. There is leisurely dancing to bands in a somewhat less formal atmosphere at such other Palm Beach locals as the *Brazilian Court* and the *Colony* (See "Hotels") and *Ta-boo* (See "Restaurants").

The disco set can be found in *Wildflower,* 551 E. Palmetto Park Rd., Boca Raton, a popular place complete with disc jockey and flashing lights, several large bars, and a lively crowd of youngsters and some middle-agers. The most popular nightspot now in West Palm Beach is *Cheers* at the new Royce Hotel, 1601 Belvedere Rd., which beginning nightly at 8:00 P.M. offers up a good buffet, disco dancers, and crowds following the beat. It's usually very crowded after 10:00 P.M., when the d.j. and flashing lights go full blast.

NORTH OF PALM BEACH TO VERO BEACH

by
JOEL A. GLASS

The Florida traveler whose journey has begun on the Gold Coast (Miami to Palm Beach) will find as he or she progresses north of Palm Beach that there is less and less commercial development, fewer high-rises interfering with and detracting from (occasionally destroying) the natural tropical environment, and more large expanses of untouched and uncrowded beaches, forests, rivers, and lakes. The generally slower-paced lifestyle, ambience, informality, charm, and neo-Southern gentility more closely resemble the Florida of a few decades ago than does the comparatively rushed pace, glamor, and glitter transported nearly intact to the Gold Coast from northern climes.

There's yet another comparison to be drawn: inland areas west of the Gold Coast are packed with tract after tract of suburban housing developments and shopping malls displacing formerly untouched lands, while inland areas north of the Palm Beaches are more heavily devoted to Florida's rural life. Citrus groves, sugar cane fields, large horse ranches, and cow farms become more the norm, and workhorses, pickups, and tractors are seen more often than the Mercedes and Cadillacs so abundant on the Gold Coast. And, you'll even hear more Deep South accents.

Singer Island

The journey into what we may call "Old Florida" (even though more newcomers arrive almost daily) begins gradually just outside North Palm Beach on a lesser-known island that offers a fine alternative to sophisticated Palm Beach.

Singer Island hasn't much to claim other than its more reasonably priced hotels, a laid-back ambience, some of the area's widest public beaches, and temperatures that are cooler in summer and warmer in winter than most of Florida; the latter attributed to the fact that Singer Island is the piece of real estate closest to the warm, tempering waters of the Gulf Stream, which often is no more than a mile off its beaches. It's a world apart in many ways from Palm Beach, including the physical: you can't even drive directly from one island to the other. You must instead drive west from Palm Beach to US 1, go north to Blue Heron Boulevard in West Palm Beach, then turn east across Lake Worth to Singer Island.

Jupiter: A "Celestial" City

Back on the mainland is a newly reemerging area of interest that 50 years ago boasted communities with such fanciful romanesque names as Juno and Jupiter. This is an area that relatively few visitors have discovered, yet it's one of the most delightful enclaves to be found, a picture-postcard jewel in a sparkling setting where the Loxahatchee River and the Intracoastal Waterway meet to thrust their waters past the historic red lighthouse of Jupiter Inlet and on out to the Atlantic Ocean.

Jupiter offers great beauty, punctuated by many parks along the Loxahatchee, the Inlet, and the Atlantic, sandy white beaches, and a delightful refuge named after Dickinson.

Hollywood Comes to Florida

Jupiter's fame in more modern times comes courtesy of a popular motion picture actor, one Burt Reynolds, a native son who has invested millions of dollars in the area with several homes, offices, and performing arts buildings, a working ranch, and the Burt Reynolds Dinner Theatre.

Note to "star-gazers": If you want to see Burt, you can try the dinner theater on opening nights, which he often attends, but it's not all that easy because when he *does* show up, it's usually in by helicopter, through a side entrance, and up to a very private box. It's a bit easier to meet some of the Hollywood and Broadway stars who often perform at the theater. They can be found after the show in the lounge at the Jupiter Beach Hilton, just down the street. If even that doesn't satisfy you, try strolling through the exclusive Jupiter Inlet Colony where Tammy Wynette and Perry Como maintain homes.

And a few words about Burt's ranch: First, he's almost never there; next, whether or not you want to visit the place anyway really depends on how devoted you are to the actor, or maybe to horses, because the BR Ranch, as it's named, really offers little for the visitor. The 168-acre horse farm is a 16-mile roundtrip from Jupiter. Once there, all you're permitted to do is visit the Tack & Feed Store and a nearby souvenir shop filled with apparel and jewelry items emblazoned with the actor's name and/or face. Photos and posters of the star hang on every wall and post. Set in an area of horse farms and citrus groves, the BR Ranch is surprisingly difficult to find. But if you're determined to go, turn west from US 1 in Jupiter at Indiantown Road (Highway 706), drive past Florida's Turnpike and, when you've clocked nearly six miles, watch carefully on your left for the small, nearly obscured BR Ranch sign at Jupiter Farms Road. Follow that road south for about two miles and you'll be at the ranch.

Stuart: "Sailfish Capital of the World"

Stuart is basically an uninteresting city of some 11,350 residents, but it's quite popular with sport fishermen, for this is the "Sailfish Capital of the World." The city's large fleet of deep-sea charter fishing boats carry thousands a year some 10 miles out into the Gulf Stream to chase a variety of challenging game fish, and a number of sailfish tournaments are held in the waters off Stuart. The city also serves as the gateway to Hutchinson Island, a stretch of land more than 20 miles long leading north to Fort Pierce, and squeezed in by the Indian River on its western side and the Atlantic on the east. Follow Highway A1A east from Stuart into Seawall's Point where it turns northward up the island. This is one of the prettiest scenic drives of eastern Florida, though not for its entire length!

Hutchinson Island: Beauty and Controversy

Just a few years ago, this island was an undeveloped, pristine stretch of sand and mangrove forests. Today, Hutchinson is heavily developed with high-rise condominiums, hotels, and the well-known Indian River Plantation resort at its southern end, and lots of single-family homes and motels of no great distinction at its northern end. But the central portion of the island boasts ecologically preserved areas immune to development—except for one man-made structure: Florida Power & Light Company's controversial St. Lucie Nuclear Power Plant.

The island's ecological preserve covers 1,132 acres, of which about 26 percent was utilized for FP&L's twin nuclear units. The balance has been retained in its original condition of mangrove swamps, marshlands, and beaches, in which 160 species of birds and 25 kinds of animals live and roam. The power company does not offer any tours of its heavily guarded, barbed-wire- and fence-enclosed facility, but the beautiful natural habitat of the area is worth seeing, particularly if you're able to ignore the towering nuclear chimneys.

Hutchinson Island is best known for its wild sea turtles, which more than anything else represent the delicate ecology. Threatened and endangered species such as the Loggerhead, Leatherback, and Atlantic Green turtles have for aeons been leaving the ocean at night between May and September to lay eggs along a 2½-mile strip of beach. Using flippers for propulsion, females weighing 200 pounds or more slowly and agonizingly crawl up the sands in search of a suitable nesting spot. The female uses her flippers as shovels to scrape out a nest, into which are deposited as many as 130 ping-pong sized eggs, which she then covers with sand and flattens out so the 45–70 day incubation period can begin. It's estimated that each year some 2,000 turtles dig out nearly 4,000 such nests along this stretch of Hutchinson Island, but the mortality rate is high. Most eggs never hatch because they're eaten by predators, such as island racoons, or dug up by humans.

If you're interested in witnessing the turtle-nesting ritual, check at the front desk of any island hotel, most of which maintain schedules of nighttime expeditions that are conducted by authorized expert guides during egg-laying season. You'll need to bring along a flashlight.

Vero Beach: The Undiscovered Resort

Vero Beach is the major city of Indian River County and, so far, one of Florida's more-undiscovered resort areas. It's current population of some 17,000 represents a sharp jump from the 3,500 in 1944. But despite that, the area receives relatively few tourists, and a large portion of those who do come are Canadian. It's a shame . . . and it's a blessing, for the area still manages to retain its Southern tropical charm and the slow, informal pace of life that goes with that attribute. Its beautiful wide sandy beaches are never crowded, traffic is light, and the chic little shops along Ocean Drive are never mobbed.

Vero Beach's prime "attraction," believe it or not, is a hotel. But the famed Driftwood Inn is not just your ordinary hotel; it's what *The New York Times* once called "the damnedest place you ever saw." And so it is! The Driftwood was built in 1932 by the late Waldo Sexton, a colorful local character who also built the nearby Ocean Grill Restaurant, as well as The Patio and Hof Brau Haus restaurants in mainland Vero. Originally, the Driftwood Inn consisted of a group of slapdash driftwood and cypress buildings on the beach that were considered eccentric at best. Hallways and rooms in the buildings were stuffed with a most eclectic collection of antiques, collectibles, and artifacts, which Waldo had picked up in his travels, and old stained glass was used at least once in every unit. Today, two of the original buildings remain.

It's a bit surprising for a town with a beach as beautiful as Vero's that there are surprisingly few oceanfront hotels.

Sebastian

The seven-mile drive north from Vero Beach on Highway A1A is pretty, terminating at the northern end of the barrier island where you'll find Sebastian Inlet State Recreation Area, a fabulous 576-acre triangular refuge where the Indian River rushes through the Inlet to meet the Atlantic Ocean. The most popular state park in Florida, Sebastian is particularly good for surfing, which draws large crowds of participants and onlookers. The Inlet's jetties are a favorite with the rod-and-reel set.

PRACTICAL INFORMATION FOR THE AREA NORTH OF PALM BEACH TO VERO BEACH

HOW TO GET THERE. By air. The only airport accepting scheduled passenger flights within this area is the small Vero Beach Municipal Airport, five miles west of the city's beachfront hotels via State Road 60. The 20-passenger planes operated by *USAir's Allegheny Commuter* operate to the airport several times a day from Orlando. Call 800–428–4253 toll-free for flight times.

Access to the southern portion of the area is via Palm Beach International Airport, three miles west of West Palm Beach via Southern Boulevard (US 98). Among major airlines serving this airport are *American, Delta, Eastern, Midway Express, Northeastern, Northwest, Ozark, PeopleExpress, TWA, United* and *USAir.* Also, commuter airlines such as *Aero Coach, Caribbean Express, Gull Air, PBA,* and *Trans Air.*

If you're heading for the northern portion of the region, the air gateway is Melbourne Regional Airport, 40 miles north of Vero Beach via US 1 and State Road 192. Among major airlines serving Melbourne are *Eastern, PeopleExpress,* and *Delta.*

For information on getting from the airport see "How to Get Around," below.

By bus. *Trailways* serves Fort Pierce; *Greyhound* stops at Jupiter, Stuart, and Vero Beach. There are a number of special fares available from various cities. Check your travel agent or nearby Trailways or Greyhound office for information on fares and special tours to this area.

By car. For rental car information, see "How to Get Around," below. The major access highways to these areas are I-95 (free) and the Florida Turnpike (toll-road), both high-speed, north-south roadways that parallel coastal areas, though both are well inland. If you plan to use I-95, you should know that there is a "missing link" between Jupiter and Fort Pierce (funds to fill in the gap dried up), so you must leave the Interstate at Jupiter, go three miles west and use the Turnpike to Fort Pierce. The most scenic, though slowest, route into and through the area is State Highway A1A, which parallels and usually is quite close to beach and ocean areas.

TELEPHONES. The area code for the entire region is 305. However, long-distance rates are applied to calls between some cities, even though they may be relatively close. If your call transcends the zone from which you're calling, a tone and recording will intercept and let you know you must "first dial 1." Local pay-telephone calls cost $.25.

HOTELS AND MOTELS in this portion of Florida's east coast, unlike more southerly areas such as Miami, Fort Lauderdale, and Palm Beach, generally are not fancy, overly expensive, high-rise, or gaudy, though there are a few exceptions. The farther north you go, the more you will find accommodations in motels or hotels of five stories or less. You will find that most places are quieter than hotels farther south because not as many large tour groups and conventions visit this region. Also, accommodation prices generally are lower than along the Gold Coast. Most visitors to this area stay in hotels on or near the beach, where prices, naturally, are generally higher than at inland hotels. But in most cases, the convenience and superior upkeep make the beach hotels a wiser choice.

The vast majority of hotels and motels lower their rates substantially during the off-season part of the year, generally April through October. All hotel rates are based on double occupancy, European Plan for the peak December to April period. Categories, determined by price, are: *Super Deluxe,* $110 and up; *Deluxe,* $90 to $109; *Expensive,* $75 to $89.00; *Moderate,* $60 to $74; *Inexpensive,* $51 to $59; and *Basic Budget,* less than $50. A state sales tax of 5 percent is added to all bills. An additional 2 percent tourist tax is added in Palm Beach and St. Lucie counties.

SINGER ISLAND TO RIVIERA BEACH

Super Deluxe

Jupiter Bay Resort & Tennis Club. 350 S. US 1, Jupiter, 33458; 305–744–0210. This is one of the Quality Inns chain's new, upscale Quality Royale properties, offering 114 suites for daily rental. The West Indies-style clubhouse with an expansive veranda for cocktails houses *Jessica's,* a stylishly pretty restaurant in pink and white. There are seven tennis courts and a complete tennis program, a pool, a six-acre manmade lake with paddleboats, and a landscaped path to nearby Carlin Park and ocean beaches.

Deluxe

Hilton Inn of the Palm Beaches. 3800 N. Ocean Dr., Riviera Beach 33404 (Singer Island); 305–848–5502. This place is a little tired, but clean, offering 126 rooms, a dining room and coffee shop, a private beach, large pool and adjoining snack bar, and two tennis courts.

Jupiter Beach Hilton. Indiantown Road & State Highway A1A, Jupiter 33458; 305–746–2511. This nicely maintained, informal property has a number of claims to fame. It's owned by Chicago newspaper czar Marshall Field, is a popular hangout for actors and actresses appearing at the Burt Reynolds Dinner Theatre down the street, and it is the only oceanfront hotel in town. There are 194 rooms, *Sinclair's,* featuring New American cuisine, lounge, swimming pool, a wide stretch of uncrowded beach, a gift shop, and a new conference center.

Sheraton Ocean Inn. 3200 N. Ocean Dr., Riviera Beach 33404 (Singer Island); 305–842–6171. The nine-story, nautically themed building has all the earmarks of a full-fledged hotel, including a large lobby, shops, two cocktail lounges, casual ocean-view dining room, pool and pool bar, tennis, 200 spacious rooms, and a lounge that is the island's most-popular nighttime gathering place.

Moderate

Rutledge Inn. 3730 Ocean Dr., Riviera Beach 33404 (Singer Island); 305–848–6621. This well-maintained two-story motel provides a nice low-key alternative to the island's flashier chain hotels. The 64 rather smallish rooms and efficiencies face a large pool area with a wide beach just beyond, and there is a restaurant and lounge offering nightly entertainment.

Inexpensive

Hobe Sound Lodge. 8605 S.E. Federal Hwy., Hobe Sound 33455; 305–546–3600. This former Days Inn offers 122 very clean rooms, a restaurant, pool, and a nice picnic area with barbecue grills, a putting green, and shuffleboard courts.

Howard Johnson's Motor Lodge. 930 US 1, Juno Beach 33408; 305–626–1531. Sitting near the ocean, this lodge offers 60 rooms in a pleasant setting, a pool, and a 24-hour restaurant. Popular with families.

STUART TO FORT PIERCE

Super Deluxe

Indian River Plantation. 385 N.E. Plantation Rd., Stuart 33494 (Hutchinson Island); 305–225–3700. This well-known and highly attractive upscale resort community offers 110 one- and two-bedroom, decorator-furnished suites and villas, just steps from the ocean. There are restaurants for formal gourmet and informal dining, a lounge with entertainment, an 18-hole, par-61 Executive golf course, pools and cabana bars, 12 Omni tennis courts, and pro shops.

Sandpiper Bay Resort. Port St. Lucie 33452; 305–335–4400. This is one of Florida's leading full-fledged resorts, a beautifully maintained 1,100-acre property on the St. Lucie River just west of US 1. More than $3 million was spent recently to spruce up an already great resort, which offers 275 quite spacious rooms, all with sitting areas, walk-in closets, refrigerators, coffee makers, and mini-bars; five restaurants ranging from formal to casual, lounges with nightly entertainment, and snack bars. There are 45 holes of championship golf, the Florida Golf School, 11 tennis courts, two swimming pools, and a children's wading pool and playground, as well as a fitness trail, waterskiing, and windsurfing.

Deluxe

Island Beach Club. 9800 S. Hwy. A1A, Jensen Beach 33457 (Hutchinson Island); 305–229–3700. Home of the popular and trendy *bj's Restaurant & Lounge,* this former Sheraton Inn was converted to provide 60 attractive one- and two-bedroom apartments that are surprisingly light and spacious. A large pool and sundeck front on the ocean and uncrowded beach.

Moderate

Frances Langford's Outrigger Resort. 1405 N.E. Indian River Dr., Jensen Beach 33457; 305–287–2411. Former singer Frances Langford and husband Ralph Evinrude of powerboat fame live in this area of Seawall's Point Peninsula between the Indian and St. Lucie Rivers and have created a quiet, peaceful resort that is particularly popular with older vacationers. There are 28 one-, two- and three-bedroom, fully furnished villas surrounding a large grassy knoll; the near-by pool and sundeck are surrounded by tropical landscaping. There's a marina, shuffleboard, and a popular Polynesian restaurant, with adjoining gift shop.

Inexpensive

Holiday Inn-Oceanfront. 2600 State Hwy. A1A, Fort Pierce 33449 (North Hutchinson Island); 305–465–6000. This expansive, family-oriented hotel offers 153 beach-view rooms, a restaurant, lounge, casual dining at the *Back Porch Patio,* and lighted tennis courts.

Basic Budget

Holiday Inn-Oceanside. 3793 N.E. Ocean Blvd., Jensen Beach 33457 (Hutchinson Island); 305–225–3000. This is a superior Holiday Inn with a super location on the beach, offering 184 rooms, restaurant, lounge with live entertainment, pool, and tennis courts across the street.

Quality Executive Inn. 3224 S. US 1, Fort Pierce 33450; 305–465–7000. Situated on the mainland four miles west of Hutchinson Island, this inn offers 170 well-maintained and surprisingly nice rooms, a pool, restaurant, and lounge.

VERO BEACH AREA

Deluxe

The Driftwood Inn Resort. 3150 Ocean Dr., Vero Beach 39263; 305–231–2800. This famous hotel, which was eclectic when first built back in the 1930s, is more so than ever. The "heart" of the resort, which offers a total of 181 hotel rooms in three major complexes, is the original *Driftwood Inn* (see "Historic Sites and Houses," below). Since changing ownership four years ago, the wooden building has been totally refurbished inside, but the original design was maintained so it retains all its charm. The primary guest facility, however, is a five-story, 108-room building north of the original inn that formerly was a Howard Johnson's, offering good-sized rooms that are nicely decorated. The resort has a beautiful wide stretch of beach, a pool, a *J.C. Hillary's Restaurant,* which opened in 1984, and *Waldo's,* a small, rustic indoor/outdoor lounge that is a local gathering spot.

Moderate

Holiday Inn-Oceanside. 3384 Ocean Dr., Vero Beach 32960; 305–231–2300. A beachfront inn with 104 larger-than-average, attractive rooms in three wings, surrounding a large, tropically landscaped pool courtyard. Adjoining are the ocean-view *Windswept Lounge,* where easy-listening music draws the middle-age crowd for dancing, a restaurant, gift shop, liquor store, and beauty salon.

Sheraton Regency Resort Hotel. 4700 N. State Highway A1A, Vero Beach 32960; 305–231–1600. Home of the popular *Arena Dinner Theatre,* this ocean-front hotel, refurbished in 1985, offers 108 standard motel rooms in two four-story wings on a nice piece of seagrape-fringed beach. There is an intimate lounge; the airy, garden-style restaurant overlooks an indoor/outdoor pool.

Inexpensive

Beach Vue Motel. 3005 S. Ocean Dr., Vero Beach 32960; 305–231–6700. This airy little motel, located just across the street from Humiston Park and the public beach, offers 15 cozy rooms, efficiencies, and one-bedroom apartments, all facing onto a stepped pool courtyard.

The Islander Motel. 3101 S. Ocean Dr., Vero Beach 32960; 305–231–4431. This snappy-looking little property also is located across the street from Humiston Park, offering 16 rooms and efficiencies, all with cypress paneling, twin double beds, ceiling fans, and color cable TV. There is a small pool and sun deck adjacent to the motel.

Basic Budget

Howard Johnson's Motor Lodge-Downtown. 1725 S. US 1, Vero Beach 32960; 305–567–7171. Nicely set back from the busy traffic and noise of US 1, this pleasant lodge provides 82 rooms, a pool, and a restaurant adjoining.

Landmark Motor Lodge. 1706 S. US 1, Vero Beach, 32961; 305–562–6591. This neatly kept, old-fashioned motor-courts-type motel offers 54 units in a one-story building next to a small pool area and a two-story building set back from noisy US 1. The motel's unpretentious restaurant is across the street.

BED-AND-BREAKFAST TREASURES. This part of Florida does not offer historic, colorful old inns such as may be found in New England—because the state just isn't that old. However, there are a few comfortable, somewhat colorful, small bed-and-breakfast places, including some near ocean areas in Jupiter, Boynton Beach, and Delray Beach. Prices average about $35 per day, double; only cash or traveler's checks are accepted. For specific details, contact Joan E. Hopp, *Bed & Breakfast of the Keys, Inc.,* 5 Man-O-War Dr., Marathon, FL 33050; 305–743–4118.

HOW TO GET AROUND. From the airport. Since the two major airports that serve as gateways to this area are quite far from most cities within it, taxis and limousines, when available, are rather expensive. (See below.) There is no public transportation from either Palm Beach or Melbourne airports into this area either. Thus, it is highly recommended that you pick up a rental car when arriving at either airport. It not only proves to be the most economical (Florida auto rental prices are the lowest in the nation), but also provides you with a means of getting around the area for sightseeing and other endeavors (see below).

By taxi. At the southern end of the area, service is provided by *A&A Yellow Cab,* 689–2222, which charges $1.25 a mile on the meter, and by *Captain's Cab,* 747–1363, which charges $1.20. At the northern end, *City Cab,* 562–3022, covers nearly all areas around Vero Beach. Rates are $2.50 for the first mile and $1 per additional mile for one person; $1.75 and $.60 per person for two or more in the cab within city limits. Outside limits rates are $3.50 for the first mile and $1.50 per additional mile for one person; $5 per person for two or more in the cab.

By limo. Since there is a lot of territory between the two main gateway airports to this region, and limousine prices are determined by distance, you can expect to pay a hefty price. If you're arriving from Palm Beach Airport, for example, *County Limousine Service,* 968–6300 (advance reservation required), will bring you to Jupiter at a cost of $32 for one or two people, or, you can take the same ride with *Air-O-Tran,* 689–2222, at a cost of only $18.90 for one or two people. There are two catches to the lower price though: you'll probably make several stops along the way for fellow passengers to disembark from the van, and the ride is not as comfortable as it is in a real limo. Air-O-Tran personnel can be found meeting all arriving flights in the terminal's baggage claim area.

By car. There are auto-rental facilities scattered throughout the area, but your best bet is to pick up a car at one of the airports when you arrive. Be sure to make advance reservations, especially during the peak season months from December to April. *Avis* (800–331–1212), *Budget* (800–527–0700), *Hertz* (800–654–3131), *Value* (800–327–2501), and *National* (800–328–4567) maintain facilities in the terminal at Palm Beach International Airport. At Melbourne Regional Airport, facilities are maintained in the terminal by *Hertz, Avis, National,* and *Budget.* If you're flying into Vero Beach Municipal Airport, you'll see counters for *National, Avis,* and *Budget,* but they're almost never manned. If you want a car, call one of those firms' toll-free numbers before arrival to reserve. You will be met on arrival by one of their representatives. If you arrive without a reservation, each desk has a direct-line telephone to their office. (See also "How to Get There," above, for information on major roadways around the area.)

TOURIST INFORMATION. Your best bets for information are the local area's various chambers of commerce, all of which are loaded with brochures for hotels, attractions, parks, events, and so on. Personnel usually are a storehouse of knowledge about their area and can show you on maps where to go to find what you may be seeking. Among the most helpful Chambers are:

Fort Pierce, 2200 Virginia Ave., Fort Pierce 33450; 305–461–2700. Open Monday through Friday, from 8:30 A.M. to 5:00 P.M.

Jupiter/Tequesta, 800 US 1, Jupiter 33458; 305–746–7111. Open Monday through Friday, from 9:00 A.M. to noon and 1:15 to 4:30 P.M.

Jensen Beach, 1910 N.E. Commercial St., Jensen Beach 33457; 305–334–3444. Open Monday through Friday, from 9:00 A.M. to 4:00 P.M.

Northern Palm Beach, 1983 PGA Blvd., N. Palm Beach 33408; 305–694–2300. Open Monday through Friday, from 8:30 A.M. to 5:00 P.M.

Stuart/Martin County, 400 S. Federal Hwy., Stuart 33497; 305–287–1088. Open Monday through Friday, from 8:30 A.M. to 5:00 P.M.

Vero Beach, 1216 21st St., Vero Beach 32961; 305–567–3491. Open Monday through Friday, from 9:00 A.M. to 5:00 P.M.

Also helpful is *Travelers Aid,* which maintains a counter at Palm Beach International Airport's main terminal, near the Northwest ticket counter and next to the gift shop. It's open daily, from 9:00 A.M. to 5:00 P.M.

TOURS. By boat. With the area so heavily water-oriented, taking a leisurely sightseeing cruise or two is the ideal way to soak up what tropical Florida is all about. *Stuart's Hy-Line of Florida* is the largest cruise operator, providing a choice of six different experiences aboard its East Chop during the November through May season. The boat has one enclosed deck and an open-air upper deck. Three-hour cruises along the St. Lucie River, past some of Martin County's most elegant homes, and to the St. Lucie Lock to see wildlife, go every Tuesday at 1:00 P.M. On Monday and Wednesday, the boat departs at 9:30 A.M. for an eight-hour journey down the St. Lucie River and Lock past alligators and lemon groves into Lake Okeechobee. Reservations are required for this cruise.

On Friday, the boat conducts two luncheon sailings: a 4½-hour cruise at noon along the St. Lucie River to Frances Langford's Outrigger Resort in Jensen Beach for a Polynesian feast, and a five-hour cruise at 10:15 A.M. for lunch and a leisurely sail north on the Indian River. On Thursday and Saturday, the East Chop goes on a 4¾-hour sailing at 10:15 A.M. around Jupiter Island, passing through the Intracoastal Waterway and the Indian River, the Stuart waterfront, and on to exclusive Hobe Sound. Since this is Hy-Line's most popular cruise, reservations are absolutely mandatory. Sunday is champagne-brunch day, conducted at 11:00 A.M. for a relaxing 3½ hours, featuring hot and cold buffet and singalong with Banjo Herbie and George. Reservations required. All sightseeing cruises leave from the dock on US 1 just north of the Roosevelt Bridge, behind the Thirsty Whale Restaurant. For information and reservations, call 692–9500.

In Vero Beach, *Vero Marine Center* operates 1½-hour sightseeing cruises on eight-passenger pontoon boats along the Indian River, past scenic portions of Vero Beach, the ritzy Riomar residential area, the city marina, and nearby islands. Boats leave Wednesday, Thursday, and Friday from the Marine Center, 12 Royal Palm Blvd. Reservations must be made by calling 562–7922.

MAJOR PARKS. *Fort Pierce Inlet State Recreation Area.* 2200 Atlantic Blvd., Fort Pierce; 461–1570. This park spans 340 acres on both sides of State Highway A1A at the southern end of a barrier island just northeast of Fort Pierce. The setting, between the Indian River to the west, the Atlantic Ocean to the east, and the Fort Pierce Inlet immediately south, consists of beach, dunes, coastal hammock, and a large spoil area in the upland portion; a submerged mangrove plant community that has been impounded for mosquito control is downland. The Area also includes Jack Island, which covers 631 acres along the Indian River just off Highway A1A. Only foot traffic is allowed; parking space is provided before you cross a narrow pedestrian bridge over the Indian River to enter the island, particularly known for its superior birdwatching. Across A1A, the Pepper Beach portion of the area offers 39 acres of beach, dunes, scrub hammock, and mangroves, bordered by the Atlantic Ocean and Indian River. Both facilities are open daily from 8:00 A.M. until sunset. Admission is $.50.

Jonathan Dickinson State Park. 14800 S.E. Federal Hwy., Hobe Sound; 546–2771. This sprawling 10,284-acre preserve, which is accessed from US 1 at a point four miles north of Tequesta, offers three scenic nature trails. One follows the Loxahatchee River through pine, mangrove, and swamp plant areas. Another meanders through sand pine scrub to a 25-foot wooden observation tower on Hobe Mountain, from which you have a very good view of the beauty in the park's east side. The third route goes through pine flatwoods to Kitching Creek. The river provides excellent opportunities for fishing and boating. Organized activities also are led by Park Rangers. There are two camping areas, one near the entrance station, the other near the Loxahatchee River. Bicycles and horses may be rented from concessionaires. The park is open year-round from 8:00 A.M. to sunset. Admission is $.50 per person.

Sebastian Inlet State Recreation Area. State Highway A1A, Sebastian; 727–1752. This truly beautiful 576-acre area on a barrier island divided by a man-made inlet seven miles north of Vero Beach includes a lagoon, coastal hammock, and mangrove swamps behind the beach and sand dunes. Straddling both sides of A1A, it's less than one mile across at its widest point, bounded by the Indian River on the west and Atlantic Ocean on the east. This highly popular recreation area, which offers an abundance of birdlife along the Inlet, river, and ocean shores attracts a lot of people, but the thing that really brings them out is the superior offshore surfing. Several major surfing championships are held here during the year, drawing tens of thousands of spectators. A long pier serves as the observation platform from which to watch the surfers; the waves are best during winter. A nearby jetty is usually filled with fishermen. The three-mile Atlantic Ocean beach area is accessed from a wooden boardwalk that crosses over fields of sea oats and other marine vegetation. Open daily from 8:00 A.M. to sunset, except for overnight campers.

BEACHES. Needless to say, all of coastal Florida is one, long beach, most of it available to the public. Some of the finest swimming areas, with parks attached, are operated by the state or by local counties. It is sometimes rather difficult to figure out if what you are visiting is a park that happens to have a beach, or a beach that happens to have a park, because most of the beaches maintained by state or local government are officially called "parks" even though the beach is their main reason for being. The farther north you go from Palm Beach, the more foresty the beach areas become. Thus, there are countless small pathways—some marked, some not—leading from main roads through forests, often over short boardwalks spanning small "rivers" of sea oats and sea grapes, to the beach. Virtually all beach parks provide parking facilities that usually are not too crowded. Smaller, more private beaches can be accessed through vegetation throughout most of this area. They do not have specific parking facilities, but you usually can just leave your car parked alongside the highway.

JUPITER TO FORT PIERCE

Coral Cove Park. Just across the southern boundary of Hobe Sound, on Jupiter Island, sits this lovely new park in a rustic grass and trees setting with a few picnic tables, changing facilities, lifeguards, and a nice piece of beach, though it does have some shells on it. It's at State Road 707 and Highway A1A. Open from sunrise to sunset.

Fort Pierce Beach. Though it's classified as a beach, the only thing you are permitted to do at this small facility is fish from its jetty. There also is a wooden boardwalk and covered picnic tables. Open sunrise to sunset, it's just north of State Highway A1A, at South Ocean Drive and Seaway Drive.

Hobe Sound Beach. This area, unfortunately, is nowhere near as swanky as the community in which it's located. Relatively small and quiet, the sandy beach is not one of the prettier ones of coastal Florida, but it's rather popular with older residents. Facilities include lifeguards, picnic tables, and changing rooms. Open from sunrise to sunset, at the corner of North Beach Road (Highway A1A) and Bridge Road.

Hutchinson Island. The southern portion of this island is in Martin County, and consists of a series of small, county-maintained beach areas with access through the trees. Most offer no facilities at all. A lot of fishermen do their thing off these beaches. To find the public accesses, look for brown signs with bright yellow lettering. The island's northern portion, in St. Lucie County (Fort Pierce), provides some larger facilities.

Jaycee Park. Stretching from State Highway A1A to the Indian River, this park is comprised mostly of a large, grassy ball field, but it's also got some covered picnic tables and parking facilities, at the corner of S. Ocean Drive and Melaleuca Drive. Open from sunrise to sunset.

Jupiter Beach Park. Adjoining DuBois Park, this facility offers a 1,700-foot-long sandy beach right at the spot where Jupiter Inlet flows into the Atlantic

Ocean. There are picnic tables along the Inlet and you can fish in its waters from a 200-foot jetty. Behind the beach is a heavily forested, relatively small area of Australian pine, which you can walk or drive through. This park can be quite crowded on weekends. Open one hour before sunrise to one hour after sunset. Take State Highway A1A from US 1 in Jupiter, then go north at Jupiter Beach Road.

Pepper Beach. This 39-acre facility that is part of the Fort Pierce State Recreation Area, one mile north of the southern end of Hutchinson Island and just east of A1A, is in a pretty setting along the Atlantic Ocean. It offers covered picnic tables, changing facilities, and a long wooden boardwalk from the parking lot over dunes and sea oats to a clean, nice, usually uncrowded beach. Open from 8:00 A.M. to sunset.

VERO BEACH AREA

Humiston Beach Park. This is a very nice park and beach sitting right in the midst of Vero Beach's shopping and hotel strip, on Ocean Drive, between Easter Lily and Camelia Lanes. The large area of grass and palm trees provides space for picnic tables and slides, swings, and crawl-through tubes for the kids. A walkway with benches overlooks the beautiful, large sandy beach. There also are changing facilities. You can park in Humiston's small parking lot or on the street along Ocean Drive.

Jaycee Park. This is a rather small but really nice municipal beach area at State Highway A1A and Mango Road, at Vero Beach's northern end. Wedged in on the north and south by low-rise condominium apartment buildings, the facility offers picnic tables with charcoal grills, three chikees for shade on the beach, changing facilities, outdoor showers, and a brand new boardwalk. Lifeguards are on duty from 9:00 A.M. to 5:00 P.M. daily. The beach is sandy with a few shells and quite wide. There also are the Ice Cream Churn, offering 28 old-fashioned flavors, and the stripped-down, Florida-informal Ernie Turco's Seaburger Restaurant, which provides snacks and is quite popular for breakfast among local residents. It's open daily when the beach is open, which is from 9:00 A.M. to 5:00 P.M.

Turtle Trail Beach Access. If you really want to get away from modern development and crowds, this is the place for you, sitting along State Highway A1A three miles north of The Village Shops. There is no lifeguard, and facilities are limited to one Porto-John, but the small sandy beach provides a real feeling of privacy. Locals do a lot of surfcasting from here.

Wabasso Beach County Park. This place at State Highway A1A and County Road 510 is really big with the surfing set, and the waves coming year-round are the reason. That sport, of course, attracts the younger crowd, but older folks in these parts get a big kick out of watching them from benches along a small boardwalk. There are changing facilities, showers, picnic tables, charcoal grills, lots of trees on the beach, and, surprisingly, some poisonous oleander. The Wabasso Beach Market provides beer, deli sandwiches, and the basic necessities of life such as suntan oil, beachwear, and tackle Monday through Friday, 7:00 A.M. to 7:00 P.M., and Saturday and Sunday from 8:00 A.M. to 8:00 P.M.

PARTICIPANT SPORTS. With lots of open space and marvelous year-round weather, this area is particularly conducive to sports participation of all types.

Boat rentals and instruction are available through *Jack's Marina,* 1 Beachland Blvd., Vero Beach, 231–0926, and *The Boat House,* 3321 N.E. Indian River Dr., Jensen Beach, 334–1416.

Diving equipment rentals and instruction are available from *Dixie Divers, Inc.,* 1717 S. U.S. Hwy. 1, Fort Pierce, 461–4488, and 1843 S.E. Federal Hwy., Stuart, 283–5588. Also from *Under-Sea World,* 521 N. U.S. Hwy. 1, Fort Pierce, 465–4114.

Fishing, of course, is a major endeavor because there are so many lakes and rivers, and, obviously, the Atlantic Ocean within the region. Deep-sea is the most popular and most challenging form of fishing in this area, particularly around Stuart, which is known as the "Sailfish Capital of the World." Among the other popular sport fishes anxiously pursued from the decks of the area's many charter boats are dolphin, wahoo, and kingfish. If you're interested in a deep-sea charter boat, reservations are a good idea, especially during winter months. Among the charter outfits are:

The Blue Heron Fleet. Jupiter Lighthouse Marina, Highway A1A at Yarlborough Road, Jupiter, 747–1200; *Lady Stuart,* Sailfish Marina, south end of St. Lucie Boulevard, Stuart, 286–1860; *Harmony & Grits,* US 1 behind J.C. Hillary's Seafood, 32 S. Federal Hwy., Stuart, 287–1451; *No Limit II,* 4609 S.E. Manatee Lane, 1 block east of Highway A1A, Port Salerno, 283–4975; *Breakwater,* Fishermen's Wharf, behind the Harbor House Restaurant, Fort Pierce, 464–6243; *Frank Williams,* Municipal Marina, 2826 Atlantic Blvd., Vero Beach, 562–3430; and, *Simbar,* 13550 Old Dixie Hwy., Sebastian, 589–4868.

If river fishing for the likes of snook, snapper, trout and bass is more to your taste, try the waters of the Indian River with *Indian River Guide Service,* Fishing Corner at Seaway Drive, 1 block north of South Bridge, 465–6104, or *Frank Williams,* Municipal Marina, 2826 Atlantic Blvd., 562–3430, both in Vero Beach.

Golf is always popular, and there are many courses in the area but most are private. Among those open to the public in Jupiter are the *Indian Creek Golf Club,* 1800 Central Blvd., 747–6262; *Heritage Ridge Golf Club,* 6510 S.E. Heritage Blvd. (Hobe Sound), 546–2800; and *Jupiter Dunes Golf Course,* 401 N. Ocean Dr., 746–6654, all 18-holers. In Vero Beach, the 18-hole *Dodger Pines,* 4600 26th St., 569–4400; the 18-hole *Indian Pines Golf Club,* 5700 Parkway Feeder Rd., 464–7018; and the 9-hole *Dodgertown Golf Club,* 569–4800.

For **surfing** equipment and rentals contact *Sun Spot Surf & Beach Shop,* 969 Beachland Rd., Vero Beach, 231–2875.

There also are a lot of **tennis** facilities but, as with golf, most are private. Among the public courts are those at *Twin Oaks Tennis Club,* 1295 6th Ave., Vero Beach, 569–2033, and the *Vero Beach Municipal Tennis Courts,* 390 Beachland Blvd., 231–4787.

If you're interested in **waterskiing,** *The Boat House,* 3321 N.E. Indian River Dr., Jensen Beach, 334–1416, can provide rentals and instruction.

SPECTATOR SPORTS. The *Dodgertown Sports & Conference Center,* 3901 26th St., Vero Beach, is a literal hotbed of major league preseason and minor-league **baseball** games. The *Los Angeles Dodgers* live and play ball at Dodgertown during March. Games begin at 1:30 P.M.; tickets are $5 each. Between April and August, the minor-league *Vero Beach Dodgers* take over with games at 7:30 P.M. and tickets priced at $2.

And there's **football** here as well when the professional *New Orleans Saints* play practice games during July and August. There's no charge to watch. The Dodgertown ticket office is open daily, from 9:00 A.M. to 4:00 P.M.; 569–4900.

The fast-paced game of **jai-alai** imported from the Basque region of Spain offers excitement along with pari-mutuel betting at *Fort Pierce Jai-Alai Fronton* on King's Highway, five miles west of US 1 or one mile north of the Fort Pierce exit on Florida's Turnpike. The season runs from mid-March through mid-September. Night matches are Monday, Wednesday, Friday, and Saturday at 7:00 P.M.; matinees, Wednesday and Saturday at noon. For information, call 464–7500.

HISTORIC SITES AND HOUSES. The *Driftwood Inn,* 3150 Ocean Dr., Vero Beach, 231–2800, dates from 1934, when a local character named Waldo Sexton (widely known as the town eccentric who never minced words, loved his whiskey, and had unusual interests) decided to build a summer beach house for his family. Having an extraordinary fondness for wood, he collected and used a large amount of driftwood from the beach along with some tidewater cypress from a barn destroyed by a hurricane. The house was immediately an oddity because of its unusual slapdash design, but it enticed acquaintances of Sexton to want to stay a night or two. The place soon evolved into an inn, the success of which grew and led Sexton to add four more rooms to one side of the house and five more to the other. Even today, you can see the result: uneven floors, rooms at slightly different levels, odd staircases. All sorts of antiques and collectibles assembled by Sexton in his travels around the world were added to the unusual building. Many of those still remain in hallways and rooms of the old building. Until a few years ago, the Driftwood continued operating as a standard hotel; now, its rooms are in a time-share vacation pool. But you still can wander in and around this most unusual building and enjoy its eccentricities.

STAGE. The *Arena Dinner Theater* at the Sheraton Regency Resort Hotel, 4700 N. Hwy. A1A, Vero Beach, 231–1600, is relatively new and the only thing of its type north of Jupiter. Broadway productions are performed by the Arena's resident theater company in a 260-seat theater-in-the-round on a small stage. Dinner is at 6:30 P.M., followed by show at 8:30 P.M., Tuesday through Saturday. The price for dinner and show is $19.95, Tuesday through Friday; $21.95 Saturday. Wednesday luncheon matinees cost $13.95. Price to see any show without meal is $10; these may be booked only on the same day you wish to see a show and are sold only if space is available.

The *Barn Theater,* 2400 S.E. Ocean Blvd., Stuart, offers intermittent local productions of Broadway shows during winter months. The box office is open Monday through Saturday from 2:00 P.M. to 4:00 P.M. and one hour before curtain time on performance days. For information on current schedules, call 287–4884.

The *Burt Reynolds Dinner Theatre,* 1001 Indiantown Rd., Jupiter, is the only place north of Palm Beach to see top-name stars of Hollywood and Broadway, as they appear in dramatic and musical performances year-round. From Tuesday through Saturday, dinner is at 6:00 P.M., and the show is at 8:30 P.M. For Wednesday and Saturday matinees, lunch is at 11:30 A.M., curtain at 1:30 P.M. The Sunday Champagne Brunch is at 11:30 A.M., followed by a 1:30 P.M. performance. The Box Office Hotline for information and reservations is 746–5566. Box office hours are Sunday and Monday from 10:00 A.M. to 5:00 P.M., and Tuesday through Saturday from 10:00 A.M. to 9:00 P.M. No refunds or ticket exchanges are permitted. Burt's Brass Rail Bar, the décor of which is sort-of spiffed-up 1890s bordello, provides showtime cocktails nightly. Jackets for men and appropriate evening dress for ladies are required.

DINING OUT. As is the case along Florida's Gold Coast, the areas north of Palm Beach are filled with residents and visitors who like to eat out, and do so quite often. There are relatively few super-expensive, fancy, dress-up restaurants in this area; most are fairly casual, some downright "come-as-you-are." Restaurants span the full range, from basic wooden shacks serving up some fine Southern dishes, such as ribs and fried chicken, to reasonably swank Continental eateries, which, in a few cases, resemble their counterparts in any major city, with service—and prices—to match, though most restaurants do offer lower priced dinner specials most nights. The most popular food, of course, is that which comes from the water, particularly from the Atlantic Ocean and nearby rivers and lakes. Among the most popular seafood dishes are grouper, snapper, flounder, shrimp, bass, crab, oysters, and lobster. In the more northerly portion of the area, around Vero Beach and environs, crab fingers are considered a local specialty. For a small town, Vero Beach has an amazingly large selection of interesting restaurants. For all restaurants in this area, except the basic, inexpensive ones, it is always a good idea to make reservations, particularly between December and April.

The price classifications of the following restaurants, from inexpensive to deluxe, are based on the cost of an average three-course dinner for one person for food alone; beverages, tax, and tip would be extra. *Deluxe,* more than $22; *Expensive,* $18 to $22; *Moderate,* $12 to $18; and *Inexpensive,* less than $12. Sales tax is 5 percent.

Abbreviations for credit cards are: AE, American Express; DC, Diners Club; MC, MasterCard; V, Visa. Most restaurants will accept Traveler's Checks but not personal checks.

Abbreviation for breakfast is B; lunch is L; dinner is D.

JUPITER TO FORT PIERCE

American

Moderate

Jake's. 423 S. Federal Hwy., Stuart; 283–5111. In New York, a place like this would seem natural; here, it's quite extraordinary. A funky, fun place with brick floor, wooden walls, book-filled library shelves, lots of stained glass, greenery, and overhead fans . . . all hidden in a building that from the outside looks like a deserted, broken-down old store. Beef and fish, simply but well prepared, are the mainstay, served in a friendly, motivated manner. If you're having lunch, you get a draft beer for only $.10 (limit 4). With lunch and dinner, everybody shares from a large black kettle filled with homemade soup. The owner calls this "a saloon with a touch of class," and so it is! L, Monday–Saturday; D, daily. All major credit cards.

Hilltop House. 4000 N. US 1, Ft. Pierce, 465–2125. Sitting atop a gentle hill three miles north of Fort Pierce, this old-fashioned family restaurant has for 35 years offered up well-prepared beef and seafood items in a friendly, homey atmosphere decorated in maroon, with picture windows overlooking a valley and the St. Lucie River. Cocktails may be taken at tables on an outdoor deck. An adjoining lounge offers piano music on Friday and Saturday from 7:00 to 10:00 P.M. L, Monday–Saturday; D, daily. AE, MC, V.

Inexpensive

Harpoon Louie's. 1065 State Hwy. A1A, Jupiter; 747–2666. Virtually everything from hamburgers to steak and seafood in a large, trendily decorated place with informal tables, lots of greenery, wood, overhead fans. You also can dine outdoors on the scenic Jupiter Inlet. Menu offerings change every six months. B,L,D, daily. AE, MC, V.

Continental

Expensive

The Inlet. 385 N.E. Plantation Rd., Stuart (Hutchinson Island); 225–3700. Though in the midst of the sprawling Indian River Plantation, this formal gourmet restaurant also has become a favorite with area residents. French versions of fish dishes prepared with local catches are a grand specialty, served in a 16-table Provincial-style room decorated in green and pink, with bamboo chairs and a quiet, refined ambience. Jackets are required for men. A 15-percent gratuity is added to all checks. D, Tuesday–Saturday. All major credit cards.

La Ruche. 10835 S.E. Federal Hwy., Hobe Sound; 546–2283. Owner/chef Claude Chateau has set a beautiful scene for fine dining inside a building resembling a small French Provincial home, with lots of greenery and candlelit tables. Despite its fine French dishes, quiches, pastries, vegetables, and ambience, dress is casual. D, Monday–Saturday. MC, V.

Restaurant Le Pavillion. 3220 S.E. Federal Hwy., Stuart; 283–6688. One of the area's most popular restaurants serves up a well-thought-out French-Continental menu in a series of cozy rooms decorated in brown, tan, and orange, separated by trellises, greenery, and light woods. Offering subdued ambience, with more than the usual spacing between tables for greater privacy, this place is casual. L, Monday–Friday; D, daily. AE, MC, V.

Moderate

The Cobblestone Cafe. 383-C Tequesta Dr., Tequesta; 747–4419. This relatively small, sometimes noisy restaurant is a bit of a delight, nearly hidden in a small cobblestone courtyard in a corner of the Gallery Square North shopping center. Blonde-wood, Scandinavian-style booths line one wall; a row of small tables line the other. The food often rises to great heights in dishes such as *fettuccine verde carbonara,* veal Française, and scampi Riviera. L, Monday–Friday; D, Monday–Saturday. AE, MC, V.

Italian

Expensive

La Caravella. 350 US 1, Jupiter; 744–1978. If inexpensive pasta is not what you care for, Raffaele Santarpia has some heady gourmet choices awaiting you in this small, brightly lit restaurant with starched white tablecloths inside and a Mediterranean-style courtyard out front. La Caravella is more formal and somewhat "stuffier" than most places in this area. It's got the usual veal, chicken, and seafood gourmet Italian dishes and—rather unusual for this area—soft shell crabs almondine. During the winter months, make your reservation at least two days in advance. L, Monday–Friday; D, Monday–Saturday. All major credit cards.

Moderate

Pasquale Restaurant. 1406 Cypress Dr., Tequesta; 746–4600. Joseph LoDuca has come up with a highly popular, neighborhood Italian restaurant; nothing fancy, just good, quality food served up in three small, cluttered but cozy rooms sporting nautical décor, hanging Chianti bottles, and other bric-a-brac, with red-and-white oilcloth on the tables. Veal concoctions and the pizza are quite special, served by waitresses who have that true, small-town friendly attitude that's getting rarer all the time. D, daily. AE, MC, V.

Polynesian

Moderate

Frances Langford's Outrigger. 1405 N.E. Indian River Dr., Jensen Beach; 287–2411. Yes, the famed singer of the 1940s is still around; in fact, she lives in Jensen Beach and owns this restaurant, which was designed by Ed Lawrence, creator of the popular Don the Beachcomber's in California. This is a large, rambling, thatched-roof, islandlike setting with picture windows overlooking the expansive Indian River. There also is an outdoor waterfront patio. All the sweet Polynesian drinks are here, along with a menu of fowl, seafood, beef, and pork prepared island-style. If you're adventurous, try the Mystery Steak—prime beef broiled and delicately seasoned with secret tropical sauce, garnished with sauteed snow peas and water chestnuts. The clientele, primarily older folks who enjoy eyeing old Langford photos adorning the walls, usually dress up a bit for dinner. L,D, daily. All major credit cards.

Seafood

Expensive

The Fish Monger. 21 Fishermen's Wharf, Fort Pierce; 465–8620. The exterior, painted in ugly Army green, is not at all noticeable, but the large selection of fresh seafood within certainly is. Most items are original recipes of owner/chef Jim Longstreet. His wife, Elouise, is a painter whose oils (for sale) adorn the walls. The place is large and quite popular, so it tends to be noisy, especially when the family crowds are in on weekends. There's a bit of history: the salad cart is a version of an old English fishmonger's cart; wall paneling was taken from the area's first seafood restaurant, which was located across the street at the turn of the century. Benches lining the walls are 100-year-old, quarter-sawn white oak church pews obtained in the area. L,D, Tuesday–Sunday. AE, MC, V.

Harbour House. 201 Fishermen's Wharf, Fort Pierce; 465–1334. This very popular place offers up some of the freshest local seafood you're apt to find, in a nice setting at the city's fishing docks. The restaurant is four-tiered, with the two rows closest to windows comprised of tables; the other two offering wooden booths, in a strictly informal, family-style atmosphere. The daily Early Bird Specials, served from 4:00 to 6:00 P.M., are a real bargain, with soup or salad, entrée, potato, ice cream, and beverage. L, Monday–Saturday; D, daily. All major credit cards.

Moderate

J.C. Hillary's Seafood. 32 S. Federal Hwy., Stuart; 286–3500. This formerly was the popular Peter's Pier 4, but it's now another of the Boston-based chain's outlets, though it's different because this one specializes only in seafood. Like the other, more meat-oriented Hillary's, this one too is large, decorated with wood, brass, and greenery, but it also offers a small outdoor area for dining while overlooking the St. Lucie River. Seafood is taken from local waters and flown in from New England. The New England clambake and Charles River Pie are specialties. L,D, daily. AE, MC, V.

Southern

Inexpensive

The Log Cabin. 631 N. A1A, Jupiter; 746–6877. As the name implies, this is a rustic old cabin in which the dining room and small lounge are quite dimly lit and the potent aroma is of things like barbequed ribs. It's sort of a redneck, but thoroughly delightful—a funky local place that's usually quite crowded. There's an "all-you-can-eat" special every night but Saturday. Aside from the ribs, try some of the local catfish and the Southern fried chicken. Also, steaks, burgers, salads, and sandwiches, onion rings, corn bread, hushpuppies. B,L,D, daily. AE, MC, V.

VERO BEACH AREA

American

Expensive

The Menu. 1517 S. Ocean Dr., Vero Beach; 231–4614. Situated in a large house, this is a highly popular, large and often-crowded and noisy seafood and beef place, one of the specialties of which is the local Indian River crab fingers. D, daily. All major credit cards.

Moderate

Skip Wright's Steak House. 780 US 1, Vero Beach; 562–9832. Skip boasts he's got "the best steak on the Treasure Coast," and lots of locals agree. They are exceptionally large (New York strip is 20 oz.; filet, 11 oz.), and they're beautiful, served in a building that from the outside looks like a large mobile home. Inside, it's informal and comfortable, with knotty pine walls, wooden floors, and candlelit tables. It's easy to overlook this nondescript place amid the tacky surroundings on US 1, but it's worth looking for. D, Tuesday–Saturday. Because of the local popularity of this place, you must reserve in advance if you hope to eat here. MC, V.

French

Expensive

Restaurant Forty One. 41 Royal Palm Blvd., Vero Beach; 562–1141. The classiest, most formal, and most expensive place to eat in the area is beautiful, with the sort of décor you'd expect to see in New York rather than in this relatively small coastal Florida town. The cozy dining room is of moderate size, with paintings on the pink walls, greenery, overhead fans, and etched glass mirrors. Menu specialties include Brittany-style sweetbreads, fresh salmon steak topped with Hollandaise sauce, and broiled fresh snapper with shallots, tarragon, and parsley butter. If you show up for dinner without a jacket, you'll be seated in the informal lounge, which overlooks a dockside patio and the river. Lunch is totally informal. L, D, daily. MC, V.

German

Moderate

Don's Hof Brau Haus. 1965 43rd Ave., Vero Beach; 567–7040. Sitting well inland just off Highway 60, this was the area's first German-American restaurant and is still the most popular because of its history, quality of food, and ambience. Built by the legendary Waldo Sexton, the red and white wooden building originally was a general store that was moved to its current location in the early 1950s. The four small dining rooms downstairs are decorated in wood and brick; one has a cozy fireplace. The restaurant is filled with antiques. The weather vane on the roof is from the stall of Sea Biscuit, the famed race horse. The ceiling over the entrance is made of cedars from Lebanon and the upstairs bar was carved from a single tree. Paintings on the walls depict the many structures created by Sexton. Specialties include sauerbraten, German pot roast, pork shanks, and Wienerschnitzel. The upstairs lounge has entertainment on Wednesday, Friday, and Saturday nights. D, Tuesday–Saturday. AE, MC, V.

Italian

Expensive

Village South. 2900 Ocean Dr., Vero Beach; 231–6727. Dominic meets, greets, and watches over you as you work your way through the relatively small selection of Italian and seafood delicacies. His crispy duck is considered by locals to be the area's best. The homey, informal restaurant offers two dining rooms with booths and tables; there's a lounge that serves as a local gathering spot at night. L,D, daily. MC, V.

Moderate

Monte's. 1517 S. Ocean Dr., Vero Beach; 231–6612. This friendly, family-style restaurant is another that's very popular with locals, thus often crowded since it has just 14 tables in a smallish room with wooden ceiling, overhead fans, and picture windows. The place offers up a very extensive menu of both gourmet and ordinary veal, beef, pasta, and seafood dishes. D, daily. AE, MC, V.

Seafood

Expensive

The Ocean Grill. 1050 Sexton Plaza, on the beach just north of the Driftwood Inn, Vero Beach; 231–5409. This is one of Florida's most popular informal seafood restaurants and has been for many years. One of the reasons is that it specializes in dishes that are unique to the Indian River area, such as flounder roll, crab au gratin made with local blue crab, coquille, and crab fingers. All breading is done with an old Southern recipe that's never too heavy, and all sauces and dressings are made daily from fresh ingredients. The large, usually full restaurant offers candlelight, wood and greenery, and large picture windows overlooking the beach, which is lit up at night. L, Monday–Friday; D, daily. AE, MC, V.

Moderate

The Patio. 1103 Miracle Mile (US 1 and Highway 60), Vero Beach; 567–7215. Another creation of the indominable Waldo Sexton, this is the oldest eating establishment in Vero Beach and one of the oldest in all Florida, though no one's quite sure exactly when it was built. Most of the wrought iron grillwork and floor tiles are more than a century old, brought to the area from Spain and France by Addison Mizener, the architect responsible for many of Palm Beach's mansions. The main dining room's Tile Bar was brought intact from Spain and bears the coat of arms of a royal family. The hand-carved wood panels above the bar in the cocktail lounge are from bridal chests carved by the Druze tribe of Lebanon. The wall below them was made from the garage doors of the Stotesbury Estate in Palm Beach. Lighting fixtures are from the Palm Beach homes of Rockefeller, Mizener, Dodge, and Stotesbury. This restaurant looks and feels like a private home: small, cozy, comfortable, and candlelit, with wood beams and greenery. You also can eat under Cinzano umbrellas on an outdoor patio. Fresh seafood and beef are the mainstays. Reservations are definitely recommended. L,D, daily. AE, MC, V.

Southern

Inexpensive

Fat Boy's Bar-B-Q. 685 S. US 1, Vero Beach; 562–8333. Downright good old-fashioned Southern barbecued pork, beef, and chicken in a locally popular, inexpensive place with undistinguished wooden booths and long tables. Meat is dipped in a secret-recipe barbecue sauce, then slowly cooked over an open-pit wood fire sprayed with water to smoke it, then served with beans or corn on the cob. Breakfasts are true, hearty, country-style. B, L, D, daily. MC, V.

NIGHT LIFE. The area from Jupiter to Vero Beach does not have what generally would be considered a "big-time" nightlife. But there are some night places that would be of some interest to the visitor who seeks a bit of what the nighttime flavor of this area is. Following is a very selective list.

JUPITER TO FORT PIERCE

The Big Apple, 1665 Old Dixie Hwy., Jupiter, 746–3939, is a relative newcomer to the Jupiter scene, offering a small dance floor for a basically young crowd on Top 40s nights, Tuesday through Saturday, and a more mature audience for the Monday Big Band night. There is a $2 cover charge Thursday through Saturday.

bj's Lounge, 9800 S. A1A, Jensen Beach, 229–3737, is a large lounge in the Island Beach Club, and one of the few such places on Hutchinson Island. It's quite popular with a basically adult crowd. Sunday and Monday are jazz nights; easy-listening is the rule on all other nights of the week. This is a comfortable, friendly, and cozy nightspot on the beach.

Bristol's, 3200 N. Ocean Dr., Riviera Beach, 842–6171, is *the* place on Singer Island, *very* New York—wood, stained-glass, and hanging plants adorn the rambling lounge. There is a small dance floor and a friendly crowd that mixes locals with tourists, who pretty much fill the place nightly and overcrowd it on Fridays and Saturdays. Free hors d'oeuvres, and drinks are two-for-one each night until 9:00 P.M.

Harpoon Louie's, 1065 Highway A1A, Jupiter, 747–2666, is a trendy, informal night spot decorated in wood, greenery, and overhead fans, and is one of the major gathering places in the area for both youngsters and adults. It sits on the Jupiter Inlet, thus allowing for cocktails on an outside patio. The atmosphere is generally low key, but it can get quite crowded here, especially on weekends.

Jake's, 423 S. Federal Hwy., Stuart, 283–5111, houses the funky but fun Train Saloon, which draws a sometimes slightly rowdy but friendly group—more than a few of them of the redneck variety. But it's a good-natured crowd in an interesting little environment. The bar's name comes from the miniature railroad that runs over the back of the bar. Called "a saloon with a touch of class," Jake's is a good place to meet the natives.

VERO BEACH AREA

Austin's, 1833 S. US 1, Vero Beach; 569–6067. Outside, you see the rear end of an old, bright red English cab protruding from the wall. Inside, you find the front end, which has fold-down tables for up to six who may wish to spend the night in the cab. This relatively new place, which soared in popularity among the middle-age crowd almost immediately, is unusually decorated for this part of Florida: the bar is black with neon figures on the wall behind it; banquettes are black and white with wicker chairs and candlelit tables. Informal, with a friendly local clientele who come to hear the nightly jazz performances.

Marvin Gardens, 3030 N. US 1, Vero Beach, 567–3939, is a true "old Florida" place that's highly informal and unpretentious, in the style of the Florida Keys, with inside/outside bars and an outdoor patio with long wooden tables. The crowd ranges from businessmen in ties to kids in jeans. The raw bar is very popular. After 9:00 P.M., the place gets very crowded, mostly with the younger set, who come for the live rock-and-roll bands, though some 1940s numbers are played to keep the more mature crowd interested.

The Outer Marker, 2625 34th Ave. (Aviation Blvd.), 562–2304, is the area's largest gathering spot for the younger set to hear and dance to live rock music, basically drawn from the Top 40s list. This night spot, which is near the Vero Beach airport and Dodgertown, gets quite crowded most every night.

Waldo's, 3150 Ocean Dr., Vero Beach; 231–9292. This rambling old-style beachfront establishment at the Driftwood Inn calls itself "the last of the Great American Hangouts." It may or may not be, but it certainly is the hangout for locals on the beach side of Vero. It's a very comfortable, informal, "do-your-own-thing" sort of place with an indoor/outdoor lounge made of driftwood in keeping with the next-door Inn. This is another great place for meeting the locals.

THE FLORIDA KEYS

by
HARRIET LA BARRE

Picture a string of 43 subtropical islands strung out in a turquoise sea from the southwest tip of Florida. These are the Floriday Keys, a paradise of water sports for vacationers. The islands are linked by the Overseas Highway (US1), and its 42 bridges, one of them seven miles long. Driving down the Keys, you have the Atlantic Ocean on your left and the Gulf of Mexico on your right, at times both a few yards away on each side of you. The effect is like sailing rather than driving.

Key Largo, best associated with the early Humphery Bogart and Lauren Bacall movie of the same name, is the first island on this string. The very last island is Key West, only 90 miles from Cuba.

The pleasures of these Keys, once the province of buccanneers, pirates, and Indians, range from sports fishing to scuba diving and snorkling, from camping to luxury-resort living, from biking to sightseeing via glass-bottomed boats. You can go birdwatching or sightseeing, jet-ski, or snooze in a hammock. And you can do most of it year-round, with temperature ranges from the 70s to high 90s in summer, 60s to 80s in winter. *All* seasons are ideal for fishing because the coral reefs protect the island from high seas; about ninety marinas dot the Keys, and international fishing prizes are won here. Informality is the rule throughout; even when deluxe dining, you'll see T-shirts.

Finding Your Way Around

When driving on the Keys, watch for Mile Markers. These are green-and-white markers on the right side of the road. They tell you the distance from Key West and end there with the zero marker. They are generally the *only* addresses you'll find along the Keys. If you ask for directions, residents will respond by telling you which Mile Marker a place is at or near.

Key Largo

In Key Largo life can be as formal as you'd like. You can stay at casual motels or the plushest lodgings. Here you can find experienced captains for Gulfstream deep-sea fishing, well-equipped charter boats, and party boats. Skindiving is wonderful all along the keys, but some feel its at its finest off Key Largo. Key Largo also has a shopping plaza where you can stock up on groceries, film, and almost anything you might need.

The John Pennekamp Coral Reef State Park, an underwater park that includes a living coral reef, runs parallel to Key Largo. The crystal-clear water allows views of the forty-one varieties of coral in their colorful, flowerlike formations, as well as an occasional glimpse of old sailing wrecks.

Tavernier

Tavernier, the Key between MM (Mile Marker) 93 and MM 91, is named for a French pirate of the 1800s and was once a port of call for vessels putting in for supplies. Tavernier (pronounced Tavern*eer*) has Harry Harris Park on the Atlantic side, with picnic grounds and a beach. At Windley Key, MM 84, you'll find the Theater of the Sea, an aquarium that is a small masterpiece of marine life. The trained sharks and porpoises are remarkable to watch. Resort motels with sailboats for rent are plentiful, and, at Whale Harbor Bridge, is one of the finest fleets of charter boats on the Keys. Holiday Isle, a resort at Windley Key, has a rooftop restaurant with a stunning view over the Atlantic.

Upper Matecumbe and Lignumvitae

Crossing Whale Harbor Bridge, you'll find yourself on Upper Matecumbe Key. The town in this area is Islamorada (in Spanish: "purple island"), named for the purple-colored sea snails that are thick in the seas nearby. Islamorada has lodges, good restaurants, gift shops, and an art gallery in its Spanish Mission House. You can take diving trips to some remarkable coral gardens offshore. Islamorada has the reputation of being one of the best fishing spots in the world; its annual fishing tournaments are internationally known.

About two miles south of Islamorada is Lignumvitae Key in the Gulf of Mexico, accessible only by boat. Lignumvitae is a 365-acre island with virgin tropical hammock and is under the protection of the Florida State Department of the Interior. Park Rangers are available to lead you on a tour of the island.

Next on your way down the Keys, at Marker 79, look to your left and see offshore Indian Key, where in a horrifying incident in 1700, Indians slaughtered 400 shipwrecked Frenchmen. In 1844 a second bloody event took place on Indian Key when the tiny settlement was sacked and burned by Seminole Indians, enraged because a resident, Jacob Houseman, had petitioned the government for a bounty on each Indian he could kill. Trips to Indian Key are available.

At Lower Matecumbe Key, MM 72 and MM 71, you can snorkel and dive among coral reefs about three-quarters of a mile offshore. Fiesta Key Resort, at MM 70, accommodates trailer and tent campers.

Long Key

Long Key, at MM 69 and 68, was the fishing favorite of writer Zane Grey, a passionate fisherman; one of the Long Key creeks is now Zane Grey Creek. The Long Key Fishing Club, which has hosted royalty and celebrities, was built by multimillionaire Henry Flagler, who also built the overseas railway to Key West. At Long Key, right on the Atlantic, you'll come to Long Key State Park. Here there are lovely palm trees and casuarinas. Vacationers with campers or trailers are welcome.

The Middle Keys

Conch Key, MM 63, has the overall atmosphere of a New England fishing village, with fishing nets spread out to dry and lobster pots piled near snug houses. If you love solitude, this is for you. Enjoy your own boat or rent one, and stay in a neat little motel. There's a small store with groceries and miscellaneous items. Duck Key, at MM 66, has expensive homes, sophisticated dining, a disco, and a super deluxe resort, Hawk's Cay. Duck Key also has a full-service marina, a golf course, and tennis. Experienced captains can take you out in pursuit of a sailfish. The Atlantic and the Gulf at this mid-Keys spot are a bonanza fishing area. Grassy Key, MM 60 and 57, is liberally sprinkled with privately owned trailer parks with full hook-up facilities. Stay overnight or for the whole season. There are also several small resorts and a sizable marina. Grassy Key also has a seaplane base. You can charter a flight to Fort Jefferson located on the Dry Tortugas—dry because the islands have no water, and tortugas (Spanish for turtles),

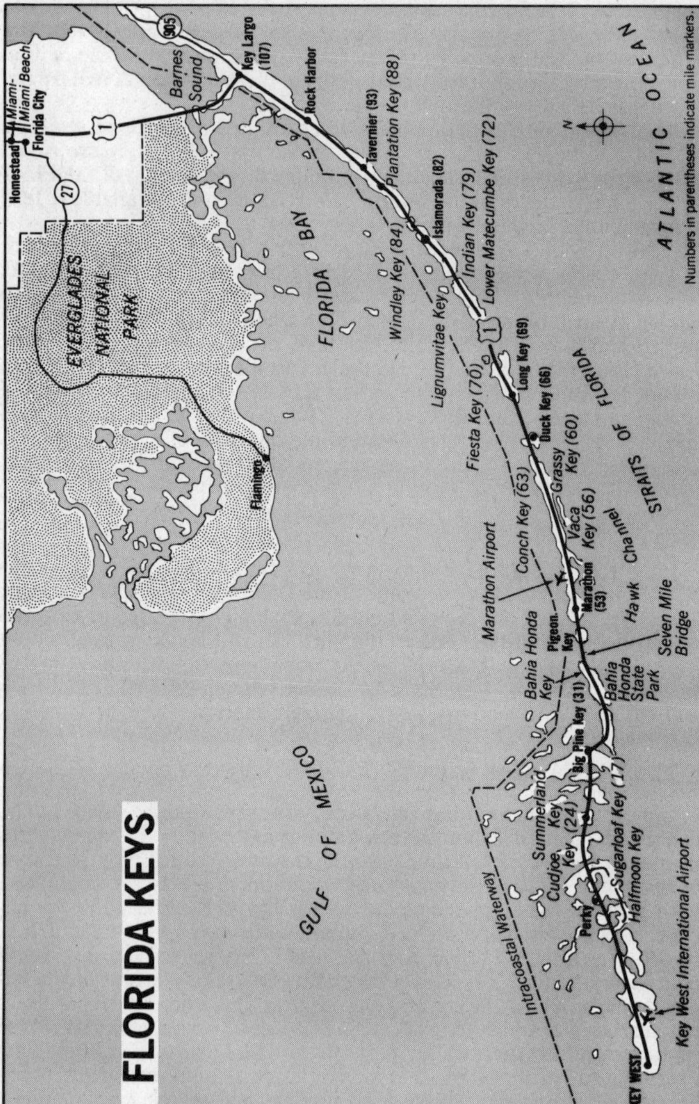
FLORIDA KEYS
Homestead
Miami-Miami Beach
Florida City
Key Largo (107)
Barnes Sound
Rock Harbor
Tavernier (93)
Plantation Key (88)
Islamorada (82)
Indian Key (79)
Lower Matecumbe Key (72)
Windley Key (84)
Lignumvitae Key
Fiesta Key (70)
Long Key (69)
Duck Key (66)
Grassy Key (60)
Conch Key (63)
Vaca Key (56)
Marathon Airport
Marathon (53)
Pigeon Key
Hawk Channel
Seven Mile Bridge
Bahia Honda Key
Bahia Honda State Park
Big Pine Key (31)
Summerland Key (24)
Sugarloaf Key (17)
Cudjoe Key
Halfmoon Key
Perky
Key West International Airport
KEY WEST
Intracoastal Waterway
GULF OF MEXICO
FLORIDA BAY
EVERGLADES NATIONAL PARK
Flamingo
STRAITS OF FLORIDA
ATLANTIC OCEAN
N
Numbers in parentheses indicate mile markers.

because of the turtles that can be found here. The Dry Tortugas were discovered by Ponce de Leon in 1513 and fortified by the U.S. with Fort Jefferson in the early 1800s.

Crawl Key through Vaca Keys, MM 56 to 47, contain the towns of Key Colony Beach, Marathon Shores, and part of Marathon, with a total population of about 8,000 residents, making this the second largest metropolis on the Keys (Key West is larger). You have your pick of charter boats, marinas, beaches, and picnic areas. Marathon has shopping centers and an airport with daily scheduled flights via PBA (Provincetown-Boston Airline) to Key West and Miami. Places to stay range from luxurious to modest, restaurants from gourmet to hamburger joints, with the accent on the best of native seafood. The good ten miles of reef offshore are a big drawing card for snorklers, scuba divers, and skin divers. From Marathon down to Key West, you can legally spear-fish one mile offshore.

Lower Keys

Passing tiny Knights Key, you now drive across the astounding Seven Mile Bridge. At the center, you'll be 65 feet in the air. The Seven Mile Bridge is 38 feet wide and is the longest continuous bridge in the United States. You are cruising by car over the seas, the Atlantic and the Gulf of Mexico meeting below you and only the sky above.

Bahia Honda Key ("deep bay" in Spanish) has Bahia Honda State Park. The park has undoubtedly the best beach on the Keys. You can picnic beneath palm trees, camp, and rent boats at the marina on the lagoon. Big Pine Key comes next. The largest Key in acreage it is surrounded by many smaller islands, some with names, some still nameless. Tiny, white-tailed deer, called Key Deer, live on Big Pine. The deer are only about 32 inches high and 38 inches long. Big Pine also has a national marine sanctuary where you are welcome to snorkel, scuba dive, and take underwater photographs. The Big Pine Key Chamber of Commerce, MM 31, will give you maps and information. There are both motels and trailer parks here. On we go through Little Torch Key, Ramrod Key, and Summerland Key, quiet, somnolent little islands with sunlit, wooded roads. Reaching Cudjoe Key, you'll find facilities for mobile homes. Cudjoe Key also has a condominium trailer park where you can buy your own site.

Sugarloaf Key, next, is bigger, but just as quiet. Little stirs here, but there is a remarkably good place to stay, Sugarloaf Lodge, at MM 17. This is a charmer, and your entertainment at breakfast, lunch, and dinner, is a porpoise show in the lagoon below. You can take a seaplane trip from here back to Fort Jefferson.

Stock Island, just outside of the island of Key West, originally had holding pens for stock: cattle and pigs destined for local markets. The pens are gone. The current activities on the island include dog racing from December to April and year-round golf. Restaurants on Stock

Island serve seafood and steaks, shrimp boats berth here, and there are marinas and docks for mooring or chartering.

Information on Key West follows the *Practical Information* below.

PRACTICAL INFORMATION FOR THE KEYS

HOW TO GET THERE. By air. *PBA (Provincetown-Boston Airline)* has several daily flights to Marathon and Key West from Fort Myers, Jacksonville, Miami, Naples, Sarasota/Bradenton, and West Palm Beach. Private planes can also fly to the airports. Marathon is an ideal spot from which to explore the Keys, since it is a midway point. At both airports, rental cars are available from Hertz, Avis, and local companies. See "How to Get Around," below.

By bus. *Greyhound Bus Lines* has regular, scheduled daily trips down the Keys from Miami and Miami Airport with scheduled stops at Tavernier, Islamorada, Marathon, and Key West. At unscheduled points on the Keys, the bus will stop to let you off, or pick you up if you flag it.

By car. The *only* route down the Keys is the Overseas Highway (US1). You can take it from Miami, pick it up at Florida City, or you can approach by way of the Card Sound Road, which joins US1 at Key Largo. Driving time from Miami to Key Largo is about 1½ hours.

By boat. You can dock your boat at any of dozens of marinas on the Keys, both on the Atlantic and the Gulf sides. The best procedure is to choose an area, then call or write the Chamber of Commerce in that area for a list of marinas (see "Tourist Information" later in this *Practical Information* section). It is wise to make a slip reservation.

TELEPHONES. The area code for all the Keys is 305 (and for all of Monroe County as well). Dialing on the Keys is a tricky business. Dialing from one Key to another a few miles away may be a long-distance call. The best procedure is to dial 0 and ask the local operator if your call will be long distance; if it is, you dial 1 plus the number. To get a long distance number outside the 305 area, dial 1 plus the area code, then the number. Information (directory assistance) is 411 if you are on the Keys. For Keys information, when dialing from outside the Keys, dial (toll-free) 1–305–555–1212. To call a toll-free 800 number, dial 1 plus 800 plus the telephone number. You can also get the telephone number of those businesses and people who have 800 numbers by dialing 800–555–1212. Pay phones cost $.25.

HOTELS AND MOTELS. You'll find informal luxury resorts, motels with resortlike luxury accommodations, and many less expensive motels complete with boat docks, boat rentals, swimming pools, restaurants, and even entertainment. Islamorada and Marathon also have a number of condominium units that are privately owned by corporations or individuals; renting information is available through the Chamber of Commerce (see "Tourist Information"), through local real estate agents, or from agents on the premises. The

Chamber of Commerce also furnishes information on the many accommodations in its area.

Peak season is from December 15th to the week after Easter, with variations from one accommodation to another. The rest of the year, rates are approximately 25 percent to 35 percent less. Rates we quote here in our selection of accommodations are peak-season rates based on double occupancy (total for two people). Add 5 percent Florida tax and 2-percent bed tax. Inquire for special seasonal, weekly, monthly, or weekend rates, Senior Citizen discounts, and the charge for children in the same room. Price classifications are as follows: *Deluxe,* $120 and up; *Expensive,* $80 to $120; *Moderate,* $60 to $80; *Inexpensive,* less than $60.

KEY LARGO

Holiday Inn. *Moderate.* MM 100; 305–451–2121. Attractive motor lodge on harbor on Atlantic. Tennis, pool, restaurant, lounge.

Howard Johnson's. *Moderate.* MM 102; 305–451–1400. Pool, restaurant, lounge, dive shop. ½ mile from Pennecamp State Park.

Gilbert's Motel-Marina. *Inexpensive.* MM 107.5; 305–451–1133. On the Bay. Pool, boat dockage, boat rentals, jet skis, Tiki Bar, restaurant, color TV.

ISLAMORADA

Cheeca Lodge. *Deluxe.* MM 82; 305–664–3651 or toll free outside FL, 1–800–327–2888. Nine-hole golf course, beach, pool, lighted tennis courts, ocean view restaurant.

Holiday Isle. *Moderate.* MM 84½, Windley Key; 305–664–2321. Pool and beach, boat rentals, party boats, wind surfing, the works.

Plantation Yacht Harbor Resort. *Moderate.* MM 87; 305–852–2381. Acres of greenery on a yacht harbor; pool, lighted tennis courts, beach, barbecue grill.

LONG KEY

Fiesta Key Resort. *Inexpensive.* MM 70; 305–664–4922. Motel accommodations are available at this KOA (Kampgrounds of America) resort that has a pool, marina, boat rental, even a pub.

MARATHON

Hawk's Cay. *Deluxe.* MM 61, on Marathon, Duck Key; 305–743–7000; toll-free in FL, 800–432–2242; outside FL, 800–327–7775. Informal but elegant, a deluxe resort with rambling, West Indies style hotel, 70-slip marina, tennis, pools, discotheque. The vacationing spot of three U.S. presidents: Truman, Eisenhower, Johnson. Lavish continental breakfast included.

Howard Johnson's Motor Lodge. *Moderate.* MM 54; 305–451–1489. Pool, 24-hour restaurant, boat rental, and waterfront views of either the Atlantic or Gulf of Mexico.

Key Colony Beach Motel. *Inexpensive.* MM 53½, 441 E. Ocean Dr.; 305–289–0411. On the Atlantic with private beach, heated pool, color TV, refrigerators.

SUGARLOAF KEY

Sugarloaf Lodge. *Moderate.* MM17; 305–745–3211. On 120 acres, all rooms with patios overlooking Gulf of Mexico. Restaurant, lounge, beach, marina. Their pet porpoise entertains in the lagoon below at breakfast, lunch, and dinner.

CAMPING. Campgrounds and RV resorts range from luxurious to extremely modest, and number about 60. Choose an area that appeals to you and write or phone that area's Chamber of Commerce for a list. (See "Tourist Information," below). Reservations are advisable. Two excellent camping resorts are:

Outdoor Resorts at Long Key, Box 816, Long Key, 33001; 305–664–4860 (collect calls accepted May through October). Olympic-size pool, tennis courts, health club, facilities for biking, boating, tennis, fishing, scuba-diving. Marina, store, health club. An Outdoor Resort of America, this is an RV resort for self-contained units. Daily rates, based on a party of two: $18 to $20. Children under 5, free. Monthly, $416 to $481.

Sunshine Key Camping Resort, MM 39, Rte. 1, Box 790, Big Pine Key, 33043; 305–872–2217. Rates based on two adults and accompanying children under 12, $21 to $25. Set in lush foliage, with its own private marina, fishing pier, boat rentals, restaurant, pool, beach, grocery, lighted tennis courts. Dog kennels available. Same rates year-round.

Camping is also available at three State Parks on the Keys. Fees are $8 per night for four persons per campsite, with each campsite restricted to the use of one family or group, $2 a night for electricity. *Bahia Honda State Recreation Area* (305–872–2353), *John Pennekamp Coral Reef State Park* (305–451–1202), and *Long Key State Recreation Area* (305–664–4815) accept telephone reservations only, year round; reservations are *not* accepted more than 60 days in advance of your check-in date. For complete brochure on State Park camping, write or telephone the *Florida Department of Natural Resources,* Bureau of Education and Information, Rm. 613, 3900 Commonwealth Blvd., Tallahassee, 32303; 904–4880–7326.

HOW TO GET AROUND. By car. You won't find city buses or taxis on the Keys. Your best bet is to drive your own car or rent a car. Car rentals through Hertz (800–654–3131), Avis (800–331–1212), and other companies are available at **Key Largo** and **Marathon.**

By bicycle: Two- and three-wheel bicycles are available at **Key Largo** at *C.J's Bicycle Shop,* $7 plus tax for 24 hours, $30 a week. Open 10:00 A.M.–5:00 P.M., seven days. Also at **Big Pine Key,** *Island Bike Shoppe,* 9:00 A.M.–5:00 P.M. Saturday 9:00 A.M.–1:00 P.M. and, in **Marathon** at *KCB Bike Shop,* 9:00 A.M.–6:00 P.M. Monday thru Sat.

By boat: To reach **Indian Key,** you must use your own boat, rent one, or connect with a trip. For rentals trips contact *Bud n' Mary's Marina,* Islamorada; 664–2461.

TOURIST INFORMATION. Booklets, maps, information about fishing, fishing guides, scheduled events for the week, and general information are available at the following chambers of commerce. All are open 9:00 A.M.–5:00 P.M. Monday through Saturday year-round.

Florida Upper Keys Chamber of Commerce, MM 105½, **Key Largo,** FL 33037; 305–451–1414. **Islamorada** *Chamber of Commerce,* MM 82½, Box 915, Islamorada, FL 33036; 305–664-4503. **Layton** *Chamber of Commerce,* Layton, FL 33001; 305–664–4129. **Key Colony Beach** *Chamber of Commerce,* Key Colony Beach, FL 33051; 305–289–1212. *Greater* **Marathon** *Chamber of Commerce,* 3330 Overseas Hwy., Marathon, FL 33050; 305–743–5417. *Lower Keys Chamber of Commerce,* **Big Pine Key,** FL 33043; 305–872–2411. *Greater Key West Chamber of Commerce,* Key West, FL 33040; 305–294–2587 (this chamber is also open on Sunday).

TOURS. The major tours on the Keys are nature walks and underwater tours, and, as you might expect, all-day and half-day party boats for reef fishing and Gulf fishing.

Discovery Undersea Tours at John Pennekamp Coral Reef State Park, **Key Largo,** at 9:00 A.M., noon, and 3:00 P.M.; $8.50 for adults, $4 for children 11 and younger. These are glass-bottom boat tours. Also *snorkeling tours,* $15 per person (includes equipment), plus a family plan available on morning trips. *Snorkeling-sailing* all-day trips are $37 a person. *Scuba* trips are $20 a person; you must have a national certificate. For further information contact Coral Reef Park Co., P.O. Box 13–M, Key Largo, FL 33037; 451–1621.

You can take an on-your-own biking or hiking tour on the *Upper Florida Keys Bike-or-Hike Trail.* The bike-or-hike trail is 20 miles. It is a one-day trip by bike, a two-day trip on foot. For an accompanying map and description of native plants, campgrounds, historical sites, and places to fish or rent a boat, write Florida Upper Keys Chamber of Commerce, **Key Largo,** FL 33037; 451–1414.

Botanical Tour of **Lignumvitae Key.** A two-hour guided tour conducted by Park Rangers at 9:00 A.M., and one-hour tours at 1:00 P.M. and 3:00 P.M., Wednesday through Sunday, $.50 a person, children under 6, free. You reach the Key in your own boat or by charter boat at nearby marinas. Only 50 people are allowed on the island at one time. For more information, contact Lignumvitae Key State Botanical Site, c/o Long Key State Recreation Area, Box 776, Long Key, FL 33001; 664–4815.

Seaplane flights, to **Fort Jefferson,** Bonefish Seaplane Service, MM 59, Grassy Key; 289–0050. Three-to-four-hour historical trip, departures at 8:00 A.M. and 12:30 P.M., seven days a week. *Snorkling* equipment available free at the Fort. $85 per person; minimum, three people. (For seaplane flights from Key West, see *Key West* section, following this Practical Information.)

Canoeing Nature Tours with Marine biologist, Stan Becker, 9:00 A.M.–4:00 P.M. Includes lunch and equipped canoes, $45 per person. Also, *canoe/camping expeditions, hiking trips,* and *snorkeling excursions* that explore Looe Key National Marine Sanctuary and other areas. For information and reservations, contact Stan Becker, Box 62, **Big Pine Key,** FL 33043; 872–2620.

STATE PARKS. The Keys have three state parks. Entrance fee is $.50 per person. The parks open at 8:00 A.M. and close at sundown.

John Pennekamp Coral Reef State Park, MM 102.5. An underwater state park that encompasses a living coral reef. The park includes 2,289 acres of land and 52,722 offshore acres. Guided underwater tours (see "Tours" above), camping, fishing, picnicking, boating, swimming, skin and scuba diving, nature trails, facilities. You can also rent masks, fins, and snorkel for a week for $8 at Key Largo, MM 102.5; 451–1621; in Florida, call toll free: 1–800–432–2871

Long Key State Recreation Area, MM 69–68. An 847-acre park. Campfire talks by rangers, nature trails, picnicking, boating, swimming on the Atlantic. Camping and trailer sites; facilities. Information can be obtained here for Indian Key. Activities accessible to the handicapped. Long Key State Rec. Area., Box 776, Long Key, FL 33001; 305–664–4815.

Bahia Honda State Recreation Area, MM 34. Camping, boating, picnicking, nature trails, a marina, recreation areas. Also the best beaches on the Keys, with swimming on either the Gulf or Atlantic. You'll also see rare species of birds and tropical plants. For information contact Bahia Honda State Rec. Area., Rte. 1, Box 782, Big Pine Key, FL 33043; 872–2353.

MARINE PARKS. Islamorada: *Theater of the Sea,* at MM 84.5, 664–2431, gives visitors the opportunity to shake hands with sea lions, touch young sharks, pet affectionate dolphins. Shows continuous 9:00 A.M.–4:00 P.M., daily. Adults $5.75, children 5–12, $3.75.

MARINE SANCTUARIES. Big Pine Key has a national marine sanctuary located on a reef called Looe Key, five miles out (up to about a hundred years ago Looe Key was an island), where you are welcome to snorkel, scuba dive, and take underwater photographs. The nearest place for rentals of scuba, snorkeling, and other underwater equipment, as well as certified instruction, is: *Underseas, Inc.,* open seven days a week, 8:00 A.M. to 6:30 P.M. At MM 31, on US 1, Box 319, Big Pine Key, FL 33043; 872–9555 or 872–2700. Underseas Inc. also offers half- or full-day diving trips to Looe Key and accepts all major credit cards.

BEACHES. Beaches are scattered like confetti all down the Keys. But they are usually small, often rocky, pebbly underfoot, and with coarse "sand" of broken coral. The best beach is at *Bahia Honda State Park,* MM 34, with soft, white sand on a long curve of beach on the Atlantic.

PARTICIPANT SPORTS. Bicycle wherever your heart desires, or else on the 20-mile Upper Florida Keys Bike-or-Hike Trail. For accompanying map, and information, write Florida Upper Keys Chamber of Commerce, Key Largo, FL 33037; 451–1414. See also "How to Get Around," above, for bike rental information.

A few resorts have **golf,** among them *Sombrero Country Club,* (743–2551) at **Marathon;** *Cheeca Lodge Resort* (664–4651) at **Islamorada;** *Key Colony Beach Resort,* (289–0411) **Marathon.**

Tennis courts are available at *Cheeca Lodge, Sombrero, Plantation Yacht Harbor* (852–2381) and several other resorts. At Windley Key, **Islamorada,** *Tennis Island* (664–9808) has four clay courts. Daily fee, $5 per person, and you can play all day if it's not crowded. In any case, you're guaranteed one hour for singles, 1½ hours for doubles. Weekly rate per person is $20. Open daylight hours; equipment and pro available.

Water sports, including **boating** and **fishing** are the main sporting activities. You can choose from over 200 deep-sea charter, drift, and guide boats. Charters include: *Ace,* Capt. Jim Taylor, Whale Harbor Marina, **Islamorada;** 652–5027 or 664–4511. Live-bait sail fishing and big game shark fishing a specialty. *Blue Chip Too,* Capt. Skip Bradeen, Whale Harbor Marina, MM 84; 852–8477. Light tackle and kite fishing a specialty. *Tallywhacker,* Capt. Ron Brack, docks at Whale Harbor Marina, MM 84, Islamorada; 664–4511. Custom 40′ Guthrie Sportsfisherman. Reef and deep-sea fishing. Families welcome. *Miss Tradewinds,* Capt. Mike Owens, Whale Harbor Docks. MM 84; 664–8341 or 852–3071. 65-foot party boat. Two half-day fishing trips daily 9:30 A.M. to 1:30 P.M., and 1:45 P.M. to 5:30 P.M. Night trips Thursday thru Saturday, 7:00 P.M. to 12 midnight. *Caloosa,* Capt. Ray Jensen. Whale Harbor Marina; MM 84; 852–3200 or 664–4511. All day deep-sea fishing, 9:30 A.M. to 4:30 P.M. Night fishing available. Holiday Isle Marina, MM 84. At Caloosa Cove Marina: *Winter Hawk,* Capt. Peter Ross. MM 73½ at Channel 2; 664–4068. 23–foot Seacraft Superfisherman. Reef fishing, offshore, light tackle, backcountry. Call Hurricane Resort, MM 49½, **Marathon,** for charter information: 743–2393.

If you'd like to **sail,** you can contact some of the following: *Channel Two Boat Rental,* **Islamorada;** 664–4068. Half-day, full-day and weekly rentals of sailing yachts. Snorkle, fish, or cruise. MM 73½, Caloosa Cove Marina. *Bird Marina South.* Sailing instructions and rentals, MM 70, Long Key, Islamorada; 664–4128. *Holiday Isle,* MM 84½, Windley Key, Islamorada; 664–2321. Sailboat rental and instruction. *Holiday Inn Resort,* **Key Largo,** MM 100, sailboat rentals from Key Largo Marine Tours; 451–2121. Sailboat School and rentals at *Gilbert's Marina,* Key Largo, MM 107.5; 451–1133.

Well over 40 dive shops will outfit you for **scuba** and **snorkeling.** Pick the area you want to be in, and the local Chamber of Commerce (see "Tourist Information," above) will furnish you with information on local guides, marinas, ramps, equipment. Dive shops include: *Atlantis Dive Center,* daily scuba and snorkel trips to **John Pennekamp Coral Reef State Park.** Instructions. 51 Garden Cove Dr., Key Largo 33037; MM 106.5; 451–3020. *Lady Cyana Divers,* instruction and rental, also daily reef trips aboard a 40-foot custom dive boat. At MM 85.9, US 1, **Islamorada;** 664–8717. *The Diving Site,* scuba-diving and snorkling trips, also instruction and rentals. Daily reef trips abroad 40-foot and 34-foot dive boats. 12399 Overseas Hwy., **Marathon,** 33050; 289–1021.

To **waterski** contact *Adventure Island,* MM 54, 12648 Overseas Hwy., **Marathon,** across from Howard Johnson's; 289–1500. Waterskiing and every other possible water sport, including jet skiing, sailboat instruction and rental, boat rental. For **jetskiing:** *Holiday Isle Resort,* MM 85, **Islamorada,** FL 33036; 664–2321. Boat and Jet Ski Rentals, at *7 Mile Marina,* 900 Overseas Hwy., **Key Largo** 33037; 743–1133. *Carribbean Watersports Inc.,* Key Largo, MM 104; 451–3113. *Gilbert's Motel-Marina,* MM 107.5, Key Largo; 451–1133. For organized scuba, snorkeling, and sailing expeditions, also see "Tours," and "Marine Sanctuaries," above.

SPECTATOR SPORTS. For information on the **dog racing** on Stock Island, see "Spectator Sports" in *Practical Information for Key West.*

STAGE. The *Tennessee Williams Fine Arts Center* is on Stock Island. See "Stage," in *Practical Information for Key West.*

DINING OUT. Seafood is king in the Keys. Yellowtail, snapper, grouper, jewfish, shrimp, stone crabs, lobster—fresh-caught, right off the boat. But there's no lack of barbecued ribs, prime ribs, and chicken a dozen ways. Don't miss the famous Key lime pie. Key limes, incidentally, are not green, but *yellow.*

The price of our selected restaurants below are based on the price of three-course dinner for one, excluding tax, tip, and alcoholic beverages. *Expensive,* $13 to $30, *Moderate,* $12 to $23; *Inexpensive,* $10. Abbreviations for credit cards are: AE, American Express; CB, Carte Blanche; DC, Diners Club; MC MasterCard; V, VISA. Most restaurants that do not accept credit cards will cash traveler's checks; many will honor personal checks if you have a major credit card.

Note: Our selection is listed by Mile Marker numbers as you drive down the Keys, so watch for the green-and-white MM (Mile Marker) signs on the right.

KEY LARGO

Italian Fisherman. *Moderate.* MM 104; 451–4471. Variety of seafood served on the water. Outdoor dining. All cards.

PLANTATION KEY

Marker 88. *Expensive.* at MM 88. 852–2381. Fine dining overlooking the Gulf. Everything from Beluga caviar to fine wines, but you can also dine on less expensive fare. All cards.

ISLAMORADA

Erik's Floating Restaurant. *Expensive.* MM 85.5; 664–9141. A floating houseboat with wonderful view, fresh seafood, and choice meats. A seafood entrée masterpiece is a three-tiered affair, $19.95, but there is a daily, low-priced $10 special. AE, V, MC.

Captain's Cove South. *Moderate.* MM 81; 664–8088. Steak and seafood, but their specialty is barbecued baby back ribs. Also famous for their loaf of french-fried onion rings. AE, MC, V.

The Galley. *Inexpensive.* MM 82.8; 664–8265. Delectable seafood and a lavish salad bar. Meats, too, and steaks out to order at $1 per ounce. CB, DC, MC, V.

MARATHON

Joe's Steak and Seafood Restaurant. *Inexpensive.* MM 49, on the Gulf; 743–6069. Sizable portions of steak and seafood, also daily specials. Popular with families.

SUGARLOAF KEY

Sugarloaf Lodge. *Moderate.* MM 17; 745–3211. Dine on fresh seafood or choice beef on the Gulf, while watching a pet dolphin play in a lagoon below. Children love it. AE, DC, MC, V.

NIGHT LIFE AND BARS. Several of the better resorts have live music, dancing, and entertainment. Among them are the **Key Largo** *Holiday Inn,* MM 100, in their Casablanca Room. **Islamorada:** *Plantation Yacht Harbor Resort,* MM 87; *Cheeca Lodge,* MM 82½. **Marathon:** *Buccaneer Lodge,* MM 49. **Windley Key:** *Holiday Isle Resort,* MM 84.5; *Whale Harbor Inn,* MM 84. *Old* **Key Largo** *Restaurant and Lounge* also has entertainment. There are local bars and lounges all down the Keys, but most of the hottest night spots in the keys are in Key West.

EXPLORING KEY WEST

Take an old seafaring town that is the farthest southern outpost of the U.S. Fill it with subtropical palms and flowers, huge, shady banyan trees, Victorian gingerbread houses with widow's walks, and tiny "shotgun" houses where Cuban cigar-makers' descendants still live. Add a handful of motels and a couple of fancy resort hotels. Add English, Irish, Scottish descendants of "wreckers" who made their living by retrieving treasure from shipwrecks of Spanish galleons (and sometimes, it is said, "arranged" those shipwrekcs with false lighthouse signals). Mix in writers and artists—many originally attracted by those famous Key West residents, Ernest Hemingway and Tennessee Williams—laid-back wanderers, tourists, "bicycle carpenters" (their offices are their bicycle) who offer their services to restore old houses and often leave behind odd-angled staircases. Complete the picture with a sprinkling of Bahamian blacks, and U.S. Navy personnel, and a sizable portion of gays, who since about 1976 have become important members of the town.

That's Key West. It is a potpourri of lifestyles, both ethnic and social, and hardly for the strait-laced. It has also what some visitors describe as "magic," perhaps having to do with the mauve-and-gold light at dusk, a light that Key West artists sometimes manage to capture on canvas.

Key West is an island 3½ miles long and 1 mile wide. The streets are narrow, and in 20 minutes you can walk the length of the main drag, Duval Street, which runs from the Atlantic Ocean to the Gulf of Mexico. This is a walking or bicycling town. A "Key West bicycle" has high handles, so that you ride sitting straight up, arms chest high.

The History

Key West's history covers close to 300 years of Indian fighting, pirate ships, Spanish rule, and the lucrative "wrecking" business. In the early 1800s, Key West was owned by a young Spanish cavalryman, Juan Salas, who had been given the island by the Spanish governor for outstanding bravery to the Spanish crown. Young Salas sold it six years

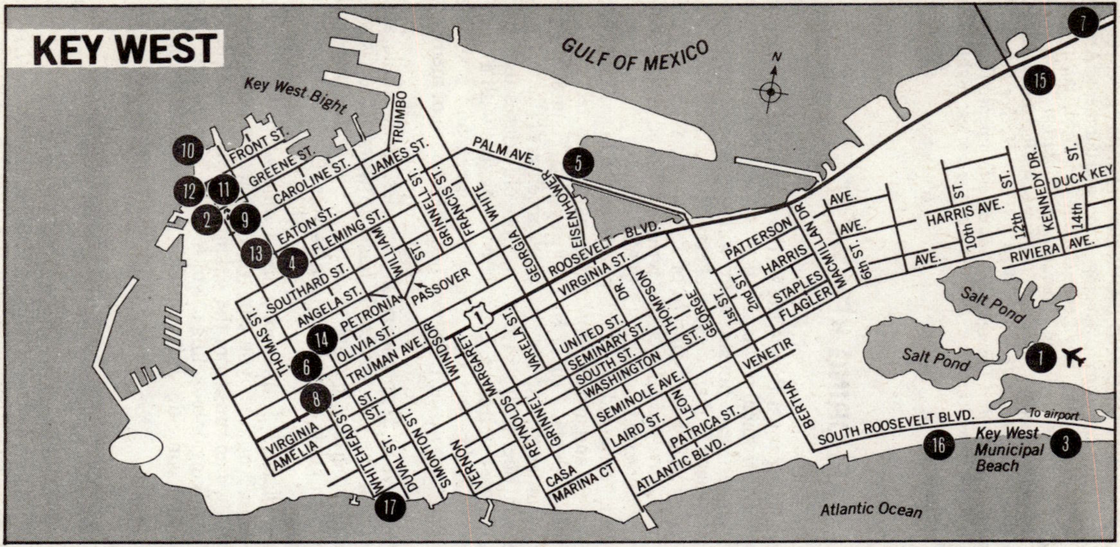

Points of Interest

1) Key West International Airport
2) Audubon House
3) East Martello Tower
4) Fast Buck Freddies
5) Garrison Bight
6) Hemingway's House
7) Key West Kennel Club
8) Lighthouse Military Museum
9) Little White House
10) Mallory Square
11) Mel Fisher's Treasure Exhibit
12) Municipal Aquarium
13) Oldest House Museum
14) Red Barn Theater
15) Searstown
16) Smathers Beach
17) Southernmost Beach

later, in 1821, to an Alabama businessman named John Simonton, for $2,000. Cubans fleeing Spain's new conscription laws in 1868 arrived in Key West and became cigar makers. In 1912, Key West was hooked to the Florida mainland via the overseas railway, and in 1915 a Key West–Havana ferry service was established. The Overseas Highway became part of the scene in 1928, in the same year, came Hemingway's enchantment with Key West. The writer paid $8,000 for the house and grounds that today, according to real-estate estimates, would bring close to $2 million. Key West was further noticed when President Truman in 1946 created the "Little White House" here because he discovered that he could take his morning walks in Key West without being bothered. To Key West "Conchs" (pronounced "konk" and meaning a native-born Key Wester) and to later residents attracted to the lifestyle on the island, everyone has a right to privacy.

Old Town

This is the heart of Key West, the main tourist attraction, with historic houses, outdoor garden restaurants, small shops, art galleries, and nightlife. It is here you'll find the two legendary bars that were Hemingway's hangouts, Sloppy Joe's and Captain Tony's Saloon. Cruise ships dock near Mallory Square, a focal point of the town's activity. Mallory Dock at sunset is the biggest free show in town, when residents and tourists stream out to the dock to watch the stunning sunset. Jugglers, tightrope walkers, fire-swallowers, the Cookie Lady selling chocolate-chip cookies, guitar-players, and magicians all vie for your attention.

The Conch Train

The best way to get a birdseye view of Key West is to take the Conch Train Tour aboard the little train of open, canopied cars. It is a narrated trip of 1½ hours that takes you around the entire island. You see some 60 historical sites—everything from Hemingway's house to the old Audubon House, where Audubon painted so many birds—and you learn about Key West's Indian and pirate days. Another option is the Old Town Trolley, which will take you on a similar trip.

PRACTICAL INFORMATION FOR KEY WEST

HOW TO GET THERE. By air. *Air Florida* has many flights every day, seven days a week, between Miami and Key West. *PBA (Provincetown-Boston Airline)* has daily flights from Miami, Fort Myers, Jacksonville, Naples, Orlando, Sarasota/Bradenton, Tallahassee, Tampa, and West Palm Beach. Private planes can also fly into the Key West airport. For information on getting from the airport; see "How to Get Around," below.

By bus. *Greyhound Bus Lines* has regular, scheduled daily trips to Key West from Miami and Miami Airport.

By car. The only route to Key West by car is down the Overseas Highway (US 1) through the Florida Keys.

By boat. You can take your own boat, and dock at Key West marinas, principally at Garrison Bight, where the major marinas are *Garrison Bight Marina* (305–294–3093) and the *Key West Yacht Club* (305–296–3446). Reservations for a slip are advisable, particularly in season.

By ship. *Commodore Lines, Chandris Lines,* and *Bahamas Cruise Lines* dock at Mallory Dock for one-day stays. Dockage for ships of other lines is currently in the works. Call your local travel agent for cruise ship information.

TELEPHONES. See "Telephones," under *Practical Information for the Keys,* above.

HOTELS AND MOTELS. Key West has a few informal, resortlike hotels, resortlike motels, more modest motels, and charming old Victorian gingerbread guest houses. There are also a few condominium units; rental information on condominiums is available from local real estate agents or on the condominium premises.

Key West is expensive. Be prepared to pay at least 25 percent more for lodging than you would at comparable accommodations on the mainland. Water is imported, electricity is generated by oil, and food must be trucked in or flown in.

Peak season is from about December 15th to the week after Easter. The rest of the year, rates are approximately 25 percent to 35 percent less. The rates we quote below in our selected list are for peak season and are based on double occupancy, no meals. Add 7 percent tax (5 percent Florida sales tax and 2 percent Key West bed tax). Inquire for special seasonal, weekly, monthly, or weekend rates; also for the charge for children in the same room and for senior-citizen discounts. Make reservations months in advance during peak season, particularly in February and March. Our selected accommodations below are listed by price and location: *Deluxe,* $90 and up; *Expensive,* $75 and up; *Moderate,* $55 and up.

CASA MARINA AREA

Marriott's Casa Marina Resort. *Deluxe.* 1500 Reynolds St.; 305–296–3535. There is a rich but laid-back wicker-and-rattan style to this resort hotel built in the 1920s and refurbished at a cost of $10 million. Private beach, lighted tennis courts, *Henry's* gourmet restaurant, lounges, entertainment.

OLD TOWN

The Pier House. *Deluxe,* Oceanfront, near Mallory Square. One Duval St.; 305–294–9541; toll free in FL 800–432–3414; toll free elsewhere in U.S.; 800–327–8340. Posh luxury leader, a chic, elegant, but informal resort with small private beach. No two rooms alike. Four bars, three restaurants. *The* Key West meeting place.

Key Lodge Motel. *Moderate.* 1004 Duval St.; 305–296–9915. Small, friendly, complimentary morning coffee in garden by heated pool. Also efficiencies and apartments.

ROOSEVELT BOULEVARD AREA

Best Western Key Ambassador. *Deluxe.* 1000 S. Roosevelt Blvd. (S-A1A), 305–296–3500; toll-free in FL 800–432–4315; elsewhere in U.S. 800–528–1234. Nine-acre landscaped resort on the Alantic. Private balconies, patio, pool, complimentary breakfast. Popular with families. Near airport.

Key Wester Resort Inn. *Expensive.* S. Roosevelt Blvd. S-A1A, on the Ocean; 305–296–5671. On the Atlantic, a resort with tennis, bicycles, free sauna, pool, restaurant. Popular with families.

Holiday Inn of Key West. *Expensive.* 1111 N. Roosevelt Blvd. 305–294–2571. Tennis, beach on Gulf, pool, gazebo dining. Popular with families.

Quality Inn. *Expensive.* 3850 N. Roosevelt Blvd.; 305–294–6681. Pool, restaurant. A friendly place that attracts families. Conch Tour Train depot on premises.

Ramada Keys' End. *Expensive.* 3420 N. Roosevelt Blvd.; 305–294–5541. Nautilus gym, Jacuzzi, pool, miniature golf. Also bar and auto rental.

Econolodge Resort. *Moderate.* 3820 N. Roosevelt Blvd.; 305–294–5511. On Gulf of Mexico. Tennis, pool, sundeck, barbecue pits.

Travelodge. *Moderate.* 3824 N. Roosevelt Blvd. 305–294–3773. Includes complimentary breakfast. Pool and attractive restaurant.

Day's Inn Motel. *Moderate.* 3852 N. Roosevelt Blvd. 305–294–3742. Pleasant, good value, good quality. Pets allowed ($4 extra). Pool, children's playground, restaurant.

SOUTHERN TIP OF ISLAND, NEAR SOUTH BEACH

Santa Maria Motel. *Moderate.* 1401 Simonton St.; 305–296–5678. Olympic-size pool, courtyard, breakfast room, and the highly rated *Queen's Table Restaurant.* Efficiencies also.

Southernmost Motel. *Expensive.* 1319 Duval St.; 305–296–6577. Heated pool, rooftop solarium, color TV. A few feet from South Beach.

South Beach Motel. *Expensive.* 508 South St.; 305–296–5611. On the Atlantic Ocean, next to South Beach. Olympic-sized pool, sundeck, balconies overlooking ocean.

GUEST HOUSES. Key West has about 40 guests houses, most of them charming gingerbread houses in Old Town. Several serve complimentary breakfast. Many have pools, sundecks, lush, shady tropical gardens. Most prefer adults only, but a few accept children. Still others cater to gay vacationists only. For the "Key West Accommodations" directory, indicating preferences, rates, facilities, write to Key West Visitor's Bureau, Box 1147, Key West, FL 33040; 305–294–2587; in FL toll-free 800–432–5330. The houses below cater to all adults, and in some cases accept children. The choices are all in Old Town, with rates from $50 to $90 double.

Cocoanut Grove. $55. 817 Fleming St.; 305–296–5107. Primarily gay, but all welcomed. Lavish breakfast included. Big, gingerbread house with balconies, verandas, a pool surrounded by tropical trees. A spacious widow's walk with a panoramic view of Key West and the Gulf of Mexico. *Adults only.*

Eaton Lodge. $70 to $90. 511 Eaton St.; 305–294–3800 Continental breakfast included. Tropical gardens, old Victorian house, hydrospa in garden. *Children accepted.*

Eden House. $50 ($47 if cash). 1015 Fleming St.; (305) 296–6868. Immaculate old house, Bermuda fans and wicker chairs, tropical plants, secluded pool. *Rich's Cafe* for breakfast. *Children may be accepted.* (if not noisy, etc.).

Heron House. $50. 512 Simonton St.; 294–9227. Continental breakfast included. Fresh and gleaming, newly restored Victorian house with pool, deck, flowering plants.

CAMPING. Two campgrounds/RV parks convenient to Key West have good facilities: *Boyd's Key West Camping* accepts tenters as well as R.V.s, has 100 sites, boat ramp, laundromat, restaurant, restrooms, fishing, swimming. On Boco Chica Channel, accessible to Gulf and Atlantic. Sites, $12 ($14 with electricity) for two persons; each additional person $2; children under 12, $1. Boyd's, Stock Island, Key West, FL 33040; 305–294–1465. *Seaside Resort,* at Mile Marker 11, is less then ten minutes from Key West. On the Atlantic, Seaside offers 200 individual oversized lots with full hookups. It has a marina, boat ramp, two pools, recreation halls, laundromats, and other conveniences. Renters can purchase sites. Double, per day, $20; extra adults $2 each; children, $1. No tents, R.V.s only. Seaside Resort, HS 1 and Boca Chica Road, Key West, FL 33040, 305–294–9515.

HOW TO GET AROUND. Key West is a bicycling and walking town, but car rentals and bus service are available. **From the Airport:** A jitney (called "the limousine") takes people into town for $3.50 a person. Taxis from airport to town are $4 a person. (See below.) You can request a limousine, about $40 to $60 an hour, in advance by calling 66666; or by calling *Lower Keys Transport Company,* 294–9457. **By bus:** There is bus service every half hour to Searstown, Key Plaza (the shopping centers on US 1), and to Stock Island. Fare, $.50. You can pick up bus schedules at many hotels or at the Chamber of Commerce (see below) or call 294–3721 ext. 160. **By car:** Car rentals available from *Avis* (800–331–1212), *Duncan-Ford,* (305–296–6547), *Hertz* (800–654–3131), *Alamo* (800–327–9633), among others. **By taxi:** Taxi service in Key West is $1.75 for first half mile, $.35 each quarter mile. Call 66666 and your taxi will arrive in five to seven minutes. **By bicycle:** Bike rental at *Bubba's Bike Rental,* 705 Duval St.; 294–2618. $5 a day, $25 a week, open 10:00 A.M. to 5:00 P.M., seven days a week. Similarly at *The Bicycle Center,* 523 Truman; 294–4556, and elsewhere.

TOURIST INFORMATION. Maps, information, booklets, folders offering discounts on various attractions are available at the *Key West Chamber of Commerce* on Mallory Square, open seven days a week, 9:00 A.M. to 5:00 P.M., 305–294–2587. Or write to *Chamber of Commerce,* 402 Wall St., Key West. You can also contact *Key West Visitors Bureau,* P.O. Box 1147, Key West; 305–294–2587; in Florida, toll-free, 1–800–432–5330. The *Welcome Center* on your left on US 1 on the corner across from the Holiday Inn as you enter Key West also provides information.

SEASONAL EVENTS. January through March. *Old Island Days,* Key West's longest annual celebration kicks off January 13th with a parade and Bahamian music. It includes more than 30 events. Highlights are *House Tours* in February and March; in February there's the *Marathon Race, Sidewalk Art Festival, Food Festival;* in March, the *Conch Blowing Contest,* and the *Blessing of the Shrimp Fleet.* **Early January:** Four-day *Key West Literary Tour and Seminar.* Authors, editors, critics, and publishers appear on panels. Poetry readings, house tours, lectures, book-and-author luncheon, a play, a meet-the-authors morning coffee, and other events. The public is invited to all. $75 for all events, but specific events are free. Write Council for Florida Libraries, 1700 E. Las Olas Blvd., Ft. Lauderdale, FL 33301; 305–525–6899. **Third week in January:** *Fort Lauderdale to Key West Sailboat Race.*

April to December. The *Annual Key West Fishing Tournament,* competition open to all; call 305–294–6098 or 296–9798.

July 20 thru 24th. *Hemingway Days Festival,* celebrating Hemingway's birthday (July 21). Street fair, Billfish Tournament, Hemingway look-alike contest, short-story contest, arm-wrestling, and more.

End of October. *Fantasy Fest,* a four-day celebration. Key West's Halloween: horror story contest, food fest, costume contest, masked ball, street fair, jazz, the *Grand Parade.*

First week in November. *International Offshore Power Boat Races.* A major, 100-mile, three-hour event on Saturday. Starts and finishes at Mallory Square. Preceded by days of qualifying races.

TOURS. *Conch Tour Train,* a little train of awninged seats takes you on a 14-mile trip of the highlights of Key West, including Audubon House, Ernest Hemingway's house, Harry Truman's "Little White House." The driver narrates the trip, and gives passengers a sense of Key West's history of Spanish conquistadors, pirates, merchants, and fishermen. 9:00 A.M. to 5:00 P.M., seven days a week, boarding at five depots. Adults $6, children 3 thru 11, $3; 294–5161.

Old Town Trolley. An old-style trolley takes you on a guided tour of Key West, historical to present—similar to the Conch Train tour. Several boarding locations; same hours, same prices as the Conch Tour Train; 296–6688.

Pelican Path, a self-guided walking tour through Old Town, beginning at Mallory Square. Map of tour available free at Chamber of Commerce, Mallory Square.

Fireball, Glass Bottom Sightseeing Boat, daily, two-hour narrated cruise, from Duval Street. Adults, $8.50; children 3 thru 12, $3.50. 296–6293

Fantasy Charters offers half-day trips, $220 for boat, up to 6 passengers, two-hour sunset trips, $90 whole boat. 296–5874.

Key West Sightseeing's *Miss Key West* departs every two hours from Mallory Square area; adults $6; youths 12–18, $3; children free. Senior Citizen discount. 296–8865.

Snorkeling trips on the *Nautilus,* a 50s dive boat. Four-hour trips, departure: 10:00 A.M. to 1:00 P.M. and 1:30 P.M. to 5:30 P.M. Adults and children, $15 each, including all equipment. Reservations and tickets at Reef Raiders Dive Shop, 109 Duval; 294–0600, or 3635.

Fort Jefferson, on Dry Tortugas. By seaplane, half-day trips of about four hours, departures 8:30 A.M. and 12:30 P.M., daily; 35-minute flight. Self-guided tour at the fort, and snorkling equipment available there, free. $85 per person round trip; under six $45; under 2, free. Key West Seaplane Service, 294–6978.

AQUARIUMS. *Municipal Aquarium.* Tropical fish and marine life. Foot of Whitehead St.; 296–2051. Adults $3.50; students $1.75.

BEACHES. Key West is not known for beaches and those that are there have no soft, white, powdery sand. *Smathers Beach,* on the Atlantic, is the municipal beach and worthy of note. It has shaded picnic areas at the quite, eastern end (best for families since the rest of the beach is active with people playing beach games). Just west of the airport on South Roosevelt Blvd. (S-A1A). *South Beach,* at the end of Duval Street, on the Gulf, is small and quiet, but pebbly underfoot.

PARTICIPANT SPORTS. Bicycling: See "How to Get Around," above.

Boating: The major marinas are *Garrison Bight* (305–294–3093) and the *Key West Yacht Club* (305–296–3446). Reservations for a slip are advised. **Sailboat** charters are available at many places. See "Tours," above, and check the Yellow Pages under "Boats-Charter."

Diving: There are a good number of places that offer diving instruction and rent equipment. Two are *Key West Pro Dive Shop,* 1605 N. Roosevelt Blvd.; 296–3823; *Reef Raiders Dive Shop,* corner Duval and Front; 294–3635. See the Yellow Pages for many others. **Fishing** is the big sport, with *Garrison Bight Marina* the big center of activity for chartering. Garrison Bight Causeway, 294–3093. **Golf** is available only at *The Key West Resort* 5201 Hwy. 1, 296–7593, which has an $8-million Rees Jones championship golf course. Fees, per person: 9 holes, $9. 18 holes, $14. Electric carts, $10 for 9 holes, $15 for 18 holes. Pull carts, $2. **Tennis** is available at some resort hotels and motels, and at the public tennis courts, Bayview Park, on Truman, just before Eisenhower Dr. going north. No reservations; you can play 45 minutes if people are waiting. Courts are lit until 10:00 P.M., Monday–Saturday. No fee. Lessons available.

Waterskiing: Equipment and instruction available at *Sky & Ski,* MM 4.5, US 1, Stock Island, 296–5165, and through *Casa Marina Resort,* Water Sports Dept.; 294–2192. **Jet Skiing** and other water sports can also be arranged here; you need not be a guest at Casa Marina.

SPECTATOR SPORTS. Dog Racing at the *Key West Kennel Club,* Stock Island, is generally December 5 through April 20th. At 8:00 P.M. daily; Saturday matinee at 1:15 P.M. Admission, $.50 but matinee is free. Ladies free admission on Tuesday night. Closed Sunday. Call 294–9517. For the current weekly events, pick up booklet at the Chamber of Commerce on Mallory Square.

HISTORIC HOUSES AND SITES. (See also "Pelican Path," under "Tours," above.) **The Audubon House.** 205 Whitehead St., at Greene; 294–2116. Where Audubon lived while studying bird life on the Keys. Open 9:00 A.M. to noon and 1:00 P.M. to 5:00 P.M. Adults, $2.50. Ages 6 through 12, $.75.

Ernest Hemingway House. Where Hemingway lived and worked for many years. 907 Whitehead St., 294–1575. Adults, $2.50; children to 12, $1.

The Oldest House Museum. Home of early merchant seaman, 322 Duval St.; 294–9502. Admission free, open daily, 10:00 A.M. to 4:00 P.M., Closed Wednesday.

STAGE. The *Red Barn Theater,* 310 Duval St., 296–9911, and *The Waterfront Playhouse,* Mallory Square, 294–5015, present plays of professional quality. Curtain time, 8:30 P.M. Red Barn tickets, $7; Waterfront $7.

The *Tennessee Williams Fine Arts Center* on Stock Island offers theater, dance, films, and concerts during the winter season. For further information, write Tennessee Williams Fine Art Center, 1 Junior College Rd., Key West; 294–6363.

ART GALLERIES. Key West is increasingly well known for producing art works. Work of quality and unusual interest range from that of the gifted primitive painter, Mario Sanchez, born in Key West, to that of many resident artists who also are exhibited in major galleries in New York, Washington, D.C., San Francisco, Boston, and elsewhere. Among the galleries showing such works are *The Gingerbread Square Gallery,* 910 Duval St., 296–8900; *Farrington Galleries,* 711 Duval, 294–6911; *Guild Hall Gallery* at 614 Duval, 296–6076; *Key West Art Center & Gallery,* 301 Front St., 294–1241; *Lucky Street Gallery* at 322 Margaret St., 294–3973; *Fred Gros Gallery,* 901 Duval 294–0545; *Jordan's,* 808 Duval, 296–2511 or 5858; *Artist Warehouse,* 814 Duval, 294–7141; *Art Unlimited,* 221 Duval, 296–5625. *Burgess/Meinster Gallery,* 810 Duval St.; 296–7382. *East Martello Gallery and Museum* also shows quality works (see "Museums). These and other art galleries are usually open Sundays as well as weekdays. Some stay open late, but you can't depend on it in Key West. Always phone first.

SHOPPING. Key West is a shopping bonanza for those who love hand-crafted work in silver, leather, and gold and boutiques with informal clothes. You'll find T-shirt shops with or without hand-painted designs, and gifts that smack of Key West, such as sponges from the *Key West Sponge Market* at 626 Duval, 294–2555; or myriads of shells, conch and otherwise, from *The Shell Warehouse,* behind Mallory Square, 294–5168.

The main shopping area is the seven blocks on Duval Street, from Petronia Street to Front Street on Mallory Square, and the few narrow little streets around Mallory Square, including Front Street, Charles, Greene, and Fitzpatrick.

The star emporium in town is *Fast Buck Freddie's,* Key West's answer to Bloomingdale's. Fast Buck's is sophisticated, fun, imaginative, and has everything from casually elegant clothes to hand-painted china, Italian espresso machines, pastel baskets woven while you watch, and ribald birthday cards; at 500 Duval, corner of Fleming. Starting at Duval, near Petronia, and heading toward Mallory Square, you'll find especially choice handmade clothes for men and women at *Machoti,* 720 Duval; the clothes are designed by two Spanish designers from Ibiza, Spain. *The Store,* 617 Duval, has informal clothes for men, as well as clever gifts. *Mirage,* 509 Duval, has fun and funky clothes, mostly for women, even washable paper overalls. *Dimitri,* 423 Duval, and *Fantazio,* 329 Duval, have dashing, stunning clothes for men and women. *Abby & Ridgley,* 111

Duval, is off-beat, stylish, chic. At *Swept Away,* 8 Charles St. off Duval near Sloppy Joe's, you'll find casual designer clothes.

A Key West speciality is aloe perfume. You'll find it at *Key West Aloe Inc.,* 524 Front St. Across the street at 529 Front St., is *Key West Hand Print Fabrics,* where you can see handsome fabrics being woven. You can buy the fabric by the yard, and clothes here as well. Next door, at corner of Front and Ann St. is *Cavanaugh's,* with everything from wicker to china imported from 27 countries.

Other delights are *Heavenly Body Kites,* 409 Greene St. Also *The Cat House in Key West,* 411 Greene St. with everything imaginable for cats.

You'll find about 30 jewelry shops, some with craftsmen working on the premises. A stand-out is *The Goldsmith Shop,* 114 Fitzpatrick St., 294–1243, with jewelry made by master goldsmith John Buzogany, whose designs have received accolades from *The New York Times* and *Vogue* magazine.

DINING OUT. In Key West you need not always eat indoors. Dine out on ocean-side decks, in tropical gardens, on balconies and porches of old houses overlooking narrow streets. You dress casually, but the cuisine is often as sophisticated as you would expect at a formal establishment. Italian, Cuban, French, American, Carribbean—they're all here, and more.

Restaurant prices in Key West are higher than elsewhere in Florida, since all food must be trucked or flown in. The prices we quote below in our selection of restaurants are for an *average* three-course dinner for one person, for food alone. Beverages, tip, and the 5-percent food tax would be extra. *Deluxe* means around $25; *Expensive* around $20; *Moderate* around $15; *Inexpensive* around $10. Except for the *Inexpensive* establishments reservations are advisable. Abbreviations for credit cards are AE, American Express; CB, Carte Blanche; DC, Diners Club; MC, MasterCard; V, VISA.

Deluxe

Cafe Des Artistes. Corner Simonton & Truman; 294–7100. French restaurant accenting fresh local seafood carefully prepared and served in the garden or indoors among original art works. All cards.

Henry's. At Marriott's Casa Marina Resort, Reynolds St.; 296–3535. The only relatively dressy place in town. Oceanside dining in elegant, candlelit, 1920s ambience. Fresh seafood specialties and continental cuisine. All cards.

Louie's Backyard. 700 Waddell Ave., 294–1061. A sophisticated gem in a gleaming old white house with a series of outdoor decks descending to the Atlantic. This "in" place has a crowded bar, and a menu that includes rack of baby lamb, Moscovite oysters, Norwegian or Scottish Salmon, smoked duckling, Beluga Malossal caviar, and many less exotic dishes. Also a simpler Key West fish-of-the-day. Indoors, the noise level is unfortunately high; on the decks, it is quieter. Service is leisurely to slow. AE, MC, V.

La Terraza De Marti (also known as "La Te Da"). 1125 Duval; 294–8435. Delightful, exotic. Outdoor dining beside pool, upper-deck bar overlooking pool (where customers have been known to swim between courses). Gourmet cooking of chicken, meats, fish. In addition, a Szechwan kitchen. Also offers special four-course prix-fixe dinner, $24, 7:00 A.M.–10:00 P.M. Everything is cooked to order, so expect *slow service.* All cards.

Pier House Restaurant. One Duval St.; 294–9541. On the Atlantic, at the Pier House. The best of American and Continental specialties. Impeccable service, fine wines, superlative desserts, including a "decadent chocolate cake." All cards.

Expensive

A & B Lobster House. Foot of Front St. on the Gulf; 294–2536. Seafood their specialty: shrimp, local fish, lobster. Also barbecued ribs, other meats. Special children's menu. View overlooking the Gulf and fishing boats. AE,CB,MC,V.

The Buttery. 1208 Simonton St.; 294–0717. Four beautiful and luxuriously comfortable rooms where you can dine on specialties such as their Gamberetti de Mare, a delectably prepared Key West shrimp. All cards.

Claire's. 900 Duval St.; 296–5558. An "in" restaurant—airy, white, attractive, great atmosphere with celebrities and beautiful people. AE,MC,V.

Las Palmas Del Mundo. 1029 Southard St.; 294–7991. A one-time cigar-maker's cottage, where you can dine indoors or in the lush little garden. The owners bake their own bread and prepare imaginative, delicious dishes, ranging from broiled swordfish with fennel to broiled tuna with mango butter. Subdued background music of the Billie Holliday variety. MC, V.

Rooftop Cafe. 310 Front St.; 294–2042. Dine on open-air deck overlooking the action on Front Street, or eat indoors to tinkling piano music. Succulent seafood, masterfully prepared chicken, and delectable beef. Sophisticated ambience. AE,MC,V.

Moderate

Casa Manana. 431 Front St.; 294–6707. Mexican delights at the Old Town Plaza, indoors and out with 15 kinds of margaritas. Burritos, nachos, pollo en molé, crab enchiladas, tostados, *big* appetizers (enough for two people), and extra-special desserts. AE,MC,V.

Half Shell Raw Bar. Foot of Margaret St. at the shrimp docks; 294–7496. Open-air waterfront raw bar and restaurant serving shrimp, fish, oysters, stone crabs, lobster, even a full dinner of lobster with crabmeat stuffing. The ultimate in informality: you sit on long benches and share a table with other diners, while gazing out at the shrimp fleet. No credit cards.

Jordan's Cafe and Art Gallery. 808 Duval St.; 296–5858. Another standout. Small garden, bar, and dining room with art works. Lots of charm, exceptional service. Charcoal-grilled hamburgers on open hearth. Limited menu with three or four beautifully prepared meat or fish entrées, good wines, desserts, AE, MC, V.

Lighthouse Cafe. 917 Duval St.; 296–7837. Southern Italian dining in a small garden or indoors, Deluxe quality, despite the price. A stunning appetizer for two, also a specialty of Ciopinno: shrimp, lobster, conch, clams, squid, in a sauce of tomatoes, peppers, onions, olives, on capellini. Hot garlic bread and tossed salad with every entree. MC, V.

Pigeon House Patio. 303 Whitehead St.; 294–1034. Here you dine on shady terraces, verandas, or indoors. Gulf shrimp in a Cajun sauce, chicken imperial, and other imaginative entrees—all served with the restaurant's homemade bread, salad, potatoes or seasoned rice *du jour.* Blow-your-mind desserts top it off. MC,V.

Inexpensive

Amy's. 7 Key Lime Sq. (off Duval); 294–9836. Pretty, tucked-away garden restaurant. Crisp, cold Gazpacho and other fresh homemade soups. Also features the freshest of native seafood and a variety of omelettes. Beer and wine. All cards.

El Cacique. 125 Duval St.; 294–4000. Spanish-Basque cuisine in an unpretentious restaurant with counter service as well as tables. Shrimp, jewfish, steak.

Specialty is *paella à la Valenciana* (must be ordered an hour in advance). Wines, desserts. Popular with locals. No credit cards.

Fleet Air Wing. 1 Telegraph Lane (next to Captain Tony's Saloon); 296–4596. Unadorned, practical-looking restaurant serving a huge, fresh salad with julienned ham and chicken. Also a variety of juicy hamburgers and exceptional chili. MC, V.

Fourth of July. 1110 White St.; 294–7553. Cuban specialties. Spanish-English menu. Delicious *paella Valenciana,* pork chunks with rice and black beans, shrimp *enchilado.* Wines and Berena Sangria. No credit cards.

NIGHT LIFE AND BARS. The two famous bars of Hemingway legend, *Sloppy Joe's,* 201 Duval, and *Captain Tony's Saloon,* 428 Greene, and a half-dozen other bars are clustered at the end of Duval and on Front Street, near Mallory Square. You can't miss them: their live, electrified group music will strike your eardrums blocks away. You'll find them packed with locals and tourists—mostly a young crowd—until 3:00 or 4:00 A.M.

For lovers of jazz, the place is *Captain HornBlower's,* 300 Front St.

For a distinctly different ambience to these brawny-type bars, Key West's most magnetic disco the gay-oriented *Copa,* 623 Duval St., draws a mixed crowd and offers new and imaginative entertainment every night. Open to 4:00 A.M. (AE, MC, V).

More traditional entertainment and dancing is at the *Casa Marina Resort's Calabash Lounge,* Reynolds St. (all cards). Also at the *Havana Docks Bar,* at the Pier House, foot of Duval (AE, V, MC).

SOUTHWEST FLORIDA

The Other Coast

by
FRED. W. WRIGHT JR.

Fred. Wright is a free-lance writer living on Florida's "other coast." He often writes about his state and has contributed to regional and national publications, including GEO *and the* St. Petersburg Times.

The sun says it the best. It is the one symbol most associated with Florida, and most especially with the stretch of the Gulf of Mexico coastline from Tampa Bay south to the Everglades. While all of Florida promotes its abundance of sunshine, this piece of the state's west coast is aptly dubbed "The Suncoast."

It is indeed "The Other Coast" as well. All the historical action seems centered around the Atlantic coast of Florida—St. Augustine, the oldest city in the country, and Miami, Miami Beach, and Ft.

Lauderdale, and all those tourist meccas so famous in literature and lore. But the Suncoast has its share of history and tourism as well; it just doesn't have the "high-profile" public image that other parts of the state have. That's a point of *braggadocio* for residents and a "find" for the hundreds of thousands of tourists who find this area by accident or will.

The three-city (Tampa, St. Petersburg, Clearwater) Tampa Bay area is fast becoming one of the nation's major markets—twenty-fourth in ranking, with a year-round population of more than 1.7-million people. Tampa was tagged by *Megatrends* author and futurist John Nesbitt as one of the ten cities of opportunity in coming years. With its Tampa International Airport luring more and more international travelers, and the success of Super Bowl XVIII in January 1984, the Tampa Bay area is on a lot more maps these days.

Tampa

Tampa, which means in Indian language "stick of fire," was largely ignored by Spanish explorers probing Florida for rumored gold and the fabled Fountain of Youth. It wasn't until 1824 that Tampa became a settlement with the establishment of Fort Brooke.

The Cuban cigarmakers moved their industry here in 1866, established Ybor City, and later flocked to join Cuban revolutionary Jose Marti against the Spanish rulers of his island home. Tourists began to come from the world over in the 1890s to stay at the Tampa Bay Hotel, then called "the world's most elegant hotel." Teddy Roosevelt set up headquarters at the hotel in 1898 and 30,000 troops were encamped in Tampa to train for the Spanish-American War.

Today Tampa is an emerging financial and business city. Its skyline is changing dramatically and quickly—and yet there are still plenty of lush areas around the city's edges that remind you daily of why people came here in the first place. Joggers can lope along the world's longest continuous sidewalk—3.8 miles—along Bayshore Boulevard, with its spectacular view of Tampa Bay.

There are other views not to be missed while in Tampa, and they can vary from the wild ways of the more than 3,000 animals and 2,500 exotic birds at Busch Garden's Dark Continent to the odd mosque-topped buildings of the area's oldest college, the University of Tampa (founded in 1933), housed in what once was the Tampa Bay Hotel, built in 1891 by railroad magnate Henry B. Plant, with rooms that rented even then at $75 a night.

Tampa also offers the Museum of Science and Industry, the largest museum in Florida and the largest science museum in the Southeast. Many of its exhibits are "hands-on"—you're encouraged to touch and to participate in ersatz hurricanes and thunderstorms.

Franklin Street Mall, through the heart of downtown Tampa, offers shops and open-air strolling and it is also the site of Tampa Theatre, a baroque survival of the old ornate opera houses so popular in the

1920s, fully restored with its twinkling ceiling stars and soft pastel clouds.

Along the city's waterfront are a World War II vintage submarine (the U.S.S. *Requin*) and the 300-ton *José Gasparilla,* the world's only fully rigged pirate ship, docked on Bayshore Boulevard and built in 1953 as the centerpiece to the city's annual Gasparilla celebration.

Ybor City in east Tampa, centering around Seventh Avenue (Broadway), is the two-square-mile Spanish city, founded in 1886 by Cubans brought to work in the cigar factories. Spanish and Italian cafés, business houses and clubs, and Spanish theaters provide the atmosphere of a city complete within itself. Ybor Square, at Eighth Avenue and 13th Street, features arts-and-crafts shows, free musical performances on some weekends, antique marts, specialty shops, a nostalgia market, and more. Some shops open daily; all open weekends. Restaurants are generally open from 11 A.M. to midnight.

Along Seventh Avenue, be sure to stop at Valencia Gardens, where Manuel Beiros has been greeting customers for more than 50 years. The Valencia, 811 W. Kennedy Blvd., 253–3773, while certainly not the only Cuban restaurant in Ybor City, still earns top honors for serving the best Spanish bean soup and hot Cuban bread in town.

Pinellas County

On the other side of Tampa Bay (connected by three slim and car-filled bridges that you don't want to go near during rush hour if you can help it), Pinellas County continues to change its image as well. Despite jokes to the contrary by talk show host Johnny Carson, St. Petersburg is not just a city of old people.

To the contrary: the median age in Pinellas County declined in the 1970s, to 45.8 average years, while the median age in some counties north of here went up. Still, Hillsborough County, where Tampa is located, is the youngster on the Suncoast—30.4 years average age.

Pinellas is the largest Suncoast county in population, with more than 725,000 people, and the smallest in land mass, 280 square miles. It is a county of small communities—a whole string of them along the county's Gulf of Mexico border, communities that sit along 28 miles of public beaches that draw tourists and residents like pilgrims during the warm winter months.

St. Petersburg is so proud of its record of sunshine that the afternoon newspaper, the *Evening Independent,* is given away if the sun doesn't shine—and that's happened less than 300 times in the past 75 years. St. Petersburg is also a city trying to rival its neighbor Tampa for public acknowledgment by getting a professional baseball stadium and team before Tampa does.

It's a wonderful rivalry between civic and business leaders—and deadly serious to many leaders in St. Petersburg, who have watched the world at large place the area's professional sports teams in Tampa alone because that's where Tampa Stadium is.

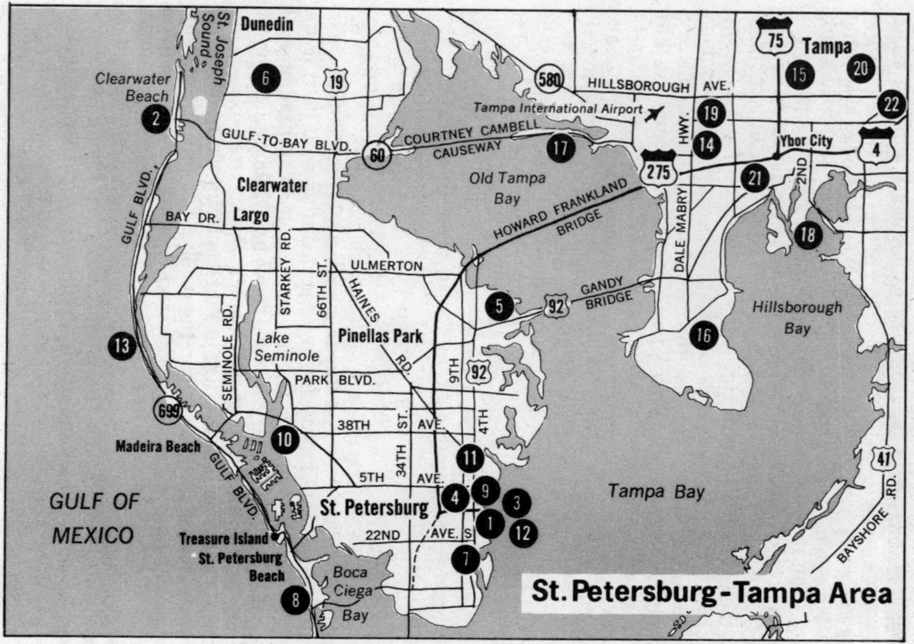

Points of Interest

St. Petersburg
1) Bayfront Center
2) Big Pier 60
3) Bounty Exhibit
4) Al Lang Stadium
5) Derby Lane (dog racing)
6) Jack Russell Stadium
7) Salvador Dali Museum
8) London Wax Museum
9) Museum of Fine Arts
10) Payson Field (baseball)
11) Sunken Gardens
12) The Pier
13) Tiki Gardens

Tampa
14) Al Lopez Field (baseball)
15) Greyhound Track
16) Jai Alai Fronton
17) Municipal Beach
18) Shrimp Fleet
19) Tampa Stadium
20) University of South Florida
21) University of Tampa
22) Busch Gardens

Otherwise, though, Pinellas likes its more laid-back, casual image. Pinellas is a county for shorts and T-shirts, for lying in the sun—even Tampa residents come over the bridge to use Pinellas beaches—for fishing and engaging in any of the other dozen or more water and sunshine sporting activities available.

A geographical digression: Pinellas has every kind of geography to be found in Florida—beaches, mangrove swamps, cattle pastures, citrus groves, and hills. In fact, one of the highest hills on the West Coast of Florida—all of 75 feet above sea level—is in Clearwater.

An Ethnic Mix

Hills or no hills, Pinellas County is as rich in variety as is its watery neighbor, Hillsborough. In the northern part of the county, a strong Scottish community lives in Dunedin, while the Greek culture thrives and attracts tourists as well in Tarpon Springs.

The sponging industry, which first pulled together the Greek fishermen and spongers into a small, close community nestled between the Anclote River and the Gulf of Mexico, has long died out. A blight killed the great sponge beds in the 1940s. But the newly rebuilt Tarpon Springs Sponge Exchange and Docks re-creates that exciting pre-forties era.

Enough sponges survive to give tourists a glimpse of once-was as daily spongers go out to bring back souvenir sponges. (For information, call the Tarpon Springs Chamber of Commerce at 937–6109.) The most famous of Tarpon Springs restaurants is Pappas, and justifiably so. Located at 10 W. Dodecanese Blvd. (the main avenue for most of Tarpon Springs's tourist-oriented shops and restaurants), the Greek salad has been a specialty there since 1925.

Working your way back south through Pinellas County means choosing from a wide selection of beaches—28 miles worth in Pinellas County alone, all open to the public—as well as restaurants. In the Clearwater area, don't miss Heilman's Beachcomber, 447 Mandalay Ave. (on Clearwater Beach, actually), owned by the same family since 1910 and featuring Sunday dinners Southern style, with fried chicken, gravy, and mashed potatoes—or seafood, if you prefer.

St. Petersburg Waterfront

The city's waterfront, however, is where life is obvious and change is constant. From blocks away, the skyline begins to move. Ship's masts pierce the horizon from the municipal marina, where scores of boats berth. To their left, the MGM exhibit, the *Bounty,* bobs quietly, a to-scale replica built for moviemaking and now used for tourist-visiting.

Along the waterfront, too, the city's two principal art museums—the Museum of Fine Arts to the north and the newer Dali Museum to the south—bracket the city's efforts to put life and energy into its downtown area. Shops along the principal waterfront road—Beach Drive—are numerous and varied. A stop at 10 Beach Dr., at the corner of Beach Drive and Central Avenue, is an occasion for food or drink. Its continental menu ranges from steak tartar to bananas Foster, and the lounge and wine bar share the same roof.

The Pier, St. Petersburg's principal downtown architectural symbol, is an upside-down, five-story, pyramid-shaped building. It is home for ethnic shops with surprisingly good prices, two restaurants, and a fifth-floor observation deck that offers a stunning view of much of downtown St. Petersburg. At night, a laser beam shoots out of the third floor, the result of a "sculpture in light" by Washington, D.C., artist Rockne Krebs.

Bradenton and Sarasota

South of Pinellas, just over the Sunshine Skyway Bridge—over the span that's still standing—Bradenton and Sarasota offer that same rich mixture of residential communities, tourist attractions, and history. It was at Bradenton that Hernando de Soto landed in 1539 looking for water, thinking he had reached the mighty Mississippi River. Wrong. But his brief step ashore is remembered, and is typical of the kind of questing that so many people do when they go south of Pinellas County into the less-populated communities on the lower West Coast of Florida.

The city of Sarasota has long been a cultural oasis, even in the younger, less affluent days of the Tampa Bay area. Sarasota has the Ringling Museum and an unparalleled reputation for art, the state's nationally known professional repertory company, the Asolo State Theater, the Ringling Bros. and Barnum & Bailey Circus, and much more. On the grounds of the Ringling Museum, just four miles north of downtown Sarasota, is the fantasy home, Ca'D'Zan (House of John), built in 1925 at a cost of $1.5-million by circus owner John Ringling and now preserved in its original glory.

Ft. Myers and Naples

Still farther south, Ft. Myers enjoys its history as a home for major-league fishing, and for a major-league inventor, Thomas Edison. He made this small coastal village his second home and typical of the inventor, he had a house built in Maine and then shipped on four sailing schooners to Ft. Myers and reassembled. This was in 1886, making the home possibly the world's first prefabricated building—an ironic footnote in Florida history.

Another favorite stop is the Ft. Myers Beach Pier, at the north end of Estero Island, in the middle of specialty shops, boutiques, and sidewalk cafés. Here visitors can fish, or just watch others vie for the more than 600 different species found in Florida waters. Freshwater fisherfolk can try the city's municipal pier, which reaches out into the wide,

wide Caloosahatchee River, where freshwater and saltwater catches, from catfish to sharks, intermingle.

Down the coast even farther, Naples is a quiet community with a great gathering of millionaires. Indeed, along serene roads lined with royal palms and coconut palms, "Millionaire's Row" and the fine, stately houses hidden behind hedges and walls, nestled against the Gulf of Mexico, is a tourist attraction all its own. Sunday brunch at the Naples Beach Hotel and Golf Club's Brassie, 851 Gulf Shore Blvd. N. (261–2222), is a great weekend experience. The ice carvings alone are worth a glance.

The Resort Islands

The three special resort islands off the coast—Sanibel and Captiva near Ft. Myers and Marco near Naples—are becoming symbols of the "New Tourist" who is discovering Florida for the first time. These small islands, once known almost exclusively for fine fishing and the best seashells in the country, are now booming into tourist meccas. Gulf-front condominiums and high-rise hotels are changing the look and pace of these communities.

Sanibel and Captiva are easily reachable from Ft. Myers via State Road 867. The winding main drive on both islands takes you past homes hidden behind Australian pine trees and hedges, homes that reflect a lifestyle before tourism. Shops and seafood restaurants are to be found, coming up quickly out of the corner of your eye as you drive the twisting two-lane roads. The Bubble Room on Captiva is a must. Its eccentric décor of old toys and model trains is offset—or complemented—by a scrumptuous menu, including homemade desserts that are worth taking home.

Marco Island shows more unrestricted growth as huge high-rises and time-share condominiums rise shoulder to shoulder along the Gulf of Mexico. Shops and restaurants are easily found and even more easily enjoyed, and great portions of the island are protected sanctuaries that will never be developed. But the island remains newly discovered, and despite the heavy growth of multi-story buildings, there are miles of beach to explore and plenty of shops to visit. The 101-year-old Old Marco Inn, on Palm Avenue (394–3131), offers old world recipes in a Victorian veranda setting.

No matter what portion of Florida's southwest coast you visit, the inevitable impression has to be one of change. The look of the land is changing. There are more buildings, taller buildings, newer buildings. It is harder to find those quaint one-family cottages that once dotted the Gulf of Mexico coastline by the hundreds. They've been sold and replaced by time-share condominiums or expensive one-family homes. The look of Florida along this stretch of the Gulf is changing.

Yet the factors that brought this progress, the very items the chambers of commerce tout in their ads—the three S's: Sun, Sand, and Surf—are still here for everyone, and will be, regardless of progress.

It will always be known as The Suncoast.

PRACTICAL INFORMATION FOR THE SOUTHWEST COAST

HOW TO GET THERE. By air. More than a score of airlines serve Tampa International Airport, including *Air Canada, American, Continental, Delta, Eastern, Northwest Orient, Pan American, Republic, TransWorld (TWA), United,* and *USAir.* In addition, a growing number of commuter airlines, as well as *People Express,* serve the smaller St. Petersburg/Clearwater International Airport in northern Pinellas County. Service is also available into the southern regions of the Florida West Coast to Fort Myers, Naples, and Venice. For information getting from the airport see "How to Get Around," later in this *Practical Information.*

By bus. *Continental Trailways* and *Greyhound* have regular service into Hillsborough (Tampa) and Pinellas (St. Petersburg and Clearwater) counties. Trailways and Greyhound both continue service down the coast as far as Ft. Myers, with stops along the way at Bradenton, Sarasota, and the like. Greyhound extends its service to Naples; Trailways does not. Check with your local Greyhound and Trailways reservation offices, or with your travel agent, for information and ticket prices.

By train. *Amtrak* has daily service into Florida aboard the *Silver Meteor* out of Washington, D.C., with connections along the way. The Silver Meteor splits at Jacksonville, with one section continuing down the east coast of Florida to Miami, Fort Lauderdale, and the area known as the Gold Coast, while the other section heads through Orlando to Tampa and the Suncoast. There is connecting charter bus service in Tampa to St. Petersburg and Clearwater, and south to Bradenton and Sarasota; but it's a nuisance. The *Autotrain* is back in business as well. It runs between Lorton, VA, which is about 7½ miles south of Washington, DC, to Sanford, FL, which is just north of Orlando. One-way fares on the Autotrain are $130 for adults, $98 for children under 12, and $200 per car. For specific fare information and reservations, Amtrak has a toll-free number: 800–872–7245.

By car. Driving to the west coast of Florida has been made very easy. While not the first mode of transportation into this part of Florida, it clearly is the foremost. The old highways—US 19 down the edge of the Gulf of Mexico or US 41, which parallels the coast a few miles inland—are still there and still offer an alternative to the high-speed billboard blur of the interstates. But I–75 cuts down the left third of the state, also parallel to the Gulf of Mexico, and temporarily ends in Tampa. Eventually it will connect in Bradenton and Sarasota for a steady run right down to the Everglades and the Tamiami Trail. As it now stands, I–75 feeds into I–275 in St. Petersburg, which carries you as far south as 54th Avenue South in St. Petersburg, just short of the Sunshine Skyway Bridge. I–75 starts up again in Bradenton and runs all the way to Naples. I–4 runs east-west and feeds traffic and tourists from the East Coast of Florida and from Orlando.

TELEPHONES. The area code for all of the West Coast of Florida from Tampa (Hillsborough County) south to Everglades City (Lee County) is 813. Information (directory assistance) is 555–1212; locally within a few miles of where you're dialing from, information is 411. Directory assistance from outside the west-coast area is toll-free by dialing 813–555–1212. And to check if there is a toll-free number for the business you want to reach, dial 800–555–1212, directory assistance for toll-free 800 numbers. Local pay phones calls are 25 cents.

HOTELS AND MOTELS. The Florida west coast indeed has hundreds of motels and hotels of all shapes, sizes, and prices, to tempt the weary or curious traveler. Many are on the miles of Gulf of Mexico waterfront that stretch from the Tampa Bay area south to the Everglades. And a growing phenomenon in Florida, and especially in this motel-rich area of the state, are time-share, or interval-ownership, units that are available for rent on a nightly, weekly, or monthly basis. Indeed, many motels along the Gulf coast have gone this route—investors buy them, renovate them, and turn each room into units that are sold like mini-condos.

Hotel and motel rates are based on double occupancy, European Plan. Categories determined by price are: *Deluxe,* $100 and up; *Expensive,* $60 to $99; *Moderate,* $35 to $59; and *Inexpensive,* less than $35.

The hotel and motel listings are organized by towns, moving generally from north to south along the coast.

TAMPA

Hyatt Regency Tampa. *Deluxe,* Two Tampa City Center; 813–225–1234 or 800–228–9000. Mirrored and elegant and expensive; 540 rooms, including 40 suites in midtown Tampa. Health club, outdoor pool on fifth floor, in-room movies; two restaurants, two lounges.

Saddlebrook Resort. *Expensive–Deluxe.* State Rd. 54, Wesley Chapel; 813–973–1111. New golf and tennis resort, 15 miles north of Tampa. Beautiful suites, restaurants, lounges. Pools, tennis courts, championship golf course, health spas, game room with bar.

Tampa Hilton. *Expensive–Deluxe.* 200 N. Ashley; 813–223–2456. On Hillsborough River, 10 minutes from airport. Restaurant and cocktail lounge. Docking facilities and patio garden.

Tampa Marriott. *Expensive–Deluxe.* 1001 N. Westshore Blvd.; 813–876–9611 or 800–228–9290. Five minutes from airport. Indoor/outdoor pool; saunas; exercise center; game room. Restaurant and lounge.

Holiday Inn. *Expensive.* Tampa International Airport, 4500 W. Cypress St.; 813–879–4800 or 800–HOLIDAY. Swimming pool stretches from outdoors into a covered atrium; weights; Jacuzzi; 482 rooms, restaurants, and lounges.

Tampa Airport Hilton. *Expensive.* 2225 Lois Ave.; 813–877–6688 or 800–432–5141. New, with 240 rooms and accessible to Tampa Stadium and interstate. Outdoor heated pool, whirlpool, ballroom, color TV (with H.B.O.).

Inn on the Point. *Moderate.* 7627 Courtney Campbell Parkway; 813–884–2000; Sauna and sunning beach around an Olympic-sized pool. A restaurant, lounge, tennis courts, putting green.

Interchange Motor Inn. *Inexpensive.* 109 E. Fowler Ave.; 813–933–6531. Close to the interstate; cable TV, movies, phones, coin laundry. Pets are $5 extra.

TARPON SPRINGS

Innisbrook Resort. *Deluxe.* Box 1088; 813–937–3124. On 1,000-acre estate, five miles south of Tarpon Springs. Lodges on property house deluxe rooms and suites. Restaurants, lounges, entertainment. Golf, tennis, heated pools, jogging trail, exercise room, lake fishing.

ST. PETERSBURG/CLEARWATER AREA

Bayfront Concourse. *Expensive.* 333 1st St. S., St. Petersburg; 813–896–1111. Downtown, on Tampa Bay. Rooftop restaurant; lounge with entertainment, swimming pool with bar. Golf, tennis, and marina nearby.

The Don CeSar Beach Resort. *Expensive.* 3400 Gulf Blvd., St. Petersburg Beach; 813–360–1881 or 800–237–8987. One of the area's finest and most unusual hotels—a huge, rococo palace in pink, overlooking the Gulf of Mexico. There are 272 rooms, 50 suites, plus Jacuzzi, health club, tennis courts, pool, and more. Four restaurants and three lounges range from the casual to the elegant. F. Scott Fitzgerald was a frequent guest here during the 20s and 30s.

Holiday Inn Surfside. *Expensive.* 400 Mandalay Ave., Clearwater; 813–461–3222 or 800–HOLIDAY. Just over two years old, the Surfside is a top-of-the-line item in this motel chain, with 428 rooms, nine suites, and such in-room items as color TV, with pay movies. Swimming pool and more. Restaurant, coffee shop, and disco.

Tierra Verde Island Resort. *Expensive.* 200 Madonna Blvd., Tierra Verde; 813–867–8611. Opened in 1962 by band leader Guy Lombardo, this resort has five interconnected two-story buildings and more than 60 condo units for rent in varying sizes and prices. Each unit has a color TV, radio, phone. The resort has pools, docks, whirlpools, bike rentals, and plenty of handy restaurants and lounges.

Admiral Motel. *Inexpensive.* 16611 Gulf Blvd., North Redington Beach; 813–398–6350. Small rooms, with color TV but no phones; pool. Nothing fancy but well located, across the street from the Gulf of Mexico.

La Mark Charles Motel. *Inexpensive.* 6200 34th St. N., St. Petersburg; 813–527–7334. Centrally located; phones, rental refrigerators, heated pool.

TREASURE ISLAND

Bilmar Beach Resort Hotel. *Expensive.* 10650 Gulf Blvd., Box 9548; 813–360–5531. Near St. Petersburg airport, on white sand beach. Heated pools, sundeck, patio, boat rental. Golf and tennis nearby. Dining room, bar, entertainment.

Quality Inn-Trail's End Resort Motel. *Expensive.* 11500 Gulf Blvd.; 813–360–5541. On beach; limo service from Tampa airport. Heated pool, surf fishing. Restaurant and lounge adjacent. Some efficiencies and small apts.

Buccaneer Resort Motel. *Moderate.* 10800 Gulf Blvd.; 813–367–1908. Rooms and apartments on private beach. Heated pool, sauna.

BRADENTON/SARASOTA

Colony Beach and Tennis Resort. *Deluxe.* 1620 Gulf of Mexico Dr., Longboat Key; 813–383–6464. With 20 acres on the Gulf of Mexico and 235 units fully equipped with kitchenettes, private balconies, and more; there's also color TV, phones, radio, and some executive suites. There are pools, Jacuzzis, tennis, valet parking, wet and dry steam rooms.

Hyatt Sarasota. *Expensive.* 1000 Blvd. of the Arts, Sarasota; 813–366–9000. Modern 12 stories in the heart of Sarasota, right on Sarasota Bay. Each of the 297 rooms has a view. Nice lobby, big banquet rooms, color TV, radios, turn-down services, in-room movies. Two restaurants and a lounge.

Longboat Key Club. *Expensive.* 301 Gulf of Mexico Drive, Longboat Key; 813–383–8821. Right on the beach, with 221 condos for rent, two 18-hole golf courses, and restaurants for guests and members only. Heated pool, 24 tennis courts, full marina facilities.

Best Western-Bradenton Resort Inn. *Moderate.* 2303 1st St.; 813–747–6465. Color TV, phones, coin laundry. Heated pool with sauna, whirlpool, miniature golf, lighted tennis courts, playground, exercise room. Reservation deposit required in season.

Cadillac Motel. *Inexpensive.* 4021 US 41 S., Sarasota; 813–355–7108. Small and accessible. Color TV, phones, heated pool. Deposit required.

VENICE

Best Western Venice Resort Inn. *Expensive.* U.S. 41 Bypass North; 813–485–5411. One-half mile from downtown, near Ringling Bros. Circus. Heated pool; lounge with entertainment; restaurant adjacent.

Holiday Inn. *Expensive.* 1660 S. Tamiami Trail, Osprey; 800–237–7554. Six miles north of Venice; three miles from beaches. Lounge and entertainment.

FT. MYERS

Ramada Airport Hotel. *Expensive.* 12635 Cleveland Ave.; 813–936–4300. One mile from Ft. Myers Airport. Tennis court, heated pool. Dining room and lounge.

Village Guest House. *Moderate.* Shell Point Blvd.; 813–466–1111, ext. 123. Located in a quiet residential community, a bit off the beaten highway but comfortable. Color TV, coin laundry, pool, phones. Deposit required.

Fort Myers Red Carpet Inn. *Inexpensive–Moderate.* 4811 Cleveland Ave.; 813–936–3229. Heated pool; Roman baths available. Restaurant and lounge.

Royal Palm Motel. *Moderate.* 70 N. Tamiami Trail; 813–262–6193. Color TV, heated pool. Reservation deposit required. Small pets $3 extra.

CAPTIVA ISLAND

South Seas Plantation. *Deluxe.* Box 194; 813–472–5111. 1856 plantation set on 330 acres, 45 minutes from Ft. Myers Airport. Private beach, pools, marina, fishing-sailing school.

SANIBEL ISLAND

Casa Ybel Resort Club. *Deluxe.* 2255 West Gulf Dr.; 813–472–3145. Nicely appointed time-share condos available, with a backyard toward the lapping surf. Good shelling on a less-traveled section of the beach. On-site restaurant and lounge. No room service, but picnic baskets available.

Song of the Sea. *Deluxe.* 863 East Gulf Dr.; 813–472–2220. Beach-front resort in garden setting overlooking Gulf of Mexico. All facilities with kitchens. Heated pool, shuffleboard, Jacuzzi, sailboat and bicycle rentals, golf nearby, tennis. Barbecue facilities. Restaurant nearby.

Konakai Motel. *Moderate.* 1539 Periwinkle Way; 813–472–1001. Thirteen units located only a few minutes from beaches. Pool and Polynesian Garden setting. Five restaurants within a block's walk. Pets $10 extra.

West Wind Inn. *Moderate.* 3345 W. Gulf Dr.; 813–472–1541. Gulf-front resort with pool, tennis courts, putting green. Motel rooms, efficiencies, suites.

NAPLES

La Playa Beach & Racquet Inn. *Deluxe.* 9891 Gulf Shores Dr., 813–597–3123. On white sand Vanderbilt Beach, 10 minutes north of downtown Naples. Heated pools; fishing dock. Gourmet restaurant and bar.

Naples Beach Hotel and Golf Club. *Deluxe.* 851 Gulf Shore Blvd. N.; 813–261–2222. 135 acres on Gulf of Mexico, five miles from airport. Private beach, golf course, tennis courts, pool. Dining room. lounge, entertainment.

MARCO ISLAND

Marriott's Marco Beach Resort. *Expensive.* 400 South Collier Blvd.; 813–394–2511. A great view and a nice, new hotel, with four restaurants and lots of shops. There's even a family of raccoons living in the bushes outside the ice-cream parlor. Suites, penthouse suites, and villas available.

BED-AND-BREAKFASTS. For information on those in the area contact Danie Bernard, *B&B Suncoast Accommodations,* 8690 Gulf Blvd., St. Petersburg Beach, FL 33708; 813–360–1753, or *Florida Suncoast B&B,* Box 12, Palm Harbor, FL 33563; 813–784–5118.

CAMPING. The west coast's abundance of beaches and public parks offer a rich choice for campers. (See "Parks," below.) State park information is available from the Department of Natural Resources in Tallahassee, 904–488–7326. There is no central clearing house for information on county parks; your best bet for information about a specific park is to consult the local telephone directory. Look in the White Pages for a page of listings for the local county municipal offices; then look under "Park Department." Camping guides also are available at local bookstores. There is no camping, short-term or overnight, in any city park along the west coast of Florida.

Camping gear is often available for rent. Try the Yellow Pages of the local telephone directory, under "Camping Equipment." Some choices in the Tampa Bay area: *Adventures-Camping & Trail,* Tampa, 870–2341; *Carter Rent-All,* Tampa, 877–4615; *Venture Out,* Clearwater, 785–8135.

HOW TO GET AROUND. From the airport. Transportation to downtown Tampa from Tampa International Airport averages $7.50. Service to Pinellas County is $8.25 to $10, depending on which transportation company you use. There is direct pickup outside the baggage claim area. All major car rental companies service Tampa International and provide free transportation from the airport to the rental office. (See "By car," below). There is no bus service out of Tampa International Airport and no subway or municipal shuttle. You get out by car or airport limousine. Major transportation agencies include *Central Florida Limousine,* 883–3730, serving only Hillsborough County; *The*

Limo, 822–3333 in St. Petersburg and Clearwater, 442–4812 in Tarpon Springs, serving only Pinellas County; *Lindo's Transportation,* 531–8923, serving Pinellas County; and *Beach Airport Transport Service* (BATS), 360–7277, serving Pinellas County. Hillsborough and Pinellas are also served by taxi companies, with fares ranging from $10 for most of Hillsborough to $20 or more for Pinellas. (See "By taxi," below.) For pickup and transportation to Tampa International (or St. Petersburg/Clearwater International), reservations are required and should be made, when possible, 24 hours in advance.

By bus. There is no municipal bus service between the two major twin cities of the Tampa Bay area—Tampa and St. Pete. Check with *Greyhound* and *Continental Trailways* for information and fares. There is a complex and not always efficient municipal bus system in both counties, as well as in all of the major communities to the south—Bradenton, Sarasota, Ft. Myers, Venice, Naples. **Around Tampa:** *Hart (The Hillsborough Area Regional Transit)* serves most areas of the county, except Plant City. During peak hours of 6:00 to 9:30 A.M. and 3:30 to 6:30 P.M., fare is $.60 and transfers are $.10. Off-peak hours (before 6:00 A.M., between 9:00 A.M. and 3:00 P.M., and after 6:00 P.M., plus weekends and holidays) fare is $.30 and $.05 for transfers. For more information, call HART at 254–4278 between 7:00 A.M. and 6:00 P.M. **Around St. Petersburg/Clearwater:** In Pinellas County, the *Pinellas County Transit Authority (PCTA)* serves all of Pinellas County. The fare is $.50 and transfers are $.10. Exact change is required. For those 65 and older and for the handicapped, a special fare is in effect weekdays between 9:00 A.M. and 4:00 P.M. and after 6:00 P.M., plus all day Saturday, Sunday, and holidays. With proof of age (a Medicare card, for example), the special fare is $.25 and transfers $.05. For information, call PCTA at 530–9911 between 7:30 A.M. and 8:00 P.M. After 6:30 P.M., PCTA buses operate only on a Dial-a-Bus schedule, Monday through Saturday only. No night service—except by reservation—is available on weekends or holidays. Reservations for night service must be made at least one hour in advance of desired pickup time. For information, call PCTA at 530–9911 between 7:30 A.M. and 8:45 P.M.

By car. There are more than 100 local and national car rental firms operating on the west coast of Florida. Quite a choice. Rates vary with the season and with the day and even with the tides, it seems. Many of the major rental agencies operating in this area have toll-free information and reservation numbers, including *Ajax* 800–421–0896; *Alamo,* 800–327–9633; *Avis,* 800–331–1212; *Budget,* 800–527–0700; *Dollar,* 800–421–6868; *Enterprise,* 800–325–8007; *Greyhound,* 800–432–1060; *Hertz,* 800–654–3131; *National,* 800–328–4567; *Payless,* 800–282–4682; and *Thrifty,* 800–331–4200.

Rush hour is traditional—7:00 A.M. to 9:00 A.M. weekday mornings, 4:00 to 6:00 P.M. weekday afternoons. St. Petersburg is a major bedroom community for Tampa's more industrial character, and the three main bridges over Tampa Bay linking the two cities—Howard Franklin, Courtney Campbell, and Gandy—are almost always heavily traveled and require concentrated driving. Interstate 275, on the other hand, offers a clean dissection of St. Petersburg and is usually quick, although some exit ramps do back up during rush hour. US 19—a north-south artery for Pinellas County—is to be avoided whenever possible.

By taxi. More than 100 major taxi companies, as well as smaller companies, service the Tampa Bay area. In addition, just about every community has its own taxi company. Rates vary according to the size of the community, but remain competitive in the larger areas. In Tampa, rates average $1.10 the minute you get into the cab and $1 a mile thereafter. That's fairly standard in St. Petersburg as well, although Yellow Cab in St. Petersburg starts at $1.70 for the first mile. In the Tampa Bay area, some cab companies to keep in mind: *Bay*

City Cab, St. Petersburg, 397–0949; *Beach Seminole Yellow Cab,* St. Petersburg, 393–9766; *Clearwater Yellow Cab,* Clearwater, 442–0464; *Dart Handicapped Transportation* (for those in wheelchairs), St. Petersburg, 895–5571; *United Cab,* Tampa, 932–5477; *Yellow Cab,* St. Petersburg, 821–7777; *Yellow Cab,* Tampa, 253–0121.

By trolley. In Tampa. A free trolley operates from parking lots on the fringe of the downtown area to the core of the city. These *Free Bee Trolleys* run two at a time, on a 20-minute round trip, 6:30 A.M. to 6:00 P.M., Monday through Friday. For more information call 254–4278.

TOURIST INFORMATION. For information on the Suncoast of Florida, also known as the Tampa Bay area and encompassing Tampa, St. Petersburg, Clearwater, Largo, and the beach communities sandwiched between St. Petersburg and the Gulf of Mexico, there are three sources. The first is just off I–275, the Ulmerton Road exit, just east of the Showboat Dinner Theatre. The *Suncoast Welcome Center* is open from 9:00 A.M. to 5:00 P.M. seven days a week, and the staff is well-armed with brochures, literature, and answers about all corners of the area. There is also a restroom at the Center. For information, call 813–576–1449. There are two other information centers operated by the *St. Petersburg Area Chamber of Commerce.* One is in the lobby of The Pier, the upside-down triangle-shaped building that juts out into Tampa Bay. It is staffed from 10:00 A.M. to 4:00 P.M. seven days a week and has info on St. Petersburg and the surrounding communities. Finally, the downtown chamber office, Fourth Street North and Third Avenue, is open from 9:00 A.M. to 5:00 P.M. Monday through Friday and has information on tourist attractions, hotels, motels, restaurants, service clubs, and activities of all kinds. Phone 821–4069 or 821–4715.

SEASONAL EVENTS. Festivals, parades, sporting events celebrate the history, the cultures, and the talents of the Southwest coast.

TAMPA

February. *Florida State Fair.* The nation's largest winter exposition, the fair includes free top-name entertainers, grandstand shows, an array of top livestock exhibitions, and a noisy midway of games, rides, and shows. *The Gasparilla Invasion and Parade.* Everybody dresses up in pirate costumes, "invades" downtown Tampa, and in general gets crazy. A tourist-oriented celebration of a once-upon-a-time invasion of Tampa by a mythical José Gaspar. **March.** Still part of the Gasparilla celebration, the *Gasparilla Sidewalk Festival* features a cross-section of artists and craftsmen displaying their wit and wares along the Hillsborough River. One of the nation's most spectacular equestrian events, the *Anheuser-Busch American Invitational Grand Prix,* is held in Tampa Stadium. Several dozen riders from all over the world compete in a world-class jumping test for horse and rider. **July.** In Riverview Park—the river is the Alafia and the view is great—Tampa holds an annual *Bluegrass Festival.* There's continuous bluegrass pickin' and singin' by both professional artists and well-known local groups, plus camping, canoeing, and workshops. **October.** Tampa's Latin Quarter, Ybor City, has a *Latin Festival on Broadway* with all the music, food, dancing, and atmosphere of an old world celebration.

ST. PETERSBURG/CLEARWATER AREA

January. The religious and the tourist blend together with the January 6 *Epiphany Celebration* in Tarpon Springs, north of St. Petersburg. The Orthodox Greek Community and the town's sponging industry offer thanks to the sea with a ritual cross-throwing to be recovered by one of the town's young men who gets good luck for a year. **January or February.** One of the most beautiful sailing races in the world, the annual *Southern Ocean Racing Conference,* brings together big boats, brawny sailors, and some stunning sailing that starts off the St. Petersburg Pier. **February.** SPIFFS—alias the *St. Petersburg International Folk Fair Society*—holds an *international gala* at the Bayfront Center in St. Petersburg. More than 40 ethnic groups offer up samples of their food, costumes, and entertainment in a two-day festival. **March.** Clearwater's big celebration of the year is its *Fun 'n Sun Festival,* with activities for young and old, highlighted by an illuminated night parade that climaxes the 10-day fest. St. Petersburg offers one of the oldest festivals around—with roots back to 1896—in its annual *Festival of States* celebration. It's a salute to springtime and there are band competitions and no less than three parades. Dunedin, a small community in north Pinellas County well-locked in Scottish tradition, holds its *Highland Games* each year with lots of Scottish revelry and rivalry, bagpipe skirling, kilted bands, boat regattas, and Highland games of skill. The biggest art show of the year for St. Petersburg is its *Mainsail Art Show* in Straub Park, on the downtown waterfront. The show attracts more than 150 artists from all over the country to compete for prizes and tourist purchases. Largo, not to be forgotten, also has a festival this time of year—a *Renaissance Festival*—with every weekend in the month filled with jousts, crafts, music, games, food, and drink all done in Medieval costumes and atmosphere. **March or April.** *Easter Sunrise Service.* A special sort of observance is held at Tiki Gardens, a small attraction and restaurant at Indian Shores. The 12-acre garden of lush tropical foliage is the site for a service that draws hundreds of residents and visitors each year. **April.** Largo reprises a few days later with something that is the complete opposite of anything Renaissance—a *Florida Cracker Supper.* Area residents come in bib and overalls for a country-style food party with lots of entertainment and southern fried chicken. Out in the Gulf of Mexico, the tarpon are the target during the annual *Tarpon Roundup.* This major fishing expedition offers the potential for big fish and big prize money, and the competition is fierce. **June.** Treasure Island, one of the beach communities along Pinellas County's Gulf-front, turns pirate sanctuary each year during its *Pirate Days.* There's the usual mock pirate invasion as well as great seafood, fireworks, and assorted contests. **September or October.** A Grand Prix auto race loops through downtown St. Petersburg for four days of high-powered cars and squealing tires. **October.** At Largo's Heritage Park, a collection of restored period houses, the *Country Jubilee* allows folks to travel back in time to an old-time country fair, complete with checker tournaments, horseshoe throwing, sack races, potato relays, and a mixture of bluegrass music, clogging, blacksmithing, sugar grinding, and more. **November.** At the start of the winter season, Madeira Beach, another community along the Gulfcoast, holds its annual *John's Pass Seafood Festival.* The food is hot and bountiful, and there are fireworks, free fish chowder, and so on. The whole thing is kicked off with a blessing of the fishing fleet that uses John's Pass as home base. **December.** The annual *Santa Parade* brings out Saint Nick and thousands of youngsters, plus more than 25 of Florida's best bands, who march in a parade of more than 100 units. What would Christmas on the Gulf of Mexico be without a *boatacade?* Madeira Beach has one—a night parade of colorfully lit boats cruising in a line in and out of the fingers and inlets.

BRADENTON/SARASOTA

March. On the grounds of the Ringling Museum of Art in Sarasota is a weekend of music, sporting events, and plays from the Medieval Age. The *Medieval Fair* features a live chess match—with live players substituting for the chess pieces. Bradenton celebrates the *landing of Hernando DeSoto*—even though no one knows for sure if he really did land anywhere near Bradenton—in a week-long binge of pageants, parades, costumed Indians, and Conquistadores. **November.** The weekend before Thanksgiving brings some of the finest artists and craftsmen in the world to the Ringling Museum grounds in Sarasota for the juried *Ringling Museums Crafts Festival.* More than 160 exhibitors display fiber, clay, leather, wood, metal, and glass works; the three-day festival draws more than 20,000 people.

FT. MYERS/MARCO ISLAND

September. The *Summerset Regatta* over Labor Day draws more than 70 boats to the Ft. Myers area, with the race culminating at Marco Island, the beach resort off the coast. It's a great occasion for photographers, sailors, and spectators.

SANIBEL ISLAND

March. The first weekend of the month is the occasion for a four-day *Sanibel Shell Fair* and celebration of the island's founding. Sanibel is one of the best shelling spots in Florida and more than 10,000 tourists show up for the weekend each year. **April.** Running through June is the *Island Open Fishing Derby,* with several grand prizes for the heaviest snook, redfish, sea trout, and cobia. Though the event is scheduled for the off-season rates, there's usually quite a crowd. Early reservations are suggested.

TOURS. Several guided tours are available in Tampa. *Around the Town Guided Tours,* 14009 N. Dale Mabry, 961–4120, takes groups of all sizes on customized tours —even groups of one or two. One of the most requested tours is the Historic Tour: through Ybor City, downtown Tampa, the residential areas, universities, museums, Port of Tampa and Davis Islands. Other tours venture to St. Petersburg, Tarpon Springs, Clearwater, Sarasota, and points in between, including all major attractions, dog races, theaters. Reservations are suggested a month in advance. *Gray Line Sightseeing Tours,* 921 3rd St. S., St. Petersburg, 822–3577 in St. Petersburg, 273–0845 in Tampa, has a variety of tours available throughout the area. *Lindo's Tours U.S.A. Inc.,* 4912 Spruce St., Tampa, and 1886 U.S. 19 South, Clearwater, 800–282–0129 or 531–8923, specializes in Florida tours as well, in and out of the west coast area. *Travel Is Fun, One Day Motor Coach Tours,* 157 3rd St. N., St. Petersburg, offers full day tours to sights and attractions in the area. Call ahead, 821–9479, for scheduled tours and prices.

By boat. Nearly a dozen different charter boat companies offer tours of short and long duration in the area. The *Spirit of Tampa Bay,* docked at the Brorein Street Bridge near Ashley Street, **Tampa,** 273–9485, offers a choice of lunch and dinner cruises including a 5:30 to 7:30 P.M. happy hour trip for $3 per person (plus drinks, of course). The *Island Adventure Excursion Boat,* Ashley St., Tampa, 251–8008, is the area's new 300-passenger, two-deck "Cabaret Fun Ship" that cruises Hillsborough River and Tampa Bay daily except Mondays. There's lunch or dinner or dancing or all three. There's even an all-day excursion to the St. Petersburg Pier across the bay. *All Seasons Yacht Charters,* 2814 Humphrey St., Tampa, 935–5676, offers a 44-foot sailing yacht for planned or spontaneous trips anywhere along the west coast of Florida. Sightseeing combined with dinner-dance are available from *Captain Anderson,* docked behind the Dolphin Village Shopping Center, **St. Petersburg Beach,** 360–2619, and from *Captain Anderson II,* **Clearwater Beach Marina,** 462–2628. *Island Adventure,* Bradenton Dock, downtown **Bradenton,** 748–7456 or 251–8008, is a 300-passenger boat that tours Manatee River and Tampa Bay every Tuesday, Wednesday, and Thursday, leaving at 10:00 A.M. and returning at 5:00 P.M. In **Ft. Myers,** the *Everglades Jungle Cruise* offers nine different cruises aboard a 600-passenger motor veseel. Choices include one and two-day Lake Okeechobee cruises and a four-hour buffet cruise, Fridays only, that sails at 11 A.M. and costs $14 for adults, $6 for children. Call 334–2743 for reservations. Private charters are available from Sanibel and Captiva Islands for short or long jaunts into nearby waters, including Cabbage Key. Try Capt. Mike Fuery, at the Tween Waters Inn, 472–5161. And in **Everglades City,** *Florida Boat Tours,* 695–3762, offers a cruise to many of the 10,000 islands that make up Florida's Gulf coast in that area. The *Fun Hunter* leaves at 10:00 A.M. every morning and roughly 90 minutes thereafter.

By air. *Suncoast Helicopters Inc.,* at **Tampa** International Airport, 872–6625, has five helicopters to choose from to service any sightseers wanting a whirlybird's eye view. Reservations are suggested a week in advance. *Topp of Tampa Airport,* 6901 State Road 54, Tampa (973–0056) and *West Florida Helicopters,* Albert Whitted Airport, **St. Petersburg,** 823–5200, also offer tours of the Tampa Bay area and the west coast of Florida.

By foot. Two walking tours are available in the Tampa Bay area. A *Clearwater Historical Walking Tour* is offered by the Beautification Council of the Greater **Clearwater** Chamber of Commerce. And a walking tour of downtown **St. Petersburg,** including points along the waterfront, is also available. Guides are available from the St. Petersburg Area Chamber of Commerce; 821–4069 or 821–4715.

PARKS. Around Tampa: *Hillsborough River State Park,* six miles south of Zephyrhills, with its entrance off US 301, is a park more fitting the interior part of the state than a coastal region. The river makes the park come alive, with its cool, lush greenery lining both banks and a running river of water that is as refreshing as it looks—although parts of the river aren't recommended for drinking. There's camping, picnicking, fishing, canoeing, hiking, and biking. For information call 986–1020. *Lowery Park,* on the corner of North Boulevard and Slight Avenue in Tampa, is a park offering a fun day for the whole family, especially the children. It holds the only traditional zoo on the west coast of Florida, as well as fairyland creatures to play among. Open during daylight hours; for information call 933–3386. *Riverfront Park,* 900 North Blvd., Tampa, offers beautifully landscaped walkways on the banks of the Hillsborough River. There are also courts for tennis, racquetball, handball, shuffleboard, and a theater-in-the-round. Open dawn to dusk; 251–3742.

Around St. Pete: *Caladesi Island State Park,* off Dunedin, in northern Pinellas County. It's only accessible by boat, a ferry running daily from the Dunedin Marina; call 443–5903. Caladesi Island itself is one of the few unspoiled and undeveloped islands left along this part of Florida's coast. No camping of any type is allowed here. *Fort De Soto Park,* located off the Pinellas Bayway (extension of 54th Avenue S.), St. Petersburg, has acres and acres of undisturbed areas for walking, resting, hiking, camping, eating, sunning, whatever. The Spanish-American War ended before the fort on Mullet Key was finished, but the cannons are still menacing. Great fishing as well. For information call 866–2484. *Phillipe Park,* 2355 Bayshore Dr., Safety Harbor, is where the very first grapefruit tree in Pinellas County was planted in the 1800s by Count Odet Phillipe, an early settler. The Park, the county's oldest, also holds an old Indian mound. Call 726–2700.

Around Ft. Myers: *Cayo Costa State Preserve,* on Pine Island Sound near Charlotte Harbor, just north of Captiva, is one of the largest undeveloped barrier islands remaining in Florida. The area looks much as it did 500 years ago when the Spaniards arrived looking for gold. *Collier-Seminole State Park,* on US 41 just east of State Road 92 junction, features an 1,100-foot nature trail and the Blackwater River. It also has a tropical hammock dominated by trees characteristic of coastal forests of the West Indies and Yucatan, and an extensive mangrove swamp fills the rest of the space.

THEME PARKS. Tampa: *Busch Gardens,* 3000 E. Busch Blvd., Tampa. The second most popular theme park in the state—after Walt Disney World—Busch Gardens is also known as "The Dark Continent." The African theme is carried throughout, and the animals are spectacular. They are allowed, for the most part, to run wild in a manmade "veldt." Also to see: a Moroccan village, an orangutan and bird show, flume rides, African Bazaar, Timbuktu theme area, lots of rides, craftsmen, and, most spectacular of all, a breeding colony of rare white Bengal tigers. Rides include the Python, the Scorpion roller coaster, and the Congo River Rapids (a white water raft adventure). There are also petting zoos, exhibits for children, and shows for youngsters as well in the Stanleyville Amphitheatre, daily at noon, 2:00 and 4:00 P.M. Open-truck tours for photographers wanting to snap pictures of the Serengetti Plain leave the World of Wildlife gate 10 A.M. Saturday—providing reservations have been made in advance; call 988–5171, ext. 252; fee, $30 per person. Garden hours are 9:30 A.M. to 6 P.M. daily. Admission charged. There are plenty of special prices and packages throughout the year. Special rates for groups, senior citizens, and others. For information, call 971–8282. Also part of Busch Gardens, a few blocks east, is *Adventure Island,* offering pools, slides, picnic area, snack bar, and more. Generally open weekends in the spring and fall, daily April through September. Admission charged. For information, call 971–8282.

ZOOS. Tampa: There is only one traditional zoo in the entire seven-county area. Fortunately, *Lowry Park* is undergoing much-needed renovation. The animals seem grateful, too. Located at 7525 North Blvd., the zoo does offer 15 acres of animals surrounded by the 105-acre park. Animals currently on hand include monkeys, lions, tigers, an elephant, alligators, birds, and others. Open 10:00 A.M. to dark every day. And it's free. For information: 813–933–3386.

Naples: *African Safari Park,* US 41 and Fleischmann Boulevard. A chance to see animal acts and animals acting natural in the wild. There are rides, trails, and tours. Circus Africa features a small animal show at 11:30 A.M., 2:00 P.M., and 4:00 P.M. daily. Snack bar, gift shop, and 70 acres of jungle. Open 9:30 A.M.

to 5:00 P.M. daily. Admission charged. For information: 262–4053. (See also *Busch Gardens,* listed above under "Theme Parks.")

BEACHES. There are beaches everywhere you look in Florida. As a peninsula surrounded on three sides by water, Pinellas County boasts the most beaches of all. There are 28 miles of soft white sand along the Gulf of Mexico on Pinellas County's beachfront, and 128 miles of shoreline. Virtually all of it is public. With an average of 361 days of sun a year and an average temperature of 71 degrees, the area's beaches are a favorite gathering spot year-round.

While **Tampa** itself doesn't offer a great variety of beaches, heading southwest from the city, the first major beach area is the *Ben T. Davis Municipal Beach* off the Courtney Campbell Parkway (one of the three bridges connecting Tampa with St. Petersburg), between Tampa and Clearwater. It pales next to St. Petersburg and Clearwater beaches, however; the water tends to be as muddy-looking as the sand.

Caladesi Island, off northern **Pinellas County,** has free parking for passengers taking the hourly ferry over. There are bathrooms, showers, concession stands, and lifeguards. Call 443–5842 for ferry reservations. *Clearwater Beach,* off northern Pinellas County, has metered beach parking and lots of beach. Very popular with young people, who come to watch and be watched. Arrive before 11:00 A.M. or plan to hunt a while for a parking space. *Fort De Soto Park,* off northern Pinellas County, is another favorite, despite the $.65 toll required to get there. Plenty of space, with Australian pines, campgrounds, picnic tables and a great and eerie view of the missing center span of the Sunshine Skyway Bridge (which was struck by a phosphate freighter, killing 35 people in 1980). Another beach to consider: *Honeymoon Island* off Dunedin Beach, again off the northern edge of Pinellas County. But don't walk barefoot; there are lots of stones and shells. Young people also like *Pass-a-Grille Beach* on St. Petersburg Beach, with metered parking, concession stands, and some notable rock 'n roll bars nearby.

Danger area for waders and swimmers is *Johns Pass,* a cut in the barrier islands of Pinellas County made by a 1926 hurricane. Johns Pass is the border between *Treasure Island* and *Madeira Beach,* and both beach communities offer good, free beaches. But the pass itself is deadly and claims lives every year.

Bradenton/Sarasota: *Lido Beach* off Sarasota's coast has free parking, an unheated pool ($1 for adults, $.50 for children), and good shelling as well.

Around Ft. Myers: The best shelling of all is along the white beaches of *Sanibel* and *Captiva Islands,* a thin string of islands off the Ft. Myers coast. Shell collectors come from around the world to walk the beaches here, heads bent, often using flashlights at evening low tides to make a find.

PARTICIPANT SPORTS. There are more sports opportunities for the active visitor than you can do in a lifetime—several lifetimes. Because the area offers more than 361 days a year of sunshine and an average year-round temperature of 71 degrees, the great outdoors is always full of people.

A number of sporting goods stores offer rentals for the transient athlete. Most notable is *Bill Jackson's* in St. Petersburg (576–4169), where you can rent just about any kind of sporting equipment—*except* stuff for "ball sports" (racquetball, tennis, and so on). Bill Jackson's also has training classes for **diving, mountain climbing,** and **skiing.** Need gear for **fishing, camping, hiking?** Bill Jackson's. The Yellow Pages list numerous places that can set you up for your favorite sport.

Biking. There are no municipal bike paths along the west coast of Florida. Several parks do offer smaller bike paths for visitors. It's best to ask when planning to visit a state park, or when arriving. For bike rentals try *Bi-Sick Call,* Tarpon Springs, 937–3030; *Chainwheel Drive,* Clearwater, 441–2444; *Cap's Cyclery,* Madeira Beach, 392–0778.

Boating. Sailing is an obvious choice. There are numerous sailing charter spots along the west coast offering small and big boats, as well as instruction for the beginner. Don't forget the passive joy of watching one of the area's frequent regattas—climaxed by the annual Southern Ocean Racing Conference in early February. Excursion boats are also available. A simple jaunt out and back for a quick look at the area from a seaman's perspective can cost as little as $4.50; add in dinner, dancing, and a bit of moonlight, and the fare can go up to $17 or more. Sailing equipment is readily available. Some places to consider in Tampa Bay area are the *Annapolis Sailing School* in St. Petersburg, 867–8102, with Rainbows or Sunfishes available; *La Gringa Sailing Services,* St. Petersburg, 822–4323, with 20- to 41-foot sailboats to rent; *Suncoast Rent a Boat,* Redington Shores, 393–3425, with 17-foot Watkins to rent. If you say you can sail, most will rent to you. The only exceptions are sailboards; many sailboard rental shops ask for some proof of skill.

Other area charter boats include: *Flamingo Sightseeing Cruises,* Clearwater Beach Marina, 461–3113; *Gourmet Yacht Charters,* 425 Chippewa St., Tampa, 253–3755; *Bay Winds Charters,* 7345 Bay St., at Corey Ave., St. Petersburg Beach, 367–2721.

Powerboat rentals are also possible. Try: *Suncoast Boat Rentals,* St. Petersburg Beach, 360–1822, or *Budget Boat Rentals,* Madeira Beach, 397–6400.

Canoes—for those who like to go slow and at their own power—are plentiful. *Art's Swap Shop* in Tampa, 935–4011, rents canoes and a car rack. *Canoe Outpost,* Sarasota, has wilderness canoe trips through hundreds of primitive rivers all over Florida. Address: Rte. 2, Box 330J, Sarasota 33582; 800–342–8570.

Fishing is an obvious sport option. No license is needed for saltwater fishing. All you need is a hook, a line, and some bait. Bridge fishing is an inexpensive and easily accessible choice; for those who want to go farther out into the Gulf of Mexico, there are countless fishing boats available—for one or two people or for 30 or more. Rates run from $250 to $350 for someone who wants to fish alone to as low as $10 for a half-day on a party boat where you fish elbow-to-elbow with friends and strangers alike. Check any local newspaper or guide for a long list of boats for charter. Some are listed here: Tarpon Springs, *Dolphin Deep Sea Fishing,* 937–8257; Clearwater Beach, *Double Eagle Party Boat,* 446–1653; Madeira Beach, *Hubbard's Pass Port Marina,* 393–1947; Treasure Island, *Kingfisher Deep Sea Fishing Fleet,* 363–9800; St. Petersburg, *Isa Del Sol Marina,* 867–5907; St. Petersburg Beach, *Miss Pass-a-Grille,* 360–2082. All hotels will also have charter boat and party boat fishing information.

Or you might want to try pit fishing. Florida is known as one of the best bass-fishing states in the country, and the heart of the large-mouth bass fishing lies just a few miles north of Tampa in manmade lakes created by the state's phosphate industry. Six of these former phosphate mines have been stocked and are now open for fishing. For more information, contact the Tampa City News Bureau, 228–7777.

Fishing equipment is available for rent from numerous bait and tackle shops. If you sign up for a half-day, all-day, or overnight party boat (that means fishing with a gang of strangers), gear is also available.

Golf. There are golf courses galore in this part of Florida. Remember: Sarasota was the site of the country's first golf course early in the century and has more than a score of courses today. Public golf courses include: *Apollo Beach Club,* Tampa, 645–6212; *Babe Zaharias Golf Course,* Tampa, 932–4401; *Rocky Point Golf Course,* Tampa, 884–5141; *Clearwater Golf Park,* Clearwater, 447–5272; *Dunedin Country Club,* Dunedin, 733–7836; *Pasadena Golf Club,* St. Petersburg, 345–9329. Many golf shops near the courses will rent equipment. Also check phone directories and local chambers of commerce for golf course listings.

Rollerskates more your speed? There are rinks in Tarpon Springs—the *Astro Skate Roller Rink,* 875 Cypress, 934–8951; in St Petersburg—*Gould's Roller Rink,* 2191 9th Ave. N. 576–7108, and *Radiant Rollers* on Davis Island in Tampa, 251–0003, which every Friday and Saturday night beginning at 9:00 P.M. sponsors a 10-mile, 4½-hour skating party that stops conveniently at local watering holes.

Tennis. Many city municipal parks offer tennis courts—often with lighting for night play—and such information is available from any city parks department. It's best to call and come early, however; Florida tennis is a very popular pastime.

In the Tampa Bay area, some public tennis courts can be found at such places as: *Davis Island Tennis Center,* Tampa, 253–3997; *Riverfront Park,* Tampa, 251–3742; *Tennis Center of St. Petersburg,* 894–4378; Northwest Park, *St. Petersburg,* 893–7751.

SPECTATOR SPORTS: The Tampa Bay area offers a rich mixture of professional and collegiate sports as well as several choices of competitions accompanied by pari-mutuel wagering.

Baseball abounds in this part of Florida. The Grapefruit League means winter baseball with 10 major league teams offering exhibition games in March and early April throughout the area. For information on all the teams call 904–488–0990. Home bases for 7 of the 10 teams are in the Tampa Bay area are: Bradenton, *Pittsburgh Pirates,* McKechnie Field, 9th St. W. and 16th Ave., 748–4610; Clearwater, *Philadelphia Phillies,* Jack Russell Stadium, Seminole and Greenwood Ave., 462–6134; Dunedin, *Toronto Blue Jays,* Grant Field, 311 Douglas Ave., North of State Road 88, 733–4151, ext. 203; St. Petersburg, the *New York Mets* and the *St. Louis Cardinals,* Al Lang Stadium, 1st St. and 2nd Ave., 893–7490; Sarasota, *Chicago White Sox,* Payne Park, US 301 and Ringling Blvd, 953–3388; Tampa, *Cincinnati Reds,* Al Lopez Field, Dale Mabry and Tampa Bay Blvd.; 872–7977. Professional baseball also is offered by the Florida State League, with the *Tampa Tarpons,* a minor league team, calling Al Lopez Field (next to Tampa Stadium) home from April until August.

For pro **football** fans, there are two teams, and nearly year-round football, with the *Tampa Bay Buccaneers* of the National Football League and the *Tampa Bay Bandits* of the U.S. Football League, both using Tampa Stadium, 4201 N. Dale Mabry Hwy. For Bucs information, call 870–2700; for Bandits information, call 875–2059. Professional **soccer** is represented by the *Tampa Bay Rowdies* (877–7800), who play their indoor games at the Bayfront Center, 400 1st St. S. in St. Petersburg, and their outdoor games at Tampa Stadium in Tampa.

Gambling. You can bet a year-round playground like the west coast of Florida offers another variety of spectator sports—horse racing, dog racing, and jai-alai, with parimutuel wagering allowed on site. **Horse racing** is at *Tampa Bay Downs,* Race Track Road off State Road 580, Oldsmar, 855–4401, with thoroughbred races December through March. **Dog racing** is year-round—with races January to May at *Derby Lane,* 10490 Gandy Blvd., St. Petersburg, 576–1361, September to January at *Tampa Greyhound Track,* 8300 N. Nebraska Ave., Tampa, 932–6710, and *Sarasota Kennel Club,* 5400 Bradenton Road,

Sarasota, June to September, 355–7744. **Jai-alai** is offered at the *Tampa Jai-Alai Fronton,* S. Dale Mabry and Gandy Boulevard, Tampa, January until mid-June, 831–1411. And for people who like sedate gambling, there's the one-of-a-kind **Seminole Bingo Hall,** run by the Seminole Indians. Located at 5221 Orient Road, Tampa, the hall seats 1,400 and has jackpots of $60,000 or more. For information, call 621–1302.

Professional **softball** comes from the 40-year-old team, the *Clearwater Bombers,* who play at Jack Russell Stadium, Seminole and Greenwood Avenue, 462–6134, in Clearwater, April until September. The famous *Kids 'n Kubs* are proof you're never too old to do what you love to do; the Three-Quarters Century Softball League consists of players who are at least 75 years old. They play exhibition games each winter at North Shore Park in St. Petersburg. For information call 893–7298 or 893–7111.

Stock car racing is available March through October at Sunshine Speedway, 4550 State Rd. 688, St. Petersburg, 577–4598.

HISTORIC SITES AND HOUSES. Tampa: *Ybor City,* in north Tampa, has history as well as ethnic charm. Not only does it hold many of Tampa's finest and most popular Spanish restaurants, but it was through funds raised in Ybor City in the 1890s that José Marti lead the successful invasion to free Cuba from the Spanish, an act that culminated in the Spanish-American War. Ybor City is also the home for the cigar industry, begun when cigar makers migrated from Havana to Key West and then to Ybor City in 1885.

St. Petersburg Area: *Heritage Park,* 11909 125th St., Largo, east of the junction of State Road 688 and State Road 694 (Walsingham Road). Here you can stroll through Pinellas County's pioneer days and walk in and amid a collection of old buildings. There's Seven Gables, a 13-room home built in 1907 that reflects northern architecture standards; The Plant-Sumner House, built by Henry Plant in 1896 for the construction foreman of a hotel he was building in Pinellas County; and the McMullen-Coachman loghouse, dated around the 1850s, the oldest building in Pinellas County. Open 10:00 A.M. to 4:00 P.M., Tuesday through Sunday. Free. Guided tours available.

Bradenton Area: *Gamble Plantation,* US 301, Ellenton. Go south across the Sunshine Skyway Bridge to US 41, continue south on US 41 to the intersection with US 301, then north on US 301 to Ellenton, about 30 miles from St. Petersburg. Built in the early 1840s, the plantation home served as a refuge for Judah P. Benjamin, Confederate Secretary of State during the Civil War. Antebellum and Civil War period furnishings. Tours daily on the hour. Open 9:00 A.M. to 11:00 A.M., 1:00 to 4:00 P.M. Admission.

MUSEUMS. Tampa: *Museum of Science and Industry,* 4801 E. Fowler Ave. Clearly one of the most innovative museums in the Southeast. It's fun! There are exhibits that focus on hands-on exhibits dealing with weather, physical science, botany, and related sciences. The most popular exhibit is the Gulf Coast Hurricane, a wind tunnel that creates 75 M.P.H. winds that you lean into while your hair blows asunder. Also popular is Dr. Thunder's Magic Boom Room, which simulates a Florida thunderstorm. And, as you might expect, there's even a complete working weather station. Open 10:00 A.M. to 4:30 P.M. seven days a week. Admission: $2 adults; $1 children up to age 15; children under 5, free. For information, call 985–5531.

The *Tampa Museum,* 601 Doyle Carlton Dr., in downtown Tampa, behind the easy-to-spot Curtis Hixon Convention Center, is the city's major museum.

It's young but holds an impressive permanent collection of sculpture, ancient artifacts, and nineteenth-century oil paintings. The central gallery houses permanent works, while three additional galleries hold a variety of touring exhibits. The museum has a strong "hands-on" exhibition program for children. The gift shop has inexpensive *objets d'art* relating to current shows, Oriental kites, books, posters, etc. Open 10:00 A.M. to 6:00 P.M. Tuesday, Thursday, and Friday; 10:00 A.M. to 9:00 P.M. Wednesday; 9:00 A.M. to 5:00 P.M. Saturday; 1:00 to 5:00 P.M. Sunday. There is no admission charge. Call 223–8130 for more information.

St. Petersburg/Clearwater Area: *Haas Historical Museum,* 3511 2nd Ave. S., St. Petersburg. The museum actually is a series of houses and buildings, including the Grace S. Turner House and the Lowe House (built in 1850), as well as a historical and preserved railroad station, blacksmith shop, a real eagle's nest (sans eagle), treehouse and more. Open 1:00 to 5:00 P.M. daily except Monday. Admission: $1 adults, $.25 children 12 and under. For more information, call 894–1052.

HMS Bounty Exhibit, 345 2nd Ave. N.E., St. Petersburg, on the approach to The Pier. Owned by MGM—the movie people—this reduced-size but exact replica of the famous 18th-Century *Bounty* bobs at anchor. Used for the film *Mutiny on the Bounty* (as well as a more recent film starring the gang from Monty Python, *Yellowbeard*). Open 9:00 A.M. to 10:00 P.M. daily. Admission. 896–3117. There is a possibility that this will be moved to Miami.

Inness Paintings, at the Universalist Church, 57 Read St., Tarpon Springs. The largest single collection of works by George Inness, Jr., the landscape artist of the 1900s, whose most notable works were done in Tarpon Springs. Open 2:00 to 5:00 P.M. Tuesday through Sunday, October through May. Free, but $1 donation requested. 937–4682.

London Wax Museum, 5505 Gulf Blvd., St. Petersburg Beach. About 10 miles from downtown St. Petersburg, this museum holds more than 100 life-size figures patterned after Madame Tussaud's in London, including Disney characters and a Chamber of Horrors. Winter hours: 9:00 A.M. to 9:00 P.M. Monday through Saturday; noon to 8:00 P.M. Sunday; spring and summer hours: 9:00 A.M. to 11:00 P.M. Monday through Saturday; noon to 11:00 P.M. Sunday. Admission. For information, call 360–6985.

The *Museum of Fine Arts,* 255 Beach Dr. N.E. Small but special, with its Mediterranean-style villa as home for a growing permanent collection, the museum continues to bring in notable traveling exhibitions as well as rotating examples from its own vaults. There is a special emphasis on the French Impressionists, including works by Monet, Renoir, and others. There is also a growing collection of black-and-white photographs, pre-Colombian art, and other specialties. Each gallery represents a different style of art or period, and is decorated accordingly. The gift shop offers replicas of works of art on display plus the usual mix of posters, art books, and trinkets. There is a small and respected art library, accessible by permission; call 896–2667. Open 10:00 A.M. to 5:00 P.M. Tuesday through Saturday, 1:00 to 5:00 P.M., Sunday. Free.

Pinellas County Historical Museum, Heritage Park, 11909 125th St. N. at Walsingham Rd., Largo. Restored historic homes, with attendants in costume, craftsmen from the period, refreshments, and a modern museum of artifacts. Also a small gift shop. Open 10:00 A.M. to 4:00 P.M. Tuesday through Saturday; closed Sunday and Monday. Free.

Salvador Dali Museum, 1000 Third St. S., St. Petersburg. Truly a must-see museum for any Florida visit—the world's largest collection of works by the Spanish master, including 93 oils, 200 watercolors, and 1,000 graphics and three-dimensional objects. Valued at more than $35-million, the collection is a surrealistic tour through a one-room gallery that gives visitors ample room to view the large Dali works from every angle. The gift shop sells Dali memorabilia. Open 10:00 A.M. to 5:00 P.M. Tuesday through Saturday; 1:00 to 5:00 P.M. Sunday. Admission: $3 adults, $2 senior citizens, $1 students. For more information, call 823–3767.

Spongeorama, Dodecanese Boulevard, the Sponge Docks, Tarpon Springs. The Greeks originated the art of sponge diving and settled in Tarpon Springs, where the natural sponges in the surrounding waters provided income from diving and tourists. Life-size scenes and animated displays of sponge diving. Open daily. Free. For information, call 937–4111.

Bradenton/Sarasota Area: *Ringling Museum of Art,* 5401 Bayshore Blvd., Sarasota. The museum complex includes the *Ringling Museum of the Circus* and the *John and Mable Ringling Home.* One of the country's most extensive collections of baroque art, including a vast permanent collection of Flemish, Dutch, and contemporary paintings and sculptures, all on 68 acres of grounds. Open 9:00 A.M. to 7:00 P.M. Monday through Friday; 9:00 A.M. to 5:00 P.M. Saturday; 11:00 A.M. to 6:00 P.M. Sunday. Admission: $4.50 adults, $1.75 children under 12; free on Saturday. For information, call 355–5101.

South Florida Museum and Bishop Planetarium, 201 10th St. West, Bradenton. The permanent collection includes exhibits on archaeology, astronomy, anatomy, ornithology, ethnology, paleontology, geology, and more. There are also Indian artifacts, coin collections, costumes, and more. There are daily planetarium shows, and special astronomy classes are available. Open 10:00 A.M. to 5:00 P.M. Tuesday through Friday; 1:00 to 5:00 P.M. Saturday and Sunday. Planetarium shows at 3:00 P.M. Tuesday through Sunday; 7:30 P.M. Friday and Saturday. Admission. For information, call 746–4132.

Ft. Myers/Venice/Naples Area: *Edison Home Museum,* 2350 McGregor Blvd., Ft. Myers. A great way to spend an afternoon, puttering around Thomas Edison's very eccentric and wonderful home and workshop. There's an extensive array of Edison artifacts, including many of his inventions in their earliest form. Open 9:00 A.M. to 4:00 P.M. Monday through Saturday, 12:30 to 4:30 P.M. Sunday. Admission: $2 adults, $1 students. For information, call 334–3614.

MUSIC. One of the finest orchestras in the Southeast, recently renaming itself the *Florida Orchestra* (formerly the Florida Gulf Coast Symphony), performs a concert series throughout the Tampa Bay area each fall and winter, October through May, ten programs in all. The 88-piece orchestra, under the baton of Irwin Hoffman, plays in Clearwater's Ruth Eckerd Hall, (1111 McMullen-Booth Rd.) Tampa's McKay Auditorium (on the University of Tampa campus), and St. Petersburg's Bayfront Center (400 1st St. S.). The orchestra covers music from the baroque period through the twentieth century. It also performs numerous outdoor pops concerts and has an extensive music-in-the-schools program. For details, call 887–1013 in Tampa or 823–1870 in St. Petersburg.

Tampa Bay Chamber Orchestra came to be in 1983. The 35-member ensemble offers a series of concerts in Tampa, St. Petersburg, Clearwater, Dunedin, and Largo. The group performs works specifically written for small orchestras, and only during the Florida Orchestra's off-season. For information, call 677–0817.

Tampa Oratorio Society performs free concerts with programs consisting mostly of masses and oratorios. Performances are during the fall, winter, and spring, throughout the Tampa area. For information, call 886–1553.

Florida Opera West gives its performances at the Bayfront Center in St. Petersburg and at Clearwater's Ruth Eckerd Hall. The company produces major operatic efforts, fully staged, with soloists imported from other leading companies in the U.S. and Europe. For information, call 381–2151.

STAGE. The *Asolo State Theater* in Sarasota is the area's sole professional company—and one with a national reputation for excellence on stage. Performances by the state-supported regional theater are in an intimate setting (seating is under 300) imported from Asolo, Italy, and reconstructed on the Ringling Museum grounds. From December through July, the theater presents plays in rotating repertory. For information, call 355–2771.

Professional theater also comes to the west coast in the form of touring road companies. There are a number of municipal auditoriums that can book the touring companies. The road companies usually come in the fall and winter. Watch newspaper ads and announcements for shows at these municipal centers: Bayfront Center, 400 1st St. S., St. Petersburg, 893–7211; Ruth Eckerd Hall, 1111 McMullen-Booth Rd., Clearwater, 725–5573; and Van Wezel Performing Arts Hall, 777 N. Tamiami Trail, Sarasota, 953–3366.

Dinner theaters are also a popular feature on the west coast of Florida. There are four to check out: *Showboat Dinner Theatre,* 3405 Ulmerton Rd., north of St. Petersburg, featuring name performers in Equity comedies and musicals, 576–3818; *Country Dinner Playhouse,* Gateway Mall, 7951 9th St. N., St. Petersburg, another Equity house featuring musicals and comedies, 577–5515; *Golden Apple Dinner Theatre,* 1850 Central Ave., St. Petersburg, also Equity, also musicals and comedies, 821–6676; and its sister theater, Golden Apple Dinner Theatre, 25 N. Pineapple, Sarasota, 366–5454; *Naples Dinner Theatre,* 1025 Piper Blvd., Naples, featuring musicals and comedies, with guest artists, 597–6031.

ART GALLERIES. Tampa: The *Artists Alliance,* 1629 Snow Ave., in Hyde Park. A small but growing public gallery featuring works by Florida artists. The gallery is willing to take chances with art and artists not normally found on display, featuring everything from neo-light installations to works in progress. Open 11:00 A.M. to 3:00 P.M. Tuesday through Friday, 7:00 to 9:00 P.M. Thursday. Free. For information, call 248–1171. *GraphicStudio,* University of South Florida, Fine Arts Building, 4202 Fowler Ave., Tampa. For information, call 974–2848. The USF graphics workshop features work by some of the country's major contemporary artists who have come here to work and display. *Quest Gallery,* 1623 7th Ave., Ybor City, Tampa. This combination studio/gallery features works primarily by Ybor City artists and those building reputations. Displays include lithographs, photography, etchings, stained glass, and other media. Open 9:00 A.M. to 6:00 P.M. Monday through Friday. Free. For more information, call 248–3654.

St. Petersburg/Clearwater Area: *Dunedin Fine Arts Cultural Center,* 1143 Michigan Blvd., Dunedin. The center offers a comprehensive view of works by regional and national artists, plus theatrical productions, classes, and children's showings. Open 9:00 A.M. to 4:30 P.M. Monday through Friday, 1:00 to 3:30 P.M. Sunday. Free. For information, call 736–6731. *Florida Gulf Coast Art Center,* 222 Ponce De Leon Blvd., Belleair (north of St. Petersburg). Ongoing exhibits plus some works in permanent collection. Works by students and staff as well, plus classes and educational tours available. Open 10:00 A.M. to 4:00 P.M. Tuesday through Saturday; 2:00 to 5:00 P.M. Sunday. Free. For information, call 584–8634.

Bradenton/Sarasota Area: *Art League of Manatee County,* 209 9th St. West, Bradenton. Changing exhibits, usually of members' works, throughout the large and numerous studios. All media represented. Open 9:00 A.M. to 4:30 P.M. Monday through Friday, 9:00 A.M. to noon Saturday, 2:00 to 4:00 P.M. Sunday. Free. For information, call 746–2862. *Sarasota Art Association,* 707 North Tamiami Trail (US 41), Sarasota. Sales gallery, library, continuous showings of juried shows, plus art demonstrations and slide lectures. Open 10:00 A.M. to 5:00 P.M., Monday through Friday, 10:00 A.M. to 5:00 P.M. Saturday, 1:00 to 4:00 P.M. Sunday. Free. For information, call 365–2032.

Ft. Myers: *Four Winds Gallery,* 1167 3rd St., S., Naples. This gallery deals almost exclusively in Southwest Indian art, jewelry, weavings, sculpture, pottery, and paintings. Open 10:00 A.M. to 5:00 P.M. Monday through Saturday. Free. For information, call 263–7555.

SHOPPING. New York hasn't come to the west coast of Florida quite yet. Some of the biggest names in retailing are absent in this part of the world; but there are shopping meccas to be explored. One of the most popular ones is *St. Armand's Circle,* just off John Ringling Boulevard in Sarasota. Here, there are more than 100 exclusive specialty shops, along with some fine restaurants, surrounding a park. Stores include *Lilly Pulitzer, Polo/Ralph Lauren, John Baldwin, Jacobson's Department Store,* as well as numerous sporting and beachwear stores. Most are open from 10:00 A.M. to 6:00 P.M. Monday through Saturday. Some shops are seasonal and are closed during the off-tourist months during the summer.

Other specialty areas can be found along Beach Drive in St. Petersburg, from Central Avenue to Fourth Street North. There are women's and men's American and European designer clothes, as well as shops catering to boating enthusiasts. A few names to look for include *Clementine's, John Baldwin, Maxine's,* the *Straw Goat.* Hours are 10:00 A.M. to 6:00 P.M. Monday through Friday. Another area with lots of shops is the *Sponge Exchange,* 735 Dodecanese Blvd., Tarpon Springs. There 45 specialty shops and three restaurants on the site of the original exchange, built in 1907 and recently torn down and replaced. Shops are open from 11:00 A.M. to 9:00 P.M. Monday through Saturday, noon to 9:00 P.M. Sunday.

Off-price outlets abound, with more opening every month. There is a *Dansk Factory Outlet* at 2790 Gulf-to-Bay Blvd., Clearwater, open 9:30 A.M. to 9:00 P.M. Monday through Saturday, 10:00 A.M. to 6:00 P.M. Sunday, and *Loehmann's Plaza,* 1730 US 19 N., St. Petersburg. Open 10:00 A.M. to 5:30 P.M. Monday, Tuesday, and Saturday; until 9:30 P.M. Wednesday, Thursday, and Friday; and noon to 5:00 P.M. Sunday. The 60-store complex offers discounted name-brand and designer merchandise, ranging from lingerie to men's and women's clothing and accessories.

Finally, for the whole family, a shopping venture to be enjoyed is one of the area's flea markets. The *Wagon Wheel Flea Market,* 7801 Park Blvd. N., Pinellas Park, just north of St. Petersburg in Pinellas County, is one of the largest in the world, open year-round on Saturday and Sundays from 8:00 A.M. to 5:00 P.M. (open every day around Christmas). There are more than 1,000 booths, most covered, and a $.50 parking fee. There's even a free trolley to commute shoppers from the parking lot to booths.

DINING OUT. In a part of the country with so much sea—Gulf, actually—there's obviously a lot of seafood (or Gulffood, if you prefer), to go with it. Eating out is perhaps the most popular tourist pastime on the west coast of Florida. In addition to the ethnic foods available—Greek food in the Tarpon Springs community in northern Pinellas County, for example, and the plentiful choices of Latin and Spanish food in Tampa—seafood is the prime choice of most restaurants along this coast. Seafood prices are reasonable and competitive at many Florida restaurants.

And with the abundance of seafood comes a casual attitude in dining out dress. At just about any restaurant along the west coast of Florida, it's possible to see a range of attire—from shorts to suits, from skirts to skimpy bathing suits. It even happens at some formal restaurants that customers can be casual while the staff are dressed to the nines.

A state sales tax of 5 percent is added to all menus. A built-in gratuity of 12 percent to 15 percent is just now beginning to become popular with restaurants in this part of Florida, due in a large part to a growing influx of foreign visitors who are used to finding the tip automatically included in the bill—and who don't always remember to tip if it's not.

The price classifications of the following restaurants, from *inexpensive* to *deluxe,* are based on the cost of an average three-course dinner for one person for food alone. Beverages, tax, and tip would be extra. *Inexpensive* is less than $5; *Moderate,* $5 to $15; *Expensive,* $15 to $25; *Deluxe,* more than $25.

Abbreviations for credit cards are: AE, American Express; CB, Carte Blanche; DC, Diners Club; MC, MasterCard; V, Visa. Most restaurants that do not accept credit cards will cash traveler's checks; few will honor personal checks, even with identification.

Abbreviations for meal codes are: B, breakfast, L, lunch; D, dinner. As restaurant hours and days of closing often change, you should call first to confirm the hours open, In most instances, reservations are wise; in tourist season, November through April, reservations are almost always a must.

TAMPA

Bern's Steak House. *Expensive.* 1208 S. Howard Ave.,; 251–2421. Specialties include aged prime beef and selections from the largest wine list in the world—more than 6,000 selections, ranging in price from less than $10 to one little chateau wine for $10,000. The place is filled with odds and ends collected by owner and chief chef Bern Lexer. Even the vegetables are special—grown in Bern's own organic farm. The finest *chateaubriand* steak this side of Paris. D, daily. All cards.

Brothers Too. *Expensive.* 1408 N. West Shore Blvd.; 879–1962. An art-deco décor in a garden setting offsets the noisy bustle of West Shore Boulevard just outside. A recent treat touted by one food critic: baked shrimp stuffed with crab, minced artichoke hearts, Greek salonika peppers, and Monterey Jack cheese. L, D, Monday through Saturday. AE, DC, MC, V.

CK's, *Expensive.* Atop the Tampa International Airport's Marriott Hotel, 879–5151, features the best nonwater view in the Tampa Bay area from its revolving restaurant. A great place to catch an early dinner or late snack before a late flight to somewhere. Entrées vary from stir-fried shrimp to red snapper. If you're lucky enough to see one of the Suncoast's famous afternoon thunderstorms roll in while visiting this high view, it's a sight you won't soon forget. L, D, daily. All cards.

Columbia. *Expensive.* 2117 E. 7th Ave., Ybor City; 248–4961. A landmark and a Spanish cuisine trademark in Tampa for decades. Chicken and rice are a specialty, and try the Columbia's 1905: the salad of ham, olive, and cheese named for the year this restaurant was founded. The building is charming and singers and dancers entertain with gusto. L, D daily. All cards.

Colonnade. *Moderate.* 3401 South Bayshore, at Julia Avenue; 839–7558. One of the most popular restaurants in town since 1935, it has an unparalleled and yet serene view of Tampa Bay, while serving good seafood in a pleasant atmosphere. Broiled steak and fried chicken as well. L, D. All cards. No reservations.

Valencia Garden. *Moderate.* 811 W. Kennedy Blvd.; 253–3773. Renovated in the past few years, the menu hasn't changed in decades: the Spanish bean soup is tops and this is one of downtown Tampa's oldest and most popular Spanish restaurants. D, daily. All cards.

ST. PETERSBURG/CLEARWATER AREA

King Charles Room. *Deluxe.* Don CeSar Beach Resort, 3400 Gulf Blvd., St. Petersburg Beach; 360–1881. Quiet elegance and fine service await hotel guests and nonguests on the fifth floor of this great big pink building. A harpist plays while the chefs concoct some fine, original dishes. Appetizers range from smoked salmon stuffed with crab mousse ($9.75) to Beluga caviar on ice ($45). L, D daily. AE, MC, V.

Peter's Place Cafe International. *Deluxe.* 208 Beach Dr. N.E., St. Petersburg; 822–8436. There's no other place quite like this place. The verbal menu will make your mouths water as the waiters recite the day's choices. Highlights include roast Long Island duckling, scented with Amaretto with brandied peaches, and the boneless breast of capon Lugano. A fixed price as well, with 18 percent tip included. L, D, Tuesday through Saturday, CB, DC, MC, V.

The Wine Cellar Restaurant. *Expensive.* 17307 Gulf Blvd., North Redington Beach; 393–3491. Recently voted the top restaurant in the Tampa Bay area in a reader's poll by the *St. Petersburg Times,* this popular and usually filled restaurant serves French cuisine in a Swiss decor. Recommended: Veal Oscar à la mode du Chef Karl ($15.95). You're hungry by the time you finish ordering the entrée. L, D, Tuesday through Thursday. All cards.

Heilman's Beachcomber. *Moderate.* 447 Mandalay Ave., Clearwater Beach; 442–4144. A family restaurant—since 1910—with a very special touch, this restaurant is popular as a special night out or as a family treat. Sunday dinners feature Southern-style food: fried chicken, mashed potatoes, and gravy, and all the trimmings. But there's seafood and lobster for those who want it. L, D, daily. MC, V, AE.

Pappas. *Moderate.* 10 W. Dodecanese Blvd., Tarpon Springs; 937–5101. This is the definitive Greek restaurant on the west coast, as far as most people are concerned. The Pappas Family has been here since 1925 and in this particular restaurant since 1975. With a view of the Sponge Docks, the Greek salad is a meal in and of itself. L, D, daily. MC, V, AE, DC.

Seiple's Garden Seat. *Moderate.* 1234 Druid Rd. S., Clearwater; 442–9681. A family restaurant since the 1920s, dinner is served with imagination and formality. Dessert offers a choice of more than 40 temptations in a quiet atmosphere. Sometimes even the appetizers, such as strawberry soup, aren't to be found anywhere else. The gardens are worth walking through. L, D. All cards.

Ted Peters Famous Smoked Fish. *Inexpensive.* 1350 Pasadena Ave. S., Pasadena, St. Petersburg; 381–7931. There are just two dinner choices—smoked mullet or smoked mackerel—but both come with homemade German potato salad that's a meal in itself. It's outdoor eating at its best, and the lunch-time hamburgers are huge. L, D, daily except Tuesday. No cards.

Skyway Jack's. *Inexpensive.* 6701 34th St. S., St. Petersburg. You get fishermen and stockbrokers shoulder to shoulder for one of Jack's breakfasts. He starts serving at 5:00 A.M. and the line starts earlier. Customers rallied to save the restaurant from I–275 and won. Fans recommend the Sloppy Joes as well. B, L, D daily. No cards.

BRADENTON/SARASOTA

Cafe La Chaumiere. *Expensive.* 8197 S. Tamiami Trail, Sarasota; 922–6400. The French Gastronomic Writers Association awarded owner Alain Tauler the International Trophy of Haute Cuisine, an annual award presented only to a French restaurant outside France. D, Monday through Saturday. All cards.

Cafe L'Europe. *Expensive.* 431 Harding Circle, Sarasota; 388–4415. Located on the shopping circle of St. Armand's Key, this small café has a rich variety of entrées and a dessert choice that will awe you. L, D, daily. All cards.

The Crab Trap. *Moderate.* 5611 US 19 N., Palmetto; 722–6255. Just south of the Bradenton end of the Sunshine Skyway, this family seafood restaurant draws a crowd of regulars. The menu offers the usual—and the unusual for a seafood restaurant, including alligator tail, soft turtle, wild pig, blacktip shark. L, D, Sunday through Thursday. MC, V.

Bijou Cafe. *Moderate.* 1287 1st St., Sarasota; 366–8111. Whether it's breakfast, lunch, or dinner, there is a special continental touch here—a flambé entrée. Try it for breakfast; ham and eggs will never seem the same again. B, L, D, Monday through Saturday. MC, V, AE.

FT. MYERS

Casa Lupita. *Expensive.* 8199 S. Cleveland Ave.; 939–0334. Mexican specialties such as arroz con pollo, as well as enchiladas, chimichangas, and fried ice cream. L, D, daily. Most cards.

CAPTIVA ISLAND

The Bubble Room. *Expensive.* Across from the Island Store; 472–5558. Outrageous décor by owners Katie and Jamie Farquharson, matched only by outstanding food. The collection of old toys, stuffed camels, electric trains, Santas and elves, stuffed water buffalo, and bubbling antique Christmas lights are matched by sticky buns and the African Queen entrée that mixes deviled crab, fish, and scallops wonderfully well. No reservations; plan to wait during the "season," January through April. D, daily. All cards.

SANIBEL ISLAND

Thistle Lodge. *Expensive.* Casa Ybel, Sanibel Island; 472–3145. Resident restaurant for the interval-ownership resort. Fine food nonetheless. Try the blackened grouper ($12.50), flash-fried in a 500-degree skillet for a few seconds after dipping the filets in a mixture of 23 spices and sugar—a chef Peter Harmon specialty. L, D, daily. All cards.

NAPLES

The Chef's Garden. *Expensive.* 1300 Third Street S., Naples; 262–5500. This restaurant was picked by *Florida Trend,* a statewide business magazine, for a 1984 Golden Spoon award for being one of the "12 Best." And deservingly so. The cuisine and wine list are outstanding, and the garden setting provides the perfect setting. The desserts deserve speical notice as well. L, D, daily. All cards.

Naples Beach Hotel and Golf Club. *Expensive.* 851 Gulf Shore Blvd., N., Naples; 261–2222. The Brassie is a popular and rewarding restaurant for residents and visitors at any meal. The Sunday brunch is outstanding, with carved ice statues vying with the caviar for attention. B, L, D daily. All cards.

MARCO ISLAND

The Marco Island Inn. *Expensive.* Palm Ave., 394–2121. Where Marco began, around 1883. The house was built for hunters and fishermen; now it serves German-style cuisine, including an accident—German Farmer Soup. It was a "found" recipe when a cook misunderstood instructions about letting three different soups, navy bean, lentil, and split pea, soak overnight. He did—together. The result, one of the menu's most popular appetizers. L, D, daily. MC, V, AE, DC.

NIGHT LIFE. Contrary to Johnny Carson, the sidewalks do not roll up at night in the Tampa Bay area, nor in any other part of the west coast of Florida. While many of the residents in this part of Florida may be retired, that doesn't mean they don't seek out evening entertainment. And the college and university populations of this part of Florida, particularly around the Tampa Bay area, are encouraging more and more night spots that offer all brands of music and dancing.

Certainly there is little risk of harrassment to women traveling alone at the motel or hotel lounge. The same is true for a lounge or pub sharing space with a restaurant of your choice. Nearly all of the unattached lounges are also safe to visit. If you have any doubts—or just want to play it safe—ask at the reservations desk of the hotel or motel where you're staying.

TAMPA

CC's. 1512 E. Fletcher Ave.; 977–3760. Close enough to the University of South Florida to draw heavily on the student-age crowd, but popular too for having a heavy-duty sound system with a disc jockey spinning current dance favorites. Very casual.

Confetti's. 4811 Cypress Ave.; 875–6458. You find just what you think you'd find—lots of confetti in your hair after an evening here. That's just one of the pop touches here, one of the "in" places in town to be seen and to see, with red plastic worms twisting above the dance floors, mannequins of Darth Vader and E.T. sitting on motorcycles suspended from the ceiling.

Peanut Gallery. 11329 N. Nebraska Ave.; 977–7782. In terms of music, you can find most anything here from night to night—jazz, rock, country, blues, and even comedy acts—and the performers are just as mixed—local, regional, and national. Informal atmosphere, with—what else?—peanut shells on the floor.

ST. PETERSBURG/CLEARWATER AREA

Le Club. Tierra Verde Resort, Tierra Verde (St. Petersburg); 867–8611. Soft oldies Monday through Thursday; Dixieland jazz, Friday and Saturday. The Best of Giggles—live comedy sketches—Sunday, starting at 9:00 P.M. Cover, no minimum.

Coliseum Ballroom. 535 4th Ave. N., St. Petersburg; 894–1812. Not exactly a nightclub, but dancing each and every Wednesday and Saturday night—ballroom dancing, for the most part, and increasingly popular with younger people. Customers bring their own booze and can buy set-ups.

Lenny Dee's Supper Club. 10551 Gulf Blvd., Treasure Island; 360–3660. Lenny is an organist-comedian with a following Victor Borge would envy. He is a Suncoast fixture, with scores of instrumental albums to his credit for MCA records, and a packed house every night, of mostly mature 40ish fans.

Studebaker's. 2516 Gulf-to-Bay Blvd., Clearwater; 799–4147. Bop-'til-you-drop fifties music and decor; rich in neon, noise and hostesses in wide skirts. Good food as well. Opens 4:00 P.M. Monday through Friday, 5:00 P.M. weekends.

BRADENTON/SARASOTA

Horsefeathers. 1900 Main St., Sarasota; 366–8088. Plum-colored booths, wood and brass styling, and lots of greenery set the mood for this lounge, with top-40 music and comfortable dress. Caters mostly to a professional crowd, 25 to 40.

Marina Jack's. No. 2 Marina Plaza, Sarasota; 365–4232. A dock next to the lounge and restaurant provides easy harbor and easier access for boaters and sailors. The Deep Six Lounge has piano and guitar music, and a great view of the water from the second floor. The lounge is very casual.

Playground South. 1927 Ringling Blvd., Sarasota; 366–3830. Concerts by local, regional, and nationally known groups fill the bill here regularly. One of the hit spots with the younger crowd, Playground South has four balconies and four bars on two levels. There are the usual wet T-shirt contests as well.

306th Bomb Group. 6770 N. Tamiami Trail, Sarasota; 355–8591. Definitely a theme spot, named for the first U.S. bombing wing to go to London in World War II. In peacetime, though, the lounge plays top-40, with a disc jockey at the stick. The décor features WW II vintage gear and photos.

FT. MYERS

Barzak's. Chateau Robert, Royal Palm Sq., 1400 Colonial Blvd.; 939–5151. The rich greens and brass of this contemporary lounge contrast harmoniously with the classic French design of the Chateau Robert Restaurant. A roaring fireplace—in season—and comfortable overstuffed chairs set the mood for a cozy, relaxed evening. There's usually a singer-pianist in house as well.

Club Bar. at the Shallows Restaurant, 5833 Winkler Rd.; 481–4644. An elegant club with lots of crushed velvet in a previously for-members-only room. Now there are mirrors, lighting, a piano bar for listening, and a dance floor for footwork. The sound varies as well, from 40s to jazz to Golden Oldies.

Rafferty's. Rafters Mall, 3858 College Pkwy.; 489–3500. Top-40 live band music thrives here six nights a week (except Mondays). And when the band takes a break, a DJ steps in. There are champagne nights (30 cents a glass), beach nights, and more. Informal and popular.

THE ORLANDO AREA

The World's Number One Tourist Destination

by PAUL C. RAPP

Paul C. Rapp is a former newspaperman and was a publicist at Walt Disney World. He is currently a free-lance writer based in Winter Park, Florida, from where he writes about the hospitality, travel, and entertainment industries.

The area was first known as Fort Gatlin, a military outpost established in 1838 two miles south of the present city of Orlando. Twelve years later the name Jernigan was given to the settlement, and, finally in 1875, the village was incorporated as the city of Orlando, with just 85 inhabitants. The town had no seaport or major waterway, nor was there a railroad or even a respectable dirt roadway. There was nothing to stimulate or sustain commerce. Thus, Orlando has been called the city that "had no reason to be." Because of a few determined citizens, however, the town lived and grew.

Long noted for its mild climate and natural beauty, the Orlando area has been especially attractive to the residents, who live near hundreds of clear, spring-fed lakes and enjoy the sweet aroma of orange blossoms and citrus fruit. Old timers recall a simple, friendly, and picturesque existence at a slow but charming small-town pace. Orlando was once called "The City Beautiful." And, today, because of far-sighted planning, it still is. The city itself has retained a parklike atmosphere, with hundreds of lakes in the immediate metropolitan area.

Today, the friendliness, the lakes, many of the orange blossoms, and the southern charm remain, but an explosive growth in business, electronics, manufacturing, space technology, transportation, and tourism has altered Orlando and its environs forever. The greater metropolitan area that includes Orange, Seminole, and Osceola counties now offers lifestyles that range from the quiet countryside to the excitement and hustle of a prospering metropolis.

Today, the Orlando area constitutes a giant vacation land and claims to be the number-one tourist destination in the world. In addition to hosting the $2 billion Walt Disney World, with its Magic Kingdom and the more recent Epcot Center (which attracted 22.7 million visitors in its first full year of operation) the area is also the site of several other large attractions, with more under construction or on the planning boards.

WALT DISNEY WORLD

The Development

In this part of the country, it is said that the "world" began October 1, 1971, when Mickey Mouse led the first official visitor through a turnstile and into the Magic Kingdom at Walt Disney World. When that happened, it reflected ten years of planning and building by WED (for Walter Elias Disney) Enterprises, the development arm of the Disney organization. The planning had started in the early 1960s, when Walt Disney first envisioned the theme park as a means of bringing a Disneyland concept to the eastern United States.

By 1963, Florida had been selected as the best location because the weather would permit year-round operation, and Florida was already the leading state for tourism. Eventually the site was narrowed down to the Orlando area, with its large areas of open land and major traffic arteries. By 1964, property was being quietly purchased, and the package eventually totaled more than 28,000 acres. But it wasn't until late in 1965 that it became known that the purchaser of all that property was the Disney organization, and that a mammoth Disney project was planned for the area.

At a press conference in Orlando on November 16, 1965, Walt Disney outlined his dream of a unique entertainment and innovative center, as well as a new way of life. He called it the Experimental Prototype Community Of Tommorow—EPCOT. The first phase of the entire multi-million dollar project was to be the Magic Kingdom and a huge Vacation Complex. Unfortunately, Walt Disney was never to see his dream materialize. He died in December 1966.

Site preparation and the development of a 45-mile network of water control channels was begun by the Disney organization in 1967, and actual construction got under way in April 1969. More than 9,000 workers were involved during the thirty-month construction period, and the first guest was welcomed on October 1, 1971.

With the October 1 opening, the vacation destination was an instant success, and by Thanksgiving of 1971 guests had to be turned away because the parking lots were full. Attendance at the Magic Kingdom on the following December 29 reached 69,458 in one day.

Construction activity continued during the first years of operation with additional facilities being added and new attractions being completed at frequent intervals. At the end of the first full year of operation, 10,712,991 guests had visited the Magic Kingdom.

1975 was the year to announce detailed plans for another phase of the Disney master plan—construction of Epcot. Ground-breaking ceremonies were conducted by WED October 1, 1979, and exactly three years later to the day—October 1, 1982—Epcot Center, as it is now called, was opened with a month-long celebration that included the West Point Glee Club, the 450-piece All American Marching Band, and World Showcase Festival performers representing 23 countries. With that event a new one day attendance record of 123,800 was set December 28, 1982. Some 22.7 million guests visited the park during Epcot Center's first year.

The World Today

Walt Disney World today is said to be the world's largest destination center. It is a vast entertainment and vacation complex occupying 43 square miles that include something for everyone. Included is, of course, the 100-acre Magic Kingdom with Main Street, USA, and Adventureland, Frontierland, Liberty Square, Fantasyland, and Tomorrowland. Three miles south of the Magic Kingdom is Epcot Center, a 260-acre complex of "imagineered entertainment" in two distinct dimensions: Future World, which offers new ideas in communication, energy, transportation, and lifestyles, and World Showcase, where nations share their cultures. Three vacation centers are formed around the three Disney-owned hotel resorts adjacent to the Magic Kingdom: The Contemporary, the Polynesian Village, and the Golf Resort. There are now three championship golf courses where PGA play takes place each year. A popular facility is the 650-acre Fort Wilderness Campground, with more than 1,000 campsites. Nearby is River Country, a

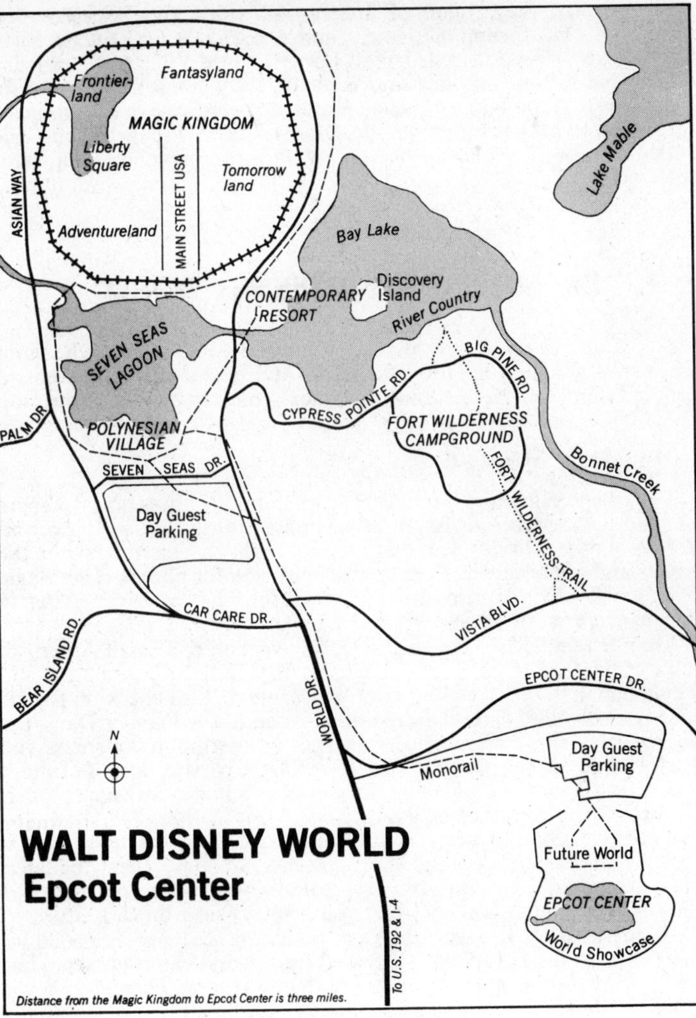
Frontierland
Fantasyland
MAGIC KINGDOM
Liberty Square
Tomorrow land
MAIN STREET USA
ASIAN WAY
Adventureland
Lake Mable
Bay Lake
Discovery Island
CONTEMPORARY RESORT
River Country
SEVEN SEAS LAGOON
BIG PINE RD.
CYPRESS POINTE RD.
FORT WILDERNESS CAMPGROUND
PALM DR.
POLYNESIAN VILLAGE
SEVEN SEAS DR.
Bonnet Creek
FORT WILDERNESS TRAIL
Day Guest Parking
CAR CARE DR.
VISTA BLVD.
BEAR ISLAND RD.
EPCOT CENTER DR.
WORLD DR.
N
Day Guest Parking
Monorail
WALT DISNEY WORLD
Epcot Center
Future World
EPCOT CENTER
World Showcase
To U.S. 192 & I-4
Distance from the Magic Kingdom to Epcot Center is three miles.

water-oriented playground of flumes, raft rides, rope swings, rock dives, the "Ol' Swimmin' Hole," and a sandy beach. Buena Vista Shopping Village, now called Walt Disney World Village, is a popular dining and gift-buying area and is particularly convenient to the six large hotels in the Disney Village Hotel Plaza and the one-, two-, and three-bedroom apartments in the Disney World Village Villas. The Villas and the Hotel Plaza form a city and entertainment complex of their own.

EXPLORING WALT DISNEY WORLD

Get your free guidebook at City Hall when you first enter the park. Then take the time to study the guide and decide how you want to proceed. Don't crisscross and backtrack; you'll be wasting time.

The Magic Kingdom

The Magic Kingdom consists of 45 major adventures on a 100-acre site and is the home of Mickey and Minnie Mouse, Goofy, Pluto, and dozens of other Disney characters. They all can be seen romping on the streets and are always willing to pose with you for photos. The Magic Kingdom is divided into six "lands" of fun and fantasy, serving to delight children of all ages from 1 to 100:

Main Street, USA. This is the Disney version of a small American town at the turn of the century. Stop at City Hall for information and a guide book to help you find your way around. Also check on parade schedules or other special events, then listen to the Dapper Dans, the Sax Quartet, the World Band, and other wandering musicians as you start down the street toward Cinderella Castle, passing dozens of shops and sidewalk activities. Ride antique cars or a horse-drawn street car, all included in the price of your ticket.

A word of advice: when you enter the Magic Kingdom, don't get too involved in the shops along Main Street, USA. Save them for later. Start your day deeper into the park before long lines form, then visit the shops in late afternoon when you want to slow down a little.

Tomorrowland. The ten shows and rides here are themed to what we might find in the future, but all geared for fun and entertainment. The Space Mountain is a must: it's more than a roller-coaster.

Fantasyland. Here's where you'll find It's A Small World. Originally created for New York's 1964–65 World's Fair, this is a boat ride around the world—the "world" here consisting of animated dolls that sing and dance. Also here: Cinderella Castle, the 180-foot-high Disney landmark of the Magic Kingdom, with mosaic interior walls and spiral domes; Peter Pan's Flight, where visitors ride in flying versions of Captain Hook's ship; 20,000 Leagues under the Sea, an underwater trip in a version of Captain Nemo's infamous submarine; Snow White's Adventure, retelling her story; Mr. Toad's Ride, a children's ride that follows Mr. Toad's adventures through a mansion; and other delights.

Adventureland. You'll want to take the Jungle Cruise, watch a pirate raid on a Caribbean town in Pirates of the Caribbean, and listen to the Tiki Birds. Or climb the Swiss Family Treehouse.

Liberty Square. Don't miss the Hall of Presidents, where all the chief executives of our nation come to life through Disney "audio-animatronics," and Mr. Lincoln makes a speech. Enter the spine-tingling Haunted Mansion and ride down the Rivers of America on a riverboat.

Frontierland. Big Thunder Mountain is a ride you'll remember and the Country Bear Jamboree is a foot-stompin' hoedown that'll get you jumping. Be sure to check for tickets to the Diamond Horseshoe Revue, a show in a recreation of a western dance hall.

There are no less than thirty-two places to eat in the Magic Kingdom, and they range from a cup of coffee and hot dog to full meals. (See "Dining Out" in *Practical Information for Walt Disney World.*) The best times to eat are when everyone else doesn't, so to avoid the crunch. Eat before 11:00 A.M. or after 2:00 P.M., and before or after the 5:00 to 7:00 P.M. dinner hour.

Epcot Center

Located three miles from the Magic Kingdom, Epcot Center is more than twice its size and consists of two completely new, different, and exciting dimensions: Future World and World Showcase.

Entrances to Epcot are off I–4 or US Route 192. They are very clearly marked, and it isn't likely you could miss them. If traveling by car, you will pass through the parking toll gates, where you pay a $2 parking fee. Attendants will direct you into a parking space in the 9,000-car lot; from there you can catch a tram ride (or walk) to the ticket windows. If the Epcot lot is full, you will be directed to park in the Magic Kingdom parking area at the Transportation Center; from there you can take the Epcot monorail for a three-mile ride to the park. Upon arrival via monorail, you'll get an elevated preview of Epcot as you make a wide swing through the park before disembarking at the ticket areas.

As you enter Epcot you will pass beneath Spaceship Earth, a 17-story sphere that marks the start of Future World. World Showcase is behind Future World. Stop at Earth Station and make your reservations for dinner; you'll need them.

A tip: when inside the gates, don't get in the first line you see at Spaceship Earth. Go deeper into the park, say to World Showcase, and save Future World for later when the mobs are at World Showcase.

Future World. Offering innovative ideas in communications, energy, transportation, lifestyles, the land, and imagination—with yet greater dimension under construction. Major activities include:

Spaceship Earth: A 180-foot-high geosphere that houses a spiral journey through the dramatic history of communications, from cave drawings to satellite technology.

Communicore: Epcot Center's "community core" of new ideas that may affect twenty-first-century lifestyles, with hands-on exhibits and displays of tomorrow's technologies.

Universe of Energy: a fast-paced exploration of the forces that fuel our lives and the universe itself. Guests ride on theater seats through a display of earth's beginnings, past battling dinosaurs, through earthquakes and beneath volcanoes into a presentation on energy's impact on twentieth-century life.

Horizons: An incredible journey into the lifestyles of the next century with robotic-staffed farms, ocean colonies, and space cities. It ends when you make your choice of what the future should hold.

World of Motion: A General Motors presentation that provides a comfortable trip through the evolution of transportation—from footsore cavemen to the wheel and into today's and tomorrow's means of getting around.

Journey into Imagination: "Dreamfinder" and "Figment" lead you through an imaginative creative process, depicting how all literature, music, art, and drama came from "one little spark" of an idea. Don't fail to see a special 3-D screen offering by Kodak.

The Land: A cruise through tropical forest, desert, American plains, and early farm life—then into state-of-the-art technology and on into future methods of producing food to feed the world's growing population.

The Living Seas: Opens in January, 1986. A six-million gallon aquarium to house the world's largest man-made coral reef filled with sea life.

World Showcase. Ten nations—more to come—open their doors to share their culture, their lifestyles, their customs, and their products. Built around a large lake, the mile-long circular promenade is serviced by double-deck buses or by launches that make stops at designated intervals. Listed in a counterclockwise manner, one starts from World Showcase Plaza and finds:

Canada: A replica of the Chateau Laurier, peopled by Royal Canadian Mounted Police, lumberjacks, Indians, and Eskimos, featuring "O Canada," an awe-inspiring 360-degree-circle-vision production of the nation's great outdoors, plus "Le Cellier," for prime rib and fine beer.

United Kingdom: Complete with authentic pub and even warm beer if you ask for it. Steak and kidney pie and corned beef sandwiches are on the menu in the Rose and Crown. And there's lots of shopping here.

France: See France in all its beauty through a 200-degree wraparound screen, then test the Au Petit Cafe or the famous "Chefs de France" gourmet restaurant. Reservations are necessary.

Morocco: Discover treasures of the Casbah, see the fine handcrafted tile work, and savor native cusine in the Restaurant Marrakesh. Reservations.

Japan: Here you'll find an exclusive collection of Japanese art and culture, plus some of the finest food in "the World." The Teppanyaki Dining Rooms specialize in seafood and grilled meats; reservations are required. No reservations needed for the Yakitori House or Tempura Kiku.

American Adventure: Ben Franklin and Mark Twain present a dramatic and inspiring account of America's origins, the struggles of early settlers, the woes of wars, and the American character. AudioAnimatronics have Ben climbing steps, Mark smoking his cigar.

Italy: Home of the popular L'Originale Alfredo di Roma Ristorante, featuring veal, seafood, chicken, and pasta, plus the world-famous fettuccine Alfredo. Reservations are a must.

Germany: Sing with the oompah band and Oktoberfest entertainment. Excellent dining on traditional German fare. Reservations, of course.

China: You can discover the mysterious East through 360-degree circle-vision, and enter the Forbidden City, see the House of the Whispering Willows, and a thousand years of Chinese culture. Try the Nine Dragons Restaurant. Reservations.

Mexico: Sail the River of Time through the Mexico of yesterday and into today. The pyramid-like pavilion also houses a collection of more than 130 art works and artifacts, some dating back to 1500 B.C. Fine dining, but reservations will be needed.

In addition to the special dining facilities mentioned above, there are at least a dozen other food outlets in Epcot that offer everything from full-course meals (The Good Turn in the Land Pavilion) to hamburgers.

PRACTICAL INFORMATION FOR WALT DISNEY WORLD

WHEN TO GO. Friday is usually a good day to visit WDW, unless it is part of a special weekend like Thanksgiving. Weekends are good, also, and, to an extent, so is Thursday. But Monday, Tuesday, and Wednesday tend to be more crowded. Of course, Easter, Thanksgiving, and Christmas holidays are the busiest times at WDW. If you can come at other times, do so.

Most guests seem to arrive from 9:30 to 11:00 A.M. If possible, get parked and be at the gates no later that 8:30 or 9:00 A.M., or wait until later in the day. An evening visit is particularly pleasant in the summer months.

HOW TO GET THERE. The four conventional methods of travel in the United States—air, bus, car, and train—will get you to Walt Disney World. But regardless of how you get there, you will probably wish you had a car once you are there. The reason? A visit to Walt Disney World is usually combined with other area sightseeing because of the vast concentration of attractions in central Florida. For example, after paying the fare to get to Disney World, it costs very little more to make a stop at nearby Sea World, Circus World, or Cypress Gardens, since all are probably within a few miles of your hotel. Likewise, Cape Canaveral and the Space Coast, with beautiful beaches, are within 50 miles on a straight shot across on the Beeline Highway. It is possible to get buses and tours to all these places, but an automobile of your own is by far the more convenient way to do it.

By air. Orlando International Jetport is 20 miles from Disney World. It is a major airport served by most commercial carriers with direct flights to 100 U.S. cities. For information on transportation from the airport see "Getting from the Airport," below. Arrivals via private aircraft have two choices for a landing site: Orlando Executive Airport, 25 miles away, or Kissimmee Airport, just 10 miles away. Both service private and corporate aircraft.

By bus. *Greyhound* and *Trailways* both offer frequent service into Orlando. For information on local buses to WDW, see "How to Get Around," below.

By car. Tourists arriving from the north, midwest, or east have a direct route into Orlando and Walt Disney World via super highways. Interstate 4 connects Daytona in the east with Tampa and the Florida west coast, and passes through downtown Orlando and WDW en route. Furthermore, Florida's Turnpike, a toll road, passes just south of Orlando en route to Miami. Another toll road, the Beeline Expressway, connects Orlando to the Space Coast and beaches at Cape Canaveral and Cocoa. In short, all roads lead to Orlando.

Getting from Orlando to Walt Disney World is simple. Take I–4 West (which is actually *south* according to our compass) for about 20 miles and you'll find first the Walt Disney World Village exit, followed by the Epcot exit a mile farther. Both peel off to the right. The turnoff to the Magic Kingdom and Fort Wilderness Campground is down the road three miles at US 192, where you bear right for another mile to the Disney entry road, also on the right. Visitors arriving from the direction of Tampa would reverse the sequence.

By train. *Amtrak* provides twice-daily service to Orlando from New York and Washington, where connections can be made for midwestern areas. Other routes connect with Miami and St. Petersburg. For information on fares call Amtrak, toll-free at 800–342–2520. The Orlando station is at 1400 Sligh Blvd., 843–7611. In Winter Park, it is at Morse Boulevard and Park Avenue, 645–5055. The *Amtrak Auto-Train* carries passengers and their cars daily between Washington, DC, and Sanford, FL, 28 miles north of Orlando; call 800–872–7245.

TELEPHONES. The area code for Orange, Seminole, and Osceola counties, which would cover all WDW areas and greater Orlando, is 305. Dial 800–555–1212, directory information, for toll-free 800 numbers to determine if there is an 800 number for the business you want to reach. Charges for local calls from a pay telephone are $.25 in most of the central Florida area, with the exception of the WDW area and the Winter Park exchange, where it is $.10. If you make a local call from your hotel room, the charges may be more.

There are two telephone numbers that can be used to obtain general information regarding Walt Disney World. One is 824–4500 and the other is 824–4321. Both are in the 305 area-code zone.

All reservations for hotels or the campground *inside* the Walt Disney World complex can be made through the Central Reservations Office; telephone 305–824–8000.

EMERGENCY NUMBERS. Within Walt Disney World, for *emergency* ambulance, security, or fire, dial 911 and remain at the telephone until the operator answers and can determine the nature of the call. All Disney World cast members can also help you obtain the right assistance.

TIPS FOR CAMERA BUGS. A camera is almost as essential as comfortable shoes when visiting Walt Disney World. And the opportunities for assembling a long-to-be-cherished album are endless whether one owns a camera or borrows one at the Vacation Kingdom. Both the Magic Kingdom and Epcot Center offer a broad range of interesting photographic subjects. To help visitors get their best shots, professional photographers familiar with the Disney parks have selected exceptional locations and marked them as photographic sites. The sites provide guests with a variety of distance views, close-ups of minute detail, and plenty of opportunities to include friends and family in set-ups.

If you do not have a camera, you can borrow one free of charge at the *Kodak Camera Center* in the Magic Kingdom and the Kodak Center at Epcot Center. You must leave a deposit, which is totally refunded when the camera is returned. All you pay for is the film. Minor repairs can also be made at the camera centers, and film can be left for processing.

HANDICAPPED GUESTS. Many special arrangements have been made by WDW management for the convenience and safety of handicapped or disabled visitors, including reserved parking areas. Ask at the toll plaza where to park, then request a copy of "The Disabled Guests" Guide Book at the Ticket Center. Wheelchairs are available at Epcot Center and the Magic Kingdom. Ask at the Ticket Booth.

HOTELS AND MOTELS in Walt Disney World can be identified in three different categories: those on Disney property *owned and operated* by the Disney organization, those on WDW property, but *not* owned or operated by Disney, and those surrounding the WDW area. Those owned by Disney, called "the resorts," may tend to cost more, but are far more convenient to the attraction and lessen the need for other means of transportation. Guests staying in Walt Disney World resorts have other advantages, such as advanced reservation opportunities for dinners, shows, and golf tee-off times. Resort guests also have unlimited access to WDW transportation systems within the park as well as reduced tennis and green fees.

The next most convenient accommodations are those on Disney property that are operated by private companies. There are six major hotels in this category, all in the WDW Village Hotel Plaza. Rates in these hotels are slightly less (in most cases) than the Disney Resorts, but tend to run higher than those on the periphery of WDW property. Again, however, the convenience of being within walking distance of the WDW Shopping Village, restaurants, and entertainment, with advance reservation rights, and with ready transportation to the Magic Kingdom and Epcot, might make the extra expense worth considering.

The third category offers accommodations in all ranges, with most of them located east and west along US 192 (the closest), some in the Kissimmee area, up to ten miles distant, and another concentration on International Drive, off I–4 East on the south side of Orlando, also some ten miles away. This latter group has another advantage in that International Drive has somewhat of a downtown atmosphere with sidewalks and attractions tying together a mile-long stretch of hotels, restaurants, night spots, and fast-food outlets. It is also closer to Orlando, which has its own array of interesting areas.

When reserving a room, be sure to check on family rates. Many hotels and motels allow up to four or five guests for the same rate as two. Some offer kitchenettes, another advantage for a large family.

There are some peak periods and some lows that might be considered when planning a visit to Walt Disney World. The busiest seasons are usually during holiday periods, such as Easter, Thanksgiving, and Christmas. The winter season is roughly from mid-December until the end of March, and the summer crunch starts in early June and fades after Labor Day. Thus accommodations are most likely easier found (and maybe even cheaper) from the post-Easter rush to the end of May, and again from after Labor Day to mid-November.

No matter where you stay in the Central Florida area, you will pay a 7 percent tax, 5 percent of which is sales tax and 2 percent is resort tax.

Many visitors planning to stay in the Disney Resorts make their reservations as much as a year in advance, although drop-ins have on occasion hit it lucky and found a fresh cancellation available. But that's gambling. When considering a visit, inquire about the many packages offered, such as the "World Adventure" which provides accommodations in the 1,046-room Contemporary or the 636-room Polynesian Resort hotels or in the unique Tree Houses or Resort Villas, plus unlimited use of all attractions in the Magic Kingdom and Epcot. Special packages for the 151-room Golf Resort are also available.

All Walt Disney World reservations can be made by calling or writing: Walt Disney World, Central Reservations Office, P. O. Box 78, Lake Buena Vista, FL 32830; 305–824–8000. All are located off the Main Entrance Road, accessible via US 192. Only American Express and Master Card are accepted at Walt Disney World facilities; most other establishments take all major credit cards. The WDW resorts can all be considered *Deluxe,* with rates ranging between $105 and $160. These apply to one room, whether single or double occupancy, and most can accommodate four to five people in a room for an additional charge. For additional accommodations in and around Orlando, see *Practical Information for the Orlando Area.*

WDW RESORT HOTELS

Deluxe

Contemporary Resort Hotel. The largest of WDW properties, with over 1,000 rooms, shops, restaurants, snack bars, lounges, a marina, a beach, and health club. The monorail stops within the building itself. Rooms in the Tower section have wonderful views and cost more than those in the North and South Garden Wings. Maximum of five people per room, additional charge of $15 for the third and fourth adults in the room. Children under 17 free with adults.

Gold Resort. Some consider this the most serene of the WDW-resort hotels. All 275 rooms have patios or balconies and views of woods or the golf courses. Two championship courses; also a pro shop, pool, restaurant and lounge, and two tennis courts. Maximum of five per room; additional charge of $15 for third and fourth adults; children under 17 free with adults.

Polynesian Village. The name describes it: a three-story garden with a waterfall in the lobby, called the Great Ceremonial House. Shops and restaurants are located here. The longhouses beside it contain the 600-plus rooms. All rooms have a balcony or patio and a view of the lagoon or one of the pools. Marina, children's playground, a game room, shops, restaurants, snack bars, lounges.

Maximum of five per room; $15 additional for third and fourth adults; children under 17 free with adults.

WDW Villas and Tree Houses. Within walking distance or a short golf cart ride of Walt Disney World Village are four types of apartment-style accommodations, most with kitchens. These units are ideal for family groups of more than five. Spread around through the woods and along the fairways of the 18-hole Lake Buena Vista Course, the apartments are roomy as well as quiet. Included are: *Vacation Villas.* One-bedroom townhouse models are $120 and can accommodate four people. The two-bedroom units will sleep six, plus a seventh small child, and go for $160 per night. *Club Lake Villas.* The smaller one-bedroom units can handle four and rent for $105 per night. The large one-bedroom suites with Jacuzzi sleep five and are $150. *Fairway Villas.* All are two-bedroom apartments and can accommodate six plus a youngster. $160. *Treehouse Villas.* Two-bedroom houses on stilts with an outside veranda arrangement. Can handle six, for $160. The kids will love it.

WDW VILLAGE HOTEL PLAZA

There are six hotels in the WDW Hotel Plaza, all within a short walk of the WDW Shopping Village. All are on Disney property, but are operated privately and have a special relationship with the Disney organization, such as use of the WDW bus system and an early shot at hard-to-get dinner reservations at Epcot or the Golf Course. Rates are based on double occupancy, European Plan, and are grouped in three price ranges: *Deluxe,* $110 and up; *Expensive,* $90 to $110; and *Moderate,* $60 to $90.

Deluxe

Buena Vista Palace. 1900 Buena Vista Dr., Lake Buena Vista 32830; 305–827–2727 (toll-free, 800–327–2990; from Florida, 800–432–2920). 870 rooms, all with balconies, in a five-story building or 27-story tower—the tallest in Central Florida. Three restaurants, two lounges, and night club. 26 suites with commanding view of WDW and environs.

Hilton at Walt Disney Village. Box 22781, Hotel Plaza Blvd., Lake Buena Vista 32830; 305–827–4000. (toll-free 800–445–8667, Florida only). 814 guest rooms, including 29 suites, in ten-story tower on 23 acres of landscaped grounds. Across street from WDW Village. Two pools, spa, sauna, whirlpool, tennis courts, self-service guest laundry, two restaurants. A special "Youth Hotel" is available for day care and even overnight care for youngsters. Room rates good for up to five in a room. No extra charge for cots.

Hotel Royal Plaza. 1905 Hotel Plaza Blvd., Lake Buena Vista 32830; 305–828–2828 (toll-free, 800–327–2990; from Florida, 800–432–2920). 400 large rooms in a 17-story tower with a pair of two story wings. Pool, tennis courts, sauna, Jacuzzi, two dining rooms, two bars, live entertainment, children's programs, barber shop, beauty salon, private balconies. Rates include up to four in a room. $8 for cots. Also offers four types of suites, each with two bedrooms, for $300 and up.

Howard Johnson's Resort at the Village. Box 22204, Lake Buena Vista 32830; 305–828–8888 (toll-free 800–654–2000). 323 rooms in a 14-story tower and a six-story annex. Atrium with glass elevators. Two pools plus kiddies' wader, Jacuzzi, and playground. Restaurant and coffee shop. No additional charge for children under 18. Extra cots $8.

Expensive

Americana Dutch Resort Hotel. 1850 Hotel Plaza Blvd., Lake Buena Vista 32830; 305–828–4444 (toll-free, 800–327–2994; from Florida, 800–432–2926). 615 rooms in a 19-story tower with two five-story wings. The Dutch theme carries over to a windmill-shaped swimming pool. One restaurant (the *Flying Dutchman*), entertainment in the *Hague Lounge.* Tennis courts, racquet-ball, shuffleboard, minature golf, playground. Rates are for up to four guests. Extra costs $10.

Moderate

Viscount Hotel. Hotel Plaza, Box 22205, Lake Buena Vista 32830; 305–828–2424 (toll-free, 800–255–3050). 325 rooms in 18-floor building, all with private balconies. Swimming pool, game room. One restaurant. The 18th floor houses *Top of the Arc Lounge* with sweeping view. No additional charge for children under 17 using existing beds. Extra cots $6.

LAKE BUENA VISTA AND KISSIMMEE AREAS

Hotel and motel listings *not* on Disney property are based on double occupancy, European Plan, and are grouped by price: *Deluxe,* $110 and up; *Expensive,* $90 to $110; *Moderate,* $60 to $90; *Inexpensive,* $40 to $60; and *Basic Budget,* less than $40. Remember, this is not a total listing of every accommodation, but an across-the-board selection. Further details can be obtained by contacting the particular property that interests you or by calling the tourist information office in that locality (see "Tourist Information" below). Remember, too, that rates can, and do, change without notice.

Deluxe

Hyatt Regency Grand Cypress. 1 Grand Cypress Blvd., Lake Buena, Vista 32819; 305–239–1234 (toll-free, 800–228–9000). 750 rooms and 75 suites in a T-shaped 18-story tower located on a 25-acre lake immediately adjacent to the WDW Village Hotel Plaza. Main features include a half-acre swimming pool, 25,000-square-foot ballroom, four restaurants, a large lounge with entertainment, three bars, 11 tennis courts, and an 18-hole golf course designed by Jack Nicklaus. Kids under 18 with parents are free. No extra charge for cots. The one-bedroom suites range from $200 to $705.

Moderate

Best Western World Inn. I–4 and SR 535, Lake Buena Vista 32830; 305–239–4646. 245 rooms, one-quarter mile from WDW Village on edge of Disney property. Shuttle bus to Disney attractions. Game room, playground, laundry, and entertainment.

Hilton Inn Gateway. 7470 W. Hwy. 192, Kissimmee 32741; 305–396–4400 (toll-free, 800–327–9170). 360 rooms, golf, two pools, sun patios, shuttle service to attractions. No charge for children in same room with parents.

Holiday Inn, Main Gate West. 7300 Spacecoast Pkwy. Kissimmee 32741; 305–396–7300. One mile from WDW; restaurant; lounge; pools; tennis courts; shuttle to WDW.

Howard Johnson's Motor Lodge, Main Gate. 7600 West Spacecoast Pkwy., Kissimmee 32741; 305–396–2500. Bus to WDW; 1¼ miles from WDW; restaurant; lounge; game room; pool.

Hyatt Orlando. 6375 West Spacecoast Pkwy., Kissimmee 32741; 305–396–1234 (toll-free 800–228–9000). 2½ miles from WDW entrance road. 948 rooms divided into four clusters, each with pool and playground. Four restaurants, two lounges, tennis courts and shopping area.

Ramada Resort Hotel. 2850 Reedy Creek Blvd., Kissimmee 32741; 305–396–4466. 386 rooms. Two pools, tennis, game room, restaurant, entertainment, and gift shop.

Inexpensive

Days Lodge. 5820 Spacecoast Parkway, Kissimmee 32741; 305–396–7900. 2½ miles from WDW. Cafeteria; restaurant adjacent; three swimming pools.

Holiday Inn, East. 5678 Spacecoast Pkwy., Kissimmee 32741; 305–396–4488. 2½ miles from WDW with shuttle to area attractions. Restaurant, lounge with entertainment, pool, tennis.

Larson's Lodge, Main Gate. 6075 W. US Hwy. 192, Kissimmee 32741; 305–396–6100 (toll-free, 800–327–9074). 128 rooms, 16 efficiencies. Gifts, game room, tennis, restaurant and lounge. 1½ miles east of WDW entry road.

Sheraton Lakeside. 7711 W. US 192, Kissimmee 32741; 305–396–2222. 650 rooms, two pools, tennis, paddleboats, playground, miniature golf.

Basic Budget

Best Western Vacation Lodge. 8600 Spacecoast Pkwy., Kissimmee 32741; 305–396–0100 (toll-free, 800–327–9151). Four miles from WDW. 300 rooms. Shuttle to Disney. Tours to other attractions.

Days Inn, Disney West. 7980 Spacecoast Pkwy., Kissimmee 32741; 305–396–1000 (toll-free, 800–325–2525). (Note: there are 16 Days Inn members in the area; the common toll-free number is 800–325–2525). 2½ miles from WDW. Restaurant, game room, pool.

Roadway Inn. 5245 Spacecoast Pkwy., Kissimmee 32741; 305–396–7700. 200 rooms. Restaurant, lounge, entertainment, playground and game room.

INTERNATIONAL DRIVE/FLORIDA CENTER

Deluxe

Sonesta Hotel Village at Sand Lake. 10000 Turkey Lake Rd., Orlando 32819; 305–352–8051 (toll-free, 800–343–7170). On lake with 250 villas. Gourmet restaurant, patio lounge, tennis, spa, beach, water sports, barbecue, and playground.

Wyndham Hotel Sea World. 6677 Sea Harbor Dr., Orlando 32821; 305–351–5555 (toll-free, 800–822–4200). 718 rooms and 64 suites in a 10-story tower built around a football-field-sized atrium lobby. Directly across from Sea World marine park and midway between Disney World and International Airport. Two large ballrooms and 24 convention rooms. Three restaurants, 400-seat lounge, piano bar, swimming pool, tennis, health club, and play areas.

Expensive

Hilton Inn, Florida Center. 7400 International Dr., Orlando 32819; 305–351–4600. 400 rooms with lush tropical gardens. Two pools, sun patios, play areas, lounge.

Holiday Inn, International. 6515 International Dr., Orlando 32819; 305–351–3500. Set on 13 lush acres with 642 rooms. Pool, lounge, game room, playground, and two restaurants.

Orlando Plaza Suites Hotel. 8250 Jamaican Court, Orlando, 32819; 305–345–8250 (toll-free, 800–327–9797). Located in Plaza International. 246 1-bedroom suites, plus buffet breakfast and cocktail hour. Pool, piano bar, exercise areas.

Sheraton Twin Towers. 5780 Major Blvd., Orlando 32819; 305–351–1000. Two 18-story towers with 592 rooms and large ballroom. Pool, three restaurants, two lounges with nightly entertainment, and game rooms. Free bus to airport and local attractions.

Moderate

Marriott Inn, Orlando. 8001 International Dr., Orlando 32819; 305–351–2420. 1079 rooms surround two tropical lagoons. Three heated pools, two poolside bars, lounges, tennis courts, play areas, meeting rooms, and Jacuzzi.

Sheraton World Hotel. 10100 International Dr., Orlando 32819; 305–352–1100. Offers 807 rooms with three restaurants, two lounges, three pools, tennis, and miniature golf.

Viscount Hotel and Justus Aquatic Center. 8444 International Dr., Orlando 32819; 305–345–0505 (toll-free, 800–752–0001). Swim-oriented. 3 pools, diving well. 300 rooms, restaurant, lounge, athletic club.

Inexpensive

Best Western Las Palmas Inn. 6233 International Dr., Orlando 32819; 305–351–3900 (toll-free in Florida, 800–432–1175; outside Florida, 800–327–2114). Across from Wet 'n Wild, with 260 rooms, restaurant, pool, playground.

Howard Johnson's Florida Center Hotel. 5905 Kirkmann Road, Orlando 32819; 305–351–3333. 260 rooms and bilingual staff. Two restaurants.

Quality Inn High Q. 5905 International Dr., Orlando 32819; 305–351–2100. A 21-story circular high rise with 293 rooms. Pool, sauna, restaurant, lounge, and game room.

Basic Budget

Continental Plaza Motor Inn. 6825 Visitors Circle, Orlando 32819; 305–352–8211 (toll-free, 800–327–2112; in Florida, 800–432–2720). 192 rooms, pool, bar, game room, gift shop, laundry facilities.

International Inn. 6327 International Dr., Orlando 32819; 305–351–4444. 315 rooms, heated pool, restaurant, lounge, game room.

Quality Inn, International. 7600 International Dr., Orlando 32819; 305–351–1600. 729 rooms. Two heated pools, restaurant, lounge, game room, and gift shop.

CAMPING Most offer full hook-ups, picnic tables, hot showers, laundry, recreation areas, and pools. Costs here are for 2 people in an RV.

Fort Wilderness Campground Resort. A Disney property, off the Main Entrance Road on WDW grounds, between Epcot and Magic Kingdom. 650 heavily wooded acres with 1,000 large, paved campsites. Full hook-ups and all the amenities. Camp store, campfire, jamborees—all the goodies that campers seek. Sandy beach, close to River Country for a dip in the Ol' Swimmin' Hole, and adjacent to Pioneer Hall and the Hoop-Dee-Doo Musical Revue. Call Central Reservations at 305–824–8000, or write Walt Disney World, Central Reservations Office, Box 78, Lake Buena Vista, FL 32830. Sites are $20–$24, depending on location. If you don't have an RV, Disney has: completely equipped Fleetwood trailers, air-conditioned and ready to occupy. Just bring your clothes. $105 a night; sleeps six.

Off-site Campgrounds: Aloha Travel Park. Hwy 17–92, Kissimmee, 32741; 305–933–5730. 112 sites. $12. **Port-O-Call.** W. Hwy 192, Kissimmee, 32741; 305–396–0110 (toll-free, 800–327–9120). 500 sites. Complete RV supplies and repair available at Camping World, next door. $18.95. **Captain Kidd's Camp-**

ground. 8550 Spacecoast Hwy, Kissimmee, 32741; 305–396–6101; 500 sites. **Outdoor Resorts of America.** US Hwy 192, Clermont 32711; 305–422–7461. West of the main Disney entrance with 980 sites. Fishing and water sports. $17.50. **Yogi Bear's Jellystone Park.** 9200 Turkey Lake Rd., Orlando 32809; 305–351–5494. Convenient to Sea World and International Drive areas. 547 sites. $16.75. **Holiday Village Campground.** 2650 Holiday Trail, Kissimmee 32741; 305–396–4598. 450 sites. **KOA Campground.** W. Hwy. 192, Kissimmee 32741; 305–396–2400. 374 sites with tenting area. **Sherwood Forest RV Resort.** US Hwy. 192, Kissimmee 32741; 305–396–7431. 513 sites. **Ramada Camp Inn.** Highway 530, Kissimmee 32741; 305–846–1201. Tenters welcome. 144 sites. **Holiday Inn Village Campground.** US Highway 192, Kissimmee 32741; 305–396–4595. Tent areas. 450 sites.

GETTING FROM THE AIRPORT: The Disney World Information Booth in the airport main terminal is a wise stop for schedules and advice on getting to WDW. **By car.** Orlando International Jetport is about 20 miles from WDW. During rush hours, 7:30 to 9:00 A.M. and 4:30 to 6:00 P.M., at least an hour should be allowed for the trip. The Beeline Expressway, Hwy. 528, is a toll road ($.25) running east and west. It connects the Florida east coast with I–4 and the Florida Turnpike, while passing in front of the airport. I–4 provides a north-south division of Orlando, past the Walt Disney World and continues on to Tampa.

Upon leaving the airport, a left turn onto the Beeline leads you past Sea World to I–4 and a left at I–4 takes you to Walt Disney World Village and Epcot or on to US 192 and the Magic Kingdom entrance. A right turn on I–4 from the Beeline takes you past Hwy. 482 and into downtown Orlando. If you want to go to International Drive, exit from I–4 to the east at Hwy 482.

US Hwy. 192 is the southern edge of Disney property and passes the main entry to the Magic Kingdom. Called the Spacecoast Parkway, US 192 has a concentration of motels and campgrounds both east and west of the Disney entrance. US 192 also leads east into Kissimmee (Kiss-im-ee), a tourist and agricultural town of 17,000. Continuing east, US 192 crosses the Florida Turnpike and ends on the beach at Indialantic.

Rental Cars: The Central Florida area has nearly as many car rental agencies as orange trees—more than fifty of them, in fact. All major rental companies have offices conveniently located inside the airport terminal, while many smaller and lesser-known agencies are found on airport approach roads. For the big ones, i.e., Avis, Budget, General, Hertz, and National, advanced reservations are essential, if you want fast service. Other visitors have found excellent rates at the peripheral agencies, although sometime should be allowed for making such arrangements. Thus, you have a wide range of choices, from a luxurious limosine to somewhat less pretentious, yet drivable, "Rent-A-Wreck." Following is a partial list. *Alamo Rent-A-Car, Inc.,* 8200 McCoy Rd. Orlando, 800–327–9633; *Avis,* 8445 Bear Rd, Orlando, 800–331–1212; *Budget,* International Airport, Orlando, 800–527–0700; *Hertz,* International Airport, Orlando, 800–654–3131; *National Car Rental,* International Airport, Orlando, 800–328–4567; *Rent-A-Wreck,* for addresses call 800–421–7253; *Value Rent-A-Car,* 3255 McCoy Rd., Orlando, 800–327–2501.

By taxi. It is approximately 14 miles from Orlando International Jetport to midtown Orlando and about the same distance to the International Drive area. A taxi to either place from the airport will cost in the neighborhood of $14 plus tip. A cab to Walt Disney World will run around $28. Most cabs are metered, but if not, be sure to settle on a price before starting out. (*City and Yellow Cab Co.,* 425–3111; *Ace Taxi,* 859–7514.)

By limousine service. Several companies provide limousine service to and from the airport and other areas, with a wide range of ammenities and prices. All are chauffeur-driven. A sampling follows: *Airport Limousine Service,* 8433 Bear Rd., Orlando, 305–859–4667 (800–432–9204); *Britannia Limousines,* 1025 S. Orange Blossom Trail, Orlando, 305–849–9722; *Carey Limousines,* 1523 Pine St., Orlando, 305–671–4488.

Continuous limousine service to WDW is available from the 2nd level of the airport, at either exit. Cost, $9 per adult, $4 per child. (*Airport Limousine Service,* Main Terminal, 859–4667.)

By bus. Bus service is provided at half hour intervals from the airport 2nd level to WDW area hotels and motels by *American Sightseeing Tours,* 859–2250. Adults, $6.50; children, $3.25.

GETTING FROM YOUR HOTEL. Many area hotels have shuttles to WDW. **By car.** See "From the airport by car," above, for the highways in the area and car rental agencies. **By bus.** Bus transportation from downtown Orlando to WDW and Sea World is provided by *Grey Lines of Orlando.* For specific schedules call 422–0744. Transportation is also available from the International Drive area and from Florida Center through *Rabbit Bus Lines,* 291–2424. Call for detailed schedules.

ARRIVING AT WALT DISNEY WORLD: No matter how you arrive to visit the Magic Kingdom, you will eventually end up at the Transportation Center. If you arrive by car or bus you must pass through the Main Entrance Gates (car parking fee $2). By bus, you will be deposited at the Transportation Center. If by car, you will be directed into the 12,000-car Magic Kingdom parking lot, where you can catch a tram ride (or walk) to the Transportation Center. There you can purchase your ticket, if you have not alrady done so, then board the monorail or take a boat to the Magic Kingdom. Or, you can do both; take the monorail over and return by boat. But be sure that at some time you ride the monorail through the 4th-floor level of the Contemporary Hotel.

If you are heading to Epcot Center, you will also pass through toll gates ($2) and into a (9,000-car) parking area. A tram will deliver you to the ticket booth area and you can walk directly into Future World from there. If, by chance, the Epcot parking lot is full, you will be directed to the larger lot at the Transportation Center from where you can ride the monorail to Epcot Center and enjoy a ride through Future World before being deposited at the ticket center.

WDW ADMISSION PRICES: General admission costs for the Magic Kingdom and Epcot Center are the same. Tickets can be purchased for a single day in either park, but are good for that particular park only. You cannot buy a single-day ticket and use it to see both attractions, which would be an impossible task at any rate. The most economical way to see Walt Disney World is to purchase a multiple-day "passport" which is good for both the Magic Kingdom and Epcot Center. The ticket also includes transportation. Multi-day passports are available in three-, four-, and five-day units. Pricing information at press time is as follows:

One-Day World Passport: adults, $18; children 3–12, $15.
Three-Day Passport: adults, $42; child, $34.
Four-Day Passport: adults, $52; child, $42.
Five-Day Passport: adults, $62; child, $50.

Guests staying in WDW hotels, villas, or the campground receive a slight reduction.

A one-day ticket is good for either the Magic Kingdom or Epcot Center, *but not both.* Multiple-day tickets are valid at either park.

TRAVELING AROUND WDW: WDW's *monorail* and *ferries* can take you to the Magic Kingdom. Monorail travel is also available from the Magic Kingdom to Epcot. Call WDW information if you have questions; 824–4321. *Water taxis* and *buses* can carry visitors around World Showcase. However, if your health permits it, don't stand in Epcot lines to get on a bus to go to World Showcase pavilions—you'll probably save time walking.

If you have small children, *strollers* can be rented. Inquire at ticket windows. Kids will tire, and the strollers are also handy for packages, camera cases, etc.

Wheelchairs are also available. Also inquire about these at ticket windows.

Most important, wear comfortable shoes! And dress casually.

TOURIST INFORMATION. For detailed information on Walt Disney World, contact: *Guest Relations Department, Walt Disney World,* Box 40, Lake Buena Vista, FL 32830; 305–824–4500. Assistance and information at Walt Disney World can be obtained from the Guest Services desks of the resort hotels, at City Hall within the Magic Kingdom, at WDW Village, at Earth Station within Epcot Center, or from Guest Relations at 824–4500. (See also "Telephones," above.)

Foreign currency can be exchanged at Sun Bank locations at WDW Shopping Village, next to City Hall as you enter the Magic Kingdom, and at Epcot. Sun Banks and Barnett Banks in downtown Orlando also have foreign exchange departments.

BABYSITTING. If you are staying at a WDW resort and are interested in seeing the nighttime sights without the kiddies, call Kindercare at 827–5437. Children 2 and over who are toilet-trained can be left at the Care Center from 6:00 P.M. to midnight. For in-room babysitting, there is no time limit, but a three-hour minimum, plus travel time, is charged. Call for rates.

SPORTS. All sports activities are available to non-staying guests as well as to hotel guests, but registered guests have a priority on starting times and equipment rental. Sport facilities include two championship *golf* courses at the Golf Resort and another at Lake Buena Vista near WDW Village, plus a 6-hole beginner's course at the Golf Resort. For starting times, call the Master Starter at 824–3625. There are 11 *tennis* courts, six at the Contemporary Hotel, 824–1000, two at the Golf Resort, 824–2200, and three at the Lake Buena Vista Club, 828–3741. *Swimming pools* are available at all resorts and at River Country, a water-related attraction with water chutes, rapids, slides, swings, beach, and the old-swimming-hole atmosphere. *Boating, water skiing, sailing,* and the full range of water-oriented fun is available through beachside attendants at the Contemporary Hotel and Polynesian Village. At Fort Wilderness, guests can enjoy *horseback riding, fishing, swimming, horseshoes, nature trails, hiking,* and *bike pedaling.* Fees for all sports vary and should be checked by calling 824–4500.

SHOPPING. For unusual and sophisticated shopping there are two main areas. One is *World Showcase,* where nine of the ten countries represented (not the USA) offer unique native merchandise that would otherwise require an overseas trip to obtain. The second area is at *Walt Disney World Village* in Lake Buena Vista, only two miles from Epcot Center and six miles from the Magic Kingdom. The Village is a collection of 29 rare and unusual shops that offer a variety of merchandise found so concentrated in very few places in the world. At all WDW shops, stores, resorts, and table-service restaurants, Master Card and American Express are accepted.

DINING OUT. Until the advent of Walt Disney World, central Florida area eateries might have been thought of in terms of chicken, black-eyed peas, hush puppies, and, perhaps, seafood. But good food has long been a trade mark of the Orlando area and the coming of Disney, and particularly Epcot Center, has only widened the gourmet diner's horizons. There are more than 100 eating places *inside* the Disney complex, and at the Hotel Plaza, plus hundreds in the surrounding areas. Thus, only a sampling can be listed. For wider area listings, see the *Practical Information for the Orlando Area* section.

Price classifications are based on the cost of an average meal for one person, not including tax, gratuity, or beverage. *Deluxe,* $30 and up: *Expensive,* $15 to $30; *Moderate,* $7 to $14; and *Inexpensive,* less than $7.

Abbreviations used for credit cards are AE, American Express, CB, Carte Blanche; DC, Diners Club; MC, MasterCard, and V, Visa. Within WDW, only AE and MC are accepted. Most restaurants will accept traveler's checks, but few, if any, will accept personal checks.

Abbreviations for meals are: B, breakfast; L, lunch; and D, dinner. Prices and operating hours change, so be sure to check first to be sure.

INSIDE MAGIC KINGDOM

Moderate

Crystal Palace. Graceful, domed setting for cafeteria. Turn left at end of Main Street, USA. B, L, and D. AE and MC.

King Stefan's Banquet Hall. Medieval theme. Prime rib, chicken, and seafood. Reservations made at door in person, L, D. AE and MC.

Town Square Cafe. A handy stop just inside Magic Kingdom on the right-hand side. Chicken, steaks, sandwiches, pies. B, L. and D. AE and MC.

INSIDE EPCOT CENTER

Reservations are necessary within Epcot Center for lunch and dinner at all listed restaurants except *LeCellier* in Canada. Because the system changes, be sure to check for current procedure upon arrival. Call 824–4321.

Expensive

Le Bistro de Paris. A delightful selection of traditional French dishes. Try the snapper prepared in a white wine. L, D. AE and MC.

Les Chefs de France. On World Showcase Promenade. Operated by three famed French chefs, who offer classic French foods. A real delight. Try the oysters baked with spinach and champagne sauce. L, D. AE and MC.

Mitsukoshi Restaurant. Japanese native cooks with authentic Far Eastern dishes. Several separate eating areas with tempura, terriyaki, and everything you'd expect to find, and more. L, D. AE and MC.

L'Originale Alfredo di Roma Ristorante. The names tells it. The specialty is fettuccine Alfredo, and you won't find anything you won't like. L, D. AE and MC.

Moderate

Biergarten. It's German all the way with sauerbraten, bratwurst, sauerkraut, dumplings, plus yodelers and a delightful oompah band. L and D. AE and MC.

Le Cellier. Canada's entry in the cuisine service, specializing in prime rib in a cafeteria format. Reservation not required. L, D. AE and MC.

The Good Turn Restaurant. A revolving full-service dining area in The Land pavilion in Future World. Rotates completely once each hour and overlooks "Listen to the Land" boat ride and a constantly changing background. Complete breakfast served, without reservations, but you'll need them for lunch and dinner. B, L, D. AE and MC.

Marrakesh. Authentic Moroccan cuisine. Try the basticca, a pastry filled with chicken and almonds. L,D. AE and MC.

Rose & Crown Pub and Dining Room. A touch of England with fish and chips, steak and kidney pie, bangers and mash, complete bar. L, D. AE and MC.

San Angel Inn Restaurant. In the Mexico pyramid. A full menu service in a relaxing setting. L, D. AE and MC.

WALT DISNEY WORLD VILLAGE

Deluxe

The Empress Room. On the upper deck of the *Empress Lily,* a concrete-embedded stern-wheeler; 828–3900. Dining at its best in luxurious surroundings with a sophisticated menu. A 20 percent surcharge is added to your bill. Men are required to wear jackets. D only. AE and MC.

Expensive

The Fisherman's Deck. On the *Empress Lilly* lower deck, overlooking the Buena Vista Lagoon. No reservations. L, D. AE and MC.

Lake Buena Vista Club. At the LBV Golf Course; 828–3735. A typical country-club atmosphere with a full menu in an informal and relaxing theme. Dinner reservations preferred. Jackets for dinner. B, L, and D. AE and MC.

Steerman's Quarters. On the *Empress Lilly.* Superior dining with special emphasis on beef dishes. No reservations. L, D. AE and MC.

Moderate

Village Restaurant. On edge of Buena Vista Lagoon. Seafoods, omelets, quiche, sandwiches, and bar service. No reservations. L, D. AE and MC.

WDW VILLAGE HOTEL PLAZA

Deluxe

Arthur's 27. L. D. Arthur's roof sits atop the 27-floor Buena Vista Palace Hotel and offers a panoramic view of the Disney complex and the surrounding countryside; 827–2727. Continental cuisine. Reservations only. Appropriate dress required. D only, 6:00–9:00 P.M. All major credit cards.

Expensive

The Flying Dutchman. In the American Dutch Resort, 1850 Hotel Plaza Blvd.; 828–4444. Features Florida and Maine lobster and veal. B, L, D. All major credit cards.

El Cid. In the Royal Plaza Hotel, 1905 Hotel Plaza Blvd.; 828–2828. International cuisine in a casual elegance. Call for reservations. D only. Major cards.

BREAKFAST AND BRUNCH SPECIALS. One of the best food buys in Walt Disney World is the **breakfast buffet** served in the *Golf Resort,* at the *Polynesian Village,* or at the *Top of the World* in the *Contemporary Hotel.* All you want for $5.50 adult, $3.75 for children under 12.

For the kids, there are **"character" breakfasts** at the *Polynesian, The Empress Lilly,* and the *Contemporary,* where Mickey, Pluto, Goofy, or any of the other Disney characters just might pop in. Prices vary, so check first.

On Sundays, a **champagne brunch** is offered at the *Lake Buena Vista Club,* the *Golf Resort,* and the *Contemporary,* featuring bloody Marys and screwdrivers as well as the bubbly wines. Prices vary. Check first.

NIGHT LIFE AND BARS. A few of the nighttime shows and activities include:

Baton Rouge Lounge. On the *Empress Lilly* at WDW Village. Continuous entertainment 1:00 A.M. nightly.

Hoop-Dee-Doo Musical Revue. Pioneer Hall at Fort Wilderness Campground. A foot-stompin' country show with barbecued ribs, chicken, corn on the cob, beans, and strawberry shortcake. Three shows nightly. Check first at 824–8000. Reservations necessary well in advance. Adults $18.50; children $12.

The Polynesian Review. In Luau Cove at Polynesian Village; 824–8000. A full dinner, luau style, with a lively South Seas revue. Adults $20, youths 12–17, $16.50; and children 3–11, $12. Hours vary. Reservations required. AE and MC.

Top of the World. "Broadway at the Top" is a dinner show, including a live musical revue and dancing, at the Contemporary Hotel. Reservations required. AE and MC.

Village Lounge. A warm and friendly club with live jazz entertainment. No cover, but there may be a minimum. AE and MC.

There are a dozen other lounges and bars in the resort hotels, most with some type of entertainment, including the *Top of the World Lounge* (not the dinner-dance-show area) where you sip your refreshment while watching the lights or fireworks at the nearby Magic Kingdom. More entertainment can be found at WDW Village. In addition, each of the six major hotels in the Hotel Plaza at WDW Village has one or two lounges with entertainment and shows.

EXPLORING MORE OF THE ORLANDO AREA

The attraction next to Disney in size and investment is the $60 million Sea World of Florida, a marine life theme park located twelve miles southwest of Orlando and ten minutes from Walt Disney world, where it offers six major shows daily and twenty-three exhibits. And there is a damp kind of fun to be had at Orlando's Wet 'n Wild amusement park: water flumes and slides, boats, swimming holes, rapids, and whirlpools.

Within an hour's drive or bus ride to the south is Florida Cypress Gardens, the home of the original water ski show and the site of beautiful botanical gardens with more than 8,000 varieties of plant life. Florida's famed beaches are less than an hour away. Only a half hour away is Circus World, featuring live circus performers, thrill rides, and animals. And there are dozens of other attractions overshadowed by the giants.

To accommodate the influx of visitors, the area boasts some 45,000 hotel rooms, and many more are under construction.

The area supports a symphony orchestra, several theatrical groups, ballet, the arts, museums, and four institutions of higher learning: The University of Central Florida, Rollins College, Seminole Community College, and Valencia Community College, plus vocational and other private schools. In addition, Orlando is the home of one of the state's finest university-affiliated research and development parks. Central Florida Research Park is adjacent to and operated in cooperation with the University of Central Florida.

Outdoor recreation plays a major role in the lifestyle of many Orlando area residents. The balmy temperature averages 72 degrees, making Orlando a perfect place for golf, tennis, sailing, fishing, and a variety of other outdoor activities. Almost every other home has either a pool in the backyard or a boat in the driveway. Lakeside living and boating are almost synonymous with central Florida. There are nearly 2,000 lakes and springs in the tri-county area.

Along Winter Park's famous chain of lakes boaters can view stately homes and the Rollins College Campus. The Winter Park chain and the Butler Chain of Lakes are popular outlets for local boaters who water-ski and fish. In nearby Sanford, Lake Monroe provides a link to the St. Johns River. Naturalists, swimmers, and canoists enjoy the subtropical woodlands and crystal waters of Wekiva Springs State Park near Longwood.

Golf and tennis are two other outdoor sports that influence lifestyle in the Orlando area, making country club living a natural. In the past several years numerous golf clubs have developed, many of them as an integral part of a residential community. These communities aspire to something called the "total lifestyle concept." They strive to make the most of central Florida living, with golf, tennis, swimming, shopping, dining, and more, all in one residential vicinity. There are currently thirty-five golf courses in the immediate area.

Thus, a once isolated village with "no reason to be" has become an ever-expanding center of tourism, industry, commerce, and agriculture, as well as a transportation hub that serves the state, the nation, and the world. In addition, it would appear that central Florida has it all—education, culture, the arts, a relaxed lifestyle, an ideal climate, forests, lakes, recreation, and outdoor activities, and close proximity to

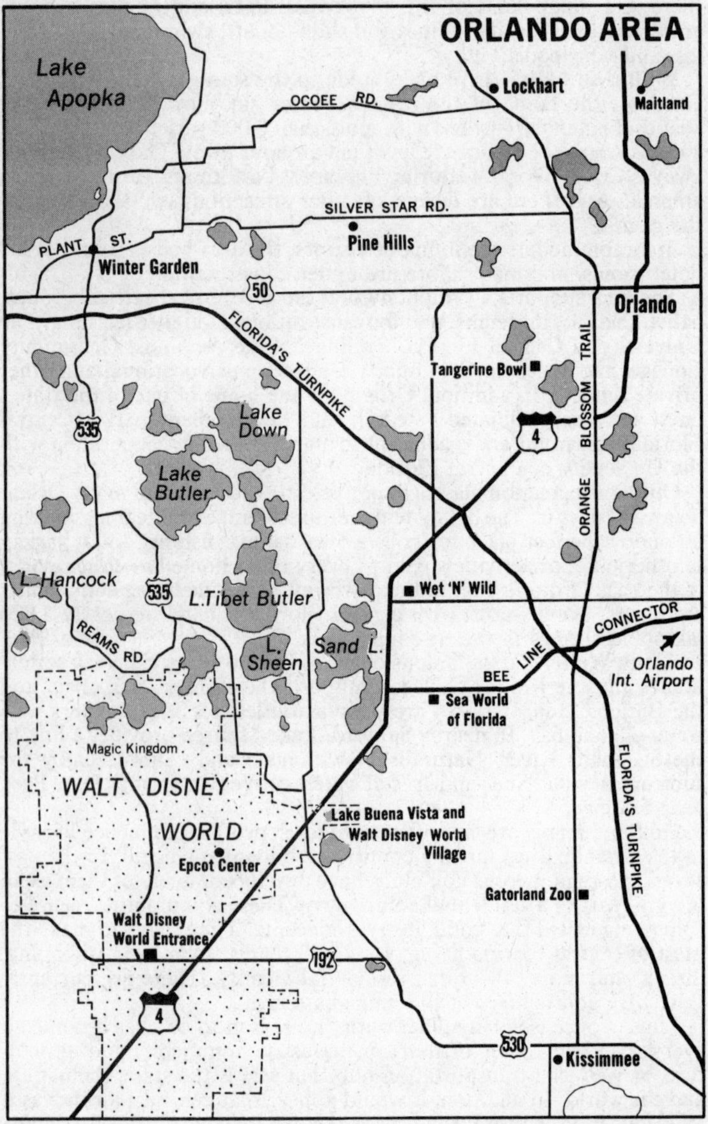
ORLANDO AREA
Lake Apopka
OCOEE RD.
Lockhart
Maitland
SILVER STAR RD.
PLANT ST.
Pine Hills
Winter Garden
50
Orlando
FLORIDA'S TURNPIKE
Tangerine Bowl
ORANGE BLOSSOM TRAIL
535
Lake Down
4
Lake Butler
L. Hancock
535
L.Tibet Butler
Wet 'N' Wild
CONNECTOR
REAMS RD.
L. Sheen
Sand L.
BEE LINE
Orlando Int. Airport
Sea World of Florida
Magic Kingdom
WALT DISNEY WORLD
Epcot Center
Lake Buena Vista and Walt Disney World Village
FLORIDA'S TURNPIKE
Gatorland Zoo
Walt Disney World Entrance
192
4
530
Kissimmee

two coastlines and beaches. Perhaps the local newspaper was not exaggerating when it formerly carried in its front-page logo the daily reminder: "It's a Privilege to Live in Central Florida."

To define the Greater Orlando area for purposes of this chapter is to include Orange, Osceola, and part of Seminole counties. Orange County, with Orlando as the county seat, includes Winter Park, Lake Buena Vista, and part of Walt Disney World. Osceola County, to the south, is also a host to Walt Disney World, and has Kissimmee as the county seat, and St. Cloud as its agricultural-oriented center. To the north of Orlando is Seminole County, which includes the bedroom communities of Maitland, and Altamonte Springs, with Sanford as the county seat. For more information on central Florida, outside of the greater Orlando area, see the following chapter: "Central Florida: East, West, and North of Orlando."

PRACTICAL INFORMATION FOR THE ORLANDO AREA

HOW TO GET THERE. By air. Orlando International Jetport is 14 miles from downtown Orlando and Winter Park, and about 18 miles from Kissimmee. It is a major airport served daily by most commercial carriers with direct flights to 100 U.S. cities. Transportation from the airport is readily available by shuttle bus, tour bus, limousine service, and taxi. Car rentals are also available. See "How to Get Around," below.

If you're traveling by private aircraft, Orlando Executive Airport is within the city, and services private and corporate aircraft.

By bus. *Greyhound* and *Trailways* both offer frequent service to Orlando. To get to a local hotel, however, will probably require a taxi. The Greyhound Bus terminal is at 300 West Amelia St. in Orlando; 305–824–4319. The Trailways terminal is at 30 North Hughey Ave., Orlando; 305–422–7107.

By car. See *Practical Information for WDW.*

By train. See *Practical Information for WDW.*

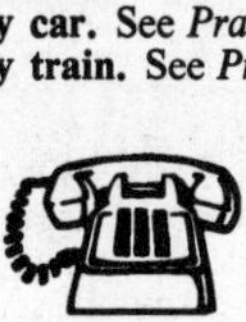

TELEPHONES. See *Practical Information for WDW.*

Emergency Numbers: In the Orlando area, the number 911 can be used to call the police, ambulance service, and fire department. Be sure to remain at the telephone until the dispatcher can determine the nature of the emergency. Remember, 911 is an *emergency* number, only.

HOTELS AND MOTELS. Accommodations in the Orlando area run the full range from deluxe to raw-bones basic budget. As a rule of thumb, the deluxe and more expensive hotel rooms are found in and around Walt Disney World area and Sea World. The farther one gets from attractions, the more likely one will be to find less pretentious (and less expensive) but probably quite comfortable accommodations.

When reserving a room, be sure to check on family rates. Many hotels and motels allow up to four or five guests for the same rate as two. Some offer kitchenettes, another advantage for a large family.

There are some peak periods and some lows, which might be considered when planning a visit to the Orlando area. The winter season is roughly from mid-December through the end of March, and the summer crunch starts in early June and fades after Labor Day. Thus, accommodations are easier to find (and cheaper) from the post-Easter rush to the end of May, and again from after Labor Day to mid-November.

No matter where you stay in the Orange County area, you will pay a 7 percent tax, 5 percent of which is sales tax and 2 percent is resort tax.

In listing accommodations, and because of the volume, only a cross section of area hotels can be included. Most accept major credit cards. The rates given are based on double occupancy, European Plan, and are arranged by districts in the following categories: *Deluxe,* $110 and up; *Expensive,* $90 to $110; *Moderate,* $60 to $90; *Inexpensive,* $40 to $60; and *Basic Budget,* less than $40. For accommodations in and closer to Walt Disney World, see *Practical Information for Walt Disney World,* earlier in this chapter.

AIRPORT VICINITY

Moderate

Orlando Airport Marriott Hotel. 7499 Augusta National Dr., Orlando 32812; 305–851–9000. 486 rooms in a nine-story tower one mile from terminal. Two restaurants, two lounges, entertainment, playground, game room, and spa. No extra charge for children; $10 per extra adult.

Inexpensive

Days Inn, Airport. 2323 McCoy Rd., Orlando 32809; 305–859–6100. 724 rooms, two miles from airport. Some efficiencies. Airport courtesy van. Two restaurants, two pools, game rooms, and gift shop. Children in room $1 extra, and $5 per additional adult. No charge for cots.

Sheraton Orlando International Airport. 3835 McCoy Rd., Orlando 32812; 305–859–2711 (toll-free, 800–325–3535). 289 rooms, 1½ miles from terminal. Two restaurants, lounge, and pool. No extra charge for children. Extra cots $6.

CENTRAL ORLANDO

Expensive

Radisson Hotel Orlando. 60 S. Ivanhoe Blvd., Orlando, 32804; 305–425–4455 (toll-free, 800–228–9822). A convention hotel in downtown area, with meeting rooms and exhibit space. The 15-story building houses 344 rooms, plus restaurant, pool, tennis courts, exercise room, sauna, and whirlpool.

Moderate

Harley Hotel of Orlando. 151 E. Washington St., Orlando; 305–841–3220 (toll-free, 800–321–2323). Located in the heart of downtown with 301 rooms. Pool, lounge, dining room, entertainment, and transportation to the airport. Extra adult, $10.

Howard Johnson's Downtown. 304 W. Colonial Dr., Orlando 32801; 305–843–8700 (toll-free, 800–654–2000). Located at junction of I–4 and SR 50 with 263 rooms, lounge, restaurant, gift shop, and pool.

Ramada Inn Central. 4919 W. Colonial Dr., Orlando 32808; 305–299–8180 (toll-free, 800–327–6908). 219 rooms with restaurant, lounge, pool, and playground; transportation to attractions and airport. $6 extra for cots or extra adult.

Basic Budget

Orange Court Motor Lodge. 650 N. Orange Ave., Orlando 32801; 305–422–5131. Offers 209 rooms and lounge. Children not accepted.

NAVAL TRAINING CENTER AREA

Moderate

Sheraton Colonial Plaza Motor Inn. 2801 E. Colonial Dr., Orlando 32803; 305–894–2741. 225 units. Lounge and pool. Discounts available.

Inexpensive

Orlando Motor Lodge. 1825 North Mills Ave., Orlando 32803; 305–896–4111. 85 units. Discounts available, kitchenettes, and pool.

Basic Budget

Flamingo Court. 1819 N. Mills Ave., Orlando 32803; 305–896–3121. Coffee shop, lounge, pool, and kitchenettes. Major credit cards.

NORTH ORLANDO AREAS

Deluxe

Errol Country Club. P. O. Box 1208, Apopka 32703; 305–886–5000. A cluster of comfortable villas off US 441 N., with two bedrooms and two baths. $137.50 per night for two; $167.50 for four. Restaurant, lounge, pool, tennis courts, and a golf course. Weekly and monthly rates.

Moderate

Altamonte Springs Inn/Racquet Club. 151 N. Douglas Ave., Altamonte Springs, 32714; 305–869–9000. Lots of tennis plus 216 rooms with pool, playground, restaurant and lounge. Extra adult, $6.

Inexpensive

Holiday Inn, Lee Road. 626 Lee Rd.; Orlando 32810; 305–645–5600 (toll-free, 800–238–8000). At junction of I–4 and Lee Road. Offers 200 rooms plus restaurant, lounge, pool, and meeting space. Extra adult, $6.

Basic Budget

Days Inn Orlando North Lodge. 450 N. Douglas Ave., Altamonte Springs 32714; 305–862–7111 (toll-free, 800–325–2525). 437 rooms, two pools, restaurants, gas station. Children, $1 each. Extra adults, $5.

ORLANDO SOUTH

Moderate

Gold Key Inn. 7100 S. Orange Blossom Trail, Orlando, 32809; 305–855–0050 (toll-free 800–327–0304). 208 rooms, pool, entertainment lounge, putting green, Piccadilly Restaurant. Also a separate Executive Club. Extra adult, $6.

ORLANDO NEAR-SOUTHWEST

Inexpensive

Best Western Catalina Inn. 3401 McLeod Rd., Orlando 32805; 305–841–6450 (toll-free, 800–327–0502). Convenient to I–4. 205 rooms, retaurant, lounge, pool.

Days Inn, 33rd Street. 2500 W. 33rd. St., Orlando 32805; 305–841–3731. (toll-free, 800–241–3400). Convenient to I–4, with 198 rooms, restaurant, and pool. Charge of $1 for each child. Extra adult, $5.

HOW TO GET AROUND. By car. An automobile is by far the most convenient way to get around, but is by no means the only way if you stick with the standard tourist attractions and reside at a sizable hotel or motel where shuttle rides are available. Getting around in the Orlando area should not be difficult. Slicing north and south through downtown Orlando is Interstate-4, which is a direct link between Daytona and Tampa/St. Petersburg. Also in the downtown area is the East-West Expressway, a toll road that carries State Road 50 traffic above the city streets and out of the heavy traffic. Farther south, the Beeline Expressway fronts the airport and connects Cocoa Beach and the east coast areas with I–4. The Florida Turnpike links northwest-Central Florida from Wildwood to the southeast and Miami areas.

Hwy. 436, also known as Semoran Boulevard, runs along the city's eastern and northern periphery and ties the airport with the East-West Expressway, Hwy. 50, I–4 East (northbound), and US 441 north to Apopka. US 441 and US 17/92 are additional north-south routes through Orlando and Kissimmee.

US Hwy. 192 is the southern edge of Disney property and passes the main entry to the Magic Kingdom. Called the Spacecoast Parkway, US 192 has a concentration of motels and campgrounds both east and west of the Disney entrance. US 192 also leads east into Kissimmee, crosses the Florida Turnpike, and ends on the beach at Indiatlantic.

There are more than 50 car rental agencies in Orlando. All major rental companies have offices inside the airport terminal, while many smaller and lesser-known agencies are found on airport approach roads. For the big ones, Avis, Budget, General, Hertz, and National, advanced reservations are essential, if you want fast service. Thus, you have a wide range of choices, from a luxurious limousine to a less pretentious "Rent-A-Wreck". For a list of rental companies, see "Rental Cars" under "Getting from the Airport" in *Practical Information for WDW.*

By taxi. It is approximately 14 miles from Orlando International Jetport to midtown Orlando and about the same distance to the International Drive area. A taxi to either place from the airport will cost in the neighborhood of $15, plus tip. Most cabs are metered, but if not, be sure to settle on a price before starting out. (*City and Yellow Cab Co.,* 425–3111; *Ace Taxi,* 859–7514)

By limousine service. See "Getting from the Airport" in *Practical Information for WDW.*

By bus. City bus #11 leaves from the airport daily at 30 minutes past the hour from 6:30 A.M. until 7:30 P.M. A bus departs from the downtown terminal at Pine and Central avenues daily at 15 before the hour from 5:45 A.M. to 6:45 P.M. The departure point at the airport is the first level escalator doors at A and B terminals. The cost is 60 cents for passengers 6 and over. For additional details call Tri-County Transit at 841–8240. For bus information to WDW see "Getting from the Airport" and "Getting from your Hotel" in *Practical Informations for WDW.*

Tri-County Transit, 438 Woods Ave., Orlando, 32805, provides service from the downtown terminal north as far as Sanford and south into Sea World, International Drive, and the Skylake Subdivision. Schedules vary. Call 841–8240 for details. Other service also makes stops in Winter Park, Maitland, Cassellbery, Altamonte Springs, Naval Training Center, Goldenrod, Colonial Town, and Pine Hills.

Bus transportation from downtown Orlando to International Drive, Sea World, and WDW is also provided by *Greylines of Orlando.* For schedules call 422–0744.

TOURIST INFORMATION. For detailed information on Orlando and the surrounding communities and attractions, the following agencies can be most helpful: *Greater Orlando Area Chamber of Commerce,* 75 East Ivanhoe Blvd., P. O. Box 1234, Orlando 32802, 305–425–1234; the *Kissimmee/St. Cloud Visitors Bureau,* Box 2007, Kissimmee 32742, 305–847–5000; toll-free 800–327–9159; *Orlando* magazine, 742 Clay St, Winter Park 32789, 305–644–3355 (ask for special "Guide to Orlando" section of current issue, $1.50). The *Orlando Sentinel* also publishes special sections on area activities.

TOURS. *Downtown Walking Tour.* Orlando. Starts at 10:00 A.M. every Thursday from the corner of Wall Street Plaza and Orange Avenue. Look for the large blue sign that marks the starting point. Sponsored by the Junior League, the free tour visits downtown areas and lasts about one hour; 843–7463.

Scenic Boat Tour. East Morse Boulevard at Interlachen Avenue in Winter Park. A 12-mile boat ride through beautiful lakes and canals with views of Rollins College, Kraft Azalea Gardens, and other scenic spots. Adults, $4; children 2–12, $2. Call 644–4056 for schedules.

Scenic Tour Drive. Do it in your own car and follow signs. One in Orlando, another in Winter Park. Both start from respective chambers of commerce and lead past most interesting city points. For details, call Orlando Chamber, 75 E Ivanhoe Blvd., 425–1234, or Winter Park Chamber, 150 N. New York Ave., 644–8281.

PARKS. The subtropical climate of Central Florida offers endless opportunities for outdoor activity. A few of the places to enjoy nature and the elements include:

Christmas Park. A reconstructed Fort Christmas, originally used in the second Seminole War, with picnic area, playground, and ball fields, located 23 miles east of Orlando off State Roads 50 and 520; 568–4149.

Genius Drive. In Winter Park, east on Fairbanks Avenue and Osceola Drive, right on Henkel to Genius Drive. Take a sandy, country lane through a tunnel of ancient oaks to view 100 or more magnificent peacocks wandering freely on a large private estate. No charge.

Kelly Park. 26,000 gallons of 72-degree water flow each minute from Rock Springs, the focal point of this 200-acre park. Picnic tables and limited camping. Located five miles north of Apopka off State Road 435. Call 889–4179 for operating hours.

Lake Fairview Recreation Complex. A 23-acre park with swimming beach, boat ramp, picnic area, and playground. Open 10:00 A.M.–6:00 P.M. US 441 at Lee Rd., on northwest side of Orlando.

Loch Haven Park. Mills Ave. and Princeton in North Orlando. Home of the Loch Haven Art Center, Orange County Historical Museum, Orlando Science Museum, and other activities. Lots of room to walk or jog.

Turkey Lake Park. A city-owned outdoor complex at 3401 S. Hiawassee Rd. in southwest Orlando; 299–5581. Covered picnic tables, barbecue grills, hiking trails, bike paths, petting farm for the kids, playground, lake swimming, and limited camping. Open 9:30 A.M.–6:00 P.M. Admission $1. Camping extra.

Wekiva State Park. North of Orlando off Hwy. 436 between Apopka and Altamonte Springs. Swimming in the Wekiva River spring boil. Canoe rentals. Call 862–1500 for information on operating hours.

THEME PARKS AND AMUSEMENTS. Florida Cypress Gardens. Located on State Road 540 near Winter Haven. In Orlando, telephone 351–6606. A botanical garden, water show, fun, and adventure for the entire family. Visit *Southern Crossroads* and step back in time to a bustling antebellum town. Arcades, shopping cinema, and magic shows, kid-sized rides, and a huge model railroad exhibit. In the *Living Forest* is a six-acre animal nature center, where visitors can meet and touch friendly critters or observe and learn about the untamed. See hundreds of exotic birds and the exciting water ski show or enjoy a relaxing stroll or quiet electric boat ride among acres and acres of unmatched floral beauty. Ascend 153 feet on the revolving Island in the Sky ride. Hotel, dining facilities, and gift shops on property. Admission: adults, $10.95; children 6–11, $7.50. Open 8:00 A.M. to dusk every day.

Gatorland Zoo. South of Orlando on US 17/92 near Kissimmee; 855–5496. 35 acres of alligators and crocodiles, viewed from walkway. Also snakes, flamingos, monkeys, and other Florida natives. Open 8:00 A.M. to 6:00 P.M. daily. Adults, $4; children 3–11, $3.

Medieval Times. P. O. Box 2385. Kissimmee, 32741; 396–1518 (toll-free in Florida, 800–432–0768). A dinner show lasting one and a half hours reviving the days of King Arthur chivalry, with brave knights on horseback, jousting, sword-fighting, and competing. Dinner starts at 6:00 P.M.; show at 7:00. Adults, $19; youths 12–17, $17; children 3–11, $12.

Mystery Fun House. 5767 Major Blvd., off Kirkman Road near International Drive; 351–3355. Magic mirrors, moving floors, laughing doors, barrels that roll, etc. Open 10:00 A.M. to 9:00 P.M. daily. Adults, $4.76; children 4–12, $3.76.

Sea World. Located 10 miles south of Orlando at the intersection of I–4 and the Beeline Expressway, 7007 Sea World Dr., Orlando 32821; 351–3600 (toll-free, 800–327–2420 in Florida, 800–432–1178). Call for operating hours. Sea World is a 235-acre marine life theme park featuring performing marine animals in seven major shows and 23 exhibits. Admission: adults, $13.95; children 3–11, $11.95. An additional $3 gets you a week-long pass. Admission price covers all shows, including:

The Shamu Celebration: A new show featuring one of the best known whales, Shamu, who teams with Namu and Kandu for a remarkable and entertaining 30-minute performance in a 5-million-gallon tank. In harmony with their trainers, the three 4,500-pound stars help trace the evolution of man's relationship with killer whales.

Whale and Dolphin Friends: A mixed species of smaller whales and dolphins demonstrate some 200 behaviors including tail-walks, rope skipping, back flips, and other antics during a 35-minute show.

Spooky Kooky Castle: Sea lions, otters, and a walrus do slapstick in a whodunit skit at a haunted castle.

Shark Encounter: Live sharks in a 600,000-gallon aquarium built above a moving sidewalk where guests get a close view of hundreds of thrashing killers.

Beach Blanket Ski Party: On a 17-acre lagoon in front of Atlantis Theatre, this is a water and ski show of breathtaking quality.

Nautilus Theatre: A 3,100-seat theatre for special guest performances. Open during peak periods only.

Undersea Fantasy: A whimsical stage production concerning a girl who is transfixed to an underwater wonderland in a mythical ocean coral reef.

Al E. Gator's: A full-service restaurant within Florida Festival with seating for 250. Menu includes conch, snapper, and alligator served in a festive, casual atmosphere.

Also in the park are large aquariums, tropical fish, otter habitats, walrus training, the Cap'n Kids' World playground, botanical gardens, a Hawaiian Village, a Japanese Village, and a 400-foot sky tower (an additional charge to enter it). There are ten food outlets, ranging from snack shops to a delightful Polynesian luau and show. For the luau, call 351–3600, ext. 442, for a reservation and for current prices. (Note: For accommodations close to Sea World, see also *Practical Information for Walt Disney World.*)

Wet 'n Wild. 6200 International Dr., Orlando 32819; 351–3200 or 351–1800. A series of water flumes and slides, rapids, whirlpools, waterfalls, swimming holes, boats, and ski-tow ride. A handy diversion for families staying at International Drive hotels. General Admission: adults, $9.95; children, 3–12, $7.95; under 3, free. Hours vary; call for information.

More local theme parks are described in the following chapter, "Central Florida."

BEACHES. The famous Florida beaches are an hour away to the east and two hours to the west. See the next chapter, "Central Florida: East, West, and North of Orlando."

PARTICIPANT SPORTS. Fishing: Lakes are everywhere you look and large-mouth bass and specks are plentiful in most of them. Some of the more popular fishing areas are found in the Winter Park chain of lakes; along the Weikiva River on the north edge of Orlando; along the St. Johns River between Sanford and Deland, some 25 miles north of Orlando; in the Butler chain southwest of the city; in lakes of the Clermont-Mt. Dora area northwest of Orlando; and at East Tohopekaliga, east of Kissimmee. Fish camps, with bait and tackle, thrive in the area. Most have boat launch ramps and nearly all have Jon boat or motor-powered fishing boats. Some offer guides. The Orlando *Sentinel* runs a daily fishing column (420–5000), as well as solunar tables, and *Denmark's Sporting Goods* stores in the area (425–2525) gladly provide free advice to visiting fishermen. Be sure to obtain a license, of course. There may also be alligators; if you spot one, stay clear and by no means attempt to harm it. For information on fishing and licenses call the Florida Game and Fresh Water Fish Commission at 295–9123.

Swimming. For visitors, the safest swimming spots are at the hotels, the WDW River Country attraction, Wet n' Wild in the International Drive area, or the city and county parks with designated swimming areas, such as Lake Fairview, Hwy. 441 at Lee Road, or the Turkey Lake Park recreation area at 3401 S. Hiawassee Rd. The most popular, of course, are the nearby ocean beaches where most native Floridians like to go (see the next chapter, "East, West, and North of Orlando"). It is not prudent to swim in unfamiliar Florida rivers or lakes and never, ever, try to swim near thick weeds or murky waters. Other swimming facilities are available at Weikiva State Park, off Hwy 436 near Apopka; Downey Park, east of Orlando at Hwy 50 and 425 in Union Park; Kelly Park, north of Apopka on Hwy. 435; Orlo Vista Park, on Nowell Avenue north of Old Winter Garden Road; Warren Park, on Daetwyler Road north of Hwy. 528; Moss Park, on Moss Road off Hwy. 15.

Tennis. There are hundreds of tennis courts available and 32 golf courses in the Orlando area. For details on locations and green fees, call the Orlando Chamber of Commerce at 425–1234 for current list.

Waterskiing can be done on most lakes, but requires some preparation. For information on rentals and instruction, call the Chamber of Commerce at 425–1234, or *Florida State Ski and Dive, Inc.* (831–3200), *Ski World of Orlando* (894–5012), or *Walt Disney World* (Ft. Wilderness, 824–2900).

SPECTATOR SPORTS. **Baseball** fans find plenty of action through two sources. Orlando's Tinker Field, downtown at Tampa and Rio Grande Aves., is the spring training ground for the *Minnesota Twins,* and fans are constant observers during early practice sessions and during the pre-season games with other American or National League teams. For spring training 1985, the Houston Astros will be in Kissimmee. In addition, the city has its own team, the *Orlando Twins,* who play in the Southern League. For schedules call Tinker Field at 849–6346.

The city also has its own professional **football** team, the *Orlando Renegades,* a USFL member that moved from New Jersey in 1984. For information or tickets, call 843–USFL. Orlando Stadium is the home field.

Orlando is the scene of the annual *Citrus Bowl football* classic at Orlando Stadium, each December. For dates and participants, call 849–2107.

College football is generating new interest in the area with the recent development of the Knights at the University of Central Florida. In time, it should become a major sporting activity. Schedules can be obtained by calling the University at 275–2000.

Golf. The Orlando area also serves as host to several PGA and LPGA events at Walt Disney World (824–4500), *Arnold Palmer's Bay Hill course* southwest of town on Bay Hill Blvd. (876–2747), Errol Estates, on the north edge of Apopka, (886–5000), Rio Pinar east of town on El Prado Blvd. (277–5520); and other golf centers in the area. For dates and locations of tournament play, call the specific golf club or the Orlando Chamber of Commerce at 425–1234.

Greyhound racing is conducted December to May at the Sanford/Orlando Kennel Club, Dog Track Road off north US 17/92 at Longwood (831–1600), and **harness racing** and **horse racing** can be seen at Ben White Raceway (293–8721) on Lee Road and US 441 in Orlando's northwest corner.

Jai-alai is played nightly during the winter season at the Jai-Alai Fronton of Orlando Seminole on Hwys. 17–92 at State Rd. 436 in Casselberry; 331–9191. Matinees on Monday, Friday, and Saturday.

Orlando and Winter Park each support a **rugby** team and take part in national and international competition. For details, call Orlando Coach Jim Millar at 857–4669 or Johnny Johnson at 629–4824.

HISTORIC SITES. See "Christmas Park," under "Parks," above.

MUSEUMS. *Loch Haven Art Center.* Also in Loch Haven Park off Mills Street at Rollins Avenue; 896–4321. This is both an art center and a musuem that houses a permanent collection of pre-Colombian, African, and twentieth-century American art. It also hosts visiting art, such as the King Tut exhibit. Admission free, except when special exhibits are shown. Open Tuesday through Friday, 10:00 A.M. to 5:00 P.M.; Saturday noon to 5:00 P.M.; Sunday 2:00 P.M. to 5:00 P.M.; closed Mondays.

The Orlando Science Center. Located in Loch Haven Park off North Mills Street at Princeton Avenue; 896–7151, it is both a museum and a planetarium. The museum contains exhibits on astronomy, health, science, and history; the planetarium offers daily presentations. Admission: Adults, $2; children under 18 and senior citizens, $1.50. Open 9:00 A.M. to 5:00 P.M. Monday through Thursday; 9:00 A.M. to 9:00 P.M. Friday; noon to 9:00 P.M. Saturday; and noon to 5:00 P.M. Sunday.

The Orange County Historical Museum. Located in Loch Haven Park, it shares a building with the Orlando Science Center; 898–8320. It offers a look at the central Florida of a century ago and an extensive collection of Black history, including a slave cabin. Early printing processes and an early American fire station are part of the collection. The museum has also hosted visiting treasures, such as the Magna Carta. Admission free. Open 10:00 A.M. to 4:00 P.M. Tuesday through Friday, 2:00 P.M. to 5:00 P.M. Saturday and Sunday.

ART GALLERIES AND ART FESTIVALS. The mild climate of central Florida has encouraged the development of outdoor arts and craft festivals. There are three outstanding festivals, plus a number of fine galleries in the Orlando area. Included are:

Autumn Art Festival. Held during October on the campus of Rollins College off East Fairbanks Avenue in Winter Park. Features Florida's most outstanding artists who exhibit in a wooded, parklike setting. For dates and other details, call 671–1886 or 644–8281.

Cornell Fine Arts Center. Located at Rollins College, East Fairbanks Avenue in Winter Park; 646–2526. The collection includes nineteenth-century American art, fourteenth- and fifteenth-century European Old Masters, the Smith Watch/Key collection, Gregorian Oriental Rugs, stone sculptures, and more. Admission free.

Loch Haven Art Center. Located in Loch Haven Park off North Mills Avenue at Princeton, it is a rapidly growing center, which houses a permanent collection of Colombian, African, and twentieth-century American Art. It also hosts changing exhibits that offer a broad spectrum of art forms and art periods. Open Tuesday through Friday from 10:00 A.M. to 5:00 P.M. Saturday from 12 to 5 P.M.; Sunday, 2 to 5 P.M. Closed Monday. Free admission. Call 896–4231 for information.

Maitland Art Center. 231 W. Packward St., Maitland (just off US 17 92); 645–2181. Admission free. Call for operating hours. The Center resembles a Mayan temple and houses a variety of exhibits thoughout the year and periodic cultural events.

The Morse Gallery of Art. 151 E. Wellbourne Ave., Winter Park; 644–3686. Admission: adults, $2.50; students, $1. Home of unique collection of Louise Comfort Tiffany, Frank Lloyd Wright, and many others. Call for operating hours.

Winter Park Sidewalk Art Festival. Park Avenue in Winter Park. A juried event held the third weekend in March. Features artists from all over the U.S.,

Canada, and Mexico, who compete for sizable prize money. Truly a multi-arts event with periodic performances by the Florida Symphony Orchestra, as well as other musical and theater groups. Admission free. For additional information, call 628–2537 or the Winter Park Chamber of Commerce, 644–8281.

Walt Disney World Festival of the Masters. Held during a three-day period in November at Walt Disney World Village. Attracts some of the best artists from all over the country. For information, call 828–1241 or 824–4500.

A number of smaller, more local art festivals are conducted in many other communities of Central Florida. For information, call the Orlando Chamber of Commerce at 425–1234 or the chamber in your particular area of interest (see "Tourist Information," above).

MUSIC. Orlando is blessed with a well-rounded taste of the performing arts and with a newly renovated auditorium well-suited for the cultural events that take place there. *The Bach Festival of Winter Park* presents an annual program of the great choral compositions of Bach, along with other works of famous composers. Held during the last week of February in the Rollins College Chapel in Winter Park, the program is presented by a 140-voice choir supported by members of the Florida Symphony Orchestra. For additional information, call 646–2110.

The Florida Symphony Orchestra is an Orlando-based group recognized as one of the outstanding organizations in the southeast. It is Florida's only full-time professional orchestra and presents a full range of classical, pop, and educational concerts in its 100-or-more performances each year. Home for the Florida Symphony is the 2,500-seat Bob Carr Performing Arts Centre on West Robinson Avenue in downtown Orlando, where it performs ten classical subscription concerts during the October–May season. Several free concerts are performed throughout the year at various locations around the Orlando area. For tickets, times, and dates, call the Symphony office at 896–0331.

The Orlando Opera Company presents three major operas each season—usually in November, February, and March—and all feature the Florida Symphony Orchestra, as well as professional and international operatic talent. The Bob Carr Performing Arts Centre, West Robinson Ave., Orlando, is the scene. For information on performances, call 896–7575, or 843–8111.

DANCE. *The Ballet Royal,* a 30-year-old nonprofessional dance company formed to enhance appreciation of ballet, presents the *Nutcracker* during the Christmas holiday season with support from the Florida Symphony Orchestra. The company also presents a spring series of classical ballet. They perform at Bar Carr Municipal Auditorium, 401 Livingston St. For information, call 647–2717.

The Southern Ballet Theater is Central Florida's only professional dance company. The group presents performances of classical, modern, and jazz, and usually offers three shows during the winter season. Performances are in downtown Orlando at the Bob Carr Municipal Auditorium, 401 Livingston St. For information on the series, call 628–0133.

Dance Unlimited formed to provide young dancers an opportunity to develop their skills. The group appears in an annual concert and at various community functions during the year. Performances are usually at Bob Carr Municipal Auditorium. For schedules, call 671–2155.

The Innovations Dance Company of the Academy of Dance and Theatrical Arts is a nonprofessional company organized to perform classical and contemporary dance and to educate the public on these dance forms. There are two groups. The Senior Company gives an annual performance in June, while the Children's Company presents an annual spring performance. For details, call 645–3847. Performances are usually downtown at Bob Carr Auditorium.

STAGE. *Central Florida Civic Theatre* produces excellent shows that range from musicals to drama at the Edyth Bush Theatre in Loch Haven Park. Located off North Mills Avenue at Princeton, the group calls on excellent local talent for six productions a year. Call 896–7365 for information. The group also supports *The Central Florida Civic Theater for Young People,* which offers a series of productions for kids from kindergarten through ninth grade.

Once Upon A Stage, a dinner theater at 3376 Edgewater Dr. in Orlando, offers imported talent in musicals and drama in a comfortable cabaret setting. For details, call 422–3191.

Zev Buffman Broadway Theater Series imports a variety of professional road shows during the winter and spring months for presentation at Bob Carr Performing Arts Centre. Major talent and current Broadway hits are seen in the five or six productions each season. For information, call 849–9935.

SHOPPING. Central Florida is a shopper's dream. It is also a major shopping center for South Americans and West Indian Islanders who often end their stateside visits or business trips with a stop at Walt Disney World and the neighboring durable goods outlets. The visitor's choice extends from the unique, world-class shopping offered at Walt Disney World Village, to the quaint boutiques of Winter Park, to the two-level stores at Altamonte Mall, or the bargains at the Factory Outlet complex. While there are no *Macy's* or *Sak's* by name, the quality is matched under different names. But wherever you shop, be prepared for a 5-percent sales tax (except for groceries). The following list is only a sample of the larger shopping centers and is by no means all-inclusive. For information on shopping WDW and WDW Village see *Practical Information for Walt Disney World.*

Altamonte Mall. Central Florida's two-level, totally enclosed and air-conditioned mall with 165 stores that offer at least one of everything. Includes huge Burdines, Jordan Marsh, Robinsons, and Sears department stores, and covers 30 acres. Off I–4 north of Orlando, and east on Hwy. 436. You can't miss it!! Open 10:00 A.M. to 9:00 P.M. daily; Sundays, 12:30 P.M. to 5:30 P.M. Plenty of parking space.

Antique Row. Not a proper name, but a collection of a dozen or more antique shops spread along several blocks of North Orange Avenue. Exit I–4 at Princeton, then one block east to Orange Avenue. Turn either way, and you'll find antiques. Most shops are open from 10:00 A.M. to 5:00 P.M., Monday through Saturday.

Colonial Plaza. Go east on Hwy. 50 to Bumby. Closest mall to downtown area. Has large Ivey's, Belk-Lindsey, and Jordan Marsh department stores, plus 100 smaller outlets and restaurants. Should have whatever you're looking for. Open 10:00 A.M. to 9:00 P.M. daily; Sunday, noon to 5:30 P.M.

Downtown Orlando. Exit I–4 at South Street, Anderson, Robinson, Amelia, Colonial, or Ivanhoe onto Orange Avenue in heart of downtown area. Most stores are open from 9:00 A.M. to 5:00 P.M., six days a week. Closed Sundays. Metered parking in most places.

Factory Outlet Mall off I–4 south of Orlando. Exit to International Drive then north on Oakridge Road. Billed as the largest discount mall in the country with 25 to 50 percent savings, the 50 stores include outlets for men's, women's, and children's clothing, glassware, shoes, china, cameras, electronics, jewelry, artwork, toys, home furnishings, and nearly everything else. Plenty of parking. Open 10:00 A.M. to 9:00 P.M.; Sunday, 1:00 to 9:00 P.M.

Flea World Market. On US 17/92 north of Orlando. Claims to be the largest flea market mall in the nation, with 750 dealer booths. Free parking and admission. Open Friday, Saturday, and Sunday, from 8:00 A.M. to 5:00 P.M.

Florida Festival, across from Sea World at I–4 and the Beeline Expressway, 10 miles southwest of Orlando. A collection of 16 specialty boutiques and 22 eateries housed beneath a tentlike canopy of Fiberglas featuring Florida arts and crafts. Open from 10:00 A.M. to 1:00 A.M. No admission charge. Good parking.

Loehmann's Plaza. A 160,000-square-foot, open-air fashion shopping center in Altamonte Springs, north of Orlando, offering designer fashions at a reputed 30 to 50 percent discount. No credit cards or returns. Take it "as is." Follow I–4 north to SR 434, then west 2 miles. Open 10:00 A.M. to 5:30 P.M. daily; Sunday, noon to 5:30 P.M.

Park Avenue, Winter Park, a tree-lined main street facing Central Park and known locally as "Little Europe" because of its quaint boutiques, specialty shops, exclusive and expensive women's finery, and gourmet restaurants. Be sure to explore "Hidden Gardens," which any native will gladly point out for you. Most stores are open from 9:00 or 10:00 A.M. to 5:00 P.M. and are closed on Sunday. To get there, follow Fairbanks Avenue east and turn left at Park Avenue near Rollins College.

DINING OUT. In keeping with Orlando's conservatism, most restaurants are moderately priced with the exception of the more exclusive hotel dining rooms. Despite moderation in prices, there is some excellent eating to be had in the central Florida area. You should find almost anything you want. Seafood is always popular, but there are excellent steak houses, as well as dinner and entertainment spots. And the nearby Walt Disney World complex is a diners' world of its own and is thus listed separately (see *Practical Information for Walt Disney World*).

Price classifications of the following restaurants, from expensive to inexpensive, are based on the cost of an average meal for one person and does not include tip, tax, or beverage. *Expensive,* $15 to $30; *Moderate,* $7 to $14; and *Inexpensive,* less than $7.

Abbreviations for credit cards are AE, American Express, CB, Carte Blanche, DC, Diners Club; MC, MasterCard; V, Visa. Most restaurants will accept traveler's checks but few, if any, will accept personal checks.

Abbreviations for meals are: B, breakfast; L, lunch; D, dinner. Since operating hours often change, you should telephone first to be sure.

AMERICAN-CONTINENTAL

Expensive

Jordan's Grove. 1300 S. Orlando Ave., Maitland, 628–0020. A tree-shaded old home turned restaurant. Fine selection of foods and wine. L, D, Tuesday through Sundays. All major credit cards.

Maison et Jardin Restaurant. 430 Wymore Rd., Altamonte Springs; 862–4410. Continental and American cuisine, with veal Oscar a specialty. Situated in a villa surrounded by statues and fountains. Excellent wine list. Cocktails.

Strolling musicians. D, Tuesday through Sunday. Also Sunday brunch. Reservations suggested. All major credit cards.

Moderate

Alexander's. 431 E. Central Blvd., Orlando; 422–5578. In Plaza Building on Lake Eola in downtown area. Varied menu. Piano accompaniment with dinner. L, Monday through Friday; D, Monday through Saturday. All major credit cards.

Cafe on the Park. 151 E. Washington St., Orlando, in Harley Hotel; 841–3220. Rose dining room overlooks Lake Eola. B, L, D daily. Sunday brunch. Cocktails. All major credit cards.

Empire Room Supper Club. Langford Hotel, New England Ave. at Interlachen, Winter Park; 644–3400. Offers full evening of entertainment. Features prime rib, steaks, and seafood. D, Monday through Saturday. Reservations recommended. All major credit cards.

Freddie's Steak House. Hwy. 17/92 in Fern Park; 339–3265. Famed for its steaks and seafoods served in gaslight setting. Piano bar entertainment. D only, closed Sundays. Reservations preferred. All major credit cards.

House of Beef. West Colonial Drive at John Young Parkway, Orlando; 295–1931. A popular prime rib and steak place. Salad bar. Fine wine list. L, D daily. Major credit cards.

Lili Marlene's. 129 West Church St. at Rosie O'Grady's, Orlando; 422–2434. French onion soup a house specialty. International selections of pork, lamb, fowl, and seafood in an atmosphere of antiques and novelties. L, D daily. Sunday brunch. Full bar service. All major credit cards.

Longwood Village Inn. 150 South East Lake St., Longwood; 834–5555. A 100-year-old Victorian Inn specializing in steaks, seafood, and veal. L, Monday through Friday; D, Monday through Saturday. All major credit cards.

Purple Porpoise. 220 N. Orlando Ave., Maitland; 644–1861. A seafood and steak house with a New England motif. Fish nets adorn the walls. Unlimited salad buffet. Lobster, raw oysters, steak. Cocktails. D daily. Reservations accepted. Major credit cards.

Smuggler's Inn. 525 E. Altamonte Springs Rd., in Altamonte Springs; 828–8125. Prime rib and king crab are house specialties. Luncheon special is "British Burger" on sour dough bread. L, D daily. All major credit cards.

Two Flights Up. 329 Park Ave., South, over Colony Gardens in Winter Park; 644–9868. Skylights, atriums, and greenery are backdrops for a well-rounded menu. Famous for its coffees. L, D Monday through Saturday. MC, V.

Inexpensive

Bakerstreet. 743 Lee Road, Winter Park; 644–8811; also 703 Orange Blossom Trail in Orlando; 851–8811. Offers a variety of fried munchies, quiche, burgers, marinated chicken sandwiches, plus steak and seafood. Nachos are the house specialty. L, D daily. Cocktails. AE, MC, V.

Johnny's Pizza Palace. 4908 Lake Underhill Rd., Orlando; 277–3452. Try the stuffed pizza—two sealed crusts covered with mozzarella and sauce stuffed with blended cheeses. L, D daily. AE, MC, V.

Kelly's. Fashion Square Mall, East Colonial Dr., Orlando; 898–6041. Fried munchies, quiche, burgers, nachos, with Polynesian chicken the house speciality. L, D daily. Late-night dancing Wednesday through Saturday. All major credit cards.

SEAFOOD

Moderate

Al E. Gators. At Sea World's Florida Festival, I–4 and Beeline Expressway; 351–3600. The specialty in this tent-covered novelty attraction is alligator tail breaded in crushed pecans. Gator's bar is 50 feet long with electric train to deliver drinks. L, D daily. All major credit cards.

Bailey's. At Sheraton World, 10100 International Dr., Orlando; 352–1100. A complete seafood bar with shrimp, oysters, clams, plus a full range of entrées from shrimp tempura to pepperloin. D daily. Reservations recommended. All major credit cards.

Bakerstreet Seafood Grill. 743 Lee Rd., Winter Park; 644–8811. Grills over mesquite charcoal. Specialties include swordfish, grouper, red snapper, and halibut. New Orleans décor. Wines and beer. D daily. Reservations accepted. AE, MC, V.

Brazil's. 701 Orienta Ave., Altamonte Springs; 331–7260. Creatively prepared fresh seafoods daily. Also prime rib, steaks, and chicken. L Monday through Friday; D daily. Cocktail lounge with live entertainment and dancing Tuesday and Saturday. All major credit cards.

Gary's Duck Inn. 3974 S. Orange Blossom Trail, Orlando; 843–0270. A tradition in Orlando. Largest seafood restaurant in Central Florida; a best buy. Features wide range of menu items, but is best known for its seafood platters. L Sunday through Friday; D Saturday. All major credit cards.

CHINESE

Moderate

Kim Wu Chinese Restaurant. 4904 S. Kirkman Rd., Orlando; 293–0752. Cantonese, Mandarin, and Szechuan in authentic style. Roast Peking Duck a specialty. Winter-melon soup and *dim sum* selections. Wine and beer. AE, MC, V.

ENGLISH

Moderate

Limey Jim's. At the Hyatt Orlando, I–4 and US 192; 396–1234. A touch of merry old England with gas lamps and pewter tableware. A broad selection, with Hyatt cheese soups a specialty. D daily. Sunday brunch. All major credit cards.

Townsend's Fishhouse and Tavern. 35 West Michigan St., Orlando; 422–5560. English-pub atmosphere. Seafood, prime rib, barbecued ribs, homemade soups, and unlimited salad bar. L, D daily. All major credit cards.

FRENCH

Expensive

La Belle Verriere. 142 Park Ave., S. Winter Park; 645–3377. French continental cuisine served in a garden setting amid a collection of Tiffany stained glass. International menu includes escargots, vichyssoise, Chateaubriand, pepper steak, and rack of lamb. L, D, Monday through Saturday. All major credit cards.

Moderate

La Normandie. 2021 East Colonial Dr., Orlando; 896–9976. Authentic French cuisine. Full menu. Cocktails. L, Monday through Friday; D, Monday through Saturday. All major credit cards.

Le Cordon Bleu. 537 W. Fairbanks Ave., Winter Park; 647–7575. Famous for gourmet French cuisine. Specialties are veal Cordon Bleu, filet *chez nous,* seafood gratinée, and sweetbreads. L, Monday through Friday; D, Monday through Saturday. All major credit cards.

Le Coq au Vin. 4800 S. Orange Ave; 851–6980. Classical, traditional, and modern French foods, plus a broad but moderately priced wine list. L, D, Tuesday through Saturday. AE, MC, V.

ITALIAN

Moderate

La Scala Ristorante. 205 Loraine Dr., Altamonte Springs; 862–3257. Gourmet Italian restaurant specializing in veal dishes. L, Monday through Friday; D, daily. All major credit cards.

Villa Nova. 839 N. Orlando Ave., 644–2060. Winter Park's restaurant of tradition. Full range of Italian dishes, plus seafood, beef, and veal. L, D daily. Reservations preferred. All major credit cards.

JAPANESE

Moderate

Arigato Japanese Steak House. 3911 E. Colonial Dr., Orlando; 896–9696. Japanese setting and Japanese-born chef. Chicken, shrimp, scallops, steak, lobster served in authentic Japanese style. D daily. Reservations suggested. All major credit cards.

Tokyo House Restaurant and Lounge. 649 N. Primrose Dr. (across from Colonial Plaza); 896–5849. Japanese and Chinese cuisine served in relaxed surroundings. Shrimp tempura and porterhouse teriyaki are specialties. L, Monday through Saturday; D daily. All major credit cards.

MEXICAN

Moderate

Casa Gallardo Mexican Restaurants. 277 W. Hwy. 436, Altamonte Springs; 869–9191; 8250 International Dr. 352–8121; E. Colonial Dr., Orlando; 896–2167. A bit of old Mexico with family-oriented dining. L, D daily, plus Sunday brunch. All major credit cards.

Paco's. 1801 W. Fairbanks, Winter Park; 629–0149. Just about anything you could want and in true south-of-the-border style. L, D Monday through Saturday; closed Sundays. No reservations. No credit cards.

MEDITERRANEAN

Moderate

Epicurean Restaurant. 7900 E. Colonial Dr., Orlando; 277–2881. Try the gourmet delight, alligator tail. A full complement of steaks and Mediterranean specialties, served in a quiet atmosphere. L, Monday through Saturday. D daily. All major credit cards.

POLYNESIAN

Expensive

Sea World Luau. Hawaiian Punch Village; I–4 and the Beeline Highway; 351–3600. Polynesian buffet in a tropical setting at lakeside. Sweet and sour pork, fried rice, chicken aloha, banana creme tart, vegetables, and Hawaiian punch. Hula entertainment. Reservations advised. All major credit cards.

THAI

Moderate

Bangkok Restaurant. 260 Douglas Ave., Altamonte Springs; 788–2685. Beautiful Thai showcase in a reproduction of a Thai temple. Bangkok roast duck a specialty. Seafood, shrimp curry, red snapper topped with sweet sauce, and many chicken, beef, and pork items. L, D daily. All major credit cards.

NIGHT LIFE. Orlando and the surrounding communities provide all varieties of night life, ranging from dinner theater to nightclubs to disco bars, and even the sleazy. *American Sightseeing Tours* (859–2250) offers a number of night life tours that visit leading spots, usually including dinner and some drinks. Prices for conducted tours range from $24 to $26 per person. See also *Practical Information for Walt Disney World.*

DOWNTOWN LOCATIONS

Cafe on the Park. 151 E. Washington St. in the Harley Hotel; 841–3220. Dining and dancing nightly.

Church Street Station. Church Street at I–4; 422–2434. Includes *Rosie O'-Grady's Goodtime Emporium,* featuring the Goodtime Jazz Band with a New Orleans style that gets you jumping and singing. *Apple Annie's Courtyard* offers country and folk sounds, while the disco group finds its fun in *Phineas Phogg's Balloon Works.* Lots to keep you entertained. $5.95 admission also gets you in the *Cheyenne Saloon,* a western bar with country and blue-grass music.

Shakespeare's Tavern. 15 W. Church St.; 841–4144. Old English cooking and comedy, but don't expect to hear the Bard. $24.95. Reservations required.

WINTER PARK AREA

Empire Room Supper Club. In the Langford Hotel on New England Ave.; 644–3400. Dinner, dancing, and live entertainment.

Villa Nova. 839 N. Orlando Ave,; 644–2060. Dinner, dancing, and jazz. Cover charge.

J. J. Whispers. 5100 Adanson St.; 629–4779. A group of rooms with varied entertainment including big bands in the *Whispers Lounge,* stand-up comics in the *Rascals Room,* a sound and video room called *Shouts,* an *Art Deco* room where you watch all the other action on video, and the *Alexander Graham Bell* room where each table has a telephone so you can dial persons at another table. $3 admission.

KISSIMMEE

Medieval Times. Hwy. 192, at Oren Brown Road; 396–1518. A castle-dinner-show lasting 90 minutes. Displays of jousting by knights in armor, complete with wenches, footmen, and a cast of 150. A fun night that costs $19 for adults, $17 for youths 12–17, and $12 for children. Major credit cards.

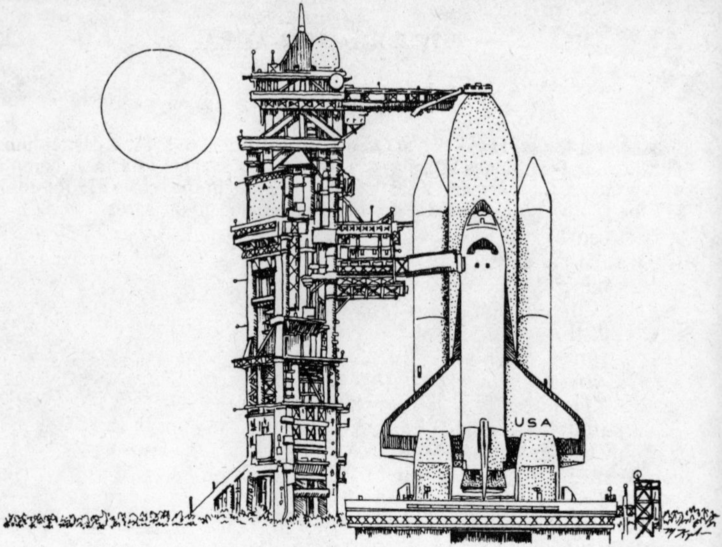

CENTRAL FLORIDA

East, West, and North of Orlando

by
JOHN RUTHERFORD

To best discuss the Central Florida area outside of Orlando, we are dividing it into two sections. The first is the area east of Orlando—that is, the area east of I–4 and the Florida Turnpike all the way to the Atlantic. This area includes the beaches south to Cocoa Beach in Brevard County and north to Ormond Beach in Volusia County, covering the Kennedy Space Center and Daytona Beach.

The second section of the chapter covers the area north and west of Orlando. More wooded than the eastern area, this is a landscape of forest, farmland, rivers, and lakes.

EXPLORING EAST OF ORLANDO

Between Cocoa Beach and Ormond Beach lie miles of generally wide, hard-packed beaches. In Volusia County, in fact, beaches are so stable that cars and light trucks are permitted to drive on them. In Brevard County, more traditional beachgoers park just shy of the beach and walk the remaining few feet to the Atlantic. Either way you can see why on a beautiful day Florida's beaches remain her most alluring asset. If you drive onto the beach, remember that old but still applicable saying: "Time and tide wait for no man." Many a bather has returned to his car after a day of swimming and sand castle building to discover that low tide has given way to high with grievous consequences for the car. Remember, too, that the beaches' 10 M.P.H. speed limit is strictly enforced.

Between Orlando and both coasts are dozens of small towns, some virtually unchanged in decades, others showing the outward push from growing beach and inland cities. In these small towns, such as Sanford and Deland, visitors begin to sense what Florida was like before air conditioning made the state more suitable for development. Agriculture, not tourism, was the state's dominant industry in those days, and even though farming never enters the mind of many tourists, it remains the industry that shapes the Sunshine State personality.

East Central Florida Beaches

For the sake of convenience, we've divided east coast beaches easily accessible from Orlando into those which fall in Brevard and those which fall in Volusia County. If you need to ask a local for directions, be sure to specify Daytona *Beach* or Cocoa *Beach,* or you may find yourself directed to the mainland towns know simply as Daytona or Cocoa. The beachside development took place after the mainland villages were settled along the Florida East Coast Railroad built by Henry Flagler.

Residents in both counties divide them into three parts: Volusia, is divided into Ormond Beach, Daytona Beach, and New Smyrna Beach; Brevard, which bills itself as the Space Coast, divides into three sections known simply as north, central, and south. We cover the central and northern beaches in this chapter. The brackish rivers that divide mainland towns from their beachside namesakes form part of the Intracoastal Waterway, a protected water highway along the Florida peninsula. Fishing, pleasure boating, and skiing are among the popular watersports you'll see in the Indian, Banana, and Halifax rivers and the many bays and inlets that characterize this coastline.

All of the beaches offer an irresistible view of the sun rising—it looks like an egg yolk over the Atlantic. Man offers an equally irresistible view of his own achievements—launches from the Kennedy Space Center on Brevard County's Merritt Island. On a good day you can see a rocket from as far inland as Orlando and north or south 40 to 50 miles. And if you're close enough to the Space Center when the shuttle lands, you'll hear a deafening noise as it breaks the sound barrier. The boom rattles windows even in towns west of Orlando. Equally overwhelming on the audio scale is the roar of high performance cars and cycles racing for high-stake purses at Daytona International Speedway.

Most beaches in Brevard and Volusia fall due east of A1A, a common designation for the main north-south artery in beach towns up and down Florida's east coast. US 1 and I–95, also major north-south routes, are inland. All three roads are easily reached from Orlando via a number of east-west arteries. Beaches are most crowded on weekends beginning in later winter or early spring when inland residents join coastal residents and tourists. They stay busy until cooler weather begins, usually in November. Don't be surprised if the locals seem disturbed by your plans to wade into the Atlantic on a 65-degree January day. Like beach residents everywhere, they think tourists are desperate. While hard freezes do occur in Central Florida, you'll rarely need more than a heavy sweater. And even if the water temperature falls to 65 degrees or lower, you'll find sunbathing enjoyable, particularly if you build a wind barrier of beach towels or blankets.

Cocoa Beach

Merritt Island stands between mainland Cocoa and Cocoa Beach. To orient yourself, pick up a free official Florida transportation map, distributed at chambers of commerce and visitor information all over the state. Cocoa Beach is nearly as popular with surfers as it is with bathers and "sunners." In fact, surfing's popularity draws its adherents to beaches all along the Brevard Coast. Be especially careful if there are surfers around; their loose boards can be dangerous.

Kennedy Space Center

To see the rockets and learn about the space program, you want to go to the Kennedy Space Center, *not* Cape Canaveral. The Kennedy Space Center features a free museum and rocket display at the new Spaceport USA, but to get the real feel of the Space Center, you may wish to take a tour of the reservation, available through the information center. Access is possible from Merritt Island, but the best route from Orlando is across the NASA Causeway from the mainland. Once again, be sure to follow directional signs to the Kennedy Space Center's Spaceport USA.

Canaveral National Seashore

One of the great ironies of the high technology of the space center is that it's made possible the preservation of one of the most pristine beaches on Florida's east coast, The Canaveral National Seashore. To assure human safety in the event of a launch failure, land around the launch sites was left undeveloped. Thanks to that foresight, the public may now visit the Merritt Island National Wildlife Refuge and the adjoining Canaveral National Seashore. Fresh water is limited to that available at the headquarters building from the Wildlife Refuge, so plan ahead if you visit either the refuge or the seashore preserve. Be especially careful to check if you plan to visit during a launch period; access is generally limited a few days in advance as well as the day of a launch. In addition, access is limited when a shuttle landing is scheduled. Check local newspapers or chambers of commerce if you're not sure. In addition to swimming and sunning, visitors may view the Florida manatee, which migrates comfortably between salt, fresh, and brackish water.

Numerous birds, including the bald eagle, make their home in the wildlife refuge, as do alligators and marine turtles. If you're lucky, you may see a pod of dolphins cavorting offshore. But the turtles, oddly enough, are probably the greatest drawing card for the locals. Each summer they come ashore to bury their eggs, then depart, leaving the eggs to be hatched. By instinct the hatchlings head straight for the ocean. Most turtle species, some birds, all dolphins, and manatees are protected by federal statute, which means you may not interfere with them in any way. If you find an injured animal, call the Florida Marine Patrol or the staff of the preserve. The law also forbids collecting remains of any protected species. Note: the only access to the National Seashore is via SR 402 in North Titusville.

Daytona Beach

Beached in east central Florida are on narrow barrier islands or peninsulas separated from the mainland by rivers whose salinity waxes and wanes with the tide. Daytona is no different in that respect. Its chamber of commerce may overstate the matter when it refers to the beach as the "World's Most Famous Beach," but it is forgivable hyperbole. In Daytona's early days, its fame spread, thanks to automobile racing on hard-packed sand beaches. The races are now run at the Daytona International Speedway on the mainland, but millions of bathers have indeed carried word of Daytona Beach to the hinterlands. Not least among those emissaries are the college crowds that migrate over spring and Easter break to beaches all over Florida—especially Daytona and Fort Lauderdale. In recent years, producers of such goods as sun-tanning potions and beer have mounted enormous promotional campaigns during the stay of the college crowd, trying hard to induce brand loyalty by staging parties and other giveaways.

While the beach may be world famous, the undisputed king of the man-made attractions in Daytona is the Daytona International Speedway. Races began modestly in Ormond Beach, but they apparently offended the sense of propriety then at large in Ormond, so they were moved south to Daytona. The rest is history. Races now are scheduled throughout the year and feature modified production-line cars, as well as motorcycles and high-performance race cars. If you're within a few miles of the oval track on a race day, you'll hear the unmistakable sound of wide tires roaring around the pavement.

The areas to the south and north of Main Street offer accommodations for every pocketbook. Ormond Beach (to the north) and Daytona Beach Shores (to the south) are also heavily built up with condominiums and cater to a somewhat more affluent clientele.

The Inland Towns

Although Florida is one of the nation's fastest growing states, much of the growth is confined to the coasts. Some inland towns such as Orlando, Lakeland, and Ocala also have experienced what seem to some residents to be runaway growth. If you've seen the theme parks and had your fill of the beaches, we recommend day trips out from Orlando. Understand that by northern standards, 100-year-old towns aren't especially old, but they retain a charm and appeal unique to Florida.

DeLand

The DeLand area offers some of the best offbeat recreation in the state. At nearby Blue Spring, the endangered Florida manatee congregates each winter just off the St. Johns River. Springs up and down the river, with names such as De Leon Spring, so called because it's believed to have been the spring that Spanish explorer discovered while in quest of the fountain of youth, evoke the mystery and history of the region. Among the most appealing offerings are the rental houseboats that you may pilot on the river yourself. Fishing is first rate, not only on the river but in local lakes as well. Two nearby towns also bear mention: Cassadasga, which is home to a number of spiritualists. Palm readings are available by practitioners who keep somewhat erratic hours in this tiny village. North of DeLand in Astor, an equally tiny village, wildlife lovers thrill to the sight of viable osprey nests just west of the St. Johns and SR 40.

PRACTICAL INFORMATION FOR THE AREA EAST OF ORLANDO

HOW TO GET THERE AND HOW TO GET AROUND. By air. The nearest airport is *Orlando International Airport.* See "How to Get There" in *Practical Information for the Orlando Area.*

By bus. *Trailways* offers service to Daytona Beach, Cocoa Beach, Ormond Beach, DeLand, and Sanford; call 305–422–7107 for fares and schedules. A number of tour bus companies offer service to the Kennedy Space Center, Port Canaveral, and other beachside destinations from Orlando area hotels. Inquire at the guest services desk in your hotel or call *Florida Tour Lines* at 305–282–7400; or *Gray Line of Orlando,* 305–422–0744.

By car. A car is probably your best means of getting around this area. There are numerous car rentals that can be picked up in Orlando. See "How to Get Around," in *Practical Information for the Orlando Area.* Remember that the beaches described above are the eastward side of barrier islands just off the mainland. The principal east-west roads serving the Orlando area and the east coast are I–4, State Road (SR) 50 and SR 528 (the Bee Line Expressway), a toll road. The principal north-south roads serving the coastal region are I–95 and US 1; on the beachside, the principal north-south route is A1A. Caution: A1A is on the islands and peninsulas and does not run continuously from Ormond Beach to Cocoa Beach. Select carefully the best route to your destination. Otherwise, you may find yourself on the beachside miles from where you wish to be and have to return to the mainland to get back on the right course.

To reach central and north Brevard County destinations from Orlando, take SR 528 east. (Take a dollar or so in change to avoid waiting in lines at toll booths.) To reach Cocoa Beach, stay on SR 528, which becomes A1A. Or head south on I–95 or US 1 to SR 520 eastbound. To reach the Kennedy Space Center, take SR 528 east to SR 407 north; stay on SR 407 until it intersects with SR 405, then head east across the NASA Causeway to Spaceport USA at KSC. Such mainland towns as Cocoa and Titusville are accessible from either I–95 or US 1. Canaveral National Seashore is accessible only via SR 402 from US 1 in North Titusville. To reach New Smyrna Beach from Orlando, take I–4 east to SR 44, then head east on 44 until it becomes A1A. To reach Daytona Beach, take I–4 east to US 92, which crosses the Indian River to the beachside. (Note: there are several incorporated towns south and north of Daytona Beach, but the area is generally lumped together simply as Daytona Beach.) To reach Ormond Beach, which is contiguous to Daytona Beach, take I–4 east to I–95; take I–95 north to SR 40, then go east until you reach the beachside. To reach DeLand, take I–4 east to SR 44, then take SR 44 west. Sanford is accessible from Orlando by taking I–4 to SR 46, then heading east on SR 46.

By train. Train service is not available to any city covered here, except Sanford and DeLand, both of which are within an hour's drive of Orlando. Call (800) 872–7245 for schedules and fares; long distance rates apply if you're outside the immediate Orlando dialing area.

For information about the *Amtrak Auto Train,* which can take you and your car to Sanford call toll-free (800) 872–7245.

TELEPHONES. The area code for Orange, Seminole, and Brevard counties is 305; for Volusia County, it's 904. Because the area-code boundaries do not follow precisely the boundaries we've established for this chapter, we've included area codes for all phone numbers. In some cases cities that appear to be within the Orlando dialing area are in fact long distance. Try the number first and if it's long distance, an operator will tell you to dial a "1" before dialing your number. Pay calls cost from $.10 to $.25.

HOTELS AND MOTELS. In general, hotels along the beaches cater to middle-income families. Even in the high season, beachside properties are a bargain for vacationers. The high season runs from about mid-January to the end of April; some hotels retain high-season rates through Labor Day and some require deposits and/or minimum stays. You should have confirmed reservations if you intend to visit during that period. If you're unable to find a room during a particularly crowded period, call the nearest chamber of commerce. Be careful to reserve a room if you visit during a launch, races at Daytona, or a holiday weekend. Rooms are usually available over the Thanksgiving and Christmas holidays, but if the weather is especially nice, you should reserve a room before heading for the beaches. We categorize rooms as: *Deluxe,* $60 and up; *Expensive,* $45 to $60; *Moderate,* $40 to $45; *Inexpensive* $15 to $30. Rates are for double occupancy in season. Off-season rates drop around $5 to $15. Oceanview rooms may cost slightly more.

In recent years, time sharing of condominuns has supplanted hotel occupancy to a degree. Many times shares are available to transient guests. Unfortunately, there are no central clearing houses to determine availability. Chambers of commerce and boards of realtors will refer you, but generally only to properties owned by their members. If you know of one you'd like to use, the best bet is to call the resident manager directly.

CENTRAL AND NORTH BREVARD

Cocoa, Cocoa Beach, Titusville, Kennedy Space Center

Deluxe

Howard Johnson's. 2080 N. Atlantic Avenue., Cocoa Beach; 305–783–9481. Restaurant, lounge, pool, pathway to beach, no pets.

Expensive

Holiday Inn. 260 E. Merritt Island Causeway (SR 520), Merritt Island; 305–452–7711. Pool, restaurant, lounge, whirlpool, tennis, shuffleboard, pets under 20 pounds allowed.

Ocean Landings Resort and Racquet Club. 900 N. Atlantic Ave. (A1A), Cocoa Beach; 305–783–9430. Pool, tennis, racquetball, restaurant, lounge, no pets.

Quality Inn. 1275 N. Atlantic Ave. (A1A), Cocoa Beach; 305–783–2252. Across street from beach. Restaurant, pool, $25 non-refundable pet deposit.

Wakulla. 355 N. Atlantic Ave. (A1A), Cocoa Beach; 305–783–2230. All two-bedroom suites, pool, shuffleboard, no pets.

Moderate

Crossway Inn and Tennis Resort. 3901 N. Atlantic Ave. (A1A), Cocoa Beach; 305–783–2221. 300 feet from beach. Lighted tennis courts, kiddie playground, pool, shuffleboard, volleyball, barbecue pits, game room, efficiencies available.

Econo Lodge. 5500 N. Atlantic Ave. (A1A), Cocoa Beach; 305–784–2550. Pool, efficiencies available, small pets only.

Inexpensive

Scottish Inn. 4150 W. King St., Cocoa; 305–632–5721. Guest laundry, pool, 24-hour restaurant.

VOLUSIA COUNTY

Daytona Beach, Daytona Beach Shores, Ponce Inlet, Ormond Beach, New Smyrna Beach, Holly Hill

Lodging costs in the Daytona Beach area are slightly higher than those in Brevard County to the south. For that reason, we define *Deluxe* as costing $75 to $100; *Expensive,* $60 to $75; *Moderate,* $40 to $60; and *Inexpensive,* $20 to $40. When northern schools break for spring and Easter, the town is inundated with college students, a fact to which most hoteliers alert prospective guests. Like the weekends when racing fans are in town, spring breaks are high-volume, good-time party periods.

Deluxe

Daytona Hilton. 2637 S. Atlantic Ave. (A1A) Daytona Beach Shores; 904–767–7350. On sandy beach. Rooftop dining, lounges, pool, free parking, tennis, sauna, exercise room, no pets.

Holiday Inn Oceanside. 905 S. Atlantic Ave. (A1A), Daytona Beach; 904–255–5432. On the beach. Pool, restaurant, lounges, guest laundry, no pets.

Inn at Indigo Lakes. US 92 at I–95, Daytona; 904–258–6333. 600-acre resort with golf, tennis, fitness trail, Nautilus fitness center, restaurants, lounges, suites available, no pets.

Plaza of Daytona Beach. 600 N. Atlantic Ave. (A1A), Daytona Beach; 904–255–4471. Oceanfront. Headquarters hotel for college students during spring break, pool, lounges, restaurant, tennis, basketball, shuffleboard, no pets.

Expensive

Acapulco Inn. 2505 S. Atlantic Ave. (A1A), Daytona Beach; 904–761–2210. Overlooking Ocean. Heated pool, cable TV and in-house movies, restaurant and lounge, pool bar, in-room refrigerators, shuffleboard, no pets.

Americano Beach Lodge. 1260 N. Atlantic Ave (A1A), Daytona Beach; 904–255–7431. Minimum stay at certain times of year, pool, restaurant and lounge, pool bar, tennis privileges, two restaurants, lounges, no pets.

Castaway Beach Motel. 2075 S. Atlantic Ave. (A1A), Daytona Beach; 904–255–6461. On 7 acres, with beach. Efficiencies available, room refrigerators, sauna, exercise room, game room, home of the *Barn* nightclub.

Perry's Ocean-Edge Motel. 2909 S. Atlantic Ave. (A1A), Daytona Beach Shores; 904–255–0581. Indoor garden, indoor/outdoor pools, Jacuzzi, shuffleboard, putting green, volleyball. No pets. Known for its complimentary homemade donuts.

Sheraton Inn. 3161 S. Atlantic Ave. (A1A), Daytona Beach Shores; 904–761–2335. On beach. Efficiencies available, dining room, lounge, shuffleboard, transportation to Disney World, deposit on small pets.

Treasure Island. 2025 S. Atlantic Ave. (A1A), Daytona Beach Shores; 904–255–8371. Two penthouses, beachside barefoot bar, game room, efficiencies available, no pets. Home of *Billy Bones Tavern.*

Moderate

Best Western Daytona Airport. US 92 at I–95, Daytona; 904–253–0643. Pool, lounge, closest to airport, near speedway, jai-alai, dog track, no pets.

Biltmore Beach Lodge. 187 S. Atlantic Ave. (A1A), Ormond Beach; 904–677–2331. On 3-acre beach. Pool, restaurant, lounge, shuffleboard, no pets.

Holiday Inn-Speedway. 1798 Volusia Ave. (US 92), Daytona; 904–255–2422. Pool, restaurant, lounge, HBO, small pets OK.

Islander Beach Lodge. 1601 S. Atlantic Ave. (A1A), New Smyrna Beach; 904–427–3452. Pool, dining room/lounge, shuffleboard, Jacuzzi, miniature golf, no pets.

Voyager Beach Motel. 2424 N. Atlantic Ave. (A1A), Daytona Beach; 904–677–7880. On ocean. Two pools, shuffleboard, tennis, golf privileges, coffee shop, transportation to Disney World.

Inexpensive

Daytona Beach Youth Hostel. 140 S. Atlantic Ave. (A1A), Daytona Beach; 904–258–6937. Dorm-style and private rooms available, game room with weights.

Ormond Hotel. 15 Granada Ave. (SR 40), Ormond Beach; 904–677–1881. Space for transient guests is limited, at this Victorian-style old hotel. An elevated veranda wraps around the wooden building.

CAMPING. Nowadays, camping is more often defined as taking your home with you in the form of a recreational vehicle. There are backpacking trails in the *Ocala National Forest;* if that's your preference, write to: Forest Supervisor, National Forests in Florida, P.O. Box 13549, Tallahassee, FL 32308. For information on camping in state forests, contact Bureau of Information and Education, Marjory Stoneman Douglas Bldg., 3900 Commonwealth Blvd., Tallahassee, FL 32003. call 904–488–7326. (See *Practical Information for North and West of Orlando* for additional information on camping in Central Florida.) Facilities mentioned below cater generally to the R.V. traveler as opposed to backpackers. Fees for sites range from about $7.50 to $10.

Cocoa Beach Area: *Jetty Park Campground.* 800 E. Jetty Park Rd., Port Canaveral; 305–783–7222. Full-service campground, shaded location on water, good location to watch launches from Kennedy Space Center. No pets. *Space Coast KOA.* 820 Barnes Blvd., Rockledge (south of Cocoa on the mainland); 305–636–3000. Full-service facility, pets allowed on leash.

New Smyrna Beach; *New Smyrna Beach KOA.* Mission Road on the mainland near US 1; 904–427–3581. Full-service facility.

Daytona Beach Area: *Ocean Village Campgrounds.* 2162 Ocean Shore Blvd., Ormond Beach; 904–441–1808. Full-service facility on ocean. Pets OK on beach. *Orange Isles Campground.* 3520 S. Nova Rd., mainland, Port Orange; 904–767–9170. Full-service facility. *Seaside Trailer Park.* Two miles north of SR 40 on A1A, Ormond Beach; 904–441–0900.

TOURIST INFORMATION. Practically anyone can tell you how to reach major attractions and destinations such as the beach. Chambers of Commerce and hotels are generally well prepared to tell you more than you ever wanted to know about Florida. *Orlando* magazine and *See* magazine publish good local guides. The *Daytona Beach News-Journal* publishes "Go Do" on Saturday, a comprehensive guide to local events. *Cocoa Today* also publishes a weekend guide to local happenings. Chamber addresses and phone numbers follow: *Cocoa Beach Area Chamber of Commerce,* 431 Riveredge Blvd., Cocoa 32922; 305–783–3650. *Daytona Beach Area Chamber of Commerce,* City Island, Daytona Beach 32014; 904–255–0981. *DeLand Area Chamber of Commerce,* P. O. Box 629, DeLand 32721; 904–734–4331. *New Smyrna Beach/Edgewater Chamber of Commerce,* P.O. Box 129, New Smyrna Beach 32069; 904–428-2449. *Orlando Area Chamber of Commerce,* 75 E. Ivanhoe Blvd. (I–4 at Ivanhoe Blvd.), Orlando 32802; 305–425–1234. *Ormond Beach Chamber of Commerce,* P.O. Box 874, Ormond Beach 32074; 904–255–0981. *Greater Sanford Chamber of Commerce,* P.O. Drawer CC, Sanford 32772; 305–322–2212. *Titusville Chamber of Commerce,* 2000 S. Washington Ave. (US 1), Titusville 32780; 305–267–3036.

SPECIAL INTEREST TOURS. *Kennedy Space Center Tours.* Be sure if you ask directions to this federal installation that you specify Kennedy Space Center Spaceport USA. There seems to be substantial confusion between it and Cape Canaveral, although they are miles apart. The visitor center offers free admission to an excellent museum featuring displays and movies on the history of space flight, equipment that actually has flown in space, and even a few rockets used to lift payloads beyond the reach of the earth's gravitational pull. In addition, there are demonstrations of various technologies developed in support of the space program. You should budget at least an hour to see all elements of the museum; two would be better.

Once you have toured the Spaceport, take the bus tour of the reservation. Your guide will show you the shuttle if it's in port and detail the various launch programs currently underway. You'll also see a presentation on how the astronauts were trained to land and walk on the moon. In addition, the tour takes you as close as you can get to the gigantic vehicle assembly building and the crawler transport, which moves spaceships from the assembly building to the launch pad. It takes about two hours to complete the tour. Tours may be curtailed immediately before and following launches. Spaceport USA also provides timetables on scheduled launches. If you can possibly arrange your visit to coincide with a launch, do so. Few things are more awesome, even from a distance of several miles. That's about as close as most laymen can get to a launch site, but the unbelievable noise and the earth shaking beneath your feet confirm that a truly incredible phenomenon is taking place. Launches take place almost monthly. Call 800–432–2153 for launch information; for other information, call 305–452–2121. Tour price is $4 for adults and $1.75 for children 3 to 12. Group rates are available.

CRUISES. Take a river cruise for lunch or dinner up the St. Johns River, or board a ship in Central Florida for three- and four-day cruises to Nassau. *Dixie Queen.* P.O. Box 623, Holly Hill, FL 32017; 904–255–1997. Dinner and dancing cruises on the Halifax River between the Daytona Beach peninsula and the mainland. *S/S Royale,* Premier Cruise Line; 3- and 4-day cruises to Nassau. Prices start at $275. Frequent specials. Call travel agent for booking. *Star of Sanford.* 433 N. Palmetto Ave., Sanford; 305–321–2627. Lunch and dinner cruises up the St. Johns to Dutchman's Bend. *Viking Sun.* 841 Ballough Rd. (near the Seabreeze Bridge), Daytona Beach; 904–255–1997. Moonlight dance cruises.

STATE AND NATIONAL PARKS AND FORESTS. User fees for state and national parks vary from park to park. Where there is an entry fee, it ranges from 50¢ to $1. Camping fees begin at $6 for inland sites and go as high as $8 for coastal sites. While there are no fees for hunting and fishing, licenses are required.

Blue Spring State Park. Camping and swimming. Manatees congregate near the spring boil during cold weather. Two miles west of Orange City, off I–4 and U.S. 17. Call (904) 775–3663 for additional information.

WILDLIFE. Florida's wildlife is as appealing as her beaches. The endangered *manatee,* a relative of the elephant, migrates throughout inland rivers and streams and brackish coastal waters. If you're boating, be especially mindful of these extremely slow-moving, very gentle creatures. There are fewer than 1,000 remaining and most have propeller scars as a result of their encounters with boaters. Fishermen should be careful about disgarding monofilament line; it can wrap around a manatee's flippers and in severe cases cause the limbs to atrophy. Birds, too, often are victimized by fishing line and plastic packaging materials. The best time to see the manatees is during the winter months, when they congregate around warm springs, such as that in Blue Spring State Park, or at power plant outfalls, such as those on the Crystal River.

Few things so delight youngsters as discovering coastal wildlife. *Giant sea turtles* come ashore in the summer to bury their eggs in the sand. Tiny saltwater snails called *periwinkles* wash in with the tide and burrow into the sand as the water retreats, only to emerge again in search of microscopic food when the next waves washes up. Periwinkles occur by the thousands on New Smyrna Beach. Offshore, you can often see *dolphins* cavorting; they're especially visible in the Indian and Banana rivers in the Cocoa Beach area. You may want to book passage on a sightseeing or fishing charter to get a closer look. Quite social, dolphins have been known to trail boats for miles.

You can also spot a variety of *ray* species offshore. Like whales and dolphins, they'll often breach—leap completely out of the water—and hit the surface with an audible smack. Despite its reputation as a stinger, the ray is a beautiful creature to watch. It seems almost to fly underwater. *Whales,* too, are frequently sighted in coastal waters. They occasionally beach themselves in populated areas, a cause of great concern to bathers. If you happen onto a beached animal, do not touch it, since by law that's considered harassment. Instead, call the local office of the Florida Marine Patrol or the U.S. Fish and Wildlife Service; both agencies have personnel trained to deal with beachings. It's also illegal to take the remains of a beached animal or any protected species, including a number of birds, such as the pelican.

ZOOS. *Central Florida Zoological Society (Central Florida Zoo).* On US 17/92 just east of I–4, Sanford 32771; 305–323–6471. Built completely with contributions, the zoo features more than 200 animals including reptiles, big cats, primates, and hoofed stock. Elephant and pony rides, feeding demonstrations, nature trail, strollers, birthday parties by reservation. Hours: 9 A.M. to 5 P.M. daily except Christmas. Admission: $1 children 3–12, $3 adults, $1.50 seniors 60 and over.

BEACHES. With two exceptions, the entire coastline from Ormond Beach to Cocoa Beach is open to the public. The exceptions are the beach on Cape Canaveral, which is permanently off limits because of the space program, and Playlinda Beach in the Canaveral National Seashore, which is closed before, during and after launches and landings. Ormond Beach, Daytona Beach, Daytona Beach Shores and Ponce Inlet are all on the Daytona peninsula and contiguous; all are accessible from U.S. 1, I–95 and A1A. New Smyrna Beach is also accessible from each of those north-south arteries, but A1A (the main beachside drag in most of eastern coastal Florida) is not a continuous road. In short, to reach New Smyrna Beach from beaches to the north or south, you must return to the mainland, drive to Smyrna, then re-cross the Indian River on SR 44. Likewise, to reach Playlinda and Cocoa Beach from more northern beaches, you must return to the mainland, drive south on U.S. 1 or I–95, then cross the Indian and Banana rivers on state roads 402, 520 or 528. Except for Playlinda, all beaches here have on-beach food concessions or immediately adjacent restaurants and bars.

Cocoa Beach. Popular with Florida residents, Cocoa Beach's hotels draw their share of tourists as well. Pace is somewhat less frantic than Daytona and the fact that cars aren't permitted on the beach makes Cocoa a good beach for families with small children or senior relatives who prefer not to dodge cars. Limited bathroom and shower facilities; no pets; no fee; no alcohol; pier with food and beverage service; very popular with surfers. Take SR 520 or 528 from U.S. 1 or I–95 to beach.

Daytona Beach. Unless you see the sign marking the boundary, you won't know you've driven into this jurisdiction. Driving at 10 m.p.h. (strictly enforced) is permitted on this and all Volusia County beaches. Bathrooms and outdoor showers available; no pets; no entry fee; boardwalk with games and food outlets; lifeguards; food, bicycle and moped concessions on beach; no alcohol.

Daytona Beach Shores. Like Ormond Beach to the north of Daytona Beach, this beach town caters to a somewhat more affluent crowd. Limited restroom facilities; lifeguards; no pets; no beach fee (although a court test case is in progress); driving and parking on beach; no alcohol; on-beach food, bicycle concessions.

Ormond Beach. Condominiums, time shares and new hotels appeal to the middle and upper-middle-income travelers who headquarter here. Ormond is the northernmost beach in this coverage area on which cars are permitted to drive and park. Limited bathroom and outdoor shower facilities; fishing pier; no pets; no beach fee; some surfing; lifeguards; no alcohol.

Playlinda Beach. In the Canaveral National Seashore, Playlinda is closed before, during and after launches and landings at the nearby Kennedy Space Center. A wilderness beach, its facilites are limited to those available at the headquarters building at the entrance to the preserve. Off-beach parking. Note: on the northern reaches of Playlinda, there is discreet nude bathing and sunning, both frowned on by local authorities who arrest its practitioners; a court test case is underway. Entry only via SR 402 in north Titusville.

Ponce Inlet. The southernmost beach on the Daytona peninsula, Ponce Inlet retains the flavor of a small Florida beach town. The extremely wide beach around the lighthouse at the southern tip of the peninsula is especially popular with families. The jetty on the north side of the inlet appeals to fishermen; in fact, a roving bait vendor works this territory. Historic lighthouse; lifeguards, portable bathrooms during high season; pets permitted on leash; alcohol permitted; float, food and bicycle concessions; no entry fee; beach driving and parking permitted.

New Smyrna Beach. At present, there's no bridge across the inlet to New Smyrna Beach, so to reach New Smyrna from Ponce Inlet, you'll have to return to the mainland and drive south on US 1 or I–95. Easily the least commercialized of the beaches in this coverage area, its lodging consists mainly of time shares and condomiuniums. A great favorite with Florida residents, New Smyrna appeals to surfers and sailors. Entry fee of $1; limited bathroom and shower facilities; lifeguards; no pets; no alcohol; beach driving and parking permitted; on-beach food, float, bicycle, moped concessions. Note: sailboats and power put in at mainland or riverside marinas, then pass through Ponce Inlet to the open ocean.

PARTICIPANT SPORTS. Canoeing. Canoe rentals are available in most state and national forests; some counties and cities that abut inland rivers also lease rental concessions. This is one sport that chambers of commerce don't seem to promote very heavily, so your best bet is to call county or city park departments. For additional information on canoe rentals, write *Canoe Outpost of Florida* at Rte. 1, Box 1462, Ft. McCoy, FL 32637, or call 904–236–4606. Canoe Outpost is a franchise operation with canoe rentals on 10 Florida rivers; it publishes a brochure detailing routes as well as day and overnight outings. If you're interested in seeing undeveloped Florida at its best, we recommend a canoe trip. It's inexpensive (rentals start at about $9 per person per day), even a novice can peddle a canoe downstream (which is how most canoe runs are structured), and it can be done practically year round. Besides all that, it's a blissfully peaceful way to spend the day. Be sure to pack a picnic. Canoe Outpost will also rent camping gear for overnight trips; package rates start at $45 per person for all equipment except food, although rates are lower if you take your own tent.

Fishing: See below.

Golf. There are more than 500 courses in Florida, many of them of championship caliber. We've listed here only those facilities that are open to the public. Local chambers of commerce and the Yellow Pages publish lists of private clubs (which may have reciprocal agreements with your hometown club) and semi-private clubs. Fees range from $8 to $15. Expect to pay about twice that if you use a cart. **Cocoa Beach Area:** *Cocoa Beach Municipal Golf and Country Club,* Tom Wariner Blvd. at Minuteman Causeway, Cocoa Beach; 305–783–4911. **New Smyrna Beach Area:** *Fairgreen Country Club,* Fairgreen Ave., mainland, New Smyrna Beach; 904–427–4138. **Daytona Beach Area:** *Daytona Beach Golf & Country Club,* 600 Wilder Ave., mainland, Daytona Beach; 904–255–4517. *Indigo Lakes Golf Club,* I–95 at US 92, mainland, Daytona Beach; 904–254–3602. One of the newest and nicest. *Riviera Golf & Country Club,* 500 Calle Grande Ave., mainland, Ormond Beach; 904–677–2464. *Tomoka Oaks Golf & Country Club,* on Nova Rd. (SR 5A) just west of US 1 and north of SR 40, Ormond Beach; 904–677–7117.

Sailing. For rentals you can contact: *Shannon's Hobie Center,* 3466 S. Atlantic Ave., Cocoa Beach; 305–783–9763. Catamarans by hour and day.

Surfing. The rule of thumb is that you can surf wherever there's good wave action. But some restrictions may apply in areas heavily populated by bathers. Beaches are marked if surfing is prohibited. Locals surfers tend to congregate in New Smyrna Beach and Cocoa Beach. For surfing supplies and information on local events, call *Ron Jon Surf Shop,* a huge emporium with every imaginable surfing accessory: 4151 N. Atlantic Ave. (A1A), Cocoa Beach; 305–784–1485.

Tennis. Anyone determined to play tennis can find a court within reasonable distance just about anywhere in the state. Besides municipal courts, many school districts also allow non-students to use their courts during off hours. In addition, many hotels either have courts on their property or agreements with nearby clubs. The best bet is to check with the guest services desk at your hotel or call the local recreation department. Courts listed below are free to the public in most cases; where there is a fee, it is only a few dollars. **Cocoa Beach Area:** *Cape Canaveral Recreation Complex,* N. Atlantic Ave. (A1A) at Filmore St., Cape Canaveral; 305–783–1126. Also has handball courts. *Cocoa Beach Recreation Complex,* Minuteman Causeway, Cocoa Beach; 305–783–4911. Also has handball courts. **New Smyrna Beach:** *Detwiler Park,* Horton at Oakwood, beachside; 904–427–5450. *Faulkner St. Courts,* just off Canal St. (SR 44) in downtown New Smyrna; 904–427–5450. **Daytona Beach Area:** *City Island,* Orange Ave. at the Halifax River, Daytona Beach; 904–257–4060. *Indigo Lakes Racquet Club,* I–95 at US 92, mainland, Daytona Beach; 904–254–3603. *Ormond Beach Racquet Club,* 38 E. Granada Blvd. (SR 40), Ormond Beach; 904–677–0237.

HUNTING. As in other states, hunting in Florida is rigidly regulated. In addition to different seasons for different species, there are different seasons for different types of weapons. Some species—the manatee and Florida panther, for example—may not be hunted under any circumstances since they are protected by federal legislation. Other protected species, such as the alligator, may be hunted only with special permits. For details on seasons, permissible weapons, and hunt sites, contact: *Florida Game and Fresh Water Fish Commission,* Tallahassee, FL 32301, or call 904–488–1960. The commission publishes a hunting handbook useful in planning hunting trips; it also provides information on bag limits according to species and season.

FISHING. Despite the threat of growth-related pollution, Florida's rivers and lakes remain some of the most productive in the world. You need only a hook and line to fish in the ocean, but a permit is required for freshwater fishing. Many fish camps will sell you a license starting at $6 for a five-day permit, going to $11 for an annual license; some operators are required by county statute to tack on a surcharge that goes to maintaining public docking facilities. You can rent anything from some operators; others provide only boats and bait. Expect to pay $15 to $25 daily for a motorized boat for freshwater fishing. It costs about the same to deep-sea fish aboard what the locals call a "party boat," which carries upwards of 100 people.

Equipment rentals start at $5 for rod and reel and go up, so if you can take your equipment, do so. Cleaning services are extra. If you want to fish for a particular species or in a small group, consider chartering a small boat by the half or full day. Prices for deep-sea game fishing charters for parties of up to six start at about $150 a day. The best bet if you want just to dabble or try your hand as a novice is to book passage on a boat carrying lots of people. Some operators are listed below: *Coghill's Marina,* Port Canaveral; 305–783–9535. Base for a number of small charters that specialize in taking smaller parties. Ocean fishing. *Critter Fleet,* 4950 S. Peninsula Dr., Ponce Inlet (on the Halifax River); 904–767–7676. Departs at 8:00 A.M., returns at 4:30 P.M. Ocean fishing. *Lone Cabbage Fish Camp,* SR 520 at the Orange/Brevard county line; 305–632–4199. Freshwater fishing on the St. Johns River. *Miss Cape Canaveral,* Port Canaveral; 305–783–5274. Daily year-round; night fishing during the summer. Ocean fishing. *Osteen Bridge Fish Camp.* SR 415 at the St. Johns River, Sanford; 305–322–3825. Freshwater fishing on the St. Johns. *Tradewinds V,* Port Canaveral; 305–784–0535. Specializes in ocean fishing for grouper and snapper.

SPECTATOR SPORTS. Jai-Alai. In its modern form, this fast-paced game was developed by the Basque population in the Pyrenees Mountains of Spain and France. It resembles handball, but the players use a basket called a *cesta* to throw and retrieve the rock-hard ball called a *pelota.* The ball travels at speeds in excess of 150 M.P.H. Each match lasts from twelve to twenty minutes and may be played singly or in doubles. General admission is $1 and prices go up to $3 for clubhouse seats, where dressier attire is requested. Almost as much fun as betting (and winning) is watching the spectators cheer for their favorites. The fronton is on Volusia Avenue (US 92) just east of I–95. Call 904–255–8333. The season runs from February through July. Noon matinees are scheduled on Monday and Saturday; games begin at 7:15 nightly except Sunday.

Racing: *Daytona International Speedway.* US 92 at I–95, P.O. Drawer S., Daytona Beach, FL 32015; 904–255–5301. If you're in Daytona on a race day, it'll be hard to miss the incredible noise generated by custom and stock cars or motorcycles making rounds on the oval track. Races begin in early February and continue on and off through December. You can watch the action firsthand from both the grandstands and the infield. If you're driving an R.V. into the infield, you'll have to use a special entrance and pay a fee of $15 per day. Per-person prices start at $15 for single-day events and go up to $55 for the choicest seats at the biggest race of all, the Daytona 500. Wherever you sit, you'll be at one of the world's biggest, non-stop parties. Be patient when entering or leaving the Speedway; the staff moves thousands of vehicles onto and off of the property efficiently, but it still takes time.

Daytona Beach Kennel Club. West Volusia Ave. (US 92), just east of I–95 on the mainland; 904–252–6484. **Greyhound racing** season begins in May and runs through September (call for exact dates). Pari-mutuel betting nightly except Sunday; matinees on Monday, Wednesday, and Saturday. Admissions: $.50 general admission; clubhouse seats $1 and up. Group rates available.

HISTORIC SITES. *The Casements.* Granada Blvd. (SR 40) at Riverside Dr., Ormond Beach; 904–673–4701. As the railroad pushed south along Florida's east coast, wealthy families like the Rockefellers built winter "cottages" like The Casements. It's an especially appealing wooden house, lately restored for use as a community center by the City of Ormond Beach. Restoration continues on the formal gardens, which stretch from the house to the Halifax River.

Ormond Hotel. 15 E. Granada Blvd. (SR 40), Ormond Beach; 904–677–0881. A splendid and sprawling resort built toward the end of the last century, the wooden hotel is wrapped with an elevated (and elegant) veranda. Now used mainly as a residential hotel, its owners welcome visitors who appreciate the Victorian flavor of this wonderful old hotel. When space is available it still accepts transient guests at a rate considerably lower than the newer properties along the beach.

Turtle Mound. On the Indian River at the south end of Atlantic Avenue (A1A), New Smyrna Beach. This fifty-foot-high mound of shells, pottery shards, and other evidence of early Indian inhabitants is one of the last in the state. Others were destroyed for use as a roadbed base. Nearby sand mounds are thought to have been Indian burial grounds. If you visit, be sure to wear light clothing that covers as much skin as possible or take an insect repellent; the mosquitoes are very determined.

ART GALLERIES AND MUSEUMS. (See also "Special Interest Tours," above, for information about the *Kennedy Space Center* museum.) While local musuems and galleries lack the scope and polish of their big city kin, they are nonetheless important cultural assets in the communities they serve, bringing in a number of rotating shows and in some cases, establishing residencies for nationally and internationally known artists. Predictably, most focus on indigenous culture, history or wildlife. Admissions, when charged, are tax deductible and under $2.

Atlantic Center for the Arts. 1414 Arts Center Blvd. (near the airport and just off US 1), New Smyrna Beach; 904–427–6975. Probably the most ambitious undertaking on behalf of the arts in eastern coastal Florida, the Atlantic Center is situated on a wooded tract to whose cottages prominent American and foreign artists are invited for "creative residencies." Undisturbed by phones, patrons, or other disruptions, the painters, sculptors, writers, and musicians are free to practice their art. James Dickey, Edward Albee, Duane Hanson, and Lowell Nesbitt are among those who've conducted workshops, lectured, performed, or exhibited their work at the center. Write 1414 Arts Center Ave., New Smyrna Beach, FL 32069, for further information. Center also features exhibits by local, regional, and national artists that change monthly. Open 9:00 A.M. to 5:00 P.M., Monday through Friday and 2:00 P.M. to 5:00 P.M. Sunday.

Birthplace of Speed Museum. 160 E. Granada Blvd., Ormond Beach; 904–672–5657. Features racing memorabilia and Racing Hall of Fame.

DINING OUT. As you'd expect, seafood fairly dominates the restaurant scene in Florida's coastal towns. If you're accustomed to $35 to $40 per-person tabs, you'll like the generally affordable prices in local restaurants. You can still run up a tab that high if you have wine and a few cocktails with your meal, but you can eat very well in the best local restaurants for under $20 a person.

Each restaurant listed has items above and below their average entrée price; we classify *Deluxe* as $12 to $15; *Expensive,* $9 to $12; *Moderate,* $6 to $9; and *Inexpensive,* under $6. Prices noted are for one person, excluding drinks. Master Card and Visa are accepted, unless otherwise indicated; AMEX, Diner's Club, and Carte Blanche are also accepted, although less widely.

COCOA BEACH AREA

Deluxe

Bernard's Surf. 2 S. Atlantic Ave. (A1A), Cocoa Beach; 305–783–2401. Probably the best known of all local restaurants, Bernard's has its own fishing fleet. In addition to well-prepared local fish, it serves steaks and a number of exotic foods, such as rattlesnake meat. Homemade onion bread and fruit muffins are especially good.

Black Tulip. 207 Brevard Ave., Cocoa; 305–631–1133. A continental house serving lobster, veal, steaks, Florida lobster (quite different from Maine lobster), grouper, kingfish, scallops. The Tulip is recommended by the locals on the basis of its attentive service, which is generally regarded as equal to the chef's efforts.

Capt. Ed's. SR 401 at Scallop Dr. (north of Cocoa Beach in Port Canaveral); 305–783–1580. Every coastal resort has its version of Captain Ed's., a big, shiny place which serves a huge volume of food. This one is right by the docks that fishing boats use to unload their catch, so the freshness is indisputable. Try one of their more unusual offerings, such as tiger shark.

The Phoenix. 7073 N. Atlantic Ave., Cape Canaveral; 305–783–4466. White-glove service. The Phoenix specializes in veal, but also does a number of poached fish dishes. It serves steaks and chops as well.

Expensive

The Mousetrap. 5600 N. Atlantic Ave. (A1A), Cocoa Beach; 305–784–0050. This stylish restaurant is especially popular with the locals, who frequent the place for late-night steaks and seafood. Its active lounge explains part of its popularity.

Moderate

Buccaneer Bill's Oyster Bar. SR 401 at Port Canaveral; 305–784–4777. Raw bar with good homemade chowders and fish stews. Bill's is one of several restaurants right on the water within Port Canaveral.

Pedro's Capri. 260 N. Orlando Ave., Cocoa Beach; 305–783–0107. Pedro's advertises itself as specializing in Italian, American, and Spanish cuisine, but despite that lack of focus, it comes well recommended by the restaurant community. It's especially well known for its Cuban sandwiches.

Inexpensive

Alba's Italian Villa. 969 N. Cocoa Blvd. (US 1), Cocoa; 305–632–1913. Homemade pasta, fresh pizza dough, first-rate subs, and carryout service make Alba's a hit with the locals. It serves traditional Italian dishes.

Inky's Bar-B-Q. 1341 N. Cocoa Blvd. (US 1), Cocoa; 305–636–6160. Simply put, it's some of the best barbecue around.

DAYTONA BEACH AREA

The Daytona area appealed to tourists by building thousands of hotel rooms rather than condominums, so there are far broader choices among local restaurants. Daytona's market is middle income, which also determines in part its restaurant offerings. You can find well prepared food, but with few exceptions, restaurants cater to simple tastes. We define *Expensive* here as $12 and above (per person); *Moderate,* $7 to $11; and *Inexpensive,* under $6.

Expensive

Chez Bruchez. 304 Seabreeze Blvd., beachside; 904–252–6656. You'll sense from the décor that Chez Bruchez's specialty is provincial French cooking. It's not fussy or prissy, but when a dish demands a subtle sauce, the chef delivers. Chicken dishes are especially good, as are such stews as beef burgundy. Closed Sundays.

La Crepe en Haut. In Fountain Square on Seabreeze Blvd., just east of Atlantic Ave. (A1A), Ormond Beach; 904–673–1999. Crêpes, naturally, are the house stalwarts, but the chef also prepares several specials each meal, generally with locally caught fresh fish. Ormond Beach caters to a more upscale crowd that nearby Daytona, and it's reflected in restaurants like this one.

Hilton Roof Restaurant. 2637 S. Atlantic Ave. (A1A), beachside, Daytona Beach Shores; 904–767–7350. Oddly enough, not many restaurants in the Daytona area take full advantage of their oceanside location. This one does. Again, beef and seafood are the mainstays of the menu. Also has a rooftop lounge.

King's Cellar. 1260 N. Atlantic Ave. (A1A), beachside, Daytona Beach; 904–255–3014. The Cellar occupies one floor of a former beachside mansion. Still elegant, it features beef and seafood dishes, and in addition to the usual salad bar, has a dessert bar. Entertainment in adjacent lounge.

Moderate

Aunt Catfish's. 550 Halifax Dr., on the Halifax River, Port Orange; 904–767–4768. Forget everything else and order a platter of fried catfish with cole slaw and hushpuppies. Be prepared for a wait, exacerbated by the wonderful smells from the kitchen.

Julian's. 88 S. Atlantic Ave., beachside, Ormond Beach; 904–677–6767. Julian's makes no apologies for its emphasis on charbroiled, prime western beef. Nor should they; the steaks are outstanding. Seafood available.

Marko's Heritage Inn. 900 S. Ridgewood Ave. (US 1), two miles south of Port Orange Bridge; 904–767–3809. Go early or late to Marko's or be prepared to wait; service is attentive and Southern-style cooking is excellent, but there's nearly always a line. Homemade breads, good prime rib, seafood.

Riccardo's. 610 Glenview Ave. (one block north of Seabreeze Blvd. and one block west of Atlantic Ave.), Daytona Beach; 904–253–3035. A family restaurant that makes its own bread and pasta. Complimentary antipasto with each entrée. This Italian eatery specializes in variations on a veal theme. Veal Marsala is especially good.

Inexpensive

Hog Heaven Bar-B-Q. 37 N. Atlantic Ave. (A1A), beachside, Daytona Beach; 904–257–1212. Your nose will tell you that this place turns out compelling barbeque. Your tastebuds will confirm it. Chicken, pork, and beef are expertly and slowly cooked. Call ahead for large orders. No cards.

DELAND AND SANFORD

Moderate

Blair's Jungle Den. Alice Drive (on SR 40 at the St. Johns River), Astor; 905–749–2264. The restaurant operation of a fishing camp, Blair's imports some seafood for its buffet, but the best fish are those caught right outside in the St. Johns.

Lake Monroe Inn. On Seminole Blvd. (US 17/92) between downtown and I–4, Sanford; 305–322–3108. A country inn setting as unpretentious as they come, but which serves local freshwater fish expertly prepared.

NIGHT LIFE. Live entertainment in area pubs leans very heavily to rock 'n roll and country/western. In fact, aside from an occasional jazz room, some video parlors, a Polynesian show here and there, and a single comedy club, there's little else. Live music is consistently available from Thursday through Saturday, and a number of establishments listed here are dark or offer limited (recorded) entertainment on Sunday. Where cover charges apply, they're in the $2 range. When name actors are appearing, expect to pay according to reputation of the group.

Cocoa Beach Area: *Brassy's.* 501 N. Orlando Ave., Cocoa; 305–784–5414. R&R live bands, name acts.

County Line Saloon. 4650 New Haven Ave., Melbourne; 305–724–8830. Local and big name acts in a country/western vein.

Diamond Ginny's 8625 Astronaut Blvd., Cape Canaveral; 305–783–5374. Country/western music.

Holiday Inn. 1300 N. Atlantic Ave., Cocoa Beach; 305–783–2271. Reggae bands, dancing.

Daytona Beach Area: *Beachcomber.* 2000 N. Atlantic, Daytona Beach; 904–253–1178. Raw bar, bands, patio dancing.

Big Daddy's. 21 S. Ocean Ave., Daytona Beach; 904–255–8810. Five-level oceanview lounge with live bands, dancing.

Club Mocambo. 637 N. Atlantic, Daytona Beach; 904–258–9413. Live music from the 50s and 60s.

Julian's. 88 S. Atlantic Ave., Ormond Beach; 904–677–6767. More adult crowd, live bands.

Kings Cellar. 1260 N. Atlantic Ave., Daytona Beach; 1–904–255–3014. Easy listening music.

Mac's Famous Bar. 2000 S. Atlantic Ave., Daytona Beach Shores; 904–252–9239. One of the granddaddies of R&R bars.

Ocean Deck. 127 S. Ocean Av., Daytona Beach; 904–253–5224. Reggae bands, dancing.

Ocean Pier. Main Street at the Atlantic, Daytona Beach; 904–253–1212. Live bands in a huge dance hall on the pier.

Other Place. 2000 N. Atlantic Ave., Daytona Beach; 904–672–2461. Game room, live R&R bands, dancing.

PJ's. 400 Broadway, Daytona Beach; 904–258–5222. R&R bands, dancing.

600 North Club. 600 N. Atlantic Ave., in the Plaza Hotel, Daytona Beach; 904–253–1730. Light and video shows, Top 40s dancing.

EXPLORING NORTH AND WEST OF ORLANDO

Just as visitors to Orlando's theme parks and east-coast beaches see two facets of Florida's character, so do those who tour the area north and west of Orlando. First, it is less developed than Orlando and the beaches, although some towns are catching up quickly. Because it's generally rural, it's retained more of what the locals call Florida's "cracker" heritage. That could mean—depending on whom you talk to—tiny clusters of white clapboard bungalows ambitiously called "villages," roadside watermelon stands, or a third- or fourth-generation native. Second, this great inland expanse of farmland and forest is replete with activities for the outdoors set. From camping and canoeing in state and national forests to marveling at the wildlife and clarity of dozens of warm water springs and streams, it is a region of subtle, fragile beauty. The struggle to preserve that beauty goes on in the public and private sectors at every level, addressing the complexities of a groundwater pollution, wetlands development, traffic, and urban services in general. Some towns seem to cope better than others. Ocala, for example, has improved its traffic patterns greatly to keep up with growth, while small towns such as Inverness and Brooksville (low on the state's priority list and financially unable themselves to contend with the surge) seem to be choking on traffic. But between the two extremes lie dozens of little towns largely unchanged in decades. They bespeak the Florida that existed before air conditioning and energy crises. Several rather spectacular resorts complement those small towns.

Florida's west coast, incidentally, differs greatly from its east coast, at least in the area of our coverage. Whereas the east is characterized by sandy beaches, the west coast we cover here is marshy and wooded. Water sports are centered on inland rivers and lakes, although the Gulf of Mexico attracts many fisherman and pleasure boaters. We define north and west of Orlando as that area falling west of I–4, I–95 and the Florida Turnpike all the way to the Gulf of Mexico, where New Port Richey defines our territory on the south and Yankeetown on the north.

Ocala

Like so many Florida towns, Ocala takes its name from the Indians who were thought to have been the first inhabitants of the area. In the sixteenth century, the Timucuans were supplanted by the Spanish, who later occupied Florida until the Monroe administration acquired it in 1819. Federal troops skirmished with the Indians until the mid-1840s, when a peace was established. They called their garrison Fort King, now the name of a prinicipal street in the historic district. Unhappily, many significant buildings already have been bulldozed, including a rambling resort hotel on the downtown square. The consolation is that Ocala is increasingly populated with urbane newcomers who have joined native preservationists in the effort to reclaim the historic residential and commercial districts.

There are some wonderful success stories. The Marion Block Building, which in various incarnations served as an opera house and drugstore, now houses professional offices and an exceptional eatery called O'Neal Bros. The original tile floors from its life as a drugstore are intact and, like the roof detailing, are evidence of craftsmanship now too costly to duplicate or altogether unavailable. Just off the town square is the old Marion Hotel, which for years was a derelict property and is now put to pleasing reuse as an office center. In the 55-block residential neighborhood recently designated a historic district, attorneys and other professionals are restoring wonderful old Victorian structures to their former glories. A commercial district with antique shops and the like usually comes hand-in-glove with the preservation movement. Ocala is making the transition slowly, but the fever is beginning to catch on. There are already a dozen or so antique shops in the Ocala area, most of them concentrated in or near downtown. Artists have begun to inhabit lofts above commercial buildings, too, another factor that points to the fact that the district will one day rival Park Avenue in Winter Park.

If any group can make a real contribution to the preservation movement in Ocala, it is the growing community of horsemen and women. What began as winter pastures and training centers for a few owners has today become a major center for the horse business. Thoroughbreds, Arabians, Quarter Horses, Walkers, and Appaloosas are among the more than 30,000 registered horses in Marion County. Take a drive out from downtown in any direction and you'll encounter the fenced pastures that announce horse country.

Tourism is another vital factor in Ocala's economy. Just to the east is Silver Springs, a thriving attraction that in addition to its natural beauty features a well-maintained antique car museum and a manmade version of the old swimming hole called Wild Waters. The Ocala National Forest, a paradise for the outdoors family, lies just east of Ocala. Its proximity is a decided advantage for tourist and resident alike. For the most picturesque approach from Orlando take US 441 north. For the expeditous route, take the Florida Turnpike north to I–75, then follow 75 north to SR 200 or SR 40 eastbound, both of which will take you right into town.

Dade City

Dade City (follow US 98) is a citrus town that lately has been getting an inordinate amount of attention from the culinary media. The focus of that attention is a tiny restaurant seating fewer than fifty people. Called Lunch on Limoges (after the china-producing region of France), this outstanding, anything but run-of-the-mill restaurant has gotten rave reviews from every critic who's made the trek. The restaurant is housed in what used to be the men's section of a turn-of-the-century, rural department store. These days, it specializes in stylish women's apparel, unusual gifts, and extraordinary food. As the name suggests, Lunch on Limoges serves lunch mainly. But every fortnight or so, the owners turn on the creative circuits and produce lavish, themed dinners. And when we say themed, we mean the music, the flowers, the linens, even the sashes on the waiters and waitresses conform. But the theater, germane as it is, is secondary to the excellence of the table. In a nutshell, it's one of the best in the state.

The critics say there's really no other reason to visit Dade City, but in fact the Pioneer Florida Museum, just north of town, is well worth a visit. The two make a perfect morning or afternoon outing. To reach Dade City from Orlando, take SR 50 west to US 301, then drive south about 10 miles. Or take I–4 west to US 98, then drive north about 30 miles.

PRACTICAL INFORMATION FOR THE AREA NORTH AND WEST OF ORLANDO

HOW TO GET THERE AND HOW TO GET AROUND. By air: Ocala is served by *USAIR;* call (800) 428–4322. See also *Practical Information for the Orlando Area.*

By bus. *Greyhound* (843–7720 in Orlando) offers service to Apopka, Brooksville, Clermont, Dade City, Mount Dora, Inverness, Homosassa Springs, Ocala, Weeki Wachee, and Zephyrhills. *Trailways* (422–7107 in Orlando) offers service to Clermont, Inverness, Ocala, and Weeki Wachee. Local bus service within those cities is all but nonexistent. Only Ocala has any significant service.

By car. The only practical way to tour the area north and west of Orlando is by car. *Hertz,* 800–654–3131; *National,* 800–328–4567; *Avis,* 800–331–1212; *Budget,* 305–855–6660; and literally dozens of other smaller companies maintain rental offices in the Orlando area, some at multiple locations. Rates begin as low as $10 a day and go to $70 or more if you rent a late-model luxury car. (See also "How to Get Around," in *Practical Information for the Orlando Area.*) *Limousine* service is also available if you can afford top-drawer travel. *Florida Tour Lines* (305–282–7400) and *Gray Line Limousine* (305–422–0744) are among the dozen or so companies offering limousine service on an hourly, daily, or weekly basis.

The principal north-south routes in the area covered here are I–75, the Florida Turnpike, US 27, US 441, US 19, US 98, US 41, and US 301. The principal east-west roads are I–4, State Road (SR) 50, and SR 40. All state and federal highways are well marked, as are most county roads. If you want to see old-time Florida, we suggest consulting your map and planning your route along state roads. Be mindful of agricultural equipment, especially trucks hauling citrus and tractors used for grove maintenance. Also, trucks bearing gravel from quarries in the north central region fan out to locations all over the state; give them plenty of breathing space on two-lane roads.

TELEPHONES. The central region of Florida we cover here is served by three different area codes. In general, the area immediately surrounding Orlando is the 305 area-code zone; the area immediately north of Tampa and extending over to Orlando, then down the middle of the state lengthwise, is in the 813 area-code zone; north central Florida is in the 904 code zone. Because of the difficulty in defining service areas, all phone numbers are accompanied by area codes. If you're uncertain, simply dial the operator and ask. Toll calls cost $.10 to $.25 cents, depending on your location.

HOTELS AND MOTELS. Like accommodations in the area east of Orlando, hotels north and west of the city remain a bargain. You can book a comfortable room for two for as little as $25. Or you can check in at a number of deluxe resorts and pay $110 or more for a one-bedroom suite. Still, even the poshest resorts in this region seem cheap in comparison to room rates in the largest U.S. cities. Expect to pay $35 to $50 for a room for two in a property on par with the Holiday Inns. Moderately priced rooms in that range are the most common in our coverage area. We define *Deluxe* as $65 or over; *Expensive,* $50 to $65; *Moderate,* $35 to $50; and *Inexpensive,* under $35. Rates noted are in season for double occupancy; they'll drop $5 to $15 in the off season. Season is this area is generally defined as mid-January to late April. All properties listed take MasterCard and Visa; most also take American Express, and some take Diners Club and Carte Blanche as well.

Deluxe

Crown Hotel. 109 N. Seminole Ave., Inverness 32650; 904–344–5555. This charming hotel doesn't quite fit the bed-and-breakfast or country inn mold, being a little too large for either classification. It's best defined as a jewel of small hotel. In an unlikely location in the friendly bustling town of Inverness, it's just two hours from Orlando. It takes its name from the replicas of the British crown jewels on display in the intimate lobby. On close inspection, the jewels are clearly reproductions, but that detracts not at all from the sheer fun of studying them. Upstairs, each of the 34 rooms is individually decorated with fine antiques. The Crown has lived a varied life, first as a general store, later as the Orange Hotel, still later as the Colonial Hotel. With the royalist sympathies of its current (British) owners firmly in place, it's now the Crown. Along the way, it picked up considerably more space in the form of two additional floors; the original floor is now the middle floor. Recreation on the hotel property is limited to a swimming pool, but golf and a host of water sports are available nearby. The Crown also accepts non-hotel guests in its elegant dining room, called *Churchill's.*

Grenelefe Golf and Tennis Resort. 3200 SR 546, south of Haines City; 813–422–7511. Another of this region's renowned resorts, Grenelefe like the others is miles from nowhere. In such remote locations, which translate into cheap land for the developers, every imaginable activity is available. Grenelefe has three 18-hole golf courses, 13 tennis courts, and a program of scheduled activities with everything from a video analysis of your tennis game to fishing on Lake Marian. The tennis program is especially high-profile and includes extensive spectator seating around the center court for professional and amateur tournaments. Most accommodations are one-, two-, and three-bedroom condominium units in a beautifully wooded setting.

Mission Inn Golf & Tennis Resort. P.O. Box 441, Howey-in-the-Hills, 32737; 904–324–3101. To reach this well established resort, take the Florida Turnpike north to SR 19, then drive north a few miles ot the small town of Howey-in-the-Hills, a retreat for wealthy winter residents. Both the town and the resort are worth a visit, even if you don't stay at the Inn. In addition to its 18-hole golf course and the requisite tennis courts, the hotel offers water-skiing lessons on the nearby chain of lakes. You'll find the usual resort amenities, including beauty and barber shops, babysitting services, gift and pro shops, fine dining room, and exercise facilities.

Plantation Golf Resort. Crystal River 32629; 904–795–4211. One of the granddaddies of west Florida's resorts, the Plantation's 136 rooms and suites are priced slightly lower than those of nearby resorts. But with its colonial charm and attentive service, it remains a wonderful retreat in this beautiful region of the state. There are 27 holes of golf, a driving range, pro shop, game room, shuffleboard, tennis, swimming, and fishing. Diving is popular in the nearby springs that feed the Crystal River, an aptly named if short stream that spills into the Gulf of Mexico. There's an on-site marina if you wish to take your boat or set out on a fishing trip with a local guide. The hotel also operates a dive shop with rental gear; you must be dive qualified to rent scuba equipment. The Plantation Room is best known for its prime rib, although it serves Gulf seafood, too. One especially nice touch is that the chef will prepare the fish you've caught—if he's not too busy.

Saddlebrook, The Golf and Tennis Resort. P.O. Box 7046, Wesley Chapel 34249; 813–973–1111. A relatively new and quite stylish resort, Saddlebrook is a mile or so east of I–75 on SR 54. It gets high marks on just about every amenity from its 27 holes of golf to its bocce ball court (an Italian version of lawn bowling). Much of Saddlebrook's business comes from corporate meeting planners who understand the value of seclusion and service combined in an ably managed package. If you're staying elsewhere and wish to visit Saddlebrook for a round of golf, a set of tennis, or dinner in one of its three restaurants, the hotel welcomes outside guests. The concierge will arrange everything from a deep-sea fishing charter to outings to nearby attractions. While your spouse is attending his or her meeting, the staff stages a variety of sports clinics. The clinics are among many planned activities, including programs for children. Most accommodations are one-, two-, or three-bedroom suites, although conventional hotel rooms are available.

Moderate

Holiday Inn West. SR 40 at I–75, Ocala 32671; 904–629–0381. In the middle of horse country. HBO, pool, Finish Line Lounge, Golden Horseshoe Restaurant, senior discounts.

Holiday Inn. US 19 at SR 50, Weeki Wachee 33512; 904–596–2007. Near Weeki Wachee Springs attraction. Pool, putting green, restaurant, pets OK.

Howard Johnsons Motor Lodge. 3811 N.W. Blitchton Rd., Ocala 32675; 904–629–7041. US 27 at I–75. Pool, playground, restaurant, pets OK.

Sheraton Homosassa Springs. US 19 North, Homosassa Springs 32647; 904–628–4311. Near Homosassa Springs Nature World attraction. Tennis, playground, pool bar, overlooks water features.

Inexpensive

Big Bass Motel. 1098 N. 4th St., Leesburg 32748; 904–787–4141. Small suites and efficiencies. Good location for local fishing, boating.

Southern Host Motor Lodge, Best Western. 3520 W. Broadway, SR 40 at I–75, Ocala 32674; 904–629–7961. Heated pool, accessible to handicapped.

TraveLodge North. 4020 N. W. Blitchton Rd., US 27 at I–75, Ocala 32675; 904–732–2510. Restaurant, pets OK.

CAMPING. Commercial campgrounds in Central Florida cater generally to the recreation vehicle traveler. The *Withlacoochee State* Forest and *Ocala National* Forests both have extensive facilities for backpacking and wilderness camping. The Withlacoochee Forest is divided into two sections and is in western central Florida. The Ocala National Forest is in the central eastern part of the state. In addition to the state and national forests, there are nearly 100 state parks throughout Florida, many of which accommodate campers.

Camping fees in state parks start at about $6 for inland parks and go to $7 for coastal parks and are based on four-person occupancy. Electricity, where available, costs $2. Annual passes are available for individuals, families, and seniors. For information on wilderness camping and backpacking in the Ocala Forest, write Ocala Forest District Ranger, Rte. 2, Box 701, Silver Springs, FL 32688, or 1551 Umatilla Rd., Eustis, FL 32726. There are nine camping areas evenly distributed throughout the Ocala Forest. For information on camping in state forests and parks, write the Florida Department of Natural Resources, Division of Recreation and Parks, 3900 Commonwealth Blvd., Tallahassee, FL 32303. Commercial campgrounds listed below offer full hookup, laundry, and sanitary facilities. MasterCard and Visa are also accepted. Hookup rates begin at about $7.

Arrowhead Campsites. 1720 N.W. 39th Ct., US 27 at I–75, Ocala; 904–622–5627.

Holiday Trav-l Park. 4001 S.W. Broadway, Ocala; 904–622–5330.

Lake Waldena Resort, 8 miles east of Silver Springs on SR 40, 904–625–2851.

Ocala KOA. 3200 S.W. 38th Ave., Ocala; 904–237–2138.

KOA Kampground. SR 54 at I–75, Zephyrhills; 813–973–0999.

TOURIST INFORMATION You may think you've arrived at that great brochure rack in the sky as you visit this area. The locals are nothing if not supportive of tourist-related activities and destinations. If you don't find something that appeals to you at service stations or restaurants along the way, you may wish to contact the following chambers of commerce: *Apopka Area Chamber,* 180 E. Main St., Apopka 32703, 305–886–1441; *Hernando County Chamber,* 101 E. Fort Dade Ave., Brooksville 33512, 904–796–2420; *Greater Dade City Chamber,* Courthouse Square, Dade City 33525, 904–567–3769; *Leesburg Area Chamber,* 918 W. Main St., Leesburg 37249, 904–787–2131; *Mount Dora Chamber,* 341 Alexander St., Mount Dora 32757, 904–383–2165; *Citrus County Chamber,* 208 W. Main St., Inverness 32650, 904–726–2801; *Ocala Chamber,* 110 E. Silver Springs Blvd., Ocala 32678, 904–629–8051. Some of these chambers are staffed by volunteers, so you may have to call several times to find someone in. Local newspapers are also a good source of information on current activities.

STATE AND NATIONAL PARKS AND FORESTS. User fees for state and national parks vary from park to park. Where there is an entry fee, it ranges from 50¢ to $1. Camping fees begin at $6 for inland sites and go as high as $8 for coastal sites. While there are no fees for hunting and fishing, licenses are required.

Ocala National Forest. Lies between Daytona Beach and Ocala; (904) 625–2520. Covering hundreds of square miles, the Ocala Forest features practically every outdoor activity imaginable—hunting, fishing, camping, backpacking, canoeing, swimming, hiking.

Withlacoochee State Forest. Lies 20–30 miles inland in three separate sections, north and west of Orlando; (904) 796–5650. In addition to the usual state forest activities (swimming, camping, etc.) the Withlacoochee has a 26-mile trail for off-road motorbikes. Permit required for off-road bikes at $13 per year or $4 for a 6-day permit. Biking only in central section of forest.

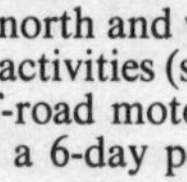

THEME PARKS AND ATTRACTIONS. Buccaneer Bay, next door to Weeki Wachee (see below), is a water themed playground featuring slides, rope rides, wading, and fun pools. Admission is $4.95 adults and $3.95 for children 3 to 11. It opens in late March and remains open until just past Labor Day. Summer hours are 10:00 A.M. to 6:30 P.M.; hours are shorter early and late in the season. Call 904–596–2062 for exact times.

Circus World, on US 27 at I–4 in Haines City (about 20 miles southwest of Orlando; 305–422–0643), is the place to go if you've ever considered running away with the circus. There are plenty of kiddie rides, but the thrill rides are among the best in Florida. For one thing, the Roaring Tiger Wooden roller coaster is the longest (3,500 feet) and fastest (speeds up to 60 M.P.H.) in the South, according to the park's brochures. Newest ride is the Wiener Looping, the fastest, highest looping roller coaster in the World. When they're not performing in the hour-long Circus Spectacular, most of the animals are on display. Among the most endearing are the baby Asian elephants, five of which have been born at Circus World. There's also a midway, a participation circus (audience volunteers walk the tight rope), a stomach-grabbing IMAX film, illusion magic show, jumbo ferris wheel (16 stories high), and the Great Western Stampede (a rodeo show). Children seem especially fond of being made up as clowns; budget 10 minutes and $3. Admission to Circus World is $12.95 for adults and $10.95 for children 5–11; ages 4 and under free. Hours are 9:00 A.M. to 6:00 P.M. Allow about six hours to see the entire park.

Silver Springs. One mile east of Ocala on SR 40, Silver Springs; 904–236–2121. The glass-bottom boats are Silver Springs' answer to Mickey Mouse and Shamu. And a pleasant alternative they are. Powered by silent electric motors, they glide over one of the largest concentrations of artesian limestone springs in the world. Boat captains pilot the jungle cruise past monkeys, giraffes, camels, zebras, gators, and other critters, while commenting on local history and free-roaming wildlife. Whoever writes the guides' speeches has a wonderful sense of humor—they are hilarious. Less amusing, but no less fascinating, are the snakes and other amphibians housed in the Reptile Institute on Cypress Point, a cypress bog laced with elevated wooden walkways. You may also pet deer, goats, sheep, and baby giraffes in the deer park. Silver Springs features a collection of beautifully maintained antique cars, which includes such automotive exotica as a 1934 Rolls Royce Phantom II Continental and a Duesenberg of the same vintage. Hours are 9:00 A.M. to 5:30 P.M.; admission is $9.75 adults and $6.95 children 3 to 11.

Wild Waters, just next door to and part of Silver Springs, is a seasonal version of the old swimming hole. Rides, slides, wading pools, and wave machines will exhaust your youngsters and give you a chance to work on your tan. Admission charge is separate from that for Silver Springs; $6.95 for adults and $5.50 children 3 to 11. Wild Waters opens in late March and stays open until just after Labor Day. Summer hours are 10:00 A.M. to 6:00 P.M.; hours are shorter early and late in the season. Call 904–236–2121 for exact times.

Weeki Wachee Springs is on US 19 at SR 50 (904–596–2062). Another of the dozens of freshwater springs around Florida, it spews millions of gallons of water daily at a constant 72 degrees. Its most renowned show is that performed by mermaids. They're actually local beauties who rely on exceptional lung capacity and occasional trips to free-floating air hoses to stay underwater for 30 minutes at a time. In its new amphitheatre, Weeki presents birds of prey shows, which include an equestrian "support cast." There are also nature trails, a raptor rehabilitation center, and a pelican orphanage in the 545-acre park. Hours are 9:00 A.M. to 6:00 P.M.; admission is $4.95 adults and $3.95 children 3 to 11.

WILDLIFE. *Homosassa Springs Nature World.* US 19 (P.O. Box 189), Homosassa Springs, FL 32647; 904–628–2311. You enter the attraction at the Sheraton on US 19, then take a jungle cruise to the spring and nature trails. The keepers of the small zoo feed the alligators and hippo and offer informal chats on the huge variety of birds which naturally congregate here.

There's also a rehabilitation pond for injured manatees. But the outstanding feature of this peaceful preserve is the observatory built almost directly over the spring boil. Thousands—maybe millions—of fish swim up to the river's headwaters when temperatures in the Gulf of Mexico drop. Even during warm weather, there's an astonishing number of freshwater and saltwater fish. When the attendant throws a small fish into the water, a veritable feeding frenzy ensues. Hours are 9:30 A.M. to 5:30 P.M.; admission is $5 for adults and $2.75 for children 3 to 11. (See also "Silver Springs," in "Theme Parks," above.)

PARTICIPANT SPORTS. Canoeing. Canoe routes in the area north and west of Orlando pass through some of the most magnificant scenery in Central Florida. Some of the best canoeing is in the *Ocala National Forest* and the *Withlacoochee State Forest.* In the Ocala Forest, the *Oklawaha Canoe Outpost* offers both day and overnight excursions. For information on Oklawaha canoeing (and on nine other Florida rivers), contact Oklawaha Outpost, Rte. 1, Box 1462, Fort McCoy, FL 32637, or call 904–236–4606. Near Orlando, *Katie's Landing* in Sanford rents canoes for trips on the Wekiva River. Call 305–628–1482 for directions. Prices for one-day outings begin at about $8. Overnight trips, for which vendors furnish all equipment except food, begin at $45. Also close to Orlando is *Alexander Springs;* call 904–759–2365. Alexander Springs is in the lower eastern part of the Ocala Forest. West of Orlando in Tampa, the *Rowlette Canoe Outpost* offers trips on the Hillsborough River; call 813–634–2228 for directions. For a list of canoe-rental facilities throughout Florida (and the remainder of the U.S.) send $1 to National Association of Canoe Liveries and Outfitters, 8600 W. Bryn Mawr Ave., Suite 720-S, Chicago, IL 60631.

Fishing. Unless you know regional rivers, lakes, and coastal waters, your best bet is to engage a local guide. They tend to make their services available through fishing camps situated on lakes and rivers where fishing is best. Guides in the more westerly part of the state usually will take you out into the Gulf of Mexico. If you have your own gear, take it, since most guides expect their guests to come equipped. Some will put ashore at midday and cook your catch for you. When you return in the late afternoon, there are cleaning and packing services nearby. Passage for groups up to four for a full-day's fishing start at $125, although hourly and half-day rates are available. Many Gulf and river guides are members of the Crystal River Guides Assn., whose president, Bob Edge, can tell you what species are running and can also line you up with a knowledgeable escort. Reach Mr. Edge at 727 N.W. 3rd Ave., Crystal River, FL 32629, or call 904–795–2465. If you wish to fish any waters in the *Ocala National Forest,* call Bass Champions Guide Service at 904–685–3177. The service is located on Lake Kerr in the north central part of the forest. Other camps and guide services in this region include: *Salt Springs Lodge* at Salt Springs in the Ocala Forest, 904–685–2742, or Rte. 3, Box 3202. Fort McCoy; *Fisherman's Cove* in Weirsdale (on the Oklawaha River, just south of Ocala), 904–821–3701; *Cypress Lodge in Inverness,* 904–726–1271; *Trail's End Camp* in Floral City, 904–726–3699; and *Turner's Camp* in Inverness, 904–726–2685. Local chambers of commerce and Yellow Pages are also good sources for guide referrals.

Golf. Ocala is one of the few cities in this area that maintains a public golf course. But there are many fine semi-private clubs which welcome non-members. In addition, area resorts will schedule non-guests after accommodating resort guests. (See also "Hotels and Motels," above.) Fees are as low as $10 on some courses; $15 to $20 is closer to average. Expect to pay about twice that if you use a cart. *Errol Estates Golf & Country Club.* On US 441 north of Apopka; 305–886–5000. *Marion Oaks Golf & Country Club.* 4260 S.W. 162 St.

Rd., Ocala; 904–245–5626. *Mission Inn Golf & Country Club.* Howey-in-the-Hills (on SR 19 east of the Florida Turnpike); 904–324–3101. *Rainbow Springs Golf & Country Club.* On US 41, four miles north of Dunnellon; 904–489–3348. *Saddlebrook, the Golf & Tennis Resort.* In Wesley Chapel on SR 54 just east of I–75; 813–973–1111. *Whispering Oaks Golf and Country Club.* 35000 Whispering Oaks Blvd., Ridge Manor; 904–583–4020.

Horseback Riding. In light of the thousands of horses in the Ocala area, it's surprising there are so few stables where novices may learn to ride or where intermediates may rent a mount by the hour. The *Oak View Riding Stables* in Anthony (about seven miles north of Ocala) offer beginner's instruction and by-the-hour rentals for more experienced riders. Call 904–732–6451. Rates are about $8 an hour.

Hunting. As Florida's inland towns continue to grow, huntable territory shrinks proportionately. But there are still deer, rabbit, squirrel, bird, wild pig, and other populations that, if not checked by hunting, would decimate food sources to the detriment of the entire animal population. While hunting has come under increasing public scrutiny, wildlife experts still regard it as an integral part of their management program in state and national forests. For the first week or ten days of hunting season, the number of hunters permitted in public forests is limited according to the species that may be taken and the huntable area. Thereafter, hunters may secure permits for specific areas. The season opens in November and runs through January, although some species may be hunted through spring. Florida strictly controls seasons, huntable species, bag limits, types of weapons, and a variety of other factors. For details, contact the Florida Game and Fresh Water Fish Commission, Tallahassee, FL 32301, or call 904–488–1960. The commission publishes maps of hunting areas, including the Withlacoochee State Forest, one of the largest hunting preserves in the central-eastern part of the state. For information on hunting in the Ocala National Forest, write to Forest Supervisor, National Forests in Florida, P.O. Box 13549, Tallahassee, FL 32308. You may also write the Ocala Forest District Rangers at Rte. 2, Box 701, Silver Springs, FL 32688, or 1551 Umatilla Rd., Eustis, FL 32727. For information on central Florida hunting guides, you may call Denmark's Sports Travel at 843–3008 in Orlando.

Tennis. As with golf, there are limited public tennis facilities in the area north and west of Orlando. Some hotels maintain courts, and municipal recreation departments will advise you as to location and availability of their courts. (See also "Hotels and Motels," above.) Relatively few tourists take day trips just to play tennis, but if you want to drive out from Orlando, you'll find that each of the facilities listed under the golf heading above (except the Ocala Municipal Course) also has tennis facilities. Rates average $5 per hour, although they're less if you're a resort guest.

SPECTATOR SPORTS. The novelty quotient in spectator sports north and west of Orlando is high, even if the competitions take place on an intermittent basis. **Horse shows** and **parachute meets** in Ocala and Zephyrhills, respectively, are worth the trip to those cities. Also in Ocala is the *Ocala* **Jai-Alai** *Fronton,* whose season runs from January-March and again from mid-June through October. The fronton is ½ mile east of US 441 on SR 318 and features nightly games (except Sunday) and noon matinees on Wednesday and Saturday. Call 904–591–2345 for reservations and information.

MUSEUMS. (See also "Theme Parks and Attractions," above.) Few of the small agricultural towns in this area can afford to support museums on a grand scale. But one whose focus is especially noteworthy is the *Pioneer Florida Museum* in Dade City. In addition to the main building, there are several structures that have been moved to the site, including the old rail terminal from nearby Trilby. The museum also produces two festivals, the Old Time Music Championship in April, when instrumentalists gather to play on historic instruments, and Pioneer Florida Day on Labor Day, when the vital crafts of early Florida are re-created for visitors. The museum is on US 301 just north of the Dade City limits. Hours are 1:00 to 5:00 P.M., Tuesday through Saturday, and 2:00 P.M. to 5:00 P.M. on Sunday. Admission is $1 for adults and $.50 for children 4 to 12. Call 904–567–0262 for additional information.

SHOPPING. Residents in the area north and west of Orlando tend to do their major shopping in Orlando, Ocala, and Tampa—all of which have a number of huge malls. But there are some intriguing shopping opportunities in the area, one of the most unusual being the *Webster Flea Market.* If it's not the world's largest, it's certainly *one* of the world's largest. The market is open for business only on Monday and draws vendors and customers from about a 150-mile radius. You'll see the usual assortment of discontinued merchandise lines, but one-time vendors sell everything from immaculately maintained tool sets to antique rockers. Local farmers also sell their just-picked produce. Be careful to check retail prices before you go if you're looking for a specific item; sometimes the flea market price is not a bargain. To reach Webster from Orlando, take SR 50 west to SR 471 at Tarrytown (watch for the "Dangerous Intersection" sign), then drive north on 471 a few miles. Parking is $1.

Rogers Christmas House and Village is farther west on SR 50 at the eastern edge of Brooksville. The Rogers family for years ran a small department store in Brooksville before opening the Christmas specialty shop in a comfortable old house. One by one, more buildings were acquired and the thousands of Christmas decorations were supplemented with fine gifts and accessories. Today, there's a bride's house, which stocks linens, china, crystal and other quality merchandise, all uniquely displayed. The shops are arranged around a charming garden, where walkways are inscribed with the names of local children invited to leave their mark on posterity. The village is on SR 50 just east of downtown. Call 904–796–2415 for further information. Closed Christmas.

Brooksville also has a number of *antique shops* within a few blocks of the Christmas House. Ocala antique shops publish a map to fourteen stores in and around Ocala. In Mount Dora, about 30 minutes northwest of Orlando, a number of antique shops and galleries are located on the town square and nearby side streets. This shopping district is looking more and more like Winter Park's fabled Park Avenue and is well worth the trip. Shopping in other cities in this coverage area is centered in downtown commercial districts and in strip centers just outside town.

Williams on Courthouse Square in Downtown Dade City also got its start as a small-town department store. Its merchandise mix would drive a dry-goods chain crazy, but its customers love its unusual gifts and stylish apparel. Within the store is *Lunch on Limoges,* easily the best restaurant in Central Florida outside Orlando or Tampa. Call 904–567–5685 for further information.

DINING OUT. The many top drawer resorts north and west of Orlando in part determine the multitude of very-good-to-excellent dining rooms in this region. But there are some standouts, which exist only because some enterprising host has decided there ought to be a decent restaurant in his town. We define *Deluxe* as a meal for one at $15 or more, although a few entries under that heading are there simply because the food and/or service make them memorable. *Expensive,* $10 to $15; *Moderate,* $5 to $10; and *Inexpensive,* under $5. Each restaurant could, on the basis of one or two entrées, move up or down a category; prices noted exclude cocktails and desserts. All restaurants take MasterCard and Visa unless otherwise noted; most also accept American Express and some take Diners Club and Carte Blanche as well. In general, the less expensive the food, the less likely is an operator to accept a multitude of credit cards.

Deluxe

Blueberry Patch. On SR 50 just east of Brooksville; 904–796–6005. This cheerful little tearoom isn't really that expensive; you can eat for about $5 to $8. But the service, atmosphere, and food are so good we've included it in this category. A favorite with shoppers at the Rogers' Christmas House across the street, it serves filling lunches and suppers of salad Nicoise, salmon loaf, and quiches. But the best menu items are the delicious desserts, such as Kentucky Derby Pecan Pie (laced with bourbon and chocolate). Each dining room is decorated with antiques. Closed Sunday.

Churchill's. In the Crown Hotel, 109 N. Seminole Ave., Inverness; 904–344–5555. Like the hotel, Churchill's is decorated with elegant period furniture that matches the chef's offerings. They include Chicken Madras (tomatoes and mushrooms in a cream sauce with chicken), a wonderful grilled pork Française, and an exceptional shrimp dish prepared with mangoes and curry. Dress for this dining room.

Cypress Room. At Saddlebrook Resort in Wesley Chapel, just east of I–75; 813–973–1111. Jackets are requested in this handsome dining room, which overlooks the Saddlebrook golf course. The Caesar salad is excellent, as are the seafood buffets and Sunday brunches. Saddlebrook accepts non-resort guests at its more informal Little Club and, when it's not reserved for private parties, at the Gourmet Room. Reservations are suggested.

El Conquistador. In the Mission Inn, just north of the Florida Turnpike on SR 19 in Howey-in-the-Hills; 904–324–3101. A quiet retreat in a small wealthy town north of Orlando. Chicken tarragon and veal Madeira are good bets. Jackets and reservations required.

Green Heron. At Grenelefe Resort, 3200 SR 546, south of Haines City; 813–422–7511. The Sunday brunch in Tuck's Table is a great local favorite, but the chef performs throughout the week, creating memorable dishes from grouper, snapper, and various forms of beef. Wine list includes entries from California, Germany, France, and Italy. Jackets are not required, but reservations are suggested.

Lunch on Limoges. Courthouse Sq., Dade City; 904–567–5685. Part of this restaurant's charm is happening onto it in such an unlikely location. It serves mainly lunches and the specials vary according to what's available from local farms and seafood markets or how the chef feels. Once a month or so, the owners do French, Mexican, Italian, or other themed dinners, which run about $35 a person and are worth every penny. The desserts are in a class by themselves. Closed Sunday. Complex includes dress and gift shops.

Plantation Room. In the Plantation Golf Resort, Crystal River; 904–795–4211. The resort is on the Crystal River and most of the public rooms take sensible advantage of the location. Prime ribs and steaks are house specialties, but the kitchen also does an excellent job with local fish. In fact, if he's not too busy, the chef will prepare the fish you've caught that afternoon. The Plantation Room's staff is very friendly and attentive.

Expensive

Coach 'n Paddock. 2677 N.W. 10th St., Ocala; 904–732–5256. An exuberant dining room that always seems to draw a crowd celebrating something. It specializes in steaks and seafood and is heavily patronized by members of Ocala's horsey set. Reservations suggested.

Lamplighter Steak Pit and Tavern. 1016 S.E. 3rd Ave., Ocala; 904–732–5339. Don't be put off by the down-home name; this place serves expertly prepared prime western beef and a commendable onion soup.

Petite Jardin. 2209 E. Silver Springs Blvd., Ocala; 904–351–4140. Reservations are mandatory for this very small, unassuming dining room, which nonetheless turns out a laudable Cornish hen and lamb loin. Closed Sunday.

Seaport Inn. 11217 US 19 N., Port Richey; 813–863–5402. Frequently recommended by the locals, this French-leaning restaurant dresses local fish with subtle sauces and also serves well-prepared beef dishes.

Moderate

Captain Appleby's. US 441 at SR 44B, Mount Dora; 904–383–6622. Emphasis in this eatery is on Atlantic seafood. Also serves a better-than-average prime rib. Senior menu.

Caverns at Cascades. 1515 E. Silver Springs Blvd., Ocala; 904–629–1616. Steaks and seafood are the mainstay of this quite attractive restaurant in the Cascades shopping center.

Vecchio's Italian. 2023 S.W. Pine Ave., Ocala; 904–629–6080. A favorite with the locals, this restaurant is especially well known for its lasagna and ravioli. Also bakes its own breads.

The Yearling. CR 325 (north of Ocala), Cross Creek; 904–466–3033. The name of the restaurant does more than recall Marjorie Kinnan Rawlings; it also alludes to her beloved "cracker" cuisine, which includes frog legs, soft-shell turtle, and alligator. Closed Monday.

Inexpensive

Lake Kerr Bar-B-Que. East Rd. 314 (Salt Springs Road) on the western edge of the Ocala National Forest. Outstanding barbecue pork, chicken, ribs, and turkey.

NORTHERN FLORIDA

by
MARY LOU NORWOOD

The area being considered here as Northern Florida is a large and diverse section of the state—including the cities and beaches of the northeast coast and stretching west across the Panhandle's cities and gulf beaches. Clearly we cannot cover everything of interest here, but instead have tried to focus on those areas that seem to have the most to offer a visitor.

The discussion of Northern Florida begins in the northeast section of the state, covering the Jacksonville Area, including Fernandina Beach, Amelia Island, and St. Augustine. Then the text covers North Central Florida: specifically Cedar Key. The final section of this chapter contains information on Florida's Panhandle: Tallahassee and west—the "Miracle Strip" beaches of Panama City Beach, Destin and Fort Walton Beach, Pensacola Beach, and finally, the historic city of Pensacola itself.

EXPLORING THE JACKSONVILLE AREA

Jacksonville is a big city by population and even bigger by land area. It is the commercial hub of north Florida, southeast headquarters for many national companies, a busy port, and in the top-ten auto and air destinations for Florida visitors.

Such popularity with tourists seems unusual for a hard-working business town until you consider its beautiful and majestic St. Johns River and the sparkling Atlantic Ocean beaches that sweep to the horizon and beyond. To this add its Southern character and scenery, relaxed lifestyle and climate, cosmopolitan and cultural offerings, and a history that has left a romantic imprint.

Cultural Firsts

Many of Jacksonville's cultural activities and organizations were Florida firsts and provided a base tradition for recent flowering in the visual and performing arts. Area theaters, concert halls, museums, and galleries—many new and others venerable—are busy and well attended. Jacksonville University, the University of North Florida, Edward Waters College, and Florida Junior College extend the cultural scene.

Sports

But the culture devotee had best check the sports calendar before winging to Jacksonville. Such events as the Gator Bowl football classic, the annual Georgia-Florida football game, the 15-K River Run, the Tournament Players Championship at Sawgrass, and Women's Tennis Association Championships at Amelia Island Plantation affect accommodations. Professional football and baseball, plus college basketball and year-round greyhound racing, fill the spectator's appointment book.

The big participant sports are golf, tennis, boating, and sailing. Public links and courts are good and the area's several world-class sports resorts feature outstanding facilities for their guests. Boating and sailing are as ubiquitous as the sunshine. Just head for nearby waters, and chances are there will be a public launch ramp, a private marina with rentals, or both.

Ocean and river, lagoons and lakes, bayous and creeks mean fishing is not so much a sport as an integral part of life. Visitors will find it great sport indeed. The opportunities and quarry are almost endless, from deep-sea extravaganzas on charter boats to cane-poling from a bank or bridge.

Though Jaxons relish their Southern heritage, they have never been parochial. A great infusion of corporate executives, Navy brass, college and university faculties, and young professionals augment the native sophistication. A happy result for visitors is a broad choice for dining and entertainment.

The North Side of the St. John's

Touring Jacksonville and its beaches means driving, in either your own car or in a rented one. It also means following the river and crossing some spectacular bridges—six in all—and one ferry. A drive west and then south from downtown on the north side of the St. Johns, along Riverside Avenue, St. Johns Avenue, Herschel Street, Ortega Boulevard, and finally Roosevelt Boulevard (US 17), provides a residential economic history. The canopy of live oaks and Queen Anne mansions of Riverside (the oldest money) change to the sprawling lawns and mini-estates of Ortega (established money) and at last to the woodsy retreats off side roads in Orange Park (more recent affluence). Farther south along this bank, on and off US 17 (off is more fun), are old river towns such as Hibernia, Magnolia Springs, and Green Cove Springs, whose fortunes rose and fell with the paddlewheelers and their tourist passengers.

To tour east along the north bank, take I-95 or US 1 north to Heckscher Drive and then turn east (right) on Heckscher. This route goes by the Jacksonville Zoo, crosses several creeks and small rivers with good fishing opportunities, crosses the Intracoastal Waterway, and pulls up in Fort George, where an obscure side road to the left leads to Kingsley Plantation State Park. From Fort George, A1A north continues to Little Talbot Island State Park, with its uncrowded beaches and wild marshes, while on A1A south you take the ferry across the river to Mayport, Mayport Naval Station, and the Jacksonville beaches.

Across from Downtown

Immediately across the St. Johns from downtown are modern hotels and office towers, Friendship Fountain, the Jacksonville Museum of Arts and Sciences, splendid open spaces that invite public festivities, and the Riverwalk. Elsewhere the southside is just as handsome—Regency Square, University of North Florida, Jacksonville University, Jacksonville Art Museum, some of the best restaurants, campuslike office blusters, and affluent residential areas along the river and its tributaries.

The Beaches

Three routes going east from south Jacksonville lead to the beach communities, but use Atlantic Boulevard (SR 10) to stop by Fort

Caroline National Monument on the way (take Monument Road from Regency Square). After visiting the monument return to Atlantic Boulevard to cross the Intracoastal Waterway and reach the beaches. Beach Boulevard (US 90) and Butler Expressway ($.25 toll) are the other two routes that span the Intracoastal. All three end at SR A1A, which is the ocean-hugging road that links not only Jacksonville's beaches but Florida's beach communities from Fernandina Beach to Miami Beach.

North on A1A are Kathryn Abbey Hanna Park, Mayport Naval Station, Mayport, and the ferry. Atlantic Boulevard dead-ends at Atlantic Beach and Neptune Beach, the favored, quiet residential areas of the beaches. Beach Boulevard ends in Jacksonville Beach, which is more tourist oriented with accommodations, restaurants, night spots, and a seasonal boardwalk, and an amusement park. Ponte Vedra to the south is one of those classic understated communities of wealth and a prestigious resort. Some say that April in Paris is gauche compared to spring in Ponte Vedra.

Fernandina Beach and Amelia Island

This quiet beach community north of Jacksonville has been almost a family vacation secret among North Floridians and South Georgians until recent years. Then a world-class resort popped up followed by resort condominiums; newcomers have chosen to emphasize the island's off-the-track character rather than change it.

Fernandina's heyday came in the late nineteenth century as a railhead and lumber port. This was the crystallized moment when shipping agents and lumber barons built their Victorian and Queen Anne edifices. When a thirty-block area was named a National Historic District, there was little to do except apply some paint to the well-preserved buildings and put up signs.

At the north end of Amelia Island is 1,000-acre Fort Clinch State Park—admission $.50. The huge nineteenth-century fort never had much strategic importance, but it's delightful to explore. Beneath its walls fishermen cast into Cumberland Sound, which separates Florida from Georgia, and around toward the ocean they fish from the 2,000-foot pier and great stone jetty.

On its ocean side, the island has 13 miles of beautiful white sand beaches with driving allowed on part of it. Across the island from the port is the longtime family beach section of summer cottages and small apartments. Most newer facilities are farther south on the beach, with Amelia Island Plantation resort encompassing much of the island's southern end. On the inland side are broad salt marshes cut by convoluted creeks and tidal rivers that make this an island.

St. Augustine

St. Augustine, south of Jacksonville, is the oldest city in the United States. It is a rare blend of great natural assets and historic quaintness —mild climate, wide sweeping beaches, narrow streets with overhanging balconies, and little shops. The old Spanish fort on the bayfront, Castillo de San Marcos, still protects the town that is both historic district and everyday workplace for residents. Across the bay on the beaches, the contemporary joys of sunning, swimming, surfing, and shelling at the ocean's foaming edge take over. It is a dichotomy of strong tourist magnetism.

At least six Spanish expeditions to Florida failed in the half century after Ponce de Leon's discovery in 1513. Then in 1564, French Huguenots established Fort Caroline near the mouth of the St. Johns River. The Spanish could not tolerate this threat to their treasure routes. Pedro Menendez de Aviles was sent to drive out the French and establish a colony. Thus on September 8, 1565, Menendez and his company of 600 men came ashore on a bay they had discovered on August 28, the feast day of St. Augustine. The bay and the subsequent settlement were named for that popular saint. Forty-two years prior to the English at Jamestown and 55 years before the Pilgrims at Plymouth, Spain founded St. Augustine.

Menendez succeeded in driving out the French, overrunning Fort Caroline, and killing the shipwrecked survivors of the French relief fleet at an inlet still called Matanzas, Spanish for "slaughter." That crisis passed, and Menendez built a settlement. However, more crises lay ahead.

There were Indian troubles, and the soldiers mutinied in 1570. In 1586 Sir Francis Drake, the English privateer, burned the town and stole its treasury. But he delivered more serious blows by defeating a Spanish fleet at Cadiz in 1587 and assisting in the destruction of the Spanish Armada in 1588. As Spain's naval power weakened, so did the flow of supplies and assistance to St. Augustine. Hunger, even famine, resulted.

Another English buccaneer attacked and looted the town in 1668, killing 60 people. As Virginia colonists pushed southward in the Carolinas, conflicts between the Spanish and English occurred more often and the stone castillo was begun in 1672. By 1696 it was practically finished, and none too soon. Governor James Moore of Carolina arrived for a two-month seige in 1702, and townspeople took refuge within the thick walls. It was, however, the only structure that survived.

Georgia's General James Oglethorpe brought stronger fire power in his seige of 1740, but again the fort withstood the steady bombardment. Again the seige failed. Then British diplomats did what British colonials could not: they took the castillo and all Florida at the treaty table in 1763. The castillo has never been taken by assault.

During the twenty years of British rule, second stories and gabled roofs appeared in St. Augustine. Florida was promoted in the other American colonies and a very tiny seed of tourism was planted. During the American Revolution, the visitors were refugee Tories, as St. Augustine and Florida remained loyal to Great Britain.

The 1783 Treaty of Paris gave Florida back to Spain, but "the sick old man of Europe" could not police it. Americans began settling in the borderlands and a U.S. military force once spent weeks camped just outside St. Augustine. Spain gave under the pressure, and on July 10, 1821, St. Augustine and East Florida became U.S. territory. West Florida was exchanged a week later.

Americans found the 250-year-old Spanish town charming, but outbreak of the Seminole War in 1836 interrupted its evolution into a winter haven. The famous Seminole warrior Osceola was briefly imprisoned in the castillo.

St. Augustine's people had divided sympathies during the Civil War. When Florida seceded local Confederates seized the castillo, only to abandon it in 1862 when Union blockaders appeared and demanded surrender. Union forces occupied St. Augustine for the rest of the conflict, but a native son, Edmund Kirby-Smith, was the last Confederate general to surrender. The end of the war and St. Augustine's 300th anniversary coincided in 1865.

In the Reconstruction Era, St. Augustine boomed. Railroads, big wooden hotels, and popularity as a winter resort came all at once. Among the visitors was Henry Flagler, co-founder of Standard Oil. His career in railroads and hotels, which opened the whole Florida east coast to tourism, began in St. Augustine with the construction of the Ponce de Leon Hotel in 1888. This was Florida's first multi-million-dollar tourist facility. He immediately added the Alcazar and Cordova hotels and St. Augustine's skyline—red-tiled Spanish Renaissance towers poking through a canopy of green live oaks—was born.

Great fires in 1887 and 1917, plus an impetuous rush to build a modern tourist resort, destroyed many old Spanish houses. However, the significance of these losses was gradually realized and the trend was not only stopped but reversed. Much of St. Augustine's older area is within the historic district, where centuries of living produce a quaint architectural mix. In a special section of the district, San Augustin Antiguo, restoration and reconstruction have brought the Spanish colonial village of the 1700s back to life. A million and a half visitors enjoy St. Augustine's rare blend of history, beaches, and sunshine each year.

The Sights Today

In St. Augustine sightseeing doesn't break down into categories. You see and do things all together. You may want to start at the Visitor Information Center, 10 Castillo Dr. Just a short distance away are the gates to the old city. The Castillo de San Marcos is also nearby. This

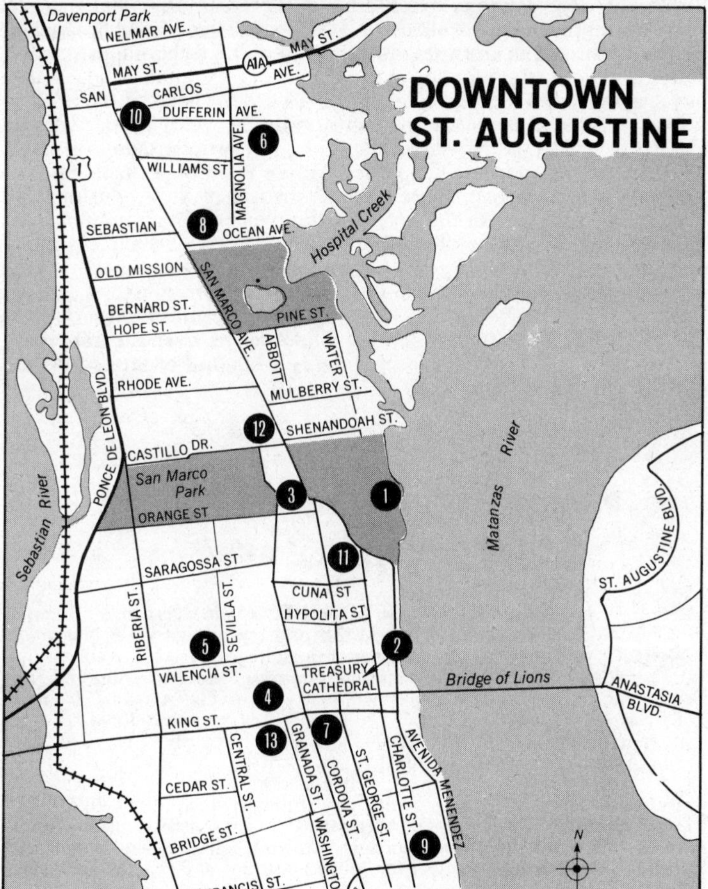

Points of Interest

1) Castillo de San Marcos
2) Cathedral of St. Augustine
3) City Gate
4) Flagler College
5) Flagler Memorial Presbyterian Church
6) Fountain of Youth
7) Lightner Museum
8) Mission of Nombre de Dios
9) Oldest House
10) Old Jail
11) San Agustin Antiquo—Restored Village
12) Visitors Information Center
13) Zorayda Castle

fort is the city's landmark; construction began in 1672 and took 15 years to complete. On a walk down St. George Street in old St. Augustine you visit restored houses, and the oldest U.S. schoolhouse, watch craftsmen work, shop for souvenirs and crafts, examine antiques, and buy snacks or meals in ancient settings. This is the heart of the restoration area. Around the plaza you can admire the beauty of the Catholic Cathedral, go to the movies, walk through a war museum, or rest a while in the old market. The Oldest House is on St. Francis St.

Over on King Street, there's the Cathedral of St. Augustine, the ebullient architecture of the hotels of the Flagler era, a museum filled with special collections of almost everything, and a unique antique mart in an old swimming pool. A stroll on Aviles Street takes you past art galleries, gift shops, a turn-of-the-century store museum, and an eighteenth-century house that was a nineteenth-century inn. Ponce de Leon's Fountain of Youth is on Magnolia Avenue. Even the train tours and carriage rides are multifaceted. Only a handful of attractions are outside the historic district.

PRACTICAL INFORMATION FOR THE JACKSONVILLE AREA

HOW TO GET THERE. By air. Jacksonville International Airport, the primary air entry for the whole northeast corner of the state is served by *American, Delta, Eastern, People Express, Piedmont,* and *TWA.* For information on getting from the airport see "How to Get Around," below.

By bus. *Greyhound Bus Lines,* 10 N. Pearl St., Jacksonville, 356–5521 (plus 4 other terminals in city), and 100 Malaga St., St. Augustine, 829–6401, and *Trailways Bus System,* 410 W. Duval St., Jacksonville, 354–8543, provide intercity transportation along major highway corridors.

By train. Jacksonville is the entry city through which four daily *Amtrak* trains connect the city with the northeastern U.S. and southeast and southwest Florida. For reservations and schedules, call the toll-free Amtrak number: 800–872–7245. The local number for Amtrak's station at 3570 Clifford Lane is 731–1600.

By car. Major highways through Jacksonville north and south are I-95, US 1, and US 17. The latter takes a general southwesterly route from Jacksonville into Central Florida. I-95 runs just west of St. Augustine; US 1 goes right through the city. Major east-west highways are I-10, which connects with I-75 about 90 miles west of Jacksonville and has its eastern terminus here, and US 90, which continues through Jacksonville eastward to the Atlantic beaches. Florida's popular coastal highway, SR A1A, begins in Fernandina Beach, the state's northernmost town, and parallels the ocean east of Jacksonville and through its beach communities along the Atlantic. A1A crosses the St. Johns River near its mouth via the *Mayport Ferry,* Florida's only state-operated ferry, which runs on a half-hour schedule from 6:20 A.M. to 10:15 P.M. and costs $1.50 per car. A1A passes right through St. Augustine.

TELEPHONES. The area code for Jacksonville and all North Florida is 904. Dial 800–555–1212 for directory information on toll-free 800 numbers to see if there is an 800 number for the business you want to reach. A call from a pay phone is $.25.

HOTELS AND MOTELS. The range is enormous—world-class resorts to budget mom-and-pops. Summer is high season at the beaches; spring high season at the resorts. Rates between Labor Day and February 1 are lowest. Elsewhere rates tend to be year-round. However, rates throughout the area are affected by big events such as the Gator Bowl and Georgia-Florida weekend in Jacksonville. Availability is affected by those activities, as well as by appearances of major artists and festivals. Reservations are always wise; you just might arrive when "no vacancy" signs are up everywhere.

Many tourist-oriented properties offer special season and off-season packages that you should check out in advance. Rates change and should not be considered firm. Those quoted are for European plan per night, per room, double occupancy. *Super deluxe,* more than $100; *Deluxe,* $80 to $100; *Expensive,* $60 to $80; *Moderate,* $40 to $60; *Inexpensive,* $30 to $40; *Budget,* less than $30.

AMELIA ISLAND

Because this is a vacation community and not just an overnight stop, many (perhaps most) rental units are efficiencies or apartments. However, there are adequate overnights available. Rooms at the top and bottom of the price range are plentiful, but middle-range rooms are harder to find. Rental agencies play a major role in handling apartments, single cottages and condo units.

Amelia Island Plantation. *Super deluxe.* Amelia Island 32034; 904–261–6161, national toll-free 800–874–6878, Florida toll-free 800–342–6841. A world-class 900-acre resort set in oak forests, salt marshes, and sand dunes; 14 pools, five restaurants and lounges, health club, beach club, tennis center with 21 courts and stadium (site of WTA Championships each April), 27-hole golf course, nature trails, youth programs.

Amelia Surf & Racquet Club. *Deluxe to super deluxe.* 800 Amelia Pkway. S.; 904–261–0511. Multi-tower beachside condo complex, with 60 rental units, pools, tennis courts.

Amelia Landings. *Moderate to expensive.* 76 Sadler Rd.; 904–261–0050. Forty-eight acres, with 60 condo units, pool, and beach cabana.

Beachside Motel. *Inexpensive to Moderate.* 3172 S. Fletcher Ave.; 904–261–4236. On beach, pool, kitchenettes, no pets allowed.

Amelia Motel & Apartments. *Inexpensive to moderate.* 1997 S. Fletcher Ave.; 904–261–5735. Across from beach. Pool, kitchenettes, no pets allowed.

Surf Motel. *Budget to Moderate.* 3199 S. Fletcher Ave.; 904–261–5711. Across from beach. Pool, kitchenettes, restaurant, no pets allowed.

JACKSONVILLE

Downtown, Airport, and Interstates

Sheraton St. Johns. *Deluxe to Super Deluxe.* 1515 Prudential Dr. 32207; 904–396–5100, downtown on the river. Facilities and services include 350 rooms, outdoor pool, tennis, restaurants, lounges, entertainment, and airport shuttle. Pets allowed.

Jacksonville Hilton. *Expensive to Super Deluxe.* 565 S. Main St. 32207; 904–398–8800, downtown on the river. Facilities and services include 292 rooms, outdoor pool, restaurant, lounge, entertainment and airport shuttle. Pets allowed

Holiday Inn Airport. *Moderate.* I–95 N. at Airport Rd. 32229; 904–757–3110, Near airport. Facilities and services include 340 units, indoor recreation center, tennis, restaurant, lounge with entertainment, airport shuttle, car rental office. Pets allowed.

Thunderbird Resort Hotel. *Moderate.* 5865 Arlington Expressway 32211; 904–724–3410, national toll-free (800) 874–3000, Florida toll-free (800) 342–2357. East of downtown across Matthews Bridge. Facilities and services: 273 units, outdoor pool, restaurant, lounge, entertainment. Pets allowed.

Ramada Inn East. *Inexpensive to Moderate.* 6237 Arlington Exway. 32211; 904–725–5093. Between Gator Bowl and beaches. Facilities and services: 145 units, outdoor pool, restaurant, lounge entertainment, dancing, near golf and tennis. No pets allowed.

Emerson Inn. *Inexpensive to Expensive.* 3558 Phillips Hwy. 32207; 904–398–6961. Facilities and services: 59 units, outdoor pool, no pets allowed. Southside on US 1.

JACKSONVILLE

Beaches

Holiday Inn Oceanfront. *Moderate to Super Deluxe.* 1617 N. First St. 32250; 904–249–9071. Outdoor pool, tennis, sailboating, restaurant, lounge, entertainment, 150 rooms, pets allowed.

Howard Johnson's on the Ocean. *Moderate to Deluxe.* 1515 N. First St. 32250; 904–249–3838. Outdoor pool, restaurant, lounge, entertainment, 186 rooms, pets allowed.

Ramada Resort. *Moderate to Deluxe.* 1201 N. First St. 32250; 904–241–5333. Outdoor pool, sailboating, restaurant, lounge, entertainment, 140 rooms, pets allowed.

Sheraton Beach Resort. *Moderate to Deluxe.* Oceanfront at 11th Ave. S. 32250; 904–249–7231. Outdoor pool, restaurant, lounge, entertainment, 156 rooms.

Sea Turtle Inn. *Moderate to Expensive.* One Ocean Blvd. 32233; 904–249–7402, national tollfree (800) 874–6000, Florida toll-free (800) 831–6600. Outdoor pool, restaurant, lounge, entertainment, 202 rooms, no pets.

Golden Sands. *Inexpensive to Moderate.* 127 1st Ave. S., 32250; 904–249–4374. Pool, picnic area, 18 units. No pets.

MARINELAND

Quality Inn. *Moderate to Deluxe.* SR A1A S., Rte. 1, Box 122; 904–471–1222. 125 rooms all oceanfront, two adult pools, two child pools, tennis courts, surf fishing.

PALM COAST

Sheraton Palm Coast. *Expensive to Deluxe.* Oceanfront off SR A1A South, P.O. Box 4000, Palm Coast 32037; 904–445–3434. 130 guest rooms, five miles of beach, pool, restaurant, lounge, entertainment, lighted tennis courts, hydro spa, game room. No pets allowed.

PONTE VEDRA

Sawgrass. *Super deluxe.* P.O.Box 600, Ponte Vedra 32082; from outside Florida toll-free 800–874–7547, within Florida call 800–432–1270. The 4,800-acre resort is the permanent home of the Tournament Players Championship and includes the PGA's Tournament Players Club among its 63 championship holes of golf. The 13-court Sawgrass Racquet Club is among America's top tennis resorts. Swimming pool, beach club, nature trails, water sports (canoeing, sailing), bicycling, horseback riding, shopping, 3 restaurants, live entertainment in lounge.

Ponte Vedra Inn and Club. *Expensive to Super deluxe.* Ponte Vedra Beach 32082; 904–285–6911. The grande dame of area resorts, formerly operated as a private club, became an all-public facility in 1985, with 50 years tradition in elegant resort living. Full facilities for dining and shopping on premises. Two 18-hole golf courses, 15 all-weather tennis courts, 3 swimming pools, and a 12-mile stretch of white sand beach.

ST. AUGUSTINE

Mainland

Ponce's By The Sea and Marina. *Moderate to Deluxe.* 57 Comares Ave., 904–829–8646. 20 units, waterfront, private beach, fishing pier, restaurant, lounge, pool, dockage and moorings, charter boats. No pets.

Monson Motor Lodge. *Inexpensive to Deluxe.* 32 Avenida Menendez, 904–829–2277. 50 units, on bayfront, restaurant, lounge, pool, home of Bayfront Dinner Theatre. Small pets allowed.

Holiday Inn Historic Area. *Moderate to Expensive.* 1300 Ponce de Leon Blvd., 32084; 904–824–3383. Northwest of historic area; restaurant, lounge, cable TV and HBO. Pets allowed.

Ponce de Leon Lodge and Country Club. *Moderate.* US 1 N., P.O. Box 98; 800-824-2821 outside Florida, 800–228–2821 inside Florida. 200 units, pool, restaurant, lounge, 18-hole golf course, putting greens, tennis courts.

Anchorage Motor Inn. *Inexpensive to Moderate.* Anastasia Blvd.; 904–829–9041. Just across Bridge of Lions, 38 units, bayfront view of St. Augustine skyline, pool, fishing pier, yacht dock. Pets allowed.

Red Carpet Inn. *Budget to Moderate.* Intersection I–95 and SR 16; 904–824–4306. 103 units, pool, restaurant. No pets allowed.

Whetstone Bayfront Inn. *Budget to Moderate.* 138 Avenida Menendez; 904–824–1681. 37 units, overlooking Matanzas Bay in historic district, pool.

ST. AUGUSTINE BEACH

For a complete list of condominiums that offer daily, weekly, or monthly rentals, contact the St. Augustine/St. John's Chamber of Commerce, P.O. Drawer 0, St. Augustine 32085.

Beach Club Resort. *Inexpensive to Super Deluxe.* SR A1A S. at Ocean Trace Rd.; 904–471–2626. 59 motel and condo units, oceanfront, pool, tennis, Jacuzzi.

Holiday Inn Beach. *Moderate to Deluxe.* 1061 A1A S.; 904–471–2555. 150 rooms, oceanfront, pool, restaurant, lounge, entertainment, game room.

La Fiesta Motor Lodge. *Inexpensive to Expensive.* 1001 A1A S.; 904–471–2220. 38 units, pool, restaurant. No pets.

Sheraton Anastasia Inn. *Inexpensive to Expensive.* A1A South at Pope Rd.; 904–471–2575. 144 units, near ocean, restaurant, lounge, entertainment, pool. No pets.

Surf Village Motel & Cottages. *Budget to Expensive.* A1A S. at 16th St.; 904–471–3131. 26 units, pool.

BED-AND-BREAKFAST. Increasingly popular, bed and breakfasts offer accommodations that allow guests to become acquainted with residents as well as fellow visitors.

AMELIA ISLAND

The Bailey House. 28 7th St.; 904–261–5390. A landmark Victorian house on the National Register, in the heart of the Historic District. Guest rooms are furnished with antiques; private baths.

The 1735 House. 584 S. Fletcher Ave., 904–261–5878. On the beach; 7 one-bedroom and two-bedroom suites, $55 to $65, and a model lighthouse nearby, $85.

JACKSONVILLE

Manor Inn. 1630 Copeland St. at Oak St., Jacksonville, 904–384–2919, is a converted old mansion in the historic Riverside neighborhood. Reminiscent of the old-time Southern guest house, the facility has 13 units, $25. Lunch and dinner available to guests staying week or longer.

ST. AUGUSTINE

Casa de Solana. 21 Aviles St.; 904–824–3555. Renovated 1763 colonial home in historic district. Full breakfast. Walking distance to restaurants. Use of bicycles for touring historic district. Double occupancy, $50 to $65; suites $75.

Kenwood Inn. 38 Marine St.; 904–824–2116. Victorian house (1886) in historic district. Pool, no small children or pets. $35 to $50.

St. Francis Inn. 279 St. George St., 904–824–6068. 1791 structure in heart of historic area, including 10 one- and two-bedroom suites ($30 to $50) and a two-bedroom/two-bath cottage ($70). Full breakfast; swimming pool.

Victorian House. 11 Cadiz St.; 904–824–5214. In historic district, rooms restored and furnished with antiques, and canopy beds. Continental breakfast served from 8:30 A.M. to 10 A.M. No small children or pets. Rates start at $25.

HOW TO GET AROUND. From the Airport. Car rentals and limousine service are available at the Jacksonville airport. (See below for rental-car information.) It will cost about $8 by limo to downtown Jacksonville; $30 to Jacksonville beaches ($17 if 2 or more passengers); $50 to St. Augustine; about $30 to Amelia Island. Some of the fancier resorts have airport pickup.

Amelia Island. Cars are necessary here; see Jacksonville, below, for rental companies in the area.

Jacksonville. By bus. Jacksonville Transportation Authority operates the public bus system. Fares on locals are $.50, $.75 for express buses. Express to the beaches is $1.10. Schedule information available from 633–7330 or printed schedules by stopping by J.T.A.'s headquarters at Forsythe and Hogan downtown. **By car.** This is really the best way to get around Jacksonville. Normal rush hours prevail: weekday mornings 7:30 to 9:30 and weekday afternoons 4:30 to 6:30. The downtown core area has many one-way streets. Downtown parking is primariliy at private pay lots and many of the spaces are leased; outside the downtown area parking is generally good. Six major bridges and an expressway system move suburban traffic rapidly. On sunny summer weekends the beach-and-back traffic is bumper-to-bumper, so plan accordingly. A variety of auto rental plans and rates means a little shopping around can save money but there will usually be a convenience sacrifice. Check the ads in the telephone directory yellow pages. Reservations are not absolutely necessary except around major event dates but are always wise.

Alamo Rent A Car: national toll-free, 800–327–9633; airport area, 904–757–7414.

Avis Rent A Car: worldwide toll-free, 800–331–1212; airport, 904–757–2327; beaches, 904–241–4932.

Budget Rent A Car: national toll-free, 800–527–0700; airport, 904–757–3555; southside, 904–737–5353.

Dollar Rent A Car: worldwide toll-free, 800–421–6868; airport, 904–757–0614.

Hertz Rent A Car: worldwide toll-free, 800–654–3131; airport, 904–757–2151; downtown, 904–354–5474.

National Car Rental: worldwide toll-free 800–227–7368; airport, 904–757–7580; Hilton Hotel, 904–396–9491.

By taxi. Rates for all cabs are the same: $1 when you enter the cab and $1 for each additional mile. *Checker Cabs,* 764–2472; *Gator City Taxi,* 355–8294; *Yellow Cab,* 354–5511.

St. Augustine. There's no problem getting around the historic district and its many attractions. Tour trains offer one-day unlimited stop-offs and most sites are on or just off the train routes. So many points of interest are concentrated that walking and browsing is very popular. Outside the historic district you must tour by car. There is no public bus system. **By car.** Parking within the historic district is limited and demand exceeds supply. There is a metered parking lot on Hypolita Street just east of St. George Street. The best bet is the huge free parking lot at the Visitors Information Center on San Marco Avenue, and there is a free lot for visitors at the castillo. Driving in the historic district is an adventure of narrow one-way streets, blind corners and horse-drawn carriages. Go slow and keep a sharp eye for one-way and stop signs. Auto rental: *Avis Rent A Car,* Municipal Airport, 904–829–3700 or 800–331–1212; *Hertz Rent A Car,* 353 San Marco Ave., 904–829–5313 or 800–654–3131. Several local automobile dealers also offer day, week, and longer leasing. **By taxi.** *Ancient City Cab,* 222 San Marco Ave., 904–824–8161; *Yellow* Cab Co., 904–829–2256, and *Bass* Cab Co., 904–829–3454, both at 30 Granada St.

TOURIST INFORMATION. The best source of information for the whole Jacksonville area is the *Convention and Visitor Bureau,* 206 N. Hogan St., Jacksonville 32202, 904–353–9736, which produces a variety of maps and brochures and distributes material for other tourism-oriented organizations. The bureau is open from 8:30 A.M. to 5:00 P.M. weekdays. The *Jacksonville Beaches Area Chamber of Commerce,* P.O. Box 50427, Jacksonville Beach 32250, 904–249–3868, and the major resorts are also good sources. When writing or calling ahead it is helpful to state the dates of your proposed visit and any special interests.

The Friday and weekend issues of the local newspapers and the *Jacksonville* magazine contain features, listings, and advertising related to leisure activities.

Once you're in **St. Augustine,** stop by the *Visitor Information Center,* 10 Castillo Dr. 32084, just across the greensward from the castillo; 904–824–3334. In addition to folders on almost every attraction, motel and restaurant, a hostess will answer your questions. There is also a 20-minute film on St. Augustine, $2 for adults and free for those under 16 accompanied by an adult. You can also contact *St. Augustine and St. Johns County Chamber of Commerce,* P.O. Drawer 0, St. Augustine 32085–0119; 904–829–5683. Chamber offices are in the Lightner Bldg., 75 King St.

TOURS. From Jacksonville.: The *Convention and Visitors Bureau,* 206 Hogan St., 353–9736, distributes a brochure outlining five self-guided tours of Jacksonville and the Northeast Florida area. *Gray Line Tours,* 396–8687, conducts four-hour tours every day of Jacksonville, St. Augustine, and Fernandina Beach. Cost is $15 for any of the three tours and reservations should be made a day in advance.

St. Augustine: *St. Augustine Historical Tours,* 167 San Marco Ave., 829–3800. Trolleys leave The Old Jail on the hour and half hour for a seven-mile, one-hour tour with stop-off privileges at all attractions for $4 for adults (13 years and older) and $2 for children (6 to 12), under 6 free with parent. For $6 adults, $3.25 children, a second package includes the one-hour tour plus admission to the Old Jail and the Old Drugstore.

St. Augustine Sightseeing Trains, 3 Cordova St., 829–6545, leave the station every 15 to 20 minutes from 8:30 A.M. for a 7-mile, one-hour tour with stop-offs at all attractions *and* points of interest; $5 for adults and $2 for children, under 6 free with parent. Four package tours featuring various combinations of attractions and sites range from a three-hour $9.95 package to a six- to eight-hour marathon for $21. The one-hour tour ticket is good for 24 hours and package tour tickets are good for the length of your stay.

Colee Sightseeing Carriage Tours, P.O.Box 604, 829–2818, may be the oldest continuous tourism enterprise in Florida. The company hauled passengers from train to hotel in the Flagler era. The horse-drawn carriages leave from the bayfront near the castillo on demand and tour most of the sights, stop at Flagler Memorial Church, and go into some of the historic district streets the tour trains can't maneuver. The drivers narrate as they go, a delightful melange of fact, near fact, mis-fact and gossip. Rates are $5 for adults, $2 for children.

Victory II Scenic Cruise, City Yacht Pier, 824–1806, tours Matanzas Bay and adjoining waterways on 75-minute cruises. The first cruise usually leaves at 1:00 P.M., but check for current schedules.

PARKS. See also "Beaches," below.

Three state properties near St. Augustine are of interest to visitors. *Anastasia State Recreation Area* on Anastasia Island across Matanzas Bay from St. Augustine has broad ocean beach backed by picturesque sand dunes and also encompasses the quarries from which the huge coquina blocks for the Castillo de San Marcos were taken. *Faver-Dykes State Park,* off US 1 about 10 miles south of St. Augustine, consists of 752 acres bordering the tidal marshes along Pellicer Creek. The wild landscape appears much as it did to the Spanish explorers of the sixteenth century. Wading birds, waterfowl, alligators, otters and raccoons are often seen along the creek. There is a $.50-per-person entrance fee. *Washington Oaks State Gardens,* about five miles south of Marineland on A1A, has an outcropping of coquina rocks on its oceanfront where limpets, mussels, anemones, starfish, and tiny crabs can be observed at low tide. On the Matanzas

River side are the home and gardens of the late Owen D. Young, former chairman of the board of General Electric. The whole park was part of Belle Vista Plantation, owned by General Joseph Hernandez, a Spanish Floridian who became an American. There is a $.50-per-person entrance fee.

ZOOS AND MARINE PARKS. *Jacksonville Zoo,* 86806 Zoo Rd., 757–4466, has more than 700 animals from all over the world (including a herd of rare white rhinos) on its 61 acres. Hours are 9:00 A.M. to 4:45 P.M. daily. Admission is $2.50 ages 12 to 64, $1 ages 4 to 11 and over 64, and free to those under 4 or handicapped.

Gatorland Alligator Farm on US 1 N. Features alligators and other reptiles, exotic animals, and birds. Open daily 9:00 A.M. to 5:00 P.M. Admission charge. 824–1700.

Marineland, 18 miles south of St. Augustine on SR A1A; 471–1111. This was the world's first oceanarium. Two huge tanks with viewing windows and a porpoise-show pool. Open daily, 9:00 A.M. to 5:30 P.M.; admission charge.

St. Augustine Alligator Farm, A1A S. on Anastasia Island; 824–3337. Tourists have been ogling huge gators at this attraction since 1893. Alligator wrestling, shows on the hour. Open daily, 9:00 A.M. to 5:00 P.M. Admission.

BEACHES. Amelia Island has 13 miles of beach. Summer-cottage and small-apartment residents use the stretch across from the port. Most newer facilities are farther south. Amelia Island Plantation encompasses most of the southern end.

Miles and miles of clean, sandy ocean beaches for sunning, swimming, shelling and fishing are probably the **Jacksonville** area's greatest tourist asset. They are about 12 miles east of downtown both north and south of the St. Johns River estuary via several routes. All beaches in Florida are public, though access can sometimes be a problem. Alcoholic beverages and glass containers are prohibited on all beaches in Duval County.

Little Talbot Island State Park. On State Road A1A north of the St. Johns, the park can be reached by using Hecksher Drive along the north shore of the river or by using Atlantic Boulevard (SR 10) south of the river and then the Mayport Ferry on A1A to cross over. The park has five to six miles of beaches with parking, changing facilities, restrooms and showers at several places. Admission is $.50 a person. Picnic areas have no grills. Dogs not allowed.

Kathryn Abbey Hanna Park. South of the river just below the Mayport Naval Station, the park has several miles of ocean beach and a freshwater lake where windsurfing lessons are a warm-weather feature. There are picnic facilities and camping. Dogs must be leashed. Admission is $.50 a person. Take Atlantic Boulevard (SR 10) from downtown and turn left on A1A.

Atlantic Beach. Northernmost of Jacksonville's four beach communities, Atlantic Beach is quiet and residential with good beach access. From downtown take Atlantic Boulevard. Local surfers prefer this and Neptune Beach, just to the south. Catamaran rentals and instructions are available at the Sea Turtle Inn during warm weather. Lifeguards are on duty at five locations from 10:00 A.M. to 6:00 P.M. during the summer. Dogs on leash are permitted.

Neptune Beach. Like its norther neighbor, this is a quiet residential community with good beach access. It is also popular with local surfers. Reached via Atlantic Boulevard. Lifeguards are on duty in the summer from 10:00 A.M. to 6:00 P.M. Unlike Atlantic Beach, however, no dogs are allowed on the beach proper. Actually, no dogs and few visitors can tell when they cross city limits as all four beach communities are fused.

Jacksonville Beach. This is the liveliest of the great sweep of beaches that start south of the St. Johns River and run unbroken down to St. Augustine Inlet, almost 30 miles. Here is the traditional beach boardwalk with T-shirt shops, souvenir stands, hot dog and hamburger vendors, and a summer amusement park. Lots of small bars give respite from the sun during the day and rock at night. The Jacksonville Beach Pier extends about 1,000 feet over the beach and surf. It costs $3 to fish and $.50 to stroll and spectate. Rental tackle and refreshments are available on the pier. At intermittent sites along public beach areas are lifeguard towers with lifeguards on duty during the summer season from 10:00 A.M. to 6:00 P.M.; daily service locations vary according to crowd concentrations and surf conditions. No dogs are allowed on the beach. From downtown take Beach Boulevard (US 90) or Butler Expressway ($.25 toll).

Ponte Vedra. This southernmost of the beach communities is actually in another county, but much more a part of the Jacksonville area than the St. Augustine scene. It is a very affluent residential and resort locale—the Ponte Vedra Club and Sawgrass. Access to the beach is quite limited, which makes it nice for residents and guests of the resorts. Big dunes and an unspoiled coastline give a glimpse of Florida past.

St. Augustine's beaches are as big an attraction as its history, and the city's home county has 43 miles of them—white, wide, almost level, and suitable for driving much of the time. State Road A1A N. crosses over North River to Vilano Beach. There is public access if you go straight ahead where A1A takes a sharp turn left or north in Vilano.

North of A1A are it is difficult to park along the highway and walk through the dunes to the beach. If you choose to try, however, exercise caution, for it is easy to get your car stuck in the sand, and most of the property is private and posted.

The southern stretch of beach is on Anastasia Island across the Bridge of Lions of A1A S. The highway goes through *Anastasia State Park,* where there is public access, and then curves right and south through St. Augustine Beach. There is a public parking lot at the pier just south of the curve. Several of the east-west cross streets have ramps to the beach.

Words of caution: tides come in as well as go out, so leave your possessions well up on the beach when you go swimming and check periodically to see if the distance between them and the surf is narrowing. When driving, stay on the damp sand and where there are tire tracks of other cars. However, tire tracks are not an infallible sign of safety as they may be those of a 4-wheel-drive vehicle.

PARTICIPANT SPORTS. Jacksonville is an all-seasons and all-sports city. For information on **jogging trails, bicycle routes, boat ramps,** and such, contact the *Parks and Recreation Dept.,* 633–2540. The *Convention and Visitors Bureau,* 353–9736, keeps tabs on what's doing where for a spectrum of participant sports. The area's large resorts have their own golf, tennis, and swimming facilities for their registered guests and some hotels and large motels have courtesy arrangements.

Public **tennis** facilities include: *Boone Park Tennis Courts,* 3730 Park St., 384–8687; *Huguenot Park,* 200 16th St. S., Jacksonville Beach, 249–9407; and *Whalen Tennis Center,* 6009 Powers Ave., 737–8800.

Among **golf** courses open to the pubic are: *The Dunes,* 11751 McCormick Rd., 641–8444; *Fort George Island Golf Club,* off SR A1A in Fort George,

251–3132; *Hyde Park Golf and Country Club,* 6439 Hyde Grove Rd., 786–5410; and *Jacksonville Beach Golf Club,* Penman Rd., 249–8600.

Boating. You can rent catamarans from a concessionnaire at the Sea Turtle Inn, One Ocean Boulevard, Atlantic Beach; 249–7402. Instructions available here, too.

Fishing is the biggest participant sport and so good that outdoorsmen are drawn to the area just to try their luck. The combination of freshwater and saltwater habitats provides a broad selection of fish, and geography provides good access. Indeed, the access is so good that a lot of fishing can be done without a boat—surf, jetties, bridges, banks, and the long Jacksonville Beach pier. Both sides of the river from its mouth through the city "S" curve and up river as far as you want to go are sprinkled with fish camps, marinas, boat liveries, and bait and tackle shops.

Charter and party boats for saltwater fishing dock at Mayport and several other places down river or on the Intracoastal. Inshore charter trips run $150 to $225 a day, offshore trips for up to six people are around $450, depending on distance and time. Day trips on party boats, which take 40 to 60 people out bottom fishing, cost about $30 and rental tackle is available.

Monty's Marina, Mayport, 246–7575, arranges charters.

Florida has no saltwater fishing license requirement. However, out-of-state and out-of-county fishermen must have a freshwater fishing license. They can be purchased at most fish camps and bait and tackle shops or from the county tax collector's office.

St. Augustine. The bay, tidal creeks, Intracoastal Waterway, and St. Johns River offer hours of **boating** pleasure. Sailboats and small motor boats are rented by the hour or day at local marinas, which also have maps and charts. See local Yellow Pages. Windsurfing instruction and rentals are available through *Windsurfing St. Augustine* at the Surf Station, 1020 Anastasia Blvd., 471–9463. **Fishing** is a popular activity and pursued in a number of ways—surf, bridge, pier, small boats on inland waters, and charter and party boats for deep-sea. Fish camps, bait and tackle shops, and marinas are the places to get fitted and are the best sources of information on where and how. The *Camachee Cove Charters,* 824–3328, is headquarters for charter and party boat fishing. For **surfing** information and rentals, check with the Blue Sky Surf Shop, 517 Anastasia Blvd., 824–2734.

The **golf** course at *St. Augustine Shores,* 794–0303, is open to the public. It is a par 60 exective course with $7 greens fee and $10 for electric carts. Reservations are taken no more than 48 hours in advance.

There are 22 public **tennis** courts in various locations, many lighted for night play, and the St. Augustine-St. Johns County Recreation Dept. has details.

SPECTATOR SPORTS. The sports fan has a full engagement book in the **Jacksonville** area. **Baseball** in Wolfson Park features the *Jacksonville Expos,* class AA farm team of the Montreal Expos. The Jacksonville Coliseum down the block provides the big indoor space for college basketball, other court games, and special sports spectaculars; call 633–2900 for information. **Greyhound racing** is year-round with dates split among three tracks: *Bayard Raceways,* 18 miles south on US 1, 268–5555, September through November and March through May; *Jacksonville Kennel Club,* 1440 N. McDuff Ave., 388–2623, May through September; and *Orange Park Greyhound Track,* US 17 at I-295, 264–9575, November through March. Call for schedules and post times. Admission is $.50 grandstand and $2 clubhouse. Florida law excludes anyone under 18 years of age.

The *Gator Bowl,* 633–2900, not only hosts the New Year's **football** classic and annual Georgia-Florida rivalry, but is home field of the USFL's *Jacksonville Bulls.*

St. Augustine: *Bayard Raceways,* US 1 N., 268–5555, has **greyhound racing** dates from September through November and March through May. The facility has undergone recent renovation and refurbishment and is one of the best. Check for exact dates and post times. No one under 18 admitted.

HISTORIC SITES AND HOUSES. Clearly there can be more to a vacation in the Jacksonville area than relaxing on the beaches. The rich history here can make for days of fascinating sightseeing.

JACKSONVILLE

Fort Caroline National Monument, 12713 Fort Caroline Rd., is most directly reached by Monument Road off Atlantic Boulevard at Regency Square. A small museum tells the bloody story of the 1564 French Huguenot fort (the first Protestant settlement in the New World) and European's first struggle for control of North America. High on a bluff overlooking the St. Johns is a replica of the stone column Jean Ribaut erected in 1562 when he claimed the land for France. Below the bluff on the river's flood plain is a replica of the fort overrun in the 1565 massacre led by Spain's Pedro Menendez de Aviles. The monument is open daily from 9:00 A.M. to 5:00 P.M. and there is no charge; call 641–7155.

Kingsley Plantation State Historic Site, on Fort George Island off SR A1A, (251–3122) was home and headquarters of Zephanish Kinglsey, the richest plantation owner of his time and operator of a worldwide slave trading empire. Slaves fresh from Africa were schooled here in agricultural and plantation skills, thus increasing their already considerable price following the slave embargo of 1808. Kingsley built the plantation house in 1817. The story-and-a-half house behind it, built by the original plantation owner, was the kitchen and house of Anna Jai, Kingsley's African princess wife. Tours of the kitchen house and plantation are conducted daily at 9:30 and 11:30 A.M. and at 1:30 and 3:00 P.M. Admission is $.50, under 6 free.

ST. AUGUSTINE

Castillo de San Marcos, One Castillo Dr., St. Augustine's dominant landmark and the only structure to survive the English seige of 1702 virtually intact. Construction began in 1672 from huge coquina blocks quarried on Anastasia Island. A national monument administered by the National Park Service. Open daily from 8:30 A.M. to 5:15 P.M. Small admission.

Cathedral of St. Augustine, 35 Treasury St. Most impressive landmark on the plaza. The present building was dedicated in 1797 to replace a church ruined during British Period. The parish register goes back to 1594 and is the oldest written record in the U.S. Open daily, 5:30 A.M. to 5:00 P.M. Monday through Friday, 5:30 A.M. to 7:00 P.M. weekends. Donation.

City Gate, San Marco Ave. Part of the defense perimeter and only entrance to the city from the north in colonial times. Present stone gate replaced earlier log structures in 1808; remains open as welcome to the city. Free.

Dr. Peck House, 143 St. George St. Stone walls of lower story date from 1750, restored and maintained by Women's Exchange in early territorial style when occupied by physician and family. Open 10:00 A.M. to 4:00 P.M. Monday through Saturday. Free; 829–5064.

Flagler College, 70 King St. Former Ponce de Leon Hotel built by Henry Flagler and opened in 1888, Florida's first multi-million-dollar tourist hotel, now a private college. Front courtyard is open to public. Free.

Flagler Memorial Presbyterian Church, 36 Sevilla St. Highly ornate building of Venetian Renaissance architecture was a gift from Henry Flagler, who is entombed here. Completed in 1889. Open daily 8:30 A.M. to 4:00 P.M., guided tours. Free.

Government House, west block of the plaza. On the site of the Spanish governor's residence. Present building was once post office and customs house, and now offices of Historic St. Augustine Preservation Board. Exhibits on first floor. Open daily. Free.

Fountain of Youth, 155 Magnolia Ave. One of the oldest commercial attractions, large globe shows routes of the explorers and planetarium shows the sky of that time. Indian burial ground and village. Open daily 9:00 A.M. to 4:45 P.M. Admission; 829–3168.

Lightner Museum, King St.; 824–2874. Former Alcazar Hotel built by Henry Flagler, three floors of Victorian and turn-of-the-century art objects and artifacts collected by former editor of *Hobbies Magazine,* also serves as city hall and chamber of commerce office. The *Antique Mall* is housed in the former hotel's swimming pool. Museum open daily 9:00 A.M. to 5:00 P.M.; admission charge. The mall is open 10:00 A.M. to 5:00 P.M. Wednesday through Sunday; free.

Mission of Nombre de Dios, San Marco Avenue and Ocean Avenue. Site of first mass in America, 1565. Here there is a 208-foot stainless steel cross, Prince of Peach church, Our Lady of La Leche Shrine. Open daily, 9:00 A.M. to 6:00 P.M. Donation.

Museum of Yesterday's Toys, 52 St. George St. More than 1,500 dolls and antique toys in a restored house. Open daily, 9:00 A.M. to 6:00 P.M. Admission.

Oldest House, 14 St. Francis St. A National Historic Landmark owned and restored by the St. Augustine Historical Society. Believed to have been occupied first in 1727; enlarged by British officer. Adjoining museum. Open daily except Christmas 9:00 A.M. to 5:00 P.M. Admission; 824–2872.

Oldest Store Museum, 4 Artillery Lane. Former C. F. Hamblen Store operated on this site in the 1800s. Many displays are found in the store's warehouse. Open Monday through Saturday, 12:00 to 5:00 P.M. Sunday. Admission; 829–9729.

Oldest Wooden Schoolhouse, 14 St. George St.; 824–0192. Building appears on 1763 city map, used as a school in Second Spanish Period. Exhibits include school materials of the times. Open daily 9:00 A.M. to 5:00 P.M. Admission.

Old Drug Store, Orange and Cordova Streets. Lotions and potions used in yesteryear. Open daily, 9:00 A.M. to 5:00 P.M. Admission. Tour trolley stop.

Old Jail, 167 San Marco Ave.; 829–3800. A fun look at City of St. Augustine's former jail. Open daily from 8:00 A.M. to 5:30 P.M. Admission. Tour trolley station.

Old Sugar Mill, 254 San Marco Ave.; 829–2244. Mill and tools used in mid-1800s, antique museum. Open daily, 8:30 A.M. to 5:00 P.M. Free. Tour train station.

Plaza de La Constitution, King Street and bayfront. Laid out in accordance with royal decree soon after St. Autustine was established. Contains old market and monument to Spanish Constitution of 1812. Free.

San Agustin Antiguo-The Restored Village, St. George Street. An eighteenth-century Spanish Colonial village authentically reconstructed and restored *in situ,* with guided tours. Craftsmen demonstrate traditional skills, re-create daily life in 1750s. Operated by St. Augustine Preservation Board.

Information and tickets across from Ribera House. Open daily, 9:00 A.M. to 4:30 P.M. Admission. Call 824–6363.

St. Photios Shrine, 41 St. George St. National Greek Orthodox Shrine commemorates America's first Greek settlers, who became part of St. Augustine during British Period. Chapel is in ornate old Byzantine style; audio-visual presentation of the immigrants' story. Open daily, 9:00 A.M. to 5:00 P.M. Free.

Trinity Episcopal Church, King Street on plaza. Oldest Episcopal church building in Florida, begun in 1825.

Ximenez-Fatio House, 20 Aviles St.; 829–3575. Constructed about 1797, became a boarding house for tourists in the nineteenth century. Maintained by the Colonial Dames of American. Open Monday through Friday, March 1 through August 31, 11:00 A.M. to 4:00 P.M. Free.

Zorayda Castle, 83 King St.; 824–3097. Reproduction of a portion of the Alhambra in Granada recalls the days of Spain's Moorish kings. Collection of Oriental art. Built during city's Flagler era. Open daily, 9:00 A.M. to 5:30 P.M. Admission.

In addition, many restored structures throughout the historic district are occupied as homes and shops, or, in the case of the St. Francis Barracks, by the headquarters of the Florida National Guard. Little shops are scattered throughout the district on side streets both north and south of the plaza.

MUSEUMS. See also "Historic Sites and Houses," above. **Jacksonville:** *Cummer Gallery of Art,* 829 Riverside Ave., 356–6857, is built in the gardens of the former Cummer mansion (lumber millionaires), and one room of the mansion is preserved in the museum. Permanent exhibits lean toward the traditional—medieval, Renaissance, baroque, American, and a stand-out collection of the early Meissen porcelain. Hours are 10:00 A.M. to 4:00 P.M. Tuesday through Friday, noon to 5:00 P.M. Saturday, and 2:00 to 5:00 P.M. Sunday. Closed Monday, Christmas Day and New Year's Day. Free admission.

Jacksonville Art Museum, 4160 Boulevard Center Dr., 398–8336, is the area's exponent of contemporary art although it has permanent exhibits of oriental porcelain and pre-Colombian artifacts. Hours are 10:00 A.M. to 4:00 P.M. Tuesday, Wednesday, and Friday; 10:00 A.M. to 10:00 P.M. Thursday; 1:00 to 5:00 P.M. Saturday and Sunday. Closed Monday and the month of August. Free admission.

Jacksonville Museum of Arts and Sciences. 1025 Gulf Life Dr., 396–7061 and 396–7062. Permanent exhibits focus on Egypt, health, Florida Indians, pioneer life, wildlife; planetarium and science theater shows are included in museum admission. Hours are 9:00 A.M. to 5:00 P.M. Tuesday through Friday; 11:00 A.M. to 5:00 P.M. Saturday; 1:00 P.M. to 5:00 P.M. Sunday. Closed Monday. Admission is $2 adults, $1 children ages 4–17, and free for children under 4. On Friday and Saturday nights the planetarium presents Cosmic Concerts, blending rock music with special effects, at 9, 10, and 11 P.M.

St. Augustine: *Potter's Wax Museum,* One King St.; 829–9056. Features 243 figures of famous people from the past in authentic costumes. Open daily except Christmas, 9:00 A.M. to 5:00 P.M. winter, 9:00 A.M. to 9:00 P.M. summer. Admission.

Ripley's Believe It Or Not Museum, 19 San Marco Ave; 824–1606. Curiosities collected by Robert Ripley fill 14 galleries on three floors. Open daily 9:00 A.M. to 6:00 P.M., summer, 9:00 A.M. to 9:00 P.M. Admission.

PERFORMING ARTS. Jacksonville: The Arts Assembly of Jacksonville makes the area's very rich music, dance, theatre, and film activity accessible through one-stop information on schedules and ticket availability. The 24-hour *Artline Hotline,* 353–1405, delivers an up-to-date recorded message on current cultural events. The *Arts Assembly,* Florida Theater Building, 128 E. Forsyth St., Suite 505, Jacksonville 32202, 358–3600, and the Convention and Visitors Bureau produce an events calendar quarterly.

The Jacksonville performing arts tradition is long and strong. The *Friday Musicale* is probably the oldest music group in Florida. The Friday Musicale auditorium is at 645 Oak; 355–6851. *Theater Jacksonville* is the oldest community theater in the country. Their address is 2032 San Marco Blvd.; 396–4425. The *Jacksonville Symphony,* 354–5479, and *Florida Ballet of Jacksonville,* 353–7518, are regional leaders. Several cultural series bring international artists to area stages. Notable among these stages are the modern *Civic Auditorium* on the riverfront and the *Florida Theater,* one of those grand silent movie and vaudeville palaces of yesteryear lovingly restored and renovated in 1983.

The *Alhambra Dinner Theater,* 12000 Beach Blvd., 641–1212, is an Equity troupe with nationally known headliners in popular light fare. The buffet, which even area food critics laud, and play are about $20 per person. Reservations are a must. See "Dining Out," for other dinner theaters.

St. Augustine: *Cross and Sword,* is the state's official play, telling the story of St. Augustine's early years with a huge cast of authentically costumed players and dramatic lighting and music. Performed mid-June to Labor Day in the St. Augustine Amphitheater, Route A1A; 471–1965.

The resident repertory company, the *Saint George St. Players,* present Spanish comedies in translation May to September, Thursday-Monday nights by torchlight in the St. George St. Restoration Area.

SHOPPING. St. Augustine: The *Antiques Mall* in the Lightner Museum is located in what was once the Alcazar Hotel's indoor swimming pool. It's open 10:00 A.M. to 5:00 P.M., Wednesday-Sunday. The craft shops in the historic district are well worth browsing through.

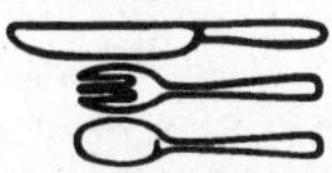

DINING OUT. The price classifications of the following restaurants, from inexpensive to deluxe, are based on the cost of an average three-course dinner for one person for food alone; beverages, tax and tip would be extra. *Deluxe* is more than $25; *Expensive,* $15 to $25; *Moderate,* $7 to $15; and *Inexpensive,* less than $7.

Abbreviations for credit cards are: AE, American Express; CB, Carte Blanche; DC, Diners Club; MC, MasterCard; V, Visa. Most restaurants that do not accept credit cards will cash travelers' checks.

AMELIA ISLAND

1878 Steakhouse. *Moderate to Expensive.* N. 2nd St.; 261–4049. Very good steaks and seafood in a converted 18th-century warehouse. Dinner daily, lunch Monday to Friday. AE, MC, V.

The Bamboo House. *Moderate.* 614 Centre St.; 261–0508. Cantonese food. Open for lunch and dinner weekdays, Saturday for dinner. Closed Sundays. AE, MC, V.

Brett's Casual Fine Dining. *Moderate.* 501 S. 8th St., 261–2660. New restaurant whose name reflects its fine foods and casual atmosphere. Veal, seafood, fettuccine. Lunch Tuesday through Friday, dinner Tuesday through Saturday. AE, MC, V.

The Sandbar. *Moderate.* Off A1A S.; 261–4185. Follow the red arrows to this seafood tradition since 1932, original family management. Closed Monday. MC, V.

The Surf. *Moderate.* 3199 S. Fletcher Ave.; 261–5711. Across from beach, full service for three meals daily, extensive wine selection. AE, MC, V.

Marina Restaurant. *Inexpensive to Moderate.* 101 Centre St.; 261–5310. Right next to the docks at the foot on Centre St. Seafood is featured, early hours accommodate anglers. Open daily 6:00 A.M.–9:00 P.M.

JACKSONVILLE AND ITS BEACHES

American

Woody's. *Moderate.* 1638 University Blvd.; 721–8836; 5930 Powers Ave.; 731–0490; and 9825 San Jose Blvd., 262–3955. Barbecue ribs, Brunswick stew, and peanut butter pie draw local crowds, especially at lunch. Sunday to Thursday, 11:00 A.M.–10:00 P.M., Friday and Saturday, 11:00 A.M.–11:00 P.M. No credit cards.

The Homestead. *Inexpensive to Moderate.* 1712 Beach Blvd.; 249–5240. Huge portions of chicken and biscuits, and steak dinners. Monday to Saturday, 5:00 P.M.–10:00 P.M., Sunday, noon-10:00 P.M. AE,MC, V.

Beach Road Chicken. *Inexpensive.* 4132 Atlantic Blvd.; 398–7980. Generations of Jaxons have lined up for home-style chicken dinners with biscuits and gravy, cole slaw, and rice or fries. Fried shrimp recently added. Open Tuesday to Saturday, 5:00 P.M. to 10:15 P.M.; Sunday and holidays, noon to 9:45 P.M. No credit cards. No reservations.

Continental

Le Gueridon. *Moderate to Deluxe.* Costa Verde Plaza, 2429 S. Third St., South Jacksonville Beach; 241–2426. Attentive service and outstanding cuisine in a gracious setting. Dinner Mon.-Sat., 6–10 P.M. Reservations accepted but not necessary. AE, MC, V.

Andre's. *Expensive.* 1435 N. University Blvd.; 743–7167. Highly acclaimed for its imaginative and sometimes unique preparation of dishes in the Continental style. Lunch Monday–Friday, dinner daily. AE, MC, V.

Wine Cellar. *Expensive.* 1314 Prudential Dr., Southside; 398–8989. Pleasing décor, excellent service, and outstanding veal and seafood dishes make this one of the most acclaimed restaurants in town. Outdoor tables in good weather and extensive wine list are other features. Lunch and dinner. Tues.-Sat. Closed Sun. and Mon. Reservations definitely for dinner. AE, MC, V.

Italian

La Pasta Fresca Ristorante. *Moderate to Expensive.* 556 Kingsley Ave., Orange Park, 269–5738. A wide selection of fresh pasta dishes and sauces of distinction, fresh-baked crusty breads, and a way with veal and chicken make this tops in Italian cuisine. Dinner only, 6:00 P.M.–10:00 P.M., Tues.-Sat.

DeFranco's. *Moderate.* 4224 Blanding Blvd.; 778–3174. A westside favorite with homemade pasta and crusty bread. House specialties really are special. Open daily, 4:30 P.M.–11:00 P.M. MC, V.

Oriental

Ieyasu of Tokyo. *Moderate.* 25 W. Duval St.; 353–0163. Sit on floor or in chairs for authentic Japanese cuisine. Very good tempura. Lunch Mon.-Fri., dinner Mon.-Sat. Closed Sun. AE, MC, V.

Mr.. Hu's. *Moderate.* 5849 University Blvd W.; 739–1461. Very extensive menu and a choice of degrees of hotness on Szechuan dishes. One of the area's very best ethnic restaurants. Lunch and dinner every day. AE, MC, V.

Seafood

Chart House. *Moderate to Expenisve.* 601 Hendricks Ave., next to the Sheraton at St. Johns Place; 398–3353. A handsome part of Jacksonville's new waterfront, the Chart House could be listed under steakhouses except that its seafood is so good. Dinner only every day. All major credit cards.

Diamond Head. *Moderate to Expensive.* 823 Gulf Life Dr., 396–6414. Another new restaurant that takes advantage of the revitalized river view. Seafood shares honors with veal and beef dishes. Valet parking. Dinner only Mon.–Sat. AE, MC, V.

Ragtime Tavern and Seafood Grill. *Moderate to Expensive.* 207 Atlantic Blvd., Atlantic Beach; 241–7877. Seafood done up Creole style with a dash of Cajun seasoning and a lively atmosphere. Open 11:30 A.M.–10:30 P.M. Sun.–Thurs.; 11:30–11:00 Fri.–Sat.; Sunday New Orleans–style brunch 11:00–4:00. AE, MC, V.

Sea Turtle Inn and Restaurant. *Moderate to Expensive.* One Ocean Blvd., Atlantic Beach, 249–7402. This is the oceanside dining room of a beach landmark inn with a great view and atmosphere. Breakfast, lunch, and dinner daily. Major credit cards.

Crustaceans. *Moderate.* 2321 Beach Blvd., Jacksonville Beach; 241–8238. Very popular waterfront spot with an excellent raw bar as well as regular dining room. Dinner only Mon.-Sat., Sun. 1:00 P.M.–11:00 P.M. AE, DC, MC, V.

Sliders Oyster Bar. *Inexpensive to Moderate.* 218 First St., Neptune Beach; 246–0881. The crowds tell you this is the place for broiled and baked seafood despite appearances. Be prepared to wait, since they don't take reservations. Weekdays from noon to 10:00 P.M., Saturday to 11:00 P.M. Closed Sundays. MC, V.

Steaks

The Tree Steakhouse. *Moderate.* 942 Arlington Rd.; 725–0066. Reputedly the area's best place for steak, which is all they serve. Steaks are cut to your order tableside. Dinner daily, from 5:30 P.M. AE, DC, MC, V.

Spindrifter. *Moderate.* Best Western Motel on US 17 in Orange Park; 264–1211. An all-purpose restaurant—breakfast, lunch, and dinner—that has earned a reputation for excellent prime ribs. Dinner, 5:00–10:00 P.M. daily. All major credit cards.

ST. AUGUSTINE AREA

Bayfront Dinner Theatre. *Moderate to Expensive.* Monson Lodge, 32 Avenida Menendez; 829–2277. Menu features prime rib, roast beef, and chicken; playbill features modern comedies for a general audience. Dinner and play are $17.95, play only $9.45. Reservations. MC, V.

Chart House. *Moderate to Expensive.* 46 Avenida Menendez; 824–1687. In a prominent restored house on the bayfront. Seafood, steak, and chops. Open daily from 5:00 P.M. for dinner. All credit cards.

Le Pavillion. *Moderate to Expensive.* 45 Avenida Menendez; 824–6202. Good continental food in French country décor, specialties include lamb and roast duck. Open daily for lunch and dinner. MC, V.

Cap's Seafood Restaurant. *Moderate to Expensive.* Off A1A north of Vilano Beach; 824–8794. On the Intracoastal Waterway above North River Bridge. Family recipes are the secret to this restaurant's success. Expect a wait even with reservations. Open for lunch on weekends, open for dinner Wed.-Sun. AE, MC, V.

Columbia Restaurant. *Moderate to Expensive.* 98 St. George St.; 824–3341. New branch of Tampa's noted restaurant for Cuban cuisine; located in heart of historic area. Open daily, lunch and dinner. AE, DC, MC, V.

Raintree. *Moderate to Expensive.* 102 San Marco Ave.; 824–7211. An honored restaurant among Florida food critics, continental-style cuisine in a restored Victorian house. Dinner daily. Reservations accepted. DC, MC, V.

Aldo's Restaurant. *Moderate.* 60 San Marco Ave.; 824–0373. Excellent Northern Italian cooking in an old (non historic) house in St. Augustine. A regional favorite. Dinner only, Tues.-Sun. AE, MC, V.

Chimes Restaurant. *Moderate.* 12 Avenida Menendez, 829–8141. Small restaurant with a big view—Castillo de San Marcos. Nice lunch spot while sightseeing. Seafood, steak and chops. Open for breakfast, lunch and dinner daily. Credit cards.

Cafe Alcazar. *Inexpensive to moderate.* Antique Mall, Lightner Museum Bldg.; 824–2618. Ever lunch on the bottom of a swimming pool? Charming setting for light French country lunches. Open 11:00 A.M.–4:00 P.M., Wed.-Sun.

Scarlett O'Hara's. *Inexpensive to moderate.* 70 Hypolita St.; 824–6535. Tourists love it by day, the young crowd by night. Sandwiches, beer, and drinks in a rambling old house. Open daily, 11:30 A.M.–1 A.M. MC, V.

NIGHT LIFE. Amelia Island: No trip to Fernandina is complete without stopping by *The Palace.* 117 Centre St., 261–9068, though it need not be at night. This is Florida's oldest saloon, built in 1878, comlete with hand-carved bar and murals. If you get the nibblies, order the boiled shrimp.

Jacksonville: On shining new riverfront where the *aprés*-concert crowd goes, entertainment tends to the smooth and mellow. On the beaches (excluding Ponte Vedra, of course) the atmosphere is casual and sometimes downright familiar. Around the naval stations you can find raunchy, if that's your choice. There's an abundance of live music everywhere, but no big-time nightclub shows. Headliners appear in concert instead.

Applejack's, 1402 San Marco Blvd., Southside, 398–2111, presents jazz, rock, and blues.

Brandy's Good Time Emporium, 602 Atlantic Blvd., Neptune Beach, 246–1755, has well-known rock groups on weekends and uses budget and gimmick drink rates to attract a mixed crowd.

Fantasy World, 749 Cesery Blvd. in Arlington, 723–3730, promises girls, girls, girls, and an amateur go-go contest every Tuesday night.

J. P. Peppercorn's, University Blvd. at I-95, 731–5412, has a 400-seat pub with live rock music Tuesday through Sundays and snacks until 1:30 A.M.

Malabar Lounge, 9801 Beach Blvd., 641–5033, features bluegrass.

Shucker's Beach Club, 222 N. Oceanfront, Jacksonville Beach, 246–7701, features small combos and raw oysters along with bargain drink specials.

TC's. Holiday Inn-Oceanfront, 1617 N. First St., Jacksonville Beach, 249–9071, is the only rooftop lounge on the beaches.

Two nightspots that draw the young crowd are *Playground South,* 945 Arlington Rd., which books name bands, and *Big Daddy's Lounge,* 9278 Arlington Expressway, which has a New Wave night every Tuesday, with wild styles and colors of clothes and hair.

A favorite of more mature fun-seekers is the *Alhambra Dinner Theater,* 12000 Beach Blvd., 641–1212. Nationally known headliners are supported by a professional cast of Equity troupers. The buffet dinner fare is rated good, as is the stage fare of popular and musical comedies.

St. Augustine: In the summer, both *Cross and Sword* and the *Saint George Street Players* trod the boards. The *Bayfront Dinner Theatre* year-round. *Scarlett O'Hara's* has the young folks, while the *Columbia Restaurant and Lounge* suits a more mature audience (see "Dining Out," above).

EXPLORING CEDAR KEY

Cedar Key is the quintessential nineteenth-century fishing village. Every narrow street and lane ends in a seascape of docks and boats and islands. Most buildings wear a touch of gingerbread or other signs of bygone eras. It is quaint, picturesque, friendly, and guaranteed to charm you right out of your vacation timetable.

As residents like to say, Cedar Key isn't off the Gulf of Mexico but in it. A three-mile stretch of keys and bridges reach out from the mainland to the island village. This is the end of SR 24, which crosses US 19 about 20 miles east at Otter Creek and connects with I-75 at Gainesville, some 50 miles distant. You can also come by private boat or land your private plane on the 2,400-foot runway, but the tiny town is not served by any commercial transportation—a fact that perhaps contributes to its appeal.

On the south side of the island, a unique semi-circular dock (with one-way auto traffic) extends a block or more from shore before curving back to land by a public beach. Fish houses, gift shops, art studios, restaurants, and bait shops on pilings abut the dock. A fishing pier juts still farther seaward. Altogether, much of the town's social, recreational, and business activities take place on the dock.

The major business, of course, is fishing. Area waters produce a rich harvest of fish and shellfish for the commercial fisherman and good sport for outdoors enthusiasts. Fishing guides often double as sightseeing guides to such nearby islands as Sea Horse Key, with its 1855 lighthouse.

In the nineteenth century, Cedar Key boomed as a steamship port, gulf terminus of Florida's first cross-state railroad, and source of red cedar slats for making pencils. Then a second cross-state railroad reached Tampa, the customs house moved, and the cedar trees ran out. Cedar Key returned to quieter ways and became the picture-postcard fishing village, artists' colony, and vacation retreat it is today.

The Sidewalk Art Festival on the third weekend in April and the Seafood Festival on the third weekend in October are major events that draw mixed crowds of Floridians and out-of-state tourists.

PRACTICAL INFORMATION FOR CEDAR KEY

HOW TO GET THERE. By air: Closest airports to Cedar Key are **Gainesville Regional,** 56 miles northeast, served by *Eastern* and *Aerocoach* and *Skyways* commuter lines; and **Ocala Regional,** 72 miles east, served by *Allegheny* and *Skyways* commuter lines. Northern connection point is *Jacksonville International Airport;* see *Practical Information for the Jacksonville Area.*

By bus. Although *Greyhound Bus Lines* and *Trailways Bus System* do not offer service into Cedar Key, their closest access points are **Chiefland,** 28 miles away (Greyhound/Trailways: 493–4954); **Bronson,** 33 miles (Greyhound: 493–4954, Trailways: 372–6327); **Gainesville** (Greyhound: 376–5252, Trailways: 372–6327); and **Ocala** (Greyhound: 732–2677).

By train. *Amtrak's* service goes through Waldo (in the Gainesville area), Ocala, and Wildwood (about midway between Ocala and Orlando). Schedule information (it changes with the seasons) is available toll-free from 800–877–7245.

The most practical, and least complicated, way to get to Cedar Key and move around the North Central Florida area is **by car;** see rental car listings in "How to Get Around," below. SR 24 leads from Gainesville directly to Cedar Key; US 27 N from Ocala intersects with SR 24 at Bronson. A three-mile stretch of bridges at the terminus of the mainland spans a series of uninhabited keys and leads to Cedar Key.

TELEPHONES. The area code for Cedar Key and all North Florida is 904. The emergency number is 911. A call from a pay phone is $.25.

HOTELS AND MOTELS. Most accommodations in Cedar Key are efficiencies or apartments and modest but nice. Several new establishments with fancier amenities have appeared and there will be others. At the other end of the scale are fishing camps that should be seen before registration (see "Participant Sports" below).

Price categories for double occupancy per night are: *Expensive,* more than $60; *Moderate,* $40 to $60; *Inexpensive,* $30 to $40; *Budget,* less than $30.

Island Place. *Moderate to expensive.* 1st St.; 904–543–5307. 22 condo units fully furnished for cooking and dining, pool, waterfront.

Cedar Cove. *Inexpensive to expensive.* Box 508; 904–543–5332. Rooms, studios, lofts; full kitchen and dining area, pool, marina, canoe rentals, restaurant.

Beach Front Motel. *Inexpensive.* Box 400; 904–543–5113. 23 units, some efficiencies, pool.

Bon Air Cottages. *Budget.* 904–543–5360. 8 efficiencies; standard accommodations.

HOW TO GET AROUND. Private **car** is the only practical way to do much moving about. See "How to Get There," above.

Closest car rental sites to Cedar Key are Chiefland, which offers *Ford Rent A Car System* (N. Main St., 493–4297), and Fanning Springs, which has a local firm called *G&D U-Save Auto Rental* (US 19 N, 463–2626). Ocala offers more than a dozen local firms in addition to five national companies: *Avis* (1550 SW 60th Ave., 237–2714, national toll-free 800–331–1212), *Budget* (1016 N. Magnolia Ave., 732–3322, national toll-free 800–527–0700), *Hertz* (809 E. Silver Springs Blvd., 629–3672, national toll-free 800–654–3131), *National* (SW 60th Ave., 732–2494, national toll-free 800–227–7368), and *Thrifty* (SR 40 W, 351–2050, national toll-free 800–331–4200). Gainesville offers an array of firms, both local (check the Yellow Pages if you want to shop around on prices) and national firms including: *Avis* (airport 376–8115, toll-free 800–331–1212), *American International* (4304 NW 13th St. 372–0537, toll-free 800–527–0202) which offers pick-up at airport and Amtrak station in Waldo; *Hertz* (airport 373–8444, 376–5600, toll-free 800–654–3131), *National* (airport 377–7005, toll-free 800–227–7368), and *Dollar* (airport 375–0077, toll-free 800–421–6868).

TOURIST INFORMATION. *Cedar Key Chamber of Commerce:* Box 610, Cedar Key 32625; 904–543–5600 (open Monday, Wednesday, Friday 10:00 A.M.–2:00 P.M. only).

MUSEUMS AND HISTORIC SITES. *Cedar Key Historical Society Museum,* SR 24 and 2nd St. The society gleaned attics and city council minutes to assemble its collection and produce a series of well-documented historical pamphlets. *Cedar Key State Museum,* on SR 24, has additional historical exhibits; open 9:00 A.M.–5:00 P.M. daily, entrance fee $.25.

Marjorie Kinnan Rawlings' House, State Historic Site, Cross Creek, 21 miles southeast of Gainesville on SR 325. This is the "cracker" farmhouse where the author lived while writing the novels, including *The Yearling,* that drew on the characters and life of Florida's scrub country. It is as she left it and the park ranger does a fine interpretive job. Open daily 9:00 A.M.–5:00 P.M. Entrance fee $.50, under 6 free with adult.

DINING OUT. The average dinner for one, exclusive of drinks, tax and tip will be about $10 (though *The Yearling* might be an exception). Lunches are less. Reservations are usually necessary on Friday and Saturday.

The Captain's Table. On the dock; 543–5441. Lounge.

Helen's Place on the dock serves hamburgers with all the fixings for about $3.

The Heron. On 2nd St.; 543–5666.

Johnson's Brown Pelican. On the dock; 543–5428.

Richburg's Breakfast Cove on 2nd St. will get fishermen off to a good early start with $2 breakfasts and keep them going with $4 lunches.

Seabreeze-on-the-Dock. 543–9227. Lounge.

The Yearling. Cross Creek, about 21 miles from Gainesville on SR 325; 466–3033. An honored restaurant near Marjorie Kinnan Rawlings' old farmhouse. Features Florida "cracker" dishes such as alligator tail, frog legs, "cooter," and soft shell crabs but also serves standard entrees of beef, chicken, and seafood. Lunch and dinner Tues.-Sun., closed Mon. AE, DC, MC, V. Dinners run anywhere from around $7 to $20.

EXPLORING THE PANHANDLE

Tallahassee, the Capital

Tallahasse enjoys the same attributes that it did in 1824 when chosen to be Florida's capital—a pleasant prospect on rolling hills, well watered by lakes and streams, fertile soils, and a location about halfway between St. Augustine and Pensacola. The last fact was most important. With delegates being shipwrecked or lost for weeks on wilderness trails, the new territory's Legislative Council abandoned the original scheme of meeting alternately in the two old capitals of East and West Florida and sought a compromise. A location in former province of Apalachee was chosen and the area's occupants, then Seminole Indians, reluctantly agreed. The Seminole called the site "old fields," or "tallahassee," and that name was retained.

A lot has been added to the pleasant old fields of the Apalachee in the intervening 160 years. A large complex of white state buildings around the 22-story new Capitol now crowns the original hill. From the Capitol's top observation deck you can look out over a city of more than 100,000 which includes two state universities, Florida State and Florida Agricultural and Mechanical. But except for the red brick buildings of the universities and whiteness of the regional medical center, what you see mostly are trees—spreading live oaks, tall pines, and bright-leafed pecans—and lakes. On a clear day you can spot the tiny white finger of the St. Marks Lighthouse 26 miles to the south on the Gulf of Mexico, and 17 miles to the north, under the carpet of pines, Florida changes to Georgia.

The high-rise Capitol designed by Edward Durell Stone looks down on the Old Capital, originally built in 1845 but restored to its 1902 form and decor. Both Capitols are open to tours.

The Florida Legislature meets for 60 days each spring and both chambers have visitor galleries. The nearby R.A.Gray Building houses the Museum of Florida History, the State Library with its special Florida collections and the State Archives.

In Tallahassee's older section, hard by the capital complex, many old buildings have been restored and converted to new uses. Adams Street Commons with its upscale eateries, new-old inn, and parklike treatment has turned senile commercial buildings into handsome mall. On tree-lined perimeter streets, fine old homes are now professional offices. Park Avenue with antebellum First Presbyterian Church and houses, one now used as the chamber of commerce, is particularly attractive.

West Along 98

Moving west of Tallahasse, off US 98, is St. George Island, one of the few "untouched" beaches in the state. The island, accessible by toll bridge, is about 30 miles long, and bordered by near-primitive beaches, where you can find some wonderful shell. Some of the sand dunes are spectacular, rising to 30 feet or more. Here birdwatchers can spot long-billed marsh wrens, snowy plovers, ospreys, pelicans, and many others. O n Little George Island, accessibly by boat only, a lighthouse (over 150 years old) guards the secret of buried treasure in the sands.

On the narrow spit extending north in St. Josephs Bay, visitors are delighted with the recreational facilities on the more than 2,000 acres peaked with dunes, extend for at least 20 miles, with the Gulf of Mexico on the west and the bay on the eastern shores. Pine-studded woodland and surf-tipped beach combine for a scenic collage. Overnight camping is delightful here, and there are rental boats, picnic facilities, snack vars, everything for beachcombers.

Panama City and Panama City Beach

Panama City is the seat of Bay County and no county is more appropriately named. There's East Bay, West Bay, North Bay, and St. Andrews Bay—all distinctly separate bodies of water but all connected. They are fringed by scenic bayous and points of land, many with grand old live oaks. The sparkling bays, bayfronts beaches, and excellent sports fishing made Panama City attractive to visitors from its early times. But when a good bridge spanned St. Andrews Bay some 50 years ago to the snowy beaches, tourism moved there.

This is the beginning of a 100-mile stretch of beaches, from here to Pensacola, with sand so white and waters so turquoise it's called the Miracle Strip. From the ship channel into St. Andrews Bay westward to Philips Inlet, about 27 miles of unbroken white sand beaches, is Panama City Beach. Running that length are motels, hotels, restaurants, lounges, stores, shops, amusement parks, and every service a beach vacationer needs and wants. The amusement parks alone can occupy days: roller coasters and carousels, water rides, Old West towns and haunted houses. All this is strung along the Miracle Strip Pkwy., 98-A to most and officially US 98 Alt.

Toward the east, where the highway turns to Hathaway Bridge (the connector between Panama City and Panama City Beach), an arm of St. Andrews Bay called Grand Lagoon runs behind the beach. Along here is newer development characterized by condominiums, big restaurants, and marinas for charter, sightseeing, and party boats. The area's easternmost section is St. Andrews State Park and Bay Point Resort, separated from each other by Grand Lagoon.

Though Panama City Beach has enjoyed great popularity as a summer beach resort for Southern families, the trend is toward year-round tourism and broader appeal. New multi-million-dollar tourist facilities already up and others underway indicate that many investors feel the trend will become a landslide.

For the tourist, life is on the magnificent gulf beach. Trips to town are usually centered on conventional shopping at the modern malls, the first-run movie houses, restaurants and cultural events. Shell hunters won't want to miss a trip to Shell Island—boats leave from Capt. Anderson's Marina on Thomas drive.

Destin and Fort Walton Beach

Destin and Fort Walton Beach are in the middle of the snow-white beaches and turquoise waters of the Miracle Strip. By unusual geography each community has four distinct waterfronts. There is the Gulf of Mexico on the outside, then each has a barrier island protecting a lagoon or sound. Next is a narrow mainland section and inland from that huge Choctawhatchee Bay, named for the Choctaw Indians and literally meaning Choctaw water. The bay, 29 miles long and eight miles at its widest, is unusually clear.

A map only confirms what the eye beholds; there's water, water, water. This is a watersport capital—fishing, sailing, scuba diving, swimming, skiing. It's also one of Florida's hottest tourist markets. Building cranes are as much a part of the skyline as wading birds are of the shoreline.

East Pass, which connects Choctawhatchee Bay with the Gulf of Mexico, is Destin's western boundary and may be the most beautiful short stretch of water in Florida. Destin itself perches high on an ancient line of sand dunes at the western tip of a 23-mile-long peninsula. Holiday Isle, which protects the harbor from the gulf, isn't really an island but another skinny peninsula. (Once, however, it was an island before errant tides and winds of a long-ago hurricane closed the eastern end of Old Pass Lagoon.)

Across East Pass is the eastern tip of a barrier island that runs west parallel to the mainland for 50 miles. This eastern part is called Okaloosa Island, but for most of its length it's Santa Rosa Island and Santa Rosa Sound is the narrow body of water behind it. The sound connects with Choctawhatchee Bay, and at the connection is Fort Walton Beach. East Pass and six miles of sand dunes on Okaloosa Island, piled up like whipped cream, separate the two Miracle Strip resorts.

However, Destin and Fort Walton Beach are separated by more than geography. Fort Walton was a popular summer resort and bustling Air Force town when Destin was still just a fishing village. That distinction in character remains even though Destin now has 1,000 motel rooms and 6,000 condominium units. The ratio in Fort Walton Beach is reversed.

Fort Walton is the big town, the place for ordinary shopping—Sears, Penney's, a variety of supermarkets, a broad choice of everything. Destin's charter fleet is very active, and the town is considered by some to be the sport fishing capital of the Gulf. Tournaments are frequent and there is no problem for anyone to arrange a fishing expedition. Nightlife and movies are in Fort Walton Beach. Destin's 10-mile stretch of open beach east of town is preferred by many. Fort Walton has more of the fun accoutrements of a seaside resort—the fishing pier, jet ski rentals, gaggles of bright-sailed hobies, and giggles of funny T-shirt shops. Fort Walton is bouncy: Destin is easy. No matter where your accommodations are, you'll spend time in both towns. The two make a total resort.

Pensacola

To reach Pensacola take US 98 and enter the city via a four-lane bridge, which residents have named "the world's largest fishing pier."

Downtown, by the port, you will discover the historic heart of beautifully restored Old Pensacola, complete with romantic gaslights on the Spanish-accented streets. It's a good idea to stop first at the Tourist Information Center at the foot of Bay Bridge, where the friendly staff has a variety of free, informative literature, including a mapped guide for an automobile tour. This begins at the information center and ends in a walking tour of the Seville Square Historic District. Of course, if you need any information at all, the center is glad to be of assistance, and you can call them locally at 800–874–1234 (800–343–4321 in Florida).

Going to jail to see art is rather unusual, but that's what happens when you visit the Pensacola Museum of Art, 407 South Jefferson Street, at the Historical District. When the city built a new jail in 1954, the old, two-story Spanish-designed edifice was converted to an art gallery named the Pensacola Art Center. Now it is an important museum with ever-changing major art exhibits and a permanent collection of work by Florida artists. The remaining bars on windows and inside doors lend an interesting effect. The museum is free.

It's a delightful step back into another age when you visit the Seville Historic District with old brick streets, shaded by majestic trees. Shops and boutiques are housed in 18th- and 19th-century mansions and cottages, and the old-fashioned, friendly service is a pleasure. In Pappagallo's, there is hot coffee to drink, while you look around. Dining is fun in atmospheric places and some are just for drinking and relaxing —Rosie O'Grady's Good Time Dixieland Emporium, Coppersmith's, Palace Oyster Bar, Lili Marlene's, End O' The Alley Bar. Parking is free and unrestricted in this charming historic district, where residents still live in the stately mansions. This is where the first settlement began in 1752.

If you are interested in Black history, don't miss some of the important landmarks, which include the Julee Cottage, built around 1790. The owner, Julee Panton, was a freed slave, who invested in real estate and also loaned money to slaves so that they could buy their freedom. The Bonifay House, built about 1812, is on property owned by Mary

J. Bonifay, a free black woman. Many of the homes in Old Pensacola, as you will note, were built or owned by women, both black and white, long before Women's Liberation or integration.

It would be impossible to list all the historic sites, but you will want to see where Spanish headquarters were situated at Plaza Ferdinand VII, now on Palafox at Government and Zaragoza streets; the Panton trading post at Barcelona and Main streets; Old Christ Church, now Pensacola Historical Museum. If you are interested in things nautical, do visit the Pensacola Historical Museum, with a ceiling made from the hull of a boat. Should you decide to stay in the Seville district, the Sheraton and Ramada Inns are close by.

The North Hill Preservation District, bounded by LaRua, Palafox, Blount, and Reus streets, deserves the attention of anyone interested in old Southern mansions that have remained virtually unchanged for a century. The Visitors Information Center can provide you with a map of the area.

The Naval Air Station also plays a major part in Pensacola's economy, and is an interesting blend of new and old. Take Garden Street to Navy Boulevard from downtown to Fort San Carlos and Fort Barrancas, where the Old Pensacola Lighthouse (dating back to 1825) still functions. You can visit the Naval Aviation Museum; Sherman Field, home of the precision flying team, the Blue Angels; and the giant aircraft carrier U.S.S. *Lexington.* When she's in port, you can go aboard "Lady Lex," as she is affectionately called by her 1,400 crew members.

Water-skiing is very popular in the calm bay and bayous. As for fishing, four major tournaments are held every year with thousands of dollars in prizes. The old bridge over Pensacola Bay is a fishing pier, and you can park anywhere you think that the fish are biting. Gulf Pier at Pensacola Beach is another lucky fishing spot. Party fishing boats leave bright and early from piers and marinas and head out to the "snapper banks" in the Gulf for the famous red snapper, also scamp and grouper. Billfish Alley is about a two-hour run away, and you can charter a boat with an experienced captain.

You may want to take a side trip to the state park in Milton, north of Pensacola, for more water sports and camping. No beachcomber should miss the Gulf Islands National Seashore. Fort Pickens is here, incidentally, and at last the fort is seeing some action—visitors who come to enjoy the miles and miles of glorious beaches, extending across to the eastern shores of Mississippi, massive sand dunes crowned with swaying golden sea oats.

At the park, you can rent a cabin or pitch a tent, and enjoy an *alfresco* lunch in the picnic pavilion. Park activity headquarters is called the Sandbox, where National Park Service rangers oversee the daily schedule of events from discovery walks to creating souvenirs from shells and driftwood. At the amphitheater, interesting nature films depict the sea around us.

For unwinding, there is nothing like the stroll along the Dune Nature Trail, bordering the blue-green Gulf. The Rangers at Fort Pickens will be glad to recommend where you can do some scuba diving and spear fishing, charter a fishing boat, where to fish from the beach or pier, best places to swim.

PRACTICAL INFORMATION FOR THE PANHANDLE

HOW TO GET THERE. By air. The closest airport to **Destin** and **Fort Walton Beach** is the Okaloosa County Air Terminal on SR 85, served by *Delta ASA, Eastern Metro, Republic Airlines* and *Air New Orleans,* a commuter line. These same carriers serve Panama City-Bay County Airport, the airport closest to **Panama City** and **Panama City Beach. Pensacola** Regional Airport is about five miles from the downtown area. It is served by *Continental, Eastern, Delta,* and some commuter lines. **Tallahassee's** airport is served by *Atlantic Gulf, Delta, Eastern, PBA,* and *Republic;* nonstop service from Miami, Fort Lauderdale, Orlando, and Tampa. For information on getting from the airports see "How to Get Around," below.

By bus. *Greyhound* and *Trailways* connect with **Fort Walton Beach** (Greyhound: 60 Beal Pkwy., 904–243–1940; Trailways: 105 Chestnut Ave. SE, 904–243–6156), **Panama City** (Greyhound: 310 W. 5th St., 904–785–7861; Trailways: Harrison Ave., 904–785–6111), **Pensacola** (Greyhound: 201 N. Baylen St., 904–432–5196; Trailways: 301 N. Baylen St., 904–433–5047), and **Tallahassee** (Greyhound: 112 W. Tennessee St., 904–222–4240; Trailways: 324 N. Adams St., 904–224–3101).

By car. US 98, Florida's scenic gulf highway runs east-west through Destin and Fort Walton Beach, Panama City and Panama City Beach; some 30 miles north I-10 also takes an east-west route, through the northern suburbs of Pensacola (a connector I-110 extends to downtown), brushing Tallahassee. US 331, US 231, US 29, and US 319 reach I-10 from the north. 331 brings traffic to US 98, about 17 miles east of Destin; or take SR 85 from I-10 right into Fort Walton Beach. 231 brings traffic from I-10 near Panama City; 29 carries visitors to Pensacola from I-10, and 319 brings northern travelers into Tallahassee. (For rental car information, see "How to Get Around," below.)

By water. The *Gulf Intracoastal Waterway* can take private yachts to Destin, Fort Walton Beach, Panama City area, and Pensacola.

TELEPHONES. Area code is 904. Pay phones cost 10¢ in Destin, Ft. Walton Beach, and Tallahassee, 25¢ in the Panama City area and Pensacola.

TIME ZONES. Tallahassee is on Eastern time; central time is observed west of the Apalichicola River, which includes Panama City, Destin, Fort Walton Beach, and Pensacola.

HOTELS AND MOTELS. The quoted price categories are based on summer rates. The price categories are for one room double occupancy per night or in the case of condos for the smallest unit: *Super deluxe,* $100 and up; *Deluxe,* $80–$100; *Expensive,* $60–$80; *Moderate,* $40–$60; *Inexpensive,* $30–$40; *Budget,* under $30.

The condo unit is a fully (sometimes elegantly) furnished apartment usually with amenities such as dishwashers and trash compactors. Whether occupied by two people or a group, the rate is the same. Seasonal variation in condo rates is extreme: winter rates are about $25% of summer rates and fall and spring rates about 50% of the summer high. Motel and resort rates vary much less.

DESTIN

Destin has luxurious sports resorts down to a few simple cottages from an earlie era. Its forte is luxury condominiums and it has many more of these than the usual motel rooms. For individual condos, apartments, and cottages, two companies offer free services, even down to toll-free numbers: *Abbott Realty Services, Inc.,* 114-B Amberjack Dr., Fort Walton Beach 32548; toll-free 800–874–8914 (904–244–0899 in Florida)—a central reservation system for both Destin and Fort Walton Beach; *Gulf Coast Vacation Advisors,* Box 1804, Destin 32541; toll-free 800–874–6390 (904–837–3211 in Florida), locates suitable rentals, makes reservations and calls you back.

Jetty East. *Super Deluxe.* 500 Gulfshore Dr.; 904–837–2141. On tip of Holiday Isle, 198 units, 900-foot beach; private balconies, pool, lighted tennis courts, covered beach pavilion, 24-hour security.

Sandestin Resort. *Deluxe to super deluxe.* US 98 East; 904–837–2121, toll-free 800–874–3950 out-of-state. Ten miles east of Destin on a vast property that runs from Choctawatchee Bay to the Gulf of Mexico; 514 villas, suites and rooms; 45 holes of championship golf; 14 tennis courts, grass and composition, 5 lighted, 2 covered; marina; 6 pools; restaurants; lounges; private beach; variety of water sports. Also on the property is the new 400-room **Sandestin Hilton** (904–837–7430), *deluxe to super deluxe,* with oversize rooms, indoor and outdoor pools, sauna, Jacuzzi, game room, and amphitheater.

Seascape Resort. *Deluxe to super deluxe.* US 98 East, P.O. Box 970, Destin 32541; 904–837–9181, toll-free 800–874–9141. Located 8½ miles east of Destin on property that extends from Choctawhatchee Bay to the Gulf of Mexico; 220 condo units; 1,500-foot beach; 18-hole golf course; 8 tennis courts, Hard-Tru and Rubico; 4 pools; steam and sauna rooms; restaurants, lounges; beach club.

Beach House Condominiums. *Expensive to deluxe.* US 98; 904–837–6131. On the beach, seven-story 106 condo units, nine miles east of Destin Bridge; balcony or patio overlooking gulf; kitchens with dishwasher, ice-maker, disposal, compactor; laundry each floor; 2 tennis courts, adult pool, children's pool, club house, beach gazebo; rec room with pinball machines.

Holiday Inn. *Expensive to Deluxe.* US 98, Box 577; 904–837–6181. On the beach, round 9-story with 206 rooms; indoor and outdoor pools, sauna, health facilities, 2 restaurants including revolving rooftop, 2 lounges, game room.

Best Western Village Inn. *Moderate.* 215 US 98 Box 757; 904–837–7413. New 100-unit motel across from Destin charter boat fleet, pool, cable TV.

Silver Beach Hotel-Motel-Cottages. *Moderate.* US 98, Box 1025; 904–837–6125. On gulf, 112 units, pool, tennis, breakfast room, 1,000-foot beach, chair and umbrella rentals, lifeguards during summer.

Seaview Cottages. *Inexpensive.* US 98, Box 283; 904–837–6211. On Destin Harbor, 10 family cottages with kitchens, private boat and fishing dock, cable TV.

FORT WALTON BEACH

Bluewater Bay Resort. *Deluxe to Super Deluxe.* SR 20 E., Box 247, Niceville 32578; 904–897–3613, toll-free from out-of-state (800) 874–2128. This luxury resort is across Choctawhatchee Bay from Destin and Fort Walton Beach on the bay's northern shore. The wooded terrain gives a feeling of seclusion to the 150 studio, townhouse, patio, and villa units. Olympic swimming pool, 18-hole golf course, lighted tennis courts, 2 restaurants, 2 lounges, sailing, fishing, marina.

The Breakers of Fort Walton Beach. *Deluxe to Super Deluxe.* 381 Santa Rosa Blvd.; 904–244–9127, toll-free (800) 874–8937. On the gulf, 160 units, beach, pool, wading pool, tennis court.

Coronado/Sheraton Beach Resort. *Deluxe.* 1325 Miracle Strip Pkwy, US 98 East; 904–243–8116, toll-free (800) 874–8104. On the gulf, 154 units, beach, heated pool, wading pool, playground, restaurant, lounge.

Holiday Inn. *Expensive to Deluxe.* US 98 and Santa Rosa Blvd.; 904–243–9181. On gulf, 400 units, beach, 2 lighted-heated pools, kiddie pool, lighted tennis courts, restaurant, lounge, game room.

Marina Bay Resort. *Moderate to Expensive.* 80 Miracle Strip Pkwy, (US 98); 904–244–5132. On Santa Rosa Sound, pool, boat slips, restaurant, lounge, entertainment, game room.

Greenwood Motel. *Inexpensive to moderate.* US 98 E.; 904–244–1141. On bay, 56 units, beach, private fishing pier, pool, across street from gulf state park.

Days Inn. *Inexpensive.* 135 Miracle Strip Pkwy.; 904–244–6184, toll-free (800) 241–2340. 62 units, pool, restaurant.

Marina Motel. *Budget.* US 98 E., Okaloosa Island; 904–244–1129. On Choctawhatchee Bay, 38 units, beach, pool, private fishing pier, boat dock, laundry.

PANAMA CITY BEACH

Though a number of motels on the beach close during the winter, the trend is toward year-round operation as Canadians and Northern retirees are discovering Panama City winters are not that cold. All of the accommodations in the sample listing are open year-round. Another trend is condominiums and several realty management companies that handle condo rentals:

Condo World Realty, Inc., Box 9456, 8815-A Thomas Dr., Panama City Beach 32407; 904–234–7364, 234–9255. *Royal American Management, Inc.,* 7006 Thomas Dr., Panama City Beach 32407; 904–235–3267, toll-free (800) 824–1883. *Sunspot Management,* 16428 W. 98, Panama City Beach 32407; 904–234–7151, toll-free (800) 874–6001.

Landmark Holiday Beach Resort. *Super Deluxe.* 17501 W.98 Alt. 32407; 904–235–3100. On the beach, 95 condo units, indoor pool, tennis, golf, cable TV, HBO.

Holiday Inn Beachside. *Deluxe to Super Deluxe.* 12907 W. 98 Alt. 32407; 904–234–1111, toll-free (800) 238–5510. Near beach, 350 rooms, 2 pools, golf and tennis club, game room, 3 restaurants, 6 lounges, disco, whirlpool.

Bay Point. *Expensive to Deluxe.* 100 Delwood Beach Rd., 32407; 904–234–3307, toll-free (800) 874–7105. This is a luxury resort community on a point of land between Grand Lagoon and St. Andrews Bay with residential homes as well as vacation homes and condominiums. Facilities include 36 holes of golf, tennis courts, pools, restaurants, lounges, entertainment, cable TV and HBO.

Fontainbleau Terrace. *Expensive.* 14401 W.98 Alt. 32407; 904–234–6581, toll-free (800) 874–8025. On the beach, 124 units, indoor pool, restaurant, efficiencies, cable TV.

Miracle Mile Resort. *Expensive.* 9400 S. Thomas Dr., 32407; 904–234–3484, toll-free (800) 874–6613. This is four separate establishments—Barefoot Beach Inn, Gulfside Inn, Sands Inn, and Sheraton Inn—under one management umbrella and side by side. On the beach, 640 room and kitchenettes, lighted tennis courts, pools, beach equipment, pools, sailboat rentals, restaurants, lounges, entertainment.

Ramada Inn. *Moderate.* 3001 W. 10th St., Panama City 32401; 904–785–0561, toll-free (800) 228–2828. On St. Andrews Bay, 150 units, pool, restaurant, lounge, entertainment, dancing, adjacent to fishing fleet.

Bay Villa Motel. *Inexpensive.* 4501 W. 98 32407; 904–785–8791. Near beach overlooking St. Andrews Bay, 31 units, 400–foot pier, pool, efficiencies, cable TV.

TALLAHASSEE

Football weekends mean rate hikes and minimum stay requirements throughout most of the city. Establishments that by location or tradition are popular with government visitors tend to boost rates during the annual legislative sessions, roughly April, May, and early June.

Governors Inn. *Deluxe to Super Deluxe.* 207 S. Adams St. (Adams street Commons) 32301; 904–681–6855. 32 rooms and suites individually decorated and furnished with antiques incorporating a converted 100-year-old carriage house, units named for deceased Florida governors, room refrigerators, some fireplaces, valet parking.

Tallahassee Hilton. *Expensive.* 101 S. Adams St. 32301; 904–224–5000. Two blocks from Capitol, 245 rooms, dining room, coffee shop, lounge, nightly entertainment, pool and sun deck, parking garage.

Wakulla Springs Lodge. *Moderate.* SR 61 and SR 267, Wakulla 32305; 904–224–5950, 640–7011. An old-fashioned hotel in a nature preserve by the world's deepest spring, 13 miles from Tallahassee, dining room, suites available in moderate range.

Executive Inn. *Inexpensive.* 522 Scotty Lane 32303; 904–386–2121, just off US 27 N., 116 units, pool, restaurant, lounge, some rooms with whirlpool, non-smoking rooms available.

Lafayette Motel. *Budget.* 1525 W. Tennessee St. 32303; 904–224–1145. On US 90 W., 38 units, pool in summer.

PENSACOLA

New World Inn. *Deluxe to Super Deluxe.* 600 S. Palafox St.; 904–432–4111. Part of the New World Landing complex in the restored Quayside area. A small luxury inn with 16 units all differently furnished with 18th-century antiques; restaurants and lounge.

Pensacola Hilton. *Deluxe to Super Deluxe.* 200 E. Gregory St. 32501; 904–433–3336. Opened in summer 1984, 210 rooms and suites, 2 restaurants, 3 lounges. English tea served in the lobby, live entertainment, dancing, free valet parking, airport pickup, car rentals.

Perdido Bay Resort. *Expensive to Deluxe.* SR 292, One Doug Ford Dr. 32507; (904) 492–1212. Seventy-five luxury units in a sports resort of 2,800 acres. Championship golf course is the site of PGA Pensacola Open and among nation's top courses; lighted tennis courts; pool; private beach with cabanas; biking; restaurants; lounges.

Holiday Inn North. *Moderate to Expensive.* 6501 Pensacola Blvd.; 904–476–7200. 216 rooms, pool, restaurant, lounge, babysitting service, airport pickup.

Seville Inn. *Inexpensive.* 223 E. Garden St.; 904–433–8331. 172 rooms, pool, restaurant, lounge, airport pickup.

Scottish Inn. *Budget.* 1801 W. Cervantes St.; 904–434–1301. 66 rooms, pool, kitchenettes.

PENSACOLA BEACH

Holiday Inn Pensacola Beach. *Deluxe.* 165 Fort Pickens Rd.; 904–932–5361. 144 rooms, heated pool, restaurant, lounge, babysitting service, golf, tennis, courtesy transportation.

Dunes Motel. *Expensive to Deluxe.* 333 Fort Pickens Rd.; 904–932–3536. 117 rooms, pool, restaurant, lounge, babysitting service.

Gulfside Resort. *Expensive to Deluxe.* 14 Via De Luna; 940–932–5331. 216 rooms total for four one-management properties—Barbary Coast, Holiday Townhouses, Howard Johnson's, Tiki House Motel. 4 pools, restaurant, 2 lounges, kitchenettes, tennis.

Sun Ray Motel and Cottages. *Moderate to Expensive.* 20 Via De Luna; 904–932–2130. 62 rooms, pool, oyster bar, kitchenettes.

Gulf Aire Motel. *Moderate.* 21 Via De Luna; 904–932–2319. 20 rooms, kitchenettes.

BED AND BREAKFAST TREASURES. *Bed 'n Breakfast Central Gulf Coast,* P.O. Box 12561, Pensacola, 32573; 904–455–2148 is a booking service for the **Pensacola** area, and *Tallahassee Bed and Breakfast, Inc.,* 3023 Windy Hill Ln., Tallahassee 32308; 904–385–3768, offers facilities in and around the capital city. Write them for more information on the accommodations they represent.

HOW TO GET AROUND. Private car, your own or a rental, is the only practical way to get around, and if you're in a big motel/hotel complex with all the amenities you may not want to. Most people do, however, and thereby hangs a 27-mile bumper-to-bumper crawl during the summer season. The Miracle Strip Pkwy., US 98 Alt. West, is the mainstreet of the beaches. Several blocks north and parallel is US 98 without the Alt., so find out which cross streets are convenient to your accommodations and use US 98, called the Back Beach Road, when traveling any distance.

Destin and Fort Walton Beach: There is no public transportation. **From the airport,** limousine service is provided by the *Florida Cab Company* (892–2903), *A-1 Taxi* (678–2424), or the *Yellow Cab* (244–3600) will take up to five passengers to a single destination for one fare.

Several auto rental firms have airport booths and others provide pickup. *Avis Rent A Car,* County Airport, 904–651–0822 toll-free 800–331–1212. *Budget Rent-a-Car,* 11 Eglin Pkwy. S.E., 904–244–5488, toll-free 800–527–0700. *Dollar Rent A Car,* 394 Mary Ester Cut-off, 904–244–0212, provides airport, hotel and office pickup. *Economy Rent-A-Car,* 282 Washington Ave., 904–678–6223, operates the Rent-A-Heap Cheap, provides customer pickup. *Hertz Rent A Car,*

County Airport, 904–651–0612, toll-free 800–654–3131. *National Car Rental,* County Airport, 904–651–1113, toll-free 800–328–4567.

Panama City Area: There is limousine service at the airport operated by the *Yellow Cab Co.,* 763–4691. From the airport to downtown Panama City is about $6 and to Panama City Beach about $14, depending on pickup and drop-off points. The taxi companies, which operate by system of zones in calculating fares, are *Central Taxi Co.,* 785–7586; *North Side Taxi Co.,* 763–9860; and *Yellow Cab Co.,* 763–4691. There is no public bus transportation.

Rental cars are available at the airport, which is about 5 miles from downtown and 12 from the beaches. Some firms without an airport counter provide pickup service. One firm has a beach location. *Avis Rent A Car,* Municipal Airport, 904–769–1411, toll-free 800–331–1212. *Dollar Rent-a-Car,* 3132 Airport Dr. (1 blk. from airport), 904–785–1924. *Hertz Rent A Car,* Municipal Airport, 904–763–2262 or 763–6673, toll-free 800–654–3131. *National Car Rental,* Municipal Airport, 904–769–2383, toll-free 800–227–7368. *Ugly Duckling Rent-a-Car,* 428 Thomas Dr., Panama City Beach, 904–234–6175.

Pensacola: Several accommodation facilities, including the new Pensacola Hilton, are within walking distance of Seville Square, Quayside and downtown. Though the city bus system is geared to residents, it does include a route to the Pensacola Regional Airport. *Escambia Transit System,* 1515 W. Fairfield Dr., 904–436–9383, operates the public bus system and will assist with route information. The bus fare is 60¢ and transfers 15¢. Airport transportation is additionally provided free by a number of larger hotel/motel establishments.

All the taxi companies regularly meet incoming flights and the fare to downtown is about $5. Taxis in the Pensacola area are: *ABC Taxi,* 438–8650; *Airport Brown & White Taxi,* 477–8119; *Black & White,* 432–4151; *Blue & White Taxi,* 438–1497; *East Hill Taxi Stand,* 433–9211; *West Hill Taxi,* 417 W. Belmont, 438–5621; *Yellow Cab,* 433–1143.

Rental cars are also available at the airport and some rental car companies at other locations offer airport pickups for their customers.

Airport Thrifty Rent-A-Car, 5800 Tippin Ave., 904–477–5553, toll-free 800–367–2277, airport and hotel pickups. *Avis Rent A Car,* airport, 904–433–5614, toll-free 800–331–1212. *Budget Rent A Car,* airport, 904–478–8445, toll-free 800–527–0700. *Hertz Rent A Car,* airport, 904–432–2345, toll-free 800–654–3131. *National Car Rental,* airport, 904–432–8338, toll-free 800–328–4567.

Tallahassee: The airport is about six miles from downtown and there is limo service with rates varying depending on point of pickup or drop-off, but averaging $5–$7. Taxis from downtown to airport are $8–$9. Taxi cabs are metered and set for $1.60 for the first mile and 80¢ for each additional mile with a $2 surcharge for trips outside the city limits. *Tallahassee Taxi,* 683 W. Tennessee St., 224–8313. *Yellow Cab,* 508 W. Gaines St., 222–3070.

Rental cars are available at the airport. *American International Rent A Car,* 1530–1 Capital Circle S.W., 904–575–8166, airport pickup. *Avis Rent A Car,* Municipal Airport, 904–576–4133, toll-free 800–331–1212. *Budget Rent A Car,* Municipal Airport, 904–575–9191, toll-free 800–527–0700. *Hertz Rent A Car,* Municipal Airport, 904–576–1154, Monroe and Tennessee Sts., 904–222–1686, toll-free 800–654–3131. *National Car Rental,* Municipal Airport, 904–576–4107, toll-free 800–227–7368.

TOURIST INFORMATION. Destin Chamber of Commerce, P.O. Box 8, Destin 32541, 904–837–6241, office on Miracle Strip Pkwy. (US 98) in mid-town.

Fort Walton Beach Chamber of Commerce, P.O. Drawer 640, Fort Walton Beach 32548, 904–244–8191, office on Miracle Strip Pkwy.

The Panama City Beach area does a good job in assisting visitors. Besides the *Bay County Chamber of Commerce,* P.O. Box 1850, Panama City 32402, 904–785–5206, which handles mail and telephone requests and walk-in business at its 235 W. 5th St. offices, the *Visitor Information Center* at 12015 W.98 Alt. on Panama City Beach is a cooperative project of area tourism interests; P.O. Box 9473, Panama City Beach 32407. For calls originating in Florida or Canada, the number is 904–234–6575. For calls originating in the other states use toll-free 800–874–7107. Office hours for both chamber and beach center are 8–5 Mon.-Fri. and from Memorial Day through Labor Day the Visitor Information Center adds 9–5 Sat. The *Bay County Motel & Restaurant Association* operates a referral service for its members from the Visitor Information Center, beginning in April through Labor Day. The service number is 904–234–3193. After office hours an outside terminal at the Visitor Information Center will respond with information and directions.

The Pensacola Area Chamber of Commerce operates Visitor Information Center at 1401 E. Gregory St. 32501, in the Wayside Park at the foot of the Pensacola Bay Bridge. The center has two toll-free numbers: for calls originating outside Florida the number is 800–874–1234; for calls originating within Florida the number is 800–343–4321. For local calls use 434–1234. The center responds to mail, phone, or drop-in requests and distributes a wide range of materials on the Pensacola area.

The Tallahassee Area Chamber of Commerce, 100 N. Duval St. 32301; 904–244–8116, produces and distributes helpful brochures and will respond to mail or phone requests. One brochure covers a windshield tour of Tallahassee, and the route is marked by distinctive signs. When requesting information it is advised to mention the dates of your prospective visit and any specific interests. The building in which the chamber of commerce is located is a restored historic home called The Columns, open 9:00 A.M.–5:00 P.M. weekdays.

TOURS. Destin/Fort Walton Beach: Seasonal scenic cruises of the area's beautiful waterways are provided by *Capt. Anderson II,* 1150 US 98 E. at Brooks Bridge, Fort Walton Beach, 243–DINE (see also "Dining Out"). Call for schedules, fares and reservations. *Love Bus Tours,* Suite 106, 13 Memorial Pkwy., P.O.Box 1793, Fort Walton Beach, 244–2222, offers land tours and sightseeing of local and surrounding area points of interest. These are different tours each day, so call for schedule.

Panama City Area: Sightseeing, shelling, dolphin-feeding, sunset, and dinner cruises are offered, as are full and half-day cruises to Shell Island and Hurricane Island Beach Club. Firms include *Capt. Anderson/Capt. Davis Queen Fleet,* Anderson Pier, 234–3435; *Gulf Charter Service,* Treasure Island Marina, 235–2809; *Treasure Island Charters,* Treasure Island Marina, 234–8944.

Pensacola: A windshield and walking tour of Pensacola's historic sites is presented in a brochure available from the *Visitor Information Center,* 1401 E. Gregoory St., 434–1234. The windshield part of the tour covers the North Hill Historic District which was the fashionable section of town in the latter half of the 19th century. Several of the homes are occupied by descendants of their builders. The preservation district is a 50-block area and can take as much or little time as you want.

The walking part of the tour is *Seville Square,* where extensive restoration efforts have brought the early half of the 19th century back to life. A brochure distributed by area merchants will take you around the square and radiating streets through a mix of cottages and mansions serving now as museums, gift shops, restaurants, and professional offices.

Capt. Anderson II (432–6999), headquartered in Fort Walton Beach during the spring/summer period, also sails from downtown Pensacola on Thursday evenings for dinner/dance cruises.

PARKS AND GARDENS. See also "Beaches," below. North Florida has many state park properties, and overall information can be secured from the Division of Parks and Recreation, Florida Department of Natural Resources, Marjory Stoneman Douglas Building, 3900 Commonwealth Blvd., Tallahassee 32303.

Eden State Gardens, SR 395 N., Port Washington; 231–4214, is a restored antebellum-style mansion of a late 19th-century lumber baron. It sits among moss-draped live oaks and magnolias on the shore of Choctawhatchee Bay. The spring bloom of azaleas brings special beauty to the scene. The house is filled with antiques and open for tours, but the schedule varies. A call ahead will avoid disappointment at the end of the 30-mile drive from **Destin.** Admission to the house is $.50. The grounds are open daily from 8:00 A.M. to sunset year-round.

Blackwater River State Park, northeast of Pensacola off US 90, is a popular wilderness park in the midst of the 180,000-acre Blackwater River State Forest. A major feature of the park (Rt. 1, Box 57-C, Holt, FL 32564, 904–623–2363) is the river and canoeing its clean wild route. Adventures Unlimited, P.O.Box 40, Bagdad, FL 32530, 904–623–6197 rents canoes and arranges canoe and tube trips on the Blackwater and other wild streams in the western panhandle. The park is open 8:00 A.M. to sunset every day, and admission is 50¢.

THEME PARKS AND AMUSEMENTS. Destin/Ft. Walton Area: *The Gulfarium,* Okaloosa Island, US 98; 244–5169, features scuba divers, trained porpoises, sea lions, harbor seals, and many, many species of fish. Operating hours and show times are seasonal, so call first. Admission.

Just across US 98 from the Gulfarium is another seasonal attraction, the *Okaloosa Amusement Park.* It includes thrill rides, games of skill, and other carnival activities.

Commercial attractions and amusement parks are a large facet of **Panama City Beach.** *Castle Dracula,* 12390 W.98 Alt.; 234–0125, is a spook show, wax museum and arcade. Seasonal.

Gulf World, 15412 W.98 Alt.; 234–5271, is an oceanarium plus. Four shows —porpoise, sea lion, parrot, and scuba—plus sharks and other live exhibits and tropical gardens. It is seasonal, open in March every day 9–3 and added evening hours during the summer. Admission is $6 for adults, $4 for 12–19, $3 4–12, and free under 4.

Miracle Strip Amusement Park, W.98 Alt.; 234–5810, contains just about everything in the amusement park lexicon. It is seasonal and hours vary so check by phone, but it's open, generally, weekends March through May, and every day (and night) during the summer. Admission is $10.50 for adults and $8.75 10 and under.

Ship Wreck Island, 234–0368, is Miracle Strip Amusement Park's separate water park with water slide, wave pool, etc. It is seasonal, open spring weekends and every day in summer, 10:30 A.M. to 5:00 P.M. Admission is $9.95 for 11 and up, $7.75 for 5–10, 4 and under free.

Pensacola Beach Area: *Gulf Marine World,* 944–3700, at Lafitte's Landing, is home for a variety of sea creatures and shows. *The Zoo,* off US 98 east of Gulf Breeze (932–2229), houses hundreds of mammals, birds, reptiles, and amphibians in open settings among its 20 acres of botanical gardens.

BEACHES. Destin/Fort Walton Beach: There are miles upon miles of sugar-white gulf beaches washed by the blue-green Gulf of Mexico and miles of narrower beaches on the protected waters of Choctawhatchee Bay, Destin Harbor, and Santa Rosa Sound.

Gulf Beaches are right out your front door if your condo or motel is on the Gulf of Mexico. For those with accommodations away from the gulf beaches there is parking and access on *Okaloosa Island* at the Wayside Park (picnic facilities, showers, restrooms, guarded beach in summer and the 1,216-foot Okaloosa Island Pier) and *John C. Beasley State Park* (boardwalk to beach, covered picnic tables, playground, freshwater showers, changing rooms and lifeguards in summer). Also on Okaloosa Island is the *Elgin Reservation Beach* of 5 miles where the public is allowed except where posted.

The most beautiful sweep of gulf beach is east of Destin on US 98, centered around *Crystal Beach Wayside Park* (picnic tables, shelters, restrooms and changing facilities, and lifeguards, in summer). For the 5 miles on either side of the Wayside Park (the *Henderson Beach* area recently purchased by the state) there is roadside parking to be used carefully. State ownership means changes in access and facilities will be coming soon.

Grayton Beach State Recreation Area, SR 30A, P.O.Box 25, Santa Rosa Beach 32458; 904–231–4210, is about 28 miles east of Destin. This 356-acre park, well off the beaten track, gives an impressive look at the marvelous dunes and Gulf coast before any development. There's picnicking, swimming, changing and restroom facilities, surf fishing, skin and scuba diving. Admission is 50¢ and the park is open daily 8:00 A.M. to sunset.

Choctawhatchee Bay Beaches are popular with boaters and families with small children. In Fort Walton Beach there are two waterfront parks on the bay off Eglin Pkwy. Laguna Park on Cinco Bayou is reached by Yacht Club Rd. Garnier Park farther north features a wooded area, diving tower, bath house, playground, and lifeguards in summer. On the bay side of Destin, Clement Taylor Park on Calhoun Ave. has shade trees, picnic tables, and restrooms.

Santa Rosa Sound is accessible from accommodations along its shore and Lisa Jackson Park, 3 miles west of downtown Fort Walton Beach on the Miracle Strip Pkwy. (US 98). Besides the Sound beach, the park has extensive playground equipment, shaded picnic and grill areas, boat launches, and a pavilion.

Destin Harbor is accessible from accommodations along its shore and from a parking area at its western tip at East Pass.

Panama City Area: If your accommodations are on the beach, just step outside. If your accommodations are across the road, access walks are between beachside properties. If you drive to the beach, public parking is at the county and city piers, on the roadside, and in St. Andrews State Park (see below). In the summer and on sunny weekends year-round, these fill up quickly. Shower and changing facilities are provided at the Wayside Park opposite the city pier. There is a flag warning system for swimming conditions that should be observed. A red flag means dangerous undertow, a yellow flag means be careful of undertow, and a blue flag means calm seas. However, the lack of a flag does not mean safe seas.

St. Andrews State Park is on Thomas Dr. at the east end of the Panama City Beach area. It is one of the most popular recreation spots in Florida, over a thousand acres of beaches, dunes, pinewoods, and marshes. Two swimming areas, the Gulf beach, and a protected area behind a jetty have bathhouses and picnic shelters. Fishing is from the beach, the jetties, a 450-foot pier on the Gulf and a 200-foot pier on Grand Lagoon. A boat ramp is located on Grand Lagoon and rental boats are available in summer. The park is open 8:00 A.M. to sunset year-round, and admission is 50¢.

Pensacola: Santa Rosa Island and Perdido Key offer many miles of famous Miracle Strip snow-white sands and turquoise waters. There is public parking and changing facilities at *Pensacola Beach,* across the Pensacola Bay Bridge. Facilities there also include a fishing pier and on the Santa Rosa Sound side of the island concessions and picnic tables. *The Gulf Islands National Seashore* now preserves many miles of Santa Rosa Island and Perdido Key in their natural state and provides environmentally protective access to pristine Gulf beaches. Included in the seashore program are *Fort Pickens* at the western tip of Santa Rosa Island and *Fort San Carlos de Barrancas* on the Naval Air Station grounds. Fort Pickens is open daily 9:00 A.M.–5:00 P.M. April–October, 9:00 A.M.–4:00 P.M. rest of year; guided tours at 1:00 P.M. and self-guided tours and brochures other hours. Fort Barrancas is open 9:00 A.M.–5:00 P.M. during summer, 9:00 A.M.–4:00 P.M. September–June 1; guided tours at 1:00 P.M. and self-guided tours and brochures other hours. Both forts are closed Christmas Day and open from noon to 4:00 P.M. on Thanksgiving and New Years.

Perdido Key is reached by SR 292, the Gulf Beach Hwy.—a trip of about 20 miles from downtown Pensacola. The Johnson Beach here (part of the national seashore) has parking, restrooms, picnic facilities, and lifeguards seasonally.

PARTICIPANT SPORTS. See "Beaches," above. **Destin-Fort Walton Beach Area:** The area may be the best saltwater **fishing** spot in the nation. Sports anglers land about 4,000,000 lbs. of fish annually and Destin's nickname as "The World's Luckiest Fishing Village" is well earned. During the fishing season, roughly March through October, Destin Harbor is port for well over 100 charter boats. In addition, thousands of fishermen trailer their own rigs here or come by the Intracoastal.

Offshore the deep De Soto Canyon is a billfishing paradise, best on the Florida Gulf Coast. Reefs and wrecks provide hot spots closer to shore, and inshore trolling is the most popular charter fishing trip.

Charter boats that go 35 miles offshore to the billfishing grounds looking for sailfish and white or blue marlin cost $600 to $650 a day and take up to six people. Overnight charters can be arranged, but the day trip of 10–12 hours is the usual. Charter boats are also used for inshore trolling, close in along the beach for cobia, king and Spanish mackerel, bluefish, dolphin, and bonito. The trip lasts 4 to 6 hours. The costs for a boat are $245–$300 for a half-day and $440–$550 for a full day.

Bottom fishing from a charter boat permits more fishermen per trip; some boats can handle 20 or 24, and more people means lower individual cost. An all-day trip runs $440–$550, and it takes 6 to 8 hours. Electronic gear locates the best areas.

Charter operations include *Barbi-Anne* (837–6059) and *Windwalker* (837–2930), docked next to Bayou Bills; and *Reville II* (837–6714), at Kelly Docks.

Party Boats that accommodate 25 to 100 fishermen leave at 7:00 A.M., return at 5:00 P.M., and are always greeted by crowds. The cost per person is $35 and includes tackle, bait, and ice. Species caught are snapper, grouper, triggerfish, amberjack, and plenty of surprises. Among the boats using the Destin Harbor docks are *Her Majesty II,* Capt. Ben Marler, P.O.Box 277, 837–6313, and *New Florida Girl,* Capt. Dave Marler, P.O.Box 487, 837–6422.

Non-boat fishing is not to be looked down upon just because it's the most economical. You may land a pompano or two, a highly prized table fish. The *Okaloosa Island Pier,* a 1,216-foot concrete structure at the Wayside Park on the island is open 24 hours a day during the fishing season. The charge is $2.50 for fishermen and 50¢ for observers. You can call 244–1023 to be sure it's open and find out what's biting. The *Destin Bridge* catwalk runs for 3,000 feet along the south side of the bridge and over the most beautiful pass in Florida. If the fishing slows you can always admire the spectrum of colors—it's unparalled.

On either side of East Pass on the Gulf end are jetties, popular with local nonboaters. The Destin Chamber of Commerce, 837–6241, will supply information about fishing from the bridge, the jetties, and also on surf fishing along the miles of beaches wherever fishing and swimming won't conflict. Sand fleas, fiddler crabs, dead shrimp or cut bait can be used to take pompano, whiting, redfish, and flounder.

Fishing tournaments are scattered throughout the season and begin with the *Destin Cobia Tournament,* which in turn begins whenever the first cobia of the year is landed. That usually happens about March 20 and the tournament runs through April 30. The annual migration of cobia (also called ling and lemon fish) along the coastline just beyond the breakers is one of the fishing year's most exciting times.

Early in July, the annual *Destin Shark Tournament* is a six-day event with daily prizes, overall prizes and species and special prizes for tigers and hammerheads. In early August is the *Fort Walton Beach-Destin Open Billfish Tournament,* with prizes for blue marlin, white marlin, sailfish, wahoo, dolphin, tuna, and swordfish.

In mid-September, the *Marlin International Tournament* offers over $50,000 in prizes. This is the biggest blue marlin event on Florida's Gulf coast.

The entire month of October is the *Destin Fishing Rodeo* with more than $75,000 in bonds, prizes, and trophies. There is no entry fee, and all types of saltwater gamefish are eligible so everyone has a chance whether they troll, bottom fish, or fish offshore. Summer vacationers are gone and sportsfishing, which is at its best, rules the town.

Golf: See "Golf and Tennis," below.

There should be a **sailing** adventure in every Destin-Fort Walton Beach vacation. You can be a total passenger, learn how to handle small boats, or rent sailing yachts—bare boat or skippered.

Abbott Charter Enterprises, 114 B Amberjack Dr., Okaloosa Island, Fort Walton Beach, 244–0922. Skippered sailing and charter service; half-day, day or longer; sunset/cocktail cruise by reservation.

Blue Gulf Beach Service, Box 1215, Destin; 837–2427. Rentals of 16-foot hobie cats along the beaches, free lessons with rentals, about $20 an hour, special rates for long-term rentals.

The Boat, 32 Miracle Strip Pkwy., Fort Walton Beach; 244–2722. Sailing and windsurfing lessons and rentals, charters.

Friend Ship Charter Fleet, Nautical Inn, 500 US 98, Destin; 837–2694. Cruises of half-day, day, evening or overnight trips for one to six people; sailing and navigation instruction, bare boat rentals.

Golden Circle Charters, Fort Walton Beach; 244–2628, 243–2628. Skippered cruises for half-day, day, evening or extended charters; rentals, instruction.

S & S Sailing, Deckhands Marina, US 98, P.O. Box 2232, Fort Walton Beach; 243–2022. Skippered cruises for half-day, day and overnight; bare boat rentals, sailing school.

Sailing South, 600 US 98, P.O.Box 282, Destin; 837–SAIL. Bare boat and skippered charters, sailing school.

Scuba. The clear waters of the Deston-Fort Walton Beach area have an underwater visibility range of 40 to 100 feet and a number of artificial and natural reefs and shipwrecks to explore. If you are a certified diver you can rent equipment and join scuba trips. Dive shops also rent snorkel equipment to explore the shallows.

Half-day charters for 4 to 6 people cost about $30 a person. Trips last about 4 hours and include 2 dives. Equipment rentals are $30–$45 a day. Snorkel equipment, of course, is much less.

Aquanaut Scuba Center, 24 US 98, P.O.Box 651, Destin; 837–0359. Scuba trips, service, instruction, air, and rentals; shell collecting, photography, spear fishing, reef, wreck, night.

Fantasea Scuba Headquarters, 1 US 98, P.O.Box 63, Destin; 837–6943 and 837–0732. Daily charters, air, scuba and snorkel equipment rentals.

The Scuba Shop, 230 N. Eglin Pkwy., Fort Walton Beach; 863–1341 and 862–4944. Dive trips and charters, instruction, equipment rentals, service, air.

Golf and Tennis. Among the six facilities open to the public under various schemes are the three luxury resorts.

Bluewater Bay, SR 20 East, Niceville; 897–3241. Semi-private, heavily wooded, rolling greens, some bay front; 18 holes; green fees $15, carts $18.

Fort Walton Beach Municipal Golf Club, Lewis Turner Blvd. and Mooney Rd., Fort Walton Beach; 862–3314. Public, large greens, water, well-trapped, wooded, open fairways; 18-hole and 9-hole courses; green fees $8, carts available.

Indian Bayou Golf and Country Club, Airport Rd. Destin; 837–6191. Guest privileges, large greens, open fairways, sand traps; green fees $16, carts $15; 18 holes.

Sandestin Resort, US 98 E., Destin; 837–2121. Semi-public, large greens, lots of waters, bunkers; 36 holes; green fees $25 for non-guests, $15 for guests, carts $16.

Seascape Golf & Racquet Club, US 98 E., Destin; 837–9181. Semi-public, rolling, tight fairways, medium greens, sand traps; 18 holes; green fees $15 for 18 holes, $9 for 9, carts $7 for 18 holes, $5 for 9 holes.

Shalimar Point Resort Golf and Tennis Club, Shalimar; 651–0116. Public, wooded, sand traps, water, on the bay; green fees $13, cart $13; course reconditioning will make 9 of the course's 18 holes inaccessible until July 1986.

Tennis courts are available at all the courses above except Indian Bayou. Other court facilities are listed below.

Fort Walton Beach Municipal Tennis Center has 12 courts and another 12 at various locations throughout the community. Contact the Parks and Recreation Dept., 132 Jett Dr., Fort Walton Beach; 243–3119.

Destin Racquet Club, Airport Rd., P.O.Box 1255; 837–8548. Open to the public, hours begin at 9:00 A.M., racquetball courts also.

Panama City: The most popular participant sport is **fishing** by a wide margin and for a good reason; it's exceptional. Public fishing piers in the Panama City Beach area are the 500-foot county pier on the beach which is free, the 450-foot Gulf pier, and 200-foot lagoon pier in St. Andrews State Park for the 50¢ park admission, and the 1,600-foot city pier on the beach which is $2 adults, $1.50 children for fishing (3 rod limit) and $1 for spectating. The city pier, open 24 hours daily, has a bait and tackle shop open 7:00 A.M.–5:00 P.M. 7 days a week.

Party boats for bottom and reef fishing are approximately $16 for half-day trips (spring/summer only), $25 for 10-hour trips, and $43 for a marathon 2:00

A.M. to 5:00 P.M. trip that includes a bunk. Food, soft drinks, bait, and tackle are available on board.

Charter boats, usually for up to six people, are priced by the boat and cost approximately $200 for four hours, $400 for eight hours and $550 for 12 hours. Longer trips can be arranged. Bait and tackle are furnished but food is not. Reservations are a necessity for charter boats and it is advisable to contact individual boat captains to work out details. Some captains and chartering services will assist in making up groups so the cost can be divided among more people.

Capt. Anderson/Capt. Davis Queen Fleet, 5550 N. Lagoon Dr.; 234–3435. Party and charter boats.

Bob Zales Charters, Treasure Ship Docks; 235–2628 or 763–7249. Charters, all types of fishing.

Gulf Charter Service, Treasure Island Marina, 3605 Thomas Dr.; 235–2809 or 234–9889 after 6:00 P.M. Charter boats.

Treasure Island Charters, Treasure Island Marina, 234–8944. Half-day fishing trips, charters.

There are three regulation **golf** courses and one nine-hole par-3 in the beach area open to the public, and one regulation private club in the Lynn Haven area that extends guest privileges on certain days.

Bay Point Resort, 100 Delwood Beach Rd., Panama City Beach; 234–3307, is a 36-hole course that is open to non-guests on an availability basis. Green fees are $24 and carts $10.

Green Valley, 14414 W.98 Alt.; 234–9289, is a 9-hole par-3 course lighted for night play. Clubs and balls furnished.

Holiday Golf & Racquet Club, 100 Fairway Blvd., Panama City Beach; 234–1800, is an 18-hole course at the Holiday Inn Beachside. Green fees are $17 for 9 holes, $22 for 18 holes; and **tennis** is $6 an hour.

Panama Country Club, 100 Country Club Dr., Lynn Haven; 265–2911, is an 18-hole private club offering guest privileges on some days. Green fees $15, carts $12.60.

Signal Hill Golf Course, 9615 N. Thomas Dr., Panama City Beach; 234–3218, is an 18-hole par 70. Play Mon.-Fri. is by reservation a day in advance; Sat. and Sun. open. Green fees are $4 for 9 holes, $7 for 18, and carts $4.50 for 9 holes and $9 for 18.

A variety of watersports such as **sailing, jet skiing, and para-sailing** are offered from concessions along the beach during the summer. Rates for the hobie sailboats are $20 first hour, $35 2 hours, $60 a half-day and $85 a day (free instructions). Jet skis are $20 for 30 minutes, and $35 an hour. Para-sailing is comparably priced.

Scuba and **snorkeling,** are popular because of the area's clear waters. Dive trips on boats with experienced personnel are about $30 for a half-day 2-tank dive and $50 for a full-day dive. Rental of scuba equipment is about $30. Of course, you must be a certified diver.

Diver's Den, (2 locations) 4720 Bus. US 98 E., P.O.Box 10606, Panama City 32401; 871–4777, and 1 Harrison Ave. (City Marina), Panama City Beach 32407; 769–6621.

Hydrospace Dive Shop, (2 locations) 1216 Beck Ave., Panama City 32401; 769–0441, and 3605 Thomas Dr. (Treasure Island Marina), Panama City Beach 32407; 234–9463.

For **tennis,** check with *Bay Point Resort* for availability and with *Holiday Golf and Racquet Club,* see "Golf," above. Some of the beach motels and hotels have their own courts.

Pensacola: Of all the many participant sports to be enjoyed in the Pensacola area, the nod has to go to **fishing.** Pensacola's snapper fleet made this delicacy a popular item on the nation's tables and sports fishermen were quick to backtrack the fish to its source. Then some years ago marine biologists discovered the De Soto Canyon at the 100 fathom line and big time billfishing came to the Miracle Strip. Modern electronic devices to locate wrecks and reefs almost makes bottom trolling and bottom fishing an exact science. But before these developments and devices came along it was the bridge, pier, and surf fishing that drew anglers to the area—and these are still the most popular.

The trip for billfishing takes about 12 hours and costs approximately $600 for a charter boat for six people. An eight-hour day of trolling costs about $400 for six. Bottom fishing on a charter boat runs about $250 for four hours, $300 for six hours and $400 for eight hours. When bottom fishing, a charter boat can accommodate more people but costs $35 extra for each person over the first six.

Bouey One Charters, 217 S. Alcaniz St.; 434–5072, half-day and all-day charters.

Capt. Red's Fishing Center, 655 Pensacola Beach Blvd.; 932–8193, half-day and all-day charters.

Lo-Baby Charters, 935 Fairway Dr., Pensacola 32507; 455–4892, will put together individuals to make up a full charter.

Lafitte Cove Marina, 1010 Fort Pickens Rd., Gulf Breeze; 932–5150, half-day and all-day charters.

Rod & Reed Marina, Gulf Beach Hwy.; 492–0100, half-day and all-day charters.

Southwind Marina, Gulf Beach Hwy.; 492–0333, half-day and full day charters.

Party boats take many individuals bottom fishing. No need to get up a group, just join the crowd of 20 to 60 people. The boats usually leave at 7:00 A.M. and return at 5:00 P.M. The boat furnishes bait, rents tackle, and there's usually a concession on board. The cost is $35 to $40 for the day.

The *Pensacola Beach Pier,* Pensacola Beach Blvd.; 932–0444, rents tackle, sells bait, has a restaurant and is lighted for night fishing. The old bridge across Pensacola Bay to the beaches is one of the longest fishing piers in Florida and makes fishing a drive-in entertainment. Just load up your car with everything you need for a day's outing, drive out, and start fishing. The cost is 75¢ for the car, 50¢ per person, with kids under 10 free.

The two public **golf** courses are *Carriage Hill Golf and Country Club;* 944–5497, and *Osceola Municipal Golf Course;* 456–2761. These have the lowest greens fees, $6–$7, but you may have difficulty getting a tee time. The semi-private courses include: *Perdido Bay Resort,* 492–1223, *Scenic Hills Country Club,* 476–0611; *Santa Rosa Shores Country Club,* 932–3527; and *Tigerpoint Golf and Country Club,* 932–3955.

Certified **scuba** divers find the gulf's clear waters and offshore reefs and wrecks fascinating. Several area firms provide service, air, and arrange dive trips.

Dive World, 3090 N. Pace Blvd., 438–5485; *Ray Manuel Diving,* 3624 W. Fairfield Dr., 455–2929; *Scuba Shack,* 719 S. Palafox St., 433–4319.

Action center for **sailing, sailboarding, parasailing** and **jet skiing** is Pensacola Beach Blvd. along the causeway. Rentals for all these sports are handled on the spot and for novices free instruction usually goes with the rental. If you want further lessons those can be arranged too. Companies in that locale include: *Bonifay Water Sports,* 932–0633; *Key Sailing,* 932–5520; *Pensacola Beach Sailing Center,* 932–0621; *Port Side Sailing Rentals,* 932–2000; *Surf & Sail Boardsailing,* 932–7873.

All of the semi-private golf facilities mentioned above have **tennis** courts. Additionally, the *Roger Scott Tennis Center,* 432–2939, is a municipal public park. *Holiday Inn Pensacola Beach,* 932–5361, and the *Pensacola Racquet Club,* 434–2434, are open on an availability basis.

Tallahassee: Lake Talquin, Lake Jackson, and Lake Miccosukee are popular freshwater **fishing** spots with rental boats, bait, and fishing camps. Freshwater fishing requires a license, available at most fishing camps or the county tax collector's offices. Saltwater fishing enthusiasts head for St. Marks, Shell Island, Spring Creek, and Panacea where marinas, rental boats and guides are available. There is no saltwater fishing license. The 18-hole *Hilaman Park Golf Course,* 2737 Blair Stone Rd.; 878–5830, is a public **golf** course. The City Parks and Recreation Dept., 912 Myers Park Dr.; 222–7529, has information on public **tennis** courts, **swimming** pools, and **jogging** trails.

SPECTATOR SPORTS. The *Washington County Kennel Club* at Ebro, on SR 79, about 40 miles north of Panama City has a May to September season; 234–3943. Races are nightly except Sun., matinees Sat. and Mon. Grandstand admission is $1. Parimutuel wagering means all persons 18 and younger are excluded.

The **Pensacola** *Greyhound Park* has meet dates that start late in April and end early in October. The park is on US 98W. and the number to call for exact post schedule and clubhouse reservations is 455–8598.

Tallahassee: FSU's **baseball** team is a frequent contender for the national title. Home **football** games are almost every weekend during the fall with the FSU *Seminoles* and FAMU *Rattlers* considered powerhouses at their respective levels of competition. The FSU Athletic Ticket Office; 644–1830, and FAMU Athletic Ticket Office; 599–3141, handle all sports at the two universities.

Pro **golf** comes to the capital city each April with the PGA-sanctioned Tallahassee Open, held at the Killearn Country Club; 893–2144.

The *Jefferson County Kennel Club* in nearby Monticello offers **greyhound racing** with parimutuel betting May–Oct. Call 904–997–2561 for exact dates and post times.

The *Big Bend Jai Alai Fronton,* south of Quincy off I-10 W., 904–442–4111, brings jai alai and parimutuel betting to the Tallahassee area Nov.–May. Call for exact dates and game times.

MUSEUMS. See also "Historic Sites," below. *The Temple Mound and Museum* is right in the heart of downtown **Fort Walton Beach,** and, praise be, the people saved it from early developers. The mound has been thoroughly investigated and excavated by archeologists, and the top bears a reconsttruction of the temple. Alongside the mound is the museum containing artifacts from the mound, and from other archaeological sites, some now under Fort Walton's streets and buildings. The museum's treasures include a unique four-legged effigy urn and examples of six-sided ceramic bowls found nowhere else. Admission to the museum is 50¢, open 11:00 A.M.–4:00 P.M. Tues.–Sat. and 1:00 P.M.–4:00 P.M. Sun.

HISTORIC SITES AND HOUSES. **Pensacola** itself seems to be one great big historic site. The best way to find out what will interest you is to get the free brochure called *Tour Guide Historic Pensacola* from the Visitor Information Center, 1401 E. Gregory St.; 434–1234. This covers sites in the North Hill Historic District, along Palafox St., and the Seville Square area.

The two old forts, Pickens and Barrancas, are under the care of the Gulf Islands National Seashore. *Fort Pickens* at the western tip of Santa Rosa Island was begun in 1829 and completed in 1834. *Fort Barrancas,* on the Naval Air Station grounds, was begun in 1839 and completed in 1844. Both are American forts, outmoded by the invention of the rifled cannon shell almost as soon as they were built. Both are on sites originally fortified by the Spanish—the Barrancas site in 1698 and the Pickens site in 1719. Both were involved in Civil War action; the Federals held Pickens and the Rebels occupied Barrancas.

CULTURAL EVENTS. **Pensacola** has tradition in the fine and performing arts. The *Pensacola Symphony* is approaching its 60th anniversary and the *Pensacola Little Theatre;* 432–2042, its 50th. The *Choral Society* is one of Florida's oldest.

The *Pensacola Arts Council* keeps up with the doings of these groups and many more. It issues a quarterly calendar of events that can be obtain by writing the council at P. O. Box 731, 32594 or by calling 432–9906. The "Weekender" section of each Friday edition of the *Pensacola News Journal* also contains information on current and coming events of a cultural or popular character.

The *Saenger Theater* on S. Palafox St.; 438–2787, is the site of performances of national touring companies, concerts by renowned performing artists and popular musical groups. The grand old movie and vaudeville palace was built in 1925, purchased and restored by the city and reopened in 1981.

SHOPPING. **Pensacola:** The *Quayside Theives Market* 712 S. Palafox St., is a large indoor-outdoor antique mall and flea market open every Fri. and Sat. 9–5. The *Quayside* and *Seville Square* are both delightful places to browse for arts and crafts, unusual gifts, gourmet foods, and many custom specialty items.

DINING OUT. Price categories are for an average dinner for one, exclusive of drinks, tax, and tip: *Expensive,* over $15; *Moderate,* $7–$15; *Inexpensive,* under $7. AE—American Express; MC—Master Card; V—Visa; DC—Diner's Club; CB—Carte Blanche.

DESTIN

Les Saisons of Destin. *Expensive.* US 98 just east of Destin Bridge; 837–3747. French cuisine including lamb, beef, veal, and seafood. With a day's notice the chef will prepare a special off-menu dinner. Open for dinner Mon.–Sat. from 6:00 P.M.; also on Sundays from Easter to Labor Day. Reservations required. AE, MC, V.

Captain Trammell's Outrigger Five Restaurant. *Moderate to expensive.* 327 US 98; 837–2001. Seafood and steaks; house specialties are stuffed scamp and grouper Parmesan. Open daily for dinner from 5:00 P.M. during summer season, closed Mon. off-season. All major credit cards.

Constellation Room. *Moderate to expensive.* Holiday Inn; 837–6181. A full-service restaurant in a revolving rooftop location; menu includes prime rib, veal Oscar, Coquilles St. Jacques, and other seafood. Table-side salads and desserts. Open daily for breakfast. lunch and dinner—dinner from 5:00 P.M. Sunday brunch. All major credit cards.

Indian Bayou Golf & Country Club. *Moderate to expensive.* Indian Bayou Dr.; 837–6192. Off Airport Rd. overlooking course and lakes. Dinner menu features Beef Wellington, veal Oscar, broiled Snapper, and flaming desserts. Open for dinner Tues.–Sun from 6:00 P.M. Reservations suggested. All major credit cards.

Bayou Bill's. *Inexpensive.* US 98 near charter docks; 837–0945. Open-air seafood restaurant with patio overlooking Destin Harbor and charter boats. Smoked mullet, crabs, barbecue. Open every day 6:00 A.M.–9:00 P.M.

Lantern II. *Inexpensive.* 419 Mountain Dr. (1 blk. off US 98); 837–2822. Pizza, spaghetti, lasagna, sandwiches, and salads. Homemade chili a specialty. Open Mon.–Sat. 10:30 A.M.–10:00 P.M., Sun 4:00 P.M.–10:00 P.M.

FORT WALTON BEACH

Captain Anderson II. *Expensive.* US 98 E. at Brooks Bridge; 243–3463. Dinner cruise and dancing. June through September 1. Days sometimes vary, so check. Also reservations suggested.

The Seasons. *Expensive.* Bluewater Bay Resort, Niceville; 897–2186. Genteel dining on fresh seafood and prime beef, good wine selection. Reservations requested. Open for dinner Tues.–Sat. from 6:00 P.M., for lunch Tues.–Fri. All major credit cards.

Liollio's Restaurant. *Moderate to expensive.* Miracle Strip Pkwy.; 243–5011. A regionally recognized restaurant specializing in seafood with Greek flavor and steaks. Lunch and dinner Mon.–Sat., closed Sun. Second restaurant at Navarre Beach. All major credit cards.

Nikko Inn. *Moderate to Expensive.* 310 Perry Ave., downtown; 244–4188. Authentic Japanese cuisine in an Oriental atmosphere. Open for dinner from 5:00 P.M. daily in summer, closed Mon. off-season. Reservations suggested. All major credit cards.

Perri's Ristorante. *Moderate to expensive.* 300 Eglin Pkwy.; 862–4421. Italian cuisine, veal dishes, house specialties are saltimbocca alla Romana and chicken alla Bolognese. Open for dinner Tues.–Sat. from 6:00 P.M. All major credit cards.

Staff's Restaurant. *Moderate.* 24 Miracle Strip Pkwy.; 243–3482. A downtown fixture for 50 years, seafood and steaks. Dinner daily from 5:00 P.M. All major credit cards.

PANAMA CITY

The Breakers. *Moderate to expensive.* 12627 W. 98 Alt.; 234–2239. This is a new beach spot and very popular, though whether for the food or the entertainment is moot. The music and usually a floor show start at 10:00 P.M. There's a $3 cover if you come for the show and not the dinner. Open daily 5:00 P.M. AE, DC, MC, V.

Capt. Anderson's Restaurant. *Moderate to expensive.* Dockside at Grand Lagoon and Thomas Dr.; 234–2225. A three-time winner of an all-Florida award and a Panama City tradition. Seafood, charcoal broiled fish, Greek salads. Dinner Mon.–Sat. from 4:00 P.M. No reservations. AE, MC, V.

The Treasure Ship. *Moderate to expensive.* Treasure Island Marina, 3605 Thomas Dr., 234–8881. Every vacation to Panama City should include a visit to this landmark, a bigger-than-life pirate ship. The higher you go the fancier the food and the price. The main dining room serves seafood and steak at family prices and does not accept reservations. The top of the Ship serves French cuisine by candlelight and requires reservations. Dinner daily. AE, DC, MC, V.

Allen's Seafood Restaurant & Oyster Bar. *Moderate.* 4200 W. 23rd St.; 785–4389. Dine on fresh seafood in a waterside setting. Closed Wed., open all other days at 4:00 P.M.

Harbour House. *Moderate.* 3001 W. 10th St., St. Andrews; 785–9053. A full-service restaurant on the old St. Andrews waterfront. Luncheon buffet; dinner features fresh gulf seafood and prime rib. Open daily 6:00 A.M. to 10:00 P.M. AE, DC, MC, V.

Pasta Peddler. *Moderate.* 448 Harrison Ave., downtown Panama City; 763–0059. Authentic Italian cuisine, homemade pasta and patries. Lunch and dinner Tues.–Sat., closed Sun. AE, MC, V.

Bob's Family Steak & Seafood House *Inexpensive.* Hwy. 77 across from the Panama City Hall; 785–5602. Choice western beef and fresh gulf seafood, salad bar, children's menu. Open 11:00 A.M. to 10:00 P.M. daily. MC, V.

Pier 77. *Inexpensive.* 3016 Thomas Dr.; 235–3080. Seafood restaurant, market, and oyster bar. Very casual, eat in or take out. Open 7 days. MC, V.

PENSACOLA

Angus Steak Ranch. *Expensive.* 1101 Scenic Hwy. E.; 432–0475. On Pensacola's eastern shoreline, a cozy fireplace setting for prime and choice steaks, Greek salads, and fresh seafoods. Open for dinner from 5:00 P.M. Mon.–Sat. Reservations suggested. Major credit cards.

Cezanee's. *Expensive.* Perdido Bay Resort, SR 292; 492–1212. French cuisine and seafood in an elegant country French setting. Duck, lamb, and beef from an a la carte menu. Sunday champagne brunch. Open for lunch and dinner daily. Dinner reservations advised. Major credit cards.

Driftwood Restaurant. *Expensive.* 27 W. Garden St.; 433–4559. A distinguished and honored restaurant in the heart of downtown, very elegant atmosphere. Seafood and steak. Lunch and dinner Mon.–Sat. Dinner reservations suggested. AE, DC, MC, V.

Flounder's Ale House. *Moderate to expensive.* 800 Quiet Water Beach Rd., Gulf Breeze; 932–2003. "Eat, drink, and flounder" is the motto of this fun restaurant that makes its specialty, hickory-grilled seafood, very special. Waterfront view of Santa Rosa Sound. Open daily at 5:00 P.M., Sun. champagne brunch. All major credit cards.

New World Restaurants. *Moderate to expensive.* 600 S. Palafox St.; 432–4111. Part of the historical New World Landing complex in the Quayside area. Three separate dining rooms reflect Pensacola's history. International cuisine of seafood, beef, veal, and fowl; extensive wine list. Lunch and dinner daily. Dinner reservations suggested. All major credit cards.

Skopelos Restaurant. *Moderate to expensive.* 1842 W. Cervantes St.; 432–6565. An award-winning restaurant and a Pensacola tradition, gulf seafood and choice steaks, broiled snapper, and baked oysters. Dinner daily. AE, MC, V.

Jolly Roger's Seafood. *Moderate.* One Marina, 47 Gulf Breeze Pkwy.; 932–5068. Relaxing atmosphere of an old galleon, seafood from pier to table, steaks. Come by car or boat. Lunch and dinner Mon.–Sat., closed Sun. AE, MC, V.

McGillivray's Restaurant and Tavern. *Moderate.* 300 S. Alcaniz St.; 438–4535. On Seville Square in a restored house, turn-of-the-century dining in the traditional manner; lamb, veal, smithfield ham, and seafoods. Open for lunch and dinner Tues.–Sun., closed Mon. All major credit cards.

Sam's Seafood. *Moderate.* Corner Main and S. "A" St.; 432–6626. Sam serves seafood straight off his own smacks (fishing boats). Lunch and dinner Mon.-Sat. All major credit cards.

Surfside Marina Restaurant and Lounge. *Moderate.* 400 Pensacola Beach Blvd.; 932–7954. Greek style broiled snapper and Greek salads, other seafoods and steaks. Docking. Dinner daily spring/summer, closed Tues.–Wed. off-season; lunch during peak season. All major credit cards.

Darryl's Restaurant and Tavern. *Inexpensive.* 7251 Plantation Rd.; 476–1821. Good port and beef barbecue in a great place for nostalgia buffs, old carrousel, and double-decker bus. Lunch and dinner daily. All major credit cards.

Hopkins Boarding House. *Inexpensive.* 900 N. Spring St.; 438–3979. No fancy decor at this family-style eatery where you sit at big tables with whomever and pass the ever-full platters and serving bowls. Breakfast 6:30 A.M.–9:00 P.M., lunch 11:15 A.M.–2:00 P.M., dinner 5:15 P.M.–7:00 P.M., no dinner Sun., closed Mon. No credit cards.

TALLAHASSEE

Andrews 2nd Act. *Moderate to expensive.* 102 W. Jefferson St.; 222–2759. Around the corner from the Adams Street Commons. Fine continental cuisine; special entrees can be a real bargain; valet parking. Lunch Mon.–Fri. dinner daily. Reservations required for dinner. All major credit cards.

Jacques Restaurant. *Moderate to expensive.* Carriage Gate Center, 3425 Thomasville Rd.; 893–5913. Fine classical French cuisine served with style. Lunch Tues.–Fri., dinner Tues.–Sat. Reservations suggested for dinner. All major credit cards.

The Silver Slipper. *Moderate to expensive.* 531 Scotty Lane, between N. Monroe St. and John Knox Rd.; 386–9366. A Tallahassee tradition: steaks and seafood. Reservations accepted. Dinner daily. All major credit cards.

Chez Pierre Pastry & Restaurant. *Moderate.* 115 N. Adams St.; 222–0936. Good French food and delicious pastries. Lunch Mon.–Sat., dinner Fri. and Sat. only, and reservations required. Pastries sold 10:00 A.M.–5:30 P.M. AE, MC, V.

Lucy Ho's Bamboo Garden. *Moderate.* 2814 Apalachee Pkwy.; 878–3366. Lucy's personal immigration program has got the whole family cooking Oriental food all over town. This is the flagship place. Lunch and dinner Mon.–Sat. Closed Sun. MC, V.

Talquin Inn. *Inexpensive to moderate.* 2759 W. Tennessee St.; 576–9193. A landmark for good seafood—hasn't changed it's decor in fifty years. The food is prepared to order, and the management likes reservation. Dinner Tues.–Sat. No credit cards.

The Bird Cage. *Inexpensive.* 2nd floor Rheinauers, Northwood Mall; 385–0203. A tea room for luncheon only. Salads, soups, and super desserts. Lunch Mon.-Sat. MC, V.

NIGHT LIFE. Destin/Fort Walton. Time was when Destin rolled up its streets at night while Fort Walton danced in its streets. It's still quieter in Destin after dark, but *Nightown* is changing that. In the number of night spots, Fort Walton Beach is still the winner because nearby Eglin furnishes a year-round clientele. Entertainment ranges from the very nice to the very naughty.

Faux Pas Lounge, 106 Santa Rosa Blvd.; 244–2274. A college-crowd hangout with live entertainment and a waiting line.

Hog's Breath Saloon, 1230 Siebert Okaloosa Island; 243–4646. Any place that advertises "hog's breath is better than no breath at all" deserves investigation.

The Last Hurrah, Coronado/Sheraton Beach, Okloosa Island, 243–8116. Dancing to the nostalgic sounds of favorites from the 40s, 50s, and 60s.

Nightown, cor. of Palmetto and Azalea 2 blks. north of US 98, Destin; 837–6448. Books a variety of big names on the contemporary music scene from rock to jazz to reggae.

Victor's Corner, 113 Eglin Pkwy S.; 243–1227. Disco with dancing every night 8:00 P.M.–4:00 P.M. Listening music in deli.

Panama City. Can you imagine a vacation resort where people ride the waves by day and the roller coasters by night? In the summer season the amusement parks run well into the evening hours and are quite popular. Florida State University's Musical Theater moved to Panama City Beach in the summer of 1984 after many successful seasons on Jekyll Island to present a repertoire of popular musical comedies at Gulfside Miracle Mile (shows/dates announced in spring). The cornball comedy of the Ocean Opry has become a beach tradition.

Then there are the more conventional nightspots and plenty of them, probably one or more in your hotel/motel complex or right next door. Popular combos and acts move from place to place and new headliners emerge each year.

Boar's Head Tavern, 17290 W.98 Alt.; 234–6628. A favorite beach spot and usually on the quiet side, but check for the current booking. Live entertainment Tues.–Sat.

The Breakers, 12627 W.98 Alt.; 234–2239. The music starts at 10:00 P.M. and usually includes a floor show. There's a $3 cover for those who don't come to dine first. Phone for reservations.

C Shell Lounge, 3001 W. 10th St., St. Andrews; 785–0561. Next to the Harbour House overlooking the romantic St. Andrews waterfront. Live band Tues.–Sat.

Montego Bay Club, 1227 Beck Ave., St. Andrews; 785–9891. Old St. Andrews rocks and pops to live bands. Dancing. Some funk, some top 40, you name it.

Ocean Opry, 8400 W.98 Alt.; 234–5464. A country music and comedy stage show. Plays five nights a week in May, every night during the summer season and weekends most of the remainder. Check with the box office for dates and reservations. It's a family show, adults $5.50, under 12 $3.

The Spinnaker II, 8813 Thomas Dr.; 234–7882. For the college crowd, this is the place to go. Live music and dancing every night.

The Treasure Ship, 3605 Thomas Dr., Treasure Island Marina; 234–8881. The Quarter Deck offers quiet entertainment and dancing. The Brig whoops it up with rock and disco.

Tourism and the U.S. Navy make **Pensacola** night life a mixed bag. Pensacola has a reputation for being very lively after dark.

Holly's Lounge, Lenox Inn, 710 N. Palafox St.; 438–4922. Dancing and live music Tues.–Sat. in a Victorian—yet lively—setting.

King's Inn Lounge, 14th and Gregory St.; 432–3332. A supper club with live entertainment, music, and dancing Mon.–Sat.

McGuire's Irish Pub, 600 E. Gregory St.; 433–6789. Irish entertainment until the wee hours.

Seville Quarter, 130 E. Government St.; 433–7436. A complex of eating, drinking, and entertainment establishments dripping with bits and pieces of collectabilia. *Rosie O'Grady's* is Dixieland jazz and singing waiters and waitresses, *Lili Marlene's* features easy-listening piano, *Phineas Phogg's Balloon*

Works combines disco with a light show, and *End of the Alley* Bar has changing entertainment usually on the quiet side. This is a tourist's must.

Tallahassee. It's a college town and most night life is designed for that age group. However, there are a few places where a mature person doesn't feel ancient. One bonus is a lot of live talent, perhaps a by-product of the collegetown environment. The Friday section of the *Tallahassee Democrat* gives a run-down of who's where.

Brothers 3, 2696 N. Monroe St.; 386–4193. Live entertainment every night except Sun. Country, top 40, and contemporary; dancing.

Capital Inn's Bonaparte's Retreat, 1027 Apalachee Pkwy.; 877–6171. Quiet contemporary guitar for easy listening, Tues.–Sat.

Lillie Langtry's, Tallahassee Hilton, Adams and Park; 224–5000. Live entertainment and dancing every night except Sun.

Radcliffe's, 114 E. Jefferson St.; 222–6013. Pop and folk acoustical guitar singles and combos, different entertainers every night. Closed on Mon. and every other Sun.

INDEX

General Information and Facts at Your Fingertips

The letter H indicates hotels, motels and other accommodations.
The letter R indicates restaurants.

Geographical & Practical Information